Enterprise Mac Security

Mac OS X Snow Leopard

■ ■ ■

Charles Edge
William Barker
Beau Hunter
Gene Sullivan

Apress®

Enterprise Mac Security: Mac OS X Snow Leopard

Copyright © 2010 by Charles Edge, William Barker, Beau Hunter, and Gene Sullivan

All rights reserved. No part of this work may be reproduced or transmitted in any form or by any means, electronic or mechanical, including photocopying, recording, or by any information storage or retrieval system, without the prior written permission of the copyright owner and the publisher.

ISBN-13 (pbk): 978-1-4302-2730-4

ISBN-13 (electronic): 978-1-4302-2731-1

Printed and bound in the United States of America 9 8 7 6 5 4 3 2 1

Trademarked names may appear in this book. Rather than use a trademark symbol with every occurrence of a trademarked name, we use the names only in an editorial fashion and to the benefit of the trademark owner, with no intention of infringement of the trademark.

President and Publisher: Paul Manning
Lead Editor: Clay Andres
Developmental Editor: Michelle Lowman
Technical Reviewer: Graham Lee
Editorial Board: Clay Andres, Steve Anglin, Mark Beckner, Ewan Buckingham, Gary Cornell, Jonathan Gennick, Jonathan Hassell, Michelle Lowman, Matthew Moodie, Duncan Parkes, Jeffrey Pepper, Frank Pohlmann, Douglas Pundick, Ben Renow-Clarke, Dominic Shakeshaft, Matt Wade, Tom Welsh
Coordinating Editor: Kelly Moritz
Copy Editor: Tracy Brown Collins
Compositor: MacPS, LLC
Indexer: John Collin
Artist: April Milne
Cover Designer: Anna Ishchenko

Distributed to the book trade worldwide by Springer-Verlag New York, Inc., 233 Spring Street, 6th Floor, New York, NY 10013. Phone 1-800-SPRINGER, fax 201-348-4505, e-mail orders-ny@springer-sbm.com, or visit www.springeronline.com.

For information on translations, please e-mail rights@apress.com, or visit www.apress.com.

Apress and friends of ED books may be purchased in bulk for academic, corporate, or promotional use. eBook versions and licenses are also available for most titles. For more information, reference our Special Bulk Sales–eBook Licensing web page at www.apress.com/info/bulksales.

The information in this book is distributed on an "as is" basis, without warranty. Although every precaution has been taken in the preparation of this work, neither the author(s) nor Apress shall have any liability to any person or entity with respect to any loss or damage caused or alleged to be caused directly or indirectly by the information contained in this work.

To my wonderful wife Lisa and sweet little Emerald, with all of my love!
– Charles Edge

To my family and friends, who incessantly inspire me to follow my passions, and to my Jill who demonstrates more patience with my creative pursuits than anyone should ever have to.
– William Barker

To Dana, Maya, and Owen, who put up with a lot.
– Gene Sullivan

Dedicated to my wife Monica who, despite completely losing me to the world of bits and bytes for the last six months yet again, has been a source of perpetual support.
– Beau Hunter

Contents at a Glance

- Contents at a Glance iv
- Contents v
- About the Authors xv
- About the Technical Reviewer xvi
- Acknowledgments xvii
- Introduction xviii
- Part I: The Big Picture 1
- Chapter 1: Security Quick-Start 3
- Chapter 2: Services, Daemons, and Processes 29
- Chapter 3: Securing User Accounts 49
- Chapter 4: File System Permissions 79
- Chapter 5: Reviewing Logs and Monitoring 113
- Part II: Securing the Ecosystem 137
- Chapter 6: Application Signing and Sandbox 139
- Chapter 7: Securing Web Browsers and E-mail 183
- Chapter 8: Malware Security: Combating Viruses, Worms, and Root Kits 213
- Chapter 9: Encrypting Files and Volumes 233
- Part III: Network Traffic 275
- Chapter 10: Securing Network Traffic 277
- Chapter 11: Setting Up the Mac OS X Firewall 299
- Chapter 12: Securing a Wireless Network 325
- Part IV: Sharing 351
- Chapter 13: Part IV: File Services 353
- Chapter 14: Web Site Security 377
- Chapter 15: Remote Connectivity 401
- Chapter 16: Server Security 423
- Part V: Securing the Workplace 483
- Chapter 17: Network Scanning, Intrusion Detection, and Intrusion Prevention Tools 485
- Chapter 18: Backup and Fault Tolerance 505
- Chapter 19: Forensics 537
- Appendix A: Xsan Security 559
- Appendix V: InfoSec Acceptable Use Policy 563
- Appendix C: CDSA 571
- Appendix D: Introduction to Cryptography 573
- Index 577

Contents

- **Contents at a Glance** iv
- **Contents** v
- **About the Authors** xv
- **About the Technical Reviewer** xvi
- **Acknowledgments** xvii
- **Introduction** xviii

Part I: The Big Picture 1
Chapter 1: Security Quick-Start 3

Securing the Mac OS X Defaults 3
Customizing System Preferences 4
Accounts 4
Login Options 6
    Passwords 7
    Administrators 8
Security Preferences 9
General 9
FileVault 11
Firewall 13
Software Update 14
Bluetooth Security 16
Printer Security 18
Sharing Services 20
Securely Erasing Disks 21
Using Secure Empty Trash 23
Using Encrypted Disk Images 24
Securing Your Keychains 25
Best Practices 27

Chapter 2: Services, Daemons, and Processes 29

Introduction to Services, Daemons, and Processes 29

Viewing What's Currently Running 31
    The Activity Monitor 31
    The ps Command 35
    The top Output 36
    Viewing Which Daemons Are Running 38
    Viewing Which Services Are Available 39
Stopping Services, Daemons, and Processes 40
    Stopping Processes 41
Stopping Daemons 43
Types of launchd Services 44
GUI Tools for Managing launchd 44
Changing What Runs At Login 45
Validating the Authenticity of Applications and Services 46
Summary 47

Chapter 3: Securing User Accounts 49

Introducing Identification, Authentication, and Authorization 49
Managing User Accounts 50
    Introducing the Account Types 51
    Adding Users to Groups 53
    Enabling the Superuser Account 54
    Setting Up Parental Controls 56
    Managing the Rules Put in Place 62
Advanced Settings in System Preferences 64
Working with Local Directory Services 65
    Creating a Second Local Directory Node 68
    External Accounts 68
Restricting Access with the Command Line: sudoers 69
Securing Mount Points 74
SUID Applications: Getting into the Nitty-Gritty 75
Creating Files with Permissions 77
Summary 78

Chapter 4: File System Permissions 79

Mac OS File Permissions: A Brief History of Time 80
POSIX Permissions 81
    Modes in Detail 82
    Inheritance 84
    The Sticky Bit 87
    The suid/sguid Bits 87
    POSIX in Practice 88
Access Control Lists 91
    Access Control Entries 91
    Effective Permissions 94
    ACLs in Practice 95
Administering Permissions 97
Using the Finder to Manage Permissions 103
Using chown and chmod to Manage Permissions 104
The Hard Link Dilemma..107

Using mtree to Audit File system Permissions	109
Summary	111

Chapter 5: Reviewing Logs and Monitoring ... 113

What Exactly Gets Logged?	113
Using Console	115
Viewing Logs	115
Marking Logs	116
Searching Logs	117
Finding Logs	118
Secure.log: Security Information 101	119
appflrewall.log	120
Reviewing User-Specific Logs	121
Reviewing Command-Line Logs	123
Reviewing Library Logs	124
Breaking Down Maintenance Logs	124
daily.out	126
Yasu	127
Weekly.out	128
Monthly.out	129
What to Worry About	129
Virtual Machine and Bootcamp Logs	130
Event Viewer	130
Task Manager	131
Performance Alerts	132
Review Regularly, Review Often	133
Accountability	133
Incident Response	134
Summary	135

Part II: Securing the Ecosystem ... 137

Chapter 6: Application Signing and Sandbox ... 139

Application Signing	139
Application Authentication	141
Application Integrity	143
Signature Enforcement in OS X	144
Signing and Verifying Applications	153
Sandbox	156
Sandbox Profiles	158
The Anatomy of a Profile	161
Sandbox Profiles in Action	166
The Seatbelt Framework	178
Summary	180

Chapter 7: Securing Web Browsers and E-mail ... 183

A Quick Note About Passwords	184
Securing Your Web Browser	185
Securing Safari	185
Securing Firefox	189
Securely Configuring Mail	196

Using SSL	196
Securing Entourage	199
Fighting Spam	202
Anatomy of Spam	202
Desktop Solutions for Securing E-mail	207
Using PGP to Encrypt Mail Messages	207
GPG Tools	207
Using Mail Server-Based Solutions for Spam and Viruses	207
Kerio	208
Mac OS X Server's Antispam Tools	210
CommuniGate Pro	211
Outsourcing Your Spam and Virus Filtering	212
Summary	213

Chapter 8: Malware Security: Combating Viruses, Worms, and Root Kits 213

Classifying Threats	213
The Real Threat of Malware on the Mac	216
Script Malware Attacks	217
Socially Engineered Malware	218
Using Antivirus Software	218
Built Into Mac OS X	219
Antivirus Software Woes	220
McAfee VirusScan	220
Norton AntiVirus	220
ClamXav	221
Sophos Anti-Virus	226
Best Practices for Combating Malware	227
Other Forms of Malware	228
Adware	228
Spyware	228
Root Kits	230
Summary	232

Chapter 9: Encrypting Files and Volumes 233

Using the Keychain to Secure Sensitive Data	234
The Login Keychain	234
Creating Secure Notes and Passwords	237
Managing Multiple Keychains	240
Using Disk Images as Encrypted Data Stores	243
Creating Encrypted Disk Images	245
Interfacing with Disk Images from the Command Line	251
Encrypting User Data Using FileVault	257
Enabling FileVault for a User	260
The FileVault Master Password	263
Limitations of Sparse Images and Reclaiming Space	264
Full Disk Encryption	266
Check Point	267
PGP Encryption	269

TrueCrypt 270
WinMagic SecureDoc...271
Summary 272

Part III: Network Traffic 275

Chapter 10: Securing Network Traffic 277

Understanding TCP/IP 277
Types of Networks 280
    Peer-to-Peer 280
    Considerations when Configuring Peer-to-Peer Networks 281
    Client-Server Networks..282
Understanding Routing 283
    Packets 283
Port Management 285
DMZ and Subnets..286
Spoofing...287
Stateful Packet Inspection 287
Data Packet Encryption..288
Understanding Switches and Hubs 288
    Managed Switches 289
Restricting Network Services 291
Security Through 802.1x..292
Proxy Servers..293
    Squid...295
Summary 297

Chapter 11: Setting Up the Mac OS X Firewall 299

Introducing Network Services...300
Controlling Services 301
Configuring the Firewall..304
    Working with the Firewall in Leopard and Snow Leopard 304
Setting Advanced Features 307
    Blocking Incoming Connections...307
    Allowing Signed Software to Receive Incoming Connections.................................308
    Going Stealthy..309
Testing the Firewall 310
Configuring the Application Layer Firewall from the Command Line 312
Using Mac OS X to Protect Other Computers 313
    Enabling Internet Sharing 313
Working from the Command Line 315
    Getting More Granular Firewall Control 315
    Using ipfw 317
    Using Dummynet..321
Summary 324

Chapter 12: Securing a Wireless Network.. 325

Wireless Network Essentials 325
Introducing the Apple AirPort...327
Configuring Older AirPorts 328
    AirPort Utility 330

Contents

Configuring the Current AirPorts 330
Limiting the DHCP Scope 333
Hardware Filtering 334
AirPort Logging 336
Hiding a Wireless Network 337
Base Station Features in the AirPort Utility 338
The AirPort Express 339
Wireless Security on Client Computers 339
Securing Computer-to-Computer Networks 340
Wireless Topologies 341
Wireless Hacking Tools 342
KisMAC 342
Detecting Rogue Access Points 343
iStumbler and Mac Stumbler 344
MacStumbler 346
Ettercap 347
EtherPeek 347
Cracking WEP Keys 347
Cracking WPA-PSK 348
General Safeguards Against Cracking Wireless Networks 349
Summary 350

Part IV: Sharing 351

Chapter 13: File Services 353

The Risks in File Sharing 353
Peer-to-Peer vs. Client-Server Environments 354
File Security Fundamentals 354
LKDC 355
Using POSIX Permissions 355
Getting More out of Permissions with Access Control Lists 356
Sharing Protocols: Which One Is for You? 357
Apple Filing Protocol 357
Setting Sharing Options 359
Samba 359
Using Apple AirPort to Share Files 362
Third-Party Problem Solver: DAVE 366
FTP 372
Permission Models 374
Summary 375

Chapter 14: Web Site Security 377

Securing Your Web Server 377
Introducing the httpd Daemon 378
Removing the Default Files 379
Changing the Location of Logs 379
Restricting Apache Access 380
Run on a Nonstandard Port 380
Use a Proxy Server 381
Disable CGI 381

Disable Unnecessary Services in Apache 382
PHP and Security 382
    Securing PHP 383
    Tightening PHP with Input Validation 383
Taming Scripts 384
    Securing Your Perl Scripts 384
Securing robots.txt 386
    Blocking Hosts Based on robots.txt 387
Protecting Directories 388
    Customizing Error Codes 389
    Using .htaccess to Control Access to a Directory 389
Tightening Security with TLS 391
Implementing Digital Certificates 392
Protecting the Privacy of Your Information 392
    Protecting from Google? 394
    Enumerating a Web Server 395
Securing Files on Your Web Server 396
    Disabling Directory Listings 396
    Uploading Files Securely 397
Code Injection Attacks 398
    SQL Injection 398
    Cross Site Scripting 398
    Protecting from Code Injection Attacks 399
Summary 399

Chapter 15: Remote Connectivity 401

Remote Management Applications 402
    Apple Remote Desktop 402
    Screen Sharing 402
    Implementing Back to My Mac 404
    Configuring Remote Management 405
Using Timbuktu Pro 408
    Installing Timbuktu Pro 408
    Adding New Users 409
    Testing the New Account 410
Using Secure Shell 412
    Enabling SSH 412
    Further Securing SSH 413
Using a VPN 414
    Connecting to Your Office VPN 414
    Setting Up L2TP 415
    Setting Up PPTP 416
    Connecting to a Cisco VPN 417
    PPP + SSH = VPN 419
Summary 422

Chapter 16: Server Security 423

Limiting Access to Services 423
The Root User 425

Foundations of a Directory Service..425
    Defining LDAP 425
    Kerberos 426
Configuring and Managing Open Directory 428
    Securing LDAP: Enabling SSL 431
    Securing Open Directory Accounts by Enabling Password Policies.........................432
    Securing Open Directory Using Binding Policies 435
    Securing Authentication with PasswordServer 437
    Securing LDAP by Preventing Anonymous Binding..439
    Securely Binding Clients to Open Directory 441
    Further Securing LDAP: Implementing Custom LDAP ACLs 444
    Creating Open Directory Users and Groups 444
    Securing Kerberos from the Command Line 448
    Managed Preferences..449
    Securing Managed Preferences...451
    Providing Directory Services for Windows Clients 453
    Active Directory Integration 454
Web Server Security in Mac OS X Server..459
    Using Realms 459
    SSL Certs on Web Servers 461
File Sharing Security in OS X Server 463
    A Word About File Size..465
    Securing NFS 465
    AFP..466
    SMB 470
    FTP 471
Wireless Security on OS X Server Using RADIUS 471
DNS Best Practices 473
SSL..474
    Reimporting Certificates 475
SSH 475
Server Admin from the Command Line 477
iChat Server 477
Securing the Mail Server 478
    Limiting the Protocols on Your Server 479
Proxying Services 480
Summary 481

Part V: Securing the Workplace..483

Chapter 17: Network Scanning, Intrusion Detection, and Intrusion Prevention Tools..485

Scanning Techniques...485
    Fingerprinting 486
    Enumeration...488
    Vulnerability and Port Scanning...489
Intrusion Detection and Prevention..492
    Host Intrusion Detection System 493
    Network Intrusion Detection 494

Security Auditing on the Mac 497
    Nessus 497
    Metasploit 501
    SAINT 503
Summary 504

Chapter 18: Backup and Fault Tolerance 505

Time Machine 506
    Restoring Files from Time Machine 510
    Using a Network Volume for Time Machine 511
SuperDuper 512
Backing Up to MobileMe 513
Retrospect 517
    Checking Your Retrospect Backups 528
Using Tape Libraries 530
Backup vs. Fault Tolerance 531
    Fault-Tolerant Scenarios 531
    Round-Robin DNS 532
    Load-Balancing Devices 533
    Cold Sites 533
    Hot Sites 534
Backing up Services 534
Summary 535

Chapter 19: Forensics 537

Incident Response 538
MacForensicsLab 539
    Installing MacForensicsLab 539
    Using MacForensicsLab 544
    Image Acquisition 546
    Analysis 548
    Salvage 551
    Performing an Audit 554
    Reviewing the Case 554
    Reporting 555
Other GUI Tools for Forensic Analysis 556
Forensically Acquiring Disk Images 557
Tools for Safari 557
Command-Line Tools for Forensic Analysis 558
Summary 558

Appendix A: Xsan Security 559

Metadata 560
Fibre Channel 561
Affinities 561
Permissions 561
Quotas 562
Other SAN Solutions 562

Appendix B: InfoSec Acceptable Use Policy 563

1.0 Overview 563

2.0 Purpose 563
3.0 Scope 564
4.0 Policy 564
    4.1 General Use and Ownership 564
    4.2 Security and Proprietary Information 565
    4.3 Unacceptable Use 566
    4.4 Blogging 568
5.0 Enforcement 569
6.0 Definitions 569
    Term Definition 569
7.0 Revision History 569

Appendix C: CDSA 571
Appendix D: Introduction to Cryptography 573
Index 577

About the Authors

Charles S. Edge, Jr is the Director of Technology at 318, the nation's largest Mac consultancy. At 318, Charles leads a team of the finest gunslingers to have been assembled for the Mac platform, working on network architecture, security, storage, and deployment for various vertical and horizontal markets. Charles maintains the 318 blog @ www.318.com/techjournal, as well as a personal site at www.krypted.com. He is the author of a number of titles on Mac OS X Server and systems administration topics. He has spoken at conferences around the world, including DefCon, Black Hat, LinuxWorld, MacWorld, MacSysAdmin, and the Apple WorldWide Developers' Conference. Charles is the developer of the SANS course on Mac OS X Security and the author of its best practices guide to securing Mac OS X. He is also the author of a number of whitepapers, including a guide on mass deploying virtualization on the Mac platform for VMware. After 10 years in Los Angeles, Charles has hung up his surfboard and fled to Minneapolis, Minnesota, with his wife, Lisa, and sweet little bucket of a daughter, Emerald.

Gene Sullivan is a geek, writer, musician, and father. He's been an Apple user since first laying hands on an Apple IIC in 1985, and he's been managing Macs professionally since 1998. Gene is currently a consultant at 318, where he deploys, administers, and supports Mac OS X, Windows, and Linux for a wide variety of clients. He contributed to *Digital Video Hacks*, available from O'Reilly and Associates. You can reach him at gene@curiousgene.com

William Barker is a freelance writer and project manager. Having worked with some of the leaders in the technology and music industries, including Apple, Microsoft, and Sony, he's been able to somehow carve out a career in both of his passions: music and technology. He also occasionally moonlights as an actor in local community theater. He lives in Southern California.

Beau Hunter has been working professionally with Apple technologies since 1999, and has been supporting businesses running the Mac OS for over 10 years. Throughout this time, he has developed a strong skill set supporting and securing Apple OS X Server in multiple capacities: clustered web and database solutions, cross-platform integration, high-performance SANs, high-capacity backup systems, automation, and cross-platform mass deployment and integration. Beau has spoken at numerous events, including Macworld 2009 and 2010. In his free time he can be found writing Python and PHP, playing PC games, and rooting for the Seahawks with his wife, Monica, in their home city of Seattle Washington.

About the Technical Reviewer

Graham Lee is an independent developer who specializes in security on the Mac, iPad, and iPhone. He has written anti-virus and disk-encryption software for the Mac, and has consulted or contracted on numerous Cocoa and Cocoa Touch applications. Graham also speaks and writes on Apple-related security issues, and maintains a blog at http://blog.securemacprogramming.com. He lives in Oxford, UK, and in his spare time wonders where his spare time went.

Acknowledgments

Charles Edge

I'd like to first and foremost thank the Mac OS X community. This includes everyone from the people that design the black box to the people that dissect it and the people that help others learn how to dissect it. We truly stand on the shoulders of giants. Of those at Apple that need to be thanked specifically: Schoun Regan, Joel Rennich, Greg Smith, JD Mankovsky, Drew Tucker, Stale Bjorndal, Cawan Starks, Eric Senf, Jennifer Jones, and everyone on the Mac OS X Server, Xsan, and Final Cut Server development team. And of course the one and only Josh "old school game console ninja" Wisenbaker! Outside of Apple, thanks to Arek Dreyer and the other Peachpit authors for paving the way to build another series of Mac systems administration books by producing such quality. And a special thanks to the late Michael Bartosh for being such an inspiration to us all to strive to understand what is going on under the hood.

The crew at 318 also deserves a lot of credit. It's their hard work that let to having the time to complete yet another book! Special thanks to JJ and to KK for holding everything together in such wild times!

And finally, a special thanks to Apress for letting us continue to write books for them. They fine-tune the dribble I provide into a well-oiled machine of mature prose. This especially includes Clay Andres for getting everything in motion; not only for this book, but also for the entire series and, of course, to Kelly Moritz for pulling it all together in the end with her amazing cracks of the whhhip (yes, that's a *Family Guy* reference). And I'll just include my co-authors in the Apress family: William, Beau, and Gene, thanks for the countless hours to make the deadlines and looking forward to the next round!

Gene Sullivan

I'd like to thank Jeff Conn and Josh Paul, along with Charles, Beau, William, and everybody at 318.

Introduction

A common misconception in the Mac community is that the Mac is more secure than any other operating system on the market. Although this might be true in most side-by-side analyses of security features right out of the box, what this isn't taking into account is that security tends to get overlooked once the machine starts to be configured for its true purposes. For example, when sharing is enabled or remote control applications are installed, a variety of security threats are often established—no matter what the platform is.

In the security sector, the *principle of least privilege* is a philosophy that security professionals abide by when determining security policies. This principle states that if you want to be secure, you need to give every component of your network the absolute minimum permissions required to do its job. But what are those permissions? What are the factors that need to be determined when making that decision? No two networks are the same; therefore, it's certainly not a decision that can be made for you. It's something you will need to decide for yourself based on what kinds of policies are implemented to deal with information technology security.

Security Beginnings: Policies

Security in a larger organization starts with a security policy. When looking to develop security policies, it is important that the higher-level decision makers in the organization work hand in hand with the IT team to develop their policies and security policy frameworks. A security policy, at a minimum, should define the tools used on a network for security, the appropriate behavior of employees and network users, the procedures for dealing with incidents, and the trust levels within the network.

The reason policies become such an integral part of establishing security in a larger environment is that you must be secure but also be practical about how you approach security in an organization. Security can be an impediment to productivity, both for support and for nonsupport personnel. People may have different views about levels of security and how to enforce them. A comprehensive security policy makes sure everyone is on the same page and that the cost vs. protection paradigm that IT departments follow are in line with the business logic of the organization.

On small networks, such as your network at home, you may have a loose security policy that states you will occasionally run security updates and follow a few of the safeguards outlined in this book. The smaller a network environment, the less likely security is going to be taken seriously. However, for larger environments with much more valuable data to protect, the concern for security should not be so flippant. For example, the Health Insurance Portability and Accountability Act (HIPAA) authorizes criminal penalties of up to $250,000 and/or 10 years imprisonment per violation of security standards for patient health information. The Gramm-Leach-Bliley Act establishes financial institution standards for safeguarding customer information and imposes penalties of up to $100,000 per violation.

Everyone in an organization should be concerned about security policies, because everyone is affected to some extent. Users are often affected the most, because policies often consist of a set of rules that regulate their behavior, sometimes making it more difficult for them to accomplish their tasks throughout their day. The IT staff should also be consulted and brought into the decision-making process since they will be required to implement and comply with these policies, while making sure that the policies are realistic given the budget available. In addition, you must notify people in advance of the development of the policy. You should contact members of the IT, management, and legal departments as well as a random sampling of users in your environment. The size of your policy development will be determined by the scope of the policy and the size of your organization. Larger, more comprehensive policies may require many people to be involved in the policy development. Smaller policies may require participation by only one or two people within the organization.

As an example, a restrictive policy that requires all wireless users to use a RADIUS server would incur IT costs not only from the initial install but also with the installs and configurations necessary to set up the RADIUS clients on each of the workstations. A more secure RADIUS server would also cause additional labor over other less secure protocols such as WEP. You also need to consider IT budgeting and staffing downtime.

When developing your actual policy, keep the scope limited to what is technically enforceable and easy to understand, while protecting the productivity of your users. Policies should also contain the reasons a policy is needed and cover the contacts and responsibilities of each user. When writing your policy, discuss how policy violations will be handled and why each item in the policy is required. Allow for changes in the policies as things evolve in the organization.

Keep the culture of your organization in mind when writing your security policy. Overly restrictive policies may cause users to be more likely to ignore them. Staff and management alike must commit to the policies. You can often find examples of acceptable use policies in prepackaged policies on the Internet and then customize them to fulfill your organization's needs.

A Word About Network Images

Whether you are a home user or a corporate network administrator, the overall security policy of your network will definitely be broken down into how your computers will be set up on the network. For smaller environments, this means setting up your pilot system exactly the way you want it and then making an image of the setup. If anything were to happen to a machine on your network (intrusion or virus activity, for example), you wouldn't need to redo everything from scratch. If you're in a larger, more corporate environment, then you'll create an image and deploy it to hundreds or thousands of systems using DeployStudio, NetInstall, Casper Suite, LanDESK, or a variety of other tools with which you may or may not have experience.

Risk Management

By the end of this book, we hope you will realize that if a computer is plugged into a network, it cannot be absolutely guaranteed secure. In a networked world, it is not likely that you will be able to remove all of the possible threats from any networked computing environment. To compile an appropriate risk strategy, you must first understand the risks applicable in your specific environment. Risk management involves making decisions about whether assessed risks are sufficient enough to present a concern and the appropriate means for controlling a significant risk to your environment. From there, it is important to evaluate and select alternative responses to these risks. The selection process requires you to consider the severity of the threat.

For example, a home user would likely not be concerned with security threats and bugs available for the Open Directory services of Mac OS X Server. However, in larger environments running Open Directory, it would be important to consider these risks.

Risk management not only involves external security threats but also includes fault tolerance and backup. Accidentally deleting files from systems is a common and real threat to a networked environment. For larger environments with a multitude of systems requiring risk management, a risk management framework may be needed. The risk management framework is a description of streams of accountability and reporting that will support the risk management process for the overall environment, extending beyond information technology assets and into other areas of the organization. If you are managing various systems for a large organization, it is likely there is a risk management framework and that the architecture and computer policies you implement are in accordance with the framework.

All too often, when looking at examples of risk management policies that have been implemented in enterprise environments, many Mac administrators will cite specific items in the policies as "not pertaining" to their environment. This is typically not the case, because best practices are best practices. There is a reason that organizations practice good security, and as the popularity of Mac based network environments grows, it is important that administrators learn from others who have managed these enterprise-class environments.

As mentioned earlier, managing IT risk is a key component of governmental regulations. Organizations that fall under the requirements of Sarbanes-Oxley, HIPPA, or the Gramm-Leach-Bliley Act need to remain in compliance or risk large fines and/or imprisonment. Auditing for compliance should be performed on a regular basis, with compliance documentation ready and available to auditors.

Defining what is an acceptable risk is not something that we, the authors of this book, can decide. Many factors determine what is an acceptable risk. It is really up to you, the network administrator, to be informed about what those risks are so that you can make an informed decision. We will discuss options and settings for building out secure systems and a secure networked environment for your system. However, many of the settings we encourage you to use might impact your network or system in ways that are not acceptable to your workflow. When this happens, a choice must be made between usability and performance. Stay as close to the principle of least privilege as much as possible, keeping in mind that you still need to be able to do your job.

How This Book Is Organized

The first goal of this book is to help you build a secure image, be it at home or in the office, and then secure the environment in which the image will be used. This will involve the various options with various security ramifications, but it will also involve the network, the sharing aspects of the system, servers, and finally, if something drastic were to happen, the forensic analysis that would need to occur.

Another goal of this book is to provide you with the things to tell users not to do. Adding items to enforce your policy and security measures will help you make your network, Mac, or server like a castle, with various levels of security, developed in a thoughtful manner. To help with this tiered approach, we've broken the book down into five parts.

Part 1: The Big Picture

First, an introduction to the world of security on the Mac comprises Part 1:

> **Chapter 1, "Security Quick-Start"**: If you have time to read only one chapter, this is the chapter for you. In this chapter, we cover using the GUI tools provided by Apple to provide a more secure environment and the best practices for deploying them. We give recommendations and explain how to use these various features and when they should be used. We also outline the risks and strategies in many of their deployments.
>
> **Chapter 2, "Services, Daemons and Processes"**: In this chapter, we look at the processes that run on your computer. We look at the ownership, what starts processes and what stops them. This is one of the most integral aspects of securing a system and so we decided to look at it early in the book.
>
> **Chapter 3, "Securing User Accounts"**: Mac OS X is a multiuser operating system. One of the most important security measures is to understand the accounts on your system and when

you are escalating privileges for accounts. This chapter explains how to properly secure these users and groups.

Chapter 4, "Permissions: POSIX and ACLs": Once you have secured your user accounts, you'll want to secure what resources each has access to. This starts with the files and folders that they can access, which we cover in Chapter 4.

Chapter 5, "Reviewing Logs and Monitoring": What good are logs if they aren't reviewed? In this chapter, we discuss what logs should be reviewed and what is stored in each file. We then move on to various monitoring techniques and applications and the most secure ways to deploy them in typical environments.

Part 2: Securing the Ecosystem

Part 2 gets down to some of the essential elements of security on a Mac:

Chapter 6, "Application Security: Signing and Sandbox": Apple has built a number of sophisticated security controls into Mac OS X. These give you the ability to control exactly which resources applications have access to. By controlling resource accessibility you can limit the damage that can be done by a rogue application or process.

Chapter 7, "The Internet: Web Browsers and E-mail": Safari, Firefox, Internet Explorer, Mail.app, and Entourage—with all these programs to manage, how do you lock them all down appropriately? In this chapter, we discuss cookies, Internet history, and browser preferences and when you should customize these settings. We also give some tips for third-party solutions for protecting your privacy. In addition, this chapter provides readers with best security practices for the mail clients that they likely spend much of their time using.

Chapter 8, "Malware Protection": Viruses, spyware, and root kits are at the top of the list of security concerns for Windows users. However, Mac users are not immune. In this chapter, we go into the various methods that can be used to protect Mac systems against these and other forms of malware.

Chapter 9, "Encrypting Files and Volumes": Permissions can do a good job in protecting access to files unless you have a system that has dubious physical security. An additional layer of security that you can take on top of permissions is to encrypt data. In Chapter 9 we look at encrypting the files, folders and even the boot volume of Mac OS X.

Part 3: Securing the Network

Part 3 describes how you secure a Mac network:

Chapter 10, "Securing Network Traffic": As useful as securing the operating system is, securing the network backbone is a large component of the overall security picture. In this chapter, we explore some of the techniques and concepts behind securing the network infrastructure. This includes the common switches, hubs, and firewalls used in Mac environments and the features you may have noticed but never thought to tinker with. We also cover how to stop some of the annoying issues that pop up on networks because of unauthorized (and often accidental) user behavior.

Chapter 11, "Firewalls: IPFW and ALF": The firewall option in Mac OS X is just a collection of check boxes. Or is it? We discuss using and securing the Mac OS X software firewall, and we go into further detail on configuring this option from the command line. We also discuss some of the other commands that, rather than block traffic, allow an administrator to actually shape the traffic, implementing rules for how traffic is handled, and mitigate the effects that DoS attacks can have on the operating system.

Chapter 12, "Wireless Network Security": Wireless networking is perhaps one of the most insecure things that users tend to implement themselves. In this chapter, we cover securing wireless networks, and then, to emphasize how critical wireless security is (and how easy it is to subvert it if done improperly), we move on to some of the methods used to exploit wireless networks.

Part 4: Securely Sharing Resources

One of the biggest threats to your system is sharing resources. But it doesn't have to be. Part 4 covers the most common resources shared out from a Mac OS X computer, including the following:

Chapter 13, "File Services: AFP, SMB, FTP and NFS": What is a permission model, and why do you need to know what it is, when all you want to do is allow people access to some of the files on my computer? Knowing the strategies involved in assigning file permissions is one of the most intrinsic security aspects of a shared storage environment. It is also important to understand the specific security risks and how to mitigate them for each protocol used, including AFP, FTP, NFS, and SMB, which are all covered in this chapter.

Chapter 14, "Web Security: Apache": Apache is quite possibly the most common web server running on the *nix platform. Entire books are dedicated to explaining how to lock down this critical service. In this chapter, we focus on the most important ways to lock down the service and some Apple-centric items of Apache not usually found in discussions about Apache on the *nix platform. We also provide you with other resources to look to if you require further security for your web server.

Chapter 15, "Securely Controlling a Mac": One of the most dangerous aspects of administration is the exposure of the very tools you use to access systems remotely. Many of these programs do not always need to be running and can be further secured from their default settings. In this chapter, we cover many of the methods for protecting these services and some of the ways that vendors should change their default settings to make them more secure. We also cover some of the ways you can secure these tools, and we help administrators make choices about how to best implement remote administration utilities to counteract these shortcomings.

Chapter 16, "Basic Mac OS X Server Security": Mac OS X Server is very much like Mac OS X Client, without many of the bells and whistles and with a more optimized system for sharing resources. This is true with many server-based operating systems. Because a Mac OS X server fills a different role in a networked environment, it should be treated differently from Mac OS X Client. For this reason, we cover many of the security options that are available as well as those that are crucial to securing Mac OS X Server. We also cover many of the security options from Mac OS X that should specifically not be used in Mac OS X Server.

Included with server security is directory services, which are critical to expanding technology infrastructures. By interconnecting all the hosts of a network, you are able to better control the settings and accounts on systems. In this chapter, we also focus on the ways to securely deploy Mac OS X clients to various directory services and point out the items to ask for (if you are in a larger network infrastructure) or to set up in order to help make the directory service environment as secure as possible.

Part 5: Securing the Workplace

How secure is your work environment's network? This part explores security as it pertains to environments with multiple Mac computers connected on a network:

Chapter 17, "Network Scanning, Intrusion Detection, and Intrusion Prevention Tools": Host-based intrusion detection systems (IDS) are quickly becoming a standard for offering signature-based and anomaly-based detection of attacks. Some of these tools allow for augmenting the operating system settings to further secure the hosts on which they run. In this chapter, we provide a best practices discussion for deploying and using IDSs. We also cover the various attacks that have been developed over the past few years against IDS systems and explore add-ons for IDSs that provide rich aggregated data about the systems.

Chapter 18, "Backup and Fault Tolerance": If you don't have a backup plan now, then you will after you read this chapter. Backups are the last line of defense in a security environment. Backups are critical and should be provided in tiers. In this chapter, we describe some of the strategies for going about implementing a backup plan, from choosing the right software package to properly implementing it. We also cover some of the more common techniques for providing fault-tolerant services and the security risks that can be introduced by doing so.

Chapter 19, "Forensics": What do you do when your systems are compromised? What happens after the attack? In this chapter, we cover the basics of computer forensics and how a user can be their own digital sleuth. The goal is not to have you testifying in court on large-scale network attacks but instead to help first responders get comfortable with safely imaging Mac systems for investigations without contaminating evidence.

Appendixes

The following are the appendixes:

Appendix A, "Xsan Security": Here we provide tips on securing your Xsan.

Appendix B, "Acceptable Use Policy": This appendix contains an acceptable use policy from the SANS Institute that has been reprinted here with their consent.

Appendix C, "Secure Development": Here we give a brief rundown of Apple's development architecture.

Appendix D, "Introduction to Cryptography": In this appendix, we give a brief history of cryptography and look at some of the protocols used today and how they came about.

The Big Picture

Part I

Chapter 1

Security Quick-Start

Ready to start securing your Mac? Let's get right into it. Keep in mind that this chapter is meant to be a quick-and-dirty start to securing your Mac, for the "I don't have time to dive into the nitty-gritty, I need to get my Mac secured right away" readers. This chapter will give you just the basics to get your Mac secure quickly, and although it will leave you with a fairly secure system, it's not as comprehensive as the subsequent chapters, where we fine-tune your Mac's settings. For a more thorough understanding of Mac OS X security and the tools you can use to secure your Mac, we urge you to continue reading beyond the basics. From Chapter 2 on, you'll be introduced to all the other intricacies surrounding securing the Mac OS, diving deeper into the larger concepts of what is covered here in this quick-start.

Securing the Mac OS X Defaults

Because it is built on a Unix architecture, Mac OS X is a fairly secure and stable operating system right out of the box. Unix, at its core, is designed for high-end server architecture, web servers, and the like. Therefore, it was designed with security needs in mind. However, it is a commonly held misconception that the Mac cannot be made any more secure in the graphical user interface (GUI) of the operating system and can only be further secured through the Unix command line. On the contrary, there are a number of security settings to configure right in the System Preferences Security section. And there are many ways in which Mac OS X can and should be made more secure without dabbling with the command line.

In fact, right out of the box, there are many security holes within the Mac OS, and this is done intentionally. Why? In the world of operating systems, there is a balancing act between an operating system's ease of use and how secure it is. If you've tinkered with various operating systems, you've seen that the more cumbersome of the lot tend to be those that require a larger number of verification windows to make sure you really want to do what you're trying to do. This can prove rather frustrating when performing even the most basic of tasks. When the engineers at Apple redesigned their OS from the ground up, they considered security very heavily, but they also considered usability. In many cases, they decided to err more on the side of user-friendly interaction than obtrusive "allow" and "deny" windows, establishing a reputation as being one of the most user-friendly computer systems available. Many security features are disabled by default. This gives the user an easy-to-use machine while providing the ability for the user to implement more advanced security measures at their discretion, but it can also leave the machine open to exploits through these security holes.

Many of the features of Mac OS X are already fairly secure without changing anything, with little or no trade-off to functionality. In fact, certain features should not be changed unless changing them is absolutely required; for example, you should not enable the root account unless you need to run a process that requires it, as is the case with programs such as Carbon Copy Cloner. Root is a very powerful feature, and enabling it is a huge security risk if other security measures are not implemented to offset the activation, such as disabling root after using it. Many security breaches occur because users forget to put security settings back the way they were.

Now that we've got that out of the way, let's start discussing some of the places that we can improve the Mac's security right away.

Customizing System Preferences

Probably the best place to start is in your computer's System Preferences pane, located in your dock or under the Apple menu. Believe it or not, seemingly innocuous settings can actually be used to exploit some of the Mac's core features. By optimizing System Preferences, we can provide a higher level of protection than what is provided to us right out of the box. Let's start with the Accounts pane.

Accounts

One of the most important concepts to understand with OS X security is that a Mac running OS X is running a multiuser operating system. Every machine has at least one user account and one local administrative account (sometimes referred to as the *root* account), which, if enabled, has the ability to take ownership of all the files on the system as well as kill any processes on the computer without giving anyone a chance to save their work (i.e., via the kill command). As with any multiuser operating system, multiple accounts on the machine create multiple points of entry for potential breaches in security. Therefore, it is important to make sure each point of entry is properly secured.

The first way to do that is actually quite simple: by using strong passwords. Let's say that again one more time for emphasis: *use strong passwords*. Your system is only as secure as your passwords are strong. All too often, machines are compromised because the passwords on the machine are simply *password* or the user's first name or the name of their company. In Mac OS X, Apple created the Password Assistant to counteract this alarming trend by assisting the user with some fairly advanced password techniques (more on that in a bit).

If you haven't set your password yet, let's do that right now. To set a password, open the Accounts preference pane and click on your account name. (Make sure the padlock at the bottom of the pane is unlocked. If it isn't, you'll need an administrator account and password to unlock it.) To the right, you'll see a Change Password button (see Figure 1–1). The name is typically your full name or the full name you may have entered when the account was created. The short name is a shortened version of the name (the first letter of the first word and the full second word by default).

> **NOTE:** We'll discuss users and groups in detail in Chapter 3, but we will touch on a few of the important points in this section: disabling login items, setting account types, and basic user security.

Figure 1–1. *The Accounts preference pane*

To change the password, click the Change Password button on the Accounts preference pane. A smaller window will appear, requesting that you enter the old password once and the new password twice (see Figure 1–2).

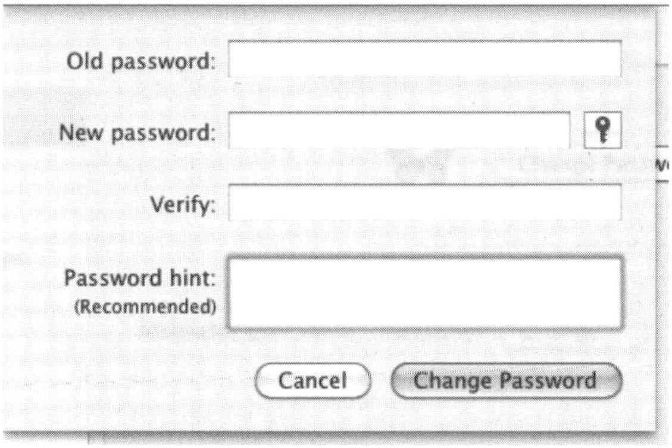

Figure 1–2. *Changing a password*

Clicking the key icon in the Change Password window opens the Password Assistant (see Figure 1–3). The Password Assistant is a random password generator that can be used to help create a more secure password. It's a great utility if you need suggestions for more complex passwords.

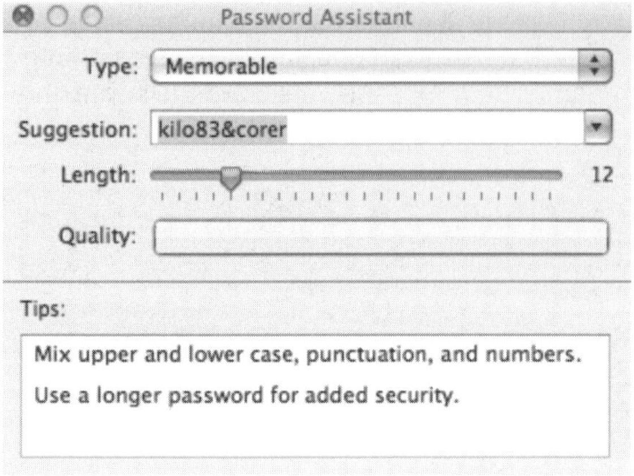

Figure 1–3. *Password Assistant*

If your password is still *password* or your name or the name of your company, it's time to change your password. Right now. We'll wait.

> **TIP:** When setting passwords, it's a good practice to make them as complex as possible by including numbers, letters, or special characters, such as !, @, #, or $. The more complex the character selection, the more secure the password can be. This is where the password assistant really comes in handy.

Login Options

You can further refine the security options in the Accounts pane by customizing the default settings of the Login Options button in the Accounts preference pane. To change the settings, click the Login Options button, which is located underneath the various accounts. (Again, you may need to click the padlock icon and access this screen as an administrator.) The first option to change here is the "Automatic login" option. If it's currently set to on, we'd recommend setting it to off. This gives you some control over who can access the computer when it's first turned on.

The Login Options screen is where you'd enable the root user (which we recommend here only to enable a certain security feature called "Display login window as," which we'll describe shortly). To enable the root user, click on the Join button next to Network Account Server. Click on the Open Directory Utility button (make sure to click the lock in the Directory Utility window) and then click on Edit in the top menu and click on Enable Root User. Now, you'll see the option to "Display login window as." This will give you the ability to have either a list of users or a blank field for the username and password at login. Quite often, users use their photo and real name when configuring their user account, which can be a security concern if an attacker were able to grab control of the machine (they'd know what they look like and what their real name is). We highly suggest that you enable root and configure the option to require a full name and password be typed in to log in (then disable root access once you're finished by following the procedure above, but instead look for the option to Disable Root User).

If the computer is in a workgroup setting and more than one user needs to access it, we'd also recommend turning off the "Show the Restart, Sleep, and Shut Down Buttons" option (see Figure 1–4), which is enabled by default. By disabling this option, these buttons will be hidden at the login window if the computer were to be logged off due to inactivity or by another user. Some systems provide services for other users and disabling that option helps to ensure that users have access to those services.

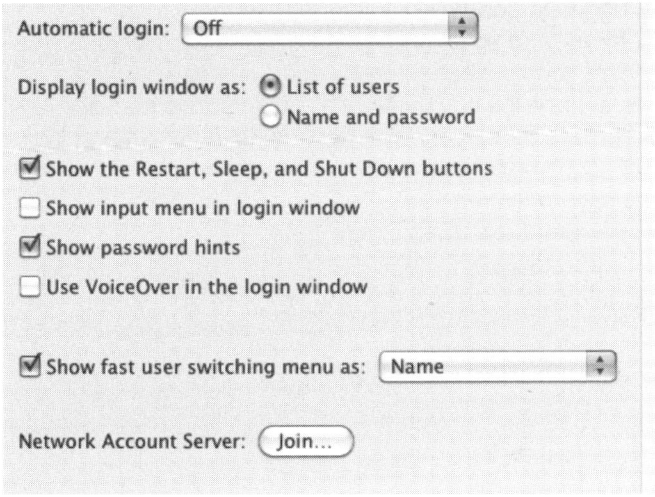

Figure 1–4. *Login options*

Passwords

The Show Password Hints option can be helpful if you need a hint to remind you of your password. But use caution here: this is a prime example of a security hole that can be easily exploited. While the hint box can help you to remember your password, it can also give someone trying to guess your password valuable insight into what the password may be. Put some thought into it and use an obscure connection to the password, something only you would know.

For example, "My dog's name," may seem harmless enough, but an acquaintance familiar with you and your pets would find it extremely easy to guess your password. Something like "bone sleuth with numbers" might jog your memory and be obvious to you, but not so obvious to others. Again, there is no substitute for the use of strong passwords. And whatever you do, do not enter the actual password into the password hint field (trust us, it happens all the time). One-word answers are guaranteed to be the first words that will be attempted when guessing your password.

> **NOTE:** You should also change your password routinely. But given the choice between a somewhat secure password and never rotating your password, we recommend a somewhat secure password. Not everyone can do both, but when you can, you should.

Administrators

The administrative user should be logged in only when administrative tasks (changing passwords, configuring network settings, and so on) are necessary, not for everyday work. This is a key component of Unix system administration and a good way to keep users from accidentally harming the system. Limit the administrative access to the machine only to the users who absolutely need it (this includes your own account if you use the machine regularly). To remove administrative access for a user, click on the Login Options button in the Accounts pane and click on the user for whom you'd like to change access. Uncheck the box "Allow user to administer this computer." (See Figure 1-5.)

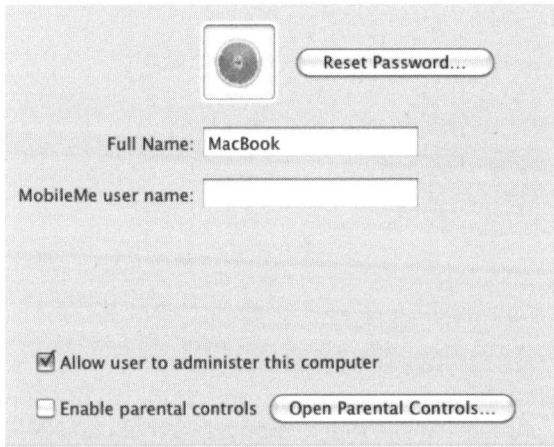

Figure 1-5. *User Settings*

Fast User Switching is a convenient way to allow a user to log in to multiple accounts concurrently. It poses a security risk, however, because it is possible to access or alter processes (and files not in the user's home directory) run by other users. Fast User Switching should only be used for specific reasons, such as testing different versions of software. As a security precaution, it should not be left running unattended.

Another way to safeguard against abuse is to limit administrative access to those who absolutely need it. Better yet, if Fast User Switching is a feature you are not likely to use, disable it by unchecking the "Show fast user switching" menu option (see Figure 1-4).

Security Preferences

Another place to change the default settings to make the machine more secure is in the Security preference panel (see Figure 1–6). Here, you will find options for enabling many of the miscellaneous security features that Apple has developed, as well as disabling some less secure features. This panel has become the default place to look for security features that don't fit into any specific section of System Preferences.

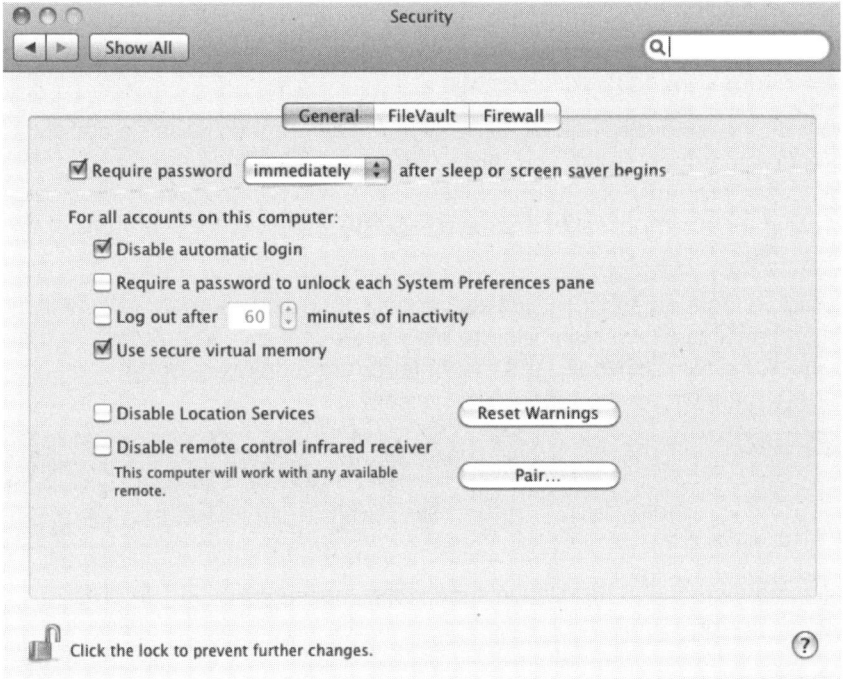

Figure 1–6. *Security preference pane, General tab*

General

Under the General tab, the first and most important of these options is the "Disable automatic login" option. Automatic login, which will remember your password and automatically log you in, is enabled by default. While this may sound incredibly convenient, it really should be disabled. Anyone with physical access to your computer would be able to restart the computer and, if the password is remembered, not be required to enter a password in order to get access to your files. With automatic login enabled, few security measures will stop someone from accessing your files if your Mac were to fall into the wrong hands.

Also under the General tab is the option to "Require a password [time interval] after sleep or screen saver begins." This will require that a password be used to wake the computer after it has gone to sleep or after the screen saver has been activated. This is absolutely critical and is not enabled by default. You can also specify a time when the password can be required after the machine has woken up. We cannot overstress the importance of enabling this option and specifying that the machine require a password immediately. Using the Exposé application to assign a key or hot corner (moving the cursor to a corner of the screen to activate the display) to put a system to sleep allows you to put your machine to sleep when you are finished using it. Later in this chapter we will review setting up automatic sleep, Exposé, and screen saver options.

The option "Log out after [number] minutes of inactivity" will automatically log users out whenever they are left inactive for a period of time. This setting is useful for machines that are used by multiple users in public locations, such as schools or libraries, where users can sometimes forget to log themselves out.

Selecting to "Require a password to unlock each System Preferences pane" is certainly a way to further secure your machine. If you rarely find yourself in the System Preferences pane, this is probably one to check. If you find yourself frequently changing system preferences, you should probably uncheck this one, as it might pose more of an inconvenience than a help.

You should also disable location services, unless you are absolutely sure that you will need them. Location services allows your Mac to be tracked in its time and place in the world. If someone were to gain access to the machine, through spyware or other means, they'd be able to determine where the machine physically is.

> **NOTE:** It's worth mentioning that half of the authors of this book use this feature and the other half do not. This is an example of usability vs. security.

Virtual memory is a means of using hard drive space as temporary memory in order to allow the computer to perform more work than the computer has available memory for. Virtual memory creates virtual chunks of memory in files called swap files on your hard drive. When this transitory memory is no longer needed, the swap files are deleted (which doesn't always happen immediately). Valuable information can be gleaned from a system by viewing the virtual memory swap files and reconstructing user operations. The option to secure virtual memory encrypts the swap files, preventing others from using them to gather private data. This is an important feature to enable.

Apple is now shipping infrared remote controls with many of its new computers, including MacBooks, MacBook Pros, and iMacs. As of this book's publication, there is little that can be done to damage systems with the infrared remote controls; however, theoretically it does allow someone to walk by the machine and launch menu options by use of a remote, which can be rather annoying. (If you do not have an infrared receiver, then you will not have this option in your Security Preferences.) Once the technology is more thoroughly utilized, there is also the theoretical chance that it could be used to exploit the system. This is a concern, thanks to the release of the wifi exploit at DefCon 2006 by David Maynor, which we cover further in Chapter 12.

Noticing this as a possibility, Apple introduced the ability to enable and disable the remote control infrared receiver in the Security preferences General tab. To turn off the ability to use an infrared receiver, click the Security pane in System Preferences, and select "Disable remote control infrared receiver." If infrared is enabled, then you can pair your remote with your machine, which keeps any old remote control from invoking applications on your computer. If at a later date you choose to unpair the remote (because you have a new remote or lost your old one), simply click on the Unpair button in this window (Pair turns into Unpair when the remote is paired with the machine). It's also worth noting that once a remote has been paired with a Mac, no other remote can operate in this function, which can help minimize the "drive-by" effect.

FileVault

Let's face it: we're human, and with the number of passwords we have to remember on a day-to-day basis, we can very easily forget them. But what happens when you forget your computer's password and you are the only one with an account on the machine? There is a system that websites use when users forget their passwords. It's called a *self-service password reset* and can be used to reset a password on its own (usually by answering a secret question on a web prompt and then receiving a new temporary password via e-mail). For a machine with many users, this would certainly be a handy feature to have, and would significantly reduce the volume of calls to the help desk. Luckily, Apple supplied Mac owners with this feature via the password reset utility included on the Mac OS X CD. By booting a computer to the CD (holding down the C key at boot), you can reset the password. A very handy feature indeed.

But what if your computer fell into the wrong hands, and you wanted to limit someone's ability to access your data if they were able to reset the password? Many of us travel with laptops that, if stolen and their passwords reset, would give users access to data they shouldn't be able to access. If a teacher's computer were rebooted by a student, they'd have access to tests, children would have access to their parents website viewing habits, employees would have access to confidential data about other employees, and so on—all if they were able to get physical access to our computers while we were away. The ability to easily reset a password introduces you to a feature of the Mac OS X security preferences that protects data, even if the password is reset using the CD: FileVault. FileVault removes the ability to access data in a user's folder, even if the password is reset, by encrypting the contents of a user's home folder into a secured disk image.

> **NOTE:** The FileVault feature is only as strong as the password protecting the home folder.

FileVault is not for everyone. It can certainly cause some inconveniences. By enabling FileVault, Windows file sharing and printer sharing are disabled, and when sharing files through Apple file sharing (AFP), users won't be able to access files you're sharing from your home folder until it is unlocked. By enabling FileVault, you will break these connections if another user is relying on them, and they will not be able to access resources in the future, so be cautious. It can also slow down the logout process, because it encrypts the data in the home folder during the logout process. FileVault can also have complications with certain applications, such as Adobe Illustrator. If you suspect that FileVault is causing an application to be problematic, then turn it off to see whether that fixes the issue. Even with these inconveniences, FileVault is an excellent way to secure the data on your machine.

To use FileVault, you will need to set it up in the Security preference pane. Open System Preferences, and click Security. Then click the FileVault tab to see a screen similar to Figure 1–7. Next, click Turn On FileVault. At this point, you will need to give the system a master password. The master password can unlock any FileVault on a computer, so it needs to be a strong one. To enable the master password, click the Set Master Password button and type the password you want to use, twice. Then, enter a hint to help you if you forget it at a later date (do not enter the password itself!), as shown in Figure 1–8.

Figure 1–7. *Setting up FileVault*

> **NOTE:** If you suspect that others will enable FileVault to encrypt their home folders, such as students, children, or employees, then setting up a master password before they can enable FileVault will help ensure that you will always be able to log into any FileVault disk images that are created by other users on the system.

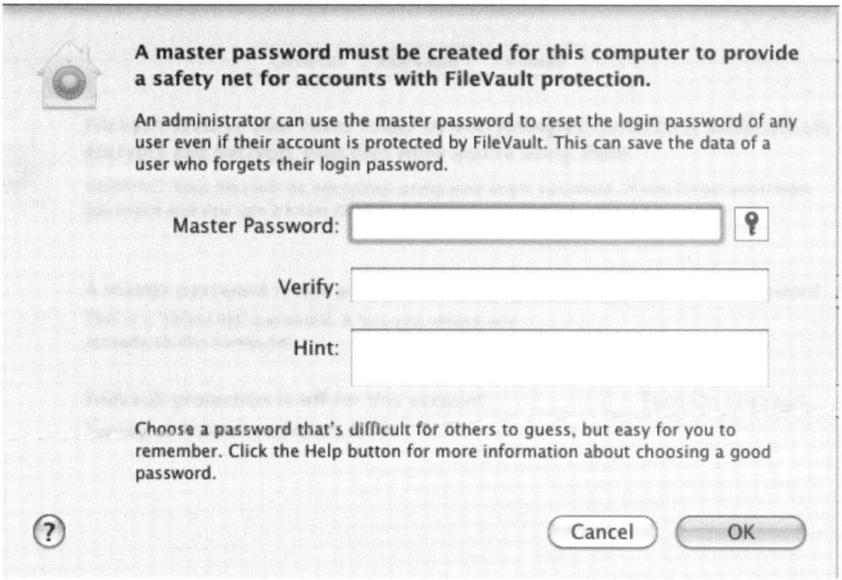

Figure 1-8. *Setting the master password*

At this point, you will be prompted for the password of the account you are currently logged into. You can stop the process of encrypting the user's home folder and just enable a master password by clicking Cancel, or you can encrypt the user's home folder by entering the password for the user and clicking OK. Keep in mind that the amount of time the encryption takes depends on how large the home folder is. It can take a while, so be patient. Interrupting the process can cause corruption or cause you to have to start the process again.

If you want to change FileVault settings later, you can do so by returning to the Security preference pane. You can change the master FileVault password or turn off FileVault completely (if the home folder is large, be prepared to wait a while for it to decrypt).

> **NOTE:** FileVault only encrypts the user's home directory. If you have sensitive information outside of the home directory and would like to encrypt the whole disk, there are third-party software packages made by PGP and Check Point that will encrypt the whole disk. Keep in mind that Full Disk Encryption (FDE) will occupy a significantly larger amount of hard disk space than the additional hard drive space required for encrypting with FileVault.

Firewall

The Mac OS X firewall (see Figure 1-9) is a software-based application firewall built into the operating system designed to block unwanted network traffic. It is disabled by default, and unless you know that enabling it causes incompatibility issues with other operating systems or file systems, you should enable it.

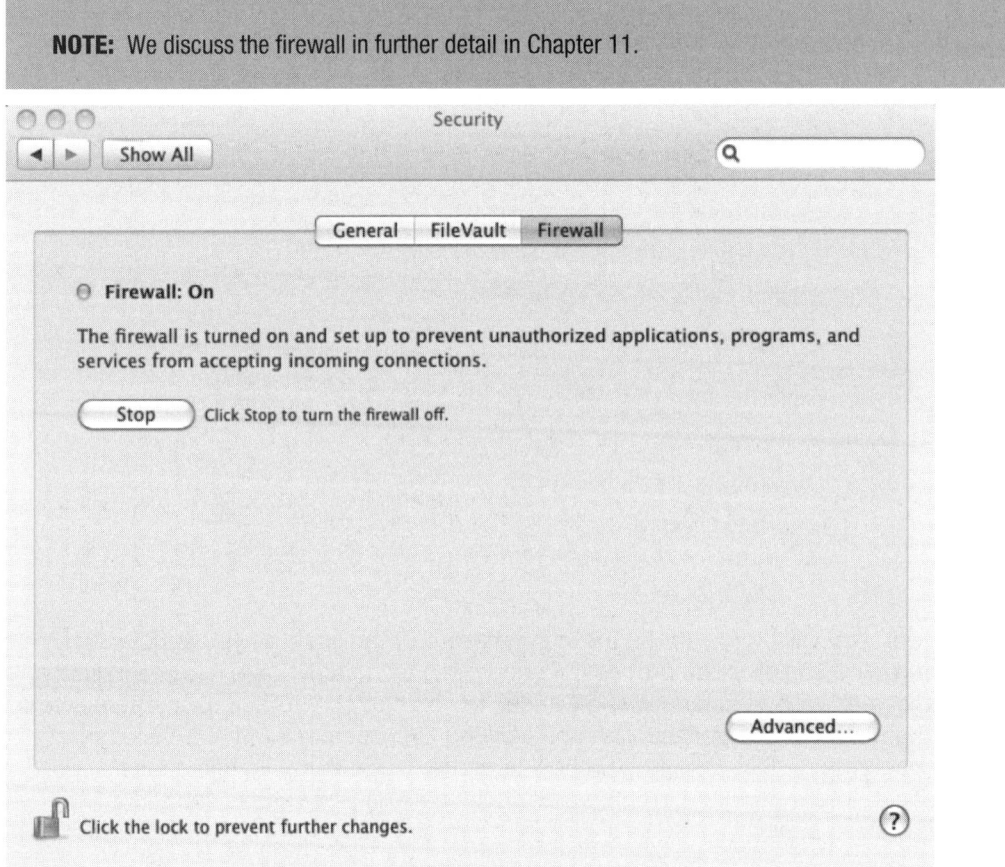

Figure 1-9. *Enabling the firewall in the Security preference pane*

Software Update

You can use the Software Update preference pane to keep your system updated with the latest Apple updates and security patches (see Figure 1-10).

Figure 1–10. *Software Update preference pane*

By default, the Software Update feature is turned on, which means that the system will automatically search for updates on a weekly basis. There are rare situations where you will not want to run certain software updates because they can cause conflicts with other installed software, as has been the case with Apple QuickTime updates and the Final Cut software on multiple occasions. But for most users, Software Update is one of the best ways to keep the latest and greatest security patches on the system, so it should be enabled.

Before running any software updates on mission-critical systems, you should test them in a lab environment. Typically, security updates will not cause issues with other applications, but it is still wise to test them in a lab environment before installing them on mission-critical machines.

> **NOTE:** To manually run the Software Update feature, open the Software Update preference pane and then click the Check Now button on the Update Software tab.

For many of you, using the Mac OS X Software Update preference pane will be adequate enough to keep your computer updated. However, if you have multiple systems on your network that need updating, you can quickly bottleneck your Internet pipe if multiple users are downloading updates all at the same time. You will most likely want to deploy a solution to help you conserve your bandwidth by managing these updates. The Software Update Server feature in Mac OS X Server is a great solution for controlling Apple software updates. However, this is not going to be the right solution for everyone because it requires an OS X Server to use.

> **NOTE:** There are ways to run the Software Update Server feature without having it run on a Mac, but it is best to run it on Mac OS X Server for simplicity's sake.

Security updates should always be taken seriously and be run when possible. One unique aspect of the Apple Software Update preference pane is that security updates are always deployed independently from other updates. Security updates rarely force a restart of the computer, and almost invariably contain a comprehensive description explaining what they fix and why they were written.

Occasionally a software update will fail. When this occurs, it is possible for the update to become stuck in the software update cache. To clear these out or retrieve them, browse to the /Library/Caches/com.apple.softwareupdate/swcdn.apple.com folder, and find the update on your system. The update will be located in the folder with the corresponding month and date. You can delete the update or run it again from this location. If the update is not located in these folders, then you should be able to run the Software Update feature and have it install again after a restart. You can also utilize this technique to save the update and burn it to optical media or a network drive for future installations.

Bluetooth Security

Bluetooth is a globally unlicensed short-range radio frequency for wireless networks, also known as IEEE 802.15.1. It is a wireless technology that provides a way to connect and exchange information between devices such as personal digital assistants (PDAs), mobile phones, laptops, PCs, printers, and digital cameras. The Apple Bluetooth keyboard and mouse are popular Bluetooth devices in Apple environments.

Bluetooth works by pairing two devices. While two devices are paired, they are able to freely exchange data. To pair a device with an Apple computer, you will need your computer to be *discoverable*, or awaiting a pairing. You are also required to accept the pairing in most cases. However, there are a variety of attacks that can force a pairing if your system is set to be discoverable without using a password. Once a connection is established, files can be shared over Bluetooth creating a security vulnerability that can be prevented by not having Bluetooth enabled.

Bluetooth is enabled and discoverable by default. If you don't have a need for Bluetooth on your system, you should disable it. To do this, open System Preferences and select the Bluetooth preference pane. Once you have this pane open, uncheck the On button to disable Bluetooth on your system (see Figure 1–11). If you want to use Bluetooth, but do not want your system to be discoverable, then you can disable discoverability by unchecking the Discoverable box on this pane. Keep in mind that by disabling discoverability, you'll be able to continue to use your Bluetooth devices; you just won't be able to add any new Bluetooth devices to the system.

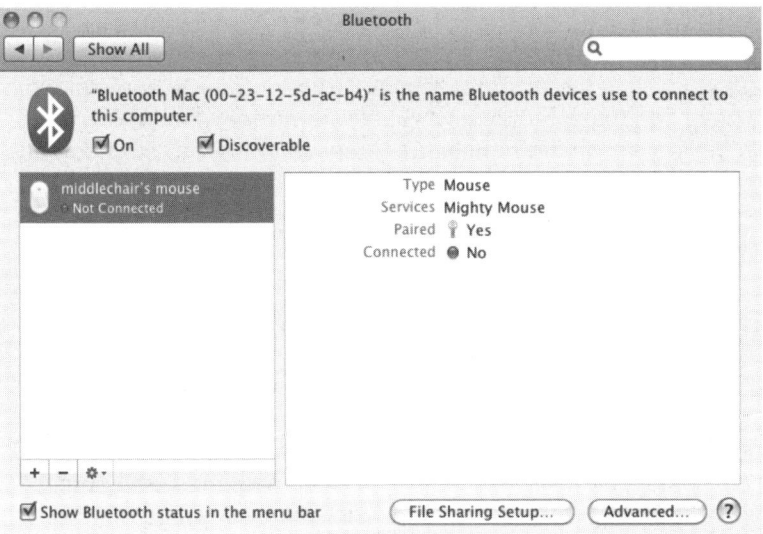

Figure 1-11. *Bluetooth preference pane*

The left side of the pane shows the various devices that have been paired with your Mac. Here, you will be able to configure each device with its appropriate settings.

The Advanced button allows you to change some settings associated with Bluetooth (see Figure 1-12)

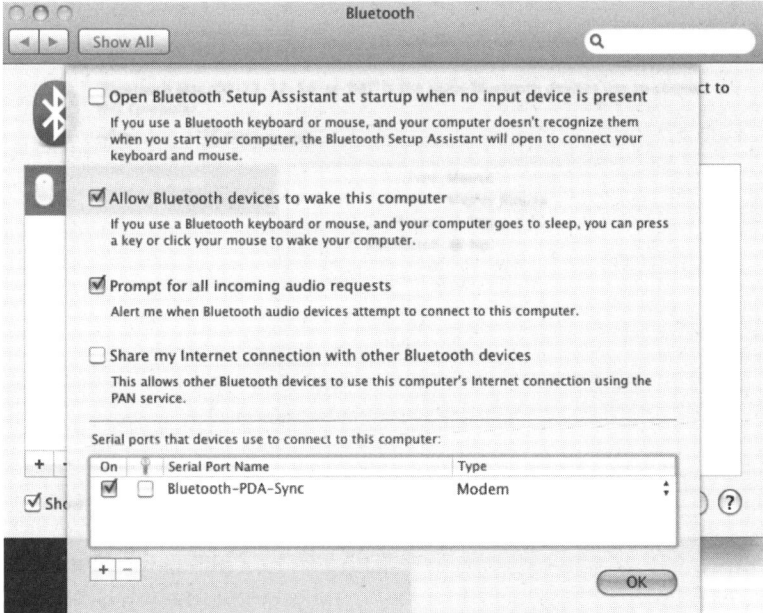

Figure 1-12. *Advanced Bluetooth Settings*

Bluetooth-PDA-Sync allows administrators to perform PDA synchronization using Bluetooth. Serial ports are often used to synchronize Palm Pilots, Blackberrys, and other devices. Bluetooth can operate as a wireless serial port. As a potential point of entry, if it's not used, it should be disabled. To disable it click the On button next to the Bluetooth-PDA-Sync feature. Check the box that asks to "Prompt for all incoming audio requests." Bluetooth hackers can masquerade as a Bluetooth device, and having your Mac prompt you when a device is trying to connect is a very smart way to stop potential Bluetooth hijackers. You should also uncheck the "Share my Internet connection with other Bluetooth devices" option whenever it's not being used to share the Internet as it presents a potential point of entry to your system.

Printer Security

The Print & Fax preference pane in System Preferences offers a few options for configuring access to shared printers and faxes. When sharing printers, only the printers that the user needs should be configured. Allowing a user to print to a printer that they shouldn't be using can cause confidentiality issues if the documents they are printing land in the wrong hands. To disable printers not in use, uncheck each printer on the Sharing tab (see Figure 1–13).

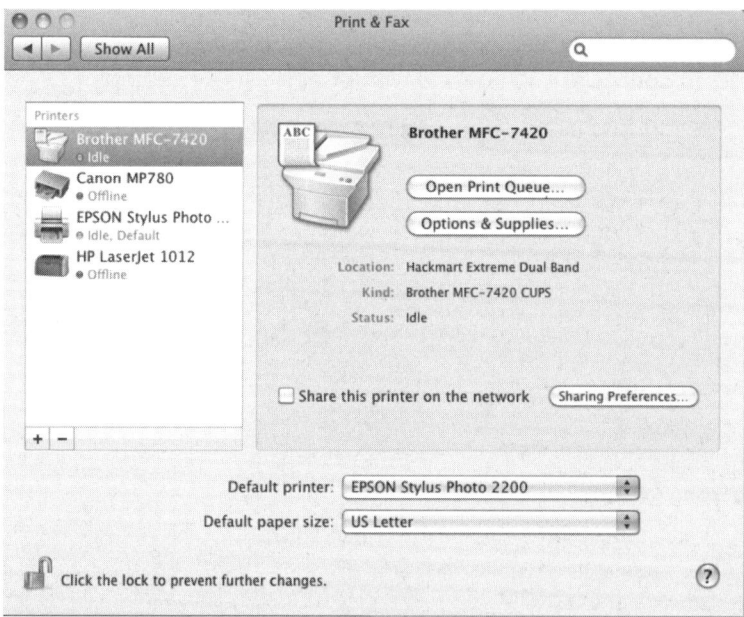

Figure 1–13. *Printer sharing*

If you do not need to allow access to printers installed on your computer, it is best to leave printer sharing disabled. If, however, you do need to give access to printers on the computer, but you want to limit this access, Printer Sharing can be configured via the Terminal or through the CUPS web interface. CUPS, or Common Unix Printing System, is the Unix printing system at the core of the Mac's printing services. CUPS uses HTTP as its transport protocol to provide printing services to users and has a built-in web interface to allow configuration of the service. To access the web interface, type the address **http://127.0.0.1:631** into your web browser (see Figure 1–14).

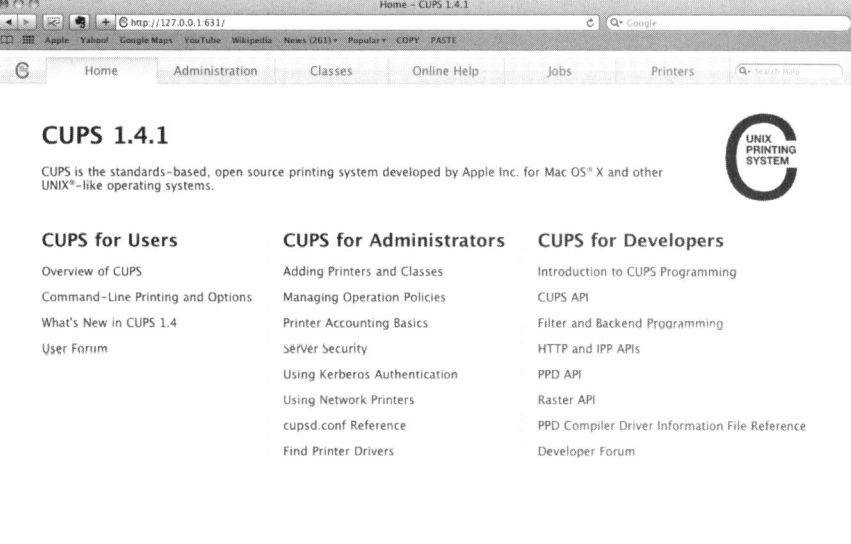

Figure 1–14. *CUPS web interface*

Click on the Administration tab at the top to perform basic printer configurations (see Figure 1–15). If you'd like to get more refined (and you know how to properly edit config files), the CUPS server has a configuration file that is editable from within the CUPS web interface. To access this file, select the Administration tab and click on the Edit Configuration File button under the Server heading. Security settings that can be altered by editing this file include the following:

- MaxCopies
- Port
- BrowseAllow
- BrowseAddress
- SystemGroup
- The Location's directive's Allow option

NOTE: The Location directive has an Allow option that can be used to dictate which addresses are allowed to access shared printing and remote administration.

- AuthType
- AuthClass
- The Limit directive's Require User option

NOTE: The Limit directive has a Require User option that dictates what access various users have. You should limit users' access to an "as-needed" basis.

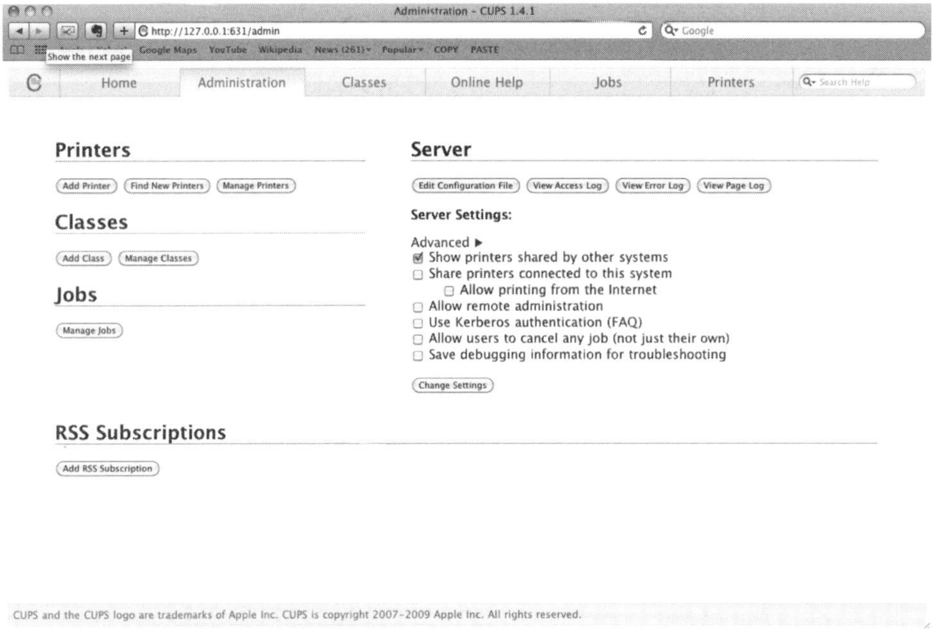

Figure 1-15. CUPS web interface Administration screen

Sharing Services

If you are not sharing any resources on your computer, disable any sharing services that might be running. To do this, open the Sharing preference pane, and review the items on the Services window on the left that are being used to share resources (see Figure 1-16). In Snow Leopard, Apple introduced the additional Shared Folders window to show you which folders you're sharing out on your computer and which users are able to access them. It's a nice feature for us security folks who would like to see at a glance which folders are getting shared.

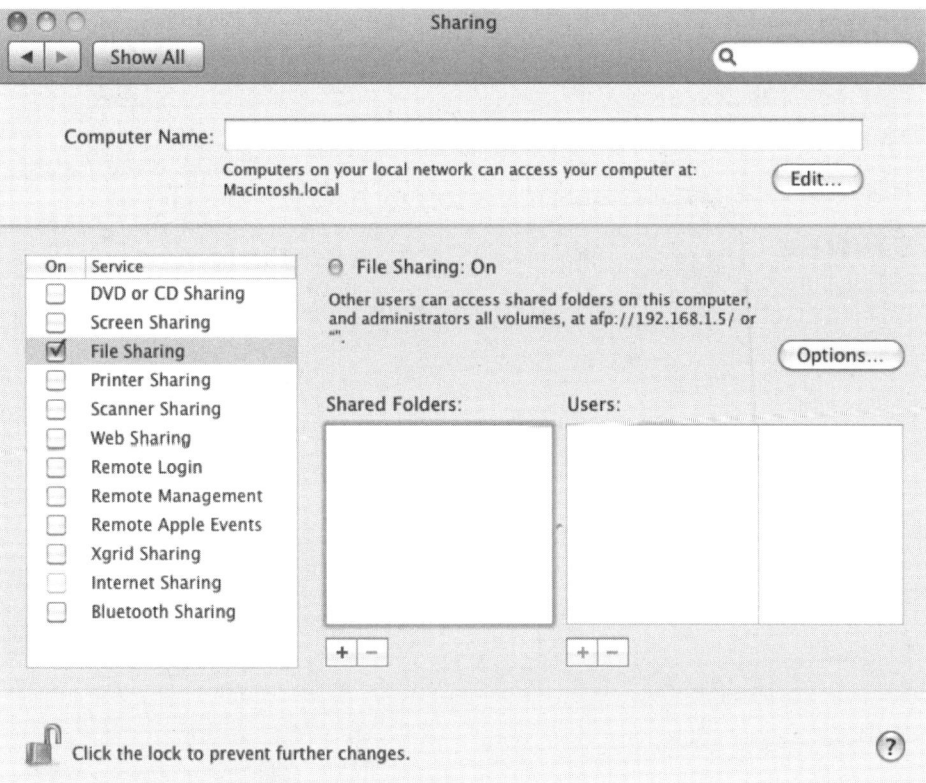

Figure 1-16. *Sharing preferences*

> **TIP:** Disable all services that are not needed by the user for whom you are configuring access. These services are more comprehensively discussed in Chapter 13, Chapter 14, and Chapter 15.

Securely Erasing Disks

When you delete a file from a hard drive, the file is marked for deletion, but is often kept by the file system until the system needs to free up space for new files. Quick formatting a hard drive does the same thing. To ensure that data isn't accessed by malicious users, always securely erase a disk before disposing of it or repurposing the drive.

To securely erase a disk, open Disk Utility, and click the drive in the left column. Next, click the Erase tab, and then click the Security Options button (see Figure 1-17).

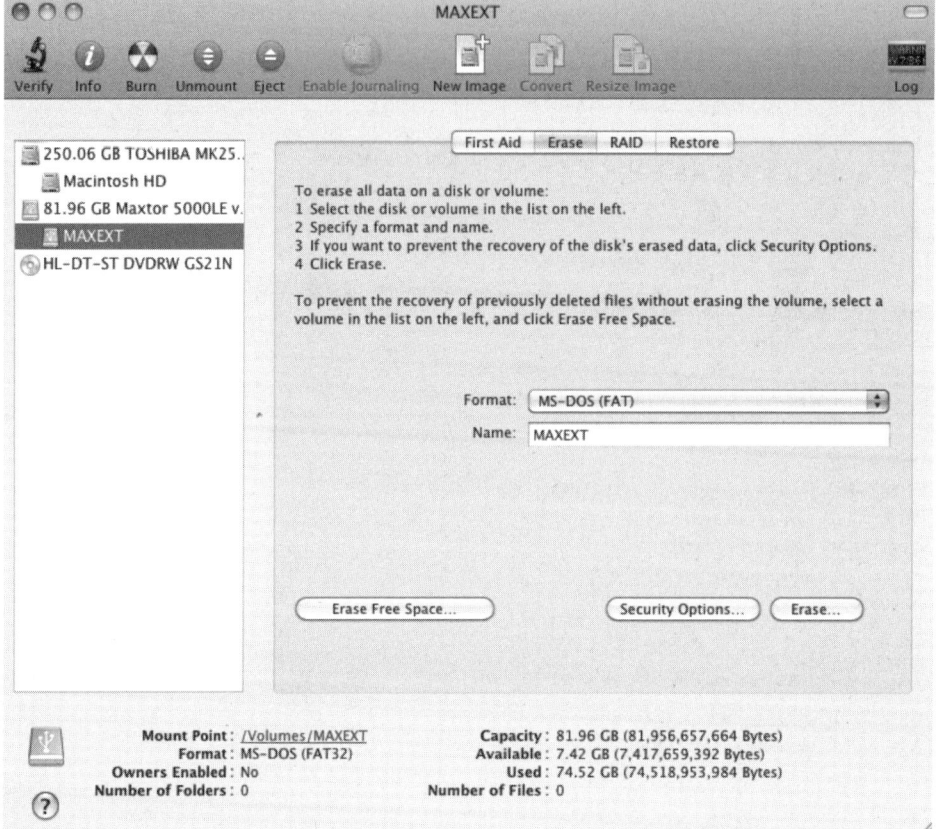

Figure 1-17. *Erase feature of Disk Utility*

This will display a list of secure erase options (see Figure 1-18). The Zero Out Data option will write zeroes over the entire hard drive. This can take minutes to hours, depending on the size of the drive. For those needing a more secure erase option, Mac OS X also has a 7- or 35-pass erase available. These options will write data onto every sector of the drive in the number of passes selected. This can take tens of hours for larger drives but will yield a more secure removal of your data, rendering it virtually impossible to extract data from the drive if it were sent to drive recovery.

Figure 1-18. *Secure Erase window*

> **NOTE:** Make sure there is no data that is needed on the disk you're securely erasing. Once you have erased data securely, the cost of retrieving the data will be great, if even possible.

Using Secure Empty Trash

The Secure Empty Trash feature works much the same way as the Secure Erase feature. This is more secure than simply emptying the trash in that it also overwrites the location of the hard drive where the data in the trash was stored with random data. This will cause the data to be much harder to recover if it were to fall into the wrong hands. To securely empty the trash, in Finder, click Secure Empty Trash (see Figure 1–19).

Figure 1-19. *Secure Empty Trash menu item*

Then click the OK button to make the files unrecoverable. It is worth noting that there are a variety of popular applications to help undelete files. As Figure 1-20 warns, by clicking the OK button to securely erase your trash, you will not be able to recover the files at a later date, even with these data recovery applications.

Figure 1-20. *Secure Empty Trash confirmation*

Using Encrypted Disk Images

Encrypted disk images offer you a place to keep files in an encrypted form. Let's say for speed or compatibility reasons you don't want to keep your entire home folder encrypted as you would by using FileVault, but you do want to keep certain folders encrypted. You can employ the use of encrypted disk images, which are much like ZIP files that compress a bunch of files into one file. Anyone attempting to access the data within them will need a password to do so.

To create an encrypted disk image, open Disk Utility and click New Image in the toolbar. The resulting screen (see Figure 1-21) will have a wide variety of options. The Volume Size and Encryption settings are the most important to consider when creating the disk image. The volume size determines the size limit of the disk image. The encryption type can be 128-bit or (for more security) 256-bit; 256-bit images are harder to crack, but they are slower to create and to open when created. They will also take up more disk space than 128-bit. It's important to consider whether 256-bit encryption is worth the performance hit and disk space increase you will experience from using it.

> **TIP:** If you are unsure what the size of your disk image should be and are not worried about limiting its size, choose Sparse Disk Image from the Image Format options, and the image will automatically grow as it requires more space (such as when you add files to it).

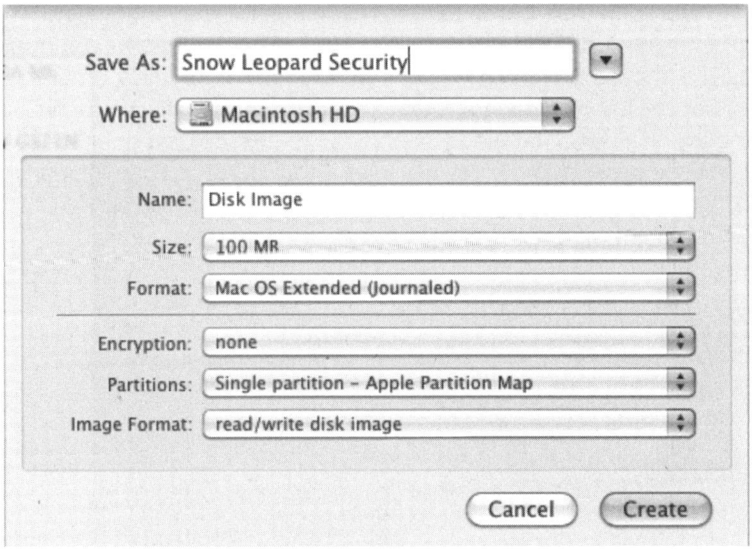

Figure 1–21. *Encrypted Disk Image options*

When you click the Create button, you will be asked for a password. Next you will click the Create button, and OS X will create a file using the encryption parameters you have selected. Once you have created an encrypted disk image, you will need the password anytime you need to access the image.

Securing Your Keychains

Mac OS X uses encrypted keychains to keep track of commonly used passwords and certificates that are accessed regularly. It is meant to make your life easier by automating the manual re-entry of this information every time you need to access it. One keychain password can be used to unlock a number of passwords, allowing your computer to keep track of credentials, saving you time, and allowing you to not have to keep track of them yourself. This is also helpful in that it allows a single service to maintain a centralized database of passwords, rather than having each application ask for passwords.

This provides a substantially secure way of caching passwords for future use. But it's really only as secure as the complexity of the password used to access it. When setting the keychain password, make sure to use a difficult password to crack that is unique from all the other passwords on the machine. To change the keychain password, open Keychain Access in the Utilities folder. Click on the login open padlock on the upper right (see Figure 1–22) and then click on Edit at the top of the screen. Select the option for Change Password for Keychain "login" and change the password. You can also lock keychain access in the Change Settings for Keychain "login" option.

There are always multiple keychains on Mac OS X computers. This includes the system keychain and the user keychains, which appear as Login for each user (by default). With multiple users on a machine, there are inevitably multiple user keychains as well. Each user has a default keychain stored in their home folder. These can be managed using Keychain Access (at /Applications/Utilities/Keychain Access), which can help further secure multiple keychains. To access Keychain Access, from your Finder, click on Go and then click on Utilities. Locate the Keychain Access folder within the Utilities folder, open it and then locate the top left panel, labeled Keychains. The Keychains panel displays all the keychains on the system known to the user. From here you can lock and unlock keychains by clicking them and clicking the lock icon at the top of the screen (see Figure 1–22). This will require a password every time an application or service attempts to access the keychain.

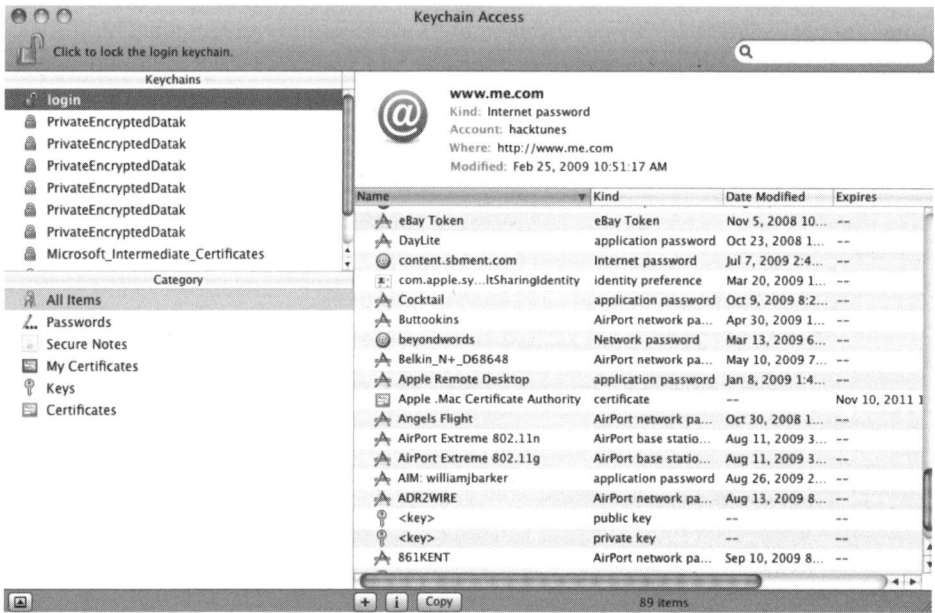

Figure 1–22. *Keychain Access options*

You can create new keychains by clicking Open Keychain Access and clicking the + sign on the next screen. This essentially creates an encrypted file containing other information that needs to be secured, such as cached passwords to web sites. This is similar to an encrypted disk image. The password assigned to each keychain will decrypt the keychain file, thereby unlocking the keychain. Each keychain can and should have a different password.

Best Practices

Here is a quick "cheat sheet" of important practices you should employ in keeping your Mac secure, followed by the chapter numbers that explore these security practices further:

- Install antivirus software (see Chapter 8).
- Always install Apple's security updates (as discussed in this chapter).
- Open files only from known sources (see Chapter 9).
- Use a standard account for everyday work (see Chapter 3).
- Disable automatic login, and assign a password for every user (see Chapter 3).
- Lock your screen when you step away, and require a password to unlock it (as discussed in this chapter).
- Give your keychain its own password, and lock it when it is not in use (see above).
- Use a firewall (see Chapter 11).
- Encrypt important files (see Chapter 9).
- Protect your wireless network with WPA, and use VPNs when using public wireless (see Chapter 12).
- Protect sensitive e-mail from prying eyes using encryption (see Chapter 7).
- Practice private surfing (see Chapter 7).
- Encrypt your chat sessions (see Chapter 7).

Chapter 2

Services, Daemons, and Processes

A computer is never entirely at rest unless it's shut down. Even when you move to another room to watch television and your computer's display has gone to sleep, there might be a dozen or more things at work in the background that you can't immediately see happening. The services, daemons, and processes responsible for all of this activity keeps your system running smoothly and able to handle regular chores such as backups, checking mail, and listening for incoming web clients.

This chapter helps you understand how these services, daemons, and processes provide the backbone of your operating system and how they function. By understanding what these essential elements are and how they interoperate, you will best be equipped to protect yourself from intruders attempting to turn these otherwise helpful programs against you.

Introduction to Services, Daemons, and Processes

The terms service, daemon, and process are frequently used interchangeably. However, each of these terms has a slightly different meaning, and understanding the difference between them is essential to properly securing and troubleshooting your system. Some of the terms defined in this section might seem a bit basic, but we feel it's important to review them to provide the proper context for understanding how they all fit together.

A Mac's hard drive contains hundreds of computer programs, or *applications*. These programs are written in a variety of programming languages, some of which are compiled into binaries, or source code that has been translated from the program's originating programming language, such as Objective-C or C++. Others are in non-compiled languages (often referred to as scripting languages) that remain as they are, such as PHP and Perl; these are typically considered *scripts*. You can usually read the source code of a script, but not a program (unless it is based on a scripting language, such as AppleScript).

When you manually start a program or script (or the computer starts the program, because it's been configured to do so), you're launching a *process*, which is any running application that takes up resources on the system. That process may consist of a single entity or a collection of entities, all working together in what are called *threads*. A thread is a stream of instructions that the computer can perform in sequence. A process can also have other processes that it invokes, known as *child processes*. Because you cannot have children without parents, the originating process is called the *parent process*.

Most modern operating systems, such as Mac OS X, can run multiple processes simultaneously, because they are multi-threaded operating systems.

If the process is running in the background and isn't directly under your control, it's often referred to as a *daemon*. Common daemons running on an OS X system include cupsd (for printing), syslogd (for logging), and blued (for interfacing with Bluetooth). Although the daemons running on your system often may have names ending in the letter d, they don't always. Daemons interact more often with other programs than they do with the user, and they sometimes have additional controller programs (in Mac OS X, many of them rely on scripts) that are used to provide various instructions to the daemon.

> **NOTE:** Whether an item is a daemon or a process can be a bit of a complicated topic. Many daemons can be run in non-daemon modes (interactively). You can take most programs or scripts and convert them to daemons to have them run in the background.

The definitions we've provided here for processes and daemons work with most of the Unix family of operating systems (Linux, OS X, Solaris, and so on). A *service*, however, is specific to Mac OS X. The Mac Developer Connection's Mac OS X Reference Library's Services Implementation Guide states that services in Mac OS X are "features exported by your application for the benefit of other applications." This means that services allow applications to communicate with one another by passing information through a shared pasteboard (not shared memory). You may have seen Services in your menu options in each application's main menu. Each application that offers a service advertises what operations its services can apply to data. It's these advertisements that make up the contents of your Services menus.

Putting it all together, it's easier to think of each of the three this way: a process can be a daemon if it's running in the background; a daemon can be a service if its purpose is to act as a helper tool to interchange data between other programs. If you do not directly invoke a process, then it's typically considered a daemon. Apple recommends that daemons not use AppKit, so they're unlikely to be services. But not all developers are in tune with Apple's best practices, and this is not a recommendation that is always respected.

The final aspect to review of these core underpinnings of the operating system is the *application bundle*. Applications appear to be single files, but in fact, they're more than that. An application bundle is a collection of programs and supporting files for those programs that are displayed as a single application to the end user. A good example of an application bundle native to the Mac operating systems with Tiger and above is Automator. If you were to navigate to your Applications folder, control-click on the Automator icon, and click on Show Package Contents (or cd into it from the command line), you would discover that it's actually a directory of files. Inside this directory are a number of files and binaries. To actually run Automator from within the directory structure, you would need to navigate to the Contents folder and then into the MacOS folder to run the Automator binary. You will typically find binaries in the MacOS folder, and within the Resources you will find the supporting graphics, icon files, and compiled nib files that make up the application.

Viewing What's Currently Running

There are a number of ways to view what's currently running on your Mac, both from the command line and using graphical tools. We'll start with the handy GUI utility, Activity Monitor, and then show you how to view things programmatically for those times when you feel like getting your geek on with the commands ps and top from the command line.

NOTE: Before you can ps and top, you'll need to open a Terminal window (/Applications/Utilities/Terminal.app).

The Activity Monitor

To view the processes running on your Mac (along with other information related to those processes), go to Applications, select Utilities, and open the Activity Monitor application, as shown in Figure 2–1. Activity Monitor will show you a variety of resources in use on your system in real time. Activity Monitor has many uses. From disk activity to memory utilization, Activity Monitor provides a dashboard of sorts into what is going on in your computer. Our focus here, though, is specifically on which processes are running on the computer and learning a bit of information about each.

By default, you'll only see what you're running under the account with which you're logged in. If you know the name of a given process, you can click in the Filter field and type the name of the process to constrain the view. You can also change which processes appear by going to the Show drop-down list box (see Figure 2–2). You can stop each of these processes, however, if you need to stop one that is owned by a user other than yourself. You'll need to provide an administrative password to do so. This is because each process is started by a user, and only has access to files and folders to which the user who started the process has access. When analyzing system processes, remember that processes should be run by the user with the least amount of privileges possible.

CHAPTER 2: Services, Daemons, and Processes

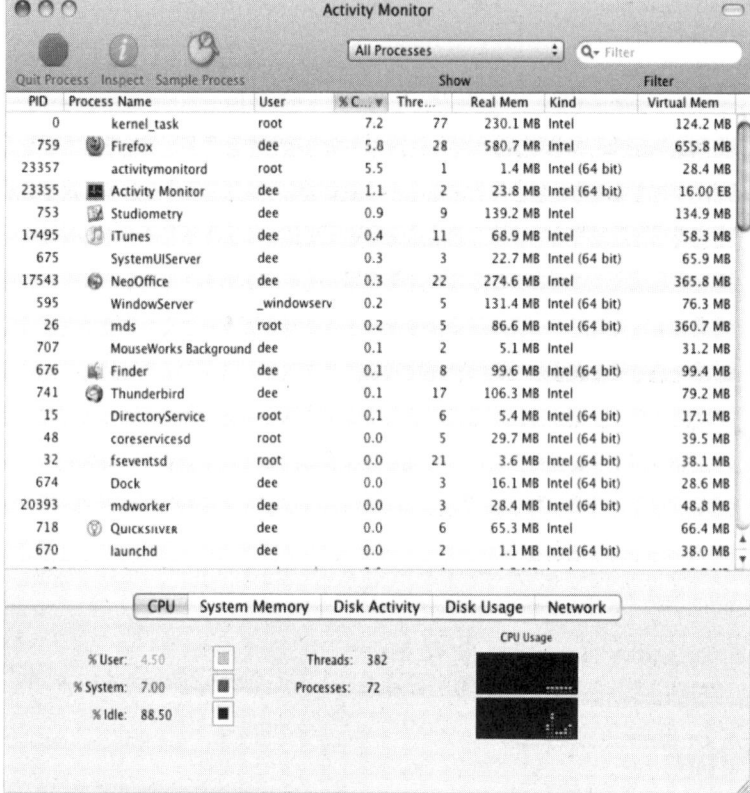

Figure 2-1. *Mac OS X's Activity Monitor*

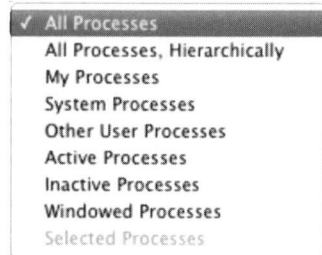

Figure 2-2. *The Activity Monitor's Show list.*

Activity Monitor's Show options break down as follows:

- All Processes: Displays every process running on the system.

- All Processes, Hierarchically: Displays every process running on the system in a tree format, where child processes appear beneath their parent processes.

- My Processes: Displays processes running under the account with which you're logged in.

- System Processes: Displays all processes run by your OS X administrator account.

- Other User Processes: Displays all processes run by other user accounts (not the account you're currently logged into, or the administrator). Expect to see processes running in this section even if you're the only person using your computer. OS X has a variety of internal users who were created only to run particular processes, such as the user _mdnsresponder to run the mDNSResponder multicast DNS service.

- Active Processes: Displays processes that are actively doing things rather than just idling and waiting for something to happen.

- Inactive Processes: Displays those processes that are currently in a waiting state and aren't actively doing anything.

- Windowed Processes: Displays all processes that are attached to windows on the desktop.

- Selected Processes: Displays only those processes that are currently selected. To choose a consecutive list of processes, click the first, and then Shift-click the last in the list. If you want to choose a non-consecutive list, Command-click each process.

To help you understand what you're looking at here, let's also look at the process listing columns from left to right, starting with PID. The PID, or Process ID, is a unique number assigned to each process when it's started. When viewing the listing in the All Processes, Hierarchically mode (see Figure 2–3), you'll notice that PID number 1 is always assigned to launchd, and PID number 0 is always assigned to kernel_task, as this is the order in which they are invoked at boot time.

CHAPTER 2: Services, Daemons, and Processes

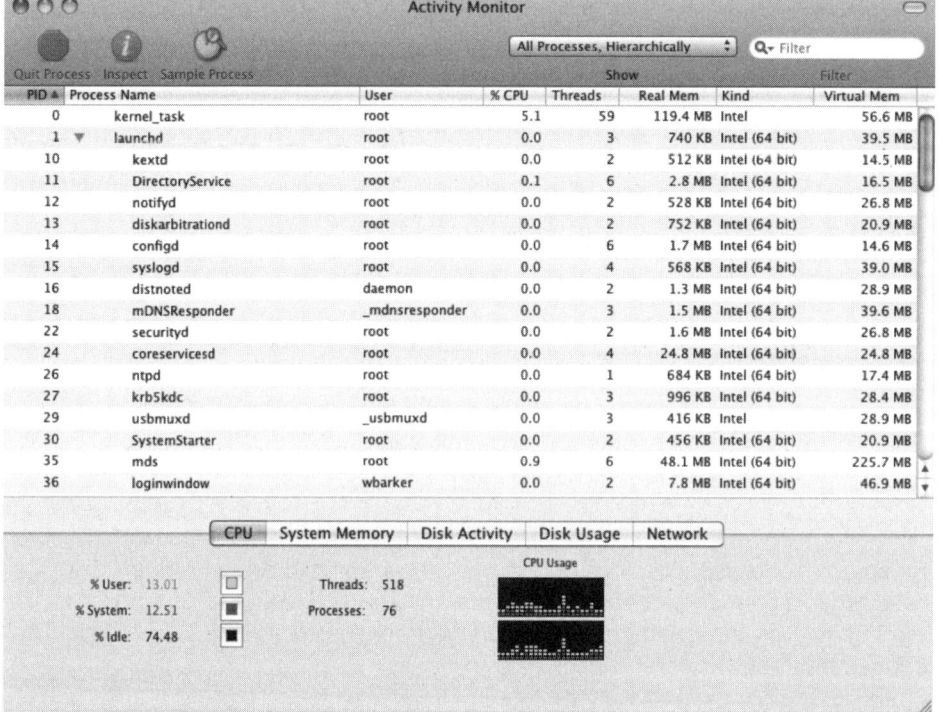

Figure 2-3. *Mac OS X's Activity Monitor*

Note that launchd in OS X is similar to init in other Unix flavors (if you are familiar with other Unix-based operating systems). OS X also has its own form of init, mach_init.d which is located in the /etc directory. The launchd daemon starts first as the system boots, and calls every other process to start. The kernel_task process is a memory manager for the OS X kernel (a kernel is the heart of any operating system).

> **NOTE:** Aside from launchd and kernel_task, PIDs will be assigned differently every time the machine is booted, and you can't typically assume other processes will get the same PID every time.

Continuing with the Activity Monitor columns from left to right, we have:

- PID: The Process ID.
- Process Name: The name of the process associated with this PID.
- User: The user the process is running under.
- % CPU: What percentage of your CPU the process is currently using.
- Threads: The number of threads (sub-processes) associated with this process.

- Real Memory: How much RAM the process is currently using (you can compare the size of virtual memory (swap) with the actual Virtual Memory size using Activity Monitor, allowing you to see the discrepancy).
- Kind: The architecture for which the process was written. Today, you're likely to see Intel or Intel (64 bit) in this column.
- VSIZE: How much virtual memory (probably swapped onto your hard disk) the process is using.

The ps Command

Sometimes we crave the flexibility of the command line, or need to work with text output to feed information to scripts. The ps command allows you to view the processes on your system using an extensive list of options and flags to specify which information you want to see and how it should be formatted. An entire chapter could easily be written on how to use this tool. But, we'll focus here on common option combinations.

ps command will show you something similar to the following:

```
PID TTY       TIME CMD
60250 ttys000  0:00.01 -bash
60263 ttys001  0:00.01 -bash
60272 ttys001  0:00.03 ssh catherine
```

Let's analyze what we're looking at here:

- PID: This is the same information we discovered in the Activity Monitor.
- TTY: This is the terminal controlling the process. A full list of available TTYs appears in the /dev directory, with all of the file names beginning with tty (for example, /dev/ttyp0).
- TIME: How much CPU time the process has used.
- CMD: Which command launched this process.

Used by itself, the ps command doesn't give you a lot of information. To see more information about the processes, you're going to want to invoke other options. When running the ps command, the following options are the most frequently used:

- a: Show all users.
- u: Can show user names instead of user IDs. (If you do not see the user name, try the –f option).
- x: Show processes that don't have a controlling terminal.

Here is an example of this output of running all of these options together, as ps aux, formatted and with the command paths truncated for easier reading:

```
USER   PID  % CPU %MEM    VSZ     RSS TT STAT STARTED   TIME      COMMAND
dee    37783  40.8  16.1 1382764 676328 ?? R    Fri02PM 1784:51.31 /Applications/...
```

```
root          21   2.7    3.7   951712 157036 ??  Ss   30Oct09   37:39.45↵
   /System/Library/...
dee        86042   2.5    1.3   543076  54328 ??  S    13Nov09   85:57.91↵
   /Applications/iTunes.app/...
```

> **TIP:** When using `ps aux`, it's a good idea to resize the Terminal window to as wide as you can manage. Many of the program paths are quite long, and the output can be visually confusing with all of the line wrapping.

The %MEM column shows you the percent of your RAM being used by this process. In STAT, you'll find the state this process is in, which is typically one of the following:

- I: Idle.
- R: Runnable.
- S: Sleeping for less than 20 seconds.
- T: Stopped.
- U: In an uninterruptible wait
- Z: A zombie, (the walking dead)

> **NOTE:** There are additional characters that can appear as well. For example, notice that the second process in the code listing above is in the state `Ss`, meaning that it's sleeping and a session leader. See the `ps` man page for more information about this and other identifiers.

Because the output of `ps aux` tends to scroll off of the screen due to the number of processes running, most command line aficionados use the following command to view the output one screen at a time:

`ps aux | less`

The top Output

While we could say the top program is a simplified version of the Activity Monitor, it's really more accurate to say that the Activity Monitor is a fancier version of top. Open a terminal session and type top to take a look (when you're done with top, press q to stop the program).

If you're used to top from other flavors of Unix, you'll find that OS X's top output is slightly different than you'll find elsewhere. As shown in Figure 2–4, top's output is divided into two major sections: the upper portion of the screen shows a variety of system state information, while the lower part shows processes.

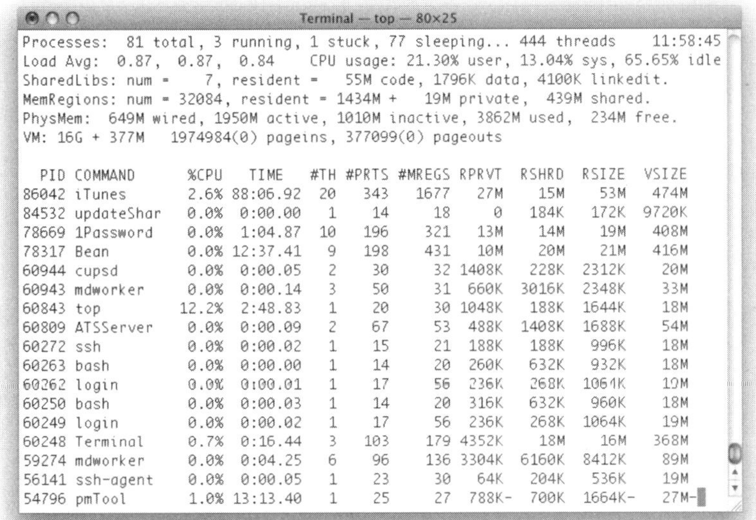

Figure 2–4. *The top program in Terminal*

The first line in the upper portion shows us a summary of how many processes are running and in what states. The lower portion's columns contain information that you're mostly familiar with: PID, COMMAND, %CPU, TIME, and #TH (number of threads). Items you might not recognize include the following:

- #PRTS: The number of Mach ports (secure pipes used for inter-process communication) in use by this process.

- #MREGS: The number of memory regions in use by this process.

- RPRVT: The amount of resident private memory in use by the process.

- RSHRD: The amount of resident shared memory in use by this process.

The `top` command has many flags and options available for controlling what information is displayed and how it appears in the window. Of particular interest is the ability to change what information `top` is using to sort its output. To sort on a column, press o and then enter the keyword for the information you're interested in. Most users will sort one of the following:

- cpu: Sort on what percentage of your CPU power the process is using.

- pid: Sort on process ID.

- vsize: Sort on how much virtual memory (swap) the process is using.

- time: Sort on how much CPU time the process is using.

- uid: Sort on the user ID associated with the process.

- username: Sort on the user name associated with the process.

See the top man page for more information on sorting top columns.

Viewing Which Daemons Are Running

You can view which daemons are running by looking at processes. Most daemons are processes that end in d; however, you can't trust that every process that ends in a *d* is a daemon, or that every daemon's process name ends in a *d*. One place to find those daemon-related tasks that are enabled and share data over your network is the Sharing section of your System Preferences, as shown in Figure 2–5.

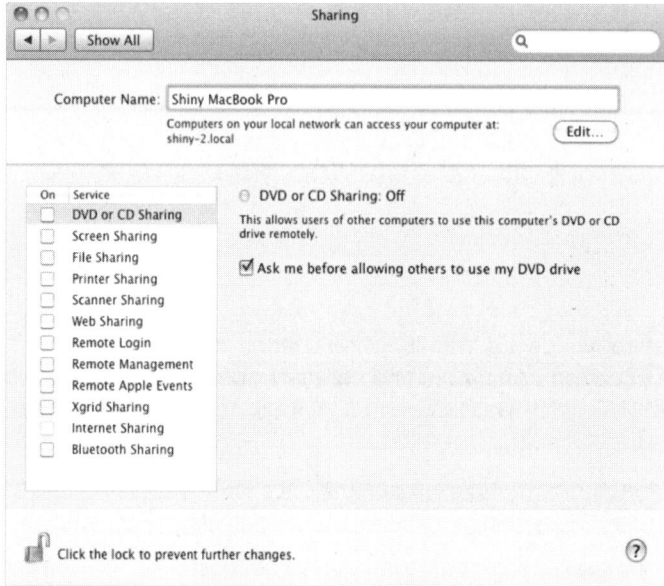

Figure 2–5. *Turning daemons on or off in the Sharing system preferences pane.*

The Services listed here (not to be confused with the services discussed in the next section) each correspond to a daemon or set of daemons that run a specific type of sharing; only that which is critical should be enabled. Some of these services include the following:

- DVD or CD Sharing: Enabling this option starts the ODSAgent, which is the service that handles remote disk features. This daemon lives here: /System/Library/CoreServices/ODSAgent.app.

- Screen Sharing: Enabling this option starts RFBRegisterMDNS, VNCPrivilegeProxy, and AppleVNCServer, with VNC being the main back end solution that allows for screen sharing. Securing this service is covered in Chapter 15.

- File Sharing: Consists of three types of sharing. When FTP is enabled, ftpd is invoked through launchproxy. When AFP is enabled, /System/Library/CoreServices/AppleFileServer.app/Contents/MacOS/AppleFileServer is invoked, which listens for network traffic on port 548. Securing this service is covered in Chapter 13.

- Printer Sharing: The cups process is running all the time, but is altered when sharing printers.

- Web Sharing: Launches multiple threads of httpd. Securing this service is covered in Chapter 14.

- Remote Login: Remote login is Apple's way of indicating that sash is enabled and invokes sshd. This can be controlled with the systemsetup command, using the -setremote login option, which can start or stop these daemons. Securing this service is covered in Chapter 15.

- Remote Management: Starts AppleVNCServer and VNCPrivilegeProxy as with Screen Sharing, but also starts the AppleVNCServer process. Securing this service is covered in Chapter 15.

- Xgrid Sharing: Enables xgridagentd and xgridagenthelper, allowing a server to use the processing power on the client for High Performance Computing (HPC).

- Internet Sharing: Starts the InternetSharing daemon, a basic Network Address Translation (NAT) implementation.

- Bluetooth Sharing: Uses blued. Bluetooth and also to share Bluetooth.

Viewing Which Services Are Available

As we discussed earlier in this chapter, determining which services are available depends on which applications you're running and have installed. To see which services are available for a particular application, select the application's main menu (for example, in iCal, you'd click on the iCal icon next to the Apple icon) and hover your mouse over Services. As of Snow Leopard, this menu has been streamlined to show you only the services that apply to a particular application. If you're using an earlier version of OS X, you'll see the full list of services. (This section assumes you're using Snow Leopard).

Services can be grouped into two major types: *processor* and *provider services*, (a single service can actually belong in both groups). Processor services act on the currently selected data (say, a chunk of text you've selected with your mouse) before sending it to another program (say, into a new document within your default text editor). Provider services give data to the application that called them, often by calling another application to grab the data. For example, say you're editing a web page in your favorite WYSIWYG (What You See Is What You Get) HTML editor and want to copy and paste a screenshot of your desktop. If your editor supports the services you need, you might go to the application's main menu at the top of the screen and then click on Services. Then if you click Grab (or its equivalent) and then Timed Desktop to take a screenshot, you would then open your favorite HTML editor and paste the image into a location in the menu.

> **TIP:** You can create new services through Automator.

The first thing you'll notice if you start looking at various programs' Services menus is that many programs don't support any services at all. When this is the case, the Services menu displays a notice that No Services Apply, and also offers you the Services Preferences menu, which we'll discuss later in this chapter.

> **NOTE:** One notable exception to the built-in services in Mac OS X is Microsoft Office. If you notice, Office has no Services advertised. Microsoft's developers have decided not to leverage these options that Apple has made available to developers.

For an example of an application that does support services, check out the humble Finder. There, you'll see a Services menu containing what's shown in Figure 2–6. As you can see, many of the related services revolve around image handling in this case.

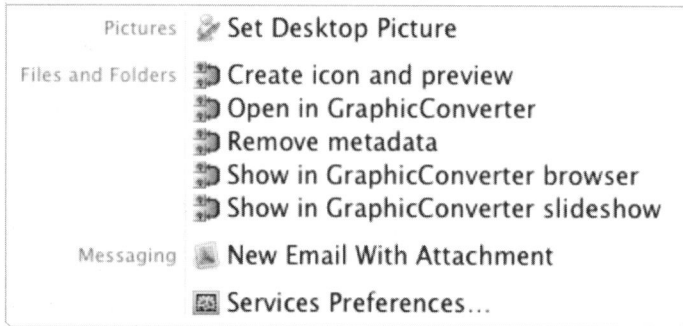

Figure 2–6. *The Finder Services menu in Snow Leopard*

> **NOTE:** The New Email With Attachment service is only useful if you use Apple's Mail client.

Stopping Services, Daemons, and Processes

Imagine that each of the running services, daemons, or processes on your system have their own door. Some of the doors are well secured, made of steel with a complex system of locks that only a true master could finesse their way through. Others are made of flimsy gauze and might as well have big flashing lights that say, "Waltz on in!"

Notice that neither extreme refers to a 100% safe door. There's no such thing. The reality is that most of the services, daemons, and processes fall somewhere between the two extremes, where each running item presents a risk that a script kiddy, hacker, malware-writer, phished, spammer, scammer, thief, or other type of malcontent will jimmy a specific door open. When that happens, they're one step closer to having full access to your system.

The more concerned with security you are, the more work you should put into identifying everything running or listening on your computer. If you discover something you don't need, stop or disable it. When there's no door, there's no way in. Let's apply what we learned in the previous sections to start to control these processes.

> **CAUTION:** It's easy to seriously damage your system by stopping the wrong process. For example, if you stop launchd, that's it, you've stopped the daemon that rules them all. Be sure you understand what each item does before changing it, or make careful backups so that you can revert to a stable state if something goes horribly wrong.

Stopping Processes

It's happened to all of us: we're working in Microsoft Word or some other program, and all of a sudden it stops responding. You click around on a menu and you just can't get it to do anything. Usually this happens to us when we try to put a joke into one of our chapters (guess it just does not compute). If you have a program that becomes unresponsive and will not quit, then you may need to force quit it.

You will have two ways to do this. The first is to simply click on an application icon for an application that is in use in your dock until you get a menu that will give you the option to Force Quit (if Mac OS X has determined that the application is hung), or simply Quit (if Mac OS X has not determined that an application is hung). The second is to use the Command-Option-Escape keystroke to bring up the Force Quit Applications screen, which you can see in Figure 2–7. If Mac OS X considers the application to be hung, then the title for the application will appear in the list in red. You will then be able to click on the application and then click on the Force Quit button, whether the application is hung or not. The one exception is the Finder. If the Finder needs to be Force Quit, because it is your interface to the computer, it will give you a button to Relaunch, which you can click and after a time, the Finder will likely lower.

> **CAUTION:** If you Force Quit an application, you will not have the opportunity to save data for that application.

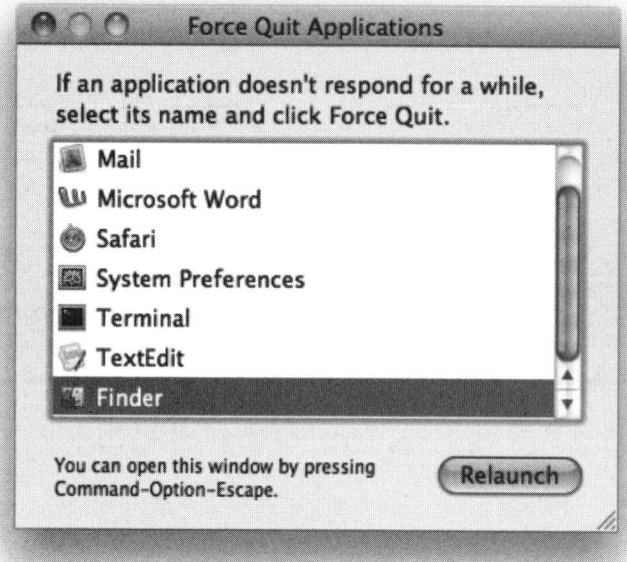

Figure 2-7. *Force Quit Applications*

Not all processes will appear in the Force Quit dialog box, but the applications that you interface with graphically should. For those that are not in the list, you can use the Quit Process button in Activity Monitor, which we covered earlier in this chapter.

You can also use the process ID to terminate a process from the command line. This is most commonly done using the `kill` command, which terminates a process. To use the `kill` command, look up the process ID using one of the methods mentioned throughout this chapter. Once you know the process ID, simply run `kill` followed by the process ID. For example, if Safari would not stop using the Force Quit Applications screen and it had a process ID of 57072, then you would run the following command to stop it:

Kill 57072.

Once you attempt to `kill` the process, it should terminate. If you continue to see the process running, then you can run `kill` more forcefully by sending different signals to the processes. For more information on those, see the man page for `kill`.

In addition to `kill`, you can also use `killall`. The `killall` command will terminate processes based on the name of the process. This can be a fairly dangerous step, considering that many processes can have multiple instances of the process running. The `killall` command works similarly to `kill`; simply place the `killall` command in the line followed by the string that you would like to match. To continue on with the Safari example, you could use Killall safari.

Stopping Daemons

While `kill` and `killall` are very useful for stopping some services, others will start right back up. This may be because they are launchd items and were told by the property list (.plist) that launched them to restart. Launchd is the first process started in Mac OS X, and starts a process that starts every process in Mac OS X. The most common way to manage (and troubleshoot) launchd is using the `launchctl` command.

A fairly simple example of using `launchctl` to troubleshoot and manage a daemon can be seen with something as seemingly innocuous as the clipboard. The `com.apple.pboard` process is the process that makes up the clipboard (or the pasteboard). If you unload the `pboard` entry using `launchctl` you will no longer be able to cut, copy, and paste. `pboard` relies on the accessibility to the user that initiated `pboard` (such as root, if root is enabled) to have access to the /tmp folder. Therefore, `pboard` will not work correctly without /tmp, and without `pboard` you won't be able to paste things. When troubleshooting cut, copy, and paste issues, first verify that /tmp exists and then verify that `pboard` is running using the following command:

`launchctl list | grep com.apple.pboard`

And if it isn't running, start it with:

`launctl start com.apple.pboard`

There are other, more complicated processes in Mac OS X whose process names end up being dynamically generated. The `diskarbitrationd` is the process that handles mounting disks when they are inserted into the computer (such as firewire, USB, and the like). Diskarbitrationd runs in the background, is always on (by default), and is started by `launchd`. New disks inserted into the computer are automatically mounted with `diskarbitrationd`; however, you might not want this and will want to disable it for any of a number of reasons (you might be forensically imaging a system, investigating malware on a device, attempting to fix corruption, simply trying to keep users that don't know how to manually mount a disk from accessing one, just to name a few).

There are a number of ways to stop `diskarbitrationd`. One of the easiest (and least intrusive, because it doesn't require a restart) is using `launchctl`. First, run `launchctl list` to obtain a list of currently running launchd-initiated processes, however, that command alone is going to output a few too many so let's constrain our search to those that include the string `diskarbitrationd`:

`launchctl list | grep diskarbitrationd`

You'll now see a PID and the name of the process. You'll notice that it has an alphanumeric string in front of it, appearing similar to `0x10abe0.diskarbitrationd`. You may also notice com.apple.diskarbitrationd, but if you see the alphanumeric string then launchd should not be managing the process. Next we will go ahead and stop this process, again using `launchctl`, but this time with the stop option:

`launchctl stop 0x10abe0.diskarbitrationd`

Once stopped, let's verify that `diskarbitration` is no longer running using `ps aux`. Once you have completed your tasks and want to re-enable disk arbitration, you can restart it using the start option in `launchctl`:

```
launchctl start 0x10abe0.diskarbitrationd
```

Finally, this process is not persistent across reboots. If you will be rebooting the system you are mounting the disk on, you might want to unload `diskarbitrationd` and then move the plist from /System/Library/LaunchDaemons/com.apple.diskarbitrationd.plist. For example, to move it to the desktop, use the following command:

```
mv /System/Library/LaunchDaemons/com.apple.diskarbitrationd.plist ~/Desktop/com.apple.diskarbitrationd.plist
```

Types of launchd Services

Now that we've looked at programmatically managing launchd, let's look at the two types of services that launchd manages: LaunchAgents and LaunchDaemons.

LaunchAgents run on behalf of a user and therefore need the user to be logged in to run. LaunchAgent configuration plist files are stored in the /System/Library/LaunchAgents and /Library/LaunchAgents. User launch agents are installed in the ~/Library/LaunchAgents folder.

LaunchDaemons can run without a user logged in. Launch daemons cannot display information using the GUI. Much like LaunchAgents, LaunchDaemon configuration plist files are stored in the /System/Library/LaunchDaemons folder (for those provided by Apple et al) and /Library/LaunchDaemons (for the rest).

GUI Tools for Managing launchd

There is also a free third-party tool called Lingon that can be used to manage launchd. Lingon is available at `http://sourceforge.net/projects/lingon/files`. Lingon, shown in Figure 2–8, provides users and administrators with the ability to interface with launchd graphically. While Lingon's future is in flux, it is unfortunately the only mature tool that can manage launchd as it does.

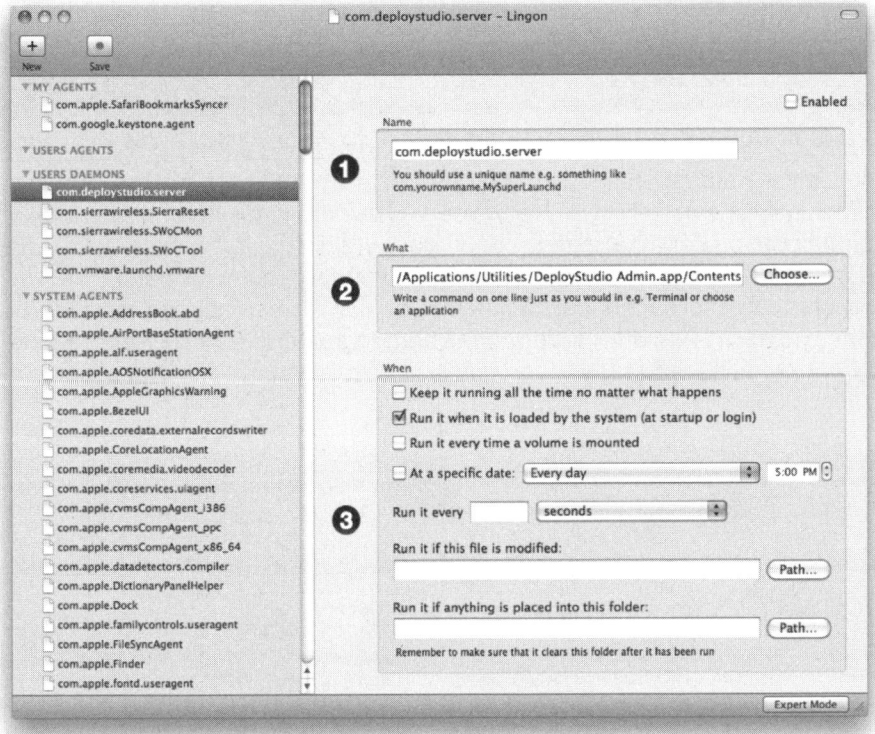

Figure 2–8. *Using Lingon to Manage Launchd.*

Changing What Runs At Login

Launchd manages processes. However, there are other tools that traditional Unix or Mac engineers may look to for managing processes. These are all, in fact, going to be started by launchd. For example, SystemStarter is a tool that can automatically start items stored in /Library/StartupItems and /System/Library/StartupItems. As Mac OS X continues to transition much of the previous functionality of other facilities, such as the cron daemon, into launchd, development has also reduced the reliance on StartupItems (also known as SystemStarter, an older technology that has arguably been around since before Mac OS X 10.0). Even though many third-party applications still use StartupItems, Apple development prefers the launchd facility, and will continue to rely more heavily on it in 10.7 and beyond.

One of the easiest ways to set up a startup item is dropping items (or shortcuts to items) into those traditional folders that Apple computers have been using for some time (such as /Library/StartupItems or /System/Library/StartupItems). But in addition, you can also create startup items for each user in the User's Accounts System Preference pane. To do so, open the System Preferences and click on Accounts. Click on the user you would like to create a startup item for. Then, click on the Login Items tab.

> **NOTE:** You should not be using /Library/StartupItems or /System/Library/StartupItems for processes. It is included here as another place to look when you are trying to determine how a process was invoked.

Here, you will see any startup items that have already been added to the list, as you can see in the list of Login Items in Figure 2–9. If you find startup items here, take a look at what they do before you become alarmed. A number of third-party tools create a startup item as part of their installation process. However, if you feel you don't need to automatically start the application, delete it here. You can also create one manually by clicking on the plus sign (+) and browsing to the item to be added. While Applications are most commonly launched at login, you can also have documents automatically opened.

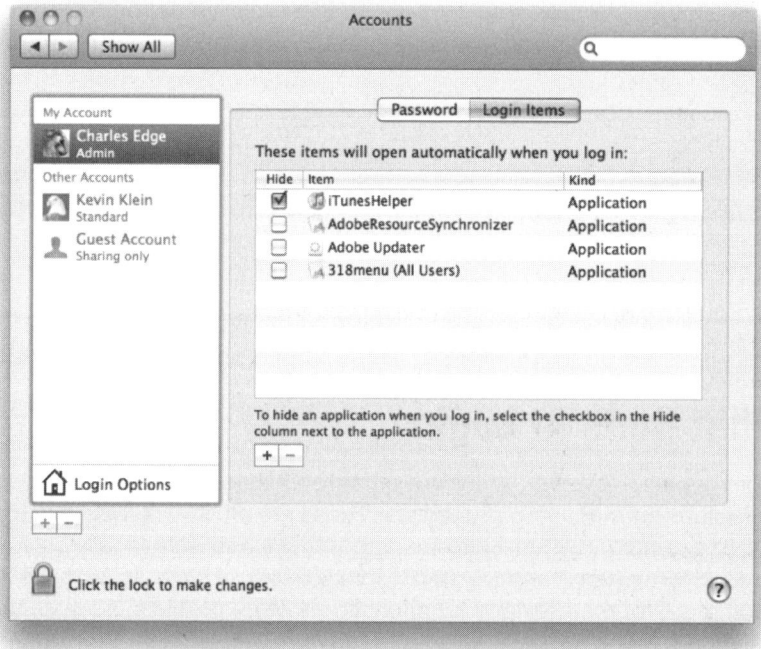

Figure 2–9. *Adding login items with the Accounts System Preference Pane.*

Validating the Authenticity of Applications and Services

We've spent much of this chapter describing how to categorize processes, how to identify information about a process, and how to interact with the processes. Finally, it's important to look at which processes should and should not be running on your systems. Every process should be reviewed for merit, either by running a quick search through sites you trust on the Internet or consulting trusted publications for validation. If a process is found not worthy it should be removed. Those processes that are worthy should also be authentic.

What do we mean by authentic? Virtually any application or service can be plucked from an operating system, altered, then put back into the OS, and run. And it would appear to be a valid service or application if you were to only look at the name of the service. But if a file has been edited, then usually the date and time of creation and/or last modification will change. To add insult to injury, date and time stamps can also be faked. So another good place to look for changes is in its default file size. These are two quick and easy ways to tell if a file has been altered, but they can both be faked (although it is rare that both would be faked at the same time). Therefore, a better method was devised to determine whether an application or service is authentic by having it signed by a Certificate Authority. The signatures of files and folders cannot be faked, and therefore the application becomes signed using PKI. That signature then becomes a means to determine that the application is therefore authentic.

Leveraging application signing allows the operating system itself to then validate the authenticity of applications. Because the applications come from vendors, the packages that install applications and the applications themselves should be able to be validated with PKI as well. For more on application signing, see Chapter 6.

Summary

Throughout this chapter, we have looked at how services, daemons, and processes are started in Mac OS X. Each of these will take up resources on a computer and according to which account invokes them they can each be dangerous. In order to mitigate some of the damage that can be done by a process, we will now turn our attention to managing these users in Chapter 3.

Chapter 3

Securing User Accounts

Over the years, Apple has gone to great lengths to make OS X strong by hardening its user security. *Hardening* means strengthening a component in a system to make it more secure. User accounts can be hardened in OS X by limiting the resources users can access. You can accomplish this two ways: by using the built-in GUI tools, or by using the command line. In this chapter, we will go deeper into securing the Mac by focusing first on restricting user access and then on more advanced command-line security that can be used to harden user accounts.

Introducing Identification, Authentication, and Authorization

Identification is determining who a user is, or what something is. *Authentication* is an operating system's attempt to verify the digital identity of someone or something attempting to communicate with the computer, such as a request to log in to the system. The sender attempting to be authenticated might be an actual person using a computer, a computer itself attempting to authenticate, or a computer program looking to run software on the machine. For example, if you were attempting to install software, authentication is the act of your Mac asking for your username and password and verifying that you are who you say you are.

> **NOTE:** Because authentication is the act of establishing or confirming something as authentic, a key security component of authentication is to protect authentication attempts, such as passwords or key pairs in transit.

Authorization is a process that determines whether a user has access to a given resource. All modern multiuser operating systems include an authorization process. This gives the operating system the ability to identify users and then verify whether they have the appropriate credentials to access a resource. Permissions are generally defined by a system administrator, either on the computer itself or in a networked environment. On

Mac OS X, the authorization process starts with the /etc/authorization file, which contains rules used when authorizing users.

Authorization can also be extensible using pluggable authentication modules (PAMs), which were initially developed by Sun Microsystems. A PAM allows multiple authentication schemes to be integrated with new software so that programs that rely on authentication can be written independently of the underlying authentication scheme.

Verifying that the person sending you information is really who they say they are is obviously desirable all the time. Authentication, however, is time-consuming, and can inconvenience users while resulting in overhead on the authentication services. To make situations like this more convenient and efficient, many systems use a method of *Identification*, a procedure that verifies the person or entity authenticating is the same one it communicated with when they last authenticated. The means of identification can be established through the use of a ticket or token issued when authentication is complete. This saves the user from being required to authenticate on each communication with the server.

WHEN IS SECURE TOO SECURE?

One example of a situation where security and usability often collide is in the deployment of one-time passwords. A one-time password is a password that must be changed each time you log in to your computer. This effectively makes any intercepted password good for only the brief interval of time before the legitimate user logs in the next time. This way, if someone intercepts a password, it would probably already be expired or be on the verge of expiration within a matter of hours.

For nearly every situation, this is too much security and impacts the ability of users to remember passwords. In our experience, when one-time passwords are deployed, it typically means users are writing passwords down. Anytime your password policy causes users to have to write down their passwords, it is a good idea to review whether you are being too strict with password policies. For example, if passwords are too complicated to remember, people will invariably write them down. This is how the kid in the movie *War Games* got into his school computer, thus sparking an entire generation of hackers.

Managing User Accounts

Mac OS X is a multiuser operating system, therefore every file on the system is owned by a user, and every process is run by a user. One great way to analyze the processes in use on your system, along with the name of the users running them, is to view them using the Activity Monitor, accessible via the Utilities folder on the machine. As you can see in Figure 3–1, a variety of accounts are listed in the User column, each running separate processes. Activity Monitor has permissions to manage processes that the user can access. Therefore, processes are restricted from accessing data they should not be able to access. This security extends to files and other system resources on your computer.

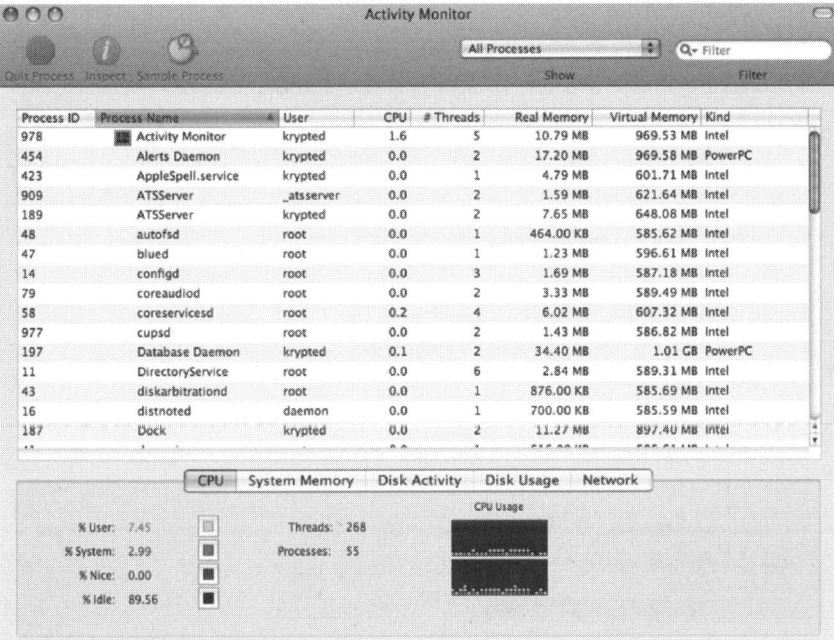

Figure 3–1. *Activity Monitor*

Key to being able to secure an operating system is understanding what actions each of the user accounts are capable of performing on the operating system. Next, we will discuss varying types of accounts within Mac OS X.

Introducing the Account Types

Limiting the capabilities of users in a standard operating environment is one of the first and most important steps in securing a system or a network, no matter which operating system you're running. Traditionally, Mac OS X has had only three user account types: administrator, standard, and root (superuser). In Leopard and Snow Leopard, Apple expanded that number to six: standard, managed, administrative, sharing, guest, and root.

The first and default user of a system is an *administrative* user; this user has almost unlimited access to the system. Administrative users can use many of the configuration utilities and change permissions of files to gain access to other users' folders if need be.

With all the power that an administrative user has, it is easy to accidentally damage the operating system. Best practices for operating in a secure environment dictate that once a Mac is set up, the administrative account should not be used for everyday use, and a *standard* account should be used instead. When the system needs more privileges than what a standard account allows, such as installing applications or making system preferences changes, you will be prompted to authenticate as an administrator. Standard users can operate basic applications, access their own files, and change some of their settings. They cannot make global configuration changes or changes to other accounts. The reasoning behind this is that it is easy to accidentally perform inappropriate actions on the system as an administrator without asking for authentication to confirm the action. As a standard user, the likelihood of malware activity and misconfiguration on the system is almost nonexistent.

Sharing accounts were added to give other users access to log into shared resources over the network on your computer without giving them physical access to the machine locally.

To set up a sharing account, follow these steps:

1. Open System Preferences from the Apple menu.

2. Click Accounts to open the Accounts preference pane, and authenticate if needed by clicking the lock icon.

3. Click the plus (+) sign on the lower left side of the pane.

4. Select Sharing Only in the Type field (see Figure 3–2).

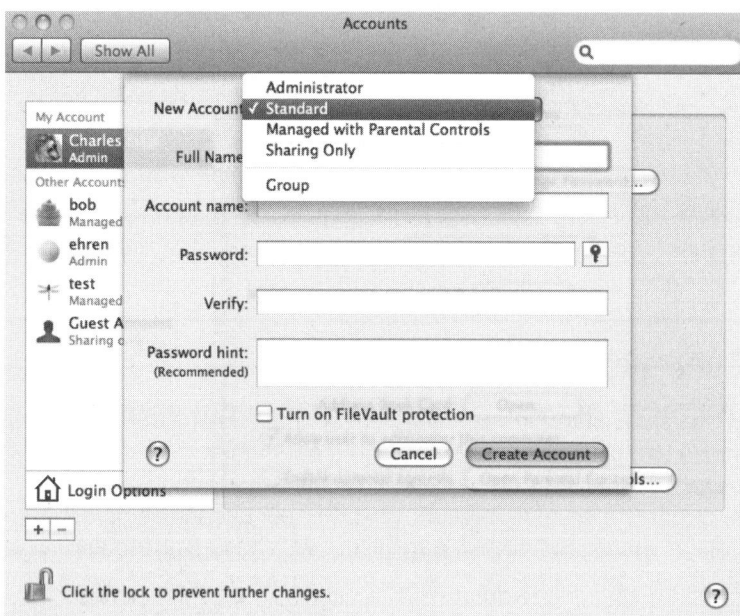

Figure 3-2. *Sharing Only account*

5. Enter a name for the account in the Name field. This is the full name of the user who will be logging in.

6. Enter a short name for the account in the Short Name field (keep in mind that this will be difficult to change at a later date).

7. Enter a password for the account.

8. Enter the password again in the Verify field.

9. Enter a hint for a password reminder.

10. Click the Create Account button.

Guest accounts allow users to perform basic functions such as surfing the Internet and checking email. Once the guest user logs off, their account's settings are deleted. If you need to give someone access to your computer but would like to keep your data private, enabling a guest account is a quick and dirty way to give them access without going through the trouble of setting up another user account on the machine.

> **NOTE:** Clicking on the guest account will allow you to enable the "Allow guests to connect to shared folders" option, which should only be used in extremely rare cases where you want to allow users without passwords to connect to your computer.

Root accounts, or superusers, are powerful user accounts that have full access to the entire filesystem on a Mac. More on root accounts in a bit.

Adding Users to Groups

You can grant access to resources based on group memberships. In Leopard and Snow Leopard, Apple has introduced a new account type to the GUI of Mac OS X called a *group*. Groups contain users who are created on the Accounts preference pane. To create a group, follow these steps:

1. Open System Preferences from the Apple menu.
2. Open the Accounts preference pane by double-clicking Accounts.
3. Click the plus (+) sign on the lower left side of the Accounts preference pane.
4. Change the account type to Group.
5. Give the group a name (see Figure 3-3).

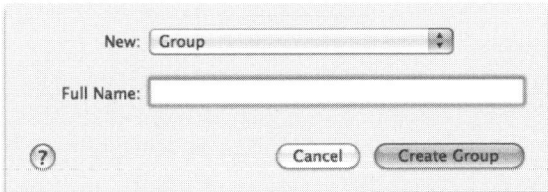

Figure 3-3. *Creating a group*

6. Add users to the group by selecting the check boxes for each user you want to include as a member (Figure 3-4).
7. Close the window to save the group settings.

Figure 3–4. *Adding users to groups*

Enabling the Superuser Account

Some items in this book will require the superuser, often referred to as the *root user*, to be enabled. The root account is disabled by default (for a reason) and has unbridled access to everything on the computer. This level of access is different from the level of access an administrative user has. For example, while logged in as a root user, one can incorrectly type commands that can erase important files in the operating system. Root is rarely required as a permanently accessible user account. Unless you are using the root account for specific tasks, such as running Carbon Copy Cloner, disable it for the majority of the time.

To enable the root account, follow these steps:

1. Open the Directory Utility located in the /System/Library/CoreServices/ folder.

2. Click the lock icon to authenticate as an administrator.

3. Click the Edit menu, and select Enable Root User from the menu (see Figure 3–5).

4. Once you've enabled root, make sure to change the root password by clicking on Change Root Password in the same menu.

5. Save the settings by closing the Directory Utility.

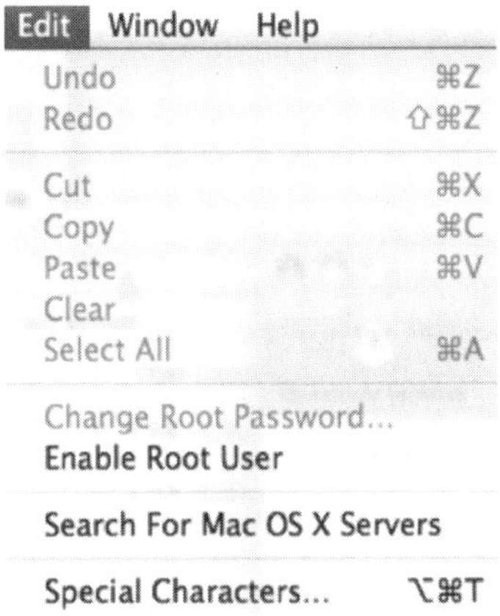

Edit	Window	Help	
Undo			⌘Z
Redo			⇧⌘Z
Cut			⌘X
Copy			⌘C
Paste			⌘V
Clear			
Select All			⌘A

Change Root Password...
Enable Root User

Search For Mac OS X Servers

Special Characters...   ⌥⌘T

Figure 3-5. *Enabling root*

To disable the root account, follow these steps:

1. Open Directory Utility by following the previously explained procedure.
2. Click the lock icon to authenticate as an administrator.
3. Click the Edit menu, and select Disable Root User in the menu (see Figure 3–6).
4. Save the settings by closing the Directory Utility.

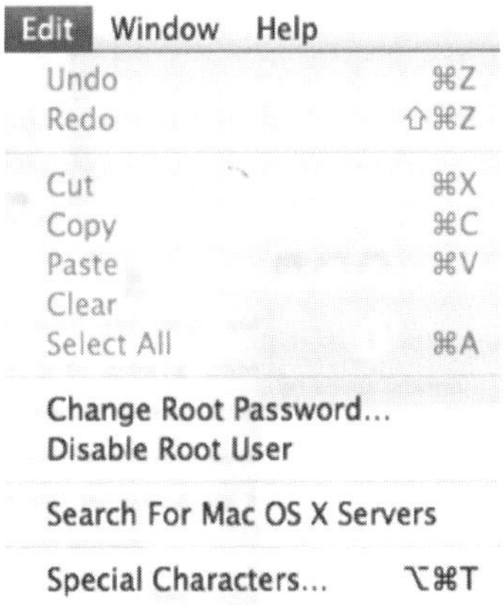

Edit	Window	Help	
Undo			⌘Z
Redo			⇧⌘Z
Cut			⌘X
Copy			⌘C
Paste			⌘V
Clear			
Select All			⌘A

Change Root Password...
Disable Root User

Search For Mac OS X Servers

Special Characters...   ⌥⌘T

Figure 3–6. *Disabling the root account*

You can also enable the root account using the command line. The `dsenableroot` command can be used to enable the root user and assign it a password. To enable root:

`Dsenableroot.`

First you will be prompted for the current user password; this user must be an administrative account. You will then be prompted twice for a password to assign the root account and then to verify the password. If you were successful, you'll see the following success code:

dsenableroot:: ***Successfully enabled root user.

To then disable the root account:

dsenableroot -d

> **TIP:** For security reasons, it is best to leave the root account disabled when you do not need it. If you do enable it, then do so temporarily. You can also use the sudoers file and sudo to manage which users can elevate privileges and how they are able to do so. We will cover the sudoers later in this chapter.

Setting Up Parental Controls

With Leopard, Apple introduced a rich set of ways to limit user access on a Mac. Included under the umbrella of empowering parents with the ability to limit their children's access, Parental Controls also gave administrators the ability to fine-tune their users' access to resources. Some of these parental controls existed in Tiger, but did not use the same techniques for management, such as a dedicated preference pane and the command sandbox. Using the new Parental Controls preference pane, you can configure controls for any user with the account type of Managed and have control over what they can do with `Mail.app`, iChat, and web browsing with Safari.

To use Parental Controls, open Mac OS X's System Preferences and click the Parental Controls preference pane. Click the account you want to control, and then click the Enable Parental Controls button (see Figure 3–7). If the account is not in the list, then go to the Accounts preference pane and verify that either the Enable Parental Controls check box is checked or that the account is not an administrative account.

Figure 3–7. *Enabling the Parental Controls feature*

Once you have enabled Parental Controls, you can control whether the user is forced to use Simple Finder (a limited way of interacting with the Finder where most of the command keys are disabled and many Finder options are also disabled), control which applications a user is able to access, control whether they can burn CDs and DVDs, place limits on how long they can use the computer, limit access to whom the user is able to converse with over iChat and Mail, restrict access to web sites they can navigate to, and even review logs of attempted violations of these rules from another computer.

To specifically restrict access to applications a user is allowed to access, open the Parental Controls preference pane, open the user you want to control access for, click the System tab, and choose "Only allow selected applications" (see Figure 3–8). Then go through the list of applications and place a check mark next to the application the user should be able to access. Other settings, such as enabling Simple Finder, disabling the user's ability to manage printers, disabling the user's ability to change their password, and disabling a user's ability to change the contents of their dock can all be configured using Parental Controls.

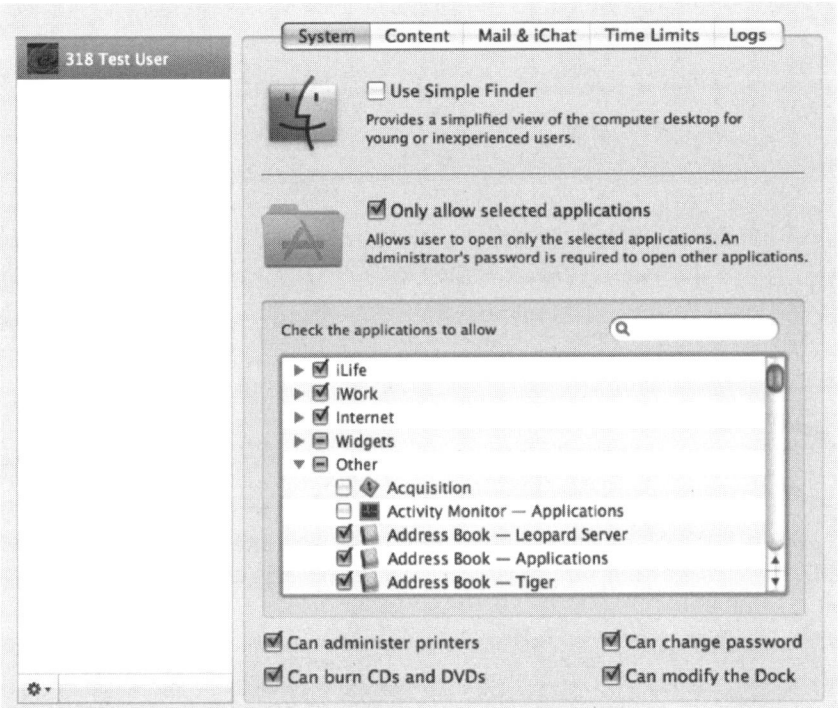

Figure 3–8. *Parental Controls, allowing access to selected applications*

You can also block web sites or dictionary items that have specific words in their names. The "Hide profanity in Dictionary" option (see Figure 3–9) sets restrictions on the words in the dictionary that users can look up.

NOTE: The Hide profanity option is the only graphical control to customize words users are allowed to look up in the Mac dictionary.

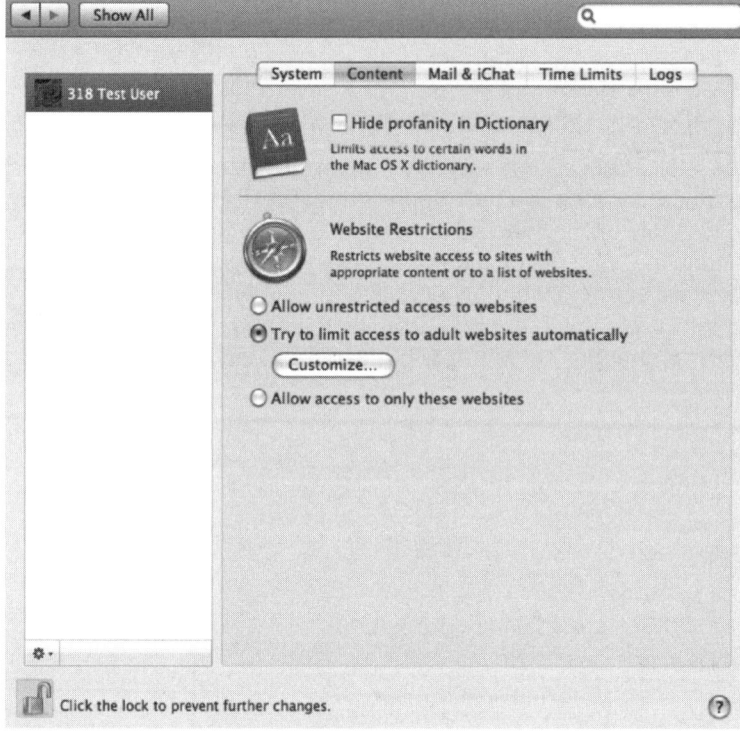

Figure 3–9. *Parental Controls, limiting the content*

Limiting access to certain web sites is a very nice feature in the core feature set of an operating system. Traditionally, operating systems relied on external devices such as firewalls with content filtration to block adult web content. Now it can be done within Leopard and Snow Leopard using predefined filters from Apple's servers. To limit access to web sites prefiltered by Apple, click the Content tab of the Parental Controls preference pane, and then click "Try to limit access of adult web sites." This will automatically enable a web site filter that will block sites Apple has chosen as inappropriate due to adult content.

> **NOTE:** If you would like more features for limiting access to sites for children, then definitely consider a product such as NetNanny if an opt-in list will not work for you. NetNanny can be found at www.netnanny.com/mac.

You can also set up an opt-in list of web sites that the user is allowed to visit. Access the list by using the Content tab on the Parental Controls preference panel to allow sites (see Figure 3–10) in the Website Restrictions section. If this is enabled, even though the prebuilt list of sites has restricted access, the sites listed in the "Always allow these sites" section will still be accessible. If a user with this control enabled attempts to go to a site not in the list of allowed sites, then the user will have to enter an administrative password to be allowed to visit the site. You can also add sites to the "Never allow these sites" section. Sites listed in this section will not ask for an administrator password when requested, and access to the sites in this list will be denied, whether or not they are allowed by the adult content filter.

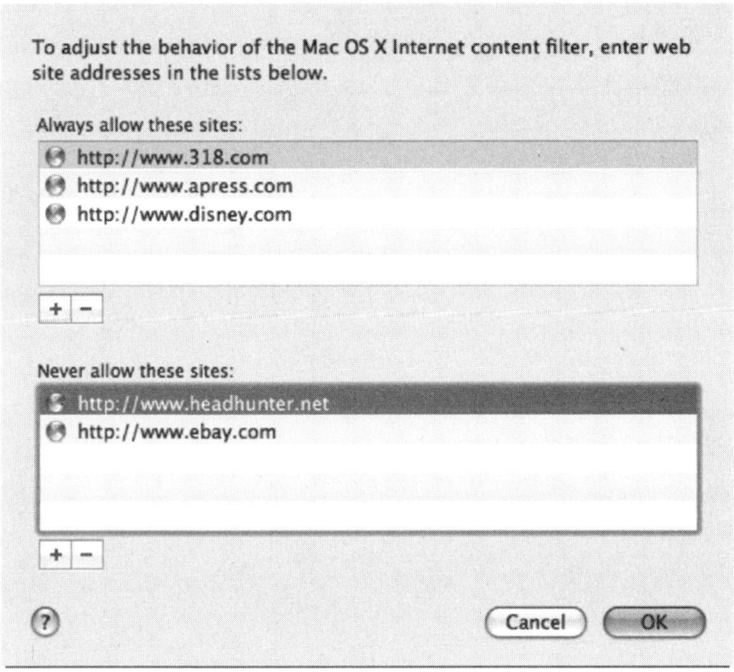

Figure 3-10. *Allowed and disabled web sites*

The Parental Controls feature can also limit who can be communicated with via Apple Mail and iChat. Keep in mind that if you choose to use Parental Controls to manage iChat and Mail, then you will need to build a list of users with which the managed user will be able to communicate. To limit access to Mail, open the Parental Controls preference pane, click the managed user, and check the Limit Mail box (see Figure 3–11). To limit access to iChat in the same manner, check the Limit iChat box.

Once you have set the managed user to limit mail and/or iChat access, you'll want to build a list of people with whom the user is allowed to communicate. By clicking the + box, the users included in the Add Users screen (see Figure 3–12) will automatically be added to the user's list of people you have deemed safe for them to instant message and communicate with via email.

Figure 3-11. *Limiting Apple Mail and iChat*

Figure 3-12. *Adding allowed accounts in Parental Controls*

You can also set up permission requests in such a way that when communication is attempted by users not in the accepted list, an email is sent to the address indicated in the "Send permission requests to" field (shown in Figure 3-11). This allows you to know when changes need to be implemented in the list to further limit or grant access. You can also add users to the screen based on their entry in your Address Book. To do this, click the disclosure button to the right of the Last Name menu (see Figure 3–13), and browse to the user you would like to add. Select multiple people by holding down the Cmd key while selecting each person, or by holding down the Shift key when selecting a group of people. Once you are satisfied with all of the users in the list, click the Add button, and the new entries will populate the list.

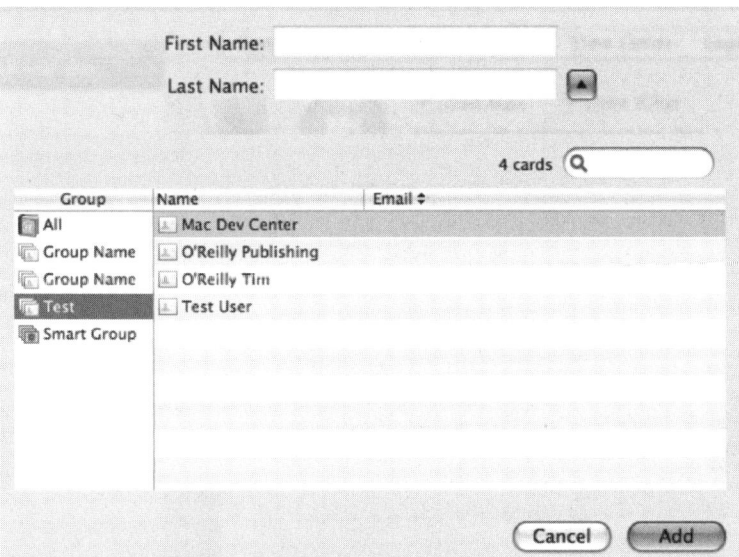

Figure 3–13. *Adding addresses from Address Book*

Once you have configured your Parental Controls for messaging protocols, you can set time limits. Time limits allow you to restrict access to the computer at specific times, or limit the total amount of time the computer can be used. You will also be able to set a period for bedtime or certain time periods when the computer cannot be used. To access time limits, click the Time Limits tab of the Parental Controls preference panel. From here, you will be able to set time limits in hours for weekdays as well as weekend days (see Figure 3–14).

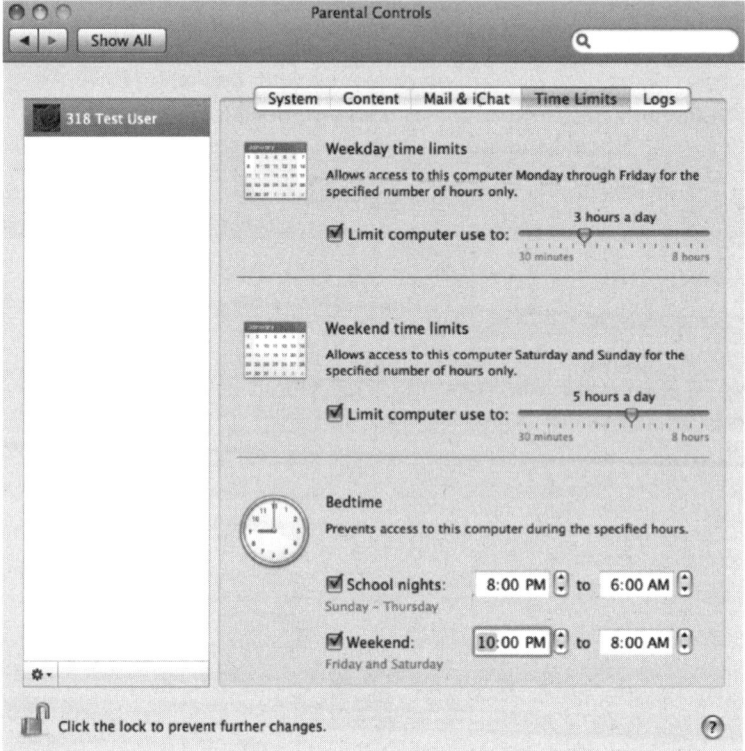

Figure 3-14. *Setting time limits*

Managing the Rules Put in Place

Once you have set the controls for your managed users, you will be able to review logs on traffic, allowing you to find users attempting to breach the rules you have put in place. You can do this using the Logs tab of the Parental Controls preference pane.

You can also copy Parental Controls settings from one user to another. This makes it easy to set up multiple accounts on a system and quickly assign the same settings to new accounts. To do this, click the account with the settings you would like to copy, click the cogwheel icon at the bottom left of the screen, and choose the Copy Settings for "<Username> Test User" option (see Figure 3-15).

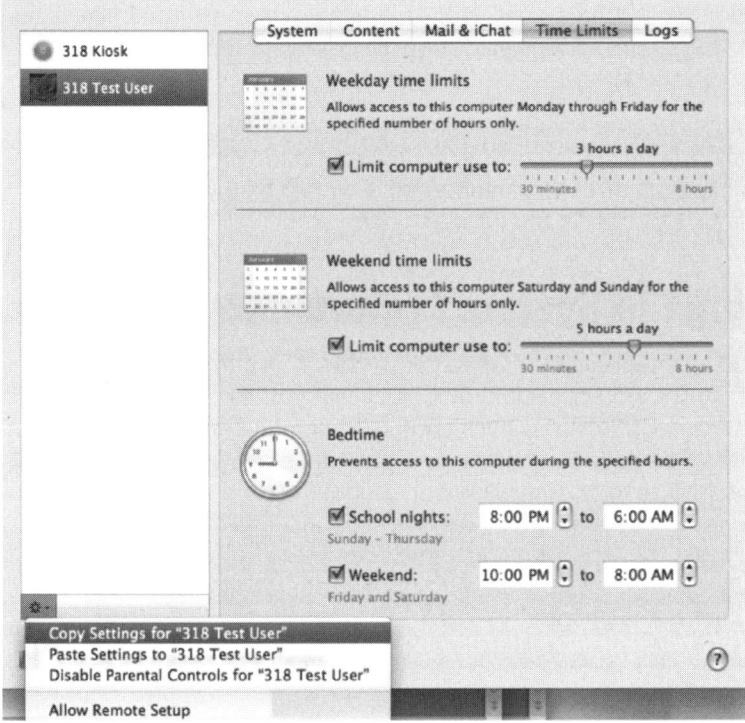

Figure 3–15. *Copying user settings in Parental Controls*

Then select the user to whom you would like to copy the settings, select the Paste Settings option, and verify that the settings have been applied (see Figure 3–16).

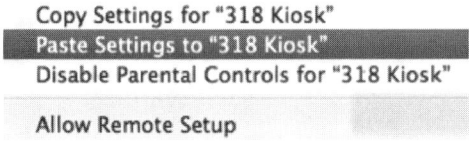

Figure 3–16. *Pasting settings to another user*

Parental Controls is not just for parents to control access to resources for their children. Although Parental Controls existed in Tiger, it has been expanded to include the options in the new sandbox system and provide a more granular control of managed settings in Leopard. Sandbox represents a giant step forward from the options in Tiger, and as such, it's a powerful new feature in Leopard that can be used in the workplace to limit what managed users can access, be it web sites or contacts used for iChat. It can even limit when a computer can be accessed, and in a manner that is not easily circumvented.

Open Directory on Mac OS X Server is a powerful way to provide administrators with more granular control of user access to resources. For example, with Open Directory, you can limit access to global settings on systems such as other System Preferences, Bluetooth, Fast User Switching, and Login Items. (For more on Open Directory, see Chapter 16). Parental Controls used in conjunction with Open Directory can push out these granular settings to many systems concurrently. It is an extremely attractive option to use these technologies together in schools or large corporations that have hundreds or even thousands of workstations.

The new Parental Controls is missing some features that we would like to see, such as an online database that is updated with acceptable sites, but overall it is a big step in the right direction for limiting access to local resources. You can expect that Apple will continue to build on Parental Controls in the future.

Advanced Settings in System Preferences

You can also edit some slightly more advanced settings from within the Accounts System Preference pane. These are accessible by Ctrl-clicking on the account name and then clicking on Advanced Options. This will bring up a screen similar to that shown in Figure 3–17. This screen allows you to change a number of values for various attributes of the accounts, including Account name, UID, default group, path to the home folder, default shell, and the GeneratedID for the account. You can also add aliases using the plus (+) sign. This will allow the same account to authenticate using multiple names in the authentication dialogs throughout the operating system. We will discuss these attributes later in the chapter.

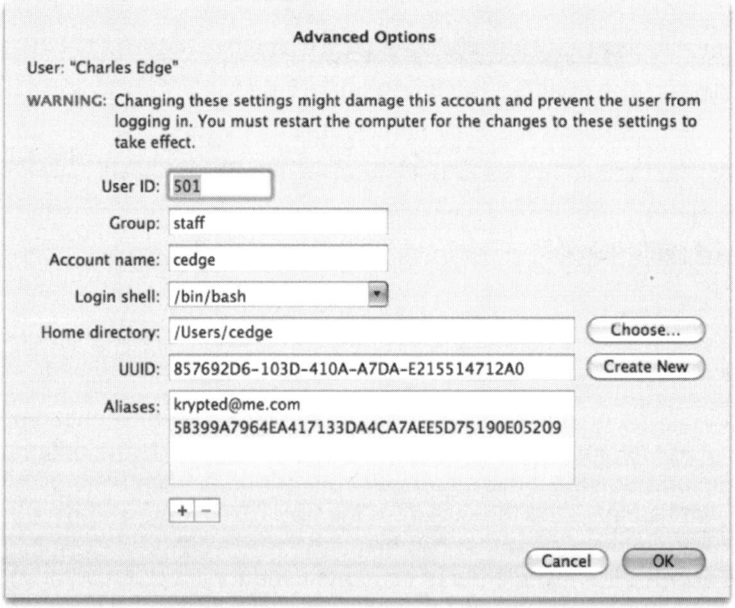

Figure 3–17. *Advanced Account Options*

Working with Local Directory Services

Users accounts in Mac OS X client can come from a variety of locations. But by default, they all reside in what is known as a local directory service. The local directory data resides primarily in the folder found at /private/var/db/dslocal. This folder, which will require elevated privileges to access, contains numerous files pertaining to the computer's directory service configuration. For instance, accounts for Users and Groups are stored in flat property list (.plist) files nested in the /private/var/db/dslocal/nodes/Default directory. Users are stored in property lists located in the /private/var/db/dslocal/nodes/Default/users folder, while groups are stored property lists in the /private/var/db/dslocal/nodes/Default/groups directory. Every local user and group account has a corresponding .plist file found in these directories. Accounts that begin with an underscore (_) are hidden service users and groups. For example, the web server uses the _www account, which obtains user settings from the _www.plist file. The _www user does not have the ability to log into the machine, because the account has no terminal access, nor does it have a password. Creating a new user in the /private/var/db/dslocal/nodes/Default/users directory will create a .plist file with a name that corresponds to the new users short name.

Inside a .plist file there are a number of attributes containing data about a given user or group. Readers with a Microsoft Windows background will notice that files in the local directory node more closely resemble registry keys for local accounts. Examine the .plist file for the user created earlier and look for the key called authentication_authority.

```
<key>authentication_authority</key>
    <array>
        <string>;ShadowHash;</string>
    </array>
```

This authentication key specifies the service that will be utilized to authenticate the user. Notice that it mentions ShadowHash, which indicates that the system will utilize a local file called a "hash" file to authenticate the user. Mac OS X password hash files contain copies of a users password in multiple formats. This allows for different services to authenticate a user with their own native password encryption type. The ShadowHash means is that passwords are stored outside the directory service, in another location (one that "shadows" the directory). Going back to the concepts introduced earlier in this chapter, identification is done through the directory; authentication to the account is done through the shadow.

> **NOTE:** In Snow Leopard, users by default also have a ;Kerberosv5; authentication authority with a generated principal on the local KDC; accounts can be authenticated against the KDC or the shadow hash.

In the user's plist file, you will also see a generateduid key. This key is used to track the user account, even if their shortname is changed. GeneratedUIDs are based on a standard called the Universally Unique IDentifier (UUID), which is a complex programmatically-generated string of characters that are never duplicated. A UUID is unique across time and space for all users.

Unless full disk encryption is being used on the local boot volume of the computer, once you know a users GeneratedUID it is possible, in single user mode, to swap password files with another user and log in to their account. To guard against this, you can require a password to enter single user mode. To do so, open /etc/ttys and then find the line that reads as follows:

```
console "/System/Library/CoreServices/loginwindow.app/Contents/MacOS/loginwindow"↵
    vt100 on insecure onoption="/usr/libexec/getty std.9600"
```

Next, change this line to:

```
console "/System/Library/CoreServices/loginwindow.app/Contents/MacOS/loginwindow"↵
    vt100 on secure onoption="/usr/libexec/getty std.9600"
```

Once saved, attempting to boot into single user mode will require a password.

If you were to look in the /private/var/db/shadow/hash directory, you would find a file that is named using the value of this key. This means that even in the event of a user account's username changing, their password would still be tied to their account. This also prevents the collection of stale password files that would accumulate if they were based on the shortname.

In this example, the authentication_authority record, which has a value of ;ShadowHash;, tells the local directory service to consult the user's local hash file when the user attempts to authenticate. This hash file will contain at least a sha-1 salted hash for the user, which is a secure unrecoverable password type. If windows file-sharing services are enabled for the user, it will also contain the respective ntlm hash for that user, which is used by windows file sharing components. Over the years, Apple has struggled to balance security and functionality as it pertains to password hashes. Although hashes for Windows file sharing require ntlm, the ntlm hash type is more susceptible to common password attacks, which makes its recoverability more feasible. To solve this, Apple only enables the ntlm hash when windows file sharing users are specifically configured for SMB/Windows sharing access in the sharing pane of the system preferences. Storing a password in a hash file allows for a consistent password file location with flexible extensibility for other password hashes such as ntlm.

The data from the account plists can be managed by altering the text files directly. For example, if you preferred to change a user's image for their profile pic without using System Preferences, then you would simply alter the picture key. However, editing property lists directly can be pretty cumbersome, and so Apple has provided a plethora of commands that can be used to manage and query data from the local directory node and other directory services plug-ins without needing to read raw XML-style property list data. Some have GUI equivalents while others do not. These commands include the following (you can learn more about these commands using their manuals, i.e., "man 'command'"):

- **dscacheutil:** Look up information stored in directory services cache and flushes various caches.

- **dscl:** Interactive command used to edit and browse directory services settings, such as user accounts, group accounts, and search policies (the order with which Mac OS X looks up account information in each directory service). The closest GUI equivalent would be twofold: the Accounts System Preference pane and the Directory Utility. This command is covered in more depth in the next section.

- **dseditgroup:** Used to edit, create, and delete groups, or to add or remove group members.

- **dsenableroot:** Controls the root user account (enable, disable, and reset the root password). The GUI equivalent would be the "Change root password", "Enable root user" or "Disable root user" options in the Edit menu of Directory Utility. (This command was covered earlier in this chapter.)

- **dserr:** Prints a description of directory services-related errors, example "dserr 14090." Once you have the error code, you can then use the man page for DirectoryService to look up the meaning of each error (or search Google for more information on the specific errors; if there is a – in front of the number, put quotation marks around the errors).

- **dsexport:** Exports directory services data. Similar functionality is available using the Export feature of Workgroup Manager, a tool distributed as part of Mac OS X Server.

- **dsimport:** Imports directory services data. Similar functionality is available using the Import feature of Workgroup Manager.

- **dsmemberutil:** Looks up UUIDs and group information and flushes group cache (example: "dsmemberutil flushcache").

- **dsperfmonitor:** Runs performance monitors of the directory services plug-in, useful with debugging operations (example: "dsperfmonitor -dump").

- **id:** Looks up a user identity, including the group memberships (example: "id cedge").

When administrators from other platforms migrate to using Mac OS directory services, one of the first things they notice is that, by default, domain administrators from a directory service are not administrators of local Mac OS X client. To mimic this functionality, it is possible to nest a network directory service group inside the local administrators group, thereby propagating local administrator rights to all network members of that group. This is very handy in large environments where administrator access may need to be limited to subsets of administrators.

Many still choose to maintain a dedicated local administrative account on Mac OS X systems, useful for desktop support, automated patch management, and other administrative tasks. There are three ways to go about creating those local administrative accounts. The first is using the Setup Assistant or the Accounts System Preference Pane, common in monolithic imaging environments but not entirely scalable in large deployments. The second is by taking the .plist and the password hash files that comprise an account and dropping them into the default directory domain's hierarchy (as explained previously). The third way is by creating a script to automate the account creation. Scripting account creation is beyond the scope of this chapter, but there are many resources available on the Internet and in other books in this series that describe this process.

Creating a Second Local Directory Node

Now that we have a better understanding of how the local directory service works, let's look at how to create a second instance of that local directory service database. This is useful for hiding administrative accounts and, if you have a rogue account running on your system, it can also be useful for finding the source of that account. To create another directory node, first make a copy of the local directory services information store that we've been working on throughout this chapter. For this example, we're going to copy it into the same nodes folder that Mac OS X uses by default, but rather than call our node Default, we're just going to call it NEW:

`sudo cp -prnv /var/db/dslocal/nodes/Default /var/db/dslocal/nodes/NEW`

When it is started, the DirectoryService daemon will look in the nodes directory for any newly created nodes, which we want it to do. Let's restart the daemon with the following:

`sudo killall DirectoryService`

Now go ahead and open up Directory Utility.app (as described previously in this chapter) and click on the Search Policy tab. Authenticate using the lock in the lower left-hand corner of the screen, and then change the Search: field to Custom path.

External Accounts

External Accounts are similar to Mobile Accounts (which we will cover in more depth in Chapter 16). With an external account, you can store the user profile, password, and account information on removable media, making it portable across computers without a network. To do this, we're going to do some crafty manipulation of the createmobileaccount command located in the /System/Library/Coreservices/ManagedClient.app/Contents/Resources directory. This command is normally used when a Mobile Account logs into the computer. Rather than let the operating system decide whether it wants to invoke the createmobileaccount dialog at the loginwindow, we're going to force it to manually run it now. The -n, -p, and -h flags define the username, password, and home directory of the account. Assuming your USB drive is called JUMPDRIVE, the following will set up your external account on the removable media (by the way, this is not in your default path, which means you must always type the full path to the command or modify your shell preferences to make it your default path):

```
./createmobileaccount -n mobileadmin -p 'MYSECRETPASSWORD' -h
/Volumes/JUMPDRIVE/Users/mobileadmin
```

That's about all there is to it. If we wanted to, we could also enable FileVault by using the -e flag and/or run the command verbosely (great for troubleshooting issues during account creation) by using the -v flag. Next, use ls -al to verify that your new external account can write to the volume.

Restricting Access with the Command Line: sudoers

By editing the sudoers file, you can take a much more granular approach to securing users' access to resources. *Sudo* stands for "su do," and *su* stands for "substitute user." sudo is a command-line utility in Unix, Linux, and Mac OS X that allows users to run programs as though they were another, more powerful user. By default, sudo will run as a system's superuser, or root account (although this can be changed using the runas_default setting in the sudoers file). The syntax sudo will run *one* command as another user. The syntax su will run *all* commands that follow it as the administrative user who is invoked. su and sudo are useful tools, but they are also very powerful and can be used to accomplish almost anything once invoked, so take precautions. You should use su and sudo in as limited a fashion as possible. In fact, you should use su with even more caution than sudo, because it maintains the elevated permissions for the duration of a Terminal session, and its use is generally not recommended.

> **NOTE:** Sudo keeps a record of every command executed through it, while su (and sudo -s, sudo /bin/sh etc.) let users evade auditing once they have elevated.

As stated earlier, by default the root, or superuser, account is disabled in Mac OS X, but can be enabled using Directory Utility. In Mac OS X Server (as opposed to Client), the root account is enabled by default, and automatically is given the password of the first administrative user who is created during installation (more about root access in Mac OS X Server in Chapter 16).

> **NOTE:** By default, any administrative user can use the sudo command.

The sudoers file is located at /private/etc/sudoers. Editing the sudoers file is a direct way to add or remove the ability for users and groups to run certain commands and perform certain tasks from the system without having to use the GUI. Before editing the sudoers file, you should always back up the file. The following code is the default content of the sudoers file on a system (the lines that start with # are inactive):

```
# sudoers file.
#
```

```
# This file MUST be edited with the 'visudo' command as root.
#
# See the sudoers man page for the details on how to write a sudoers file.
#
# Host alias specification
# User alias specification
# Cmnd alias specification
# Defaults specification
Defaults    env_reset
Defaults    env_keep += "BLOCKSIZE"
Defaults    env_keep += "COLORFGBG COLORTERM"
Defaults    env_keep += "__CF_USER_TEXT_ENCODING"
Defaults    env_keep += "CHARSET LANG LANGUAGE LC_ALL LC_COLLATE LC_CTYPE"
Defaults    env_keep += "LC_MESSAGES LC_MONETARY LC_NUMERIC LC_TIME"
Defaults    env_keep += "LINES COLUMNS"
Defaults    env_keep += "LSCOLORS"
Defaults    env_keep += "SSH_AUTH_SOCK"
Defaults    env_keep += "TZ"
Defaults    env_keep += "DISPLAY XAUTHORIZATION XAUTHORITY"
Defaults    env_keep += "EDITOR VISUAL"
# Runas alias specification
# User privilege specification
root   ALL=(ALL) ALL
%admin  ALL=(ALL) ALL
# Uncomment to allow people in group wheel to run all commands
# %wheel  ALL=(ALL)   ALL
# Same thing without a password
# %wheel  ALL=(ALL)   NOPASSWD: ALL
# Samples
# %users ALL=/sbin/mount /cdrom,/sbin/umount /cdrom
# %users localhost=/sbin/shutdown -h now
```

In the following lines (part of the original file), root and users in the admin group are given access to a Host_Alias of ALL to Runas_Alias for all users and run Cmnd_Alias of ALL. This is unlimited access to the system, and it is what makes root the powerful account that it is. If you want to reduce the access that administrative users (users defined as administrators in the Accounts preference pane) are given, you can edit this setting. Let's take a look at the following two lines that are in the default sudoers file:

```
root   ALL=(ALL) ALL
%admin ALL=(ALL) ALL
```

> **NOTE:** In a Unix file, when you see an item with % in front of it, you are typically looking at a variable. Thus, %admin is the administrators group. If you create a new group called pirates on the Accounts Preference pane, then you would refer to it as %pirates here.

Table 3–1 lists some of the flags that you can use to define privileges in the sudoers file.

Table 3–1. sudoers *Flags*

Flag	Description
mail_always	Sends mail to the mailto user for every sudo event.
mail_badpass	Sends mail to the mailto user if the password is entered incorrectly.
mail_no_user	Sends mail to the mailto user if the user is not in the sudoers file.
mail_no_host	Sends mail to the mailto user if the host disallows the user.
mail_no_perms	Sends mail to the mailto user if a disabled command is run.
tty_tickets	Users must authenticate per shell instance.
authenticate	Users must authenticate before running commands.
root_sudo	Disables users from invoking a shell using sudo.
log_host	Adds the hostname to logs.
log_year	Adds the year to logs.
set_home	Sets the HOME variable (~) to the target user's home.
always_set_home	Always sets the HOME variable (~) to the target user's home.
path_info	Disables prompts that a command is not in a user's path.
fqdn	Puts fully qualified hostnames in the sudoers file.
insults	Insults users when they enter incorrect passwords.
requiretty	Disables running visudo unless a Terminal session is present.
env_editor	Allows other text editors to edit the sudoers file. This is useful if limiting to pico or vi.
rootpw	Prompts for root password versus invoking a user's password.
runaspw	Prompts for the password of the user defined by runas_default.
targetpw	Prompts for the password of the user specified when using -u.
set_logname	Logs sudo events using the invoking user's name.
stay_setuid	Runs sudo as the real UID of the invoking user (same as set_logname).

To edit the sudoers file, you will be using the visudo command. This command will lock the file so that it cannot be written to by multiple programs. It will also verify that the file is complete with all its necessary parts and will check the file for syntax errors before allowing you to save it. Because the visudo command uses the vi text editor to edit the sudoers file, you will likely want to become familiar with vi before editing your sudoers file. For more on using the vi command, see the man page by entering the following from a command prompt (/Applications/Utilities/Terminal):

man vi

> **TIP:** Before editing the file, it is also a good idea to read the man page for visudo by entering man visudo at the command line. man will go into full detail on the uses and syntax for the program as well as any other command you're curious about.

If the file is not edited properly, it should not allow you to save it when you are finished editing. You can use the -c option with visudo to run a check of the file's syntax and ensure it is able to parse properly. The -c stands for "check mode." You can run the command by entering the following:

visudo -c

This should return with the following line provided that the file parses correctly:

/private/etc/sudoers file parsed OK

Now that you know how to check the file, let's take a look at the -f option, which is used to specify an alternate sudoers file in a different location, leaving the live sudoers file untouched. There are a variety of reasons for wanting to work with the file in a separate location, such as transferring the file to another system or changing its configuration to then have it to go live at a later date with that changed configuration. For example, you can use the following command to create a temporary sudoers file called sudoers.inprogress:

visudo -f /etc/sudoers.inprogress

You can use aliases in the sudoers file to indicate a variable that contains a user, multiple users, a group, or multiple groups. When working with multiple users or groups on a system, it is always a good idea to create aliases on the system to apply attributes to multiple users or groups at once. If you need to apply the same access rights to a group of users, you can do this by using an alias membership rather than by applying permissions for each user individually. When referencing an alias or group of users in sudoers, you will notice that % will be placed in front of the group name. To be clear, the % character is not used to signify the name of a new group, but is used to reference groups. For example, by adding the following line to the sudoers file, you could create an alias called powerusers that contains members of a group called admin, the user called cedge, and a user called MyCompany. We will also create an entry that simply lists those who the webmasters are:

User_Alias   powerusers = %admin, cedge, MyCompany
User_Alias   webusers = mark, joel, michael

Setting up a Runas_Alias for a user or group will define the user or system daemon that a user or alias can run as when using the sudo command. In the following line, we will tell the system that the webusers defined previously are able to run commands as the apache system user:

Runas_Alias   webusers = apache

The Host_Alias allows you to define a group of computers, also called *hosts*. You can reference hosts by name, by IP, or by a range of either. When defining a range, rather than specify every element within the range, it's preferable to use wildcards as catchalls. Wildcards that can be used are similar to those available in shell scripting, as shown in Table 3–2.

> **NOTE:** When using wildcards, you will not be granting access to commands in subfolders of those you define. You will need to specify those separately.

Table 3–2. *Wildcards*

Wildcard	Description
?	Matches a single character.
*	Matches multiple characters.
[...]	Matches a character in a range.
[!...]	Matches a character that is not in the range.
\x	Escapes characters, similar to regular expressions.

For example, if you want to create an alias list of all your servers, which are named afpserver1, afpserver2, odserver1, odserver2, adserver1, and adserver2, then you could use *server? for the Host_Alias. Additionally, you can use specific IP addresses or IP addresses with a subnet defined. The Host_Alias comes in handy when you are pushing out a sudoers file to a large number of machines and want to have different options for different hosts. An example of a Host_Alias configuration might include the following:

Host_Alias   Servers = *server?, 10.0.1.0/255.255.255.0
Host_Alias   Workstations = 10.0.2.0/255.255.255.0

The next portion of the sudoers file defines the commands that aliases or users can access. Cmnd_Alias is used to set them. For example, if you want to give a user access to run all the commands in the /usr/sbin directory and all the commands located in the /usr/bin folder, you would use the following line:

Cmnd_Alias = /usr/sbin/*, /usr/bin/*

The final portion of the sudoers file is where access to resources is granted to users or aliases. In previous sections of the sudoers file, we defined lists of groups, computers, and commands. Now you can take all of this and put it together by listing the group of users that has access to run specified commands on specified machines. The basic syntax of the sudoers file would read like this:

<User_Alias>   <Host_Alias> = (<Runas_Alias>) <Cmnd_Alias>

To put this into a real-world example, you can look at allowing the web scripters who were defined earlier to access the /private/etc/httpd program on servers. Here you will also introduce NOPASSWD and PASSWD into the sudoers file. This tells the system whether to prompt a user for a password when they are attempting to sudo the command that is being called. Keep in mind that, when using the NOPASSWD tag, you will not be prompted for a password. Once you've written in a section and you're committing a password to authenticate, it's a good idea to give it a once-over to catch any errors with the line before submitting the password to the system.

The section of the sudoers file for webscripters is as follows:

```
User_Alias   webscripters = mark, joel, michael
Runas_Alias  webscripters = apache
Host_Alias   Servers = *server?, 10.0.1.0/255.255.255.0
Cmnd_Alias   web = /private/etc/httpd
Webscripters Servers = (webscripters) NOPASSWD: web
```

Once you have written a good sudoers file, you can push it to other users on your network. You can do this a variety of ways; most notably through ARD, radmind, the Casper Suite, or SSH. These technologies are a bit beyond the scope of this book, but they're definitely worth researching for their administrative abilities. You can find more information on ARD at www.apple.com/remotedesktop. You can find more information on radmind at http://rsug.itd.umich.edu/software/radmind. You can find more information on the Casper Suite at www.jamfsoftware.com/products/casper5.php.

> **NOTE:** If rules in sudoers conflict, the last rule applied will be activated.

Securing Mount Points

Navigating the file system through the Finder or through Terminal on a mounted drive is one of the most common tasks a user will do on their computer. It is also one of the most common things an attacker who is actually looking for information will do. You never want your system to be compromised, but when it does happen, you want to limit the access that an unauthorized user will have. Restricting access to disks, volumes, and RAIDs using mount options is one way to accomplish this.

> **NOTE:** Each disk in a computer has a collection of disks that are mounted. This can be seen and controlled easily in the Disk Utility application. However, you will often need more granular controls, such as mounting a volume in verbose mode.

Once a disk is mounted, it is typically considered a *volume*. Running the df command, a command used exclusively for mounting disks, will show you all the volumes mounted on the system. Another command, the mount command, will also display mounted disks but can further be used to mount disks with different options, giving administrators a higher level of control over those disks. Until a disk is mounted, it will be listed in /dev/diskname (disks are often listed sequentially, as disk0s2, disk0s3, and so on). The mount command will be active only until the first reboot.

Common options for the mount command include the following:

- -t Specifies the file system type.
- -r Mounts the file system as read-only.
- -f Forces the file system into a read-only state.
- -a Mounts all the file systems available in the fstab file.
- -d Uses all the options in a dry run.
- -v Uses verbose mode with the mount command.

Administrators can mount drives that have disabled the ability to write to them or enabled other access options by mounting a disk using the -o flag in the command. The proper syntax for this command is to put the option in front of the o, such as -fo or -do. One example of using the option with the mount command is using the -ro command to make a disk read-only (or more specifically revoke-write access), often used when forensics are being performed on a system.

It is also possible to stop Mac OS X from automatically registering and mounting drives that are inserted into it by disabling diskarbitrationd, the system process that polls for new disks. There are multiple methods for doing this, which will force users to use the mount command in order to register a new disk with the operating system. One way is to kill the process and then remove the /usr/sbin/diskarbitrationd file, completely removing the daemon. Another is to move the /System/Library/LaunchDaemons/com.apple.diskarbitrationd.plist file to another location, such as the Desktop. Removing or renaming the property list (plist) file is typically the best choice. You can also control the mounting and unmounting of disks using Disk Utility or the Terminal diskutil framework.

> **NOTE:** Disk arbitration and forensics are covered in further detail in Chapter 19.

SUID Applications: Getting into the Nitty-Gritty

There are a variety of applications running on your system, and not all run as your user. When you open Activity Monitor from /Applications/Utilities and change the filter option to Administrator Processes, you will see all the processes running on the system as root. Applications that are running as root often have the SUID bit set, causing them to be run as the owner of the file, which for many of these applications is root. To view whether a file has the SUID bit set, you can run an `ls -l` command in a given directory to look for any file with a listing that has an s listed rather than an execute bit in the permissions line for owners of the file. For example:

```
-r-s--x--x  1 root root 19809 Jan 14 14:05 ps
```

Binary files (executables) that are not written well can cause SUID bits to allow for privilege escalation to an administrative user. Although you might not want to allow SUID files on your system, it's not realistic to remove the SUID bit from all files, because some applications will require certain files to be SUID, such as login. Most SUID applications exist to specifically let users perform privileged operations or gain access to resources that require root privileges when they are not logged in as the root user. Therefore, the root user owns most SUID applications.

Many applications that are not written specifically to allow manual privilege escalation actually provide a way to execute a command. Vi allows users to run commands from within the interactive text editor. Many other commands, such as less and more, allow commands to be executed by pressing the ! key while viewing a file that takes up more than one page of content. Knowing whether each SUID application is dangerous requires knowing the details of using each of these applications, and whether a shell command can be run from within the command or some binary file can be invoked receiving root access. To find all SUID applications, use the following command for a listing of all SUID or SGID files:

```
sudo find / -type f \( -perm -04000 -or -perm 02000 \) -ls
```

> **NOTE:** Mac OS X allowed SUID shell scripts until the 10.3.9 software update, so if you are running an operating system prior to Tiger 10.4, consider SUID shell scripts while auditing your system.

To fix the SUID scenario, set the UID for a user. In our example, the user will be test. If the file is executed, it will now run with the rights of the user invoking the file and not with the rights of the user who runs it:

```
chmod u+s test
```

If you are in a SGID (group SUIDs) scenario rather than a SUID scenario, set the GID for test. If executed, the file will now run with the rights of the group of the file and not with the rights of the group that runs it:

```
chmod g+s test
```

If an SGID is set on a directory, all newly created files inside this folder won't inherit the main group ID of the creator. Instead, they will be created with the group ID of the folder. For example, the SGID is set for the test folder `folder1`, and it has the group ID for www. Now, if the root user creates a file inside `folder1`, the group ID for this file will not be root but www. SUID and SGID can be set at the same time.

Creating Files with Permissions

By default, when creating a new file, the default permissions of that file are determined by the umask variable. You can work with the umask to edit the default permissions of new files. You can configure the umask setting by using the umask command. Of course, we advise that you only perform the following commands if you have a pretty good idea of what you're doing here. Fixing disk permission mistakes can be a time-consuming and costly endeavor.

First, run the command umask from a Terminal screen by typing umask at a command prompt. When you do this, you will get a number as your response. The umask variable is subtracted from the total permissions number possible for securing Unix files, 777. This leads to a umask of 0022 creating new files on a hard drive with permissions of 755.

> **NOTE:** For more information on POSIX permissions, see Chapter 4.

If you enter umask 0002 at the command line, then you will be telling the system to create new files with permissions of 775. However, if you use a umask of 077, then you will cause all new files to be readable only by the user who creates and subsequently owns the files.

Using the umask command to set default file permissions only applies to the umask setting for your session. This means the next time you restart your system, this setting will be lost. To permanently reset the permissions for new files, you will need to edit the globalpreferences. plist file on a per-user basis by inserting an NSUmask override setting in the file ~/Library/Preferences/.GlobalPreferences.plist. Insert these lines using your favorite plist file editor (Property List Editor is a tool built into Mac OS X and shown in Figure 3–18) or using the defaults command:

```
<key>NSUmask</key>
<integer>0</integer>
```

Replace the 0 with the decimal conversion of the octal umask you want to set. A decimal NSumask of 0 gives the octal umask value of 007, meaning that we allow only owners and users in a files group access to newly created files. The recommendation from Apple is to use /etc/launchd-user.conf, with a line containing "umask nnn."However, a user can then set their own umask using ~/.launchd.conf. The umask can also be defined in /etc/launchd.conf, but that sets it for all processes including system daemons which can potentially cause unexpected results.

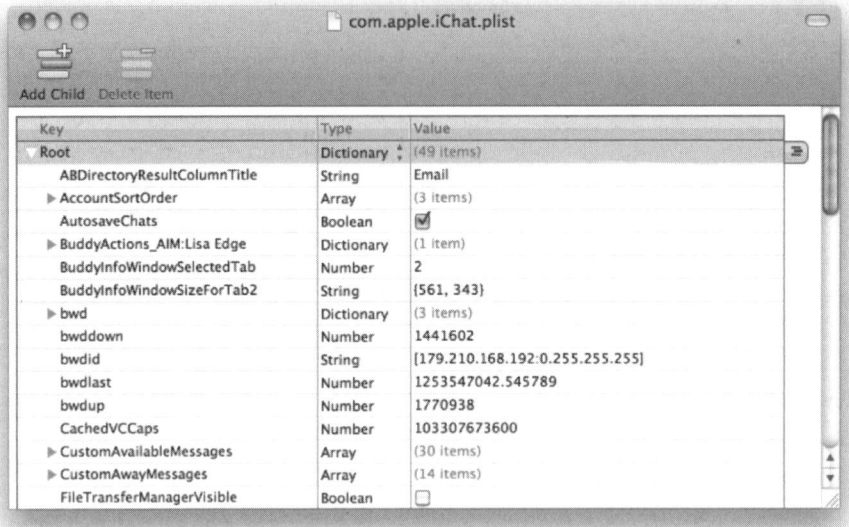

Figure 3-18. *Editing a plist using Property List Editor*

> **NOTE:** To edit this globally, insert the same setting into the file
> `/Library/Preferences/.GlobalPreferences.plist`.

Summary

We started this chapter with securing accounts using graphical tools such as the Accounts System Preferences. Once we looked at the options available through graphical means, we switched gears and started looking at those available only from the command line (such as visudo). You'll notice that the granularity of control over accounts goes far beyond that which has been provided in those Preference panes. Once we moved through the options in the preferences, we then correlated them with how those options reflect some of the changes in the property list files that make up the local directory service. By the way, there are other locations where accounts can reside, and so in Chapter 16, we will look at how Open Directory impacts accounts.

There are a myriad of options for securing user accounts, including those that you can start to look at through local managed client preferences. However, these are beyond the scope of this book. Check out *Enterprise Mac Managed Preferences*, published by Apress. Find it at `apress.com/book/view/9781430229377`.

In Chapter 4 we will cover permissions, one of the most important aspects of securing Mac OS X, a concept that builds on the concepts explained throughout this chapter!

Chapter 4

File System Permissions

There's a lot of misinformation and confusion surrounding the proper management of permissions in OS X. Discussions on the topic have been fairly heated since the migration to OS X from OS 9, which had very loose capabilities for delegating, assigning, and managing access to files and folders. OS X, in contrast, was a native multiuser OS and, as such, permission-based restrictions were, and still are, at its heart and soul.

From a security perspective, file system permissions are your data's first line of defense in a multiuser environment. A well-managed permission scheme ensures that your data is accessible and modifiable only by the proper people. The file system, after all, is the gateway to your data. An ineffective permission scheme is the equivalent of handing your data out to anyone who would express interest in it, or even worse, allowing them to destroy it. Furthermore, poorly implemented permissions can serve a different evil, preventing honest, hardworking Joe from accessing either his own documents or documents created by his collaborators.

Thus, file system permissions covers the triad of information security: *confidentiality* (ensuring your sensitive data isn't viewed by the wrong eyes), *integrity* (ensuring that data isn't manipulated by unwanted parties), and *accessibility* (ensuring that the right parties can access data consistently and reliably). This is no light matter: a small change to permissions on a directory toward the top of your file system hierarchy can have wide-sweeping effects in all three areas. Suddenly, that chmod -R 777 command that you read about online and are about to run might not seem like a good idea, and it probably isn't (if you don't understand what this means, don't worry, you will by the end of this chapter). Too many environments take a lax view on file system permissions simply because it's easier to not have to deal with them. Unfortunately, many people don't realize the importance of data security until they have to reassemble the damage caused by poorly managed permissions on vulnerable data.

In this chapter, we will cover the ins and outs of file system discretionary access controls provided by Mac OS X version 10.6. Specifically, we will cover techniques utilizing all of Snow Leopard's tools (graphical and command line) to help ensure that your data is accessible by those who need to access it, and safe from manipulation by those who don't.

In this chapter we will also cover the impact of file system permissions on the security of an operating system itself. Permissions problems not only can lead to exposed or vulnerable data, but they can also lead to the complete compromise of your system.

Mac OS File Permissions: A Brief History of Time

For many Mac users, the concept of file system permissions is both relatively new and oft misunderstood. First introduced in OS X, file system permissions were a drastic departure from Mac OS 9's largely unprotected system, a trait revealing of the system's single-user nature.

With OS X came a true multiuser OS born of Unix roots and, as such, a POSIX compliant (**P**ortable **O**perating **S**ystem **I**nterface) file system permissions implementation. If you're scratching your head right now, don't worry; the term POSIX simply refers to a series of standards covering a number of OS conventions, of which most relevant to this chapter are those covering file system permissions. Outside of Windows, the POSIX permissions standard has been the primary permissions model used by every relevant operating system on the market today. Realistically, this boils down to all of the various Unix and Linux distributions out there. Windows does itself provide a POSIX-compliant file system in NTFS, though its primary permissions model is based around Access Control Lists (ACLs), which we will get to in a bit.

The basic premise found in a POSIX-compliant permissions scheme is that each file system object, say a file or directory, has associated controls that determine the level of access that a user is granted to that object. In such a scheme there are three different access levels (referred to as *modes*), which can be defined for an object: *read*, *write*, and *execute*. These three access levels can be applied for each file or folder at three distinct targets: the file's owner, the file's group, and everyone else. With POSIX, a file system object can have only one owner or group, so at first glance, this may seem somewhat limiting, and it certainly can be. However, you can actually establish pretty complex and workable permission schemes using POSIX alone.

ACLs were introduced to OS X in version 10.4, and provide a new approach to permission access to files. While the POSIX standard does have a working draft for ACL permissions in the form of the POSIX1.e proposed standard, the status of the standard is very much in limbo, to say the least. Apple instead chose to implement an ACL system based off of the NFSv4 standard as defined in RFC 3010. This standard is implemented in such a fashion that makes it compatible with ACL implementations utilized by Windows systems beginning with Windows NT. Other systems that include support for NFSv4 ACL include Solaris and FreeBSD9. Most Linux systems adopt the POSIX1e ACLs, which only support a subset of access controls provided by the NFSv4 system.

With OS X's ACL implementation, each file system object contains a single access control list table, which contains multiple access control entries (ACEs). Each ACE defines a subject and a set of specific access rights. In OS X, the subject can be a user or a group, and there are up to 17 different access rights that can be explicitly allowed or denied for any file system object (access control rights are discussed in detail later on in this chapter). On top of this, a particular file's access control list is completely extensible, which means that an arbitrary number of ACEs can be assigned to any particular file system object. Basically what this means is that ACL-based file system permissions allow for extremely granular and flexible management.

In OS X's early incarnations, permissions problems were common among long-time Mac users, and to a degree they still are. However, any permissions problems that persist in a 10.6 environment are, plain and simple, due to poor administration. The truth of the matter is that in the earlier days of OS X, permissions problems were abundant, not only because of user inexperience but also in a large part to significant limits of OS X's permissions implementation. Although OS X has always had a basic POSIX permission system, in the early days there were fairly decent limitations to its implementations that made it difficult to properly harness. Luckily, OS X's permissions system have continuously improved throughout the life of OS X, and now with 10.6 we have a combination of basic POSIX permissions and ACLs which provide for rock solid, flexible file system permissions structures.

POSIX Permissions

As previously mentioned, basic POSIX permissions have been with OS X since its inception. Using POSIX, you can apply access restrictions at three different classes: that of the owner, of the group, and of everyone else. A file references its owner or group based upon an ID that is stored directly with the file. In order to determine the actual owner or group of a file, the OS cross-references the files user and group id against its Directory Services database.

For instance, every OS X system out of the box has a local user "admin," created with user id 501, and the default group "staff," which has an ID of 20. Therefore, any file that is owned by the user id 501 and the group id 20 is owned by the user "admin" and the group "staff," respectively. The third class is implicit for anyone that is not user "admin" or a member of group "staff." When qualifying for access to a file or directory, OS X will first check to see if the requested file or directory is owned by the effective owner or group of the currently running process. If the system determines that the user is the owner, the user will receive effective permissions assigned to the owner class. All other classes will be ignored. If the user is a member of the group associated with the file or directory, and is not the owner, then the user will receive effective permissions assigned to the group class. If the user is neither the owner nor a member of the file/folder's group, then the user will receive effective permissions of the "everyone" class.

> **NOTE:** If the user is the owner of the file, and the file's class does not have write permissions, then the user will not have write privileges to the file regardless of "group" or "everyone" class permissions.

Modes in Detail

Each class has three possible access capabilities, represented by three different modes:

Read: The read mode, when set on a file, allows a user to read its contents. In terms of a directory, the read mode grants the ability to list its contents.

Write: The write mode allows a user to modify a file's contents. When set on a directory, the write mode grants the ability to create subfolders or files. It also allows the ability to rename or delete files it directly contains, even if the user does not have write privileges on the file she is attempting to rename or delete. If a user does not have write privileges to a directory, she will be unable to rename, move, or delete any items directly residing in it, even if she has write privileges to the item itself.

Execute: The execute mode grants the ability for a file to execute in the system. This is not the same as opening a file. Execution implies that the file contains either compiled executable binary data or scripting text, which references an interpreter via a hash-bang (#!) statement, such as a shell script. For instance, if we were to write a basic bash shell script named "Click Here For Cool Stuff," save the file, and then grant ourselves execution privileges to that file, we could simply double-click on it for it to execute. If this script were to be malicious in intent, say for instance it provided instruction to delete all data that the user can access, then that badness is only a double-click away for any user that has access to the file, and it has a fairly intriguing name that most of your users would likely freely click on. (Who doesn't want to see cool stuff ?) If that malcontent script does not have execution privileges assigned, then it's largely relegated to text or binary data file. Once execution is granted, it becomes a significant and warranted threat to your user base. This is not to say that the data is completely harmless without execution rights, but by removing the executable bit the code will not be a double-click away from execution.

When applied to a directory, the execute mode grants the ability to traverse a directory. Essentially, this mode controls the ability to access any resources that exist in this directory. When applied to a directory, the execute mode is non-discriminating and absolute; without execute permissions on a directory, you will not be able to access any items inside of that directory regardless of permissions or depth of any of its containing items.

> **NOTE:** When set on a directory, the write mode grants the ability to rename its direct descendents, even if the user does not have write privileges on the subfolder or file they are attempting to rename. This has significant security ramifications: any directory that contains directly executable code or referenced code that will operate under the root user, or otherwise in system automations or routine maintenance, should be closely scrutinized. It is a possible vector for attack; a malicious user can rename the executable or referenced code and inject his own routines, thereby compromising your system in full or part.

As an exercise, if we were to remove the execute permissions from the root directory of our volume, "/", then a significant number of critical processes, including our own user environment, would fail to properly operate due to lack of resources. By eliminating execute privileges on the root directory, we essentially cut off access to all data on the drive. Denying execute privileges is a good way to completely block users from accessing data at the perimeter of a directory structure, thus allowing you to continue to use owner, group, and everyone management on subdirectories with impunity from users that don't meet criteria further up the tree.

Contrast this to the read mode: if we were to simply remove read permissions from root, the ramifications would be far less drastic. We would not be able to view the contents directly of the root directory, but once we traversed into a subfolder, such as /Applications (possible because it is executable), we would be subject to the Application's folders permissions, and subsequently the permissions on any of the individual files in that subdirectory. Now, because we don't have read access to list the contents of the root volume, we wouldn't be able to traverse into a subfolder unless we knew that it existed and what it was named. But this type of security through obscurity can also be bypassed. What we want to emphasize here is that denying users read privileges on a directory will not prevent them from traversing into its subdirectories, where they'll have any access granted at the applicable owner, group or everyone classes, a potentially less secure environment.

Modes are established on a file through the use of a bit-flag system. To truly understand this system, it is best to look at it from a command line system (we will cover GUI permissions a bit further on in this section).

For example, consider the list of files and directories in the /Users folder that the command `ls -al /Users` produces, shown in Figure 4–1.

```
helyx:~ hunterbj$ ls -al /Users
total 0
drwxr-xr-x  10 root     admin   340 Jul 1 20:22 .
drwxrwxr-t@ 51 root     admin  1802 Jul 7 00:58 ..

drwxrwxrwt  13 root     wheel   442 Jun 29 23:54 Shared
drwxrwxr-x+ 20 demo     admin   680 May 29 18:15 demo
drwxr-xr-x+ 55 hunterbj staff  1870 Jul 8 00:57 hunterbj
```

Figure 4–1. *Output of command `ls –al /Users` with Permissions, owner, group, and folder name identified.*

As illustrated in the figure, in every line of the output, the first field (the one containing combinations of dashes and the letters *d, r, t, w,* and *x*) reports the POSIX permissions. For clarity, let's look at the hunterbj folder:

```
drwxr-xr-x+ 20 hunterbj    staff   1870 Jul 8 00:56 hunterbj
```

Here, the string "drwxr-xr-x" defines the POSIX permissions. In an `ls -al` output, the first digit, 'd', specifies the file system type, and in this case, a directory. Other common entries will include a dash '–' for a file, an 'l' for a symbolic link. The next three digits, rwx (read, write, and execute), represent the mode for the owner, who in this example is hunterbj. Thus, user hunterbj has read, write, and execute privileges for this folder. The next three digits represent group privileges: "staff" has read and execute privileges. The final three characters represent permissions for everyone else: in this case, only read and execute privileges.

On a lower level, POSIX uses bit flags to represent modes. This means that permissions are represented by a unique numerical value. The read, write, and execute modes are each represented by three separate bits. The easiest way to illustrate this is by comparing it to our previous ls output.

```
drwxr-xr-x
d111101101
```

As was explained earlier, the first three characters after the 'd' designate permissions for the owner. In this case, 'rwx' is represented in binary as 111, which has a decimal value of 7. The group also has rwx privileges, which is also a decimal value of 7. The 'everyone' class has only read and execute permissions, r-x, which is 101 in binary and a decimal value of 5. Thus, the above permissions translate to 775 in their decimal form, a common type of notation called octal notation. See Table-41 for a better representation of the permissions layout.

Table 4–1. *Permissions represented in alpha, decimal, and binary format*

Permission	String Notation (ls –l)	Binary Notation	Octal Notation
Read	r--	100	4
Write	-w-	010	2
Execute	--x	001	1
Read & Write	rw-	110	6
Read & Execute	r-x	101	5
Read, Write, & Execute	rwx	111	7

You don't really need to be able to do binary math in your head to manage POSIX permissions, but knowing the numeric values of each mode can be important, as they are commonly used when managing permissions from the command line interface, which is discussed later in this chapter.

Inheritance

Another aspect to understanding POSIX permissions in OS X is inheritance, or how the system deals with group assignment on newly created files and directories. Historically in OS X there has been absolutely no inheritance capabilities of the POSIX permissions structure. This has largely contributed to many of the issues with which administrators new to the OS X platform would struggle. Prior to OS X 10.5, when a user created a file, that file would assume the owner of the creating user, and would assume group ownership based on the creating user's primary group id. This made it extremely difficult to manage permissions for users that would collaborate in numerous distinct groups; a user only has one primary group id, but may collaborate across several different groups.

With 10.5, Apple introduced compliance with Single Unix Standard, version 3 (SUS3), which dictates that the group established to the new file will be inherited based on group ownership of the parent directory. This is a *much* better system, and produces a lot less frustration. With this change, you can now use group permissions on directories to establish group-specific collaboration areas. For instance, imagine that user jdoe creates a file in the Workgroup1 folder, which has the group "workgroup1" assigned to it. The file will be owned by user jdoe and will have a group of "workgroup1" regardless of the primary group assigned to jdoe's user account. The user can then browse into the Workgroup2 folder, and create a file under that folder. The second file will have a primary group of "workgroup2."

There's a few potential wrinkles in this plan. First, if not planned properly, the new behavior of group inheritance on files and folders may have some unexpected side effects. For instance, if you are utilizing file system quotas, it is important to note that when establishing group ownership on a directory to a group that has quota limitations, any new files in that folder will count against the group quota. Thus, if you are using quotas, you need to take this consideration into account when structuring your hierarchy. The second problem is that, by default, OS X ships with a umask value of 022. The umask is a value that is used to determine default permissions on newly created files. When a user creates a file, the files' established permissions are determined by taking the default mode of 666 (777 for new folders), and then filtering that value by the user's umask value (022). To determine ultimate privileges, you simply subtract the number representing the umask from that of the privileges. So in this case, newly created file system objects will have a mode of 644 (666 minus 022), or rw-r--r--.). It would be an extremely bad idea for all new files to be executable, so their default mode is 666. On the other hand, if folders don't have execute permissions, then no one will be able to navigate into them. Thus, folders have a default mode of 777. The umask is then used to determine final permissions for any new files or folders.

The main problem with a file that has rw-r--r-- (644) permissions is that the middle octal, the group octal (r--), assigns read (r) permissions, but no write (w) capabilities. This is a very important thing to understand: by default in OS X, newly created files are *not* group-writeable. This means that when a user creates a new file in OS X, by default, only the creating user has the ability to modify (write) that file. Although this is the most secure configuration, it immediately becomes a problem when more than one person needs to modify that file. Failing to recognize this leads to serious permissions problems when using POSIX permissions in a collaborative environment. Luckily, you can change the user's umask. To do this, we must first calculate our desired umask. In most cases, we want new files to be writeable by both the creating user, and the group owner of the file, which is represented as rw-rw-r-x visually or as 664 using octet representation. To determine the umask that we want to use, we subtract our desired mode for new files (664) from the default file mode (666). 666-664 is 002, thus our desired umask is 002.

CHAPTER 4: File System Permissions

To apply this umask in OS X 10.5 or later, simply run the umask command with the desired mode /usr/bin/umask 002.

Unfortunately, executing umask may not affect all running processes, and the result won't persist across reboots. To remedy the situation, we recommend using the launchd-user.conf file found at /private/etc/launchd-user.conf. To set this, simply run echo "umask 002" >> /private/etc/launchd-user.conf as root. That's it. Reboot and you're done. From now on, whenever your machine boots up, it will read this file and set the desired umask value for any user sessions.launchd.conf at the root of their home directory.

If you're running OS X 10.4 or earlier, the process for changing the umask is slightly different and a lot more complex. We recommend installing the program Umask Doctor and setting it to launch at login if you do not wish to do this programatically. This utility specifically performs this duty, and it works out pretty well. Alternatively, you can simply make the change via the defaults command run with root/sudo privileges:

```
defaults write /Library/Preferences/.GlobalPreferences NSUmask 2
```

Note, however, that the NSUmask value is actually a decimal value of the octal umask, so you'll have to do a conversion. In other words, instead of viewing the number 777 as three different values of 7 (owner), 7 (group), and 7 (other), it instead views it as a single number: 777.

The approach to determine the decimal umask for this command is to convert the binary representation of the umask octal to decimal, so a little knowledge of binary is required.

For example, let's examine a umask of 022. If we convert each of these octets (0,2,2) into binary, the values are 000 (0), 010 (2), and 010 (2) (when doing this conversion it's important to always use 3 significant digits). After converting each octet into binary, the next step is to concatenate the values. In this case, 000,010, and 010 become 000010010. This value, when converted to decimal is 18 ($0 \times 2^0 + 1 \times 2^1 + 0 \times 2^2 + 0 \times 2^3 + 1 \times 2^4 = 18$). This decimal value is then the number to substitute for the NSUmask value. One other note: the programs that honor the NSUmask will typically operate in an OS X GUI environment, as it is a function of the Cocoa framework. Technically, command-line applications can support this property, but typically command line apps will utilize the more traditional POSIX/umask model. Not all third-party Cocoa programs support this value, but generally the major players do.

Once you have set the umask, simply restart the computer. From then on out, that computer will freely interact in collaborative folders, and files that they create will be able to be modified by other group members without having to file a helpdesk ticket. Neat.

> **NOTE:** Fortunately if you don't know binary, OS X's Calculator.app has a programmer mode which does all the mental work for you. To access this function, open up the Calculator application found in /Applications, and then select Programmer under the view menu (or use the keyboard shortcut command+3).

The Sticky Bit

For day-to-day management of POSIX permissions, the three modes we previously discussed (read, write, execute) will be your primary weapons against those pesky permissions issues. But you do have a few more tools at your disposal. In a previous ls output we showed, you may have noticed some special permissions on the directory /Users/Shared. Here's the line again:

drwxrwx**rwt** 13 root   wheel   442 Jun 29 23:54 Shared

Under the "everyone" digits (the letters in **bold**), instead of the expected *x* (execute), we have a *t*. This is referred to as the *sticky bit*. This bit has no effect on files in OS X, but when enabled on a directory, it prevents deletion or renaming of files inside of that directory by anyone other than the file's owner. Thus, if Jimbob creates a file, then gives everyone read and write privileges (or if you modified the umask), Geraldine will be able to edit its content, but not delete it or rename the file. Only Jimbob can delete the file. It's worth noting, though, that with write privileges, nothing stops Gerry from simply deleting all of the file's contents. The sticky bit simply disables the user from completely deleting it.

To assign the sticky bit to a directory, you simply use a fourth octal number, which has a value of 001. Thus, the Shared folder in the example line above has a mode of 1777, with the 1 (001 binary) being the "sticky" directory. To actually apply this mode to a file, use the chmod command. Run it as root if you're the owner of the targeted directory:

chmod 1777 /Users/Shared
chmod -R 777 /Users/Shared/*

The second line specifies the -R flag, which will actually apply the mode 777 to all items inside of the /Users/Shared/ directory. Thus, all files in the directory will be editable by anyone, but because of the first command that was run, only the owner can delete a file.

The suid/sguid Bits

The fourth octal has two modes in addition to sticky: *set-group-ID-on-execution,* which has a value of 010, and *set-user-ID-on-execution bit,* which has a value of 100. If either of these modes is set on an executable, whenever that file runs, it will do so in the context of the owner and group assigned to it. Thus, if a program is owned by root and has setuid on, whoever runs that program will have root access (within the confines of that program). This is a bit of a scary thought, so use this capability with great care. Many a local privileged-escalation exploit has been born from the setuid bit. In the early days of OS X, it was possible to set the suid bit on shell scripts as well as other interpreted scripting languages (Python, Perl, Ruby, and the like). Shell scripts have numerous attack vectors, and Apple considered this to be a large security risk. Thus this is no longer applicable. The suid and guid bits will now only be honored on pre-compiled binary executable files. Additionally, regardless of what the man page for chmod claims, the suid and sguid bits have no affect on directories in OS X. They are simply ignored. In general, use of the suid bits should be extremely limited and rare. OS X is one of the larger offenders of this principle, as OS X has historically had a large number of `suid` programs in a default number. Thankfully, the number of programs that ship with this privilege is reduced with each iteration of OS X. It is important to note that the `setuid` and `setgid` bit are not honored on removable file systems. This is important, as it provides protection against a rogue program that is introduced from a foreign (and potentially contaminated) file system, such as a Firewire, USB, or optical drives. This prevents a malicious user from being able to introduce `setuid` and `setgid` programs into the environment.

> **NOTE:** You may want to occasionally audit which executables in your system have the `setuid` and `setgid` bits set, as any executable with such privileges are potential attack vectors by local users. To see a list of all such files on your system, you can use the command:
>
> ```
> find / -type f \( -perm -4000 -o -perm -2000 \) -ls
> ```

POSIX in Practice

So that is POSIX permissions in a nutshell. The system may seem somewhat limited, but really, you're limited only by your own ingenuity and the speed at which your fingers type. In a POSIX environment, groups and nested hierarchies are your friend to creating collaborative environments, though it is also important to pay attention to file-level permissions as well to ensure data confidentiality and integrity. To illustrate this, we'll walk through some complex permissions scenarios and discuss strategies for deploying POSIX permissions.

One environment where complex POSIX hierarchies are crucial is education. Consider the various levels of accessibility that servers in an educational institution would need configured. Education environments have needs for private file-sharing collaboration areas among faculty. Such a file share needs to have facilities to provide documents to students, facilities for students to collaborate (share files with each other), and finally it is necessary for students to privately provide teachers with documents that cannot be viewed by other students (hand-in assignments).

To fulfill these various needs, you must first examine how you want to structure your data. Do you need to isolate faculty data from student data? Should it be on a different server altogether, or is it ok to store on the same volume as the rest of the student data? What kind of faculty data should be stored on a server with student data? Will faculty only be storing class-relevant data on this data store, therefore making it okay to group faculty data along with student data? This illustrates a very important point: securing your permissions on your file system is only part of your solution. It is important that you, as the admin, educate your end users on acceptable use policy, data security policies, and practices. For instance, it would be a very bad idea for your teachers to place personal information about students, such as social security numbers, medical information, and so on, in a public location. This may seem like common sense, but as an administrator it is your duty to ensure that your users are educated and in line with company/organization security best-practices and policies.

So, with all considerations in mind, we have devised an appropriate permissions hierarchy to allow students and teachers to securely utilize their file storage, shown in Figure 4–2.

Name	Date Modified	Size	Kind
▼ Comm101	Today, 2:37 PM	--	Folder
▶ Course Files	Today, 2:20 PM	--	Folder
Hand-ins	Today, 2:20 PM	--	Folder
▶ Public	Today, 2:20 PM	--	Folder
Staff	Today, 2:19 PM	--	Folder
▼ English101	Today, 2:37 PM	--	Folder
▶ Course Files	Today, 2:20 PM	--	Folder
Hand-ins	Today, 2:20 PM	--	Folder
▶ Public	Today, 2:20 PM	--	Folder
Staff	Today, 2:19 PM	--	Folder
▼ Sci101	Today, 2:37 PM	--	Folder
▶ Course Files	Today, 2:20 PM	--	Folder
Hand-ins	Today, 2:20 PM	--	Folder
▶ Public	Today, 2:20 PM	--	Folder
Staff	Today, 2:19 PM	--	Folder

Figure 4–2. *Example course hierarchy*

In Figure 4–2 there is a top level folder MySchoolShare that contains course specific subdirectories: Comm101, English101, and Sci101. Each of these contain a folder template that is meant to securely address our access requirements. Let's take a look at an `ls -al` output for the folder "Comm101":

```
drwxr-x---   7   root   comm101        238 Jan 24 14:37 .
drwxr-xr-x   6   root   staff          204 Jan 24 14:44 ..
drwxrwxr-x   2   root   comm101staff    68 Jan 24 14:20 Course Files
drwxrwx-wx   2   root   comm101staff    68 Jan 24 14:20 Hand-ins
drwxrwx---   2   root   comm101         68 Jan 24 14:20 Public
drwxrwx---   2   root   comm101staff    68 Jan 24 14:19 Staff
```

In this template, to even be able to access the directory, the user must be a member of the 'comm101' group (as is seen on the "." entry). In this case, the 'comm101' group would contain both members from the 'comm101staff' group, and the 'comm101students' group, thus we have a group which qualifies either set of users. The Comm101 folder itself only allows for read and execute permissions to the comm101 group, which means users will not be able to add any top-level subdirectories or files, and prevents them from renaming any existing items. This allows the administrator to define a folder template structure, and ensure that users, whether faculty or students, adhere to it.

The Course Files folder is used by instructors to provide course-specific files and templates to students and thus write privileges are limited to the comm101staff group.

All users have the ability to read files from this directory as they qualify for the "everyone" class. In this particular case, the "everyone" class is guaranteed to be only members of the comm101 group that are also not in the group comm101staff. We know this because of the permissions on the Comm101 folder itself:

```
drwxr-x---   7    root    comm101     238 Jan 24 14:37 .
```

These permissions indicate that any items inside of this folder are only accessible by members of group comm101. Therefore, the "everyone" class on any subfolders or files is effectively restricted to the comm101 group, or a subset of it.

The "Hand-ins" folder is utilized by students as a drop-box: a folder where they can add their own files, but cannot read any files it contains. This allows a place for users to provide teachers with their homework assignments, and not have to worry about other students viewing those files. Because the hand-ins folder provides all members of the group Comm101staff read, write, and execute privileges, any members of the Comm101 staff group can access and view files provided by students for review. A drop box is achieved by allowing users write and execute permissions on a directory, and is indicated by the special drop-box icon, show in Figure 4–3.

Figure 4–3. *A Finder drop-box folder*

The Public folder in the example hierarchy provides a place for all users of the comm101 group to collaborate. This means both students and faculty will have the ability to modify, add, or remove files from the directory. It's a bit of the wild, wild west permission-wise, but it allows a place for everyone to collaborate, which is often desirable in a classroom setting. The public folder is possible by ensuring it is owned by the more global "comm101" group, and that all members of the group have read and write capabilities, as shown in the trimmed ls output:

```
drwxrwx---   2    root    comm101     68  Jan 24 14:20 Public
```

In this case, we may want to set the sticky bit on this folder to ensure that users can only delete their own files from this folder. Last but not least, we have the Staff folder, which is a folder where teachers/instructors can privately share files outside of the purview of students. This can be handy for substitutes, multi-instructor classes, or for professors who have to collaborate during the teaching process. To facilitate this, the comm101staff group is set as the primary group and given full read and write access. Students, who will receive effective permissions of the "everyone" class, will then have no access to any items in this directory, as made evident by the permissions on the folder:

```
drwxrwx---   2    root    comm101staff   68 Jan 24 14:19 Staff
```

> **CAUTION:** A good permissions hierarchy is only a partial solution. As an administrator, it is important that you take precautions to protect your data on a social level by educating them. If your users are not aware of the consequences of placing a sensitive file in a potentially public area (such as a folder named "Public"), you will likely have a security breach due simply to user ignorance.

Access Control Lists

Mac OS X 10.4 saw the introduction of ACLs, and Apple has continually refined them through the various iterations. For a traditional Windows system administrator, ACLs are likely easier to work with than POSIX. ACLs match the permission options almost identically. In fact, as we mentioned earlier, the OS X NFSv4 ACL format, is compatible with Windows ACLs.

A file's access control list is completely extensible, allowing you to assign very granular permissions to specific users and groups. It frees you from the constraints of the POSIX user/group/everyone paradigm, and greatly simplifies permissions management. On top of their extensibility, ACLs also define numerous different access levels and inheritance capabilities, which allow for especially effective permissions hierarchies.

Access Control Entries

There are approximately 17 different access rights that the ACL system allows you to apply to a file or directory. An access control entry, or ACE, is simply a specification which includes either a user or a group combined with an allow or deny directive, and a comma-separated list of one or more rights. These rights can be broken down into four different categories: Administration, Read Permissions, Write Permissions, and Inheritance.

Administration

The Administration category includes two permissions capabilities:

Change Permissions: Users with this right can manage privileges on a file via POSIX or ACLs. They may also delete any ACLs on the file or folder, so assign this permission with caution. When using `chmod` to manage ACLs (discussed later), you grant the change permissions with the `writesecurity` privilege.

Change Ownership: Enabling this for a user enables that individual user to assume ownership of a file. However, that person can't transfer ownership to anyone else. To do so, a user must have root access. You can grant the assume ownership privilege with the `chown` permission when using the `chmod` utility, which we'll discuss a bit later in this section.

Read Permissions

The Read category includes five specific permissions:

Read: The read privilege behaves similarly on both files and directories, letting users view the content of both. If you're working with ACLs from the command line, you grant this right using read for files and list for directories.

Execute/Search: The execute and search bits behave similarly to the execute bit in the POSIX model, though they are now given differentiating descriptions to more clearly define the delineation between 'execution' capability that it provides when applied to a file, verses the 'list/traverse' behavior that is accompanied with the attribute when applied to a folder. From the command line, you grant this privilege using the execute permission for files and the search permission for folders, though the terms can be used interchangeably when applying to either.

Read Attribute: This permission is granted, using the readattr privilege, to let a user view the data describing a file's characteristics, such as its size, ownership, mode, inode number, and file creation, modification, and access times. You enable this permission with the readattr privilege.

Read Ext Attribute: This permission allows a user to read a file's extended-attribute data: file attributes commonly utilized by the OS, such as information about the OS X quarantine system, Time Machine, disk-image checksums, and third-party software for metadata purposes. Extended attributes are also responsible for the data found under the More Info tab when you get information on a file. Use the readextattr permission to grant this right.

Read Permissions: Given this privilege, a user can view security information, such as ACLs or POSIX permissions, as well as ownership of a file or folder. To assign this right, use the readsecurity privilege.

Write Permissions

The write-permissions category allows users to create and modify file data, including file metadata stored via extended attributes. There are six specific write permissions:

Write Attributes: This permission allows a user to change a file's attribute data.

Write Ext Attributes: Granting this right lets a user edit files' and folders' extended attribute data (extra information about a file's traits) as well as create new entries in that data. You'll rarely want to make such data user accessible, though. Software behind the scenes usually manipulates this data.

Write/Add Files: The Write and Add File privileges are analogous when applied to a file or directory. Like the search/execute, the two different terms exist solely to illustrate the functional difference when applied to a directory versus a file. When applied to a directory, the add_file privilege serves as a subset of the POSIX directory write capability. The key difference is that, unlike the POSIX write capability, the add_file permission does not grant the ability to delete a file or create a new directory. These abilities are now bestowed by `delete` and `append`, respectively. When applied to a file, the user will have the ability to modify the contents of the file. When applying ACLs via the command line, you can use `write` on both directories and files, but on directories, it's ultimately interpreted as the `add_file` permission.

Delete: This capability is a subset of the POSIX write capability. With ACLs, we now have a specific right granting a user the ability to delete files or directories. This right is defined by the privilege `delete`.

Append/Add Directories: This capability is also a subset of the POSIX write capability. When applied to a directory, it allows users to create new subdirectories. When applied to an existing file, it allows the user to modify the file. Note that to create new files, a user must have write privileges. Using chmod from the command line, you assign the append/add directories privilege using append. The flag is interpreted as `add_subdirectory`.

Delete Child: This permission, which applies solely to directories, lets a user delete any file directly residing inside of it, regardless of ownership on the item. In the case of subdirectories residing in this directory, the subdirectory can only be removed if the user has the ability to also delete any files which it contains. The `delete_child` flag assigns the right.

Inheritance

This category applies solely to directories. You would use inheritance to customize how permissions are inherited by a directory's children. For instance, if you apply ACL inheritance to just the first level of subfolders and files, new folders users create will inherit their parents' permissions, but items created inside the new folders will not. Likewise, by using the `inheret_only` flag, you can assign ACLs specifically for inheritance, but not have them apply to the parent object, which can be very useful. You control inheritance with the four separate rights in the following list:

Apply to this folder: When selected, the ACL will apply to this folder. Otherwise, the folder will have `only_inherit` permission, and the ACL will be active only on children that inherit the ACL.

Apply to Child Folders: When you activate this option, newly created child folders of the directory will inherit the ACL. Use the `directory_inherit` permission to grant this privilege.

Apply to Child Files: When enabled, this privilege will cause new files created in the directory to inherit the ACL. You use the `file_inherit` permission to grant this right.

Apply to All Descendants: If you activate this option, the inheritance properties of the directory will pass on to newly created directories; allowing for automated propagation of ACLs as users create additional directories and files. Otherwise, the directory you're currently attending to will have the `limit_inherit` privilege.

The specificity of the various access writes allows you to more pointedly prescribe access writes. You can now differentiate between modification and deletion as well as differentiate various rights to files and folders. More importantly, ACLs provide multiple options to define inheritance, which can be very handy in establishing complex permissions hierarchies, such as those in education.

> **CAUTION:** If no Access Control Entries are applicable for a particular user on a file, ensure that your baseline POSIX permissions are structured in a manner to prevent unauthorized access. In some instances, it may be desirable to utilize explicit deny ACLs to ensure that access is unconditionally restricted.

Effective Permissions

One major limitation of ACLs can be found when it comes to protocol support. In order to utilize ACLs, the protocol must be built to support it. Apple has mitigated this issue by building ACL support into its first-party file systems and network protocols: HFS+ (Hierarchical File System, OS X's native file system), Xsan (Apple's cluster file system based off of Quantum/ADIC's StorNext file system), and AFP (Apple Filing Protocol, Apple's native file sharing protocol). Thanks to OS X's NFSv4 ACL implementation and the Samba open source project, OS X also includes support for ACLs via the CIFS protocol, which is used for connecting to and serving files to Windows clients.

So what about services which do not include support for ACLs? How do they handle permissions provided via ACLs? Luckily, on a standard OS X server this list is pretty short. The most notable offenders are FTP and NFS, but certainly this is not an exhaustive list. The fact that OS X's NFS daemon doesn't support ACLs might have you raising an eyebrow. After all, the ACL model utilized by Apple is based on the NFSv4 right? Unfortunately, Apple's NFS implementation supports only versions 2 and 3 of the standard, which don't yet have ACL support. Even if this wasn't an issue, there are definitely scenarios where you'll be providing file services over a nonstandard protocol that most likely does not include native support for ACLs. In any of these scenarios, the protocol in question will operate under what is referred to as "effective permissions." Essentially permissions, as defined by the ACLs, will be flattened into equivalent POSIX permissions. This means that if you have an ACL that prevents append access to user jdoe on folder folder1, then when user jdoe connects to folder1 over FTP (which does not support ACLs) and attempts to create a new subfolder, the action will fail. The same is true of NFS shares; exported NFS shares will boil down to effective permissions. The NFS implementation in OS X doesn't support ACLs, but it does honor them via effective permissions: if a user is granted read/write via an ACL, they *will* have read/write access via NFS. However, there are a few things to note here. First and foremost, granular ACLs won't translate completely. Second, although you might have effective write privileges via ACLs, if you don't have write privileges via POSIX, it will *seem* as if you don't have privileges when you do an `ls` on the mounted NFS volume; however, if you try to read or write a file, it will work without issue. Poorly written third-party software might inspect the POSIX permissions and determine that you don't have access to an asset when you really do. However, most software will attempt to read/write an asset and will only report errors when encountered (as it should).

Also, for cases such as this, ACL inheritance IS honored. For instance, an ACE on a folder ensuring that all created subfiles have write permissions will in fact appropriately apply the inherited entry to files uploaded via FTP or created via an NFS mount. You won't be able to view the ACL strictly across the FTP connection or the NFS mount, but on the backend, if you check the file on the server, you will see that inheritance is in fact applied to new files.

> **NOTE:** If you are using a third-party file service that runs as root and implements its own abstracted permission system, then effective ACL permissions will *not* apply.

ACLs in Practice

So, we have now covered all of the various rights provided by the ACL system, but how can we use these in practice? Well, the granular and specific nature of ACLs makes it a system that is a little less difficult to wrap your head around than a POSIX permissions structure. With basic POSIX permissions, you have to be somewhat clever with your folder hierarchies and group structures to create a workable system. With ACLs, the approach is much more clear and direct. Let's consider the example that we discussed earlier in this chapter, in the section "POSIX in Practice," in which we discussed a permissions hierarchy for a school that seeks to provide collaborative file sharing environments for its Comm101, Science101, and English101 classes. While we were able to accommodate the schools requirements solely with POSIX permissions, what if there were more requirements attached to that problem? For instance, let's say there is a Comm101 teacher's aide who needs access to the Staff folder for collaboration, but is not permitted to have access to student's final work delivered to the Hand-Ins folder. Likewise, this teacher's aide needs to be able to add files and directories to the Course Files folder, as well as modify existing assets in that folder. To accomplish this task in POSIX, it would be necessary to create an additional group in our Directory Service, such that we could assign privileges as follows:

```
drwxr-x---    7    root    comm101                 238 Jan 24 14:37 .
drwxr-xr-x    6    root    staff                   204 Jan 24 14:44 ..
drwxrwxr-x    2    root    comm101contributers      68 Jan 24 14:20 Course Files
drwxrwx-wx    2    root    comm101staff             68 Jan 24 14:20 Hand-ins
drwxrwx---    2    root    comm101                  68 Jan 24 14:20 Public
drwxrwx---    2    root    comm101contributers      68 Jan 24 14:19 Staff
```

To accommodate the request, we have created a special group "comm101contributers" which now has access to the Course Files as well as the Staff folders. In order to access via the comm101staff group, the comm101staff group has been added to the comm101contributers group, along with the teacher's aide user.

This solution will surely meet the need, but it's not long before you reach the practical limit of POSIX: what if the teacher's aide is to be provisioned read-only access to the Staff folder? In order to accommodate that request and ensure other students do not have access, you will need to create a subfolder that differentiates between comm101staff and comm101contributers. This is highly impractical. Instead, let's revert back to our original POSIX structure before creating the comm101contributers group, and approach the situation with ACLs in mind. The first thing to do is analyze the situation and determine whether the need to provide additional use is an edge case, or if it will become a common use-case scenario. If this will prove to be a common case, then it is recommended that we do in fact create a comm101contributers group to manage access. Access would then be provisioned in Directory Services, thereby minimizing the necessity to change permissions on the file system.

> **TIP:** In general it is best to avoid provisioning ACEs to specific users. The larger your file structure and the larger your user base, the more management overhead will be needed as you provision specific user access. Moreover, the more often that changes are made to a file system's permissions structure, the more likely that human error will result in unwarranted exposure of data. Instead, it is best to define specific groups for any common access patterns that you expect to be needed by members of your organization.

In this case, we have determined that this is a very specific edge case, and so we will go ahead and provision our access to our teacher's aid, who has a user account of "comm101aid". To provide the necessary access rights, we will assign ACLs as demonstrated by the command `ls -ael` which is run against our Comm101 folder.

```
drwxrwxr-x     7          root    comm101staff    238 Jan 24 14:37 .
drwxr-xr-x     6          root    staff           204 Jan 24 14:44 ..
-rw-rw-r--@    1          root    comm101staff   6148 Jan 24 15:05 .DS_Store
drwxrwxr-x+    2          root    comm101staff     68 Jan 24 14:20 Course Files
 0: user:comm101aid allow list,add_file,search,add_subdirectory,delete_child,readattr,
 writeattr,readextattr,writeextattr,readsecurity,file_inherit,directory_inherit
drwxrwx-wx     2          root    comm101staff     68 Jan 24 14:20 Hand-ins
drwxrwxr-x     2 root     comm101staff    68 Jan 24 14:20 Public
drwxrwx---+    2 root     comm101staff    68 Jan 24 14:19 Staff
 0: user:comm101aid allow list,add_file,search,add_subdirectory,delete_child,readattr,
   writeattr,readextattr,writeextattr,readsecurity,file_inherit,directory_inherit
```

There are a few things to note about this `ls -ael` output. First, if we examine the POSIX permissions of a particular folders output, we will see that on some folders, there is a trailing '+' at the end. For instance, the Staff folder:

```
drwxrwx---+    2 root     comm101staff    68 Jan 24 14:19 Staff
 0: user:testaid allow list,add_file,search,add_subdirectory,delete_child,readattr,
 writeattr,readextattr,writeextattr,readsecurity,file_inherit,directory_inherit
```

The '+' character means that the file has one or more access control entries. When passed the –e flag, ls also outputs each files' ACL, as seen on the Course Files and Staff folders. In each case, the user "testaid" has been allowed access permissions, which effectively provide Read and Write permissions in POSIX terms. The user testaid can read existing files and their metadata (list, readattr, readextattr) can traverse into the directory (search), add new files and directories (add_file,add_subdirectory), modify and rename existing files or directories (delete_child), and can modify file attributes and extended attributes (writeattr, writeextattr). On top of this, these permissions will inherit to any newly created files or subdirectories (file_inherit,directory_inherit). This common combination of "Read & Write" privileges is utilized by a number of Apple's administration toolsets. For a detailed table of Apple's primary access groups "Read & Write," "Read Only," and "Write Only (Drop Box)," read on to the next section, "Administering Permissions."

Through the use of ACLs we can easily adapt to various permissions needs. For instance, if the aid was only to have read permissions on the staff folder, we could apply the following ACL:

```
drwxrwx---+   2 root    comm101staff   68 Jan 24 14:19 Staff
 0: user:comm101aid allow list,search,readattr,readextattr,
file_inherit,directory_inherit
```

This ACE would allow the user "testaid" read only access to the Staff folder, and any newly created items. Keep in mind that our POSIX permissions are still playing a role in this scenario, as the "everyone" group has no capabilities. This goes to illustrate the need to ensure properly planned POSIX permissions in addition to ACLs. It is not enough to rely on only one system. If necessary, we could apply an explicit deny ACL which would override any set POSIX permissions:

```
drwxrwxrwx+   2 root    comm101staff   68 Jan 24 14:19 Staff
 0: user:comm101aid deny add_file,add_subdirectory
 1: user:comm101aid allow list,search,readattr,readextattr,
file_inherit,directory_inherit
```

In this model, even though the user has the ability to create files or directories via POSIX permissions, they will be unable to, due to the explicit deny applied to the directory. Another important characteristic to note is how the ACL system resolves conflicting ACEs. In the event of two conflicting access privileges, the first entry found in the system will be applied. So, in the above example if our allow rule (rule index #1) had an add_file flag, the user would still be unable to add a file due to the higher precedence (though lower index) deny rule.

Administering Permissions

You have a number of different tools at your disposal for administering permissions. If you prefer the command line, you can use the commands chmod and chown. We must warn you though, due to the verbosity of access control entries, using chmod to apply ACEs can be a bit hairy. The easiest way to manage ACLs on an OS X server is via the Server Admin application (Workgroup Manager in OS X 10.4) as shown in Figure 4–4, showing the File Sharing tab.

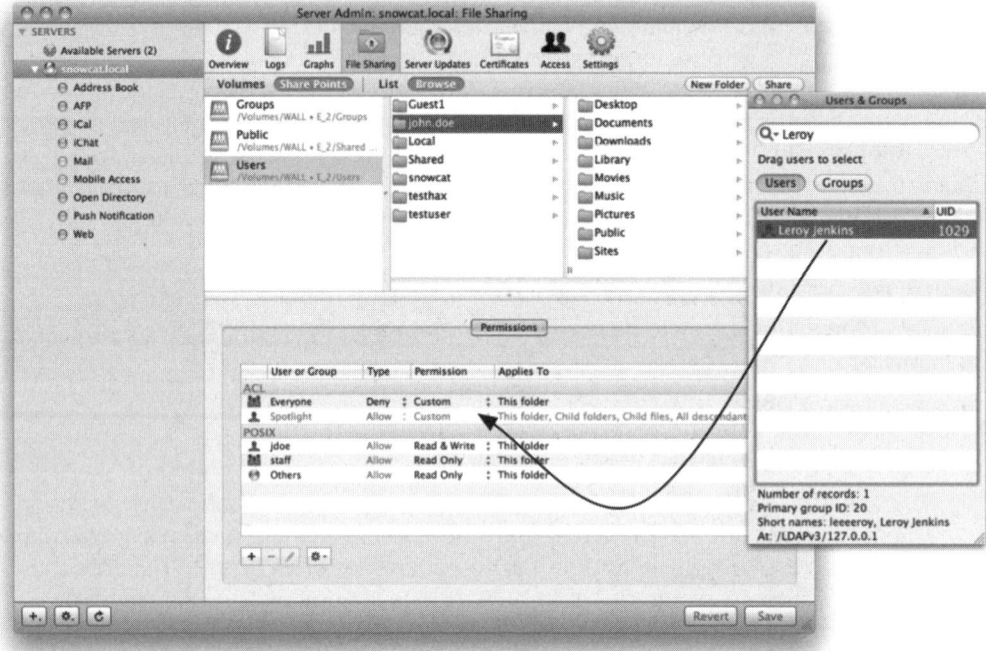

Figure 4–4. *OS X Server Admin Screen: File Sharing Tab*

You can find the Server Admin application inside the folder /Applications/Server on any OS X server box, or any client onto which you've installed the Server Admin tools (available on the downloads section of Apples support web site). Once you have the application open, you can get to the File Sharing interface by highlighting the server container in the Server Admin List, then clicking on File Sharing. Here, you can browse your file systems or share points and assign both POSIX and ACL permissions. Server Admin is a pretty good tool for modifying POSIX permissions, but it has no direct concept of "execution." There is no way to set the execution bit exclusively using this tool: if you assign Read privileges to a folder, it will include execution. When assigned to a file, the Read permission includes only read, not execution. This probably isn't a bad thing, as the number of scenarios where execution privileges need to be applied to files should be pretty rare, and the likelihood for human error would be high. Thus, the added consideration required to fire up a command line tool to grant execution rights to specific files isn't necessarily a bad thing.

You can modify POSIX owners and groups by dragging them into the respective slots and then choosing the appropriate level of permission for each. To create ACLs for users and groups, drag them into the ACL list and apply appropriate permissions. Apple has several basic presets for you to use: *Full Control*, *Read & Write*, *Read Only*, *Write Only*, and *Custom*. Table 4–2 illustrates these privileges mappings when applied to files and directories.

Table 4-2. *ACE Permissions Mapping*

Permission	File system Object	Rights
Full Control	Directory	list, add_file, search, delete, add_subdirectory, delete_child, readattr, writeattr, readextattr, writeextattr, readsecurity, writesecurity, chown, file_inherit, directory_inherit
Full Control	File	read, write, execute, delete, append, readattr, writeattr, readextattr, writeextattr, readsecurity, writesecurity, chown
Read & Write	Directory	list, add_file, search, add_subdirectory, delete_child, readattr, writeattr, readextattr, writeextattr, readsecurity, file_inherit, directory_inherit
Read & Write	File	read, write, execute, delete, append, readattr, writeattr, readextattr, writeextattr, readsecurity
Read Only	Directory	list, search, readattr, readextattr, readsecurity, file_inherit, directory_inherit
Read Only	File	read, execute, readattr, readextattr, readsecurity
Write Only	Directory	add_file, delete, add_subdirectory, delete_child, writeattr, writeextattr, file_inherit, directory_inherit
Write Only	File	write, delete, append, writeattr, writeextattr

The Server Admin utility also allows you to define custom privilege sets, which allow you to assign rights based upon four main categories, *Administration*, *Read*, *Write*, and *Inheritance*, which we discussed earlier in the section "Access Control Entries." To modify these permissions, highlight the ACE, then click on the pencil below. This will bring up a utility window, as shown in Figure 4–5.

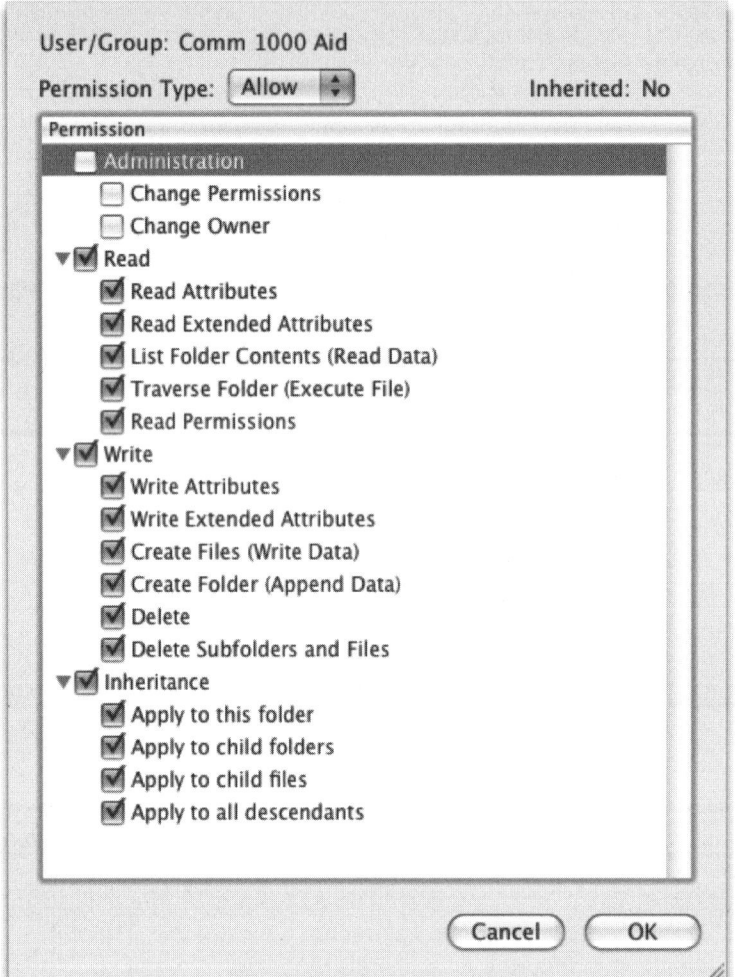

Figure 4–5. *Server Admin Custom ACE rights.*

Once you have established permissions on a directory, it is important to note that it only affects that directory. If you establish an ACE that has inheritance properties, those properties will only be inherited on newly created objects. To establish your permissions on existing files and folders, you will likely want to propagate those permissions to existing files and directories. To do so, with the desired parent folder selected, click on the Widget menu, and the select Propagate Permissions. You will then be presented with a sheet allowing you to select which permissions to propagate. As shown in Figure 4–6, choices include: owner name, group name, owner privileges, group privileges, everyone privileges, and Access Control Lists.

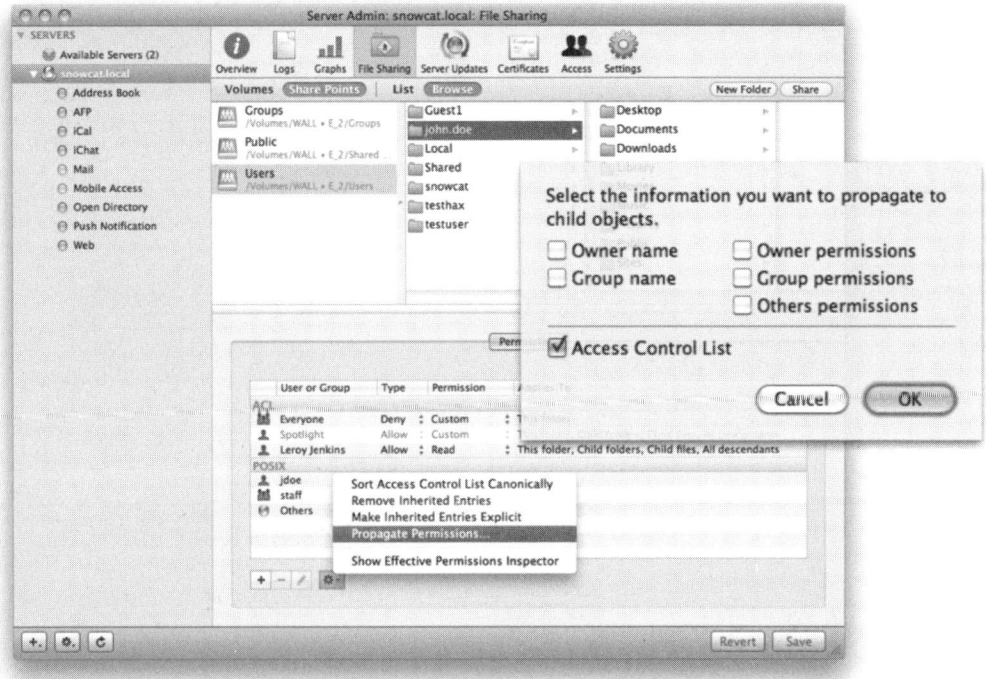

Figure 4–6. *Propagating permissions*

On a collaborative sharepoint, there will be few cases where we would recommend propagating an owner name (migrating a user's home directory is the primary use-case for that option). All other options can prove to be extremely useful when establishing permissions hierarchies. When propagating ACLs, all subfolders and files will contain an "inherited" ACL, an implicit ACL that it received based upon the directory in which it was contained. If you have propagated an ACL to a particular directory and you would like to change an ACE that was propagated, you must first make the ACE explicit. You can do this by selecting the directory in question, clicking on the widget, and then selecting Make Inherited Entries Explicit, as shown in Figure 4–7. Once you have done so, you can modify or delete the inherited entries, and then further propagate those changes using the propagation tool.

Figure 4–7. *Make Inherited Entries Explicit*

Last but not least, is Server Admin's effective permissions tool. This very useful utility allows you to examine permissions that can be effected to an individual user. To access the utility, select a directory in the Server Admin File Browser, by once again clicking on the widget menu, and then selecting Show Effective Permissions Inspector. This will bring up the Effective Permissions window. To check a specific user's access rights, just drag the appropriate user from the Users and Groups pane. As shown in Figure 4–8, the tool will define exactly which right that user will have to the specified directory.

Figure 4-8. *Server Admin's effective permissions tool*

Using the Finder to Manage Permissions

It is also possible to manage permissions using the Finder's Info pane, shown in Figure 4-9. However, this interface is fairly pared down, and the POSIX/ACL system is abstracted a bit. One large limitation is that it is not possible to change the POSIX owner or group. It is possible to change the mode for owner, group, and everyone class, but outside of that, you can only manage ACLs. For ACEs, the Finder uses the "Read & Write," "Read Only," and "Write Only" presets used by Server Admin with one crucial change: they do not set any of the inheritance properties. It is possible to propagate permissions to enclosing items using the Finder (once again found under a similar widget menu), but the propagation doesn't set any inheritance properties either. This means that newly created subdirectories or files will not inherit any ACEs that you establish through this procedure. This is a fairly significant limitation. If you are attempting to manage ACEs on an OS X client machine and wish for propagation, you'll need to set the inheritance rights yourself using the command line.

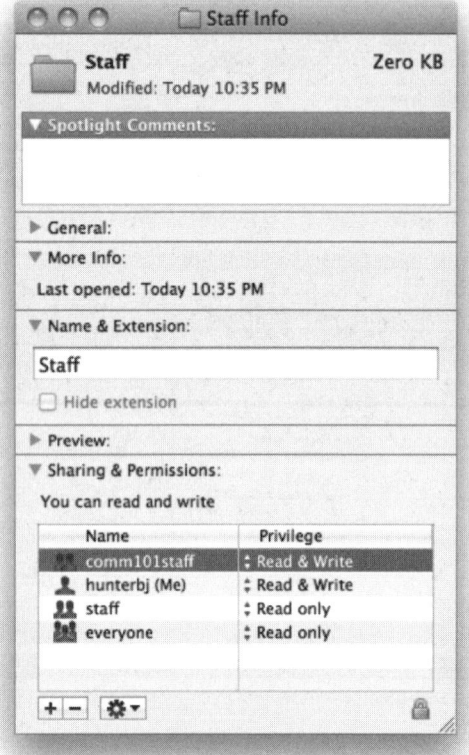

Figure 4–9. *The Finder's Sharing & Permissions window*

Using chown and chmod to Manage Permissions

You may often find yourself managing permissions from the command line. There are a few primary command line apps that you will use to do this: chown, chgrp and chmod. To change POSIX ownership of a file or folder, you use the chown utility. Its syntax is fairly straightforward:

chown owner[:group] /path to file

If all you're doing is changing ownership, you can omit the :group [the colon followed by the actual value for *group*]. Alternatively, you can use the chgrp command, which has similar syntax, but you instead provide the desired group name in the place of a user. OS X won't let just anyone change the owner of a file. To change ownership, you must either have granted the chown ACL right, or you must be running as root. However, even if you have been granted the chown ACL right, you will only be able to assume ownership of a file yourself. Only the root user can change the owner to a user other than itself. For example, the following command changes the owner of file /tmp/myfile.txt to 'hunterbj':

```
chown hunterbj /tmp/myfile.txt
```

If we also want to change the group owner of the file, we can use the following command, which assigns "admin" as the group owner. As with ownership, a user can only change the group owner to a group that the user is a member of.

```
chown hunterbj:admin /tmp/myfile.txt
```

> **TIP:** You can use the command `chflags hidden /MyFolder` to make a file or directory invisible. When run, the folder will no longer be displayed in the Finder, though it will still be visible from command line tools such as ls. To make these items invisible also from the command line, you can deny the readattr right.

You can use chmod to manage both POSIX and ACL permissions. Understand, however, that managing ACLs from the command line can be a bit hairy. It's not for the faint of heart. Having said that, let's walk you through some of the basics.

As discussed a bit earlier, you can use chmod to modify POSIX permissions. The syntax is:

```
chmod [-R] mode /path to file
```

The –R option, if used on a directory, applies the mode recursively to all descendents. To modify or create an ACE (an entry in an access control list, or *Access Control Entry*) or ACE using chmod, you would use the +a, and –a flags. For instance, to grant full control of the file test.txt to the user hunterbj, run the command

```
chmod +a "hunterbj allow read,write,execute,delete,append,readattr,writeattr,↵
readextattr,writeextattr,readsecurity,writesecurity,chown" test.txt
```

Subsequently, as discussed earlier, you can view the ACLs on that file by passing the –e flag to ls as follows:

```
ls -ael test.txt
-rw-r--r--+ 1 hunterbj staff 0 Jul 9 00:56 test.txt
0: user:hunterbj allow read,write,execute,delete,append,readattr,writeattr,↵
readextattr,writeextattr,readsecurity,writesecurity,chown
```

Likewise, if you want to grant full control of a directory, run:

```
chmod +a "hunterbj allow list,add_file,search,delete,add_subdirectory,delete_child,↵
readattr,writeattr,readextattr,writeextattr,readsecurity,writesecurity,chown,↵
limit_inherit,only_inherit" testfolder
```

To remove an entire ACE, you can use the –a# flag followed by an index number, as shown in the first example below. Or, if you wish, you can remove only specific attributes as shown in the second command, which removes only delete privileges, leaving the others in place.

```
chmod -a# 0 test.txt
chmod -a "hunterbj allow delete"
```

When first applying ACLs or when making changes, you'll likely want to propagate these changes to existing files and folders, because inheritance rules apply only at file- or folder-creation time. You can apply permissions recursively via the chmod -R +a command, but we'd recommended that you do this in Server Admin via its Propagate Permissions menu item, which you can find by clicking on the widget, shown previously in Figure 4–6 directly to the right of the pencil icon, a bit above the bottom of the screen. With this method, descendant file system objects will receive inherited, rather than explicit permissions.

When a large portion of your file system contains explicit permissions, management becomes harder. In addition, explicit permissions override implicit permissions, so you might end up with unexpected results. More care must be taken when managing such a model.

You can create inherited ACEs with `chmod` as well, which can be very useful. You do so by using the `+ai` flag instead of the `+a` flag. For example, the following commands will set a non-inherited ACE on /MyAwesomeFolder, but will then recursively copy inherited ACEs to all descendants:

```
chmod +a "hunterbj allow read,write,execute,delete,append,readattr,writeattr,
readextattr,writeextattr,readsecurity,writesecurity,chown" /MyAwesomeFolder
chmod -R +ai "hunterbj allow read,write,execute,delete,append,readattr,writeattr,
readextattr,writeextattr,readsecurity,writesecurity,chown" /MyAwesomeFolder/*
```

> **TIP:** Due to the way that the chmod utility parses the ACE, using the traditional syntax for chmod ACLs does not work correctly when used with user or group names that contain spaces in the shortname. This is primarily an issue in Active Directory environments, where users and groups routinely contain spaces. Fortunately, to get around this issue, you can use the colon as the user and rights delimiter. So, to assign an ACL for the group "MYCO\Mac Server Admins", the following syntax can be used: `chmod +a 'MYCO\Mac ServerAdmins:allow:read,write,execute' /MyAwesomeFolder`

If you do a lot of ACL management from the command line, you may wish to save the common access rights as a shell variable so that you don't have to type them out every time. To do this using OS X's default bash shell, you can simply add the following lines to your .bash_profile file found directly inside of your home directory:

```
export ACEFULLCONTROL="read,write,execute,delete,append,readattr,writeattr,
readextattr,writeextattr,readsecurity,writesecurity,chown,file_inherit,
directory_inherit"
export ACEREADWRITE="read,write,execute,delete,append,readattr,writeattr,
readextattr,writeextattr,readsecurity,file_inherit,directory_inherit"
export ACEWRITEONLY="write,delete,append,writeattr,writeextattr,file_inherit,
directory_inherit"
```

Once you have saved this file, open up a new shell or reprocess your .bash_profile (run the command `. ~/.bash_profile`) file to establish the new variables. Once done, you can establish various ACE controls with the following example commands:

```
chmod +a "user:professorbrown allow $ACEFULLCONTROL" Hand-Ins
chmod +a "group:comm101students deny $ACEWRITEONLY" Course\ Files
chmod +a "group:comm101students allow $ACEREADANDWRITE" Public
```

You can also remove all of a file or directory's ACEs via the `chmod -N` syntax. Combined with –R, you can use chmod to recurse through directories and remove all ACLs. For instance, to remove all ACEs on the Public folder, as well as nested items, the command syntax is `chmod -RN Public`.

The Hard Link Dilemma

One common issue faced with file system security is related to a low level file system capability known as hard links. A hard link in generic terms is a legal occurrence of the same file on a file system in multiple directories. When created, a hard link serves simply as a reference to an existing file, and the link maintains the exact same attributes as its source file. Thus, if ownership, mode, or even the containing data is changed on a link, those exact same changes will be realized on the source file. In OS X, and indeed most POSIX-compliant systems supporting hard links, a user can create a hard link to any file to which they have read access, as long as they have write access to the destination that they specify, and that destination resides on the same file system as the source file. As in most default OS X environments a user will have at least some file system path to which they have write access, this can present a fairly significant security issue.

For instance, consider a user who logs into a system and has a local home directory on that system. Next, consider all of the various system configuration files, which have world-readable access (hint, take a look at /etc/). Through the use of hard linking, a user with a shell account and a home directory can potentially exploit any of these world-readable files. To do so, they simply create a hard link to the file in their own home directory, using the ln command as shown here:

```
ln /etc/crontab ~/Public/Drop\ Box/crontab
```

In this particular case, the user is creating a hardlink of the file /etc/crontab in their Dropbox folder. This folder is chosen specifically, as historically it has proven to be handled insecurely by system administrators who do not fully understand how to manage POSIX or ACL permissions. In some cases, to promote collaboration, administrators will run scheduled scripts to change ownership on a directory. After all, user Leroy needs to be able to modify all files in his drop box, so why not just routinely make him the owner of everything added to this folder? Well, as we can see if we have a hard link in that folder, suddenly that routine script isn't quite so innocuous: with the linked file present in this directory, it will too be affected by the ownership change. Due to the fact that, as we learned, hard link files share all file attributes, the net result is that the crontab file at /etc/crontab will now have the ownership changes applied to it as well. Suddenly this user has the ability to modify our crontab files, which means they have the ability to create schedule tasks that can operate under any user of their choosing, including root. Combine the privilege change with the fact that cron does no ownership checks on the file, the net result is that the user now has complete access to the system, a major compromise.

> **NOTE:** Although typical OS X command line tools do not allow for creating hard links of directories, the OS does support it, and thus users can use lower level tools such as Python or Perl to create hard links to attack entire directories in a similar fashion.

So, how do we defend against such an attack? Well, one key thing to know is that hard links can only be created when the source and the destination reside on the same volume. Thus, a very easy measure to ensure system stability against hard link attacks is to ensure the separation of system data and user data via separate file systems. That is: if the users directory does not reside on the same file system as system data, then they will be unable to create a hard link to a system configuration file. Separation of user and system data in such a matter is a security and operational fundamental that should be routinely honored.

If you employ a network home directory model, then you are already provided some protections here, as the user's home directory will not reside on the same file system as any system data. The problem though is still present when used in a collaborative environment. In such a case, a user may have read only access to a particular file. By hard-linking the file to their home directory, they may be able to take advantage of any administrative tasks that deploy file system privilege modifications (whether manual or automated) to ultimately gain write access to the file. Fortunately, when a user creates a hard link, the attributes of the source file will be directly inherited from the source: any POSIX or ACL inheritance that would normally be applied to a new file will not be applied to a linked file. The security of the file remains intact: the user will have no access capabilities to the linked file that they don't have to the original. Thus, hard linking in and of itself is not dangerous. The danger comes if any administrative routines are applied to the link, and thereby the source.

So how do we protect against this? Well the truth of the matter is that there isn't a great way to protect against all possible misuses of hard links. The most approachable solution is to present access to collaboration data via protocols that do not support hard linking. For instance, neither the SMB nor the AFP protocol support hard links in default OS X configurations. Thus, any collaborative shares presented via these protocols are immune to such hard link attacks. Presenting collaborative data via a network protocol isn't always an option however, as sometimes collaboration will need to reside on a local volume. Say, for instance, an Xsan volume. In such a case, your best form of protection is to first avoid running administrative scripts which globally grant write provisions to files: lay down your file system hierarchy and a good inheritance model from the get-go, thus you can avoid having to run such routines against the data. This certainly isn't a complete answer though. Another step would be to restrict the user from utilizing tools that can be used create links. At an extreme level, this would include preventing the user from accessing a shell altogether, as well as access to AppleScript capabilities. If the user must absolutely have shell access, an alternative approach would be to utilize OS X sandboxing to restrict access to certain CLI utilities: most notably /bin/ls, but also also interpreted runtimes such as Python, Perl, PHP, or Ruby. Utilizing sandbox technology to protect an OS X environment is covered in detail in Chapter 6.

Using mtree to Audit File system Permissions

If you are reading this book we assume you have sensitive data to protect, and if so, you might want to consider routinely auditing your file system permissions. Earlier in this chapter, we learned of the dangers that can be had when permissions are poorly applied. An inadvertent write mode granted to a directory containing executables means that a malicious user can inject his own, executables, thereby granting him the ability to further exploit your system. The suid bit, when granted to an insecure program, can lead to a user subverting the program and gaining complete control of your box. If an executable must be suid to function, then there's not much you can do with POSIX or ACL permissions to prevent damage. To protect against such a scenario, consider Sandboxing your program, as discussed later on in this book, Chapter 6.

However, one thing we can do is make sure that our intended permissions structures maintain integrity. To do this, we can routinely audit our hierarchies to ensure that there are no unknown changes, and that even the files themselves have not changed. This can be used to ensure for instance that someone has not hijacked a program in your path and injected their own version. Fortunate for you, dear admin, is the fact that OS X includes by default a powerful tool for performing such an audit: mtree. Located at /usr/sbin/mtree, this command can be used to generate a "specification" file that contains information about the provided file system hierarchy. This specification can then be later referenced for comparison against the live file system. Any changes to the current structure from the specification will be reported. mtree provides the user the ability to specify the attributes to query and compare when running. "Keywords" can be specified to control exactly which statistics are saved to the specification and then which stats to compare with on the live file system. Though not an exhaustive list of mtree's keywords, we should make note of the following important attributes:

gid, gnam: The file group as a numeric value.

md5digest: The MD5 message digest of the file. Specifying this keyword will ensure that an md5digest of each file is written to the specification. If the file is modified, it will modify the files digest, and therefore our routine audits will notify us of changes in the file. Due to potential weaknesses found in the MD5 algorithm, use of the sha1digest isn't a bad idea.

sha1digest: The SHA-1 message digest of the file. This is more secure but also more CPU intensive than md5digest.

mode: The current file's permissions as a numeric (octal) or symbolic value. Monitoring this attribute will help detect any changes to POSIX permissions on the file.

uid, uname: The file owner as a numeric value and as a username, respectively. Monitoring these values can help to detect changes in directory services that might otherwise affect access.

size: The size, in bytes, of the file. Monitoring this value can help detect if any changes are made to the file itself.

link: The path that the symbolic link references. A symbolic link can be exploited by linking to a malicious program. Monitoring this keyword can help to detect against this.

time: The last modification time of the file.

type: The type of the file. This keyword detects the type of object that is at a given path, such as a file, directory, a disk or network mount.

> **NOTE:** mtree as of 10.6 does not support ACLs or other extended attributes. Changes made to either will not be detected when performing mtree audits. Depending upon your scenario, you may want to write a custom script to audit or apply appropriate permissions.

With these keywords in mind, let's venture into creating a specification file for comparison. To generate a spec file, we simply call `mtree` with the –c flag, and then point it to a path to reference for the specification with the –p flag. We use the –k flag to specify our desired keywords. And thus, the following command is born:

```
/usr/sbin/mtree -c -k 'gid gname -K sha1digest mode uid uname link ↵
type time'  -p /usr/bin > /Volumes/mtree_spec_files/myFreshSpec.txt
```

In this command, we specify our desired keywords, and then create a specification based upon the path /usr/bin. When run, `mtree` writes the specification to stdout. We capture this and redirect it to the file at path /Volumes/mtree_spec_files/myFreshSpec.txt. Preferably, once the file is written, it is then placed into a read-only state, safe from alteration or subterfuge. Once this specification file is in a secure place, preferably a read-only network mount, we can then reference it to audit the active environment. To do this, we call `mtree` with the following syntax:

```
/usr/sbin/mtree -f /Volumes/mtree_spec_files/myFreshSpec.txt -k 'gid gname ↵
sha1digest mode uid uname link type time '-p /usr/bin
```

```
        modification time expected Mon Jan 25 00:29:27 2010 found Mon Jan 25 01:16:14
tar changed
        modification time expected Mon Jan 25 00:29:27 2010 found Mon Jan 25 01:16:14
        link_ref expected bsdtar found /tmp/XEOSUHEJOUE/t4Rpwn4g3
```

When run with this syntax, mtree will output any detected change made since the specification file was generated. In this particular case, we see that the object at path /usr/bin/tar has been re-linked to a suspicious file located at /tmp/XEOSUHEJOUE/t4Rpwn4g3. Armed with this knowledge, we can repair the compromised link and begin to investigate the seriousness of the breach and the vector of the exploit.

> **TIP:** In highly sensitive environments, it may be desirable to compile a custom copy of mtree to run from read-only media. This ensures that your auditing tool itself cannot be compromised.

Consider scheduling routine checks against critical directories on your system to warn you of any issues. The default system path is a good place to start here: /usr/bin:/bin:/usr/sbin:/sbin. If you have installed programs at /usr/local, you may also want to monitor that hierarchy. The /etc/ folder also contains important configuration files which you may want to monitor for modification.

If your systems contain valuable or sensitive data, then it is always a good idea to audit your system's security. Through the `mtree` binary, OS X provides a built-in tool that does a pretty good job of accomplishing this. The `mtree` tool certainly isn't as extensive as tools such as Tripwire, but it does its job well and is fairly easy to use.

Summary

In this chapter, we discussed the various tools and facilities that are provided in OS 10.6 to allow for the management and provisioning of data access provided through the file system. You should have a good fundamental understanding of both POSIX and ACL permissions schemes, and should have enough knowledge to apply them for use in your collaborative environment. We also discussed using the `mtree` tool for auditing file system permissions and structures to help guarantee system integrity and peace-of-mind.

In the next chapter, we will discuss various logging facilities that can be used for tracking historic data, useful in forensics and non-repudiation.

Chapter 5

Reviewing Logs and Monitoring

Whether you're dealing with a car or a computer, poor maintenance habits lead to the same consequence: disaster. You're on the freeway, carefully driving at the posted speed limit, and your engine suddenly dies. You go to the mechanic, who roots out the cause: your timing belt broke. You would have replaced your timing belt, had you kept to the maintenance schedule and taken your car in for service at 60,000 miles. Airline maintenance crews who stick to a steadfast and detailed maintenance schedule rarely have this happen to them, mainly because they know precisely on what date the plane was maintained, at what time, and what maintenance was performed.

This is how many seasoned network administrators treat security. They proactively manage their systems. They log when they perform maintenance on the machine and notice when anomalies occur. They review their logs regularly. But logs often go unnoticed and unread, which is unfortunate, as they can be a great source of insight into securing your systems. Even when security has been compromised, many administrators don't think to check the logs to see what happened.

Why is this? It's simple. Logs can be complicated to the untrained eye, and some administrators just don't understand what the logs are telling them.

In this chapter, we will show you where to look for log files on the Mac (and Windows machines as well, because they can tell you a lot about security with respect to a Mac) and show you what they mean. We hope that once you realize what kind of information is stored in logs, you'll start using them a lot more effectively.

What Exactly Gets Logged?

It may seem weird to think that much of what you do on your computer gets logged. Imagine if every move you made was written down, and you could review every step you made over the course of the day. Although we may never know whether the National Security Agency (or AT&T) is actually recording our every move, logging every move on a computer is commonplace.

What gets logged can be determined by the application or by the operating system. This differs for each program, and what gets logged can be configured manually. The act of escalating your privileges is typically logged, as are failed attempts to do so. Many items are logged for the purposes of troubleshooting, but when it comes to security, any item that elevates privileges, references a password entry, or indicates the occurrence of an application failure should be logged.

A log entry can be as simple as one line indicating the deletion of a file, or as detailed as each file created during an installation or process. The following shows a portion of the output of the `install.log` file during the installation of the Mac OS X Server Admin tools. The install log shows each file created during the process as well as the corresponding date, time, and system on which each was created (or touched).

```
Oct 23 14:03:03 Gene-Sullivans-MacBook installd[137]: PackageKit: Registered bundle
   file://localhost/Applications/Server/Xgrid%20Admin.app/
Oct 23 14:03:03 Gene-Sullivans-MacBook installd[137]: PackageKit: Registered bundle
   file://localhost/System/Library/CoreServices/Server%20Assistant.app/
Oct 23 14:03:03 Gene-Sullivans-MacBook installd[137]: PackageKit: Registered bundle
   file://localhost/Applications/Server/Server%20Monitor.app/
Oct 23 14:03:03 Gene-Sullivans-MacBook installd[137]: PackageKit: Registered bundle
   file://localhost/Applications/Server/Server%20Admin.app/
Oct 23 14:03:03 Gene-Sullivans-MacBook installd[137]: PackageKit: Registered bundle
   file://localhost/Applications/Server/Workgroup%20Manager.app/
Oct 23 14:03:03 Gene-Sullivans-MacBook installd[137]: PackageKit: Registered bundle
   file://localhost/Applications/Server/Server%20Admin.app/Contents/Resources/
ServerAdminLauncher.app/
Oct 23 14:03:03 Gene-Sullivans-MacBook installd[137]: PackageKit: Registered bundle
   file://localhost/Applications/Server/iCal%20Server%20Utility.app/
Oct 23 14:03:03 Gene-Sullivans-MacBook installd[137]: PackageKit: Registered bundle
   file://localhost/Applications/Server/System%20Image%20Utility.app/
Oct 23 14:03:03 Gene-Sullivans-MacBook installd[137]: PackageKit: Registered bundle
   file://localhost/Applications/Server/Server%20Preferences.app/Contents/Resources/
ServerPrefsLauncher.app/
Oct 23 14:03:03 Gene-Sullivans-MacBook installd[137]: PackageKit: Registered bundle
   file://localhost/Applications/Server/Server%20Preferences.app/
Oct 23 14:03:03 Gene-Sullivans-MacBook installd[137]: PackageKit: Registered bundle
   file://localhost/Applications/Server/Podcast%20Composer.app/
Oct 23 14:03:03 Gene-Sullivans-MacBook installd[137]: PackageKit: Registered bundle
   file://localhost/Applications/Server/System%20Image%20Utility.app/Contents/
Library/Automator/Create%20Image.action/Contents/MacOS/AutoPartition.app/
Oct 23 14:03:03 Gene-Sullivans-MacBook installd[137]: PackageKit: Registered bundle
   file://localhost/Applications/QuickTime%20Broadcaster.app/
Oct 23 14:03:04 Gene-Sullivans-MacBook installd[137]: Installed "Server
   Administration Software" ()
Oct 23 14:03:04 Gene-Sullivans-MacBook installd[137]: PackageKit:
   ----- End install -----
Oct 23 14:03:05 Gene-Sullivans-MacBook Installer[127]: Running install actions
Oct 23 14:03:05 Gene-Sullivans-MacBook Installer[127]: Removing temporary directory
   "/var/folders/cm/cmSii-8XGFiRvFh+UL8r3U+++TI/-Tmp-//Install.127IGw3rb"
Oct 23 14:03:05 Gene-Sullivans-MacBook Installer[127]: Finalize disk "Snow Leopard"
Oct 23 14:03:05 Gene-Sullivans-MacBook Installer[127]: Notifying system of updated
   components
```

Multiple processes can be logged simultaneously, because they use such little processing power. Logging software writes entries to log files while you're performing many of the common tasks you do every day and when routine tasks are running on your system in the background. This may be some of those pesky items that cause the computer to run slowly at various times of the day, such as right around 3:15 AM (this is when the normal daily periodic Unix scripts run).

When looking at logs, try to keep in mind that reading every single line of every log file can become tedious. Rather than doing this, look for strange entries in the files. For example, if the previous log also had included a line that indicated the installation of something called `keystrokelogger`, that would be something to be concerned about.

Using Console

Trying to find and read all the system logs on a Mac used to be a daunting endeavor. With OS X, Apple has simplified this a bit by giving you a handy tool in the `/Applications/Utilities` folder called Console. In this section we'll cover how to use Console to view and mark logs.

Viewing Logs

You can use Console to review logs quickly without having to open and read each file independently. When you open Console, you are immediately viewing Console Messages. Clicking the Show Log List button gives you a listing of all the logs that Console is aware of, divided into three sections (see Figure 5–1). The Files section is a list of plain text log files, laid out according to where they're located in the file system. Any other log files you open for viewing with Console will appear in this section.

The top two sections don't show the contents of text files, but rather information drawn from the Apple System Logger database. ASL is a new logging facility that Apple introduced with Leopard, which consists of `syslogd` and `aslmanager`. The *de facto* standard for logging messages on Unix system is `syslogd`. It is historically used by the kernel to write messages to the system log, and is also used by daemons and programs such as Apache and Postfix. In Snow Leopard, messages logged by the syslogd server are stored in a binary database, located in `/private/var/log/asl/`. The files in that directory are managed by `aslmanager`. For compatibility with the many other systems that use syslogd, many of the messages are elso echoed to `/private/var/log/system.log`.

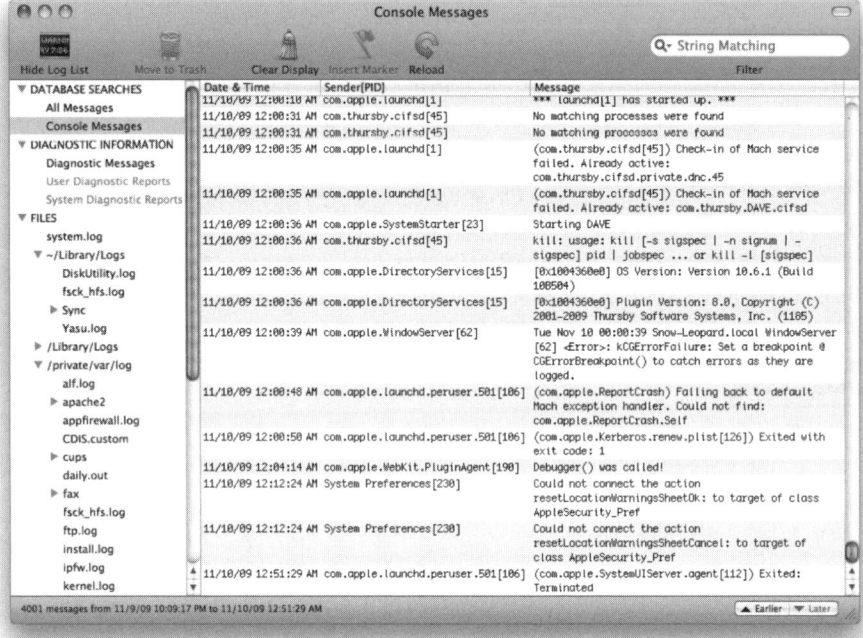

Figure 5-1. *Using Console*

Console was designed to give you an easy one-stop shop for reviewing system logs. Although this is helpful, Console doesn't show you every log on your computer. Each application logs information a little bit differently, and it would be impossible to cover every aspect of every log file ever created. Happily, many of the apps made for Mac OS X follow a fairly standard method that Apple established with its own logs. We'll point out the ones to check for most security purposes. You can then apply this knowledge to other network-aware applications in order to check their logs for issues. Before we delve into what these logs can tell you, we'll discuss how you can interact with the logs.

Marking Logs

It is sometimes helpful to mark a spot in a log, while you are reviewing them, much like using a sticky note or highlighter to mark a passage in a book. To do so, select the log in the Logs window of Console and click the Insert Marker button. It's important to note that these markers are not inserted into the log itself, but into your view of the log in Console. Clicking the Reload button, choosing another log, or quitting Console will cause those markers to disappear.

Another way to insert a marker into system.log and the ASL database is to use the logger utility, which provides an interface to `syslogd`. All entries you write will be prefaced with the date and time, and will include whatever message you send to it.

`logger Marker`

This command will insert the following line in system.log:

```
Nov  8 22:12:32 Snow-Leopard gene[1421]: Marker
```

Console also makes it easy to copy data out of the logs. When you click a log in Console, you can highlight text and copy it to TextEdit, Word, or any other program that supports pasting. To copy, you can either use Cmd-C key or select **Edit ➤ Copy**. Notice that you cannot cut text; Console does not let you modify logs.

For performance and simplicity, when you view the logs in the Database Searches section of Console, it will show you only the most recent 4,000 lines of data in the log. If there is more data in a log than Console can show, the Earlier and Later buttons on Console's status bar will become active. When viewing any of the other logs, Console will only show the most recent 16MB of messages. When a log is larger than this, the Earlier and Later buttons will allow you to view the rest of the log.

> **NOTE:** When viewing very large log files, such as `Console.log`, you might have to wait for a long time if the log size is bigger than a few megabytes.

Searching Logs

If you're looking for a specific item in a log, the Filter box in Console's Toolbar will filter the log you're currently viewing, showing you only the lines containing the text you're seeking. If you're looking for successful and failed ssh attempts, you could enter sshd in the Filter box. As you type, the messages will be filtered until you're only viewing messages containing sshd. This can be very useful for simple searches, but it can be difficult to put the results in context.

You can also search within a log by going to **Edit ➤ Find** (or pressing Cmd-F) and entering a search term. The first matching instance will be highlighted, and you can see what you're looking for while still seeing what else was being logged around that time. It's also possible to find terms within a filtered log.

Console also allows you to create saved Database Searches that will appear at the top of the Log List alongside All Messages and Console Messages. Go to **File ➤ New Database Search** (or press Cmd-Option-N), and you will be presented with the Database Search editor (see Figure 5–2).

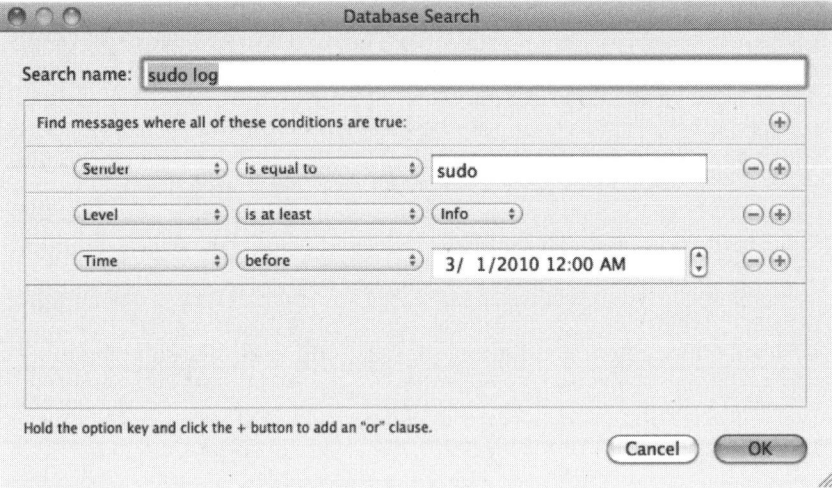

Figure 5–2. *Creating a database search*

Give your search a name and select your search criteria. You can search by the contents of the message (as with filtering, explained previously), by Sender (the name of the process sending the message), by Facility (a legacy designation of the part of the system sending the message), or by Level (the severity of the message). It's possible to create very granular searches that will be a big help in keeping an eye on your system.

Finding Logs

The /private/var/log directory is where OS X stores most of its important log files. If you write an application or script that builds its own log file, then you can write these logs to /private/var/log and they will automatically appear in Console under /private/var/log. Many developers put their logs here because the /private/var directory is used in most Unix distributions (flavors) to house logs that are not user-specific. This includes logs for open source software that has been installed by Apple such as the firewall (ipfw), the Windows sharing component (samba), the web server (apache), and many other items.

The Finder is intentionally designed to not make these folders easily accessible. To get to the /private/var folder, you need to use the Terminal application and access it through the command line, or you can use the Cmd-Shift-G keystroke and type **/private/var** (or just **/var**, which is a symbolic link) in the "Go to the Folder" field. This is a fairly standard way of accessing many of the logs we will be discussing in this chapter.

Generally you can configure third-party applications to log to wherever you want. For example, Rumpus, the popular FTP server, stores its logs by default in the /usr/local/Rumpus/Logs directory. However, you can customize this using the Log Folder field (as shown in Figure 5–3). Additionally, with third-party applications, you can usually customize the frequency with which logs are trimmed and the amount of data that is written to the logs.

> **NOTE:** To access the /usr/local folder, you need to use the Cmd-Shift-G keystroke and type **/usr/local**.

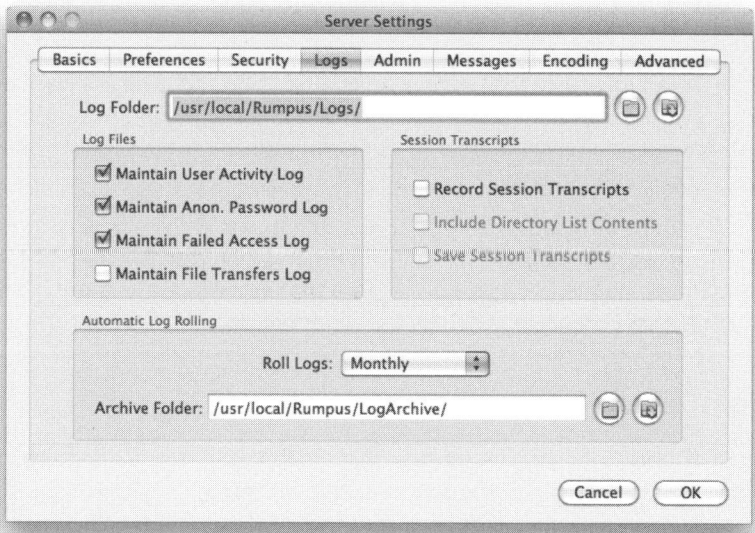

Figure 5–3. *Rumpus logging*

Secure.log: Security Information 101

The secure.log file can provide invaluable security information about your machine. This log file, found in the /private/var/log directory, tracks when passwords are entered on the computer and whether they are successful. When you turn your computer on, wake it from sleep, or enter a password to allow an installer to run, you should be required to enter a password (if you're following with the tips in this book). The secure.log file can help you determine what exactly happened when you (or someone else) did this.

For example, the following are the logs of what the system reports when you are attempting to install software. There is a date and time stamp at the beginning, followed by the account ID of the user who has run the installer. Then, you can see the module attempting to perform security. When the system asks for a password, com.apple.SecurityServer is used. The first line states that SecurityServer was invoked, and the following lines detail what tasks were performed:

```
Nov  8 21:23:20 Snow-Leopard com.apple.SecurityServer[26]: UID 501 authenticated
  as user gene (UID 501) for right 'system.install.root.admin'
Nov  8 21:23:20 Snow-Leopard com.apple.SecurityServer[26]: Succeeded authorizing
  right 'system.install.root.admin' by client '/System/Library/PrivateFrameworks/
Install.framework/Versions/A/Resources/runner' for authorization created by
```

```
            '/System/Library/CoreServices/Installer.app'
Nov  8 21:23:20 Snow-Leopard com.apple.SecurityServer[26]: Succeeded authorizing↵
    right 'system.install.admin.user' by client '/System/Library/PrivateFrameworks/↵
    PackageKit.framework/Versions/A/Resources/installd' for authorization created↵
    by '/System/Library/CoreServices/Installer.app'
```

There are two important security clues to look out for in secure.log. First, multiple bad password attempts can be an indicator that someone is attempting to guess a password by brute force, which would indicate a need for heightened security. Failed attempts can also indicate a need to have a talk with the user in question about the acceptable use policy, and the consequences of violating it.

The second item to look out for is whether someone actually ran the programs being called up in the secure.log file. For example, in the previous log snippets, you will see the string gene in the field immediately following the date that something was run. This shows that the user with a short name of gene ran this command.

appfirewall.log

Snow Leopard's built-in firewall (covered in greater detail in Chapter 11) is a feature-rich application layer firewall that is capable of logging massive amounts of data. appfwloggerd is a program built specifically for the purpose of logging firewall events to the appfirewall.log file. This file located at /private/var/log/appfirewall.log. appfwloggerd logs only those events that the Application Firewall determines are not acceptable.

```
Nov 10 00:29:44 Snow-Leopard Firewall[49]: Stealth Mode connection attempt to TCP↵
    192.168.11.3:22 from 192.168.11.4:51609
Nov 10 00:29:45 Snow-Leopard Firewall[49]: Stealth Mode connection attempt to TCP↵
    192.168.11.3:22 from 192.168.11.4:51609
Nov 10 00:30:02 Snow-Leopard Firewall[49]: Stealth Mode connection attempt to TCP↵
    192.168.11.3:80 from 192.168.11.4:51610
Nov 10 00:30:03 Snow-Leopard Firewall[49]: Stealth Mode connection attempt to TCP↵
    192.168.11.3:80 from 192.168.11.4:51610
Nov 10 00:30:03 Snow-Leopard Firewall[49]: Stealth Mode connection attempt to TCP↵
    192.168.11.3:80 from 192.168.11.4:51611
Nov 10 00:30:06 Snow-Leopard Firewall[49]: Deny cupsd data in from 192.168.11.4:631↵
    to port 631 proto=17
```

The format of the previous log entries indicates information about the network traffic, or packet, that was processed by the firewall. Log entries include the date and time stamp the source of the packet (the IP address that the packet came from), and the destination of the packet (the IP address to which the packet is traveling).

appfirewall.log can help you get a handle on the comings and goings of network traffic on your computer, but can be quite verbose. When scanning through the logs, your goal should not be to read every line, but to look for any information that seems out of the ordinary, such as a large number of rejected traffic packets. You also want to look out for repeated attempts on ports that are out of the ordinary or do not have corresponding services attached to your system.

> **NOTE:** Date and time stamps are a common theme in logs. They're invaluable correlating log entries with real-world events, or tracking a user's activities across one system or many.

Reviewing User-Specific Logs

Many user-specific operating-system components and third-party applications, such as Carbon Copy Cloner, ClamXav, and Yasu, log data into files inside each user's home directory. These logs are stored in the ~/Library/Logs folder. Because they are kept inside each user's folder, the logs are accessible only to that user (or anyone who has access to the account). This is good for the privacy of each user, but it can make troubleshooting difficult. Keep in mind that logs stored in a user's home directory are owned by that account, and could easily be modified by a proficient user. Any information gleaned from these logs should be taken with a grain of salt.

> **NOTE:** You can get around the multiuser issues with logs. Logging in with the root account will allow you to view the logs for other users.

One log of note in the ~/Library/Logs folder is DiskUtility.log. This log file stores all the activities run by the Disk Utility application, including fixing permissions, fixing the disk, and formatting and partitioning. The Disk Utility logs do not get *rotated*, or cleared out on a routine basis, which makes them particularly useful if you are investigating suspicious behavior on the system. Let's say you suspect that a hard drive was reformatted. By reviewing DiskUtility.log for each user on a system, you will find who reformatted a hard drive as well as any settings that were customized during the reformat process. The following is a sample Disk Utility log:

```
**********
2009-11-09 21:03:03 -0800: Disk Utility started.
2009-11-09 21:04:30 -0800: Preparing to partition disk: "Prolific PL3507 Combo Device"
2009-11-09 21:04:30 -0800:      Partition Scheme: GUID Partition Table
2009-11-09 21:04:30 -0800:      1 partition will be created
2009-11-09 21:04:30 -0800:
2009-11-09 21:04:30 -0800:      Partition 1
2009-11-09 21:04:30 -0800:          Size            : 30.01 GB
2009-11-09 21:04:30 -0800:          Filesystem      : Free Space
2009-11-09 21:04:30 -0800:
2009-11-09 21:04:30 -0800: Unmounting disk
```

```
2009-11-09 21:04:31 -0800: Creating partition map
2009-11-09 21:04:31 -0800: Waiting for disks to reappear
2009-11-09 21:04:31 -0800: Partition complete.
```

Another log of note is `DiskRecording.log`, which records whether any user has used the optical drive for CD burning. As you can see from the following log entries, the `DiskRecording.log` file does not indicate what data was burned, but it shows you what applications were used to burn to the optical media. This can be helpful if you are simply looking to correlate information between two different logs, such as finding instances in logs where large numbers of files were copied within a short span of burning a disc.

```
Finder: Burn started, Mon Oct 26 21:04:44 2009
Finder: Burning to CD-R media with SAO strategy in MATSHITA DVD-R   UJ-825 DAM5 via
ATAPI.
Finder: Requested burn speed was max, actual burn speed is 16x.
Finder: Burn underrun protection is supported, and enabled.
Finder: Burn finished, Mon Oct 26 21:07:54 2009
Finder: Verify started, Mon Oct 26 21:07:54 2009
Finder: Verify finished, Mon Oct 26 21:09:40 2009
Disk Utility: Burn started, Thu Oct 29 20:04:15 2009
Disk Utility: Burning to DVD-R (CMC MAG. AM3) media with DAO strategy in MATSHITA
DVD-R   UJ-825 DAM5 via ATAPI.
Disk Utility: Requested burn speed was 47x, actual burn speed is 2x.
Disk Utility: Burn underrun protection is supported, and enabled.
Disk Utility: Burn finished, Thu Oct 29 20:20:28 2009
Disk Utility: Verify started, Thu Oct 29 20:20:28 2009
Disk Utility: Verify finished, Thu Oct 29 20:28:07 2009
```

Showing the application and date stamp allows you to identify whether someone was burning a music CD or a DVD full of data files and when it was burned. As with `DiskUtility.log`, the `DiskRecording.log` file is specific to each user and will not show you disc recording activity for other users. `DiskRecording.log` does not get archived or cleared automatically. Entries will remain unless they are manually deleted from the log. If you suspect that someone has tampered with it, you can look at the last entry in the log and compare that with the most recent modification date on the file.

Launchd, the process that controls scheduled activities, also has the ability to log data. When you suspect a root kit (discussed further in Chapter 8) has infected your system as one user but isn't active for all users, take a look at the `launchd` logs for your user account to see whether any events are occurring that you should be concerned about. Things to be concerned about include non-Apple services being initiated. The log level for `launchd` is set with the `launchctl` command. `launchctl log mask notice` will configure `launchd` to log events with every severity between Emergency and Notice.

User logs can be helpful in determining what was done while logged into your account. When used in conjunction with the other logs mentioned, you can get a fairly specific idea of what was performed on the system recently.

Reviewing Command-Line Logs

DiskUtility.log lets you know if somebody burned a disk with Disk utility, but it won't show whether someone ran a reformat or repair operation from the command line. For command-line information, it is often best to look into the command-line history for each user. This information is stored in the history file. The history file is different for each shell in which a user is operating. For example, the history file for the default shell, bash, is .bash_history. It is located in the root of each user's home folder. The history files do not get rotated, but by default will only keep 150 commands. As new commands are entered, old commands will expire. You can view history by using the history command (no arguments are needed), and you can clear the history by using history -c. Although the history file can be difficult to correlate events to, it is one of the most important items to review.

When you use the su command, you are substituting your identity for that of root, the system's built-in administrative user. Any commands that are run as the root user would be captured in the root user's history, not your own. This means you need to log in to each account in order to review the account's history. Reviewing the history file can be fairly difficult if you are looking to correlate history events with other logs. Unfortunately, there are no date and time stamps available in the history file to indicate when commands were run. However, you know which commands were run, and in which order, and sometimes you can correlate this with system events from log files. To complicate matters even further, different users like to use different shells (a shell is just a different way to interface with the command line). Most users use bash (which is the default on Mac OS X), but others might use tcsh or ksh. Each shell has a different history file, and some, by default, don't log history at all. If you switch to the bourne shell, your history will be stored in .sh_history. This gives you a lot of places to look for information if you have multiple shells running in Terminal. Luckily, bash is the most commonly used shell.

The last command will show a listing of the last users who logged into the computer and how long the login sessions were open. The format of the output of a last command is the username followed by the Terminal type, then the date logged in, and finally the start and stop time of the Terminal session. ttys001 indicates the first Terminal window opened. If a second is opened, it is ttys002, the third is ttys003, and so on. This goes back to mainframe days when each terminal station had a unique identifier. This can give you a good log of recent login activity for a specific machine.

```
gene      ttys001              Tue Nov  3 23:09 - 23:15  (00:05)
gene      ttys001              Tue Nov  3 23:04 - 23:04  (00:00)
gene      ttys000              Tue Nov  3 22:35    still logged in
gene      console              Tue Nov  3 22:23    still logged in
```

Reviewing Library Logs

If you've ever helped a friend move, and that friend was a fairly efficient mover, he probably assigned someone to stay in the moving truck to arrange everything so that the maximum amount of stuff could fit. This lets everyone else maximize efficiency by moving stuff from the house to the truck without worrying about how it's packed. This idea can be translated into the ways in which software applications are programmed to work in an operating system. It often makes sense to use a shared library of items that many different applications can access. This allows more features to be written with less programming, which means greater efficiency, much like the guy in the truck allows the people moving furniture from the house to do so more efficiently.

Because the /Library folder keeps many shared application libraries (think of these as mini-applications), the types of logs stored here tend to be those generated by components that are shared across multiple applications. This includes CrashReporter, which writes application crash information into logs, and also server and directory service logs. Many application programmers also choose /Library/Logs as their log destination. This, for instance, would explain the random Timbuktu log you might notice in there.

Many applications and shared libraries communicate using data that might not make much sense to the untrained eye. In the crash logs, you will typically see hexadecimal memory segments listed, followed by the library that wrote the alert and then the path to the library. For example:

```
0x96e15000 - 0x96e2ffff libPng.dylib
/System/Library/Frameworks/ApplicationServices.framework/
Versions/A/Frameworks/ImageIO.framework/Versions/
A/Resources/libPng.dylib
```

These hexadecimal sequences in the logs can help decipher why a crash occurred if foul play is suspected. Nine times out of ten, rather than confirm irregular activity, you will instead find that there is actually a technical problem that caused the crash.

Breaking Down Maintenance Logs

Chances are you see your doctor at regular intervals. The dentist you'll see every six months, and the family physician you'll see every year. Just as your body needs to be maintained in regular intervals, so must your computer. Maintenance scripts run at scheduled times, and if one is missed, much like a doctor's appointment, it is usually scheduled for the next available time. Maintenance scripts need to be run because they log what devices were plugged into a system, they back up the user database, and they do much more. Machines can be left off at night, laptops can get closed, and power outages can disable a system, helping to explain the disparity in time stamps you may see when viewing your maintenance scripts and why you may occasionally skip the execution of a maintenance script.

One thing that maintenance scripts do is rotate and archive certain log files, which can get really big. Try to imagine how large a log file would get if it logged every step, turn, and move you made. When archiving, the log files are usually archived into compressed files using the bzip format, a compression technique commonly used to reduce the size of single files. Once archived, the file will be renamed and cleared and become ready to begin writing new data. Some people refer to archiving a log as "rotating it."

Those logs that are not rotated by the periodic scripts are maintained by newsyslog, which is run every 30 minutes by launchd. The configuration files for newsyslog are located in /private/etc/ and /private/etc/newsyslog.d/. Newsyslog.conf covers the rotation of files written by syslogd, and the files in newsyslog.d cover the rotation of files written by other processes.

The important option to configure in newsyslog.conf is count, which determines how many archive files to keep. By default, seven old versions of system.log will be kept, but only five old versions of secure.log will stick around. If you're interested in greater retention of files, change count to 10 (or even 15). Take care, though, as keeping more logs will take up more space than you might imagine.

> **NOTE:** Console will uncompress files when they are accessed. This can be time-consuming on larger files, which is why Console will, by default, show you only the first 128K of a log file.

In addition to archiving logs, maintenance scripts also perform other functions. These include removing temporary files, performing backups, reviewing drive capacity, checking how long you've been logged into your computer, and checking network statistics.

Mac OS X uses three main maintenance scripts that log data into separate files. These are known as *periodic scripts*. They include daily, weekly, and monthly. You can manually run these periodic scripts by using the periodic command. For example, to run the daily periodic script, use the following command:

sudo periodic daily

You can configure the periodic scripts to log more data than they do with the default settings. You can configure the manner with which periodic runs the daily scripts using the periodic.conf file located at /private/etc/defaults. You should make some minor adjustments to the periodic.conf file to increase the logging of events. These include the following:

- Change the NO in the lines for weekly_show_badconfig="NO" and monthly_show_badconfig="NO" to YES to have a periodic report of when there is bad configuration data found by the monthly.out file.

- Change the NO in the line containing the daily_clean_logs_verbose="NO" option to YES to have periodic show the files as they are being deleted.

daily.out

The daily.out file is an output file created by the daily maintenance scripts that run on your system. Like many of the maintenance logs, daily.out begins with a time stamp to provide you with the context of when it ran. Next, the daily.out log shows which old logs the daily script removed. For example:

```
Sun Nov  8 19:41:40 PST 2009

Removing old log files:

Removing old temporary files:

Cleaning out old system announcements:

Removing stale files from /var/rwho:

Removing scratch fax files

Disk status:
Filesystem     Size   Used  Avail Capacity  Mounted on
/dev/disk0s3   118Gi  50Gi  68Gi    43%     /

Network interface status:
Name   Mtu   Network       Address              Ipkts Ierrs    Opkts Oerrs  Coll
lo0    16384 <Link#1>                              82     0       82     0     0
lo0    16384 localhost     ::1                     82     -       82     -     -
lo0    16384 localhost     fe80:1::1               82     -       82     -     -
lo0    16384 127           localhost               82     -       82     -     -
gif0*  1280  <Link#2>                               0     0        0     0     0
stf0*  1280  <Link#3>                               0     0        0     0     0
en1    1500  <Link#4>      00:1e:c2:ab:d7:9f     4536     0     4271     0     0
en1    1500  localhost     fe80:4::21e:c2ff:     4536     -     4271     -     -
en1    1500  192.168.11    192.168.11.5          4536     -     4271     -     -
en0    1500  <Link#5>      00:1e:c2:19:fd:b0        0     0        0     0     0
fw0    2030  <Link#6>      00:1f:5b:ff:fe:2d:89:c0  0     0        0     0     0   0

Local system status:
19:41  up 44 mins, 4 users, load averages: 0.02 0.05 0.01

-- End of daily output --
```

The big thing to look out for here is that the Ipkts field is greater than the others. The Name field refers to the name of the interface that the MAC address and the other statistics will be relevant for. The Network field is similar to the Name field but states the network that the interface can run on. The MTU field is the maximum transmission unit, which means the largest "packet" size that can be transferred in one physical frame on a network. `Ipkts` refers to the incoming packets, and `Opkts` refers to outgoing packets. The `Ipkts` field should always be higher than the `Opkts` field. If anything here looks like it is out of the ordinary, such as the `Opkts` field being higher than the `Ipkts` field, it often means you need to reinstall the drivers for your network interface. Another item to look out for is high numbers of collisions (the `Col` column). If your collisions are more than 10 percent of the `Ipkts` field, then you might have issues with your network.

> **NOTE:** If the same network interface is listed multiple times, it is nothing to be alarmed about.

The final action of the daily maintenance script is to rotate the `system.log` file. The `system.log` file is often the largest log file on the system. This is discussed in further detail later in this chapter. The daily script is scheduled to run at 3:15 AM every day.

> **NOTE:** People often ask whether they should leave their computers on at night. If they have a good battery backup system, we usually tell them to do so. This allows the daily script to run when it is supposed to run.

Yasu

Yasu is a nice little free application that will run maintenance scripts if they are missed because the computer was turned off during their regular schedules (see Figure 5–4). Not only is it important to run the periodic maintenance scripts in order to view their output logs for errors, but it is equally important to run them in order to manage the size of the various log files that get archived with this script. To do this, simply open Yasu, make sure only the daily, monthly, and weekly cron script boxes are checked, and then click OK.

> **CAUTION:** If you leave the check boxes at the bottom of the Yasu screen checked, then you will erase many of the log files that you might need to review!

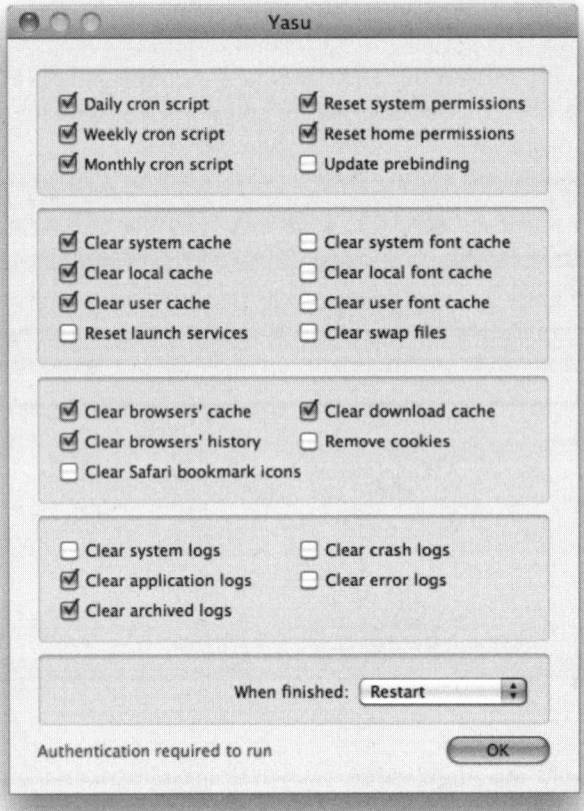

Figure 5-4. *Running maintenance scripts with Yasu.*

Weekly.out

The weekly `periodic` script runs at 3:15 AM on Saturdays. It updates the "whatis" database (used for the `whatis` command, which searches through man pages for words you provide), and little else.

```
Sun Nov  8 19:42:20 PST 2009

Rebuilding whatis database:

-- End of weekly output --
```

Monthly.out

The `monthly.out` log file is created by your monthly maintenance scripts and can be used to display what the monthly script did. As with the `daily.out` and `weekly.out` files, the `monthly.out` file will start with a date and time stamp. Monthly.out can keep track of how long a user is logged into a system, a feature unique to this file. Login accounting is useful if you suspect that a user's password has been compromised and someone is illegally logging into a machine.

```
Sun Nov  8 19:58:15 PST 2009

Rotating fax log files:

Doing login accounting:
        total       17.11
        gene        16.99
        root         0.11

-- End of monthly output --
```

The `monthly.out` script ends with a statement about the log files that it rotated. Logs that are rotated monthly generally do not get to be more than 150KB in size. The install log, for example, should be empty if you haven't installed any software in the past month. If you do see data in this file and you haven't installed software, then review what software it is and check it.

> **NOTE:** Older versions of Mac OS X will also rotate `cu.modem.log`, so you will see this noted in your `monthly.out` log file as well.

The monthly script is scheduled to run on the first of the month at 5:30 AM local time.

What to Worry About

Los Angeles can be a strange place to live. If we ducked for cover every time we heard sirens, we wouldn't get a wink of sleep or any writing done, and you wouldn't be reading this book. To some extent, much of what could be considered worrisome simply becomes normal in a big city because of all of the "white noise" to which we're exposed.

The same goes for log files. There is a lot of information in your log files, and not everything is important. This can be overwhelming for anyone, even the most senior systems administrators. We'll now cover some of the items to be on the lookout for when reviewing your logs and some of the ways to reduce the amount of "white noise" in the logs.

One way to do this is by using keywords. The words `failed`, `error`, and `incorrect` are usually important to look out for. Read the content surrounding these for more information, or use an automated analysis tool. Sorting through a log file can also be automated by using a log analyzer to help keep track of events on user systems. An excellent open source option is Swatch, which has been used by Unix systems administrators for a long time. It has been ported to Mac OS X, and can monitor just about any type of log you'll find. Other open source options are logsentry (formerly known as logcheck), a component of a security suite called Sentry Tools, and logwatch, both of which are available through MacPorts. There are also commercial options such as Sawmill, an analysis tool that can analyze hundreds of different log file formats, and Splunk, a monitoring and reporting tool that consolidates logs (as well as data from many other sources) into a searchable database.

Virtual Machine and Bootcamp Logs

It's hard to imagine that discussing the methods that Windows uses to log events would ever factor into a book about the Mac. Who knew ten years ago that two competing technologies would ever converge? But converging they are. And if your computer is running VMWare Fusion, Parallels, or Bootcamp with Windows, then security is going to be one of your top concerns. As we've discussed throughout this chapter, logs can give you a wealth of information about how secure your system is. Windows has its own tools that can help you to secure a Windows environment on the Mac.

Event Viewer

The Event Viewer is similar to the Console application on a Mac. It provides an administrator with one place to go to find information about service-oriented errors on the system itself.

The Event Viewer is split into three parts (see Figure 5–5) in Windows 7. Windows XP and the different versions of Windows Server may look different, but for the sake of discussion in this book, we will concentrate on Windows 7. Windows 7's Event Viewer is very similar to Vista's, and most Mac users are likely to be running one of those two. On the left is a list of Event categories, similar to the Log List in Console.

- Application contains events that are logged by programs. This includes database, Microsoft Exchange, and other applications that write data into logs that are not part of the core operating system.

- Security contains information about security events that have occurred when logging onto the computer. If you have enabled audit trails on file access, then this can be a verbose log. Otherwise, it is usually a very small log. Look out for anything with the word *failure* in the log because this can signify a failure with a security process.

- System shows you the events that get logged by the operating system. This includes drivers and other system components that could produce an error.

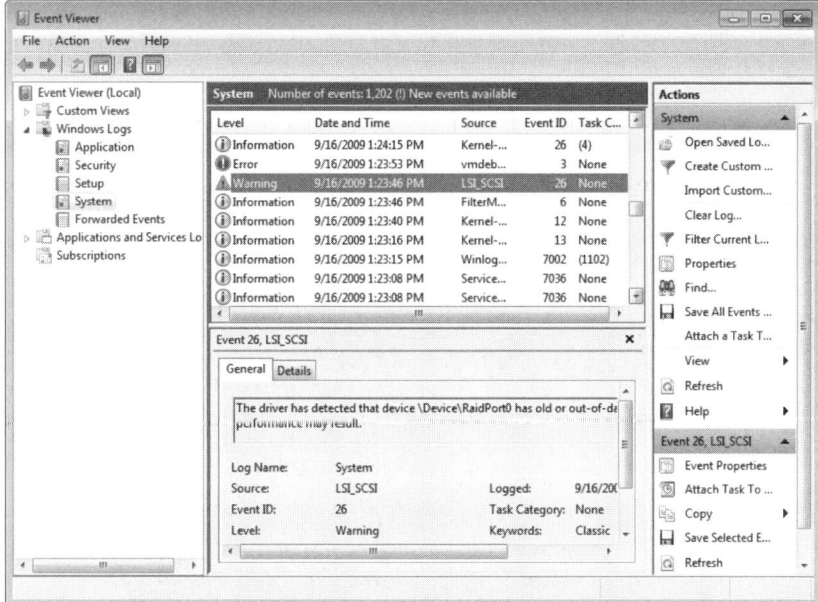

Figure 5-5. *Event Viewer*

There is a plethora of Microsoft event IDs in the Event Viewer. Microsoft has made it fairly simple to sift through these event IDs to find the errors by using color-coding. Blue means no action is necessary, yellow indicates that an item should at least be looked at, and red indicates a failure. By researching the contents of each of these entries, you will get a good handle on what Windows is having any problems with, including many events directly related to the security of your system.

Although it may seem daunting at first, you should know what every warning and error message means. The Microsoft Web site is a good place to research information about these events.

> **NOTE:** In response to the need for a more comprehensive listing of event information, EventID.net publishes information about Windows events and links to Microsoft Knowledge Base articles and third-party web sites to find more information on fixing issues you may find here. Searching for the event message, enclosed in quotation marks, on Google is also a good bet.

Task Manager

The Event Viewer is helpful for researching events that have already occurred on your system. But it doesn't go into detail about all the processes currently running on your system. The Task Manager in Windows is similar to the Activity Monitor on a Mac, and will provide you with the ability to look at what processes are currently running (see Figure 5-6).

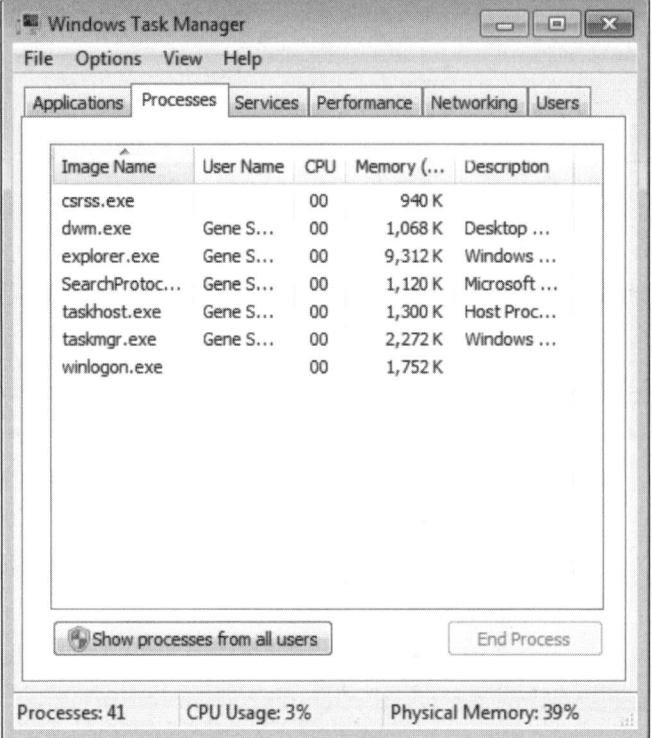

Figure 5–6. *Task Manager*

To see the Task Manager, press the Ctrl-Alt-Del keys on your keyboard, and choose Start Task Manager. Here you will see a few tabs. The first is Applications, which contains applications currently running under your account. The second is Processes, which contains the applications you have launched and any background processes that might be running, as well as the user who started the process and the CPU and memory being taken up by that application. You can use the Performance tab to check memory and processor utilization and get a chart that shows this.

To stop a process that is running, you can right-click it and click End Process. To find out more about a process, consider using Google or the Microsoft Knowledge Base at www.microsoft.com/support to research what each process is doing on the system.

> **NOTE:** You can use the Networking tab to view the network traffic running on your network interfaces.

Performance Alerts

You can use the Performance Monitor Management Console Snap-In (see Figure 5–7) to customize the amount of information that is being logged and to provide you with extremely detailed information about nearly every aspect of how your system is running.

This tool is far more advanced than those available on the Mac platform for tracking down bottlenecks in speed, levels of inbound traffic, and other items that could introduce security issues. A comprehensive discussion about this tool is beyond the scope of this book, but should definitely be consulted when trying to troubleshoot why the Windows environment on your computer is running poorly.

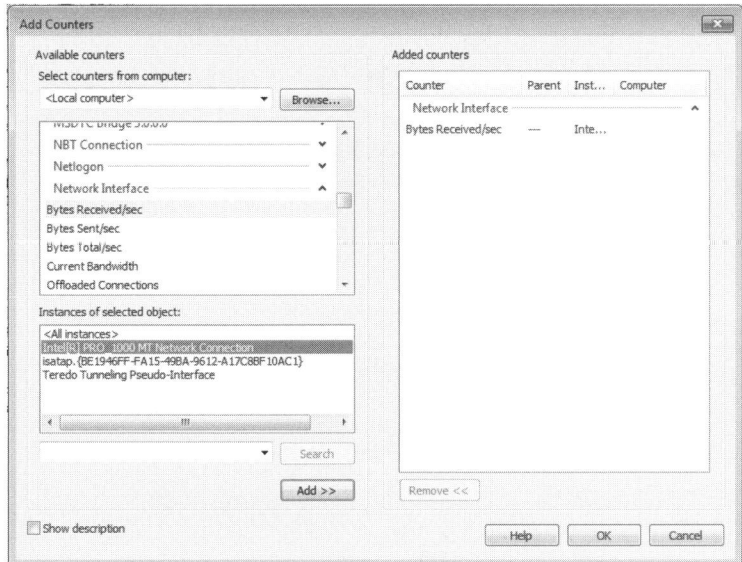

Figure 5-7. *Performance counters*

Review Regularly, Review Often

Reviewing logs is an integral aspect of security, and you should review them routinely. If you are the only person responsible for looking at logs, set up a recurring event in your calendar program to remind you to do this. This might be daily, weekly, or monthly, according to how concerned your organization is about the health and security of your system coupled with how complex your environment is.

Accountability

Establishing some form of accountability is also important. Have you ever gone to a bathroom in a gas station and seen a sign-in sheet for the attendants to mark when they've cleaned the bathroom? If a customer complains about a dirty bathroom, the manager can use the sign-in sheet to find out who forgot to clean it. Similarly, unless you establish some form of accountability, you will likely run into a situation where your logs haven't been checked in months, especially if you are dealing with multiple people in charge of log checking.

Using a spreadsheet or a sign-in sheet to indicate when log files have been reviewed is an excellent way to establish accountability for log checking. You can also track when logs are backed up to optical media (or some other form of storage) if you choose to do so.

The following are the items to include in your regularly scheduled log reviews:

- When were the `periodic` maintenance scripts (daily, weekly, and monthly) last run? You can easily find this using `ls -l /var/log/*.out` to see when their log files were last updated. Was there anything out of the ordinary in those logs?

- Were there bad password attempts? Look for repeated bad password attempts in the log for any service that accepts a network connection, such as the `smb.log` (if there are Windows computers on your network) or `ftp.log` (if you are sharing files through FTP).

- Look for any bad password attempts, and check for privilege escalations in `secure.log`.

- Review the `history` command to check for strange commands and the `last` command to look for weird user logins.

- If you're running Parallels or Bootcamp, check your Windows Event Viewer.

- The `access.log` file in the `/private/var/log /cups/access_log` folder shows all the CUPS activity on your print server.

- The logs located in the `/private/var/log/samba` directory deal with access attempts from Windows computers.

Incident Response

Smart homeowners have a disaster plan in place for what to do if their home is affected by a natural disaster or burglary. They post the phone number to the local police or fire department next to their phone. In California, earthquake country, they keep gallons of water and canned foods stored in their pantries. Whether they know it or not, they are developing an *incident response plan*.

If, in your searching through regular log files, you find something that concerns you, then you will want to also have an incident response plan for how you are going to handle these incidents. Incident response plans don't have to be very complicated, but the more people who are involved in the operations of your information systems, the more involved the incident response plan will be; therefore, the more complex the infrastructure, the more thought out the incident response plan should be.

The incident response plans can vary from location to location. For example, if you are troubleshooting your security logs at home, a typical incident response to a suspicious item in a log might be to spend an hour trying to discover what occurred. After that initial hour, if you haven't managed to discover the culprit, you will immediately reformat your hard drive and restore your data from backup. (You do have backups, right?) But at the office, you might decide that if a security event occurs and you cannot figure out what the problem is, you will open a ticket with AppleCare immediately, down the system, make a check-summed clone of it, install a new hard drive, install OS X on the new hard drive, and migrate data. Home incident response plans are typically easy to compile and really just offer you a task list of what to do in the case of a security incident. Office incident response plans are typically more comprehensive, and need to go through committees or IT groups for approval, especially because they could contain some mission-critical systems with guaranteed uptimes that need to be maintained.

We cannot stress enough the importance of implementing an incident response system. Intellectual property theft is on the rise. Companies have lost billions of dollars in revenue over the years because of stolen intellectual property. When it occurs, it is usually not a sudden occurrence; it happens over time. More often than not, the logs were giving clues to breaches in the security framework long before the actual theft occurred. Some companies have been put out of business because of security breaches. An incident response plan coupled with a tested, reliable backup plan spares everyone the heartache and devastation of stolen intellectual property and financial information.

Summary

In this chapter we looked at the various logs and logging facilities built into Mac OS X. These logs provide insight into what is happening on the inside of your computer. They can be used to guide you in troubleshooting efforts and to act as an early warning sign, even when you don't have a symptom you are looking to troubleshoot.

The logs in Mac OS X can also be used to obtain critical security information. Using the steps we laid out, you can centralize logs, or run scripts to aggregate information routinely. Those aggregated logs can enable you to see what is going on throughout an enterprise with very little work from savvy systems administrators.

Now that we have looked at logs, we'll move on to one of the aspects of Mac OS X that can place information in those logs, applications. In Chapter 6 we will jump into securing applications, with a focus on leveraging Apple's sandbox facility and rich application signing framework.

Part II

Securing the Ecosystem

Chapter 6

Application Signing and Sandbox

This chapter discusses two relatively new security features found in OS X: application signing and sandbox. These technologies were both introduced with Mac OS 10.5 and provide new facilities that help to improve the security outlook of the platform. Incidentally, both of these technologies are also heavily utilized by Apple's newest platform that you've undoubtedly heard of: the iPhone OS.

Application Signing

Application signing is a technology that Apple has implemented in OS X that seeks to address the issue of application identity and integrity. This technology provides protection to the operating system so that it can both uniquely identify an application and also determine whether the contents of the application have been modified. This includes integrity checks to both the application payload (the main function of the application) as well as the metadata about the application: its bundle identifier, version information, and the like. Once signed, if any of this information changes for an application, the OS will be able to detect that such a change has been made, and act accordingly.

From a security perspective, signing an application addresses two areas of security: authentication and integrity. By implementing these protections, Apple has a very good system to allow developers to provide a means for end users to verify the integrity of their applications, and thereby provide a method for non-repudiation. That is, when a vendor signs an application, an end user can confidently operate with knowledge that the code has not been otherwise altered by a party other than the original vendor. The concept of non-repudiation predates that of any computer system by a long shot, and seeks to provide a means for one entity to uniquely validate a piece of information.

In fact, non-repudiation has been around for centuries in one form or another. Perhaps the earliest form was the use of scarab seals, which date back as far as the Egyptian

Middle Kingdom (around 2080-1640 BC). These seals were small ornaments made of stone or clay and shaped in the form of a scarab (dung beetle). Each seal was engraved with a unique design, and could be used to authenticate documents. Another early form can be found in the Imperial Seal of China, a jade seal first used by the first Emperor of China around 221 BC. In a traditional non-computer context, consider signing a legal contract. By providing your signature to a contract, you are providing a means for the parties involved in that contract to certify that you are a participant. Once you've signed a (printed) contract, the other party can't change the wording without printing out another version, which doesn't contain your signature. However, if you only sign the last page, the other party is free to change the content of any other page, and insert or delete pages: you can repudiate the agreement to the original terms. Thus, to legally enforce non-repudiation of a contact, every page must be signed. Certainly as the world progresses, the efficacy of each various non-repudiation method has proven to be flawed, in some cases simply due to the need for better standards, and in other cases it is due to the advancements and proliferation of technology. But with that progression comes new methods for non-repudiation, with each successor becoming more and more secure.

With today's digital world, we have achieved a new level of non-repudiation, with systems that are orders of magnitude more capable than anything achievable previously. In the old days, seals and stamps could be forged, signatures could be lifted, and all of them provided rudimentary protection over the associated data as well; none of these methods provided concrete assurance that the contents or associated data had not been tampered with or manipulated.

By utilizing modern cryptography, it is possible to both uniquely identify an object and verify its contents, even when compared against millions or even billions of other entities. Such technology has seen widespread adoption in our digital age: S/MIME and PGP signatures allow a user to uniquely sign an e-mail, and allow the recipient to confidently accept that the e-mail is a valid communication, and that the contents of the e-mail are presented exactly as they were at the date of signing (the time the e-mail was sent). If at any time the e-mail's contents are manipulated by a third party, the e-mail's signature won't reflect the change and the recipient will be able to see that the content is malformed. Conversely, the third party is also unable to generate a signature that is valid for the original senders identity. This precludes an attacker from either modifying existing content or generating new content. As we will discuss in detail throughout this section, Apple's digital signing functionality utilizes this very system. Not only does it provide a very strong method for authentication, which allows developers to, in effect, put their own personal signature on their wares, it also provides a secure way to certify the content of the application.

You may be asking why this is important for an application. First and foremost, as a computer professional, you may have come to the realization that the biggest security vulnerability on many systems is that of the PEBKAC variety. That is, the Problem Exists Between the Keyboard And Chair. In the history of OS X, the majority of publicized exploits for the platform involved the utilization of a Trojan horse. Akin to the historic tale of *The Aeneid*, in computer terminology a Trojan horse is a piece of malicious software disguised as something innocuous that, when run, takes over your computer (malware is discussed in depth later on in Chapter 8). As a seasoned veteran, you know that an e-mail offering you an MS Word update available on the site `www.pwningucinz2002.ru` probably isn't a good thing to download and run, but your end user might not. Even after that, being the good Samaritan that your end user is, she might even offer it up to her coworkers. After all, it's a good idea to apply updates, right? Well, the concept of application authentication can be used to mitigate the damage this threat. Without a proper digital signature, malware can never truly masquerade as another company's product.

In this chapter we will discuss Apple's digital signing implementation. We'll delve into the nuts and bolts of the technology utilized by the system, its potential, and provide an overview of system facilities currently utilized in 10.6.

Application Authentication

Historically, the Mac OS has had only rudimentary facilities for application identification, and really no methods for application authentication. That is, an application can identify itself, but there was no way for it to absolutely *prove* its identity. With the original Mac OS, application identification was stored primarily in an application's resource fork in the form of a four-byte string called the "creator code." This creator code was then used by the operating system to associate data files with their respective application, and thus there was no need for the standard three-letter extension used by other operating systems (.exe, .doc, .txt). In the old days, this actually worked out very well, and is one of the reasons that in the early days the Mac had been considered to a be more user-friendly platform.

Unfortunately the system just didn't hold up in the modern day for a number of reasons. Four bytes of data equate to four characters, and certainly the possibility for collisions (two applications with the same creator code) is fairly high. To address this issue, Apple provided a registration system and database that ensured that all Mac OS developers' applications had unique identifiers. It was cumbersome, but it worked, and developers could reasonably assume that their application's identifier was unique.

The other problem with creator codes as a means for application identification is that there is absolutely no way to prevent your creator code from being hijacked: if an unscrupulous party wants to create an application using your creator code, there is nothing to stop them from doing so. Once that application hits the system, there is a chance that when a user double-clicks on a file meant for your application, it will, instead, open in the malicious application. There never was a great way for guaranteeing the association of data to a specific application in such an event; the Mac OS contained a database called the Desktop Database that maintained a list of all files, applications, and creator code associations. When an application saved a file, that file would be associated with your application, and the association would be saved in the Desktop Database. Such files would continue to open in your application.

The problem here is that when any files were introduced to your system from a third party (file server, e-mail, and so on), that association would not already exist, and the system would automatically try to associate the file to the appropriate application. In the event that there are two applications with this creator code (yours and the bad guys, let's say), Apple had a custom algorithm for determining which application to associate with that considered a number of factors. First it would consult all running applications. Next it would look for a qualifying application on the system volume, followed by a search of other local volumes. Finally it would check against remote volumes. The first qualifying application found for that file would then be launched and utilized, and it might very well not be yours.

With the introduction of OS X, Apple introduced a new way for an application to identify itself: the bundle identifier. A bundle identifier is a carryover from the NeXT system, upon which OS X was built, and is an application and organization unique string that allows for very specific application identification. Referred to as *reverse-domain notation*, the format of this string is essentially identical to that used by the Internet's Domain Name System, but reversed (as you may have assumed). For instance, the bundle identifier used by Apple's Text Edit application is "com.apple.textedit," Microsoft Word is "com.microsoft.Word." Like DNS, the system is very scalable and allows an application developer to uniquely identify their wares, and this alone proves advantageous over creator codes. They did not replace creator codes altogether, however, as creator codes were utilized in OS X for backwards compatibility until 10.6, which controversially killed support. If bundle identifiers are better than creator codes, then why the controversy? The controversy primarily surrounded the ability that creator codes allowed applications to associate files to themselves. That conversation is for another time though; the reality of the situation is that for application identification in OS X, the creator code as an identifying mechanism has been replaced by the bundle identifier, and the datafile/application association provided by the Creator Code has now been usurped by the UTI mechanism, which is a new system that utilizes bundle identifiers and inheritance to define association (and the primary focal point of all the creator code removal controversy). The Desktop Database as it applied to datafile/application storage has been long replaced by OS X's LaunchServices database.

An inherent problem with the bundle identifier, as with creator codes, was that there were no provisions to actually protect it. It was no longer a four-byte string (which is a good thing), but it could still be manipulated or spoofed, and malicious parties could still create their own application with your organization's bundle identifier. As such, the concept of "application authentication" was still pretty weak in OS X: we have identification, but authentication was still a complete no-show. Unauthenticated identification is akin to an airport TSA screener asking you for your name and country of origin and simply taking your word from it, rather than actually checking your documentation. Because of this, any application restrictions that were deployed on a system were suspect: even Apple's Parental Control system, or its bigger brother, MCX (Managed Client for OS X) weren't safe. Each of these systems could be trivially bypassed through the manipulation of process file names and bundle identifiers; there was no great way as a system administrator to truly restrict application usage on OS X. A disallowed application could simply mimic the identifier of an allowed application, and any access restrictions are thereby avoided.

The situation has changed with the introduction of application signing in 10.5, which allowed developers and administrators to place their own stamp on an application, certifying that it was their own creation (provided they use an identity signed by a trusted authority). For applications that aren't signed directly by the first-party company (Firefox for example), an administrator can sign it themselves using their own signing identity (for more information about signing applications, see the section "Signing and Verifying Applications"). When an administrator signs such an application, he is placing his own digital signature on the application. It's a different signature than that which would have been provided by the developer, so there is no way to certify it against the exact code that the developer shipped, but it still provides a secure way for an admin to identify *and authenticate* an application. When a signed application is provisioned to a user via parental controls or MCX, that access control is effectively incapable of manipulation: it contains a cryptographic signature of the application's bundle identifier, the contents of the application's executable, and it can be used to protect application resources. It provides full detection capabilities for any applications posing under the same bundle identifier and application name. If any such coercion exists, the MCX system will prevent the application from running.

In the end, Apple's implementation provides a very good way for a developer to provide concrete authentication for any of their applications. Likewise, it provides a way for the operating system to legitimize applications. In doing so, it opens the door for a number of powerful and very beneficial security protections that can be provided for users and administrators.

Application Integrity

Historically, the Mac OS had absolutely no ability to ensure application integrity. In the early days of personal computing, there wasn't much thought given to the possibility of malfeasance or sabotage, and as such, the concept of even needing to verify integrity wasn't a great concern in the mind of early OS designers. The fact that it could be done was known, but it wasn't thought of as a security issue (probably because no-one was thinking much of information security issues at all back then). Well, things have changed in today's modern world, and the need to verify an application's integrity is now very apparent. As we've learned, the ability to identify an application is not always enough: identities can be stolen, mimicked, and spoofed. They are fallible. In order to truly establish non-repudiation we need to be able to verify both its identity (authenticate) *and* verify the integrity of its data. If the identity is not directly associated with the data, then the system's non-repudiation factor is pretty weak.

Consider a standard computer virus, spreading mercilessly across infected computers and networks. A very common technique that viruses utilize for replication is referred to as binary data injection; a malicious piece of software, generally referred to as a "loader" (such as a Trojan horse) modifies an existing application to inject malicious code. Once an infection occurs, whenever this familiar application is launched, the malicious code is executed. This code may contain further viral function, which means that the application may spread the infection to other existing applications on the system, or even worse, the malicious code may serve as a backdoor into your computer by listening over the network for inbound connections. Suddenly any application on your computer can serve as a vector for exploitation. The limit to what an attacker can do with this is limited solely to the privileges of the executing user. If this user is an admin user, then the potential for damage is pretty high; the system will be compromised. Sadly, code signing in OS X doesn't currently prevent such an attack. It detects the attack, which permits quick reaction on the part of whoever notices the detection. Detection and reaction are important—though often overlooked—factors of a good security posture. Novel attacks are always being found, or you may have just overlooked an important risk: the only way you'll find out is if you have some detection in place.

Application signing can potentially be utilized to defend against such occurrences with its ability to confidently validate integrity. When an application is signed, that signature uniquely identifies the executable code of the application, providing a unique fingerprint. If the application's code is altered, that fingerprint changes unequivocally, and the digital signature will have been broken.

Code signing provides an additional benefit for application integrity: when an application runs, its contents are copied to memory and then executed. In the traditional sense, code signing provides the ability for an operating system to detect on-disk modifications to an application. But in actuality, it goes even further than that. Apple's code signing system actually provides the functionality to dynamically verify the validity of code running in a given process. This facility helps to verify integrity of the application on the disk and while running. Even if an application loads new code like a plug-in after it has started, code signing can detect that and update its view of the application's integrity.

Signature Enforcement in OS X

Although application signing is utilized very heavily by the iPhone and iPod Touch, it's utilization in Mac OS X is a little less prolific. As of 10.5, Apple has digitally signed all applications that it ships. However, the system facilities that actually utilize application signing is fairly minimal, and this certainly is the weak link in Apple's system: it has an excellent foundation laid that allows it to enforce extremely tight controls in the OS. When we view the iPhone OS for instance, we find a system that is 100% reliant on application signing. In such a case, Apple serves as the root authority, and as such has complete control over all applications that are allowed to run on the platform. This has proven to be a very effective system, providing a near-ironclad guard against malware on the platform. Interestingly enough, the act of "jail-breaking" an iPhone involves circumventing and ultimately disabling the signing system. This is done not by attacking the signing system itself, but by penetrating the OS through some other means to disable it altogether. Also interesting to note is that the only iPhone malware "in the wild"—the iKee and Duh worms—target jail-broken devices.

In OS 10.5 and 10.6, we have seen much more minimal implementation of the technology, and for good reason. OS X is a long-standing system, with a history of a completely open architecture; any application that is compiled on OS X can be executed and run by the user. Apple certainly couldn't get away with implementing the same measures as the iPhone with OS X, as in essence the iPhone model is the antithesis of OS X's traditional model. The iPhone itself has seen a decent amount of outcry due to its highly restrictive system; OS X certainly wouldn't be very well received if it required that *all* applications be signed. Instead, they have slowly introduced it into the system, starting with access to OS X's keychain, perhaps the juiciest (if not best protected) target on any user's system. Additional uses, as mentioned earlier, include OS X's application firewall, its parental control mechanisms, as well as the MCX system. In this section we will delve into each, and discuss exactly how the system utilizes signing to protect its end user.

Keychain Access

The keychain is a prevalent and an oh-so-important component of OS X. It is also significantly misunderstood. Its function lies much in its name: it serves a digital keychain for all of your digital keys. These keys can be a number of things, from the password of an e-mail account configured with Mail.app or Entourage, to saved credentials from your banking web page. By default, a user has only one keychain, the login keychain. This keychain has the same password as their OS X account. When a user logs into OS X, the default login keychain is then unlocked, and trusted applications can access their respective entities without user interaction or notification. The key word here is *trusted* applications, and in OS X, all applications have an inherited distrust when first attempting to access the keychain. When an application first attempts to access a keychain item, the user will be prompted to trust the application. Figure 6–1 shows the dialog box presented when an application is first fired.

Figure 6–1. *Providing keychain Access to an application. An unsigned application (left) and a signed app (right).*

In Figure 6–1, notice the difference in text on the dialog boxes (look carefully or you might miss it). The unsigned application on the left contains additional text to warn the user that its authenticity could not be verified, while the signed application simply requests access. The difference between the notices is so subtle and minimized that it's doubtful that anyone but the most experienced users will ever notice it, which is unfortunate. On top of this, there is no indication as to *who* signed the application. Camino straight from the vendor isn't signed, so some other party has done the deed, and that party may very well have injected all kinds of badness before signing it. Certainly more attention could be paid to show that an application is trusted and signed by a trusted Root Authority.

In either case, if the user selects Allow, the application will be granted one-time access to the keychain item. If Always Allow is selected, the application will have the ability to access the unlocked keychain without ever prompting the user. If the keychain becomes locked, the user will be prompted to enter his or her keychain password when any application seeks to access it. Thus, it is possible for a user to only have to remember their keychain password, and the keychain can then be used to store all of the various website and application passwords that a user may utilize. This also allows a user to follow good security practices and utilize a different password for every website they go to, yet they will only have to remember their keychain password to gain access to any of them.

Outside of this possible one-time dialog, the Keychain framework only makes benefit of application signing for one user visible feature. Without application signing, whenever an application is updated (say, a new version is released and installed), Figure 6–1 (left) would be presented to the user. If the application is signed, a developer can release updates to the software, and as long as they are signed with the same identity, you will never be prompted again to allow access to the Keychain

In older versions of OS X, this dialog was a little bit different. You may recall previously a dialog that would pop up, claiming that an application has changed and wants to access the keychain. See Figure 6–2.

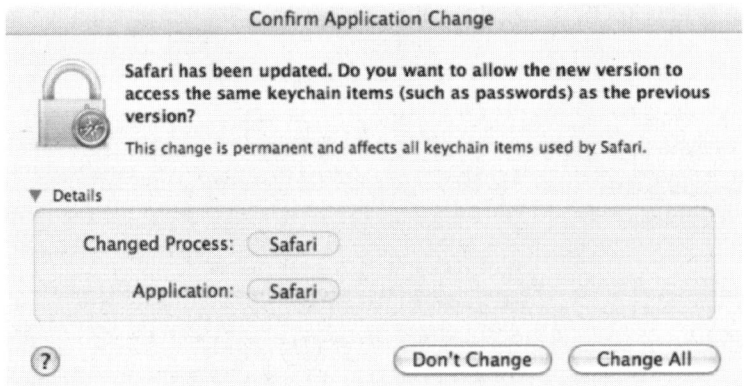

Figure 6–2. *Application change confirmation, OS 10.4*

This dialog box actually provided clear, concise information to the end user. Very specific, and very helpful. If the user is even the least bit considerate, this dialog provides enough meaning for them to understand exactly why they've been prompted: the application has changed. With the implementation in 10.6, when an application is updated, the above dialog is no longer used, instead being replaced by the same dialog pictured in Figure 6–1, which isn't very specific at all, unfortunately, and a step in the wrong direction. The good news is that with signed applications, this dialog box is actually completely eradicated. For instance, you will never see such a dialog in Safari, because any updates released by Apple will contain an identical bundle identifier "com.apple.safari," and will be signed with the same signing authority as the version of Safari that it replaces. Therefore, the update has a completely valid and non-refutable signature and can be provided access to the exact same resources as its predecessor with impunity.

The OS X Application Firewall

With OS X 10.5, Apple introduced a new software firewall that was met with pretty harsh criticism. Apple's new software firewall replaced the lower-level ipfw firewall utilized by previous versions of OS X. The ipfw firewall operates at the network layer, and allowed users to provide access provisions to specific ports and IP addresses for access. Each of these provisions were global across the system, that is, they were not associated with a particular application. The new application firewall, as its name implies, operates at a much higher level. The primary implication here is that instead of defining specific access to ports and IP addresses, restrictions are applied to specific applications. Once an application has been trusted, it is provisioned full access to any port that it might seek to open. This fact contributed to much of the controversy: it's a different take on firewalling, and power users wanted the ability to control exactly which ports could be used on their system. In the opinion of your humble authors, we feel much of the criticism is unwarranted: application firewalling is actually a much more user-friendly implementation, and considering the skill level of the vast majority of the Mac computer-using public, it is effectually more secure. On top of this, traditional firewalls can't react to Trojan horse attacks, because they allow any application access to the permitted ports.

There's much to be said for the conception that as the complexity of a software implementation increases, so also do the odds of the software being misconfigured or misused by the user. Instead of requiring a user to open up ports 24000-36000TCP and 1408TCP/UDP to host their favorite game online, the user only has to provide access to the application itself. What the user doesn't see is that when they allow network access to their game, if that game is not already signed, it will be signed by the system using an "ad-hoc" authority and will be provided access to the network. That application's digital signature then serves effectively as the key to the firewall; as long as the signature for that application is verifiable by the system, it will be granted access to the firewall. If the application is in violation of the policy, the firewall will no longer provide access to the application without user approval. Power users still have access to the powerful ipfw firewall if they want it; even as of 10.6, it's still there. There's just no GUI to configure it. For those power users who don't feel that a command-line approachable option is a good one, there are several shareware tools which provide a GUI layer for the `ipfw` tool.

As for the new firewall GUI, it is rather simplified, as can be seen in Figures 6-3 and 6-4. Found hiding under the Security System Preference Pane, the primary interface provided for the application firewall is a simple Start and Stop button, seen in Figure 6-3 specifically.

Figure 6–3. *Turning on the application firewall*

The primary firewall interface provides a lonely Advanced button, which contains such firewall features, seen in Figure 6–4.

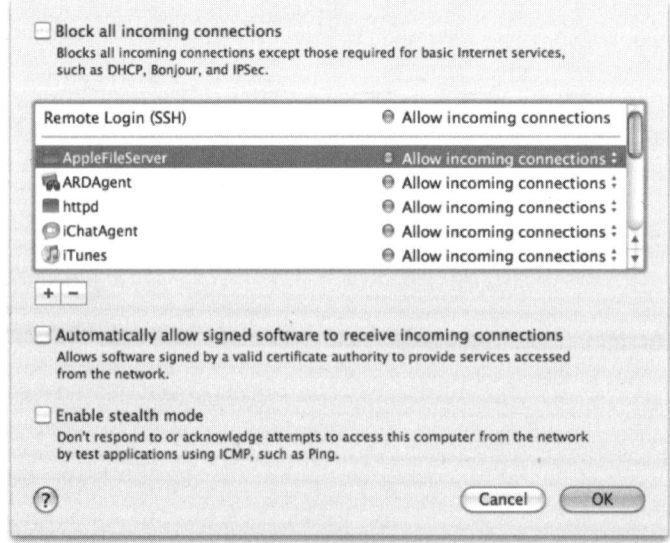

Figure 6–4. *Advanced firewall settings*

In Figure 6–4, there are only a small number of options. The first checkbox, "Block all incoming connections," allows the user to deny access to a somewhat ambiguous rule set of traffic, predetermined by Apple. However, it does an adequate job of locking down access to a computer, and exposes the computer to a network with a very minimal amount of exposure. Unchecking this box allows users to provide access to specific applications via a very basic list, with the option to allow or deny traffic to a specific application. In the event that you add an application to this list, whether denying access or allowing access, the application will be signed by an ad-hoc authority if it is not signed by it's original distributor.

The second checkbox, "Automatically allow signed software to receive incoming connections," does just what it says: if an application is signed with a digital certificate whose certificate chain is trusted by the system, the application will automatically be granted access to the network. Checking this box is equivalent to inherently trusting any application signed by a legitimate certificate authority (CA).

> **NOTE:** Just because an application has been signed by a certificate whose chain leads to a CA, it does not mean that the application is legitimate or trustworthy. Obtaining a certificate from a major CA does involve a decent amount of paperwork and vetting, but it does not absolutely guarantee the legitimacy of a company or its wares. Alternatively, the application could be perfectly legitimate but do something you don't want, like a commercial key scanner. The general point is that while a signed application carries proof of its integrity, it carries no proof of its purpose (or its fitness for that purpose). You can sign buggy applications.

The last option, "Enable stealth mode," doesn't deal with application signing, but is worthy of a brief mention: enabling it configures the client to not respond to pings, and prevents bonjour messages from being sent out. It's a pretty good way to make your computer silent on a network. For more extensive discussion on setting up the Mac OS X Firewall, see Chapter 11.

Client Management – MCX and Parental Controls

Managed preferences in Mac OS X provide administrators (and parents!) with a valuable toolset for managing many aspects of the Mac OS X computing environment. Referred to as MCX, or Managed Client OS X, its capabilities are fairly expansive, providing many functions such as managing individual userland application settings, applying user restrictions to inserted/removable media, managing iChat capabilities, and most relevant to the topic at hand, controlling application access.

OS X has two primary facilities for utilizing the MCX, to which this section is dedicated. The first that we'll talk about is more relevant perhaps to you, dear Enterprise Mac administrator. This facility is the Managed Preference system used in Open Directory to provide application restrictions to a number of users across a network, and managed with the Workgroup Manager administrative tool.

Historically, MCX application restrictions have been a bit of a moving target. 10.4 had a fairly configurable setup, allowing the option to explicitly allow applications or to specifically deny applications. Unfortunately, the system wasn't terribly resilient, and was pretty easy to bypass due to the inadequacies of bundle identifiers for application identification. With 10.5, a new take on application restrictions were put in place using, you guessed it, application signing. Restricting applications with MCX is done on an explicit allow basis. That is, once you choose to restrict applications for a user, an implicit deny will be applied to all applications that are not in the allowed applications list. Because of this, it is important to have a good understanding of the applications that will be utilized in the managed environment prior to embarking on this endeavor. If not properly planned, you will be flooded with support requests from users, claiming that they can't access their beloved applications. However, when implemented using application signing, the system proves to be extremely resilient to various hacks that might be used to subvert it.

When restricting applications with MCX, you have two primary options, both accessible from the Applications pane of the Workgroup Managers Preference interface, shown in Figure 6–5.

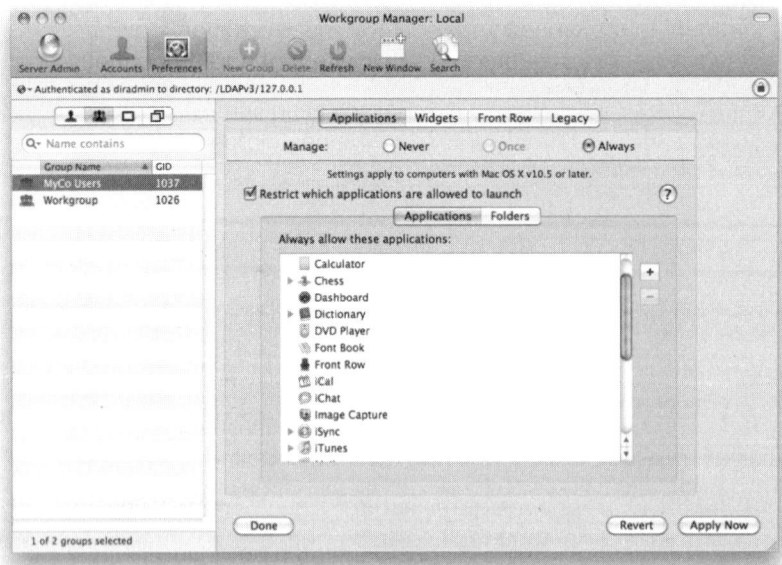

Figure 6–5. *Configuring application white listing*

Using this interface, you can allow a specific application, or you can specify a white-listed folder wherein any application that resides within it is always trusted. Specifying broad access based on folder paths is not inherently secure, and doesn't utilize digital signing protections. To utilize application restrictions to its fullest, you will want to allow specific applications in-use by your organization. This allows for fine-grained targeting of applications without the need to worry about whether file system restrictions have been bypassed or not. By utilizing application signing, the system has a very secure way to ensure that the only applications that can be launched are the intended applications. If a provisioned application is modified, it will no longer match our signature, and will thereby be treated as a foreign entity.

> **NOTE:** When adding an application to an allowed applications list, you must first specify the application from the client machine running Workgroup Manager. If the application that you wish to allow is not resident on this computer, you will not be able to select it from the list, and thereby will not be able to provision access to the app.

Likewise, when you add an unsigned application to the allowed applications list, you will be greeted with an option to sign the application, or add it to the list without signing it. If you choose the latter, the application will be allowed to launch, but it will be possible to utilize this inclusion for exploitative purposes. Because the application is not signed, it is possible to alter any arbitrary application to impersonate the application, and thereby bypass any restrictions that would otherwise be applied. As such, if any allowed application is unsigned, it represents the ability for the user to launch any application, provided they have the skills to do so. When an allowed application is not signed, it will appear with a yellow triangle next to its entry, as seen for Firefox in Figure 6–6.

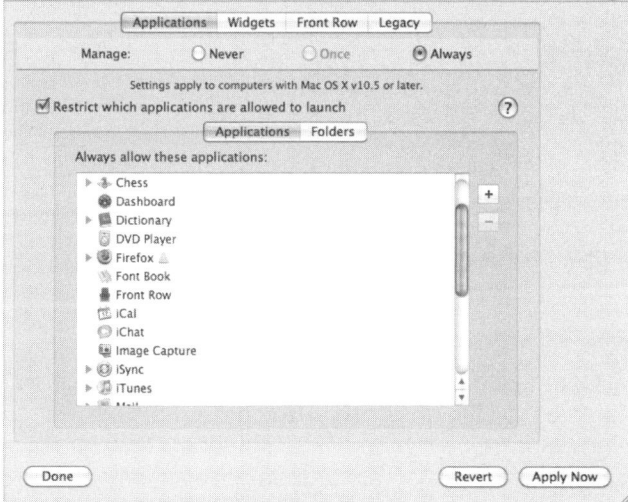

Figure 6–6. *Adding an unsigned application*

There are some ramifications for signing an application when adding via Workgroup Manager as well. Most notably, when you sign the application with Workgroup Manager, you are signing only the local copy of that application. As such, all those hundreds of copies of that application in the field remain unsigned, and therefore restricted from launching. So, in order to fulfill a securely restricted environment, it will be necessary to deploy the signed applications to all of your clients. Furthermore, you will need to sign and deploy all updated versions of the app before they work on the client systems. If the apps auto-update, you will find this becomes a significant burden on support. For developers to sign their own applications is a simple change to their build processes, so complain loudly at your app vendors to sign their applications. For more information on managing the MCX system, consult the book *Enterprise Mac Administrator's Guide*, by Charles Edge, Beau Hunter, and Zack Smith (Apress, 2009).

Parental controls utilize a very similar system to restrict application access, though its interface is greatly simplified, shown in Figure 6–7.

Figure 6–7. *Parental Controls' application restrictions*

One very notable aspect of Parental Controls: though the system can utilize application signing, the GUI does not provide facilities to sign unsigned applications themselves. Therefore, any allowed application that is not signed represents a potential hole for a user to exploit in the system; it is possible for any program to then pose as that unsigned application, and then all kinds of unscrupulous shenanigans can occur. If you intend to utilize application restrictions through parental controls, consider signing any unsigned applications yourself. We'll discuss how to do so in the next section.

NOTE: For more information about setting up Parental Controls, see Chapter 3.

Signing and Verifying Applications

We've already discussed of all the benefits of signing, and how OS X actually enforces these provisions. So let's get our hands dirty dabbling with it. To understand how signing works, it's first important to understand a little bit about the system. If you've ever used SSL, you'll have some familiarity here. Apple's implementation, like other code signing implementations, uses Public Key Infrastructure (PKI) to get the job done. Signing an application is achieved through the use of a private key, and its associated digital signing certificate. The private key, as its name implies, is to be forever protected by the organization that is performing the signing, whether it's Microsoft signing MS Word, or you, the admin, signing an application. If your private key is exposed, then the entire system is compromised. Fortunately, it is possible to revoke an identity and thereby invalidate it, but it is not a fun process and should be avoided.

The digital certificate contains less sensitive information, but nonetheless important information. It includes organizational information, such as the company name and address. It also includes information vital to decoding the signature; this includes the signature algorithm (typically the SHA-1 hash in modern-day certificates), and it includes information about the public key, the key itself, as well as the algorithm that is used. This certificate may itself be signed by a greater entity. In many cases, this will be a legitimate CA, such as VeriSign or Thawte. These are private CA organizations that establish a root chain of trust for certificates. Apple itself is a public CA of sorts, though not in the traditional sense as they only provide signing services specifically for code-signing identities to be used for iPhone applications.

In the case of the iPhone, in order to get an application to run on the iPhone (which relies heavily on application signing), your application must be signed by a certificate that is part of Apple's certificate chain. It is this certificate chaining that ultimately provides the basis for non-repudiation when utilizing digital certificates. That being said, it is not a requirement that your signing identity is signed by a chain leading to a trusted Root CA. Considering this, even a signed application could contain malware as there is no burden of evidence; the application is signed, but signed by an unknown (and potentially suspect) authority. This is not to say that an application signed by a trusted certificate cannot contain malware, it certainly can, either deliberately or accidentally (and either knowingly or unwittingly) provided by the distributor before signing. The certificate chain of an identity gives you *some* assurance regarding the identity of the signer, but none regarding the content of the product. On the iPhone, this is a show stopper, due to Apple's aggressive enforcement of code signing on that platform. In OS X, the application is simply considered untrustworthy, and the user will be prompted if the application attempts to access any security features that utilize signing protections such as access to a keychain entity or traversing the application firewall. Once the user trusts the application through this dialog, the digital signature is considered trusted from then on.

In the previous section, we discussed how to utilize GUI tools to indirectly sign applications: when an Application is allowed or denied access to the application firewall, the utility will sign any unsigned application so that the OS can properly identify it. Likewise, if you add an application to the MCX system, any unsigned application will warrant a prompt asking if you would like to sign it. Each of these systems provides fairly easy methods to sign an application, and both use Apple-provided certificates to do the signing. If you want to sign applications with your own signing identity, you must use the command line utility named `codesign`. Preferably, such a signing certificate would come from a trusted CA, however, it is possible to create your own. To do so, you can utilize the Keychain Access application found at /Applications/Utilities. With this application open, under the Keychain Access menu, select **Certificate Assistant**, and then select **Create a Certificate**…. As seen in Figure 6–8 (top left), you will be presented with the option to specify a certificate name. In this example, we use "MyCo Signing Certificate," but naturally, the name of this certificate will depend on your own organization. In this first screen, you will also want to ensure the option "Let me override defaults" is checked, and that the certificate type is "Code Signing." In this example, we are using a self-signed root identity type. You can also specify a leaf type, which you can sign by your own internal CA. In upper-right corner of Figure 6–8, you will be prompted for organizational information. For all other screens during this process, the default settings will be adequate.

Figure 6–8. *Creating a self-signed signing certificate.*

Once the signing identity has been created, it will be present in the Keychain Access utility, also seen in Figure 6–8. In this case, the certificate root has been imported into the system keychain and has also been trusted (by default it is not trusted). To trust the certificate by the system, double-click on the certificate, and under the trust pull down ensure that Always Trust is selected under the option "When using this certificate." Once the certificate is in place, you can then sign the application from the command line using the aforementioned `codesign` application using the following syntax:

```
codesign -s 'MyCo Signing Certificate' /Applications/Firefox.app
```

Upon executing this command, you will be prompted to insert credentials to access the System keychain. Upon successful authentication, the stored private key and signature will be used to sign the application.

It is also possible to use the `codesign` tool to verify the state of the application. To do so, we can run it with the following syntax, against the same application that we just signed (Firefox), as seen in this example:

```
helyx:~ hunterbj$ codesign --verify -v /Applications/Firefox.app
/Applications/Firefox.app: valid on disk
/Applications/Firefox.app: satisfies its Designated Requirement
```

It is also possible to display more information that has been signed into the application, as seen here:

```
helyx:~ hunterbj$ codesign -dvvvv /Applications/Firefox.app
Executable=/Applications/Firefox.app/Contents/MacOS/firefox-bin
Identifier=org.mozilla.firefox
Format=bundle with Mach-O universal (i386 ppc)
CodeDirectory v=20100 size=228 flags=0x0(none) hashes=5+3 location=embedded
CDHash=3928da04d4ce2480a5a077e7fe37c41750d138f0
Signature size=1566
Authority=MyCo Signing Certificate
Signed Time=Mar 4, 2010 2:33:39 AM
Info.plist entries=15
Sealed Resources rules=4 files=4
Internal requirements count=1 size=152
```

As we can see, this copy of Firefox has now been signed by an organization and deployed throughout. The signature contains information pertaining to the application, in this case, we can verify the application identifier: org.mozilla.firefox, as well as the authority that signed it: "MyCo Signing Certificate." From here on, if the application is altered in any way, its signature will fail and the user will be informed. If the application has no signature, the `codesign` operation will so state:

```
helyx:~ hunterbj$ codesign -dvvvv /Applications/Camino.app
/Applications/Camino.app: code object is not signed
```

In summary, application signing shows true promise to combat application poisoning and help developers to provide legitimacy to their application. However, the realization is that as of 10.6, application signing's enforcement in OS X is relatively minimal. Most notably, users are not warned if they launch an application whose contents have been modified! The honest truth is that users commonly identify applications based upon their filename, or even their icon. Anything that happens beyond the screen is simply magic: they click on the blue W and expect to see a word processor. The issue here, is that with the state of the system, 10.6 simply doesn't have the enforcement facilities to truly protect users like this. What is needed is for Apple to provide a clear and concise UI that can warn users if their applications are suspect. Such a system is simply just not available in the Mac OS today.

The good news is that the groundwork has been laid. OS X ships with all of its applications signed by Apple, and are thereby potentially unsusceptible to malicious modification. Likewise, third-party developers can do the same. We say "potentially unsusceptible" simply due to the fact that with no teeth the system doesn't do much good; the lack of a clear, concise and consistent UI is in my opinion the most significant shortcoming in the system. That's not to say that their current use in the Security Framework, Application Firewalling, and MCX should be ignored: in each case, they serve an important role. Users can rest assured that if they have their application firewall employed, provisioned applications won't freely be granted network if they have been modified. Likewise, system administrators who deploy signed applications have a very good system for restricting application usage on their managed networks, MCX is no longer a system easily subverted. However, the lack of communication that OS X maintains with end users minimizes the impact that all of these features have on the security situation for every day OS X users.

Apple is no doubt treading lightly here; the iPhone OS has complete enforcement of application signing. In fact, it's not even possible to run an unsigned application on the iPhone unless you jail break it (which completely disables application signing enforcement). Apple could introduce this extreme right off the bat with the iPhone OS because it was a brand new system, and it's always easier to start clean. Things aren't so cut and dry with a desktop-class OS like OS X, where dependencies on third-party vendors is more of an issue. They certainly want to avoid a Vista-like experience where security alerts are so common that they are altogether dismissed as an annoyance. As such, it's difficult to foresee a future where OS X warns users of unsigned applications. However, there's no reason why a user shouldn't be warned if a signed application is altered. Hopefully with 10.7 we'll see more user exposure and utilization of this powerful security feature.

Sandbox

In all versions of OS X previous to Leopard, access control restrictions were limited to a security model referred to as Discretionary Access Controls (DAC). The most visible form of DAC in OS X is in its implementation of the POSIX file-system security model, which was discussed heavily in detail in Chapter 4. The POSIX model establishes identity-based restrictions on an object in the form of a subject's user or group membership. Similarly, Access Control Lists are a form of discretionary control, though as we learned they are far more extensible and discrete then the POSIX model. In such models, newly created objects or processes inherit their access rights based upon those of the creating subject, so that any spawned objects are not granted access rights beyond that of their parent. The key idea behind the DAC model is that the security of an object is left to the discretion of the object's owner; an object's owner has the ability to assign varying levels of access control to that object within the confines of the DAC implementation.

For decades, the DAC model has been a staple in the management of both object/process creation and access across all mainstream computer systems due to its user-centric nature. However, there is a persistent caveat in these implementations; in all mainstream implementations of such models, there exists a superuser which has the capabilities to completely bypass access restrictions placed on objects. In POSIX-based operating systems such as Unix, Linux, or OS X, this superuser exists in the form of the root user. The existence of such a loophole presents a bit of a paradox. On one hand, it introduces several obvious security ramifications by providing capabilities to completely bypass the DAC model altogether. Any processes that are invoked by the superuser inherit the "god mode" access controls; they have free reign over the entire system. At the same time, the existence of the superuser account becomes a vital tool for the practical administration of data objects and system resources. In a perfect world, this wouldn't necessarily be a bad thing. Unfortunately that's not the world we live in, and it is not uncommon to hear about processes being hijacked for ill-will. There have been no small number of exploits that take advantage of vulnerable daemons running as the superuser. Once such a daemon is compromised, so is the entirety of your system. Likewise, environmental or binary poisoning can be used to subvert a system's integrity.

The moral of the story is that if your system has a piece of software which must run as the root user, there is an inherent insecurity built-in; your system is only as secure as your least secure piece of software which runs with such permissions. The unfortunate reality is that even in 2010, there are a large number of software implementations that need superuser access. Fortunately, such occurrences are largely relegated to the server-model, where daemonized software is a much more common occurrence.

With 10.5 Leopard, Apple has introduced a new low-level access control model, dubbed seatbelt, into their OS. Seatbelt's implementation is based upon the mandatory access control (MAC) model. Conceptually, the MAC system implements restrictions based upon actors, objects, and actions. In such a system, the actor typically assumes the form of a process, thread, or socket. The object can be any type of resource, such as a file, directory, socket, or even a TCP/UDP network port, among others. The action is simply the request of the actor to be applied to the respective object, and varies depending on the type of object involved in the request. Referring back to the file system model; the actor would be a word processor application, the object would be a .txt flat file, and the action would be a call to either read to or write to that text file. When the actor requests access to the object, the MAC authorization system evaluates security policies and decides whether the request can proceed, or if it should be prohibited. The main thing to draw from this is that in a MAC model, ownership of object or process is not generally a consideration; individual users do not have the ability to override defined policy. This applies to the superuser as well; policies are applied without discrimination.

Leopard implements the MAC model via a framework architected from TrustedBSD's MAC framework, which is designed to support U.S. Government "Trusted Computing" security requirements. This framework introduces "sandbox" access control capabilities that allow a developer or user to apply access control policies to a process, restricting privileges to various specified system resources. The restrictions are generally enforced upon acquisition, so any active file descriptors (open files) would not be immediately affected by any policy changes, however, any new open() operations would be subject to the new restrictions. In a fashion similar to the DAC model, new processes and forks will inherit the access restrictions of their parent. With 10.6, the scope and breadth of possible control points has grown, such actions include, but are not limited to, the following:

- Filesystem Access
- File/Directory read/write
- File metadata read/write
- File/Directory Extended Attributes read/write
- System sockets
- Network Access
- Inbound/Outbound control
- IP-specific controls
- Port-specific controls
- Process execution
- Forking
- Subprocess execution
- IPC (inter-process communication)
- Process signaling
- Mach-O messaging
- Shared Memory
- Low-level OS functions
- sysctl read/write
- ioctl (device/tty access)
- fsctl (file-system control:mounting/unmountIng)

In Leopard, sandbox policies can be pre-compiled into any given program, or they can be applied to any executable at runtime. The majority of this section will focus on applying sandbox profiles with the sandbox-exec command, which employs the latter strategy, though we will also cover implementing sandbox calls directly into an application. After reading this section you will be familiar with using sandbox to help secure your Mac.

Sandbox Profiles

Sandbox allows for the application of mandatory restrictions via sandbox profiles. Profiles are text configuration files defining access provisions to various System facilities. If we consider the previously discussed paradigm, where the MAC framework consists of actors, actions, and objects, a sandbox profile defines and associates actions and objects via allow or deny declarations. An individual sandbox profile contains a number of these declarations, which ultimately define the allowed behavior of an application. When a sandbox profile is applied to a process, that process will be ultimately restricted in it's function to the actions provisioned in the profile. Any attempts to access resources outside of those defined in the applied sandbox will be rejected, regardless of the operating user.

Sandbox profiles are applied at runtime to an executed process via the executable /usr/bin/sandbox-exec. By passing this command the -f key, you can specify the path to a sandbox profile to apply to an executable. The last argument passed to sandbox-exec should be the path to the executable binary. For instance, the following command launches TextEdit with the sandbox profile found at /usr/share/sandbox/lockdown.sb.

```
hunterbj$ sandbox-exec -f /usr/share/sandbox/lockdown.sb↵
 /Applications/TextEdit.app/Contents/MacOS/TextEdit &
```

Notice that, when launching a .app-based application bundle, such as TextEdit, you must supply the full path to the binary executable program, rather than the path to the .app bundle itself. Once the above command is executed, TextEdit will open and operate normally. However, until the user quits TextEdit, it will be restricted only to actions defined in the "lockdown" profile. If the user launches it again by clicking on it from Applications, it will no longer have the sandbox profile applied and will operate under normal conditions. So, it's a little harder to control access to GUI-launched user initiated applications. That being said, it serves as a great tool for performing forensics: if you're running for the first time a suspicious application, it might not be a bad idea to launch it in a sandboxed environment just in case. In conjunction with seatbelt's logging facilities (which we'll get to in a bit), it becomes very apparent to see exactly what resources the application is trying to access. Or, maybe it's not the application that you don't trust, but rather the data that it is trying to process. By wrapping Preview.app in a sandbox prior to opening a suspect PDF, should the PDF contain some payload, its effect can be largely mitigated: in such a case Preview could be restricted from writing to any file system location, from spawning processes, initiating network connections, Mach-O messaging, or other process signaling. By removing such abilities from Preview, any exploitive code executed in its guise is subject to the same restrictions.

> **TIP:** The directory /usr/share/sandbox is a built-in constant. Any profiles that reside in this directory can be called with sandbox-exec by passing the -n argument and specifying solely the profile name, without the .sb extension. Thus, 'sandbox-exec -f /usr/share/sandbox/lockdown.sb' is equivalent to 'sandbox-exec -n lockdown'

OS X ships with a number of sandbox profiles installed by default found in the folder /usr/share/sandbox. These default profiles provide a glimpse into the various interfaces provided by the sandbox system. As of 10.6, Sandbox profiles are included for system components such as Bonjour, Quicklook, Spotlight, Kerberos, ntp (Network Time), serialnumberd, syslog, and xgrid. In the purview of OS X services, this is still a pretty small number, but it's a good improvement over 10.5, and it's nice to see that many of the behind-the-scenes daemons are becoming sandboxed. For instance, Bonjour has relatively recently had an exploit that allowed for remote code execution (CERT VU#221876 www.kb.cert.org/vuls/id/221876). Bonjour functionality is provided the mDNSResponder daemon, which runs under the user root (superuser), making this a particularly dangerous exploit. Luckily, this exploit has long-since been patched, but it serves as a reminder that OS X is not impervious to attack. With 10.6, if such an exploit were to be found and attacked, the defined sandbox profile would help to mitigate (if not eliminate) the damage.

Apple also provides some built-in profiles that can be utilized by running processes. These profiles are fairly broad in their implementation, so in many cases, it will most likely be desirable to create your own precisely defined sandbox profiles. That being said, it is certainly good to know about the built-in profiles. These profiles are:

- Nointernet: Disables all TCP/IP networking
- Nonet: Disables all socket-based networking.
- Nowrite: Disables write access to all file system objects
- write-tmp-only: Disables write access to file system objects except /var/tmp and the environmental variable $DARWIN_USER_TEMP_DIR
- pure-computation: All OS services are restricted

Each of these profiles are evoked with the -n flag. For example, the following command launches TextEdit with the 'nowrite' sandbox applied and the application will not be able to make any file system writes:

```
sandbox-exec -n nowrite /Applications/TextEdit.app/Contents/MacOS/TextEdit
```

This command will launch TextEdit, but the program will have read-only access to any asset it can open.

> **NOTE:** When launching a non-Mach-O Carbon-based application, such as Microsoft Office 2004, you must actually launch the "LaunchCFM" Application found at path: /System/Library/Frameworks/Carbon.framework/Versions/A/Support/LaunchCFMApp. Thus, to open up Microsoft Word with an attached profile, the following syntax would be used: 'sandbox-exec -n nointernet /System/Library/Frameworks/Carbon.framework/Versions/A/Support/LaunchCFMApp /Applications/Microsoft\ Office\ 2004/Microsoft\ Word'

It is important to note that, outside of it's own use, Apple does not officially support sandbox profiles for use in OS X. Current access control definitions utilized by sandbox profiles are designated as System Private Interface and are therefore subject to change. That's not to say they don't work; they do. Apple uses them, and so can you. The main implication here is that if you have problems with your sandbox profile, or problems caused by its implementation, if you call Apple support they will not (be able to) help you to troubleshoot this. Likewise, as Apple makes updates available, it is possible that they will change the way that profiles work without warning. In such an event, users relying on the behavior or file format (and books that document it) will be in trouble. That being said, if you feel that your organization has a security need that can be fulfilled by applying a sandbox profile, we feel that the technology is robust and stable enough to warrant consideration for implementation. The worst thing that happens when applying a too restrictive profile is that the application cannot access necessary resources and therefore fails to run. In such an event it is possible to monitor logging to determine necessary resources and ensure access is provisioned to the application in question. Once all resource needs are properly provisioned, the application should function inside the sandbox without adverse affect. That being said, test, test, test. If you plan on deploying a sandbox to a business critical service, make sure that you have thoroughly tested all use-cases of the application under the sandbox before going live.

The Anatomy of a Profile

So, without further adieu, let's take a look at the makeup of a profile. To facilitate this, we'll walk through the creation of the previously mentioned "lockdown" sandbox profile one declaration at a time. But first, let's discuss a few basics. The first thing to know is that all declarations in a sandbox profile are encased in parentheses "()." Next, the semicolon (;) denotes an inline comment; any text to the right of a semicolon will be treated as a comment and will not be processed. Lastly, sandbox has an enforcement model such that the last declaration wins. That is, if you have two potentially conflicting access provisions, one denying access to a resource while the other allowing access, whichever declaration appears latest in the profile wins. Armed with this knowledge, let's take a look at the first line of our lockdown profile:

```
(version 1)
```

Here we are declaring the version of our profile. This is a pretty easy line as there is only one version at this point. Next, we declare our logging behavior:

```
(debug deny)
```

In this declaration, we are telling the sandbox system to debug only 'deny' activity (that is, whenever an executable attempts to perform an action that is disallowed). Alternatively (debug all) can be specified, in which case any activity tested against sandbox, whether allowed or denied, will be logged. These logs are sent to /var/log/system.log, an example 'deny' log entry can be seen here:

```
Mar 7 23:18:38 helyx sandboxd[73914]: vim(73913) deny file-write*
  /Users/hunterbj/Desktop/test.txt
```

In this example, we can see the process, (vim), the result of the action (deny), the requested action (file-write), and the requested file /Users/hunterbj/Desktop/test.txt. So, logging can be immensely helpful for determining the activity of a program. Thus, it can then be used to construct a sandbox profile for any particular program. By employing a (debug all) setting, you can start out with a very basic profile and then narrow it down based upon logged activity. After observing that no 'deny' log entries are hitting after fully vetting your program, you can switch to a (debug deny) status and then monitor the file for any disallowed behavior. In such a case, you will need to investigate any deny log entries observed to determine if they are a result of valid process activity that should be provisioned, or if they are occurring for other reasons.

> **TIP:** Once you have your sandbox profiles honed in and deployed, it may be desirable to deploy monitoring software to alert you in the event of any syslog deny entries. This will allow you to promptly respond to any unexpected behavior.

We have now declared our profile version and logging (debug) behavior. At this point, we begin with our restriction declarations. While not always necessary, it is often desirable to first declare our default behavior. To clarify, we must declare whether we allow or deny any activity that is not explicitly defined in our file. In this case, our profile is meant to prohibit all activity that we don't explicitly define as okay. Thus, our default behavior will be to deny access (this is a 'lockdown' profile after all):

```
(deny default)
```

If this were the end of our profile, we wouldn't get very far. Although this is a perfectly valid sandbox profile, we have only defined default access, and are denying access at that. So at this point, any applicable activity that our program attempts will be met with failure. To that end, we must now define explicitly what a locked-down process can do. First and foremost, we need to give it process execution capabilities. Typically this profile will be used for a very specific purpose, so we can give execution privileges to that program specifically. In this case, our 'lockdown' profile is a generic profile that can be applied to multiple processes. As such, we will allow all process execution:

```
(allow process-exec)
```

If we wanted to define this to a particular executable, so that only that executable could be used, we would do the following:

```
(allow process-exec (literal "/Applications/TextEdit.app/Contents/MacOS/TextEdit"))
```

In this case, this profile would really only work with TextEdit. We have introduced a few new concepts here that merit further explanation. In the above example we declare a basic global allow rule for the process-exec action. If we want to define specific criteria for this action, such as, say, explicitly defining the TextEdit binary, we do so by referencing the path in another subset of parenthesis. When defining these criteria, we are explicitly provisioning access based on the file path; no digital signing or application verification is done. This isn't ideal, as it means that an external process that is not sandboxed could still alter behavior of a sandboxed process, but there's unfortunately not much we can do at that point.

In any case, here we are defining a literal path of /Applications/TextEdit.app/Contents/MacOS/TextEdit. In the previous case, we were a bit extreme in granting execution capabilities on all process, but in this example, we are restricting it exclusively to the TextEdit binary. Luckily the flexibility of sandbox profiles allow us find a compromise. Considering the following declaration:

```
(allow process-exec
    (subpath "/Applications")
```

```
        (regex "^(/usr)?/(s)?bin/.*")
        (subpath "/tmp/SandboxedApps")
)
```

In this example, we have a number of file paths assigned to our `allow process-exec` right, each in their own enclosed parentheses. In this case, we separated each declaration out onto its own line; however, these can all exist on a single line as well. In this case, we are introducing two new path-testing capabilities. The `subpath` test evaluates to true for any executable found in a sub directory of the `/Applications` folder, this includes all subitems; programs in the utilities folder will also apply. We are also applying a regular expression match against the file system, in this case using the regular expression string: `"^(/usr)?/(s)?bin/.*"`. Boiled down to simple terms, this regular expression evaluates to true for directories `/usr`, `/usr/bin`, `/usr/sbin`, `/bin`, and `/sbin`. So, any executables found in this directory will properly execute given the above sandbox entry. Last but not least, we are provisioning access to the `/tmp/SandboxedApps` directory. In real-world situations, you will certainly want to avoid granting executable access to the `/tmp` directory. In fact, this is quite possibly the worst directory to allow this type of access due to its global-writeable nature. However, in this case, we will always be manually applying the lockdown profile to GUI apps for forensic purposes, so it's less of a concern. With this configuration, if you want to sandbox the application for testing, just copy it to `/tmp/SandboxedApps` and call it with sandbox-exec.

Next, because we're planning to utilize this sandbox to launch Cocoa applications, me must allow for Mach lookups. Mach is the microkernel that runs OS X at its lowest level, and it provides for inter-process communication, known as IPC. Mach IPC is used for a large number of basic behaviors, such as allowing processes to communicate with the WindowServer process to draw GUI elements, such as a window. Or say for instance allowing an application to communicate with the PasteBoard server to allow it to utilize Copy and Paste. It is also used for utilizing System services, such as looking up a contact in your address book, looking up directory services information, or even printing. Its use is prolific throughout applications that run in OS X, and its existence is somewhat of an expected truth for developers. As such, when they are unavailable, some applications will simply cease to function. For the purposes of a "lockdown" profile, we'll want to protect against these calls: just because a program doesn't directly access the network or modify contents on disk doesn't mean it can't do damage. For instance, consider an application that uses Mach IPC to query your contact list, and then send that information to a process that does have network access, and can then relay the data. If the target program allows remote calls to send external messages, this program functions as an open relay for outbound network communications, and can thereby be exploited as a means to compromise confidentiality. To allow Mach IPC to flow without restrictions, we can utilize the following declaration:

```
(allow mach-lookup)
```

However, like we said, we want to provide more protection than that in this particular profile, so we will derive a basic set of allowances:

```
(allow mach-lookup
    (global-name "com.apple.CoreServices.coreservicesd")
    (global-name "com.apple.SecurityServer")
```

```
            (global-name "com.apple.dock.server")
            (global-name "com.apple.FontServer")
            (global-name "com.apple.FontObjectsServer")
            (global-name "com.apple.distributed_notifications.2")
            (global-name "com.apple.system.notification_center")
            (global-name "com.apple.windowserver.active")
            (global-name "com.apple.windowserver.session")
            (global-name "com.apple.tsm.uiserver")
            (global-name "Multilingual (Apple)_OpenStep")
            (global-name "en (Apple)_OpenStep")
            (global-name "com.apple.pasteboard.1")
)
```

These provisions allow for basic Mach IPC that are used by most GUI applications: the security server to lookup access provisions, the Font server for fonts, the window server so that the process can attach to the GUI, and the Clip Board, to name a few. The above list is *not* comprehensive, and will certainly be too restrictive for some applications. That being said, it provides a good base for forensics work. Launch the application with the above profile, and then simply monitor the console log for sandboxd-deny log entries.

Lastly, we may want to provision some basic file system access. Remember that, due to our default deny rule, the application won't be able to make any file system writes. Depending on the application, this may or may not be a problem. Some programs do require the ability to write out support files to properly operate. In this case we will provision access to some explicitly defined directories:

```
(allow file-read-data file-read-metadata (regex "^/.*"))
(allow file-write*
    (regex "^/Users/.*/Library/Preferences/.*")
    (regex "^/Users/.*/Library/Application Support/.*")
    (regex "^(/private)?/tmp/")
    (regex "^(/private)?/var/folders/.*")
)
```

In this example, we are allowing the program to read any files on the file system. In this case, we are applying the restriction via a regular expression: regex "^/.*", but the end result would be the same as: subpath "/".

> **NOTE:** One stipulation of the subpath expression is that it cannot end with a solidus (/), as such, 'subpath "/"' is an illegal declaration. (regex "^/.*" must be used instead).

We also have a couple of file-write* provisions. In this case we are using regular expressions to allow the process to write to a user's Preferences folder, their Application Support folder, in addition to the /tmp folder. This provision allows the app to write out its preference file if needed. Keep in mind that these provisions do not usurp standard discretionary access controls: even if a process is allowed access via seatbelt, in order for it to alter a file the user responsible for running the process will need to have write access to the file as well. With the file system declarations above we are introducing yet another new concept through the use of a wild-card on our file-write action. Here, file-write* actually denotes several access provisions: file-write-data, file-write-metadata, and `file-write-xattr`, which allow for modification of a file's contents, metadata, and extended attributes, respectively.

For a large number of OS X applications, these provisions would be sufficient for operation. However, there are a number of low-level functions that certain applications may need to properly function. Such functions may include access to shared libraries, dynamic libraries, shared memory, Mach-O messaging, and so on (all those things that make GUI apps powerful). Many applications will have their usefulness (or stability) significantly diminished without access to these facilities. Thankfully, Apple has provided a basic profile, bsd.sb, which provisions access to many of these low-level functions. Sandbox profiles can be imported from one profile to another, so it's extremely easy to build off of existing profiles. In this case, we want to import the provisions specified in the bsd.sb into our current lockdown profile. We can accomplish this task with the following declaration:

```
(import "bsd.sb")
```

We place this include at the end of the file to ensure that any allow declarations that it provides are not overridden by any resource denials specified in our file. And that completes our lock down file as shown in full here.

```
(version 1)
(debug all)
(deny default)
(allow mach-lookup
    (global-name "com.apple.CoreServices.coreservicesd")
    (global-name "com.apple.SecurityServer")
    (global-name "com.apple.dock.server")
    (global-name "com.apple.FontServer")
    (global-name "com.apple.FontObjectsServer")
    (global-name "com.apple.distributed_notifications.2")
    (global-name "com.apple.system.notification_center")
    (global-name "com.apple.windowserver.active")
    (global-name "com.apple.windowserver.session")
    (global-name "com.apple.tsm.uiserver")
    (global-name "Multilingual (Apple)_OpenStep")
    (global-name "en (Apple)_OpenStep")
    (global-name "com.apple.pasteboard.1")
)
(allow process-exec
    (subpath "/Applications")
    (regex "^(/usr)?/(s)?bin/.*")
    (subpath "/tmp/SandboxedApps")
)
(allow file-read-data file-read-metadata (regex "^/.*"))
(allow file-write*
    (regex "^/Users/.*/Library/Preferences/.*")
    (regex "^/Users/.*/Library/Application Support/.*")
    (regex "^(/private)?/tmp/")
)
(import "bsd.sb")
```

This profile is a bit too generic to deploy on a daemonized program. In such a case, we would want to explicitly define all file system paths utilized by the process and allow only those. This profile is better served in a forensics role.

Sandbox Profiles in Action

So now we know what a sandbox profile looks like, but that is really only half of the picture. In the next section, we'll review some possible scenarios where sandboxing can be used to dramatically improve the security outlook. If you are an administer that provides shell access to your users, if you deploy automations utilizing pre-shared keys for passwordless authentication between machines, or if you are simply looking to provide a safety barrier from a root-run process, then the following profiles will serve as a good primer towards implementing your own sandboxes.

Using Sandbox to Secure User Shells

If you are an administrator who must provide shell accounts for your user base, hopefully you've already put a decent amount of thought into securing them. Even with only a default shell, a non-administrative user has a decent amount of access. In environments where all users are trusted, this might not necessarily impose a huge concern to administrators, but it is likely the case that security in this respect is overlooked. In environments where the user base is unknown or cannot be trusted, the integrity of the system must be carefully protected from your users themselves. One problem is that OS X does not have an extremely strong reputation in the security community when it comes to local privilege-escalation vulnerabilities.

A privilege-escalation vulnerability is an exploit employed by a user to gain access to system resources outside of those that have been provisioned to that user. In many cases, this entails a standard user gaining root privileges, and thereby having complete control of the system. In a perfect world this would never happen. Unfortunately we don't live in a perfect world, and a quick Google search for the term "os x local privilege escalation" reveals numerous security advisories for a decent number of familiar applications: AppleScript, Apple Remote Desktop, Disk Utility, System Preferences, to name a few. Even these legitimate applications have in the past provided avenues for users to subvert the system. Fortunately, Apple has addressed each of these specific vulnerabilities through various security updates. Even acknowledging that, it's a bit naïve to think that there isn't still a vulnerability out there that could potentially be exploited. If you are an OS X administrator and need to provide shell access for your user base, consider sandboxing the user's shell to reduce the amount of tools that they have access to and thereby reducing the surface area for attack.

Sandboxing doesn't only apply for user shell access though. In OS X, the sftp service is directly tied to ssh. In fact, they are provided by the same daemon. The main concern with using OS X as an sftp platform is that the daemon is not 'change-rooted' at all. What this means is that users could easily walk all over your file system. You cannot limit sftp access for a user to the user's own home directory, for example. While that can certainly be their starting point, they have full access to go anywhere that standard user's can go: your Applications folder, your /System folder, and portions of /etc are also exposed. While these resources should be impervious to damage from these users due to standard POSIX permissions, it still represents a security risk to the loss in confidentiality. Due to the blanket nature of the problem, traditional file system access control measures could not adequately address the issue. The work around to this problem is to install an alternative sftp service, whether that is a chrooted ssh-based solution, or a different product altogether, such as Rumpus. This isn't always a step in the right direction though. For instance, Rumpus itself was vulnerable to a zero-day exploit that allowed for remote code execution. The rumpus daemon runs as root, so administrators implementing this solution had exposed servers that could be fully compromised remotely. We're big fans of Rumpus and don't mean to call it out specifically. We just feel it's important to acknowledge that no software is immune to exploitation.

> **NOTE:** It is important to acknowledge that no software is immune to exploitation. While it is certainly true that properly written software will be much harder to compromise than poorly written software, the general attitude that a security administrator must hold is that all software is vulnerable.

Fortunately, with the introduction of sandboxing, we have tools to adequately address these types of problems through the use of sandbox-profiles, whether we're beefing up protections on Apple's solution or implementing a sandbox around a third-party solution.

The following profiles, base.sb and shell.sb, were specifically designed to provide reasonably secure sftp/shell services using OS X servers' built-in ssh daemon. We accomplish this by limiting available binaries to any user and limiting available utilities to those required for traditional shell functionality. It further provides protection by restricting 'read' access to any directory or file that both fall outside of our specified file system tree and also is not critical for the proper operation of a shell. Writes to /tmp are allowed for general compatibility.

base.sb

The base.sb profile provides minimal resources needed to establish a remote shell session. It contains two main privilege blocks 'shell.dependencies' and 'shell.whitelisted-apps.' Privilege blocks are to sandbox profiles what functions are to programming and scripting; they allow for the definition of predefined behavior that can be easily referenced from other profiles. To create a privilege block, you define the block by specifying the name and then encapsulating all of your standard sandbox access provisions inside of the (define) block, as shown below:

```
(define (userProcesses)
 (allow process-exec
  (subPath "/Applications")
  (subPath "/bin")
  (subPath "/usr/bin")
 )
)
```

In this example, we are creating a set of access provisions that allow for the execution of programs found in "/Applications," "/bin," or "/usr/bin." These provisions are defined but are not applied until the privilege block is referenced in the profile. This is done by enclosing the defined name on it's own line enclosed in parenthesis:

```
(userProcesses)
```

This same concept applies if this profile is imported from a different profile. To enable the access provisions provided in this shell (say we named it userProcesses.sb), we would use the following text in our own profile:

```
(import "userProcesses.sb")
(userProcesses)
```

We note this because base.sb itself only enforces a small number of access provisions, but as mentioned primarily defines two privilege blocks, shell.dependencies and shell.whitelisted-apps that can be utilized by other profiles. The former privilege block includes only resources necessary to the establishment of an interactive shell, the latter includes innocuous support apps, such as man, pagers/editors, compression utilities, and basic file operands. None of the processes established under shell.whitelisted-apps are needed for basic shell access but are rather niceties to have in a shell environment.

This profile provides security by limiting available binaries to those installed in /bin, and a select number of applications residing in other system directories. Additionally, it restricts 'read' access, in the traditional POSIX sense, to any directory or file that falls outside of our specified fs trees and is not critical for the proper operation of a shell. Writes to /tmp are allowed for general compatibility. This profile is referenced for use by several of the previously mentioned profiles and can be included in others as a way to define minimal provisions needed for a shell account.

```
(version 1)
(debug deny)
(allow default signal sysctl* mach*)
;; our global denies
(deny file-write* file-read-data file-read-metadata (regex "^/.*"))
(deny file-write* (regex "^/.*"))
(deny process* network*)
;; import the bsd profile
(import "bsd.sb")
(define (shell.dependencies)
   ;; required processes for remote shell/sftp access
   (allow process-exec file-read-data file-read-metadata
      (regex "^/bin/.*")
      (literal "/usr/bin/which")
      (literal "/usr/libexec/sshd-keygen-wrapper")
      (literal "/usr/libexec/sftp-server"))
   (allow process-fork)
   ;; our fine-grained reads.
   (allow file-read-data file-read-metadata
      (regex "^(/usr)?/bin")
      (regex "^/dev")
      (literal "/usr/lib/charset.alias")
      (literal "/private/var/run/utmpx")
      (literal "/private/etc/csh.cshrc")
      (regex "^/usr/share/locale")
      (regex "^/usr/share/terminfo")
      (regex "^/usr/libexec")
```

```
          )
          ;; Basic write access to tty and temp directory
          (allow file-write* file-read-data file-read-metadata
            (regex "^/dev/tty")
            (regex "^(/private)?(/var)?/tmp"))
) ;; end shell.dependencies
(define (shell.whitelisted-apps)
;; define our basic apps. Nothing in this block is critical for shell/sftp
;; access. Edit any of these as you see fit
          (allow process-exec file-read-data file-read-metadata
            ;; man support
            (literal "/usr/bin/groff")
            (literal "/usr/bin/grotty")
            (literal "/usr/bin/less")
            (literal "/usr/bin/man")
            (literal "/usr/bin/more")
            (literal "/usr/bin/tbl")
            (literal "/usr/bin/troff")
            ;; compression apps
            (literal "/usr/bin/bunzip2")
            (regex "^/usr/bin/bz") ;; bunzip2 binaries
            (regex "^/usr/bin/z[^print]") ;; zip binaries
            (literal "/usr/bin/gunzip")
            (literal "/usr/bin/gzcat")
            (literal "/usr/bin/gzip")
            ;; editors/interpretors
            (literal "/usr/bin/awk")
            (literal "/usr/bin/vi")
            (literal "/usr/bin/vim")
            (literal "/usr/bin/egrep")
            (literal "/usr/bin/emacs")
            (literal "/usr/bin/grep")
            (literal "/usr/bin/nano")
            ;; file operations
            (literal "/usr/bin/ditto")
            (literal "/usr/bin/rsync")
            (literal "/usr/bin/tar")
            (literal "/usr/bin/srm")
            ;; misc
            (literal "/usr/bin/banner")
            (literal "/usr/bin/clear")
            (literal "/usr/bin/cksum")
            (literal "/usr/bin/cut")
            (literal "/usr/bin/dig")
            (literal "/usr/bin/du")
            (literal "/usr/bin/env")
            (literal "/usr/bin/getopts")
            (literal "/usr/bin/head")
            (literal "/usr/bin/id")
            (literal "/usr/bin/killall")
            (literal "/usr/bin/kinit")
            (literal "/usr/bin/klist")
            (literal "/usr/bin/kpasswd")
            (literal "/usr/bin/last")
            (literal "/usr/bin/passwd")
            (literal "/usr/bin/printf")
            (literal "/usr/bin/screen")
```

```
            (regex "^/usr/bin/svn")
            (literal "/usr/bin/top")
            (literal "/usr/bin/touch")
            (literal "/usr/bin/xargs")
        )
        ;; support files
        (allow file-read-data file-read-metadata
            ;; man support
            (literal "/private/etc/man.conf")
            (regex "^/usr/share/groff")
            (regex "^/usr/share/man")
            (regex "^/usr/X11/man")
            ;; other
            (literal "/Library/Preferences/edu.mit.kerberos")
        )
) ;; end shell.whitelisted-apps
```

shell.sb

The profile shell.sb is the primary profile that we will apply to a user's shell. It provides security by building on restrictions already applied through our base.sb profile providing access to our user's home directories. When deploying this profile in your own environment you'll want to update the following line in the 'file-write*' block with the appropriate path. In the expression below, we accept both local and automounted homes:

(regex "^(/Network/Servers(/.*)?/)?/Users/")

For most server environments, this default setting will likely work out pretty well. The regular expression used here allows access to both /Users and the standard network home directory location used in OS X; /Network/Servers/server.myco.com/Users. At these locations we will rely on POSIX and ACL-based access controls to ensure users have access to only their own data. If we are providing solely sftp access to users, then we only care to import shell.dependencies from our base.sb profile. If we will be providing user shells as well, we can uncomment the line to allow applications defined by shell.whitelisted-apps also.

```
(version 1)
(debug deny)
(deny default)
;; import the base profile
(import "base.sb")
;; include our shell dependencies
(shell.dependencies)
;; and if we're not totally evil, uncomment this to our allow our app whitelist
;;(shell.whitelisted-apps)
;; specify the root of our rw branch, update this setting for your own environment
(allow file-write-data file-read-data file-read-metadata
    (regex "^(/Network/Servers(/.*)?/)?/Users/.*")
)
;; The following is needed for sftp support
(allow file-read-metadata
    (regex "^/.*")
    (regex "^/etc")
```

```
)
(allow process-exec file-read-data file-read-metadata (literal↵
"/usr/local/bin/sbshell"))
```

In this profile we apply a default deny policy, import our base.sb profile, import provisions from base.sb defined in shell.dependencies, and then provide access to our user home directories. But what about that last line:

```
(allow process-exec file-read-data file-read-metadata (literal↵
"/usr/local/bin/sbshell"))
```

Well, remember that in order to apply a profile to an environment, we do so using the sandbox-exec command. In order to do this to a user's shell, we have to create a wrapper script which performs the function. In this case, that wrapper script is defined at /usr/local/bin/sbshell and is detailed below.

sbshell

As mentioned, to apply the sandbox profiles mentioned previously to our logged-in users, we'll need to create a wrapper script to accomplish our task. We can do this by creating a very basic shell script that executes the user's normal shell program within the confines of our desired sandbox profile. As can be seen in the following, this shell simply calls the shell found at /bin/bash. This shell is passed through all parameters that were passed to the original shell (designated by "$@") to properly function with any parameters passed to the shell (utilized by commands such as ssh and rsync).

```
#!/bin/bash
PATH="/bin:/usr/bin"
## basic shell wrapper to provide sandboxed rights control.
## requires userShell.sb and shell.sb sandbox profiles to
## be installed at /usr/share/sandbox/
declare -x myShell=/bin/bash
if [ -x "${myShell:?}" ]; then
    if [ -f /usr/share/sandbox/shell.sb ]; then
        sandbox-exec -n shell "$myShell" "$@"
    else
        echo "Sandbox profile not found, cannot continue!"
        exit 2
    fi
else
    echo "Illegal shell: $myShell, cannot continue!"
    exit 2
fi
```

With this simple shell script installed at /usr/local/bin/sbshell, the next step is to ensure that it is executable with the command chmod:

```
chmod +x /usr/local/bin/sbshell
```

Once done, you can now use Workgroup Manager to configure the user's shell to reside at /usr/local/bin/sbshell. From here on, whenever the user logs in via ssh, sftp, rsync, or any ssh-based connection, their environment will be restricted to the confines of the applied sandbox profile.

Carbon Copy Cloner

Carbon Copy Cloner is a popular backup-based directory written by Mike Bombich (www.bombich.com). It has a strong group of followers due to the fact that it is a reliable piece of software that performs basic backups with minimal configuration and hassle. It even has the option to backup over a network connection to facilitate offsite backups. The facility that it uses to perform this action utilizes password-less key-based ssh authentication.

Unfortunately, there are some inherent insecurities introduced with the model. First and foremost, it creates passwordless authentication to the root user on the remote machine. This means that the host machine unconditionally trusts the backup-client; if the client machine is compromised, so is the server. Carbon Copy Cloner attempts to mitigate this issue by implementing a public key system that only works with a predefined wrapper script. That is, the key can only be used to launch a specific script which is located at /var/root/.ssh/rsync-wrapper.sh. When a remote connection is established with the pre-shared key, this script is executed. The script has some sanity checks in it to ensure that the only programs allowed to run are scp or /var/root/rsync. If neither of these commands are called, the shell will exit and the remote shell is closed. Theoretically this provides us the protection that we need, only rsync and scp can use the key, ssh isn't included, so a user can't initiate an ssh session, right?

Well, the problem is apparent when we consider the nature of the applications that are allowed, rsync and scp. Both applications are fully capable of modifying the file system, and there is nothing to prevent them from modifying the wrapper script itself. After all, the remote shell IS granted root access; what's stopping the user from using rsync to copy a new wrapper and replace the existing wrapper that applies the restrictions? Well, in truth, nothing. Say that you have several laptops that utilize this function to backup to your server. Any user of these laptops could potentially take over your server if they had the malice or intent to do so. Constructing a basic, no frills, no restrictions ssh key wrapper is pretty easy and can be accomplished with the following script:

```
#!/bin/bash
$SSH_ORIGINAL_COMMAND
```

That's it, two lines, nice and simple. Once we have this code saved into a file and that file is made executable via chmod, we can then push the new file to the server and thereby override all access controls that have been put into place:

```
cd "/Applications/Carbon Copy Cloner.app"
cd "Contents/MacOS/ccc_helper.app/Contents/MacOS/"
./rsync -e "ssh -i /var/root/.ssh/ccc_dsa" -a --rsync-path=/private/var/root/rsync /tmp/my-evil-rsync-wrapper.sh root@mybackupserver.myco.com:/var/root/.ssh/rsync-wrapper.sh
```

With this command, we are replacing the file /var/root/.ssh/rsync-wrapper.sh on the server with my own copy, located at /tmp/my-evil-rsync-wrapper.sh. Provided my rsync-wrapper contains the shell code mentioned here, we will now have full, unfettered access to the backup Server.

Game Over.

This, obviously, is a bad thing. However, we now have power to fight against this attack, using the profile defined below. In this profile, we deny write access to our rsync wrapper, preventing the above exploit from being accomplished. In the following profile, we define a sandbox profile that allows for secure remote backups with CCC. In this profile, we specify a backup directory on the remote server at "/Backups," you will likely want to change this to satisfy your environment.

```
(version 1)
(debug deny)
(allow default signal mach*)
(deny network-outbound)
;; change PathToBackupDir to the local target directory.
(allow file-write* file-read-data file-read-metadata
       (subpath "/Backups"))

;;; Static Entries, shouldn't have to mess with the below
(allow process-exec file-read-data file-read-metadata
    (regex "^(/private)?/var/root/\.ssh/rsync-wrapper\.sh$")
    (regex "^(/private)?/var/root/rsync$")
    (literal "/usr/bin/scp")
    (literal "/usr/bin/which")
    (regex "^/bin")
    (literal "/usr/libexec/sshd-keygen-wrapper"))
(allow process-fork)
(deny process*)
;; our global denies
(deny file-read-data file-read-metadata
       (regex "^/.*"))
(deny file-write*
    (regex "^/.*"))
;; our fine-grained allows.
(allow file-read-data file-read-metadata
       (regex "^(/private)?/var/root")
  (literal "/dev/autofs_nowait")
       (literal "/usr/lib/charset.alias"))
;; CCC seems to want to overwrite its copy of rsync
;; in root user's home on the server each time it runs,
;; the backup fails if the scp fails, so we add a rule.
(allow file-write* file-read-data file-read-metadata
       (regex "^(/private)?/var/root/rsync$")
       (literal "/Library/Logs/CCC.log")
  (regex "^(/private)?/tmp"))

;; import the bsd profile
(import "bsd.sb")
```

So, we now have our nice secure profile all written up, but we're missing a key piece: we still have to actually implement this profile (otherwise it's just another text file sitting idly on the server). To do this, we must modify the wrapper script that CCC uses during the remote rsync session stored at /var/root/.ssh/rsync-wrapper.sh. This wrapper is created by CCC and deploys checks to ensure that only rsync and scp applications can be utilized by its preshared key. To make the wrapper itself secure from being overwritten, we can modify a few lines in the file. Specifically, locate the following text, which appears twice in the file on its own line, as follows:

```
$SSH_ORIGINAL_COMMAND
```

Change both occurrences of this line to read:

```
/usr/bin/sandbox-exec -n ccc $SSH_ORIGINAL_COMMAND
```

From here on, all the CCC-based rsync will forever be sandboxed, and it will prevent the remote exploit from succeeding.

Securely Automating Remote rsync

While Carbon Copy Cloner is a popular Mac backup program, even more common is the old but trusted rsync utility. In fact, as we just discovered, Carbon Copy Cloner actually uses rsync on its backend to perform backups. While CCC is a great program, rsync is ubiquitous and powerful, and very handy for basic backups and data mirroring. If you're looking to automate rsync between machines, you're pretty much looking at the exact same setup that CCC deploys: a public key, and preferably a wrapper script to provide at least some baseline security. To truly understand how to secure such a setup, we'll need to walk through the entire process.

The first thing that you need to establish to provide cross-machine automation is a passwordless authentication scheme. GUI apps will often leverage the keychain for this, but this option isn't approachable from a command-line app like rsync. Passwordless authentication works through public-key-encryption, which we discussed a bit earlier in this chapter. More specifically, we set up passwordless ssh authentication by using preshared keys: to deploy this solution, you must create a private and public key, and then distribute the public key to the remote host that you want to login to. To create this key, we run the following command on our client machine from the user account that we want to have passwordless authentication from (this will commonly be "root"):

```
ssh-keygen -f ~/.ssh/id_dsa -N "" -t dsa
```

This command will create a private key named "id_dsa" in the .ssh folder found at the root of the running users home directory. This file is automatically consulted by OS X's ssh client when initiating a remote connection to a server. This command will also create a public key, "id_dsa.pub," which is the key that we distribute to our remote server. We can accomplish this by using a remote connection to the server, which for this first attempt will require you to enter your user credentials. When logging into the remote server, we specify the remote user (in this case, hunterbj) that we want to establish remote automation for: the remote user does NOT need to have the same username as the local user. In these commands, we are first creating the .ssh folder in case it's not there:

```
## Create the remote .ssh directory (password required)
ssh hunterbj@remotehost.com "mkdir ~/.ssh"
## Establish appropriate permissions (password required)
ssh hunterbj@remotehost.com "chmod 700 ~/.ssh"
## Copy the new public key into the file "authorized_keys" on the remote host
## This file is consulted by default in OS X for ssh preshared key authentication
## (password required)
cat ~/.ssh/id_dsa.pub | ssh hunterbj@remotehost.com "cat - >> ~/.ssh/authorized_keys"
## Perform a remote folder listing (no password required)
```

```
ssh hunterbj@remotehost.com ls
Desktop
Documents
…
```

So, after initiating this command, we have verified through our last command that pre-shared key authentication is fully operational. If that command failed for you, consult log files /var/log/system.log and /var/log/secure.log for hints as to why (it typically has to do with overly lax POSIX permissions on a user's home directory or .ssh directory).

So now that we have this setup, we can then perform remote rsyncs to our heart's content without requiring authentication, as long as we run the command from the user account who created the keys in the previous step (notice the remote user must also be the same as used previously):

```
rsync -av /MyAwesomeFiles/ hunterbj@remotehost.com:/Backups/MyAwesomeFiles/
```

All is well and good. Right? Well, not exactly. In this instance, the public key can be used to access *any* command, and there is no sandbox in place. How very wild, wild west of us. Well, we don't like to roll like that, so the first thing we do is put some restrictions on our pre-shared key, just like Carbon Copy Cloner does. To do this, we modify the authorized_keys file that we just copied over to the remote host. So, on this box we open up the file ~hunterbj/.ssh/authorized_keys, which will look similar to the following:

```
ssh-dss
AAAAB3NzaC1kc3MAAACBAOYUR6cON9uiyfLvGNtYtmVKOOX2AOGXmer3PJgbwR/T9Lu8kDhKOEcE6gNEZTWzeVFx
Wel6WqDRALs8bZnvPBVLLLp1yM5ntcVM3tXB9NkAQIfGghHZt/oeaayE8s9Mpq5rrndQJyg13RYpP9NcMBgm5LYh
ptvQMTr3LGAWK35DAAAAFQDhsQpzMnYd3F4pqZ/m/m2pw3kHVwAAAIEAjO3+bTcWRfqISTuTu23EoOLF4n48aWD/
rVFmgNPn7rTXd8rEOckZqY5kvL66vWBZO3ymMiN3TWf8zjR9aceLpc1MKuHZfghXOaiHNRrJgf9SVc7k7805fBXg
ex8xoppPOtXwblIO64gbTN4m66vwKzVkjppyHwOaOnIVOMAp7k4AAACBAMME9jrR2LhOAK+5pCW7jt4m5HuxJOY8
R+YbTkbRxOXtPt9OofS8xKvrQzfvb/5vZW8EDFOtnIvA6kax2h61II5ltStiEdT2T1/N8yZdfBkftwODfRPOpphj
gztjnmSgYfOHzzpz5ctT1PAPYw9pVzS4OXZMp77gb1MrcoDjHkDt hunterbj@helyx.lbc
```

It's hard to tell here, but all of that is actually on a single line of text. We can modify this file, specifically the line that contains our hosts pre-shared key (in this case the host is "helyx.lbc"). To restrict this key to a specific command, we inject it at the beginning of the line, the end result looking like this:

```
command="/usr/local/bin/sshwrapper" ssh-dss
AAAAB3NzaC1kc3MAAACBAOYUR6cON9uiyfLvGNtYtmVKOOX2AOGXmer3PJgbwR/T9Lu8kDhKOEcE6gNEZTWzeVFx
Wel6WqDRALs8bZnvPBVLLLp1yM5ntcVM3tXB9NkAQIfGghHZt/oeaayE8s9Mpq5rrndQJyg13RYpP9NcMBgm5LYh
ptvQMTr3LGAWK35DAAAAFQDhsQpzMnYd3F4pqZ/m/m2pw3kHVwAAAIEAjO3+bTcWRfqISTuTu23EoOLF4n48aWD/
rVFmgNPn7rTXd8rEOckZqY5kvL66vWBZO3ymMiN3TWf8zjR9aceLpc1MKuHZfghXOaiHNRrJgf9SVc7k7805fBXg
ex8xoppPOtXwblIO64gbTN4m66vwKzVkjppyHwOaOnIVOMAp7k4AAACBAMME9jrR2LhOAK+5pCW7jt4m5HuxJOY8
R+YbTkbRxOXtPt9OofS8xKvrQzfvb/5vZW8EDFOtnIvA6kax2h61II5ltStiEdT2T1/N8yZdfBkftwODfRPOpphj
gztjnmSgYfOHzzpz5ctT1PAPYw9pVzS4OXZMp77gb1MrcoDjHkDt hunterbj@helyx.lbc
```

Now, upon initiating a remote ssh session using this key all clients will be forced to call our sshwrapper script "/usr/local/bin/sshwrapper," rather than their default shell. This sshwrapper script, seen immediately below, is actually the script that enforces which commands are authorized, and also applies the appropriate sandbox.

```
#!/bin/bash
PATH="/bin:/usr/bin:/usr/sbin:/sbin"
```

```
#########################
##
## Basic ssh wrapper to restrict keyless authentication
## This script is meant to be called from a command declaration
## in ~/.ssh/authorized_keys
##
## All binaries are implicitely denied.
## tweak $allowedCommands to allow the execution of additional
## binaries.
##
## Beau Hunter 11/08/07 beauh@mac.com
##
###################################################################

## a space separated list of absolute paths to allowed binaries
allowedCommands="/usr/bin/rsync,/usr/bin/scp,/usr/bin/true"
## Get our command's full path, if no command was specified
## then assume default shell
if [ -z "$SSH_ORIGINAL_COMMAND" ]; then
    cmd="$SHELL"
else
    fullCmd=`printf $SSH_ORIGINAL_COMMAND`
    cmd=${fullCmd[0]}
fi
declare -x cmdPath
if [ -x "$cmd" ]; then
    cmdPath="$cmd"
else
    cmdPath=`/usr/bin/which "$cmd"`
fi
## Iterate through our allowed commands, execute the command
## if it qualifies.
OLDIFS=$IFS
IFS=$','
for path in $allowedCommands;
do
    IFS=$OLDIFS
    if [ "$cmdPath" == "$path" ]; then
        sandbox-exec -n backup $SSH_ORIGINAL_COMMAND
        exit $?
    fi
done
## Here if the command wasn't in our allowedCommand
echo "sshwrapper.sh:: Access Denied for command:'$cmd' at path:'$cmdPath'"
exit 1
```

This script enforces remote commands only to those specified by the variable "allowedCommands." We do a check against those absolute paths and if the requested program matches that path, we allow the command to proceed. On top of this, we are applying the sandbox profile "backup" to the launched process, as seen in our line that actually does the execution:

```
sandbox-exec -n backup $SSH_ORIGINAL_COMMAND
```

$SSH_ORIGINAL_COMMAND is a special environmental variable set upon remote login, and contains the text in the requested command path (be it rsync, sftp, or a standard shell).

Once we verify that this command is in our allowedCommands variable, then we launch it in our sandboxed environment.

This particular script relies on our backup.sb profile, which is responsible for securing our preshared key environment. This means restricting file system access to only directories that will be used by backups, so that the backup system itself can be used to overwrite any restrictions.

```
(version 1)
(debug deny)
(deny default)
(import "shell.sb")
(shell.dependencies)
;; specify any rw directories
(allow file-write* file-read-data file-read-metadata
    (subpath "/PathToBackupDir")
    (regex "^/var/log/backup.log$"))

;; add our allowed processes
(allow process-exec file-read-data file-read-metadata
  (literal "/usr/local/bin/sshwrapper")
  (literal "/usr/bin/rsync"))
(allow process-fork)
;; make sure we can read the user's home
(allow file-read-data file-read-metadata
    (regex "^(/private)?/var/root"))
```

As you can see, this profile utilizes our base profile, and calls the shell.dependencies block. This profile also provisions access to the root user's home directory, so that the system can read the pre-shared key information. When utilizing this profile in your own environment, you'll want to change the subpath pattern matching PathToBackupDir to specify your backup target directory. Likewise, if you utilize a user other than root on the destination, you'll want to change the last class to point to the correct user's home directory.

BIND

OS X server and client both ship with the BIND DNS server. This is a very popular DNS server that is utilized by many different UNIX and Linux variants. BIND is yet another daemon that runs under the root user, and previous versions of BIND have been vulnerable to remote exploitation. Fortunately, the shipping versions with OS X 10.5 and 10.6 have proven to be both stable and secure in the context of data confidentiality, but it never hurts to add another layer of security. Apple actually ships a sandbox profile to be used to secure BIND, found on any recent OS X box at /usr/share/sandbox/named.sb, To enable the above profile, we must modify the launchd plist that fires named (the name of the BIND daemon). This launchd plist can be found at /System/Library/LaunchDaemons/org.isc.named.plist. Helpfully, Apple has actually put some help text in this plist that explains how to enable the sandbox, so feel free to crack open for an example. The gist of it is that we need to change our ProgramArguments declaration to include a call to sandbox-exec. Thus, the default ProgramArguments block for org.isc.named.plist:

```
<key>ProgramArguments</key>
<array>
 <string>/usr/sbin/named</string>
 <string>-f</string>
</array>
```

then becomes:

```
<key>ProgramArguments</key>
<array>
 <string>/usr/bin/sandbox-exec</string>
 <string>-f</string>
 <string>/usr/share/sandbox/named.sb</string>
 <string>/usr/sbin/named</string>
 <string>-f</string>
</array>
```

These added calls to sandbox-exec ensure that named is launched with our appropriate sandbox restrictions applied.

> **NOTE:** Apple assume files in /System to be under their own control, so a future software update might revert the changes. It's likely a better idea to disable the DNS server in the Server Admin GUI, and add your own launchd plist in /Library/LaunchDaemons.

So, hopefully these profiles give you a good primer about the different ways that sandbox can be utilized, whether running it ad-hoc for forensics of an untrusted program or untrusted data, securing a background daemon, or locking down automations.

The Seatbelt Framework

As mentioned earlier, it is also possible to implement sandbox restrictions compiled directly into your application. This section discusses such an implementation. If you are not a developer, or are not interested in the lower-level functionality of seatbelt, feel free to skip this section. To introduce sandboxing to be directly built into your application, Apple has offered their own Security Policy Module dubbed "seatbelt," which is implemented as a KEXT installed at /System/Library/Extensions/seatbelt.kext. The only documented way to apply these controls in code is via the sandbox_init() function. Utilizing this function provides a way for an application programmer to voluntarily restrict access privileges in a running program. sandbox_init() is very limited at this point, providing only five pre-defined constants, which are identical in function to the pre-defined constants available for sandbox-exec, which we discussed earlier:

```
kSBXProfileNoInternet - disables TCP/IP networking.
kSBXProfileNoNetwork - disables all sockets-based networking
kSBXProfileNoWrite - disables write access to all filesystem objects
kSBXProfileNoWriteExceptTemporary - disables write access to filesystem objects
 except /var/tmp and `getconf DARWIN_USER_TEMP_DIR`
kSBXProfilePureComputation - all OS services are restricted
```

An application can utilize one of these constants to restrict capabilities in spawned processes or threads, minimizing the potential damage that can occur in the event that the process is compromised. The following shows an example implementation of the kSBXProfileNoWrite profile in code:

```c
#include <string.h>
#include <stdio.h>
#include <fcntl.h>
#include <sandbox.h>
int main() {
 int sb, fh;
 char **errbuf;
 char rtxt[255];
 char wtxt[255] = "Sandboxed you aren't\n\n";
 // init our sandbox, if we don't return 0 then there's a problem
 sb = sandbox_init(kSBXProfileNoWrite, SANDBOX_NAMED, errbuf);
 if ( sb != 0 ) {
  printf("Sandbox failed\n");
  return sb;
 };

 // open our file with read-only access
 fh = open("test.txt", O_RDONLY);
 if ( fh == -1 ) {
   perror("Read failed");
 } else {
   read(fh, rtxt, 255);
   close(fh);
   printf("FileContents:\n %s\n", rtxt);
 };
 // open the file with write access
 fh = open("test.txt", O_RDWR | O_CREAT, 0000644);
 if ( fh == -1 ) {
   perror("Write Failed");
 } else {
   write(fh, wtxt, strlen(wtxt));
   close(fh);
   printf("Successfully wrote file!\n");
 }
 return 0;
}
```

Compiling and running this code returns the following results:

```
$ ./sandBoxTest
FileContents:
 hello
Write Failed: Operation not permitted
```

So, even though our POSIX and ACL permissions allow for read/write access to the file, the sandbox prevents it, regardless of user. Running the program even with root privileges yields the same results:

```
$ sudo ./sandBoxTest
FileContents:
 hello
Write Failed: Operation not permitted
```

The key call in this code is the following, which initiates a sandbox using the standard kSBXProfileNoWrite profile, which eliminates all file system write access:

```
sb = sandbox_init(kSBXProfileNoWrite, SANDBOX_NAMED, errbuf);
```

Or, we can specify our own sandbox profile to apply more fine-grained, customized restrictions:

```
sb = sandbox_init("/usr/share/sandbox/myprofile.sb", SANDBOX_NAMED, errbuf);
```

> **NOTE:** Although providing sandbox_init with a file system path to a profile, it isn't a documented (and presumably therefore not a supported) use of sandbox_init().

If you are a developer and are looking to sandbox your application and hit problems acquiring certain resources, such as shared libraries or the like, not all is lost. A key point to realize while coding is that seatbelt's behavior does not affect already established resources. That is, any file descriptors, process executions, or other resource acquisitions that are performed prior to your call to sandbox_init() will not be restricted by the sandbox. Only resource requests after that call will be restricted. Thus, your program upon initializing can establish all of the necessary resources that it requires. Then at that point you can apply the appropriate restrictions and ensure that moving forward your program will have limited capabilities to acquire more resources. This ensures that if your program is hijacked, it will only be able to manipulate resources which you have already allocated, which can greatly limit the impact of execution hijacking.

Considering the benefits in security that can be achieved through properly sandboxing your application, we believe it would be a mistake for a developer to shrug off seatbelt as a whole. Unfortunately, the amount of information and documentation provided by Apple on these technologies is minimal at best, so approaching the technology may be a little bit overwhelming. Hopefully now armed with information presented in this chapter, this technology is now available for you to use as well. Whether you employ its use to protect your valuable data, or you are using it to run forensics on a suspect application, it can be a very useful security tool that merits consideration. The number of applications which run with root privileges these days is certainly on the decline, but they are still out there, and most likely even running on a server of yours. If this is the case for you, consider sandboxing the daemon to protect your system from its misuse.

Summary

In this chapter we discussed in detail two new security technologies in OS X. We discussed the implementation of application signing in Mac OS X both from technical and from implementation perspectives. We also discussed OS X's sandbox technology, which can be utilized to create a jailed environment around your application to limit its reach into the system. Both systems represent the future of security in OS X, as can be seen with their use (to the extreme) in the iPhone OS. Hopefully, as history progresses, Apple will find a happy medium between security and strict access measures. There's no doubt that its extensive and consistent use in the iPhone OS has helped contribute to the stability of the platform. That being said, such a model cannot simply be introduced as a replacement to an existing and established platform such as the Mac OS. Eventually, we do foresee a model that more heavily enforces a signing-required model, hopefully such a system finds the middle ground of the two platforms, utilizing the security benefits that the technology provides without the totalitarian aspects of the iPhone model.

We also discussed application sandboxing heavily in this chapter and the ways that it can be utilized to mitigate damage from rogue applications. It too is utilized heavily by the iPhone, as each individual application resides in its own Sandbox. Like application signing, Apple is taking a slow approach in regards to adopting the technology in OS X. As time progresses, it's only inevitable that more and more processes will utilize this technology to provide a more secure system.

In the next chapter we will be dealing with security on more familiar ground: web browsing and e-mail. Read on to learn how best to protect yourself against the nefarious forces thriving on the Internet.

Chapter 7

Securing Web Browsers and E-mail

Identity theft is the fastest-growing crime in the world. According to the Federal Trade Commission (FTC), identity theft is the top concern of people contacting the agency, and has now passed drug trafficking as the number-one crime in the world, affecting up to 10 million victims a year, costing the United States 50 billion dollars a year on average. Much of this can be reduced by leveraging some very practical security with regards to our Internet browsers.

One of the biggest battlegrounds in the fight against identity theft is your computer. We commonly use computers to communicate with the outside world using cell phones, web browsers, instant messaging software, and e-mail; all technologies that rely on the Internet. Identity thieves know this, and use the Internet as their tool for stealing identities through the acquisition of credit card numbers and online banking information, as well as gaining access to e-mail and social networking web sites to masquerade as someone else online. Therefore, securing our messaging systems has become a high priority to protect us from identity theft.

For the purposes of this chapter, we will concentrate on the web browser and e-mail clients as common messaging and communications systems. As we explain each of the security features of these systems and what they do, you can apply the information to other browsers, chat programs, and mail programs that you may be using, and configure them for the same level of security. Although the actual terminology may change, the concepts remain constant across applications (and platforms, for that matter).

When discussing how to secure your web browser, we will be covering Safari (Version 4) and Firefox (Version 3.6). There are other browsers out there, such as Opera and Google Chrome, but because these currently comprise a minority of browsers in use, we're going to concentrate on securing Safari or Firefox. Likewise, there are a variety of e-mail clients out there. The two most common mail applications for the Mac are Microsoft Entourage (version 2008) and Apple Mail (version 4.2), so we will discuss these throughout the chapter as well.

> **NOTE:** We spend much of this chapter discussing how to fine-tune your browser for security purposes, but we should mention that downloading and installing software from questionable sources, such as BitTorrent web sites, for example, is dangerous, and could damage your computer. It's very hard to determine the origin of the software, and there is no guarantee the software won't perform nefarious tasks on your machine. Keep this in mind when downloading software from these unknown sources.

A Quick Note About Passwords

We've mentioned it before and we'll mention it again: if you take only one tip away from this book, take this one: *use good, complex passwords*! This is a mantra that we will use repeatedly throughout this book. We cannot overstate its importance.

> **TIP:** When we refer to complex passwords, we are referring to passwords that consist of eight or more characters, contain a special character, and contain both letters and numbers where possible.

Your e-mail and online accounts are only as secure as the password you use to access them. And believe it or not, your e-mail account is quite valuable to a spammer. A resourceful spammer can make a small fortune by using insecure e-mail accounts to send spam. Because most web servers are fairly locked down with strong passwords, the spammer needs your e-mail account's password to use it. And even if they don't read your messages, they might end up getting your e-mail account disabled by your provider because of the high level of spam coming from your account. It can also be used to impersonate you to your friends and family, which can be very dangerous, especially when they ask for cash or private information. When this is used against high-profile individuals such as CEOs and celebrities, it's called *spear phishing*.

Encrypting the e-mail transport, as many e-mail servers claim to do, is good, but without a hard-to-guess password, encrypted e-mail transport is not enough. No matter how heavily you encrypt the password and its transport between client and server, if the password is too easy to guess, then you may as well have not encrypted it in the first place. A weak password can be quickly guessed, encrypted or not.

> **NOTE:** Not all providers allow the use of special characters in passwords. The characters that provide the most problems tend to be those that Unix reserves, such as ,, /, ?, and so on.

Securing Your Web Browser

A web browser is a tool used to view data that is hosted on a web server. The two most popular browsers in use on the Mac are Safari and Firefox. They are similar in security configurations; however, Firefox has more granular security controls.

When it comes to web browser security, privacy protection is the name of the game. We want to keep prying eyes away from your online purchase information, away from your passwords for web merchants, and away from the history of web sites you have visited. When securing a web browser, much of the security falls into two categories. The first is protecting your computer from the browser and any executables (such as cached scripts) that can run on the client; the second is securing the transport of data over the wire.

A NOTE ABOUT SECURE SOCKETS LAYER

The most notable form of protecting passwords and confidential information while in transit on the web and in e-mail is through the use of Secure Sockets Layer (SSL). SSL is a protocol developed by Netscape for transmitting private documents via the Internet. SSL works by using a shared session key to encrypt data that's transferred while en route to another system. Both Safari and Firefox support SSL, and many web sites use SSL to secure confidential user information, such as credit card numbers for transactions over the Internet. Most reputable banks and web sites with sensitive data require an SSL connection. You can easily tell when a web site is using an SSL connection as the URL will start with a `https`, not `http`.

> **NOTE:** Transport Layer Security (TLS) is actually the successor of the SSL 3.0 protocol. Although SSL and TLS are similar and your system can support both, it is worth noting that they cannot be used on web servers concurrently.

Securing Safari

Safari is on every Mac by default. Thankfully, securing Safari can, for the most part, be done using the dedicated Security preference tab in Safari. On this tab, you can disable features of Safari that you don't need, block pop-ups, view and configure cookies, and tell the browser to prompt you before sending insecure data over the Internet. Out of the box, Safari disables pop-ups, but all of the other features are enabled; therefore, you should make a few minor adjustments to your Safari security configuration to maintain the highest level of security (based on your own security requirements), keeping in mind that changing many of these features might cause a more interrupted browsing experience.

Setting the Safari Security Preferences

By default, Safari is set to block pop-up windows. But sometimes you may need to access features of sites that cause pop-ups, such as the address book feature of Hotmail. You can find the option to enable and disable pop-ups by clicking on Safari in the top menu and selecting Block Pop-Up Windows. Select it again to turn it off. (See Figure 7–1)

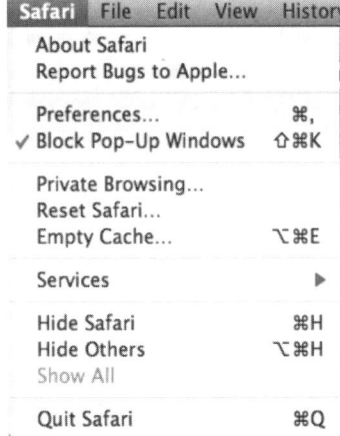

Figure 7–1. *Blocking pop-up windows in Safari*

> **NOTE:** Many sites are hip to the pop-up blocking feature and now use Flash to present overlays. Disabling Flash pop-ups can be accomplished using the ClickToFlash plug-in, developed by Jonathan Wolf Rentzsh, available at http://rentzsch.github.com/clicktoflash/.

A *cookie* is a small text file of information that certain web sites attach to a user's hard drive while the user is browsing the site. A cookie can contain information that pertains to a specific web site such as the user ID, user preferences, shopping cart information, and any other setting that can be stored on a web site. For the longest time cookies got a bad rap, mainly because they were notorious for their security concerns. But most modern-day web browsers no longer store clear-text passwords in the cookies, do not allow access to cookies between multiple domains, and many cookies expire after a certain time frame, so they are at least manageable. The important thing to remember with cookies is that you should know where they come from. Some sneaky web sites will put cookies from ad servers in your browser that can track your Internet activity. Apple has included a Show Cookies button in Safari's Security preferences so you can see the cookies on your machine. (See Figure 7–2.)

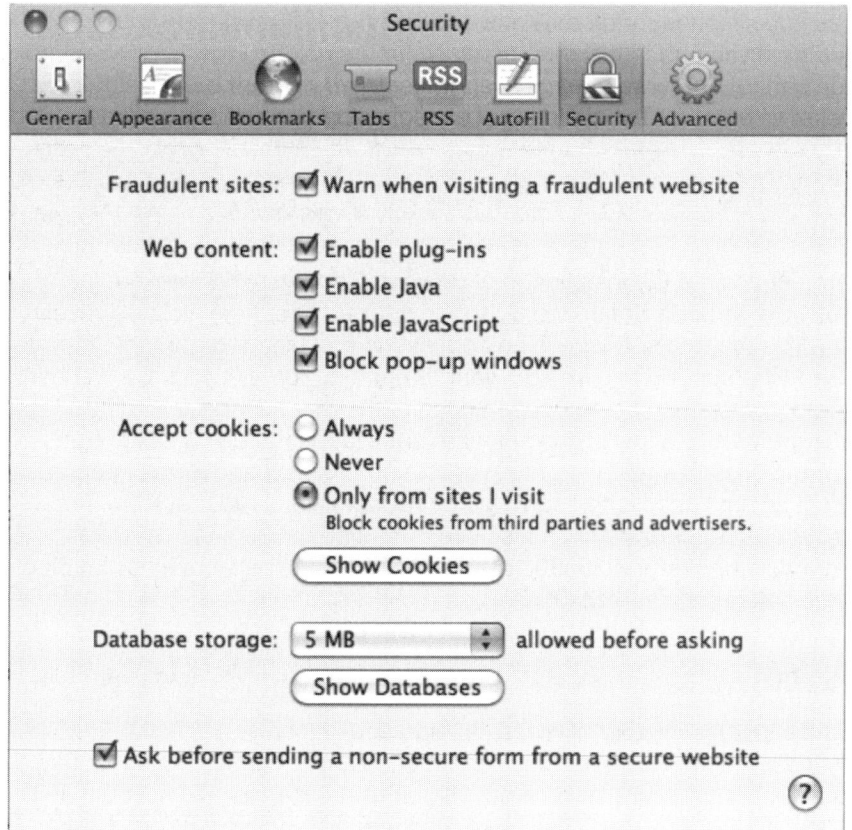

Figure 7–2. *Security preferences for Safari*

By default, Safari accepts cookies from every site that wants to give them to you. To configure Safari to accept cookies only from sites that you visit, while in Security preferences, choose "Only from sites I visit" in the "Accept cookies" section. Safari gives the user the ability to limit cookies rather than disabling them, and for good reason: disabling cookies can cause annoying compatibility issues with more advanced web sites.

Web browser attacks on the Mac (such as home page hijacking, infiltrating your file system through a web browser, or installing applications onto the workstation) are more likely than getting a virus on a Mac. Good security dictates that if there are features included in browsers that you do not use, you should typically disable them. Some features, such as Java-based plug-ins, can reconfigure your operating system. Therefore, Apple has seen fit to give you the ability to disable Java plug-ins within your browser.

Windows has had a hard time with browser plug-ins. This is one area where your surfing can seem to come to a crippling halt in a Windows environment because of plug-ins that waste system resources, including those not related to browsing the Internet. For debatable reasons, browser plug-ins have not been a huge concern on the Mac platform. You can see which browser plug-ins have been installed in Safari by clicking Help and selecting Installed Plug-ins. If you take a look at the list that appears, you'll likely notice that nearly all the plug-ins are Apple-related (for example, related to QuickTime or iPhoto). If you notice a browser plug-in that you suspect is dangerous, navigate to the /Library/Internet Plug-Ins folder in your user folder and delete it.

> **NOTE:** Some older third party plug-ins, such as the Shockwave plug-in, are already integrated into Safari.

Safari can also protect against the installation of unwanted software. When you download new software through Safari and try to run it for the first time, you will receive a message alerting you that the software is an application downloaded from the Internet. You'll also be asked whether you're sure you want to open it. You can click Cancel here, which will stop the software from being opened. One of the most dangerous things you can do on your computer is to allow rogue software applications to be installed. Pay attention to this window, as this feature (only available on Leopard and Snow Leopard) will help you protect against unsolicited software being installed on your system. For more on Malware, see Chapter 8. You can also see our article at www.afp548.com/article.php?story=20090826235425679 for a little more information on the built-in malware safeguards in Mac OS X.

Privacy and Safari

Clearing out all of the caches, history, downloads, and cookies on your system keeps prying eyes from finding them. However, this can be annoying, because it may require you to re-enter passwords for some sites, which, if you're like the rest of us, you may have forgotten. Clearing this information will also reset the history information, thus clearing out your auto-complete functionality for recently visited and non-bookmarked web sites. For security best-practices, clearing all the information is not necessary. Luckily, Safari gives us the option to be selective about what information we clear. You can reset Safari at any time by selecting the Reset Safari option in the Apple menu. You'll be presented with a menu of options to clear. (See Figure 7–3.) When clearing Mac web browsers of sensitive data, we prefer to check off the following:

- Clear history
- Remove all web page preview images
- Empty the cache
- Clear the Downloads window
- Remove all web site icons
- Close all Safari windows

Figure 7-3. *Reset Safari options*

Network Administrators Configuring Safari's Security Preferences

If you are a network administrator in charge of your company's web browser security, there is a handy free utility called the Safari Toolkit (available at MacFixit.com amongst other download sites) that will allow you to not only customize the look and feel of Safari, but also to secure the browser for individual users. If, in customizing the browser, you decide to remove any buttons that might affect security, consider setting the security options before removing those buttons.

> **NOTE:** If you are on a corporate network and you notice differences between our web browser screens and your own, your company may have a custom configured Safari installation. It can't hurt to ask your network administrator how your Safari preferences are configured.

Securing Firefox

Firefox is a free, cross-platform, graphical web browser developed by the Mozilla Foundation with contributions from thousands of volunteers all over the world. Before its 1.0 release on November 9, 2004, Firefox had already garnered a great deal of acclaim from numerous media outlets, including *Forbes* and the *Wall Street Journal*. Now in version 3.6, Firefox has become more widely used than almost any other browser on the market, in large part because of the security features built into it (and because it isn't a hacker-targeted Microsoft product). For example, Figure 7–4 displays the rather powerful encryption features found in Firefox—features you're hard-pressed to find as easily configurable in other web browsers.

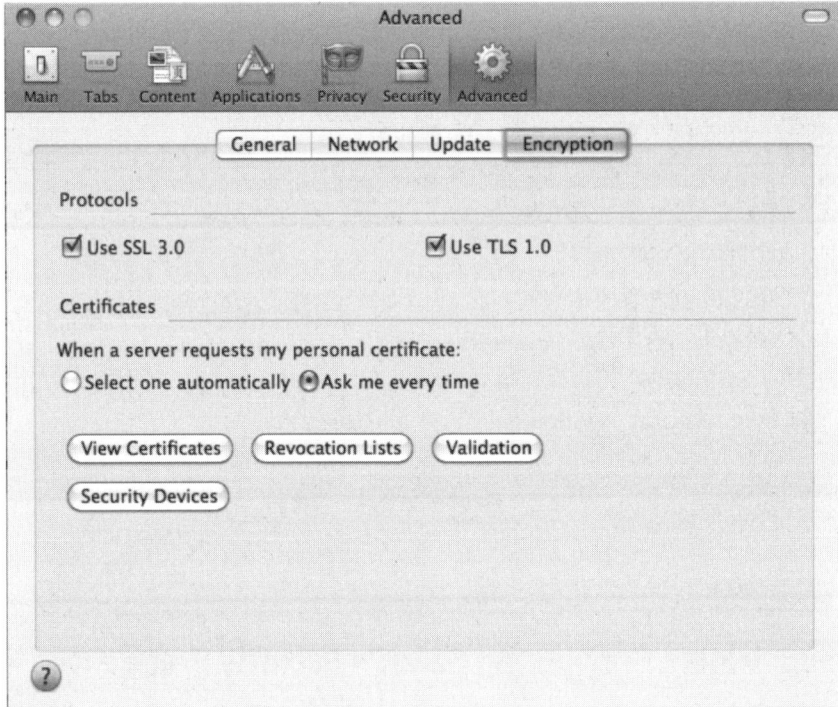

Figure 7–4. *Firefox encryption features*

Privacy and Firefox

One of the most compelling features of Firefox is its extensibility. There are numerous plug-ins available for Firefox. Luckily, the developers did not trade speed for security. Firefox gives users an impressive wide array of privacy options, allowing users to get pretty granular about configuring their privacy options. However, these options are not enabled by default. To enable them, click on the Privacy icon at the top of Firefox's preferences, and click on the drop-down menu next to "Firefox will." Select "Use custom settings for history" to change your browsing preferences.

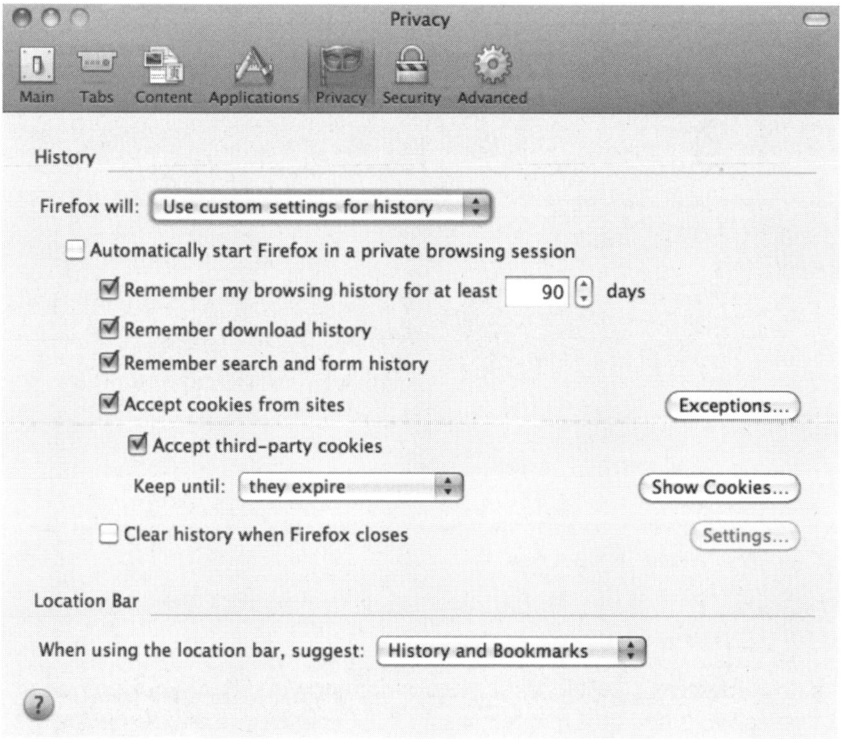

Figure 7–5. *Firefox History privacy features*

Clearing your recent history in Firefox works much like the Reset Safari feature, with the exception that it allows you to select which items will be reset, along with more fine-tuned control over what is reset. Remember, though, if you choose to reset your private data, you risk losing the information stored in the browser such as passwords, preferences, and auto-complete entries from previously viewed web sites, so make sure you choose these options carefully.

To clear private data in Firefox, click on the Tools menu and select the Clear Recent History option. This option opens the Clear Recent History screen (as shown in Figure 7–6). Click on the Details down-arrow to see a list of options for clearing data. You also have the option to select the range of time that you'd like your history deleted. This is especially useful for web sites with recent logins that you'd like to erase from the system. We recommend checking the following options: Browsing & Download History, Form & Search History, Cache and Active Logins.

> **TIP:** Selecting the Cache check box to clear your cache doesn't necessarily remove all caches, and traces of images and pages can still be left in the cache. Visit /Library/Caches/Firefox/Profiles in your user folder to check for any residual data left in your cache.

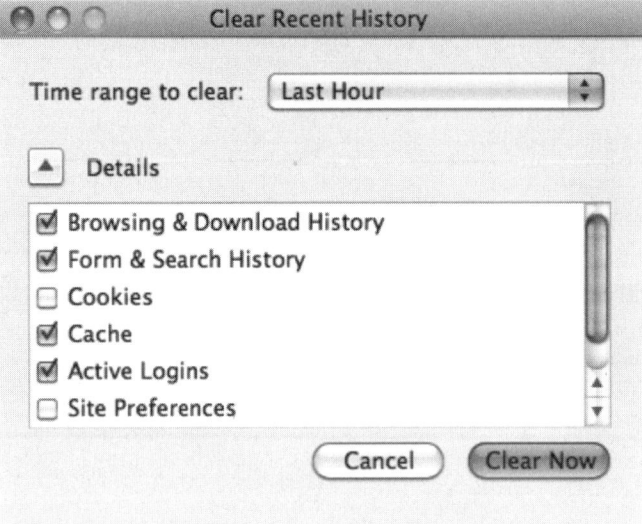

Figure 7-6. *Firefox's Clear Recent History Details screen*

Master Passwords in Firefox

If you allow Firefox to remember passwords for web sites and you share your computer with another user, you should set up a master password. Setting up a master password requires anyone visiting a web site on your computer to enter a master password every time a site tries to access your stored password information. A Firefox master password is not associated with any other program, creating a stand-alone secure environment within Firefox. This extra security layer will also keep your stored passwords safe in the event that someone else gains unauthorized access to your machine and visits web sites with highly sensitive information. If your user account is in any way compromised, your saved passwords within Firefox will not be revealed and the damage to your overall security footprint will be minimal. We highly recommend enabling this feature in your Security preferences. To do so, open Firefox's Preferences and select the Security tab. Then click the "Use a master password" check box. (See Figure 7-7).

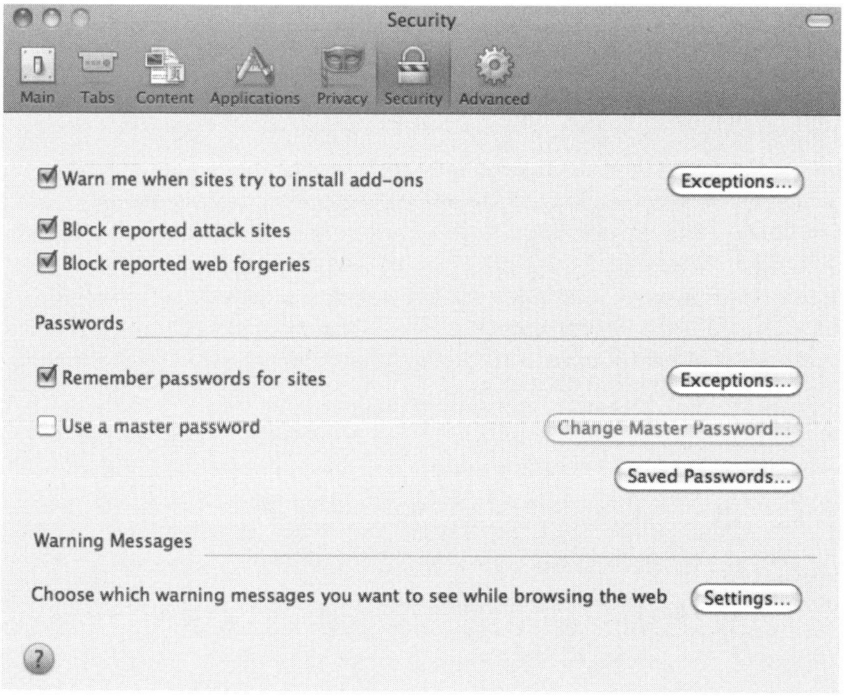

Figure 7-7. *Firefox's Security preferences*

You'll be presented with a dialog box asking for a new password and a confirmation of the new password (see Figure 7-8). Once you have set a password, you will be prompted for it the first time your system attempts to access the passwords stored by Firefox. This is similar to the keychain concept in Mac OS X, except that the password is contained within Firefox.

Figure 7-8. *Firefox Master Password dialog box*

> **NOTE:** Notice the Password quality meter that is common with many applications on this screen; this gives you constant reminders to use good passwords.

One of the dangers of Firefox is that passwords are stored rather insecurely by default if the master password option is not enabled. Firefox has the option to view saved passwords for web sites simply by opening Security preferences and clicking on the Saved Passwords button. Theoretically, it would be very easy for someone with access to your computer to open Password Manager, click a web site or fileserver for which they want to see the password, and then click the Show Passwords button to view it. Therefore, when you use the master password option, make the password a good one.

Thankfully, it is possible to stop Firefox from caching passwords for specific sites or fileservers. To do this, go to the Security preferences pane and click on the Saved Passwords button. Because you've entered a master password already, it will ask you for your master password. Once that's been entered, you'll be presented with a list of Firefox's cached information for web sites (see Figure 7–9). Then, click on the Show Passwords button at the bottom of the window to display the cached passwords.

Figure 7-9. *Firefox's Saved Passwords window*

If you see a site in the list that you don't want Firefox to cache, you can remove it using the Remove button. The next time you visit that site, Firefox will ask again whether you want to cache that password for future access. You should click the Never button if you don't want Firefox to remember the password.

Once you are satisfied with Firefox's password security, let's move on to configuring other security features, such as pop-up windows and the use of JavaScript. These features are addressed on the Content tab of the Firefox preferences (see Figure 7–10). They are similar to those found in Safari. For example, the Block Pop-up

Windows setting will cause pop-ups to be blocked, and the Java and JavaScript check boxes will disable Java and JavaScript on the sites being visited to safeguard from malicious scripts.

One unique feature here is the ability to disable Firefox's ability to load images. You can uncheck the "Load images automatically" box to disable images from loading, which will significantly speed up your browsing experience and protect you from sites that include "web bugs," which are invisible images that are used to track your visit to the site. On the other side of that coin, it can significantly damper the experience with web sites that integrate functionality into their images. As with most other features in Firefox, this can be applied to only certain sites using the Exceptions box.

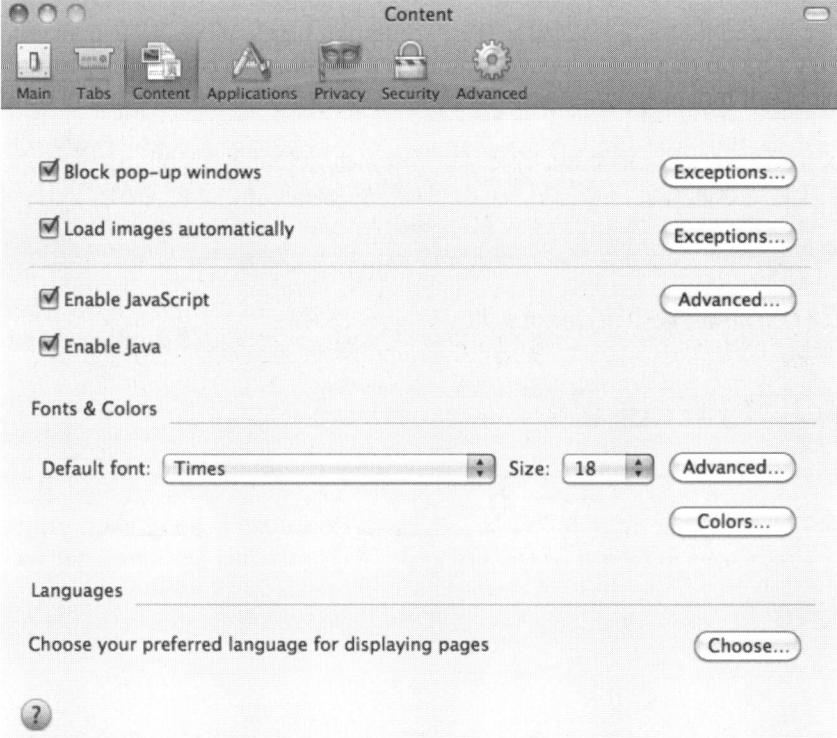

Figure 7–10. *Firefox Content tab*

There are a number of other settings that can also be configured in Firefox by visiting the about:config page (simply type about:config in the address window of Firefox). Here, you will see a granular run-down of every setting available. This provides a wealth of further customization that can be done, which goes beyond the scope of this chapter. The settings that are configured in the about:config page and in the preferences that we have covered throughout this section are then stored in a Firefox-centric profile. However, if you choose to customize these settings, you should document what you have changed because altering the settings can cause unintended consequences.

Firefox does not conform to a number of Mac OS X standards in terms of how it is developed. This can cause annoyances in a few places. First, Mac OS X is, by design, a multiuser operating system, and so the concept of having multiple profiles within a single user account, while a nice feature, can be difficult to manage. Next, the preferences for Firefox are not stored in standard Apple preferences files (called *property lists*). This can cause a number of headaches when attempting to interact with those preferences from a programming perspective, or when you are looking to perform a mass deployment. (To see how this is done, check out our tech article at www.318.com/techjournal/mass-deployments/mass-deploying-firefox-preferences-for-mac-os-x/) Therefore, you will need to edit a prefs.js file rather than a property list or, depending on the setting, perhaps even an sqlite database, all of which can be found within that profile. Finally, the profile itself isn't consistently named. Profiles are stored in ~/Library/Application Support/Firefox/Profiles; however, they are created with generic names and tracked in the profiles.ini file in that same directory. Any scripting that must be done around Firefox therefore needs to take that into account.

When working with Firefox, you can build changes into your actual application, rather than into profiles. These changes made on the application level can break during the next Firefox update, and will surely break the Application Layer Firewall's ability to interact with Firefox because the signature for the application bundle will have changed (you will need to allow Firefox to access a socket again) We discuss the Application Layer Firewall (ALF) in more depth in Chapter 11.

Securely Configuring Mail

While browsers are important, they are not the only target on your system. You also need to consider practicing good mail security. Different mail protocols have different levels of security. The default settings for most web hosts now include more secure protocols than the traditional POP and SMTP protocols. `Mail.app` has also been set up to allow for more protection of passwords in transit and more secure encryption protocols.

Using SSL

As we mentioned before, protecting passwords and confidential information while in transit is accomplished through the use of SSL. SSL should be used in the transport of e-mail as well.

> **NOTE:** Web sites typically use port 443 for SSL. However, when you are using SSL with e-mail protocols such as IMAP, the port can be different. Figure 7–11 illustrates how IMAP might use a different port when secured using SSL.

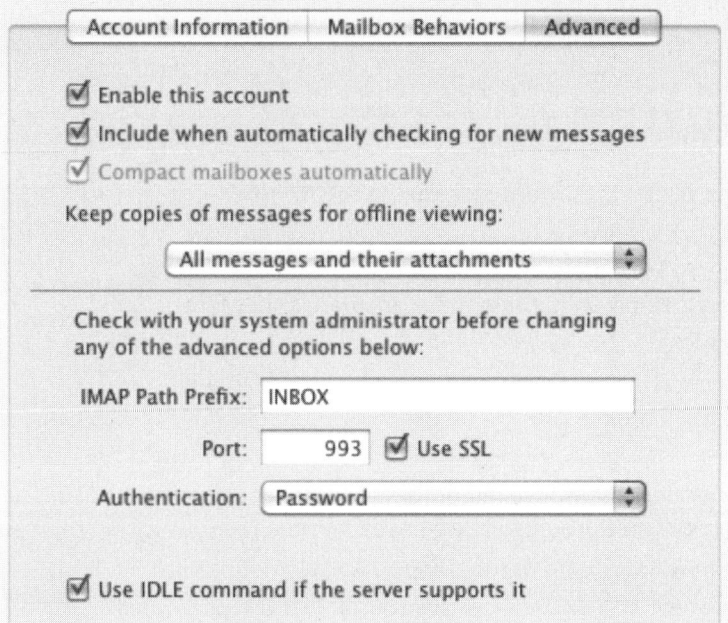

Figure 7-11. *Apple Mail's port settings for SSL*

Sometimes with SSL you'll be asked to verify the authenticity of a server every time you open your e-mail client. This often has to do with the SSL certificate of your mail host being self-signed. Self-signed SSL certificates typically need to manually be "trusted" (which means you have to click on the Trust sign when the certificate pops up) when you are visiting a site. If you choose not to trust a certificate, then SSL will not allow you to communicate over the secure channel to that host.

> **TIP:** If you are required to accept the certificate every time you visit a site, you can add the site as a secure certificate in Safari by opening the Keychain Access utility and dragging the certificate onto the Keychain Access icon in the dock. You can manage the certificate within Keychain Access.

Now that your communications have been protected using SSL, let's look at how your password is actually sent over the wire. POP is a protocol used for downloading mail from a mail server. IMAP is a protocol used to synchronize mail between a mail client and a mail server.

POP and IMAP are merely protocols for accessing data; they do not instruct a client on how to actually authenticate into the remote host. For this, there are a variety of protocols including MD5, NTLM, KPOP, APOP, GSSAPI, Kerberos, and Password (PlainText). In the realm of layered security, the most important thing to know here is that you need to contact your mail provider and find out exactly what protocols are supported. If it does not support a protocol, you will not be able to use it.

> **NOTE:** Often the only way to get your Internet service provider (ISP) to introduce support for a new protocol is to request it. When enough people request it, an ISP will find a way to support the protocol.

The options for securing your mail password include the following:

- *MD5*: Message Digest 5 (MD5) is a secure hashing function that converts an arbitrarily long data stream into a digest of fixed size. By breaking up messages and encrypting them, they are sent more securely.
- *NTLM*: This is common in more Windows-oriented environments, such as with Microsoft Exchange.
- *Kerberized POP*: POP is able to use Kerberos to access your servers. Kerberized POP can help more fully integrate your single sign-on environment. For more on Kerberos, please see Chapter 16.
- *Authenticated POP*: An extension of the POP3 protocol, APOP encrypts both the username and the password, not just the password.
- *Kerberos Version 5 (GSSAPI)*: This uses the latest version of Kerberos to encrypt e-mail passwords, authenticating the e-mail account against a directory server.
- *Kerberos Version 4*: This is similar to Kerberos Version 5, but one version back.
- *Password*: This is standard password authentication.

Some of these same authentication options are configurable in the SMTP settings, as shown in Figure 7–12. Keep in mind that if your username and password for SMTP are the same as your information for POP and you use SSL for SMTP but not for POP, then you are still potentially exposing your passwords.

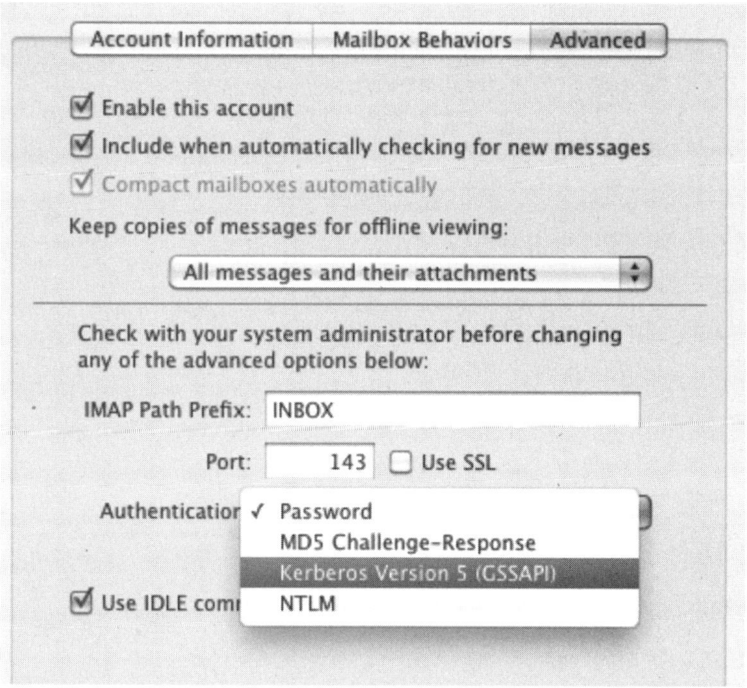

Figure 7-12. *Apple Mail's authentication settings*

Securing Entourage

You can configure Entourage to use SSL in much the same way as Mail. Open your accounts (listed under the Tools menu in Entourage), and choose the account you want to use SSL to secure. On the Account Settings screen, click the "Click here for advanced receiving options" button, and then select the "This IMAP service requires a secure connection (SSL) box."

If your service provider runs IMAP or POP on customized ports, then select the "Override default IMAP" option (or POP, if you are using POP). You can always opt to use the "Always use secure password," which will force encryption on the password when you are checking e-mail (see Figure 7–13).

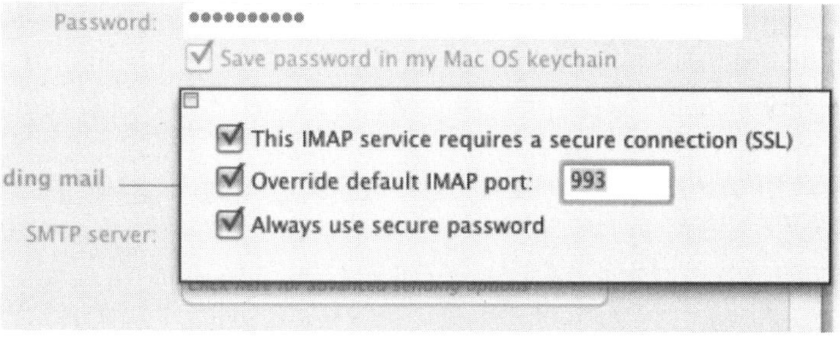

Figure 7-13. *Entourage advanced receiving options*

Once you have set SSL for your incoming mail, click the "Click here for advanced sending options" button. This opens a screen with similar options, including both options for using SSL and the default SMTP port (see Figure 7–14). Remember, both of these settings are specific to your Internet service provider's mail server settings and need to be verified with them before they can be applied.

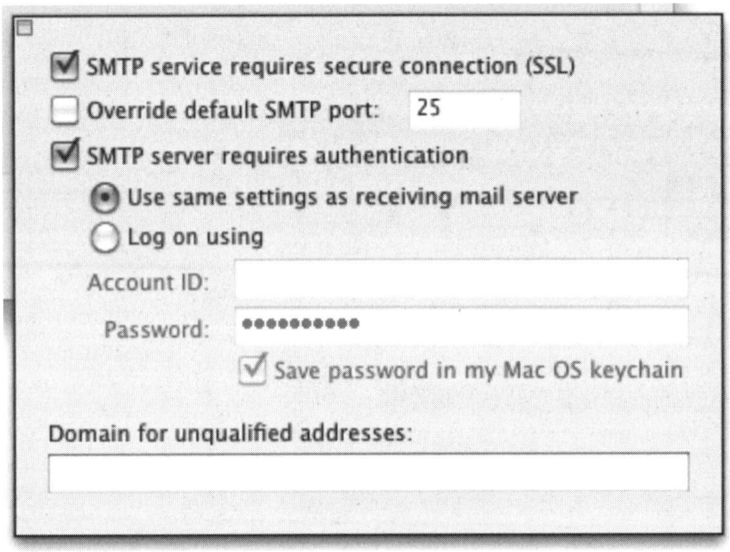

Figure 7-14. *Entourage advanced sending options*

Many ISPs are now blocking access to mail being sent over port 25, the default port for SMTP without SSL. One unintended benefit to using SSL is that, once you have set your computer to send mail over SMTP using SSL, you will often no longer run into issues with getting your e-mail blocked when trying to send mail. One unintended annoyance is that you now may have to manage certificates for your mail by accepting, denying, or importing certificates.

To add a different user's certificate to your cached certificates in Entourage, open an e-mail that has been digitally signed, click the Info Bar, and click the View Details button. This opens a screen for viewing a user's certificate data.

You can open the Certificates screen (as shown in Figure 7–15), which shows all your user certificates. By clicking a certificate and hitting the button in the certificates toolbar, you will be able to click View to see more information about the certificate. You can also click Delete to delete the certificate.

Figure 7-15. *Entourage's Certificates screen*

> **TIP:** To view the certificates for a contact, go to Entourage's address book, double-click the person's name, and then click the Certificates tab.

The Security preferences of Entourage (Figure 7-16) allow the user to be warned when an application other than Entourage attempts to access Entourage's e-mail and when an application other than Entourage attempts to access the address book within Entourage. These options limit the ability for other applications to abuse Entourage if the system is infected with some form of malware.

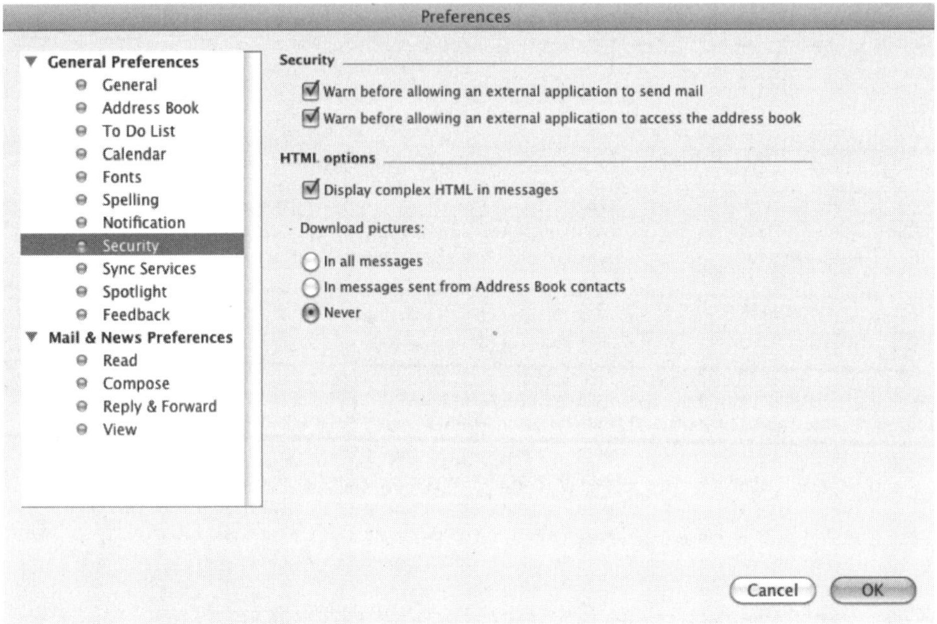

Figure 7–16. *Entourage Security preferences*

> **NOTE:** If you'd like to interact with Entourage from a programming perspective, you can do so using the options laid out in the *Enterprise Mac Administrator's Guide*, also from Apress.

Fighting Spam

Our good friends at Wikipedia said it best, "Spamming is the abuse of electronic messaging systems to indiscriminately send unsolicited bulk messages." Spam often involves sending identical or nearly identical messages to hundreds, thousands, and even millions of recipients. Addresses of recipients are often harvested from chain e-mail letters or web pages, obtained from databases, or guessed by using common names and domains. Spam is not just an irritation; it costs corporations, educational institutions, and governmental agencies in the United States alone tens of millions of dollars in lost operations and productivity each year.

An entire industry of software has risen up to help fight spam (much as an entire industry lurks to send spam). On the Mac, the products are limited, and for desktop users we will primarily focus on the built-in spam prevention of Microsoft Entourage and Apple Mail.

Anatomy of Spam

Before we move on, a bit about the structure of an e-mail as it pertains to spam: An e-mail message has a collection of headers within the e-mail. These include Sender, CC

(Carbon Copy), To, Date, and X-Spam-Status. Outside servers that perform spam filtration will assign X-Spam headers. This is meant to make it easier for mail clients to scan messages for spam quickly. The X-Spam-Status contains, among other information, a numerical score (from 0 to 10) that indicates the likelihood that a message is spam. E-mail programs that support the use of the X-Spam headers will compare this score against the score that has been determined as an acceptable risk. When configuring this setting on a mail server, it's important to set the threshold value somewhere in the middle, as it is possible for legitimate messages to get filtered out, causing what is known as a *false positive*.

The headers can be accessed using the rule sets of Entourage and `Mail.app`. Now let's discuss how to configure our mail clients to deal effectively with spam.

Filtering Apple Mail for Spam

To enable the built-in spam filter in Apple Mail, enter the Mail's Preferences and click the Enable Junk Mail Filtering checkbox. From here, you can instruct Mail on what it should do with the spam using the When Junk Mail Arrives options (see Figure 7–17). Then, select which types of messages will not be filtered. This is where you would configure the client to flag as safe, e-mail coming from entries in your address book, mail coming from people on the previous recipients list, or mail that was addressed using your full name.

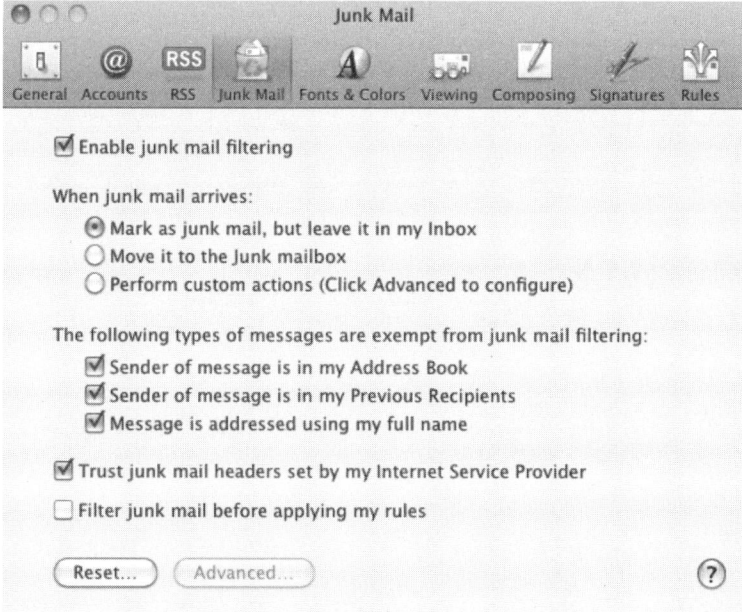

Figure 7–17. *Junk Mail filtering in Apple Mail*

Within Apple Mail, you also have the ability to select whether to trust junk mail headers. Use the Reset button of the Junk Mail preference panel of Mail preferences to reset the junk mail filter. This will undo any other settings you've made to the filter (such as marking certain e-mails as junk mall).

To make custom rules for your Junk Mail, click on the "Perform custom actions" button and then click on the Advanced button at the bottom to build custom rules (see Figure 7–18). You can also merge criteria to build very specific rule sets.

> **NOTE:** On the server side of things, the mail server will apply junk mail headers if the mail server is configured to scan mail for spam. More on configuring server spam filters later.

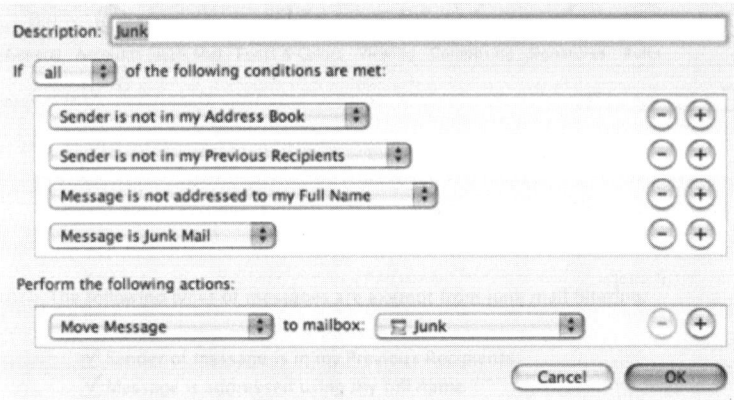

Figure 7–18. *Junk mail advanced settings in Apple Mail*

Filtering with Entourage

Entourage also has a built-in spam filter. To enable and configure the spam filter in Entourage, follow these steps (see Figure 7–19):

1. Select Tools, and click Junk E-Mail Protection.

2. At the Level screen, select the level of protection you want to use. Click OK.

Levels include the following:

- *None*: Disables the Entourage spam filter.

- *Low*: Filters out obvious junk mail, but allows some spam to come through to the user.

- *High*: Filters out as much junk as possible. This can cause some false positives, but for the false positives you should add those users to your address book in Entourage.

- *Exclusive*: Allows incoming mail only from users who are listed in the Entourage contacts list or domains listed in the Mailing List Manager (accessible in the Tools menu).

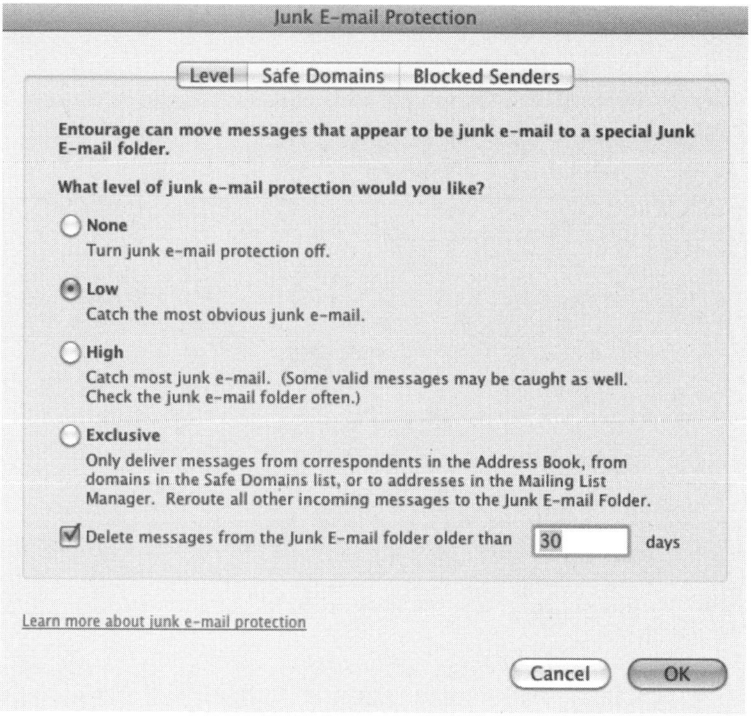

Figure 7-19. *Spam filter settings in Entourage*

Using White Listing in Entourage

The ability to establish white lists is a key component to any anti-spam application. A *white list*, also known as a *safe list*, is a list of addresses (e-mail addresses, domains, IP addresses, or server names) that will not be flagged as spam. When the filter runs and attempts to identify spam, it will skip e-mail that originates from a safe list address.

To allow all mail from a certain domain into Entourage, you can configure Entourage to allow all e-mail from that domain to bypass your spam filter altogether. To do this, click on Tools and then click Junk E-mail Protection. Click on the Safe Domains tab (see Figure 7-20) of the Junk E-mail Protection screen and enter the domain that you wish to add to the white list. When doing so, separate each domain with a comma. Keep in mind that, when white listing a domain, none of the mail sent to you from that domain will be filtered using Entourage's spam filter, so it's important to be cautious when deeming a domain safe.

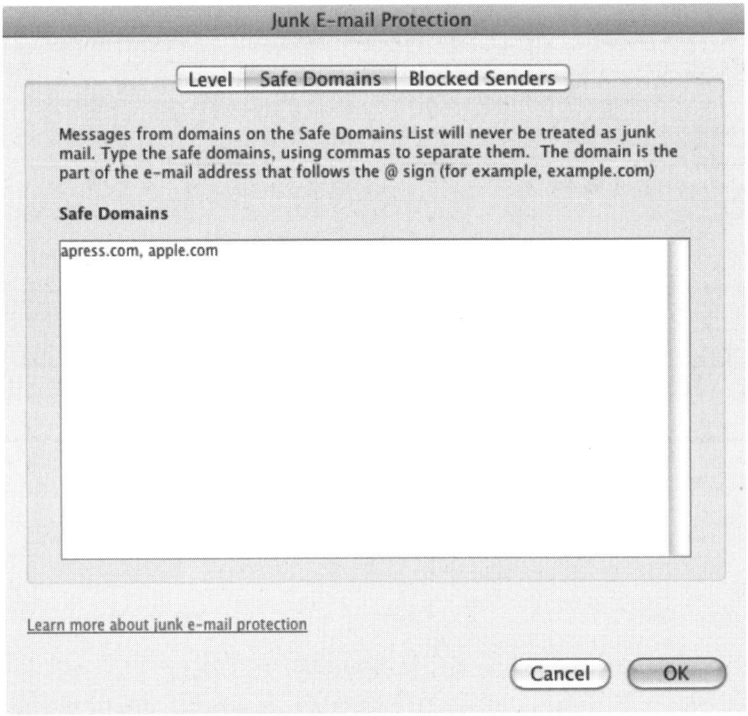

Figure 7-20. *Safe domains in Entourage*

Once Entourage's spam filter catches e-mail it considers spam, you will receive the Junk E-mail Found alert, as shown in Figure 7-21. When you first start using the Entourage spam filter, you should click Open Folder on this screen and check whether the message was really spam. If you get messages that are mistakenly marked as spam, you can click the message, and Entourage will give a few different options for dealing with the message. One of them is to add the sender to your address book. (You can always undo this later by removing the user from your address book.)

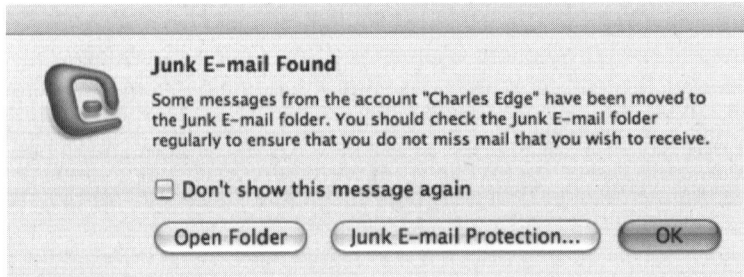

Figure 7-21. *Junk E-mail Found alert*

Desktop Solutions for Securing E-mail

There are other methods available for keeping your e-mail secure than just those included with Mac OS X. In this section, we will discuss leveraging PGP and GPG, two of the main tools used for this purpose. There are other solutions that are equally as viable, but these are the most historically used. We will start by looking at PGP.

Using PGP to Encrypt Mail Messages

PGP Desktop, developed by Phil Zimmerman, is an encryption suite (see Chapter 9 for more information on encryption and more specifically at using PGP for full disk encryption) that will encrypt e-mail messages, files, and folders before they are sent. It can be downloaded and purchased at www.pgp.com for just under $250 (the license plus a one-year subscription). PGP Desktop can also be used to encrypt instant messaging traffic in iChat beyond what is available using iChat's default security options and can also encrypt full disks.

GPG Tools

GPG (or GnuPG, downloadable from www.gnupg.org) is much like PGP; it allows users to encrypt files and e-mail. It is different in that GPG, and the suite of tools built around it, is open source. GPG is not as feature rich as PGP but does have some compelling features in that it works well with Mail.app and, of course, it's free.

To get started with GPG, you will first need to download GnuPG and install it. Once you've installed GnuPG, download and install GPGMail. The most recent releases of both are available through VersionTracker.com. Once you install them, you will see new fields in your Mail.app client when you are ready to send mail. GPGMail is currently not supported in Mac OS X 10.6; however, if you are interested in leveraging open source tools for e-mail encryption, check back with their site regularly, as it is likely that a Mac OS X 10.6 version will be released soon.

Using Mail Server-Based Solutions for Spam and Viruses

Many mail servers have the capability to thwart spam and viruses when they enter the network before they hit your inbox. The three most dominant products for mail servers on the Mac platform are Kerio MailServer, OS X Server Mail, and CommuniGate Pro. Each of these has their own strengths and weaknesses including virus and spam prevention capabilities. Each server platform offers ways to mitigate spam and viruses; however, they vary in implementation, terminology, and licensing structures.

Spam filters need to be trained. When a spam filter begins to filter spam, it may filter out e-mails that are not spam, called *false positives*. As you train your filter, you will be able to increase the intensity of the filter without increasing the number of false positives. A well-trained filter will minimize false positives while offering the best filtration available.

Make sure to spend a little time with your filter to get it configured to maximize its potential.

Kerio

To configure the spam and virus filters on the Kerio MailServer, follow these steps:

1. Open the Kerio Administration Console.
2. Open the Configuration folder.
3. Open the Content Filter folder.
4. Click Spam Filter (see Figure 7–22).

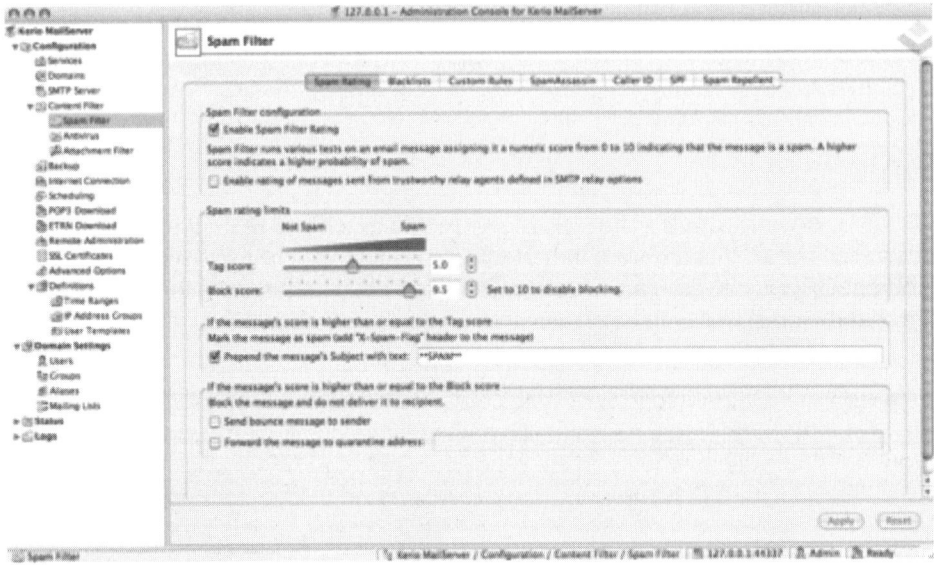

Figure 7–22. *Kerio MailServer administrative console*

5. Select the Enable Spam Filter Rating option. This will enable spam checking on incoming messages. Once a message has been scanned, it will be assigned a score. This is a rating based on the likelihood that the message is spam.

6. Rules offer Kerio administrators a way to provide more granular controls over filters. By using rules, it is possible to override the score assigned to messages with a score that will always flag those messages as spam. When creating custom rules, click the Custom Rules tab of the spam filter in Kerio. When you click Add, you will receive a screen similar to the one shown in Figure 5-31. The Description field of the rule allows administrators to keep track of what the rule is doing. The description has nothing to do with how the rule is processed.

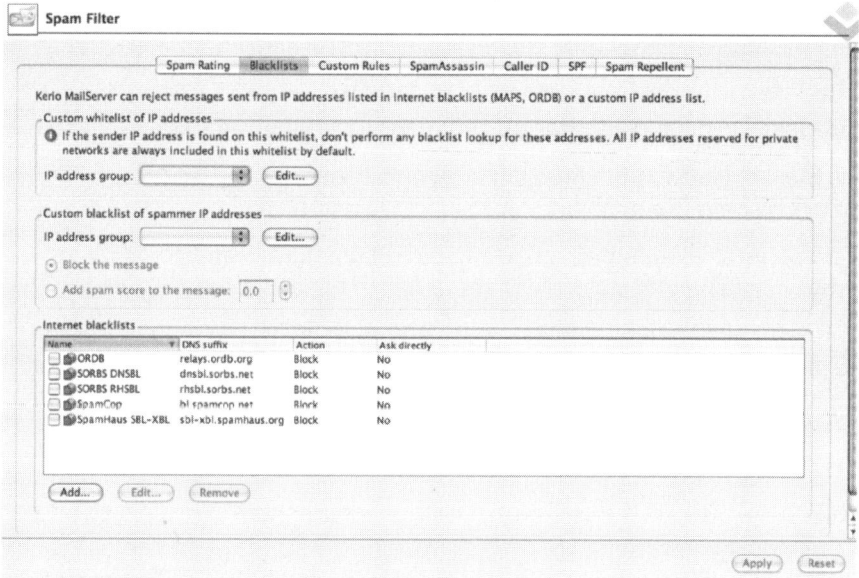

Figure 7-23. *Kerio Mail Server's spam-filtering blacklists*

The If section can teach the filter to catch all mail that matches their filter. The three fields are Header, Type, and Content. The Header field allows administrators to choose which part of the message to match to the filter. The options here are as follows:

- From
- To
- Cc
- Subject
- Sender
- X-Envelope-To
- Received

The Type field allows the administrator to define what value type is present in the header field that is being matched. Types that are available include the following:

- Is Empty
- Is Missing
- Contains Address
- Contains Domain
- Contains Substring
- Contains Binary Hex String

The Content field is not available for all types of rules. The content is the pattern that will be matched with incoming mail to trigger the rules action. The action that is taken can be one of the following:

- *Treat the message as non-spam*: Does nothing.
- *Treat the message as spam and reject it*: Allows the server to immediately discard the e-mail.
- *Add spam score to the message*: Allows you to configure clients to handle mail in a variety of ways using the X-Spam header.

Once you are finished building out a rule, you can use the If the Message Was Rejected by a Custom Spam Rule area to determine how the message is handled. Here you can select whether to bounce the message (reject it and autoreply to the message), forward it into a quarantine e-mail address, or do both (see Figure 7–24).

Figure 7–24. *Rejection action*

Mac OS X Server's Antispam Tools

Mac OS X Server has ClamAV and SpamAssassin installed by default. You can turn them on for the mail server using Server Admin, located in the /Applications/Server folder (see Figure 5-33). The GUI in Server Admin is easy to use and allows administrators to configure many of the most commonly used features of ClamAV and SpamAssassin. However, if you would like to perform advanced functions not available in the GUI such as scripting new training events, then you will need to use the command line for either ClamAV or SpamAssassin to perform them.

> **NOTE:** Common add-ons for SpamAssassin include Vipul's Razor, Pyzor, and DCC. Vipul's Razor is a distributed, collaborative, spam detection and filtering network. Many of these applications use the reputation of a server, the reputation of the IP address block, and sometimes the reputation of the owner of the server or domain to further weigh spam to indicate the likelihood that a piece of mail is actually spam.

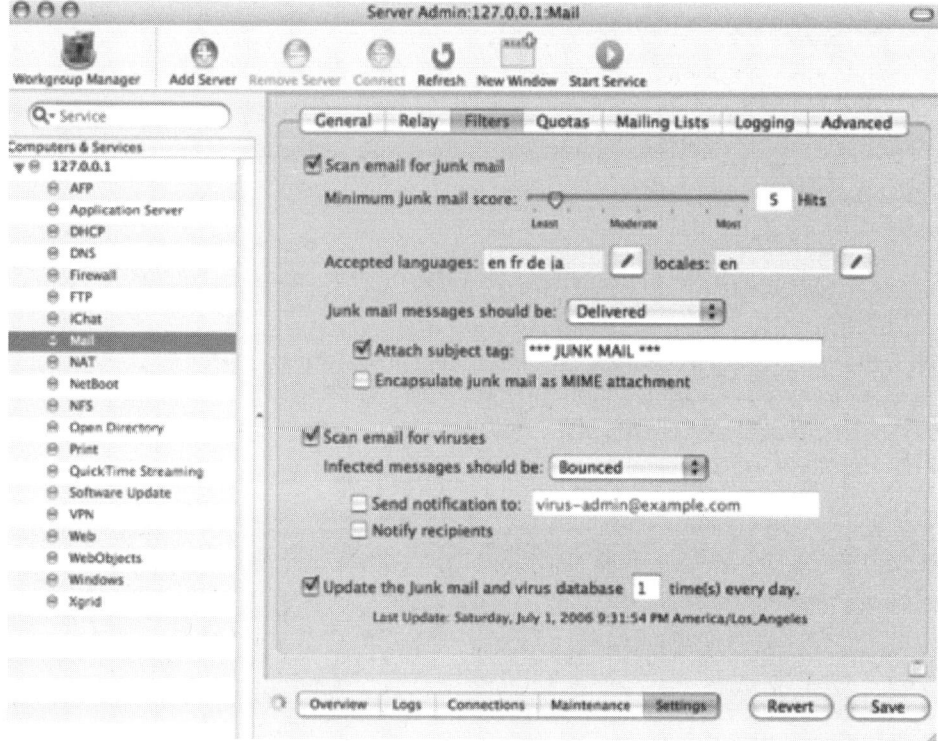

Figure 7–25. *OS X Server's admin console*

CommuniGate Pro

Stalker's CommnuniGate Pro also has the ability to scan for spam and viruses. However, these are not built-in spam and virus filtration services; they are plug-ins that can be purchased from Stalker at `www.stalker.com`. Most of these plug-ins are accessible through the use of rules on the server.

Antivirus filtration for CommuniGate can be provided using software from Kaspersky Labs, McAfee from Network Associates, and Sophos. Antispam filtration is provided using SpamCatcher from Mailshell.

It is also possible to use CGPSA with CommuniGate. CGPSA is a package from TFF Enterprises at `www.tffenterprises.com/cgpsa`. The package is free, but it does not come with support. CGPSA is tricky to configure, but once configured, it will give administrators the most bang for their buck. To install CGPSA in CommuniGate, follow these steps:

1. In your `communigate` directory, create a folder called `cgpsa`.
2. Download CGPSA from www.tffenterprises.com/cgpsa/cgpsa.tgz.
3. Download SpamAssassin at www.spamassassin.org.
4. Make sure Perl is installed on the server.

5. Install SpamAssassin on the server.

6. Place the `cgpsa` script into the `cgpsa` folder you created in your `communigate` directory.

7. Edit the `cgpsa` script to point to the Perl executable, and edit the `$cgp_base` variable to point to the CommuniGate installation on the system.

8. Place the `cgpsa.conf` file in the `Settings` folder of your `CommuniGate Pro` directory.

9. Place the `cgpsa.domainconf` file in the `Settings` folder for each domain you want to use the software with; by default this is `/var/CommuniGate/Domains/domain.com/Settings`.

10. Install the CommuniGate Pro CLI Perl Module, `CLI.pm`.

> **NOTE:** As the number of mail threats on the Internet has grown, the variety of methods used to fight spam has also grown. One popular way to fight spam and viruses is to deploy a hardware device on the network that intercepts traffic as it enters the network, scanning for mail threats. Examples of these devices include products from Barracuda, SonicWall, and Cisco.

Outsourcing Your Spam and Virus Filtering

In addition to using hardware and software on your network to scan mail for viruses and spam, you can also outsource spam and virus filtration. In fact, it is recommended for all in-house mail servers as most of these services provide some kind of perimeter failover should your mail server go down. The basic idea is that the outsourced mail filtering solution directs your MX record to the vendor's web site, and they then filter the mail for you. This reduces the bandwidth overhead coming into your network if you run your own mail server and it also helps with staffing overhead dedicated to fighting spam.

Outsourced filtration companies, such as Microsoft Exchange Hosted Solutions (EHS) and MX Logic, have gained wide adoption mainly because they require little maintenance, are inexpensive, and are fairly simple to implement.

Summary

The Internet has become crucial to our lives as a means of communicating with our friends, family and colleagues. As we've shown, securing our web browsers and e-mail from possible attackers by encrypting our communications is critical for maintaining our identities and financial information in this digital age. In the next chapter, we'll discuss the controversial topic of malware as it relates to Macs and how to combat this threat to Mac OS X.

Chapter 8

Malware Security: Combating Viruses, Worms, and Root Kits

In this chapter, we will discuss protecting your Mac from malware. But first, what do we mean by malware? *Malware* is a term used by security professionals to reference any software that is designed to infiltrate or damage computer systems without the owner's informed consent. "Informed" is the key word here. A user might consent by clicking an Accept dialog box to allow a software package to install, but might not be fully informed of the vulnerabilities that can potentially be exploited by that software package. Beta versions of new software can sometimes have potentially damaging effects on an operating system, but would not be considered malware because they generally don't intend to harm the operating system (*intend* the operative word here). What we will explore in this chapter are the ill effects that can arise from unintentionally installed software on a Mac, and how to safeguard your machine from them.

Classifying Threats

When discussing how to combat malware threats, it's important to distinguish between the different kinds of threats that can exist on a Mac. To most users, a virus is something that threatens productivity on a machine, and the term is frequently used to classify all malware. But it is important to make the distinction between the two. *Malware* is the overarching term used by security professionals to reference certain kinds of hindrances to the operating system, while a *virus* is just one form of malware. What distinguishes a virus from other forms of malware is its ability to replicate itself and spread to other files on a computer, thereby infecting them. However, a virus will infect files only on a single computer; it will not automatically copy its code and spread itself to other computers on a network. It can, however, be spread to other computers by infecting files on a network or files on a removable hard drive. This is what distinguishes a virus from a worm.

Worms are not classified as viruses. Worms spread themselves through network connections by automatically copying themselves onto other computers using the security flaws of the target computers. There is a commonly held misconception that Macs cannot be harmed by malware. However, there are indeed worms and other forms of malware that can and do affect Macs. In February 2006, OSX.Leap.A, a Mac worm, spread across the Internet over iChat and infected client computers. The distribution of OSX.Leap.A across the Internet, like many malware threats for OS X, was relatively low. But for those who were infected, the cleanup was a disaster because many applications on the infected systems were hopelessly corrupted, along with their user-specific preferences files.

> **NOTE:** Most worm threats have a *payload*, the malicious code or program carried out by the worm. If this payload is written in a language that a Mac cannot speak, then the payload will not be able to run, and the worm will not infect the computer. Some threats have a payload that will lie dormant until something triggers its release.

A *Trojan horse* is malicious code embedded within a self-contained application that becomes destructive only when an infected application is opened. Trojans closely resemble viruses because both can cause damage when a file is infected. However, a virus is added to an application after the application is written, whereas a Trojan horse is written, created, and distributed as a single application for the sole purpose of getting you to open it to then allow it to do whatever it wants to with your files. Trojan horses can be used to erase files, get passwords, and send e-mail to other users. The threat to Macs here is real. iWorkServices and Jahlav are two examples of Trojans developed specifically for the Mac. Mac systems can also be carriers of Trojans designed for PC, and can very easily pass them along to PCs through filesharing and the like.

A *logic bomb* is a threat resembling a Trojan horse, but it's architected to initiate when a specific event occurs. Logic bombs are brought into the operating system on the coattails of a virus or a worm, containing the payload that will be launched when the trigger event occurs. It is a ticking time bomb ready to go off on a scheduled date or after being resident in the operating system for a certain period of time. In some cases, programmers have been known (and have been indicted) for deploying logic bombs into their own code in order to make more work for their clients and to change the stock prices for their companies.

A *Backdoor* is an exploitable opening within an application's code. Backdoors are usually designed for the purpose of program debugging by programmers. They're similar to Trojan horses; however, they're meant to troubleshoot bugs in programming code rather than intentionally inflict harm on a machine. Typically, they are merely forgotten entryways accidentally included with the software's final release. Firewalls can sometimes stop a Backdoor from entering the system, but usually the best way to combat these vulnerabilities is to continually update the software with any updates available from the software manufacturer.

A *zombie* is a system that has been remotely triggered to perform a task. Often the tasks zombies perform allow an attacker to originate their attacks from another system undetected. An attacker can also build a virtual army of zombies to attack a target. Zombies, also referred to as *drones*, are often used to perpetrate Denial of Service (DoS) attacks and Distributed Denial of Service (DDoS) attacks. Trinoo and Tribe Flood Network are examples of DDoS attacks created for Unix variants and Windows computers.

A *retrovirus* is designed to attack a machine's backup topology. It will wait until all your backup media is infected with the virus before it performs any actions that can cause damage. This makes it impossible to restore the system to an uninfected state once the computer has been infected. Retroviruses are designed to avoid detection by antivirus software. Many of the malware types described in this chapter are available for the Mac, but we have yet to see a retrovirus for Retrospect, BakBone, or any other application used to back up a Mac. However, a few specific attacks against Retrospect have been reported, usually exploiting weak passwords.

> **NOTE:** Retroviruses are not named after Retrospect, the popular backup application from EMC. They're actually named after their biological counterparts which masquerade as a component of one's DNA.

A *macro virus* is a virus attack designed to exploit applications that have the ability to create mini-programs, called *macros*, within documents. Microsoft Word and Microsoft Excel are examples of software that can create these dangerous documents. Thus, most of the known macro viruses in existence are designed for Microsoft Office (even though there are macro viruses such as BadBunny designed for OpenOffice). And these macro viruses are cross-platform, found on both Macs and PCs and can have damaging effects on both Windows and Mac machines.

Table 8–1 summarizes the types of threats discussed in this section.

Table 8–1. *Threat Breakdown*

Threat	Description	Vulnerability for a Mac
Virus	Program that can copy itself and infect a computer without the permission or knowledge of the end user	Rare
Worm	Self-replicating computer program, often used to distribute malicious content, spreading through a computer network	Common
Trojan horse (Trojan)	Code inserted into an application that causes a program to perform actions not intended by the user	Common
Logic bomb	Malicious code triggered by a specific event such as a specific date and time	Rare

Threat	Description	Vulnerability for a Mac
Backdoor	Forgotten debugging routines that can be exploited	Rare
Zombie	Remotely triggered applications running in the background of a system used to remotely execute code	Rare
Retrovirus	Attacks against backup systems	None yet
Macro virus	A virus written using the macro feature of macro-enabled software such as Microsoft Office and OpenOffice and then deployed using office documents	Common
Rootkits	A software program written to control an operating system while remaining hidden	Common

The Real Threat of Malware on the Mac

A program called Elk Cloner is credited with being the first computer virus to spread to other computers outside of the lab in which it was created. Since then, viruses and other malware have become increasingly rampant on the Internet, in both commercial and home networks, and have caused billions of dollars in lost productivity. The MyDoom worm alone was estimated by mi2g, a global risk specialist, to have cost $43.9 billion in damages worldwide. This is equivalent to the total revenue earned by GM in the first quarter of 2007.

In March 1999, an e-mail worm named Melissa wreaked havoc across the Internet, so much so that companies unplugged their mail servers from their networks for days because of the flood of e-mail messages Melissa generated. In 2001, two more worms—Code Red and Nimda—generated so much traffic that administrators completely shut down their networks' connections to the Internet. In January 2003, a worm called, very simply, *worm*, imposed so much network traffic that it even sent ATM machines offline. Even Apple had a rather embarrassing incident where it shipped a batch of iPods that had been infected by RavMonE.exe, a backdoor that came from a Windows computer located within Apple's manufacturing line.

Malware are very real threats. And contrary to popular belief, the Mac is not immune to them. Don't believe the media hype. Get antivirus software for your Mac. Yes, it is far more likely that you will suffer from file corruption from a malware attack while working on a Windows machine, but the Mac is still prone to infection.

Macs typically are "silent" carriers of malware. Most of the time, these come in the form of macro viruses. Many Mac users won't discover that they have a macro virus until a PC user (or more likely, a network administrator) informs them that they were sent one. These viruses are typically written to exploit security holes in Microsoft application software and operating systems. Because Macs at their core are fundamentally different from Windows machines, these viruses won't have the same effect on the Mac and may go unnoticed for a while. But they will attach themselves to outgoing e-mails sent by the e-mail program and infect files sent to friends, colleagues, clients, and family. For example, many viruses are written to specifically attack Microsoft Office for Windows. When an infected file is moved from a Mac to Windows, because of the lack of some security features of Office in the Mac environment, the Mac user may "carry" the virus within the infected file and not even know it until it is passed to a Windows machine. Most commonly, the virus may infect Microsoft Word's `normal.dot` file, on which all new Word documents are based. This will cause all new Word files created by the infected computer to be infected with the macro virus. The virus may not affect the computer in any other way. This is the case with the most common virus seen on the Mac for almost a decade, the W97M virus, which is a strain of the original Melissa virus from 1997.

> **TIP:** If your machine detects the W97M virus, immediately delete the `normal.dot` file to keep future new documents from becoming infected when created.

There are ways to prevent infecting your Mac with a macro virus. For example, if you open a Word document with macros enabled, you will usually receive an alert letting you know the file has macros. If you receive a macro alert, take a minute to check that document out a little more thoroughly. In fact, check it for viruses (you do have antivirus software running on your Mac, right?) Word will even allow you to examine the macro to see what it does before opening the document. This will help you keep macros that can damage Word and Excel on your computer at bay and keep your office installation at an optimal performance level.

Script Malware Attacks

For now, Automator is probably the most underutilized and underappreciated gem of the Mac OS X operating system. It is Mac OS X's personal robot, designed to eliminate some of the repetitive tasks that we all must perform while working on our Macs by essentially "automating" them. It is a major time-saver. It can also be a huge malware headache. Automator relies heavily on workflows that are built with *scripts*, which are automatic functions that tell your computer what to do. You can probably deduce that viruses work the same way: they are scripts that tell your computer what to do. For this reason, Automator workflows are huge security risks and should be treated with caution. E-mailing workflows as attachments should be attempted only with extreme caution, simply because the potential for disastrous results from a user accidentally breaking the operating system by opening a poorly made Automator script is way too high. It is important to be conscious of what Automator workflows can do. Before running a workflow, understand exactly what it will do to the system. Only open Automator workflows built by people you trust.

The same is true for AppleScript and shell scripts (which can actually be even more dangerous, although they'd take a little more skill to perfect). Like Visual Basic in Microsoft Office, these two methods of scripting offer powerful functions that can be used to perform a variety of actions such as erasing drives, deleting files, and corrupting operating systems—dangerous operations that malware is famous for performing. With just one dangerous line of code, shell scripts can erase your hard drive while the operating system is running. Or an AppleScript might run a complicated find operation across the entire hard drive, deleting all files of a certain type. There is no undo command in the Terminal (which is where shell scripts originate), and because Terminal commands don't put files in the trash, when they're deleted, they're gone, headed for disk recovery.

Socially Engineered Malware

Gullibility and the good intentions of less-than-savvy users are the chief enablers of socially engineered viruses. These threats are completely based in social interaction. In other words, they do not spread without direct action from a user. E-mail hoaxes are prime examples of socially engineered malware. Typically, an e-mail hoax will contain a message instructing the user to perform an action on their computer, such as deleting certain key system files, which can seriously damage an operating system installation under the guise of making the computer run better. Also, users are often instructed to forward the message to others, allowing the malware to spread to other computers and to negatively impact the bandwidth demand on a network.

Here is an example of an e-mail hoax:

> TO: krypted@me.com
>
> Subject: !!!
>
> Merry Christmas everyone! Be careful out there. There is a new virus on America Online being sent by E-Mail. If you get anything called "Good Times", DON'T read it or download it. It is a virus that will erase your entire hard drive. Forward this to all your friends. It may help them a lot.

Combating e-mail hoaxes is not a no-win situation. There are excellent web sites such as About.com, the McAfee Virus Hoax page, Snopes.com, or the Symantec Latest Threats page that will generally dispel the usefulness of the e-mail right away. Also, Googling the Internet with the exact words from the e-mail in quotes should be all that is required to determine whether a specific e-mail is a hoax. Some anti-spyware software will also combat some of these e-mail hoaxes.

Using Antivirus Software

Antivirus software has one primary function: to examine a system or a network for malware and either attempt to fix the files infected or remove the infected file from the system or network. Most antivirus packages include an auto-update feature that enables them to update their definitions for new threats as soon as they are discovered. But not all anti-virus software deals with malware in the same way. A wide variety of software packages are available for scanning, repairing, and thwarting malware threats on the Mac. In the following sections, we will talk about the general state of antivirus packages for the Mac, touch on a few of the antivirus packages out there, and discuss the pros and cons of how they deal with malware threats.

discovered on February 16, 2006, and added to the Norton AntiVirus definitions that same day.

> **NOTE:** *Zero-day exploits* are released before, or on the same day as, the vulnerability—and, sometimes, the vendor patch—is released to the public. The term derives from the number of days between the public advisory and the release of the exploit.

Norton Antivirus, due to its popularity in the Windows community, is a well-known and well-documented antivirus application. Let's explore a couple lesser-known antiviral suites that pack some powerful features.

ClamXav

ClamXav is a free antivirus application for the Mac written by Mark Allan. According to Allan's website, as of this writing, the latest version is still in beta, however, we've found it to be stable enough to recommend here. It is available for free at www.clamxav.com/ in a variety of languages. Although ClamXav lacks many of the features available in some of the commercial packages available, it is a great freeware application that should be used as a first-line-of-defense warning system against malware. Although the graphical user interface (GUI) was written by Allan, the underlying code is actually developed and distributed by the open source community as part of the ClamAV project. As freeware, it can be distributed to large numbers of users to help administrators discover virus outbreaks and perform quarantine measures on infected files.

ClamXav will not clean files; it only scans and quarantines them, which can be helpful on a machine with limited infection. However, on a system where a virus or worm has been self-propagating itself for days, weeks, and even years, this could mean that every single file that the user has ends up getting quarantined. This can cause hours of lost time in rebuilding a file structure to its original hierarchy. ClamXav also does not provide scanning for incoming e-mail, which, as previously discussed, is the primary method for distributing viruses on any computer platform.

> **NOTE:** ClamXav should not be run on Mac OS X Snow Leopard Server.

ClamXav is built on open source technology. At its core, it is a command-line utility, with a GUI built on top of it, allowing administrators to control it easily. You can also configure ClamAV, the back-end package of ClamXav, from the command line.

Installing ClamXav 2.0.4 on Mac OS X is fairly straightforward:

1. Download the installer from Allan's web site at www.clamxav.com.

2. When the download is complete, double-click to open the disk image. Drag the icon from this window to the Applications folder. (See Figure 8–2.)

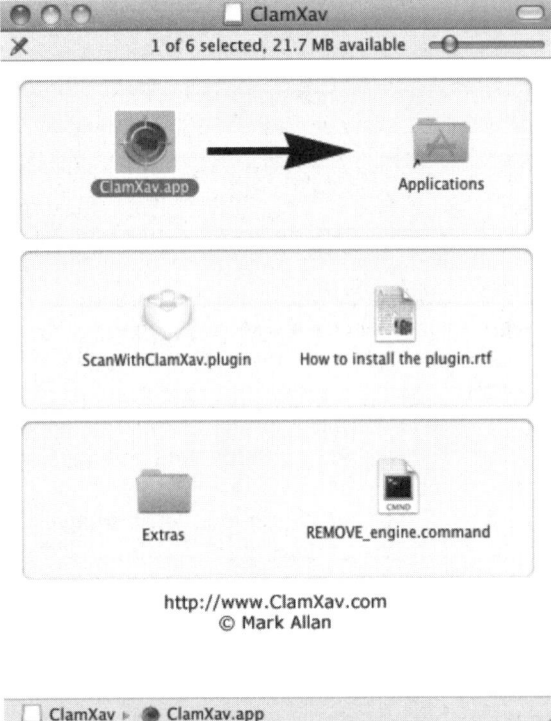

Figure 8–2. *ClamXav install*

3. Double-clicking the ClamXav icon in your Applications folder will open a screen warning that a backup of data should be made prior to running the virus scan. Click OK. (See Figure 8–3.)

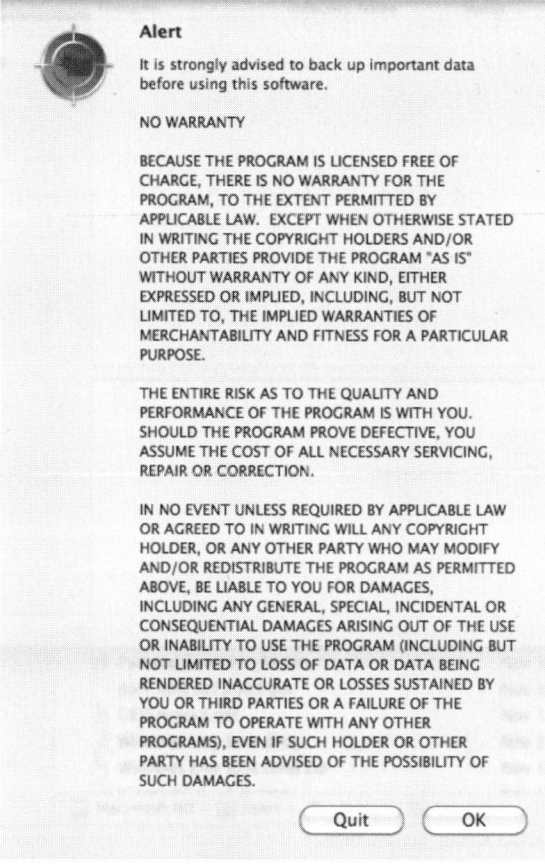

Figure 8-3. *ClamXav warning*

4. The next dialog box, shown in Figure 8-4, will ask you to install the ClamAV engine. Once the installer is finished, ClamXav is ready to run.

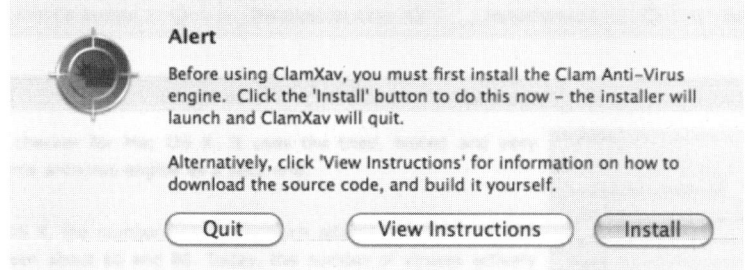

Figure 8-4. *ClamXav engine install*

5. When you run ClamXav for the first time, it will ask you to update the virus definitions. Make sure to update the definitions by clicking on Update Now. (See Figure 8-5.)

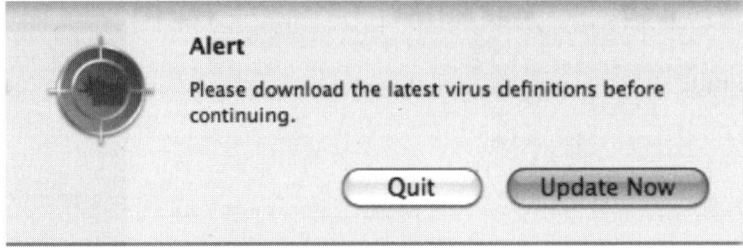

Figure 8-5. *ClamXav virus definition update*

The main ClamXav screen (shown in Figure 8–6) allows you to select items to scan, to start and stop scans, to review logs, and to set preferences for ClamXav.

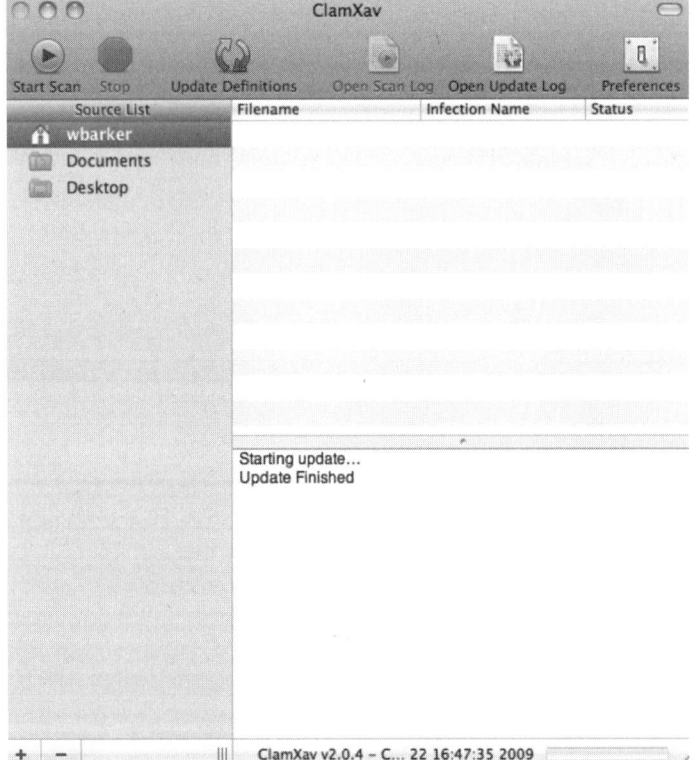

Figure 8-6. *ClamXav virus scanner*

To automate virus scanning, follow these steps (you can also automate virus definition updates here as well):

1. Click the Preferences button, and then click the Schedule tab of the Preferences screen.

2. Under the Scan pane (shown in Figure 8–7), you can either drag folder items into the pane or add items by clicking on the plus sign at the bottom to add items.

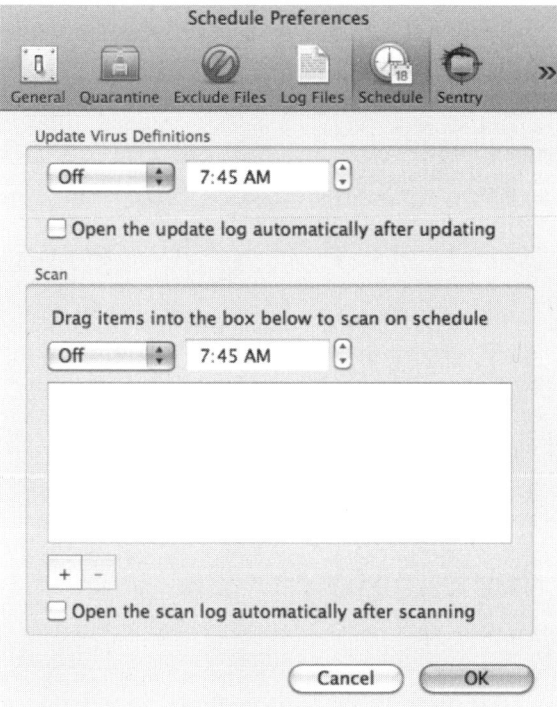

Figure 8-7. *ClamXav schedule scan preferences*

3. To schedule scans, click on the drop-down window to choose how often you'd like to scan. You can also change the time you'd like to scan. If you would like to get a report of any infected files at the end of the scan, you can check the Open the scan log automatically after scanning box.

4. Clicking OK will commit these changes the next time a scan or update is run.

The Folder Sentry is a nice feature that allows administrators to specify certain watch folders that, when changed, will automatically be scanned. This is good protection for those high-profile crucial document folders that must remain virus-free. The Folder Sentry application runs in the background and activates only when one of the watch folders has been edited. To add a watch folder, either drag the folder from a Finder window into the Folders Being Watched field or add it from the plus (+) sign below (see Figure 8–8). The "Scan inserted disks" option will scan all disks that are attached or mounted on the system. The "Launch ClamXav Sentry when you log in to this computer" option will add ClamXav Sentry to your users' Login Items, launched when the user logs in. The "Delete infected files" option will delete files that are infected automatically when they are detected. Use this option with caution because it is fairly dangerous to automatically delete files without knowing which files are being deleted. Most often, this option is best left unchecked. It's better to review your logs regularly, manually fixing files if they become infected.

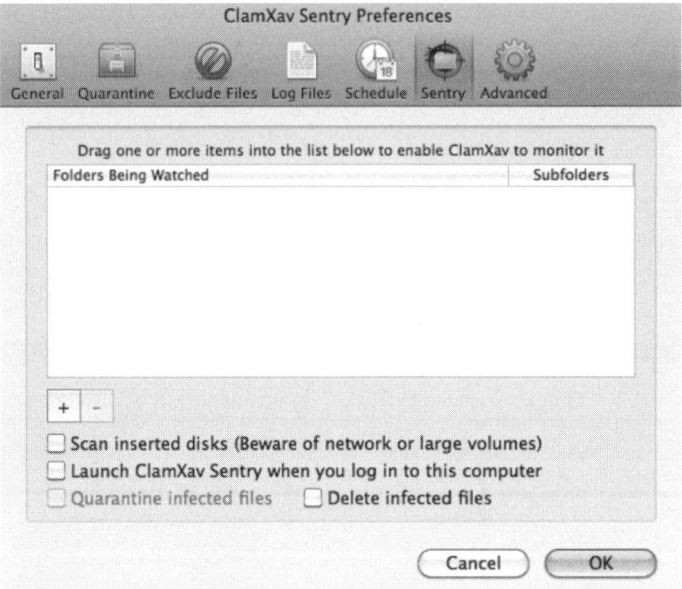

Figure 8-8. *ClamXav Sentry Preferences*

Allan has a Donate button on the ClamXav web site, and if you like the software, then we greatly encourage that you send him a donation through PayPal to help him continue to make improvements. It's a superb free product and with support from the Mac community, ClamXav will continue to grow to be an even better product than it is.

Sophos Anti-Virus

For businesses, Sophos Anti-Virus for Mac OS X is a popular and well-designed antivirus suite that can be purchased for the Mac as well as the PC. Sophos is a well-known leader in the enterprise security field, and its products, while a bit pricey, are some of the best in the industry. We like it because its virus definitions are very up-to-date, it quarantines infected files, and it has an automatic updater for virus definitions as well as disinfection capabilities, standard features for business-class antivirus programs. But what gives Sophos Anti-Virus for the Mac an edge is its unique ability to scale. It uses plug-in architecture integrated into the Sophos Enterprise Console (which requires a Windows computer) for the centralized management of client systems, allowing for cross-platform administration of antivirus protection. Sophos Anti-Virus is available as a free trial at www.sophos.com/products/es/endpoint/sav-mac.html

Once installed, Sophos Anti-Virus can be configured with a wide variety of options, such as:

- Scanning the contents of compressed files, archives, and mailboxes.
- Including non-Macintosh virus detection scans for non-Mac viruses in files.

- Instructing Sophos to perform certain actions when infected files are found.
- Specifying folders to which infected files are moved or copied.
- Many reporting options, including naming of reports and merging of reports from multiple computers.
- Giving the user the ability to configure whether alerts result in desktop prompts, what types of alerts are used, and the text of the alerts.
- Log File customizes the location and editor used in log files.

Sophos Anti-Virus licensing is flexible, if you already own licenses for the Windows platform, appropriating those licenses for a Mac is perfectly legal. While Sophos suite may be overkill for most home users, the options available for network administrators are certainly hard to beat.

Best Practices for Combating Malware

Malware is made possible by our frequent use of applications on our computers. It's the nature of the software industry that new versions of software are released regularly with new features. And with new features come bugs, which in turn means new possibilities for exploitation by pesky code. But when systems are properly defended against these threats, compromises in system integrity can be mitigated. Here is a good summation of our suggestions for best practices in combating malware.

Every Mac should have antivirus software installed on it, and you should run virus scans regularly to mitigate the damage that can be inflicted from an infection. Scheduled scans are also important to maintain the integrity of an antivirus solution. They often take a while, and it's sometimes very tempting to stop a scan while it's running, but without a regularly scheduled full system scan, you can never be 100 percent sure that a system is completely malware-free. Scanning for viruses and malware regularly, keeping the virus definitions up-to-date, and implementing the security updates regularly are all critical tasks for minimizing the likelihood of an infection.

You should also be wary of opening attachments such as Word documents, Excel spreadsheets, and even compiled applications without scanning them with antivirus software. Resist opening e-mail attachments from people you do not know. If a file requests that you enter an administrative password to your computer, it is a good idea not to open the attachment. Macs are very good about limiting the damage that can be done by malware, but once software is allowed through the administrative password gateway, practically anything can happen to the computer.

It is also easy to fall into the "false sense of security" trap that every administrator falls into after running virus scans: coming up virus-free and assuming the system is in the clear. Virus software is software like any other. As such, it can be compromised or corrupted, and it's entirely possible that the virus scanner is not catching everything. Therefore, you should test your e-mail scanner on a regular basis. There are test virus files that have no ill effects on your computer that can be downloaded and run on the machine. Web sites such as Eicar.org have good tests for anti-virus software integrity (www.eicar.org/anti_virus_test_file.htm), but they shouldn't be relied on to detect all malware threats.

A complete antivirus solution should not only include a scan and quarantine process, but should also contain a cleaning/repairing component. For example, using ClamXav might yield 30 files in the quarantine, but you'll need another application to actually repair the files. At a minimum, using any of the malware utilities is a good idea because they offer an early warning system for malware infection.

Other Forms of Malware

Malware does not end with viruses. Adware and spyware are other forms of malware that can range from mere annoyances to rather dangerous identity infiltration.

Adware

The term *adware* refers to any software that displays advertisements, whether or not it does so with the user's consent. Adware applications may display advertisements as an alternative to taking payment. These classify as adware in the sense of advertising-supported software, but not as spyware. For software to be classified as adware, it must not operate covertly or mislead the user, and it should provide the user with a specific product or service.

There is nothing unethical about adware. It is a common and valid business practice for companies to advertise via adware. However, when adware attempts to operate stealthily in the background, it becomes spyware.

Spyware

Spyware is classified as any software that covertly gathers information through an Internet connection without the user's knowledge, usually for advertising and marketing purposes. Once installed, spyware monitors Internet activity and transmits that information in the background to another party. It is usually covertly installed, allowing an attacker to gain access to your personal data or track your Internet usage and is often responsible for identity theft, password exposure, fraud, slow Internet activity, and sluggish computer performance. It is often bundled as a hidden component of free or shareware programs downloaded from the Internet.

It is a common misconception that spyware incidents on the Mac are not possible. Although it is true that they are less common and do not install themselves automatically simply by browsing certain web sites, as they do on Windows machines, spyware is a very real threat on any platform. Spyware merely needs to be installed to begin its information gathering and installation can take place using a variety of methods, most notably using files downloaded from web sites.

Because spyware attackers are rather skilled at what they do, as a community, operating system developers have been unable to completely eliminate spyware from ravaging systems. Practicing good browser security can help keep your system safe and secure. (We cover web browser security in more detail in Chapter 7.)

The most common application used to combat spyware on the Mac is MacScan. There are others, but they're not as widely distributed.

MacScan

MacScan by SecureMac is one example of a commercial program that can remove spyware and the data that spyware most commonly harvests on a Mac. MacScan checks for spyware in administrative applications running on a system and in web browser caches (see Figure 8–9), allowing the user to clean this data from the computer. MacScan is available at http://macscan.securemac.com.

Figure 8–9. *MacScan web files cleaner*

It is important to point out that MacScan is a basic application, as are many of the spyware-oriented products for the Mac. The products available for the Windows platform such as Spybot Search & Destroy, Ad-Aware, and Spy Sweeper are far more advanced and feature-rich. This is primarily because of the widespread nature of spyware in the Windows environment and the rarity of spyware within the OS X community.

Spyware attacks on the Mac is rare, but they do happen, and staying proactive against this threat takes very little work to be effective. Regularly running an antispyware program such as MacScan can help keep spyware off your computer and provide due diligence for maintaining a spyware-free Mac.

Root Kits

Root kits act like spyware, but are typically much more dangerous. The difference between Rootkits and Spyware lies in the intent. Root kits are specifically designed to allow an attacker to gain hidden unauthorized access to a computer to compromise the integrity of the system. A root kit can be installed on a computer in a variety of ways and will provide those with access unlimited access to the machine as a result. The primary objective of many root kits is to evade detection by the operating system. As such, they often masquerade as other applications in order to hide themselves.

One example of a root kit threat for the Mac is SH.Renepo.B, released in October 2004. SH.Renepo.B deletes Unix commands, deletes various log files, modifies security preferences, launches a keystroke logger, installs software, changes the `hostconfig` file, scans the system for passwords, enables file sharing, creates an invisible folder named `canned.info` in each user's Public folder, and creates a process that spikes the processor of infected hosts. The payload for SH.Renepo.B is considerable, but the file size is only 46KB.

If a root kit does find its way onto your system, then a quick comparison of the date and times that a file were created and modified based on an originally known good set of the same files will often identify the presence of a root kit. Using check sums to calculate whether any changes have occurred is a better way of detecting a root kit.

Rootkit Hunter is a GPL-based terminal application that can scan for specific known root kits. However, many root kits are not known, or they're altered so they can't be discovered by root kit scanners. Rootkit Hunter will not find SH.Renepo.B, for example, but will find variants of the FreeBSD root kit that have been found in Mac OS X environments. SH.Renepo.B may be added to future releases of Rootkit Hunter, but it is not included at this time.

You can download Rootkit Hunter from `www.rootkit.nl`. To install Rootkit Hunter, follow these steps:

1. Download the gzipped file, extract it, and run the installation script.
2. Extract Rootkit Hunter using the command `tar zxf rkhunter-<version>.tar.gz`.
3. Run `./installer.sh` from inside the rkhunter directory.
4. Change directory (cd) into the rkhunter folder, and run the command `sudo./rkhunter -checkall` to perform all the tests on the system.

Once you have Rootkit Hunter installed, you can invoke it using the following additional parameters:

--configfile <filename>: Uses a custom configuration file.

--createlogfile: Creates a log at /var/log/rkhunter.log.

--cronjob: Runs as cronjob.

--help: Shows the Rootkit Hunter manual page.

--nocolors: Doesn't use any colors in the output.

--report-mode: Limits the contents of a report.

--skip-keypress: Doesn't wait after every test (makes it noninteractive).

--quick: Performs quick scan.

--version: Shows the version.

Now we will create an example of a shell script (rkexport.sh) that will run rkhunter and append the output to a new .txt file that could be viewed from the Web, provided that the /admin directory of your site is password-protected. Once you've run rkhunter, you can build on the previous section and run a ClamAV scan of the system and dump the results into the same file:

```
Date >> /opt/apache2/htdocs/admin
Whoami >> /opt/apache2/htdocs/admin
Rkhunter -version >> /opt/apache2/htdocs/admin
Rkhunter -checkall -skip-keypress -report-mode  >> /opt/apache2/htdocs/admin
Clamscan -V >> /opt/apache2/htdocs/admin
Clamscan / -r -i -move=/Quarantine >> /opt/apache2/htdocs/admin
```

This should provide you with output similar to the following:

```
Sun May  7 18:49:04 PDT 2006
Cedge
Rootkit Hunter 1.2.8
* MD5 scan
MD5 compared            : 0
Incorrect MD5 checksums : 0

* File scan
Scanned files: 342
Possible infected files: 0

* Rootkits
Possible rootkits:

Scanning took 110 seconds

*important*
Scan your system sometimes manually with full output enabled!
Some errors have been found while checking. Please perform a manual
check on this machine called Charles.local:

----------- SCAN SUMMARY -----------
Known viruses: 52427
Engine version: 0.88
Scanned directories: 1342
Scanned files: 60046
Infected files: 0
Data scanned: 14.93 GB
Time: 19.096 sec (0 m 9 s)
```

Not all root kits need to be command line or difficult to use. One, available for a few years now, called HellRaiser (most recently called OSX/HellRTS.D) can be configured and sent to targets in only a few minutes, without the need to ever open Terminal. In order to get infected you would have to run a server daemon, and would need to install it, but it can easily be disguised as something like an iChat Smiley or a fake iLife download.

HellRaiser is a RealBasic-based trojan horse that gives control of a Mac OS X system to an attacker. The payload ends up being a root kit accessible through a graphical interface. This can give an attacker the ability to search through your file system and then transfer files, view the clipboard, send audio, send chats, view your screen, show pictures, view spotlight indexes, control mail, reboot and even send shell commands to your computer.

Most major anti-virus applications (eg - Symantec, McAfee, etc) will detect the OSX/HellRTS.D. trojan horse when using the latest definition updates, but you would need to be running one of them in order for it to root out HellRaiser.

HellRaiser is not widely distributed and so most users have a pretty low risk of being infected. If you find yourself infected. If you want to know who it is that is attempting to establish a connection to your computer then you can enable ipfw and then ipfw logging (see Chapter 11 for more on ipfw) for the port that it's attempting to connect over (by default it's 24745).

Summary

Contrary to popular belief, the Mac is not impervious to malware. Viruses, worms and rootkits are very real threats to the integrity of the Mac operating system and as such should be safeguarded against. By understanding what these threats are, how to protect yourself against them, and engaging in ways to combat them, you're that much closer to a more secure and stable computing experience. Now, let's move on to discussing how to secure your Mac's operating system through data encryption.

Chapter 9

Encrypting Files and Volumes

A common theme that you may be noticing in this book revolves around the concept of confidentiality. In a computer security context, confidentiality is the notion that sensitive data is accessible by only those users who have been approved or authorized for access to that data. For many organizations, and indeed for many malfeasants, data confidentiality is the most significant aspect of security. Certainly sabotage is a significant threat to many organizations, and often a source of incentive for many hackers, but more often than not the end-goal is to gain access to information. Whether it's personal information that facilitates identity theft, or highly valuable corporate secrets, information is highly valuable, both to you and those that would do you harm. In many corporate environments, the policy to encrypt data may be simply due to legal necessity, as there is liability involved with leaking certain data, such as personally identifiable information and payment records. Recent research indicates that loss of corporate secrets can result in an even more dangerous financial windfall for a company. Thus, protecting that data should always serve as job number one for end user's and system administrators alike.

Thankfully, OS X ships with a number of different technologies to facilitate the protection of data, as we have discussed throughout this book. In this chapter though, we will be focusing on one specific aspect of data confidentiality: encryption. Hopefully, if you're reading this book, you already have some prerequisite knowledge as to what exactly encryption is: in short, the obfuscation of data. More precisely, encryption serves as a means to obfuscate and protect data that is stored on a computer system such that it cannot be accessed without the possession of a "secret." In the broad context of data encryption, this secret can exist in many, many different forms from a simple password to a pre-shared cryptographic key, or even biometric data, such as a fingerprint or retinal scan. Certainly this isn't an exhaustive list, and technologies exist in many shapes and sizes to perform this task. Put simply, the primary role of a secret in the terms of encryption is to limit the visibility of the obfuscated data stored on a computer system. Without possession of the secret, the encrypted data is simply a mash of bits and bytes that at first glance may contain no sensible data. However, at the root of all that junk actually lies a very sophisticated mathematical algorithm that serves as a pathway to understanding that which is incomprehensible. The take away is that, without the secret, encrypted data is useless, or at least *should* be useless, assuming you are using a strong cryptographic system. The good news is that, by modern day standards, the best metric that we can hope to achieve, OS X utilizes some pretty rock-solid encryption technologies, ranging from the Keychain, to FileVault, OS X's encryption facilities that are both easy to use and transparent, but are also based upon well regarded mathematical algorithms.

In this chapter we will discuss the ins-and-outs of these technologies, endowing upon you, dear reader, the knowledge and power needed to harness them to their fullest. Without doubt each of these technologies has its own respective strengths and weakness, and it is also without question necessary to fully understand both of these aspects to ensure a truly protected environment. This chapter takes on that heavy burden so that you can confidently employ them for your own means.

Using the Keychain to Secure Sensitive Data

The keychain is an oft-misunderstood feature in OS X. This is rather unfortunate, because it is a very powerful tool for managing passwords and sensitive information. There is always a trade-off between security and accessibility, and the keychain provides a very good balance of both, providing an interface that both securely stores data and does so in an interface that is mostly seamless to the end user. We say "mostly seamless" here because there are certainly occasions where the system breaks down, and the result is end user confusion.

The keychain gets off to a bad start simply due to the fact that "password" is a four-letter word for many users; many can't even reliably remember a single password. If at any time any kind of confusion or uncertainty is thrown into the mix, for some reason these users tend to panic, and thus a help-desk ticket is launched, perhaps even followed up by a frantic call. Your job, as an administrator, is to possess a fundamental understanding of how the keychain operates so you can readily and easily dispatch keychain problems, while at the same time educating your users on its proper operation. We seek to facilitate both of these goals in this section.

The Login Keychain

Every user in OS X has a default keychain, called the login keychain. This keychain is provisioned to a user when they first log in to a workstation, and it is assigned a password identical to the password that the user provided at login. From then on, whenever a user logs into a workstation, the login password will be passed to the keychain, and the login keychain will be unlocked. As long as the keychain is unlocked, any applications that have been provisioned access to the keychain will be able to access their respective keychain password entries without user interaction.

One very key thing to know about the whole system is that each keychain utilizes a self-contained password. This keychain is stored in the user's home directory and its secret, or password, does not directly integrate with Directory Services such as Open Directory or Active Directory. The primary ramification here is that, if a system administrator resets a user's password through the directory system, typically due to the user forgetting their original password, the respective user's keychain is not updated to reflect the new password. Thus, the next time a user logs into an OS X workstation, the new login password that they used will be passed to the login keychain. According to the login keychain, which still contains the old password, the new password will be rejected. Now, whenever the user opens an application that utilizes the keychain, they will be presented with a dialog to unlock the keychain. They'll likely enter their new password again, and it will again get rejected. To the user this is very frustrating: what's the deal, did the password get reset or didn't it? Historically, OS X hasn't really had a facility to help user's recover from this: once the keychain password is out of sync, the only way around it is for the user to go to the Keychain Access utility found in the /Applications/Utilities folder. Once this application is open, the user can reset their login keychain password by selecting the "Change Password for Keychain 'login'" option found under the Edit menu. Once they manually update the keychain password to the same as their account password, the login keychain will be automatically unlocked when they login. This whole reset process is non-intuitive and the keychain password reset utility is buried inside the Keychain Access app, which most end users would never discover on their own.

A more palatable solution in OS X 10.5 was to install the excellent Keychain Minder application on every OS X desktop, and configure it to launch at user login. When ran, Keychain Minder will check to see if the login keychain successfully unlocked; if not, it will prompt the user to update their keychain password, providing fields for their old password and new password. Assuming the user can remember both, they put them in and their keychain is updated. If they can't remember their old password, they are provided the option to create a new keychain. If selected, this option will backup the old keychain, and create a new keychain using the user's updated password. Creating a new keychain obviously means that all items in their old keychain will be gone, which may or may not be problematic: if the user can't remember all of their various passwords, they're going to be locked out of at least some of their services. Their only hope to recover these passwords is to remember their old keychain password: the data is encrypted, and without the key (the user's password), that encrypted data is forever locked. The Keychain Minder dialog box, shown in Figure 9–1, is presented to the user if it detects a login/keychain password mismatch.

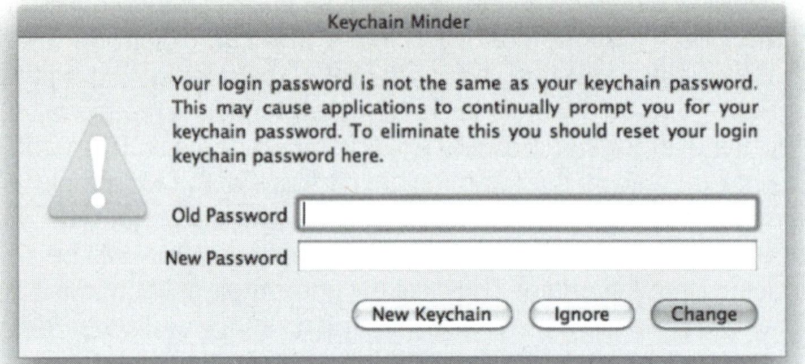

Figure 9-1. *Keychain Minder password reset dialog*

Thankfully, with 10.6, Apple introduced a functionally similar facility of its own. OS X 10.6 now prompts a user at login if the keychain password doesn't match the user's login password (see Figure 9-2). The key benefit now being of course that the facility is built in, and therefore there is no need to mass-deploy an application (and its associated fire-at-login settings) to all of your clients. Any feature that reduces management overhead is a plus in our book, so this one in particular is a very welcome.

Figure 9-2. *OS 10.6 Keychain password reset dialog*

Of course, it's probably best to avoid this whole situation if you can. Although there's no way to avoid this scenario if a user forgets his or her password, you definitely can avoid the issue if they can remember what it was. That is, if a user resets their password through client-local facilities, such as System Preferences or Login Window, then the login keychain password will be subsequently updated. The problem is that these password-reset methods require the user to know their old password, so it's not always applicable.

By default, once unlocked (typically occurring at login), the login keychain remains unlocked for the life of the user's session. This means that they will never be prompted to provide keychain access to pre-approved applications. This potentially includes Mail (Mail.app and Entourage), remote servers, Safari and Camino websites (Firefox does not utilize the Keychain), and other application passwords. For instance, if a user has his online banking credentials saved in his keychain, he will be able to go directly to his bank website and get in without ever needing to enter in a password; his banking login information will be auto filled by Safari. This can potentially lend to a security issue, because if he walks away from his computer without locking it, a malicious person could potentially sneak over to his computer and access his bank account. Likewise, if your computer is set to automatically login, then a malicious user can gain access to your accounts simply by rebooting your machine. This obviously presents a problem. Luckily, the Keychain utility has some facilities to address this very issue, which we'll discuss over the next two sections.

> **NOTE:** By default OS X also has a global keychain, the System keychain. This keychain operates behind the scenes, and is used to store low-level secure data, such as globally trusted certificates, system private keys, auto-login credentials, and trusted wireless network credentials.

Creating Secure Notes and Passwords

The keychain is used by the system to store a variety of confidential information. This includes certificates, certificate trusts, private and public keys, passwords, and secure notes. From an end user perspective, the two most prevalent objects are passwords and secure notes. Conceptually, a stored password is pretty self-explanatory: it's simply a secure object that holds authentication information consisting of the following fields:

- Name: This is an arbitrary name given to the password.
- Kind: This specifies the type of password item, which helps to identify the type of password item. For example, "Web form password," "Application Password."
- Account: This is typically the username.
- Where: This will typically contain a URI (Universal Resource Indicator) such as 'www.mycoolbank.com/login,' although the field does not always conform to URI standard.
- Comments: Miscellaneous information.
- Password: The encrypted password data.

Whenever an application needs to access to an encrypted password, it will search your keychain list for items based on its own defined criteria. This criteria will typically match using the fields: Kind, Account, Where, and Password. See Figure 9–3.

> **NOTE:** Of the above fields, only the password field is encrypted; everything else can be viewed without entering a password. Because of this, an attacker can potentially use this data for a "traffic analysis" attack; by analyzing the clear text data available in the keychain item, they may glean information that assists with gaining access to the account. For instance, an attacker can view a keychain item to gain access to your username for a website. Having access to the username may potentially open the door for them to manipulate a remote password-reset procedure. For highly sensitive sites, consider encrypting all data, including username and password, in the form a secure note, which we'll discuss more in a bit.

Figure 9–3. *Keychain Access password*

Figure 9–3 illustrates a secure password item for the site `https://store.apple.com`, and when accessed, will log in with the account jdoe. The password, as seen, is masked. By clicking on the check box "Show password," you will be prompted for the keychain password before it will present the password, even if the keychain is unlocked! This means that even if you walk away from your computer with the keychain unlocked, your nosey coworker won't be able to pop open Keychain Access and peruse your password; they'll need your keychain password for that. However, as stated earlier, they can just go to Safari, and the application will auto fill the information. So, they'll be able to login, but they won't know what your password is. So why is Safari granted full access to the password, but Keychain Access isn't? Well, this facility is made possible through the Access Control tab, shown in Figure 9–4.

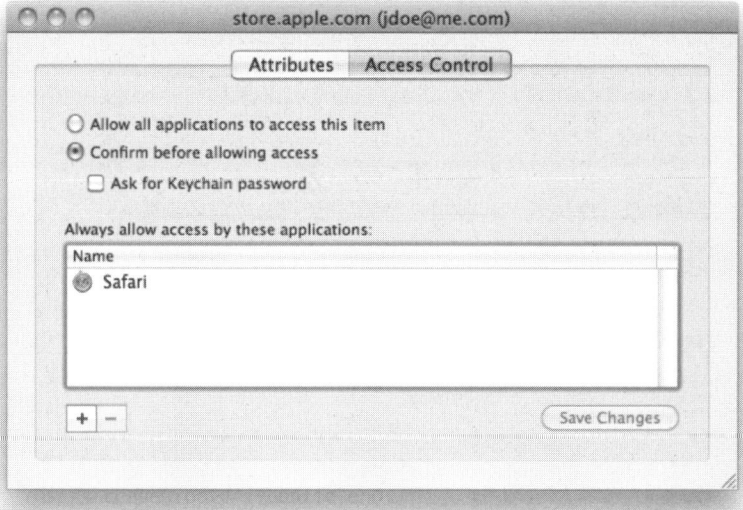

Figure 9–4. *Keychain password object access controls*

The Access Control tab allows you to specify applications that can freely access the password when the keychain is unlocked. In this case, only Safari is provisioned access, as Safari automatically provisions its own access when it creates the password item. If Keychain Access were added to this list, then you would be able to view the objects password without authentication whenever the keychain is in an unlocked state (so that naturally is a bad idea).

> **NOTE:** Regardless of Access Control settings, no application or facility will be able to freely access a password from a keychain when it is in a locked state.

The second user visible feature of the keychain system that we mentioned earlier is secure notes. Secure notes are similar to password items, but they are meant to store larger sets of data, as seen in Figure 9–5.

As Figure 9–5 shows, the interface for secure notes is much more apt to storing larger blocks of information than a standard password item. In this example, the user is using a secure note to save building access codes. Placing this information inside of an encrypted secure note is a great idea, especially if this is on a laptop or mobile machine: the chance of such a machine getting stolen is significantly higher, but the impact is greatly reduced if data is encrypted. In such an event, you might be able to sleep a little better knowing that your front door access code isn't sitting in a text file just waiting to be found. As long as your keychain password is relatively secure, your data is also secure.

Figure 9-5. *Keychain Access secure note*

Unfortunately, there are limits to what you can do with secure notes. While it's a great place to store odds and ends — building access codes, credit card information, personal information such as social security number, and so on — the text box provided supports only basic text, rich formatting is not supported. Because of this, if you have a large amount of data to encrypt, the lack of good formatting might sour your taste a bit, as it could be difficult to visually parse the information that it contains. On top of this, there isn't really a great system for organizing secure notes: there is no hierarchical system for organization; the primary method for organization is search. Unsurprisingly, there's no Spotlight support for secure notes, as allowing the system to index-encrypted note content would be counter-productive.

If these limitations become a problem for the data sets that you need to encrypt, consider using an encrypted disk image to encrypt the information, discussed later on in this chapter.

Managing Multiple Keychains

As mentioned, by default each user in OS X is provisioned a single keychain, the login keychain. That does not necessarily mean that the user can utilize only this keychain, though. In fact, the Keychain Access utility allows you to create as many keychains as you want, each with their own password, auto lock settings, and of course each can contain its own password items and secure notes. Any application in OS X that utilizes the Keychain for secure storage will automatically recognize additional keychains for use.

There are a number of key benefits that can be gained through the implementation of multiple keychains, mainly due to some security implications that are present by default in the login keychain. For instance, we learned a bit earlier that the login keychain is unlocked by default at user login, and that it has no lock timeout; that is, it will remain unlocked until the user logs out, or manually locks it. This means that if a user leaves their node while logged in and unlocked, a sneaky malevolent person could fire up Safari and gain access to any website that has its password stored in that unlocked keychain. New keychains, when created, have a default auto lock setting of five minutes. That means that a user unlocks this keychain for use, it will automatically lock itself five minutes later. If a malevolent user attempts to access a resource utilizing a password item in a locked keychain, they won't have access: the keychain must first be unlocked. Thus, utilizing a second keychain provides a bit more security in that regard.

While it is certainly possible to configure the login keychain to auto lock, or even change its password to a value different then the login password, doing so can sometimes result in an annoyance to end users, as they may complain about having to constantly enter their password. Thus, maintaining multiple passwords can help to achieve security without negatively affecting usability. In such a configuration, the login keychain can be utilized for oft-used and less sensitive information, such as casual websites or commonly used applications that utilize the keychain framework. The second keychain then could be used for data of higher sensitivity such as passwords to financial websites, secure notes containing personal information, or passwords to confidential servers.

For example, this author utilizes three different keychains on his own machine. The login keychain is fairly sparse, and contains only minimal credentials such as passwords to commonly used wireless networks, S/MIME Certificates (utilized by Mail.app to validate e-mail messages we receive from colleagues), and access to various innocuous social websites and web forums. This keychain also contains a few application passwords. For instance, we utilize MobileMe for syncing our data, so we have our MobileMe passwords stored in this keychain to avoid being prompted for a password every time it wants to synchronize. The next keychain is used solely for financial and personal data and credentials. This keychain has extremely aggressive auto-lock settings, and utilizes a password that is over 12 characters long to ensure that it is not a password that can easily be broken through a brute-force attack. The last keychain we maintain contains all credentials that we utilize professionally. This keychain also has extremely aggressive auto-lock settings, and is protected by an extremely secure and unique password. To provide additional security to all of our keychains, we have configured every keychain in our systems, including the login keychain, to lock whenever the machine sleeps. To configure this and keychain auto locking settings, select the menu option "Change Settings for Keychain <keychain name>…" found under the Edit menu in the Keychain Access application (select the appropriate keychain first). This dialog is seen in Figure 9–6.

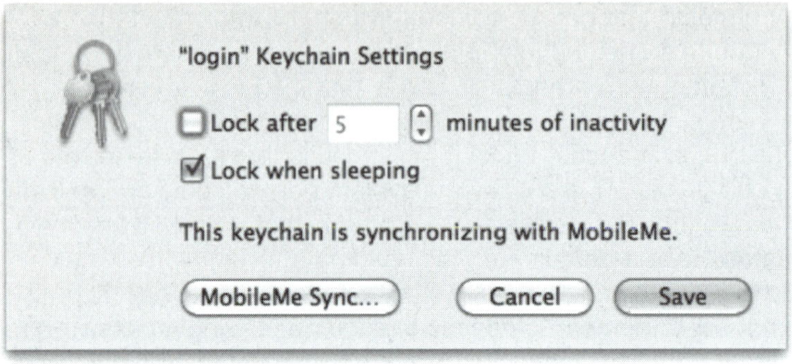

Figure 9–6. *Keychain Access keychain settings*

Maintaining multiple keychains like this allows us to organize data and assign different credentials and security policies to each keychain. This provides a very secure environment. However, there are still a few considerations that will be missed by most users. First and foremost, it's important to ensure that each keychain (outside of your login keychain) has a globally unique password: if the keychain password itself is the same as a password utilized elsewhere, it is possible that it will be compromised, especially if that password is saved in a keychain somewhere; if a password item in Keychain A has the same credentials as those used by Keychain B itself, Keychain B will be compromised if Keychain A is first compromised. If Keychain A in this example is the login keychain, then this is exceptionally bad. Because the login keychain utilizes the same password as the user's password by default, its credentials are more exposed.

Consider this: a user's login password is stored in the form of a hash on the local hard drive. On an OS X client machine by default a user's password is stored solely in the form of a SHA-1 hash inside the folder /var/db/shadow/hash. Thankfully, this file is protected with root-only access, so to access this file, a malicious user will need to either compromise your machine remotely, or gain physical access. Additionally, SHA-1 has proven to be a tough nut to crack, and is generally considered in the security industry to be a very secure algorithm. So the presence of this hash isn't a huge problem in and of itself. The problem is that SHA-1 is not necessarily the only hash format that is stored in this file. For instance, if you enable Windows file sharing for a user, an NTLM hash is then added to the user's hash file. Not all hashes are created equal, and NTLM has proven to be very susceptible to attack. In fact, a six-digit password stored in the NTLM hash can typically be cracked in a matter of minutes. Like a series of dominoes, once the login password is obtained, the login keychain is felled. If the login keychain has a single saved password containing the same password as one of your other keychains, then those keychains are also compromised, along with all of the items that they might contain. Suddenly this one small weakness has resulted in all encryption being negated.

To avoid such a chain reaction, common security practices can save the day. First and foremost, make sure that your login password is secure: at least eight characters, containing at least one alphabetic character, one capital character, one number, and one special character. The longer the password, the more secure it is from cracking. Additionally, avoid enabling Windows file services on an OS X client machine, particularly a mobile one. Lastly, as we cannot re-iterate enough, each keychain should be protected by secure, unique passwords. This is where you want to utilize those strong, harder-to remember passwords.

There is one other limitation to know about when utilizing multiple keychains to secure your data. We mentioned earlier that any application that supports the keychain framework would be able to utilize any of your keychains. While this is true, it's important to understand the default behavior when an application actually creates a new keychain item. For instance, say you browse to www.nytimes.com and log in to the website. Say it's the first time you've done so, and so the system prompts you if you would like to save your password, and you click yes. When this happens, the application saves the new password item into your default keychain: there is no way to say specifically which keychain to create the item in. So, after first creating that password item, if you wish to place it into a different keychain, you can do so by using drag-and-drop in the Keychain Access application. The good news is that the login keychain doesn't necessarily have to be the default keychain, though it is by default. To change the default keychain, highlight the desired keychain in Keychain Access, and select the menu option "Make Keychain <keychain name> Default," found under the File menu. From then on, this keychain will be utilized whenever an application creates a new entry.

The keychain, if utilized properly, can provide a way to organize and secure passwords and secure notes on multiple levels. With such a baseline system in place, it allows a user to further leverage security best practices. Users can now create many differing passwords, each unique to their own entity: they can use a different password for Facebook, Google, Twitter, a different password for U.S. Bank or Wells Fargo, for Mint.com. By utilizing a different password for each service, the user ensures that they are reducing the impact of security vulnerabilities to any of these services. If Facebook gets hacked and the user's credentials exposed, the user can maintain piece of mind knowing that that password, unique to Facebook, cannot be utilized to gain access to his other services. This is not something that most users can boast. In fact, we think it likely that most users have one password, and they use it everywhere. Someday, that user might be scratching their head to find there bank accounts emptied and their credit cards maxed, all because they trusted their credentials to a foreign entity, which could not competently protect it.

OS X's keychain empowers the end user to avoid this scenario; a user can create hundreds of different passwords, one for each site, and those passwords can now all be stored safely and securely behind the scenes. The only password they'll need to remember is that used for the keychain itself: whenever a password to a particular site is needed, the user only need ensure that the keychain is unlocked and it will be utilized by the system. This is a very powerful system: learn it and love it; it will be your friend.

Using Disk Images as Encrypted Data Stores

Although the keychain serves as a great tool for securely storing passwords and small blocks of information, it is not great for storing any type of data that requires formatting, and it has absolutely no facilities for storing files. For this type of data encryption need, we instead turn to disk images. A disk image is essentially a virtual volume that can be mounted on a computer and then used to store files. When a disk image is mounted, it appears just like any hard drive or CD would, and is accessed in the same manner as a hard drive: you simply create folders and save files to it. Disk images have been around the Mac OS for a long time, and are most commonly used today for the digital delivery of software and their subsequent updates. For instance, you navigate to http://support.apple.com and download a software package; it will be downloaded in the form of a diskimage file, as denoted by its .dmg extension. This file, when opened, will result in the mounting of a volume on the computer, typically named in a similar fashion of the disk image file itself, though that is not always the case; a disk image's volume name is independent of its file name. Figure 9–6 shows an example disk image file, in this case Apple's 10.6.2 combined updater for OS X server, named MacOSXServerUpdCombo10.6.2.dmg. When the .dmg file is opened, a volume named 'Mac OS X 10.6.2 Server Update Combo' is mounted, and a window is opened displaying the root of its filesystem.

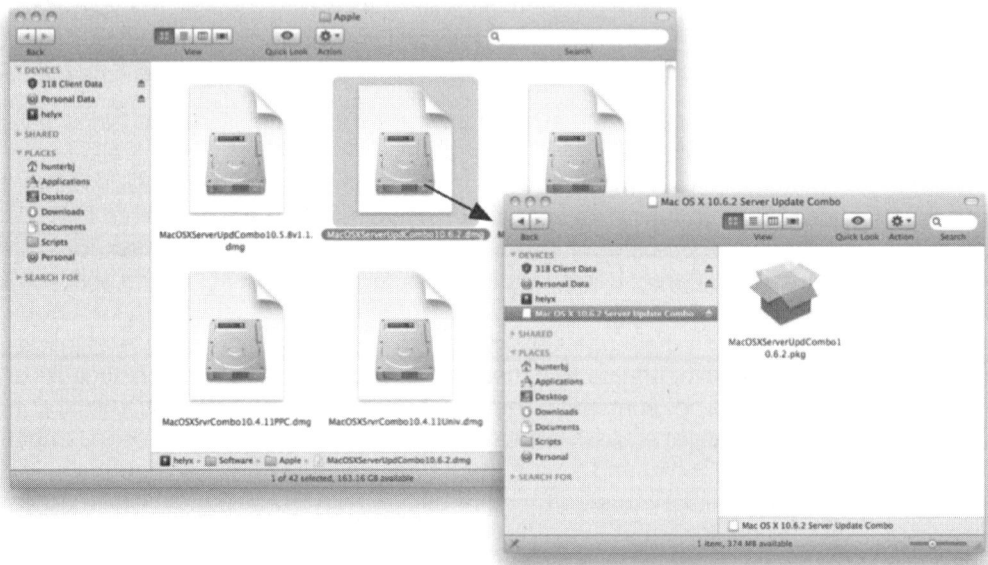

Figure 9–7. *Mounting a disk image*

In Figure 9–7, as in all scenarios where disk images are used to distribute software, the disk image presents a read-only volume. Disk images capable of modification are certainly possible, and in keeping with the tradition of this chapter, are fully capable of being fully encrypted. That is, a disk image when created can utilizes AES (Advanced Encryption Standard) encryption such that whenever a folder or file is written to its mounted volume, that data is first encrypted before being written back to the disk image's file on the disk. This allows a disk image to function as a virtual bin of folders and files that can be transported securely. In order to mount the disk image's volume (and thereby access its data), you must first enter in a password, which is then used to decrypt the data. If that password is unknown, the data will be inaccessible (though as we'll find out later in this section, there are some back-door options that can be utilized).

Throughout this section we will discuss the use of disk images to aid users in maintaining the confidentiality of their data by keeping it from unwanted interlopers. From creation to maintenance and also potential caveats, we will demonstrate effective methods to utilize encrypted disk images to achieve this end.

Creating Encrypted Disk Images

Creation of a disk image is accomplished through the Disk Utility application found in the folder /Applications/Utilities. Once open, a new image can be created by clicking on the New Image icon in the tool bar, or by selecting the menu option "**New ➤ Blank Disk Image...**" found under the file menu, as shown in Figure 9–8.

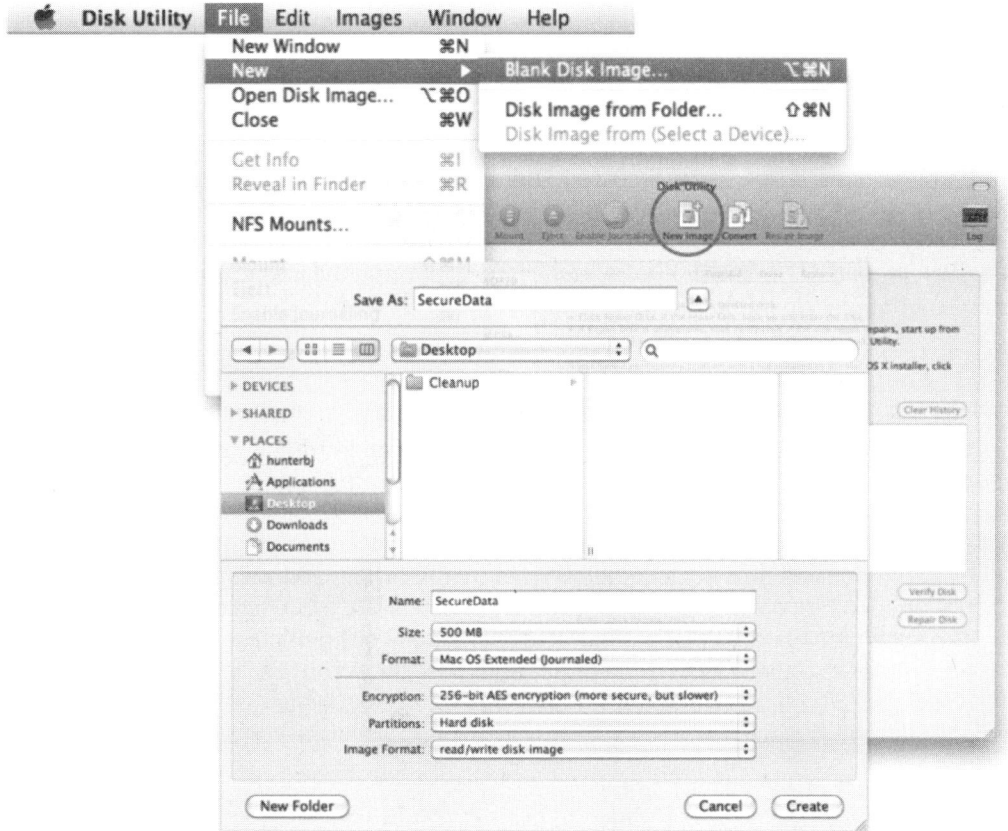

Figure 9–8. *Creating a disk image using Disk Utility*

> **NOTE:** If you have a disk selected when you click the New Image button in the tool bar, Disk Utility will create a disk image based upon the contents of the selected disk, rather than a blank image.

As can be seen in Figure 9–8, there are a number of options presented when creating a new disk image. The first and most important option for creating an encrypted disk image is of course the encryption option, where we can choose between 128 and 256 bit AES encryption. AES is generally well respected, and has been officially endorsed by the U.S. government for use with classified data. The difference between the two options presented here lies solely in the length of the key used to encrypt the data. In this case, even though the key is only twice the size of 128 bit AES, the increased level of security that it provides is an order of magnitude larger. Even though 128 bit AES is generally thought to be extremely secure, attacks on data encrypted with 128-bit AES are becoming more and more plausible. Still, even today the NSA has approved 128-bit AES for the transmission of classified data, though TOP SECRET classified data requires at least 192-bit AES. Considering this, for the vast majority of environments, 128-bit AES will provide adequate data confidentiality. Functionally, the type of encryption used operates behind the scenes, with the only user perceptible difference being in the form of computer speed. Due to the increased complexity of performing mathematics with the larger key, computer performance will be degraded when writing the data. For most day-to-day operations, the difference in speed will be imperceptible to the end user; however, when performing I/O heavy duties, the performance impact will become more prevalent in the form of high CPU utilization.

The next option to consider when creating a new disk image is the image format. This option is actually one of the more pertinent options when it comes to the long-term use and maintenance of the disk image itself. Here, we have a number of options. First, we have the option "Read/Write disk image," which is the most traditional type of disk image used by the Mac OS through the years. A read/write image is a fixed size image: the size of the image is specified at creation time, and the disk image file is allocated to disk. The disk image file, regardless of how much data its volume contains, will always occupy the specified size. Thus, a 500MB read/write disk image will immediately occupy 500MB of space on disk, and it will continue to occupy 500MB of space throughout its life. Because of the fixed-size nature of this format, it is not particularly well suited for most use-cases involving data encryption requirements. If you are only looking to encrypt data for transport, then a fixed size encrypted read/write disk image will certainly fit the bill. However, for a day-to-day encryption store that may grow indeterminably, you'll likely find this format to be limiting.

> **NOTE:** An interesting side-affect of using a read/write encrypted disk image is that someone observing the image can't tell how much encrypted data it contains.

The next option, DVD/CD Master, is very similar in function to the "Read/Write disk image" option. The primary difference is in the lower level format of the disk image file. A

DVD/CD Master formatted disk image is actually written to disk as an ISO compatible format. That is, you can change the .dmg file extension that is used on these disk images can be changed to .iso, and the image file can be processed by cross-platform disk utilities, such as those used in Linux or Windows. This does not necessarily mean that the data from such a disk image can be mounted and read on other platforms, the underlying volume format might still be the Mac-specific HFS+ format, and thereby undecipherable to a foreign OS, but the image itself can be written to CD or DVD and then read on a Mac.

The third option, "Sparse disk image," is a more approachable format. A sparse disk image is a growable image that occupies only as much data on disk as is present on its underlying volume. The image size specified at image creation time (see Figure 9–8) therefore represents only the maximum size of the image volume, not the size of the image file itself. Therefore the creation of a sparse image file that is given a size of 500MB will first result in an image file that contains only minimal formatting and partitioning data written to disk with a .sparseimage file extension (rather than .dmg). The initial file size will differ based upon the maximum size of the disk image. In the case of a 500MB volume, the initial file will be roughly 10MB. The image file will grow as data is added to it, up to a ceiling of 500MB. For a larger volume, say 2TB, the initial image size will be roughly 1GB. Because of the dynamic nature of sparse images, they are very well suited for a general-purpose file store. The disk image can be created, a defined folder hierarchy can be established on its volume, and files can be added to it on an as-needed basis. Because the image file will only consume as much space on disk as the data that it contains, a high ceiling can be set on the disk image at creation time, such as 8GB, and the disk image will grow as needed without unnecessarily consuming disk space. There are a few side effects to this aspect, but we'll dig into those details a bit later on (see section "Limitations of Sparse Images and Reclaiming Space," later on in this chapter). Because of their dynamic nature for most purposes, a sparse image file will be the go-to option.

> **NOTE:** Volumes residing on a sparse disk image cannot be resized; therefore, it is a good idea to be somewhat liberal when setting the size of the volume. It also is not a great idea to specify a size that is overly large, as it will result in lost space due to partitioning and formatting overhead on the image file.

The last option, "Sparse bundle disk image," is a different take on a sparse disk image. Like a sparse image, a sparse bundle will grow as needed based upon the content of its volume (up to the size specified at image creation). The difference between the two lies in the way that a sparse bundle is written to disk. Instead of creating a single monolithic file to represent all contents of its virtual volume as a sparse image does, a sparse bundle actually writes its data to disk in the form of directory that contains multiple files. Each of these files, referred to as a band, only contains a small subset of data within the disk image volume. As new data is written to the sparse image, new bands will be created as needed. When existing data is altered on the volume, only the bands that hold the contents of that file will change on disk.

This has a couple of benefits: first, it is more resistant to data corruption: in the event of disk corruption, the chance of a catastrophic failure of the disk image's volume is reduced. With individual bands, only the files whose data is written to that corrupted band will be lost. Contrast this with the single monolithic model of a .sparseimage file, which can be susceptible to complete data loss should that single file become corrupted. Sparse bundle disk images have another very valuable property. One significant issue found with monolithic image files is that whenever there is a change, no matter how minute, the underlying disk image file is changed.

Keep in mind that a volume isn't changed solely by your actions; there are many underlying facilities that can result in small changes in data. For instance, the Finder will commonly modify .DS_Store files in any directory that it navigates. Spotlight, if enabled, can cause changes to the volume. Quicklook can cause the generation of proxies, which can also modify the volume. Realistically this means that any time the image is mounted, the file will change.

This has an important ramification for system administrators who are backing up your system, or perhaps on you, the user, if you utilize home directory syncing or back up your own machine. Such utilities, when run, detect file changes, and in such an event will copy/backup the file, typically over a network connection. All of these utilities operate at the file level, not the block level. This means that to back up or synchronize a file, the entire file has to be backed up, not just the changes. Basically what this means is that your backup system has to work overtime to ensure these backups are performed. If you have a sparse image with only a few documents on it, this isn't likely a big deal. However, if your image contains a lot of data, then that can cause significant problems.

Consider an image with 50GB of data on it. If the image file is mounted, the effectively the underlying file will be changed. If you make a habit in opening that file, that's 50GB that needs to be backed up each time, which is a lot of data. If your backup or synchronize window isn't long enough, this could effectively act as a denial of service of your backup or synchronization process: other files might not be addressed by the system due to constant delays introduced by your huge file. This denial of service effectively acts as a breach of security in the area of redundancy. Encryption should not come at the expense of your backups, and as such, a sparse image can be detrimental at this scale. Whenever you have both encrypted files and backups, you have to make the decision of whether to back the files up in their encrypted or plain form. Backing up the plain form makes recovery easier (especially if the only person who knows the password leaves the company), but means it's easier for confidential data to leak from your backups than from the original location.

If your backups are in a secure site and your main system is a laptop or iPad, then having plain backups actually isn't so bad. Unfortunately, with a sparse image structure, backing up data in its encrypted form isn't a very plausible reality.

This is where sparse bundles really shine, and is no doubt the primary rational behind the creation of the image format. With a sparse bundle, only the bands that are actually modified will be backed up or synchronized. Thus, with the same 50GB image, if a Word document is updated on the disk, only the bands that contain that file will be affected, mounted, it is presented on the local file system as another disk. The problem with this is that if the systems runtime is compromised, then referencing the filesystem path at which the image is mounted can access the unencrypted data. This means that if the user is subjected to malware such that a foreign program is executed in his environment, then that malicious program will be able to be accessed by that program. Thus, if an encrypted disk image is opened on a compromised system, it can be assumed that the data on the mounted volume will be detected and read; confidentiality of the encrypted data will be breached. Considering this aspect of utilizing disk images for encryption, it is a good practice to get in the habit of only having secure volumes mounted explicitly when needed: mounting an encrypted disk image opens a window to the data, keeping that window closed as much as possible is key to keeping the data safe; keeping an encrypted disk image mounted at all times may expose data unnecessarily.

Interfacing with Disk Images from the Command Line

Thus far, we have demonstrated the process for creating encrypted disk images using the Disk Utility GUI application. In some cases, it may be desirable to automate the process. For instance, as an administrator, you may wish to create an encrypted disk image for the purposes of backup. Or, you may be looking to mass-deploy encrypted disk images to a multitude of users. In cases such as this, using Disk Utility to interactively create a disk image might not be the most efficient use of time. Interactive creation of disk images will severely hamper your ability to automate backups that would utilize them. Economies of scale apply to large user environments inhibiting the practicality of manually creating an encrypted disk image for each of your users. Luckily, Mac OS X offers a very capable command line suite for creating and manipulating disk images.

The primary utility for dealing with disk images from the command line is the `hdiutil` command. This command can be used to create, mount (attach), and unmount (detach) image files, among other things. Mounting and un-mounting disk images is rather trivial to accomplish with this tool. To do so, we just call `hdiutil` with the `attach` verb, and then pass in the path to our disk image file. The command and subsequent output are shown here:

```
$ hdiutil attach ~/Desktop/mySecureData.sparseimage
Enter password to access "mySecureData.sparseimage":
/dev/disk3          Apple_partition_scheme
/dev/disk3s1            Apple_partition_map
/dev/disk3s2            Apple_HFS                  /Volumes/mySecureData
```

As can be seen by the output, the user is prompted for a password, the image file "mySecureData.sparseimage" is assigned device of /dev/disk3, and is mounted at path /Volumes/mySecureData.

> **NOTE:** If you want to automate the mounting of an encrypted disk image for backups, you will need to automate the supply of the password, too, which means that the password is going to be sitting somewhere in cleartext for your script to grab. In the case of an ObjectiveC application, it is possible to utilize the keychain framework to store this value, but even then, the keychain must be unlocked at the time of use.

Once mounted, the encrypted disk image behaves just like another physical drive in the system. There are a few things to note about this. First and foremost, as stated, when an image file is attached, any POSIX permissions laid down on the volume will be effectively bypassed, due to the fact that ownership of all items on the disk image's volume is masked to the running user. On top of this, the volume is mounted to the typical OS X directory in /Volumes. This can create a security issue on nodes that have more than a single logged in user: if you mount your disk image on a computer with another active user session, they will not only be able to see that the disk was attached, but they will also be able to navigate to the volume and likely read data off of that volume. Remember from Chapter 4 that a user's default umask setting in OS X is set such that any newly created files have global read access. As such, concurrent user sessions will likely have access to the unencrypted data, which isn't good. To avoid this issue, there are a couple of options. The first is to simply ensure that the top level of the disk image volume has adequate protections. While ownership is not respected by default with disk images, the mode is. This means that, if a directory only has read and execute permissions granted at the ownership level, other users will not be able to view any data on the volume. To accomplish this, a user can simply remove all access from other users by using the Permissions tab of a Finder Get Info window. Or, you can use the chmod command as shown here:

```
$ chmod 700 /Volumes/mySecureData
```

After running this command, only the mounting user will have access to the data. While for the most part this will work out, it is possible to further secure the data on a mounted volume by passing custom mount parameters to `hdiutil` when mounting an image. Through the use of -owners option, it is possible to force a disk image to mount in a manner that enforces permissions as laid down on the image volume. On top of this, you can specify a custom mountpoint, other than /Volumes, for the mounting of your volume. Lastly, we can use the -nobrowse option to prevent the volume from being recognized as such by the Finder: instead it will treated just like any other folder on the system, and will prevent the volume from showing up in other user's devices list. To mount an image with such options, utilize the following syntax:

```
$mkdir ~/SecureData
$ hdiutil attach -owners on -nobrowse -mountpoint ~/SecureData↵
 ~/Desktop/mySecureData.sparseimage
```

After executing this command, the volume found in the mySecureData sparse image will be mounted to a folder named "SecureData" at the root of the user's home directory. You'll notice here that we are using the mkdir command to first create the directory prior to running the hdiutil command: if the designated mountpoint does not exist, then the mount operation will fail. Because we are passing the -owners flag with a value of "on," we are ensuring that any ownership on the volume is preserved, which allows you to utilize normal file system permissions to secure data on mounted volumes. For more information on utilizing file system permissions, refer to Chapter 4.

To unmount or detach the image, we simply use the detach verb and pass it the volume path:

```
$ hdiutil detach /Volumes/mySecureData
"disk3" unmounted.
"disk3" ejected.
```

Alternatively we can provide the disk path:

```
$ hdiutil detach /dev/disk3
"disk3" unmounted.
"disk3" ejected.
```

As can be seen, with either syntax the device disk3 is ejected from the system.

Creation of disk images requires a bit more lengthy syntax, and is achieved by using the create verb. The process allows for the specification of all parameters that we were presented from the GUI and more:

```
$ hdiutil create -size 100M -fs "Journaled HFS+" -volname "myImage"
  ~/Desktop/myImage.dmg
created: /Users/hunterbj/myImage.dmg
```

In this case, a 100MB image file named myImage.dmg is created on the desktop. The volume name of the image is specified by the -volname parameter, in this case "testImage." By default, the format of the image file is "Read/Write," a GUID partition scheme is used, and no encryption is used on the disk image.

To create a sparse image with encryption we can use the following syntax:

```
$ hdiutil create -size 8G -fs "Journaled HFS+" -volname "myImage" -type SPARSE
  -encryption AES-128 ~/Desktop/mySecureImage.sparseimage
Enter a new password to secure "mySecureImage.sparseimage":
Re-enter new password:
created: /Users/hunterbj/mySecureImage.sparseimage
```

Here, we were prompted for a password to use for encryption. We can also use the -stdinpass if we want to specify the password programmatically:

```
$ echo -n 'myPassword1$' | hdiutil create -size 8G -fs "Journaled HFS+" -volname
  "myImage" -type SPARSE -encryption AES-128 -stdinpass
  ~/Desktop/mySecureImage.sparseimage
created: /Users/hunterbj/mySecureImage.sparseimage
```

In both of these cases, we're encrypting the image with AES-128 bit encryption. In the first example we had to interactively enter our password; in the second example, we're passing a password of 'myPassword1$' via the echo command (the -n prevents echo from sending a trailing newline after the password), which is then read in as the password to use to encrypt the image. This is very handy in cases where you have to programmatically generate images for end users, and have a default password template or routine that should be used on new images. This password can then be changed on the image by using the Disk Utility GUI application or from the command line. To change an encrypted image's password from the GUI, you can drag the image file into the source list for disk utility, highlight it, and then from the Images menu, select "Change Password...". Or, with no image selected in the Disk Utility source pane, select "Change Password..." and you will be prompted to navigate to a disk image in the file system. To change a password from a command line using the chpass verb:

```
$ hdiutil chpass ~/Desktop/mySecureImage.sparsimage
Enter password to access "mySecureImage.sparseimage":
Enter a new password to secure "mySecureImage.sparseimage":
Re-enter new password:
```

Whether changing the password from the command line or graphical interface, the original password must be known in order to successfully complete the operation. So that begs the question: if an end user can change a password on a disk image, and that password must be known to access data on the image, what's to prevent the user from locking out you, the administrator, from accessing the data's contents? Well, nothing, and that is likely a problem in an environment that seeks to use encrypted disk images to secure company data. A loss in accessibility to company data represents a security failure, and therefore is likely unacceptable, depending on the company's attitude to risk and the impact of such unavailability. Well, luckily there are some steps that you can take to protect your organization against this scenario. Apple's disk image implementation has full support for certificate authentication based upon PKE (Public Key Encryption), which we've discussed elsewhere in this book (see Chapter 6). When creating a new disk image, it is possible to specify a certificate that can be used to authenticate an image, rather than (or in addition to) a password. When an image is created in such a fashion, as long as a user has access to the certificate's secret, its private key, then the user will have access to the data on the encrypted image. This means that as an administrator, you can generate a disk image for each of your users, and these users can access the disk image via a standard text-based password. By passing a certificate for secondary authentication, you can ensure that you retain access to the data even after the user has changed the default password. As an administrator, you are no longer a subject to the loss of data: as long as your retain the private key that corresponds to the certificate that set upon the image at creation time, then you will be able to decrypt the data and mount the disk image.

To accomplish such a task, it is first necessary to create our identity, that is, our certificate and private key. This is a standard private key + certificate combination that is used in the majority of SSL-related tasks. In the case of creating an identity for securing disk images, it is recommend to use a key/cert pair that is dedicated to this task. That is, don't re-use the same certificate that you use to secure your website or your mail system for instance. That being said, you can use these same identities if you absolutely must. The identity that you utilize for disk image authentication does not necessarily need to be signed by a trusted root Certificate Authority (CA), though if you maintain your own CA, you can sign to provide validation, we can specify that an image respect both a password as well as a certificate; if a certificate is not present in a user's keychain, then a password fallback can be used. This is perfect for our needs; we can use the certificate when creating all of our images, which will grant us global access to them all, regardless of each image's individual password. End users will continue to utilize their own password for the disk image, even changing them, and will never need access to our private key. If the end user leaves or forgets the password, we can simply recover it using our own closely guarded private key.

> **CAUTION:** By granting a single identity access to all disk images, it becomes absolutely imperative that the certificate's private key be closely guarded at all times. If this key is compromised, so too are all images created with its certificate.

To create a disk image that utilizes both a password and a certificate for authentication, we simply add an additional option, -agentpass, to our previous command. When the -agentpass flag is specified, hdiutil will prompt for an interactive password:

```
$ hdiutil create -size 8G -fs "Journaled HFS+" -volname "myImage" -type SPARSE
 -encryption AES-256 -certificate ~/Desktop/MyCo\ Disk\ Encryption\ Identity.cer
 -agentpass ~/Desktop/mySecureImage.sparseimage
Enter a new password to secure "mySecureImage.sparseimage":
Re-enter new password:
created: /Users/hunterbj/Desktop/mySecureImage.sparseimage
```

If the image is being made programmatically, then the -stdinpass flag can be used to read data in from standard input:

```
$ echo -n 'myPassword1$' | hdiutil create -size 8G -fs "Journaled HFS+" -volname
 "myImage" -type SPARSE -encryption AES-256 -certificate ~/Desktop/MyCo\ Disk\
 Encryption\ Identity.cer -stdinpass ~/Desktop/mySecureImage.sparseimage
created: /Users/hunterbj/Desktop/mySecureImage.sparseimage
```

From here on, whenever the image is mounted, disk utility will first search through all of a user's keychains for the corresponding private key; if it is not found, the user will be prompted to enter a password. If you need to mount the image from a machine that doesn't have an active console, you can specify the path to the keychain using hdiutil:

```
$ hdiutil attach -recover /Library/Keychains/MyCo\ Disk\ Encryption.keychain
 ~/Desktop/mySecureImage.sparseimage

/dev/disk1          GUID_partition_scheme
/dev/disk1s1            EFI
/dev/disk1s2            Apple_HFS                   /Volumes/myImage
```

In this example, we utilize the -recover option and specify the path to a keychain file that contains the appropriate identity. In this case, we are referencing a keychain that was made specifically for this purpose, "MyCo Disk Encryption.keychain" stored in the global library. This keychain contains solely the certificate/key pair that makes up the MyCo Disk Encryption Identity that we previously made. By creating a unique keychain for this, we can specify a very strong passphrase for this keychain and store it in a secure place. In the event that data recover is needed due to a lost password, the keychain can be imported on the administrators machine and facilitate access to the data.

> **TIP:** Or, the identity can be stored in a standard password-protected PKCS#12 container, which can be directly exported from Keychain Access, and then re-imported when needed.

Thus far, we've demonstrated how to create sparse images using `hdiutil create` and passing the -format option a value of SPARSE. However, there are a number of other formats that are worth knowing about, and each requires a specific identifier to be passed to the -format flag. Table 9–1 illustrates the available formats.

Table 9–1. *New Image Formats Used with 'diskutil create'*

Format	Comment
UDIF	This is a standard read/write fixed-size disk image.
UDTO	This is format is the equivalent of "DVD/CD Master" in the Disk Utility GUI.
SPARSE	A sparse disk image.
SPARSEBUNDLE	A sparse bundle disk image.

These options may be very familiar, and for good reason: the list is identical to the options presented in the Disk Utility GUI. However, there are a few additional properties that can be specified from the command line when dealing with sparse bundle images that are worth noting. As mentioned, a sparsebundle image is actually comprised of numerous separate files, or bands, which comprise the entire volume. By default, each band in a sparse bundle image is 8MB. Apple likely chose this default size because it is a good compromise between small and large file access. The truth of the matter is that one size doesn't necessarily fit all, and for some data sets, a small band size can adversely affect performance. This is especially true in large data sets. Consider a 500GB sparse bundle image; in such a scenario, the sparse bundle would actually contain over 60,000 bands! For instance, a backup system could process and protect 15,000 32MB bands much faster than it could process 60,000 8MB bands. Another situation where a smaller band size can adversely performance is if you plan to store larger files on your image volume. If you plan to routinely store files that are in excess of 8MB, then can be adversely affected due to the extra overhead needed for the additional I/O operations. Even though you are only accessing a single file on the image volume, the underlying file system will have to open up the individual bands that store that segment of the file. For instance, a 128MB video, just a few minutes of HD, will actually require 16 file requests. That's a fair amount of overhead, so the user may benefit from a larger band size. To create a sparse bundle with a custom band size, you use the -imagekey flag, which accepts key value pairs. For instance, to create a sparsebundle image that utilizes 32MB bands, we can use the following syntax:

```
$ hdiutil create -size 8g -type SPARSEBUNDLE -imagekey sparse-band-size=65536 -fs
"JHFS+" -volname "myImage" ~/Desktop/myImage.sparsebundle
```

With this command, we are creating a sparse bundle image with a maximum size of 8GB, a "Journaled HFS" + file system (for which JHFS+ is a shortcut), and we have specified a band size via the `sparse-band-size` key. With this key, we specify the number of 512 byte blocks that exist on a given band. In this case, we have specified 65,536 blocks. At 512 bytes per block, we have a total band size of 32MB (512 x 65,536 = 33,554,432). You might be thinking that 33,554,432 bytes is more that 32MB, keep in mind we're operating at a low level here, and thus are operating at base2. So if we were to be completely accurate, we would say that we're specifying a band size of 32 mebibytes (MiB). With such an image, we are helping to improve the efficiency of data as laid out on the sparse bundle. The negative side to this is that we have now effectively raised our minimum backup size as well. With an 8MiB band, a small file change will only result in a backup of 8MiB. On a disk image with 32MiB bands, even a small change will require the entire band to be backed up, so that the same backup procedure would be at least 32MiB. Because of this, choosing a band size that is overly large can result in inefficiencies as well. Really, the exact value will depend on the environment, and values can range from 2048 (1MiB bands) to 262144 (128MiB bands). If in doubt, just use the default values, they work out pretty well, and they are the officially supported size. If you are an administrator and feel like an 8MiB band is not optimal for your environment, then you have the power to fine-tune the size to best fit your use-case.

And that, in a (rather large) nutshell, is the landscape for utilizing disk images for data encryption. Hopefully we have laid out a good blueprint for you to follow, and have established a good fundamental understanding of their strengths and weaknesses. Likewise, we hope we have imparted upon you the knowledge required to utilize disk-image encryption to ensure confidentiality of your data, and as well as providing fail-safes in the form of certificates so that encrypted data can be retrieved in a worse-case scenario.

Encrypting User Data Using FileVault

FileVault is a technology in OS X that allows users to seamlessly safeguard their personal data vis-à-vis encryption. FileVault is configured on an account-by-account basis, and once enabled on an account, all contents of the respective user's home directory are encrypted behind the scenes. In the event that a computer is physically compromised, any accounts on the system that have FileVault enabled will maintain a rather high probability of avoiding compromise of confidentiality, subject to the strength of the password used to encrypt the data, and whether the machine was logged in and running at the time of theft. In the case of FileVault, this password is equivalent to the user's login password. Without access to the password, provided that it is of relatively secure strength (8+ characters with a number, capital letter and at least one special character), the data stands a good chance of remaining secure.

Although you may be unfamiliar with FileVault itself, you actually already possess a good deal of knowledge as to the inner workings of the technology, provided of course that you have been paying attention. In case you haven't guessed, FileVault technology is at its heart based upon the use of disk image encryption. If you skipped the previous section. Using Disk Images as Encrypted Data Stores, this would probably be a good time to stop and flip a few (dozen) pages back.

When FileVault is enabled for a user, the entire contents of the user's home directory are relocated from the standard location of /Users, and is instead transferred onto a disk image in the form of an encrypted sparse bundle and stored in at /Users/username/username.sparsebundle. When a FileVaulted user logs into an OS X workstation, the system will attempt to mount the encrypted sparse bundle image stored at this location with the password provided by the user at login, and the respective image is then mounted at the traditional home directory path: /Users/username. This technique provides for a completely user-transparent system; from their perspective, their home directory is found at the usual location of /Users/username. However, unbeknownst to them (or beknownst), any changes to files or subdirectories in there home are instead written to the sparse bundle image in an encrypted form. When the user logs out, the home directory is unmounted, at which point the data only resides on the disk in a secure encrypted form.

> **CAUTION:** When a user is logged in, whether FileVault is enabled or not, the user's data is accessible in an unencrypted form at their home directory path, and as such is susceptible to malware or other runtime exploitation: access to the data is controlled solely by POSIX or ACL filesystem access controls.

The assumption to all of this working, of course, is that the user's login password is identical to that used to encrypt the contents of the FileVault image. By default this is the case, but it is certainly not an unconditional certainty. In this respect, the situation is not unlike that which we previously discussed for the login keychain. In both situations, the ability for the OS to seamlessly access the protected data, whether contents of the login keychain, or contents of the FileVault image, is correlated to the condition that the login password be identical to that used for encryption. The scenarios for these two passwords (login + login.keychain or login + FileVault) to become out of sync are identical. Like the login keychain, if a user changes his password locally on the machine, whether through a forced password change at the login window, or through a voluntary action of utilizing the Accounts System Preference pane to manually change a password, the corresponding login keychain and FileVault disk image will be subsequently updated behind the scenes. However, just like the login keychain, if the user's password is reset by an external system, such as a web interface, network protocol (AFP or Kerberos for instance), an alternate computer, or by a network administrator, such a change will be external to the purview of FileVault, and as such, the user's login password and FileVault will be out-of-sync. When this occurs with the login keychain in 10.6, as we have previously discussed, the user will be prompted to update their login keychain password (go back to Figure 9–2), provided that they can recall their former password. In the case that they don't know or can't recall their previous password, say for instance a network admin reset their password because of this very reason, then the contents of the login keychain are unrecoverable, and the user is presented the option to create a new fresh login keychain. In a FileVault scenario though, the fail-safe isn't quite as simplistic, as after all we are talking about the entire contents of a user's home directory, rather than simply a matter of losing their stored passwords. Because of this, if a user with FileVault has their password reset, and cannot remember their old password, they will not be able to access their data without administrator intervention. When their password is reset externally, upon next login the user will be prompted to enter their own password, as shown in Figure 9–10.

Figure 9.10. *Loginwindow FileVault password recovery dialog*

Luckily, it's pretty easy to reset a user's FileVault password, provided of course that you have access to the master password, which we'll discuss in depth in just a bit. To reset a user's password, an administrator needs to login to the machine, and then can use the standard password reset facility as shown in the Accounts System Preference Pane as shown in Figure 9–11.

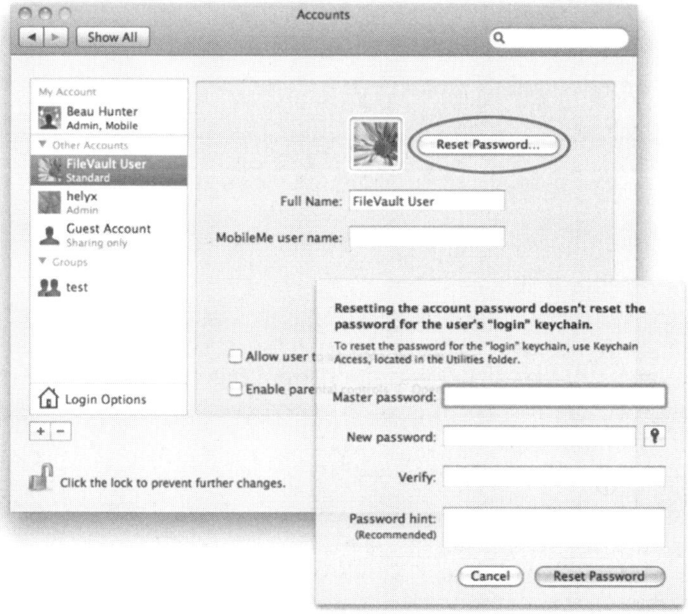

Figure 9–11. *The password reset dialog presented in the Accounts system preference pane*

Enabling FileVault for a User

Enabling FileVault for a user is a pretty easy endeavor, and is accomplished on a small scale through the Security System Preference pane. Inside of this System Preference you will find a tab labeled "FileVault," as one might expect. As seen in 9–12, the interface presented is fairly minimalistic, and provides for only two buttons: one to change the master password, and one to enable FileVault for the current logged-in user.

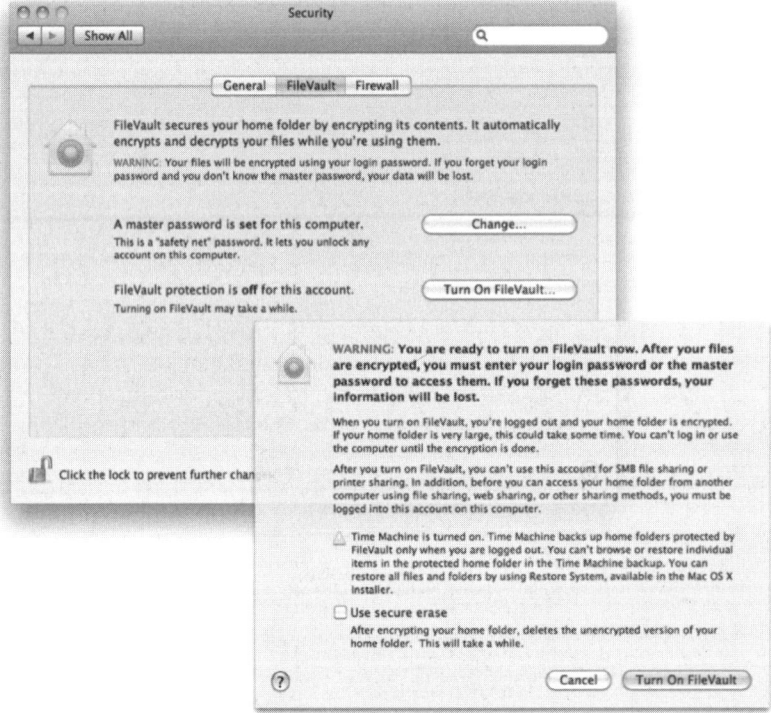

Figure 9–12. *The FileVault tab found in the Security system preference pane (back), and associated dialog when enabling the feature (front).*

We'll discuss the master password in just a bit, and the second button's function is fairly obvious though there are a few specifics that are good to know. When you click the button to Turn On FileVault, the system will convert the current user's home directory from a standard local-storage account to one that uses encryption. Upon doing so, the system will inform the user that it needs to log out to properly convert this account. When this happens, a new FileVault encrypted sparse bundle will be created, and the contents of the user's home directory will be copied to this new encrypted volume. This process involves first copying all of the user's data, and provided that that operation succeeds, will then remove the unencrypted user data from the volume. The primary implication to this process means that in order for it to succeed, there must be sufficient disk space to account for a temporary duplication of the user's data; if the user has 20GB of data in their home directory, and only 10GB of space is available on the drive, the operation will fail. In this case, the FileVault conversion will only successfully finish if at least 20GB of space is available. Bear in mind that this conversion will only temporarily occupy this space: once the users unencrypted data is removed from the volume, available space on the volume will be comparable to that before the operation took place. When enabling FileVault, the user is also given the opportunity to perform a secure erase of the existing, unencrypted home directory data (as shown in the picture above). With this option selected, the system will not only delete the existing home directory and its files from the disk, but it will also overwrite the contents of the data on the disk, preventing or at least reducing, the possibility of recovery of the data. When FileVault is enabled for a user, a few small changes are made to their directory information. OS X utilizes a few attributes in a user record that specifies the location of the user's home directory. For a normal, local user, this is limited to the NFSHomeDirectory attribute, which contains a simple path to the home directory, consider the output of the command `dscl . read /Users/hunterbj | grep -i home` :

`NFSHomeDirectory: /Users/hunterbj`

When FileVault is enabled for the user, an additional attribute, HomeDirectory is populated:

```
HomeDirectory: <home_dir><url>file://localhost/Users/hunterbj
/hunterbj.sparsebundle</url></home_dir>
NFSHomeDirectory: /Users/hunterbj
```

In this case, a URL-style path has been provided that provides the system the path to the sparsebundle image. When the user logs in, the system will mount this image at the path specified by the `NFSHomeDirectory` attribute, in this case /Users/hunterbj, the standard OS X user home directory path.

In a larger scale managed environment, it may be desirable to enable FileVault across a large spread of users, or computers. To facilitate this, FileVault fully supports MCX management. If you are unfamiliar with MCX, or Managed Client OS X, it can best be summed up as a technology supported by Mac OS X Clients and managed by OS X servers through the implementation of Open Directory. As its name implies, MCX is a system that allows for the management of various preferences and permissions applied to a user base, and can be applied to individual users, groups of users, individual computers, or groups of computers. MCX is discussed in more detail in Chapter 16.

Due to the nature of FileVault, it will most likely be desirable to deploy FileVault settings at the computer group level, in which case as an administrator you might want to make a computer group named "Mobile Computers". FileVault as a technology is typically targeted towards laptop computers after all, your companies desktop computers that perhaps utilize network home directories, or are otherwise physically secured are less apt to needing the protection of encryption (though certainly this is not the case in all environments). Thus, by enabling FileVault for all Mobile Computers, whenever a user logs into a laptop that is a member of this group, their home directory will be protected using encryption. Figure 9–13 below shows the MCX setting utilized in the Workgroup Manager application to apply FileVault settings to a multitude of users/computers.

Figure 9-13. *Deploying FileVault MCX settings Using Workgroup Manager*

For more information on using MCX management, refer to *Enterprise Mac Administrator's Guide*, by Charles Edge, Beau Hunter, and Zack Smith (Apress, 2009).

CAUTION: In order to ensure access to the FileVault encrypted image, the System will store the FileVault keys in memory. This leads to a potential problem, as certain attack vectors may be able to pull this information from memory, such as cold boot attacks or by exploiting interfaces that provide DMA (direct memory access), such as FireWire. Additionally, another feature of OS X, safe sleep, results in the contents of RAM being written to disk. Because the System memory contains the FileVault key, it is possible for an attacker to extract this information from your hard drive in the event that they can obtain your machine while it is in a sleep state. To avoid this, enable the "Secure virtual memory" option found under the Security System Preference pane, which will ensure that any memory contents, whether from standard virtual memory swapping or from a saved sleep image, are encrypted. To protect against cold-boot or DMA attacks, ensure that you log out of your computer when in transit or unattended, and that only trusted devices are plugged into your machine. Firewire-based DMA attacks can be prevented by enabling an Open Firmware password on the machine.

The FileVault Master Password

As we discussed in the previous section, there is a potential liability factor that a company assumes when deploying encryption of user data, as it means that there is a higher potential for the loss of sensitive company data, simply due to the potential loss of encryption keys. However, as we learned previously, companies can mitigate this liability by using a secondary access provision through the use of certificates. Fortunately, by default, FileVault uses such a certificate to provide a backdoor to this data. In the FileVault context, the terminology that Apple applies to this is a master password, and in fact, a master password must be set before a user can enable FileVault. If such a master password is not yet set, then an administrator will be prompted to provide one when enabling FileVault for the first time. This master password is in fact a FileVault-specific keychain whose contents consist solely of a certificate and private key identity that is used specifically for FileVault certificate-based authentication. The master password is simply the password that is used to secure the FileVault keychain itself. With this setup, the master password can be rotated without concern that existing encrypted disk images need have the new password applied to it. As we all know (hopefully?), it's a good idea in security sensitive environments to routinely rotate sensitive passwords, and certainly the backdoor password to decrypt company data qualifies as sensitive. If to change the password you needed to go out and touch every single encrypted disk image protected by this password, the ability for administrators to rotate passwords would be significantly restricted. Thankfully, this is not needed: the certificate used to decrypt data never changes, only the passcode to locally access the certificate does. There is however, another consideration that need be realized here to successfully deploy FileVault at an organization level. By default, when FileVault is enabled on a computer, the FileVault identity, the certificate and correlating private key, is dynamically generated, and stored in a keychain protected by the provided Master Password at /Library/Keychains/FileVaultMaster.keychain. Likewise, the certificate itself, which is typically public domain, is stored at /Library/Keychains/FileVaultMaster.cer. While this certificate is also available in the FileVaultMaster keychain, placing the certificate itself in the filesystem allows users to enable FileVault with the certificate backdoor without the need to first provide the master password to access the same cert that is stored in the keychain. Well, you might be noticing the problem here: if the FileVaultMaster keychain is automatically generated on each individual client machine on an ad-hoc basis, then there is a mathematical probability that no two client machines will have the same identity. This presents a significant problem when deploying FileVault on a large scale: if every machine utilizes a unique FileVault identity, which is used to recover a FileVault image, then an administrator will need to track every separate identity for every machine to ensure that they can recover the encrypted data should the user's password become unavailable. While it might not be terribly difficult to securely maintain a small number of FileVault identities, economies of scale will show it to be a detrimental strategy to provide backdoor access to encrypted data across the fleet. FileVault is at its core a client-side technology, and has no centralized key-management capabilities. Luckily, there is an easy solution to this problem, and that is to preemptively deploy a "master" FileVaultMaster keychain to all of your clients prior to enabling FileVault for any users on the system. If every machine has the same FileVault identity, then administrators need only maintain a single identity to unlock all user data across the fleet. Alternatively a number of identities can be maintained based on company logistics to mitigate the impact should the identity be compromised.

Deploying the centralized identity isn't a terribly difficult task. To accomplish this, all an administrator needs to do is to set a master password on the base image used for deployment. Alternatively, the FileVaultMaster.cer and FileVaultMaster.keychain files, found at /Library/Keychain, can be copied off of a designated machine that has had a master password set to a secure value, and then a package installer can be created for these two files and deployed. By deploying these two files to all machines in the fleet, any newly created FileVault encrypted images, regardless of the machine, will have a the common backdoor. In the event that an administrator seeks to rotate the master password, they can simply update the password used to protect the FileVaultMaster.keychain, and redeploy the keychain file with the new password to all of the machines. Because the underlying certificate and private key remains intact and unaltered, the existing FileVaultMaster.keychain can simply be overwritten by the new file. This is a very important measure to take when deploying FileVault across your organization. If you depend on the FileVaultMaster.keychain that is enabled by each individual client, management will become an arduous task, as you will need to ensure that you have access to every single machine's individual keychain, which can easily turn into a nightmare. By deploying a consistent keychain across all clients, you ensure that you have a single identity that can unlock all encrypted data across your fleet, short of individual user's keychains, for reasons discussed in the previous section.

> **NOTE:** Because a certificate backdoor is applied to a FileVault encrypted image at creation time, it is imperative that you deploy the global FileVaultMaster.keychain to a machine prior to any users having FileVault enabled on the machine. If a user has FileVault enabled prior to deploying the global keychain, if you overwrite the existing auto-generated FileVaultMaster.keychain on the client, any previously existing FileVault images will not have a backdoor access capability.

Limitations of Sparse Images and Reclaiming Space

There are some ramifications that come with using sparse images, whether file-based or bundle based, and while this discussion might belong in the previous section, these considerations are more prescient when sparse images are used in a FileVault environment, mainly due to the larger data sets that are involved when the entirety of a user's home folder is placed onto a sparse image file. We mentioned in the previous section that one benefit to using sparse images and bundle images is that, outside of minimal formatting information, they only occupy as much disk space as the data that is present on the volume. This actually is not 100% accurate. You see, as you add data to a sparse volume, the image file or bundle will grow as needed. The problem is that once the data is allocated to the image, it will remain allocated, even if the underlying data is deleted off of the image's volume. Thus, if you download a 2GB file to your desktop, your sparse bundle will grow accordingly and occupy an additional 2GB on disk. When you remove that 2GB file, the disk image still occupies that additional space, and doesn't shrink at as one might at first expect. This has important ramifications for a user home directory, especially if they begin to run out of drive space. Common user perception is that in such a case, you simply remove files and your hard drive reclaims that space. Well, with FileVault enabled (and sparse images in general), that is not the case.

To get around this, when a user logs out of their account and there is a large amount of such unnecessary waste, FileVault will automatically reclaim any missing space, in the process presenting the user with a dialog box, shown in Figure 9–14. During this operation, the sparse image will be compacted such that the image file will occupy only as much space as the data it contains. As it was in the beginning, it will again be.

Figure 9–15. *Reclaiming unused space occupied by FileVault*

It's a nice feature to have, but unfortunately, the system only executes this operation for FileVault images, and not standard encrypted disk images. For manually created encrypted images like this, it is possible to reclaim this disk space from the command line, using the previously discussed hdiutil command as seen here:

```
$ hdiutil compact ~/Desktop/myimage.sparseimage
Starting to compact...
Reclaiming free space...
................................................................................
................................................................
Finishing compaction...
................................................................................
................................................................
Reclaimed 404 MB out of 7.7 GB possible.
```

In this example, we have reclaimed roughly 400MB off the disk, though certainly the results can be much more dramatic than that when run on a FileVault image for a user hasn't logged out for a while. The amount of time needed to perform the operation will vary depending upon the amount of space needing to be reclaimed.

> **NOTE:** Due to the fact that the option to reclaim disk space unnecessarily used by FileVault is only presented when a user logs out, if the user never logs out, the system will never reclaim the lost space.

Full Disk Encryption

In some cases, the technologies we've mentioned will not meet the burden of criteria of a corporation's security policies. While FileVault on a technology level provides very strong encryption, it is not without its own limitations. At its heart, FileVault is a user-specific technology, and in fact it only seeks to protect an individual user's data. The main issue is that it leaves to chance the idea that a user will actually utilize their own home directory for document storage. In fact, users have a number of places where they can tuck away data, and certainly not all of these fall under the purview of their own home directory. Consider for instance the directory found at /Users/Shared, which is globally writeable, and to which there are no provisions preventing a user from saving data. While at first glance the obvious thought might be to prevent a user from utilizing this directory by restricting write access, and this certainly may prove to be an approachable angle in your environment. The inherent problem with this strategy is that it goes against standard system conventions where-in the expected behavior is for users to have the ability to modify this directory. Third party software therefore that relies on this expectation may then find itself non-functional or impaired with such a restriction in place. Secondly, if the user is an administrator user (which you would generally want to avoid if possible), they have the potential ability to save data on local disks wherever they please. This then, leaves the security provided by FileVault (or any encrypted disk images for that matter) up to the discretion of the end user, and invariably, this introduces a margin-for-error.

> **NOTE:** If a user is provided local administrative privileges on an OS X client, as an administrator they will have the ability to save data wherever they like. However, if standard file system permissions such as POSIX or AC's do not allow write access to the user, they will first be prompted to enter their credentials as the Finder will have to use the security framework to escalate to root and bypass them. This dialog is not available in every operation: for instance, if you try to save a document to a normally restricted folder, the save operation will not prompt for authentication and therefore the save will fail. The user can though then use the Finder to move the files wherever they would please. This applies to Xsan volumes as well: so be advised that if your user's are admins, they have potential free reign over the entire Xsan volume.

Even if your users are perfect little souls, and reliably utilize only their home directory for their data storage, OS X utilizes a number of caching mechanisms, outside of the user's control, that can result in sensitive data residing outside of the home directory. For instance, the directories /private/tmp and /private/var/tmp are commonly used as support folders for programs. Likewise, the directory /private/var/folders is utilized as a universal cache store for many Cocoa applications. If the ramifications of this aren't clear, the problem is that when an application deals with data, it may, depending on the application, store a temporary representation of the data in its cache. If this data is written to disk in a non-encrypted temporary folder, than there is a potential for that sensitive data to be recovered from the cache files themselves. While it is often a fairly technical endeavor to recover relevant data from an applications cache store, it *is* possible, and in some environments this is an unacceptable liability. For such environments, FileVault simply might not provide enough coverage.

Another problem that may arise might be in the case that you or your users are prone to using removable media for data transfer or storage. Because FileVault only protects a user's home directory, the removable media is typically outside of its purview, and therefore not encrypted. The exception here of course is if you're using OS X's external account feature, in which case the home directory and therefore the FileVault encrypted sparse bundle is stored on the removable media. Outside of that scenario, the only native facilities that OS X offers to protect data on removable media, is an encrypted disk image, but this solution is typically cumbersome, and requires the user to first insert the thumb-drive and mount the disk image, which isn't a problem for the attentive user, but in large-scale or highly sensitive environments where data absolutely must be encrypted, the extra steps to mount the disk image and intentionally save their documents in the proper folder introduces an unacceptable margin of error because it cannot absolutely guarantee that all relevant data is encrypted. The most vulnerable types of storage to theft or loss mind you are of course removable storage, and therefore encryption here is key as well.

Thus, the need may arise, depending on your requirements, for data encryption facilities outside of those found in OS X's native toolset. The good news is that there are a number of options, from respected companies, that offer current encryption solutions for the OS X platform. Naturally each product has its own strengths and weaknesses, and this fact makes it very important to choose the right product depending on your needs (which makes it important to know your needs in the first place!) In this section we'll take a look at some encryption options that you have available outside of OS X's native tools.

Check Point

Check Point is a full disk encryption (FDE) technology for OS X. By full disk encryption, we mean that any and all data written to a particular file system, regardless of where in the file system it is written to, is fully encrypted. One key aspect to Check Point's solution is that it has full support for booting OS X from an encrypted volume. To absolutely ensure that all potentially data stored on a volume is encrypted this is a key need, and the same support cannot be said for all the products that we discuss throughout this section.

Check Point accomplishes this task by utilizing a custom built boot-loader that runs prior to loading OS X. A boot loader is simply a very small, efficient program that is responsibly for initiating the Operating System boot process. It loads a small portion of the operating system into RAM, which then initiates a long number of events that ultimately leads to a running operating system. By utilizing a custom boot loader, Check Point can interject into the operation of a computer very early on in the boot sequence, in fact, before a single bit of OS X ever hits the processor. With FDE, interjecting at this early stage is the key to booting off of an encrypted disk, because at its lowest level, the EFI (extensible firmware interface) firmware found at the core of every Macintosh does not currently understand any encryption. If a disk is encrypted, then when a system first boots up, EFI will not be able to access any boot loaders written to an encrypted volume, and will therefore be unable to access the disk to boot up the system which it contains.

The key then, is to intervene in the communication process between EFI and the encrypted boot volume, and this is exactly what Check Points boot loader achieves. To do this, the Check Point software creates a tiny, unencrypted volume that contains solely an unencrypted boot loader. When the system first boots, the EFI reads in this unencrypted boot loader on the disk, and then will pass it control to begin booting the system. What EFI doesn't know is that instead of booting OS X in the normal fashion, Check Points boot loader will first provide a minimal pre-boot environment that provides a very basic interface which allows a user to authenticate and there-by gain access to the encrypted disk. If a user never authenticates, then the disks contents will remain encrypted and secure. Once a user authenticates, the system will load the standard OS X boot loader from the encrypted partition, and booting ala the standard OS X experience will commence. To facilitate writing the encrypted disk, the Check Point pre-boot environment installs a custom kernel extension (kext) that is installed into the Mac OS X environment. When booting, EFI uses the pre-boot driver to retrieve the kernel and mkext (an mkext is a bundle of kext files) cache from the encrypted disk. Mkext caches are used very early on in the boot process by the kernel to load basic functionality; in this case, it includes a driver to decode encrypted data on the main filesystem, and continues booting. With such an implementation, all OS writes or reads to and from the disk will be encrypted and decrypted at a very low level in the system; providing a high degree of transparency to the actual environment as witnessed by subsequent processes running on the system. The encryption is completely transparent to any applications, and more importantly, to the end user.

On its back-end Check Point FDE utilizes AES-256bit encryption, the same government-approved standard available for use with encrypted disk images. Authentication provided by the pre-boot environment supports a number of different facilities. Most commonly, a standard username and password can be utilized to provide access to the data. Alternatively, dynamic tokens, such as RSA or crypto card, are supported, allowing for very secure one-time token authentication. Regardless of the method used, backdoor access can be obtained by administrators or privileged users in order to gain access to the data: therefore the recovery of the data is not solely dependent on the user remembering their password. Likewise, if a user forgets their password in the field, the product has full support for remote recovery even if the laptop does not have an active connection to the Internet. This gives administrators the ability to restore access to a remote user via a standard voice-confirmation phone call. By granting temporary access, the user can regain access to the data and then reset their password. This is a pretty cool feature, and does improve accessibility, another critical component of information security.

However, remote recovery systems are not without flaws, and can open up a can of worms, allowing an attacker to socially engineer the help desk or gain permanent backdoor credentials without having to compromise the user's password or token.

In the end, Check Point is a very secure and robust product, and has very manageable features, particularly when working in large environments.

PGP Encryption

PGP, or Pretty Good Privacy, is a well-known and trusted encryption technology. Perhaps most commonly used for the purpose of encrypting and digitally signing e-mails, PGP actually offers a wealth of security and privacy features that can help users and system administrators alike ensure that their data is protected. While PGP started out as a small grassroots type of technology, it has since spawned into a wide variety of implementations, thanks largely due to its formal adoption as a standard in the form of OpenPGP, as defined in RFC 4880. A number of freeware and commercial applications have grown off of this standard, and their support and features range far and wide from digital signing of files, to encryption of remote network connections, such as network file servers or instant messaging sessions. As you may have guessed, this includes the ability for FDE provided through the commercial product PGP Whole Disk Encryption (WDE) from the PGP Corporation (www.pgp.com). Like Check Point, PGP WDE provides full support for OS X, and can be used to ensure that the volumes attached to your system are fully protected (as the name might imply!). Full disk protection is provided through a very similar approach to Check Point, and utilizes a custom boot loader that interjects very early on in the boot process to provide the ability for pre-boot authentication; just like Check Point, the user is prompted to authenticate prior to the system being able to read the OS X system on an encrypted disk, and therefore boot off of it.

PGP whole disk encryption (WDE) has a very robust feature set, and supports numerous encryption algorithms, including the familiar AES-256 algorithm that we have seen throughout this chapter. PGP also supports a very strong hashing algorithm in the form of SHA-2-256, which provides very strong encryption on the stored keys themselves. Upon first configuring whole disk encryption, the PGP system will first create a public and private key which operate in a similar manner to other PKI systems that we have discussed in this chapter: the public key is, as its name implies, a public file that can be distributed to anyone that might intend to send you encrypted data. The private key is essential to the decryption of any data generated with the public key; and therefore should be guarded with utmost care. The private key itself is protected with your passphrase, and this passphrase is required in order to utilize the private key to decrypt data. Once these keys are created, it is then possible to utilize them to begin to encrypt data stored on your local disks. Unfortunately, unlike Check Point, PGP WDE does not support encryption of individual partitions, and must instead be used to protect an entire disk. This is likely desirable in most environments anyway, as few corporate laptops will have multiple partitions, but is worth noting. For this purpose instead a separate product, PGP Virtual Disk, can be used to create virtual encrypted disks, not dissimilar in concept to OS X's encrypted disk images, though implemented in a more secure fashion due to PGP's stronger hashing algorithms.

While PGP Whole Disk Encryption provides for strong security in and of itself, the strength of the solution is greatly improved through the use of PGP management suite: PGP Universal Server. PGP Universal Server allows administrators to define and enforce various security policies, say for instance requiring any removable media to utilize encryption. Unfortunately, this is also where PGP Whole Disk Encryption on OS X falls short. While Universal Server can be used to manage OS X machines, there are a number of features that are not yet available for this platform, and unfortunately some of them are pretty key features. For instance, we just provided the example of using PHP Universal Server to enforce a policy which requires that removable media be encrypted. Unfortunately, this useful feature is only available on Windows machines. Additionally limitations include limited Directory Services integration (such as Active Directory single-sign on), no support for hardware token authentication (such as Smart Cards), and no support for password lock out policies based on failed attempts.

The lack of these features may prove to be an issue in your environment, and then again, it may turn out to be a non-issue. It really all comes down to your needs. Certainly, features found in alternate platforms but currently unavailable in OS X will slowly make their way into the product but the most important and key feature is that it provides a method to ensure that all data on your laptop or desktop's primary disk is protected with strong encrypted, and that alone provides for a good increase in security over a standard OS X system.

TrueCrypt

TrueCrypt is another product that supports full disk encryption in OS X. Unfortunately, unlike both Check Point and PGP WDE, TrueCrypt does not support encryption of an OS X system volume (this feature is limited to Windows OS), but can instead only be used to encrypt secondary volumes. This means that its use as a utility to provide full data protection of a running system is somewhat limited. However, that isn't to say that it doesn't have a use; it certainly does. One primary benefit provided by TrueCrypt can be found in its cross platform support, which includes Windows, Mac OS X, and Linux. Because it doesn't support encrypting a system volume, its usage will be primarily relegated to encrypting external or removable media, and for this it serves as a very good method for exchanging files between platforms via an external volume. For instance, consider a USB thumbdrive. In a traditionally scenario, an OS will format the thumbdrive with a file system, typically FAT32, and any data written to this volume will be completely unprotected. We mentioned earlier that you can then use an encrypted disk image stored on this volume to provide data protection. However, this can be very cumbersome, and isn't terribly transparent. A thumbdrive instead formatted with TrueCrypt will provide a much more seamless experience for a user: once they insert the thumbdrive and provide a password, the volume will be presented to the user as if no encryption is present, and any data read from or written to the volume will be encrypted on the fly.

A key feature to the TrueCrypt system when used for full disk encryption comes in the form of plausible deniability. Plausible deniability is the concept that the presence of data on a volume cannot be explicitly proven or disproven, and TrueCrypt implements a few features that make plausible deniability possible. The first such feature is really a lack of a feature: most encryption algorithms leave behind a signature, which is simply a small amount of data that identifies a block of data as encrypted data. This is typically used to identify the type of encryption used on a chunk of data. TrueCrypt utilizes no such signature and as a result, data on a volume by all accounts appears completely random when viewed at a low level. On top of this, TrueCrypt has another feature that further strengthens the ability to provide plausible deniability: hidden volumes. Using this feature, it is possible to create a hidden volume on a disk that cannot be accessed unless referenced with specific credentials. A hidden volume will co-exist inside of a standard TrueCrypt volume, which utilizes different credentials. The appropriate volume to mount then will be determined based upon the credentials that are provided. Without direct knowledge of a second, hidden volume, its presence will be undetectable to a hacker or malfeasant, and only the primary outer volume will be immediately apparent. This capability is facilitated by the fact that when TrueCrypt encrypts a volume, the entirety of the volume is encrypted and any free space on the volume is filled with random data (which is also encrypted). This random data then is indistinguishable from actual encrypted data, and therefore serves to mask the presence of this hidden volume data. The need for plausible deniability may become evident in the event that a user becomes subject to coercion or extortion. In such an event where a user is absolutely forced to provide their password, the use of a hidden volume allows the user to reveal their password, and thereby only expose data on the outer volume, which would contain files to provide the allusion of validity. Without direct knowledge of the hidden volume, the perpetrator will only gain access to the outer volume and will be operating under the assumption that the user has succumbed to demands. Because the hidden volume is written inside of the outer volume, its disk utilization will not be represented by the outer volume; so the perpetrator will not be able to induce deceit based upon missing capacity on the volume (if the outer volume only showed 512MB of space and the thumbdrive is 1GB, suspicions would likely arise). Plausible deniability becomes then a very handy feature in the event that extremely sensitive data is in transit on a disk and its presence should not only be included, but also undetectable.

WinMagic SecureDoc

SecureDoc is a promising player in the Mac encryption game, and has a compelling product. The system operates in much the same way as previously mentioned FDE products, but unlike some of them, has full support for booting of an encrypted system volume. Similar to Check Points implementation, a pre-boot authentication environment is implemented. However, SecureDoc's pre-boot authentication environment is much more feature-rich providing one, two or even three factor authentication. The system also integrates deeply with Active Directory, which can help to simplify management over its competing products.

Unfortunately, Open Directory is not supported, so if you're an all-Mac shop then you'll still be managing separate user and encryption passwords. The system does have support for other authentication schemes, such as Common Access Cards (CAC) or Personal Identity Verification (PIV), so if your environment currently utilizes such a scheme, SecureDoc should integrate well.

From a technical standpoint, SecureDoc utilizes the familiar AES-256 bit, so the data itself is well protected on disk. Unlike its competitors though, SecureDoc has support for newer drives currently shipping on the market with built-in hardware encryption, such as the Seagate Momentus FDE line of drives. Utilizing hardware encryption can offload processing power from the system, and SecureDoc's support for this feature offers a leg-up over current competition. SecureDoc can also be utilized for encrypting removable media that is attached to a computer, such as an external hard disk or a thumbdrive.

SecureDoc can be deployed to a single node, or to a fleet of nodes. If you're looking to engage in the latter, you'll likely want to deploy a SecureDoc Enterprise Server (SES), which provides a number of management and deployment capabilities that will make your life easier when trying to deploy the FDE system en masse. SES has full support for both Mac and Windows clients, and provides for platform-agnostic centralized management capabilities, which can be used for deployment and configuration of encryption identities/keys, security policies, and for provisioning user access. SES provides for centralized log collection, allowing for global auditing of security events. Lastly, the SES provides for remote password assistance capabilities.

SecureDoc has had Mac support for a few years now, and has gained a decent reputation in this time frame, as the system is generally well regarded. Its support for numerous authentication schemes, such as Active Directory and CAC/PIV, along with its support for booting off of encrypted volumes, rank it among the more capable of Mac-friendly FDE products.

Summary

In this chapter we discussed in detail methods to provide security to your data in the form of encryption. As we have learned, OS X ships with a number of encryption technologies that can be used to increase the security of a running client: the Keychain for encrypting passwords and secure notes, disk images for encrypting a subset of file system data, and FileVault can be used to encrypt the entirety of a user's home directory. While these technologies do provide a decently strong method for securing data, the protections they offer are not always enough, and additional functionality or protection may be needed. In these cases, multiple third party solutions abound that cover a wide variety of data security needs. Determining the appropriate technology to use in your environment will depend on your needs and policies, but the diversity of the options available will typically ensure that OS X can exist in your environment and adhere to your defined security policy.

For the next chapter, Securing Network Traffic, we will shift focus from protecting data physically residing on a disk to instead ensuring data confidentiality when transmitted over a less secure and more public medium: the network.

Part III

Network Traffic

Chapter 10

Securing Network Traffic

Infiltration is a very real problem for network administrators, one that can lead to confidential data being leaked outside of your controlled environment. Every day, new attacks are developed that try to breach a network's security perimeter. Building a secure network requires that a number of key software and hardware components are implemented and configured correctly. But securing a network is not just about acquiring the right network hardware to block unwanted traffic. What is more important is understanding how a network works, how Internet traffic is managed, how information flows within that network, and what services need to be secured that control the traffic. One cannot fully secure what one does not understand.

Once these crucial elements are explored, discussing how to ensure data packet protection makes sense. In this chapter, we will explore the essential concepts of network structures. Within those concepts, we will then discuss what steps you can take to make your network stronger against security breaches and unwanted network traffic.

Understanding TCP/IP

The Internet runs on a suite of communications protocols commonly known as *TCP/IP*. This stands for Transmission Control Protocol/Internet Protocol, which were the first two protocols to be defined. Over the years, the suite has expanded to include other protocols, such as User Datagram Protocol (UDP), a stateless Internet Protocol used for streaming media and DNS (the protocol used to connect names with IP addresses and the most popular protocol used on the Internet). In order to understand network traffic, it's important to understand what TCP/IP is and how it works. It is the suite of protocols upon which the majority of modern networks, including the Internet, are based. It is also one of the most common vectors exploited by network-based attacks.

This family of protocols is commonly interpreted as a set of *layers*, each comprising a different portion of the complicated task of moving data between systems. Each layer presents its own security problems, and effective security must address each layer independently.

> **NOTE:** There are several different "layer models" used to explain IP traffic. For the purposes of this condensed discussion on IP traffic, we will stick to the four-layer model laid out in RFC1122.

The path that data takes over the TCP/IP stack begins and ends at the user-level *application layer*. Here, "applications" doesn't refer to a user-level program, such as Mail.app, but refers instead to the higher-level protocols that make the network useful: HTTP for serving web pages, POP and IMAP for receiving mail, and SMTP for sending mail. Securing the application layer can consist of limiting the applications that a user has access to, as discussed in Chapter 3. It can also entail using application-level encryption—everything from manually encrypting sensitive data using PGP (explained in further detail in Chapter 9) to automatically encrypting data using a secure protocol, such as SSH, which is discussed further in Chapter 15.

Application data is then presented to the *transport layer* where a protocol, typically TCP, establishes a connection between the source and destination computers, providing reliable delivery of a stream of data from one computer to the other. In order to achieve this, TCP encapsulates the data into *packets*, manageable chunks of data with a source address and a destination address. In order to make sure the packets get to the correct application at the other end, TCP uses the concept of a *port*. This is a virtual construct that acts as an endpoint for the communication between the two computers. TCP ports are identified by numbers, and different protocols will usually "listen" in on the ports assigned to them.

> **NOTE:** This isn't strictly true, as a server will start a listener on any port you configure it to provided there isn't a listener for an application running on that port already. Some people recommend running services such as SSH on non-standard ports as an added security precaution. You can see what port each services utilizes in the /etc/services file.

One of the most important steps of securing any network is limiting the number of incoming ports to only those that are necessary. For example, If a machine is not serving web pages, it should not accept traffic on port 80, which is the default port for HTTP. Unwanted software can bind itself to commonly used ports, giving malicious activity an air of legitimacy, and so even if you are not explicitly using a port you should still block traffic to it if said traffic is not required.

Moving packets from one address to another happens at the *network layer*, and is generally handled by IP. Packets move from machine to machine via a series of intermediate steps, commonly referred to as *hops*. If we were to use the analogy of commercial shipping, this resembles packing up items into boxes and attaching shipping labels to each box. The labels have a shipping address that includes a street address (IP address) and a name (port number). There's also a return address with the same information. Once the shipping company (the network layer) delivers the packages to the appropriate building, it's the responsibility of the shipping and receiving department (the transport layer) to ensure that all packages have arrived and are accounted for, and are delivered to the appropriate resident. That resident (the application layer) can finally assemble the contents of the packages.

> **NOTE:** Packets are explained in further detail later in this chapter.

An example of security at the network layer is Network Address Translation (NAT), which presents a single IP address to the outside world, while maintaining a separate internal addressing scheme for the local network. Although it doesn't necessarily secure your network from outside attacks, the less information an outside attacker knows about your internal network, the better. This concept of "security through obscurity" increases the difficulty of exploiting vulnerabilities. Having a single incoming access point rather than a large number of systems connected directly to the Internet can make it easier to deal with certain risks, such as Denial of Service (DoS) attacks. However, this would not help protect your systems from other hosts on your internal network.

The *link layer* comprises the physical implementation of the network. For example, a wired Ethernet network consists of a Network Interface Card (NIC) in each host connected to the network, and the cabling and switches that connect them. Another example is a wireless AirPort network, accessed with AirPort cards in laptops and hosted by AirPort base stations. There are also fiber-optic ports, satellite signals, and DSL modems of the various Internet service providers, all parts of the physical layer.

The bigger your network is, the more vulnerable the physical layer. For a home user, physical security is as simple as using WPA2 encryption and a strong password on an AirPort network, as discussed in Chapter 12. For a large office, a larger number of switches and routers need to be secured. It is also important to look out for and stop unauthorized access points, spoofed MAC addresses, and Denial of Service attacks that may be launched, even unwittingly, by users.

Each layer has its own part to play, and is generally ignorant of the implementation details of the other layers, which allow the TCP/IP stack to be rather scalable. The post office doesn't tape up the package, and it isn't concerned with what is done with the contents of the package once the recipient receives it. All it cares about is moving the package from one address to another. Similarly, when you pack your boxes, you neither know nor care whether they will be put in the back of a truck and driven across the country or packed with other items into a large container and flown across the country on a cargo jet. All you are concerned with is that they get there.

However, as a security expert, you can't afford the luxury of this ignorance. You should be aware of that which you can control, and you should mitigate that which you can't control.

Now that we've run through a quick synopsis of what network traffic is, we'll discuss some of the various network topologies, management techniques for that traffic, and ways to safeguard network traffic from possible attacks.

Types of Networks

To some degree, there are about as many types of networks as there are network administrators. But they are all built using varying themes on one of two network architecture types: peer-to-peer networks and client-server networks.

Peer-to-Peer

A peer-to-peer (P2P) computer network is a network that relies primarily on the computing power and bandwidth of the participants in the network to facilitate the interactivity on the network, rather than concentrating it in a centralized set of network servers and routers. (See Figure 10–1 for a graphical representation of a P2P network.) P2P networks are typically used for connecting nodes via ad-hoc connections. Such networks are useful for many purposes: assembling marketing materials, conducting research, and acquiring digital media assets (probably the most common use).

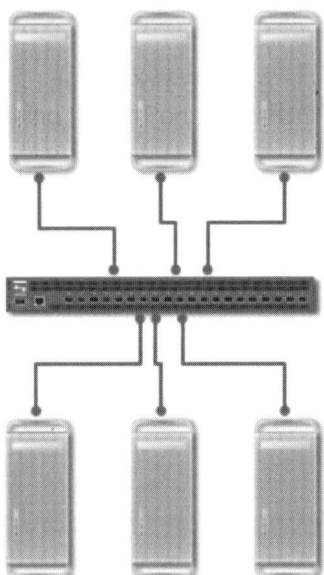

Figure 10–1. *Peer-to-peer networks*

A wide variety of peer-to-peer applications are available for use, and each has its own specific feature set that makes it popular. BitTorrent sites and other peer-to-peer networks allow you to publish music, documents, and other media to the Internet and access media published by others. However, peer-to-peer networking applications can use a considerable amount of bandwidth when they are not configured properly. Multiple computers running peer-to-peer applications can flood any network, from DSL to cable modems and even DS3s. You will also need to configure them correctly to make sure you are not sharing private information, such as your address book or financial data.

Considerations when Configuring Peer-to-Peer Networks

When configuring a peer-to-peer networking application, you will likely want to share files on your computer as well as want to download files from other computers. If you do not share files to the P2P network, then your download bandwidth can be automatically limited by the application, and some computers will not even allow you to download files from them. Sharing is an essential part of peer-to-peer networking, so you'll probably devote some bandwidth to others downloading your material. However, you should limit the bandwidth these applications are using as it can heavily affect other processes on your computer that perform their duties on the Internet.

Each application will come with the ability to limit incoming access in some way. One way to limit the bandwidth is by limiting the number of incoming connections that are allowed to access your data. Each program does it a bit differently. Look through the settings for those that allow you to configure the number of concurrent incoming and outgoing connections.

Another way to limit incoming connections is throttling bandwidth. Consider that someone accessing your computer may be running a cable modem or fiber-optic network, and might have available bandwidth of 10Mbps or more to access your files. If you are running only a DSL connection and they have FiOS, let's say, their machine could cause your connection to be saturated while your computer is trying to keep up the pace. This could also cause your Internet speed to slow to a crawl. You can limit incoming connections to make sure you always have plenty of speed available for browsing the Internet. When configuring the settings of a P2P application, look for a section that allows you to limit maximum upload and download speeds. By limiting concurrent connections, you help ensure that your network does not become flooded with P2P traffic (which can result in a Denial of Service attack on your entire network if you're not careful).

Another concern with peer-to-peer applications is limiting access to certain files. On P2P networks, users often share their entire Documents folder, exposing private data, such as their mail database and financial information, to the world. When installing a peer-to-peer application, make sure you know which folder is being shared and that the contents of that folder are limited to data you want accessible from outside your environment. For example, when using a file-sharing utility like LimeWire, you will be asked to choose a folder for shared data. Create a new folder in your home directory to share data from, and only allow Lime Wire to share from that folder. You will also be asked to select which file types you would like to share with LimeWire. You should allow it to share only those types that you actually need to share.

One administrative concern with peer-to-peer file sharing is its potential to be used for illegal sharing of copyrighted material. Although preventing this type of traffic by blocking network ports is possible, it can sometimes be a moving target because some of these P2P protocols use random ports dynamically. The Mac OS X firewall (covered in greater detail in Chapter 11) can block P2P traffic by preventing traffic generated by specific applications. Blocking P2P traffic using the firewall requires diligence. There are a number of Gnutella clients for Mac OS X, and if you block all but one, you've left a window open. Some Internet appliances and filtering packages can be configured to tag traffic that appears to be P2P, tracking the session based on these tags, and thus overcoming any reliance on blocking traffic on any specific port.

Client-Server Networks

Over the years, as networks grew, they became unwieldy, making it more difficult to keep tabs on the computers that were linked together. This led to the development of client-server networks. Client-server networks are not ad hoc. Services on client-server networks are statically provisioned and centrally managed. In this model, much of the management of the network—assigning IP addresses, warehousing data, and managing bandwidth—happens at the server level, and not on the individual workstations. Because of this, client-server networks quickly became the primary weapon in combating unwieldy networks (Figure 10–2 for a graphical representation of a client-server network).

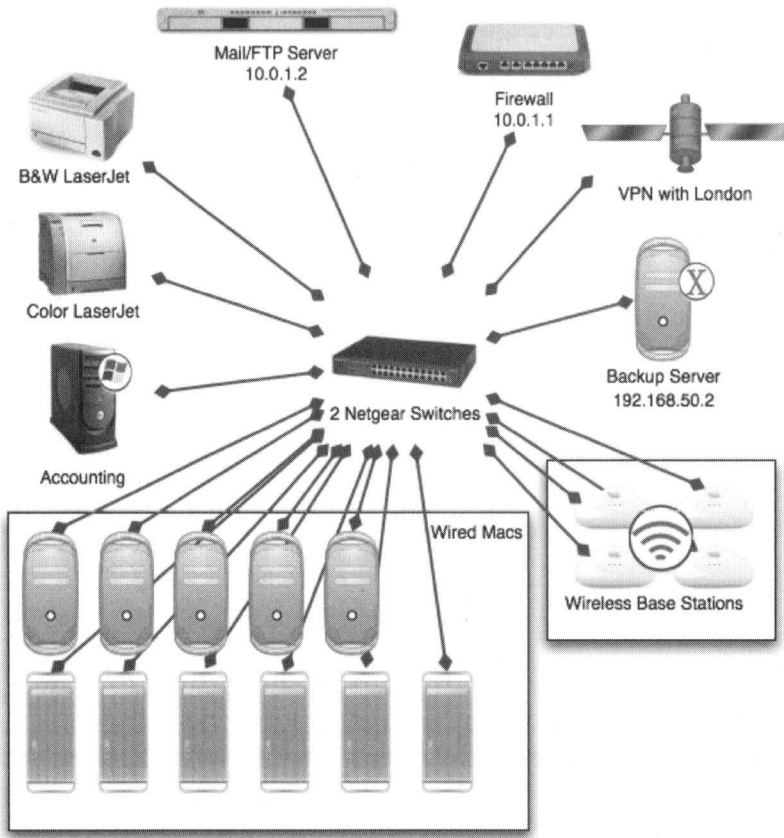

Figure 10–2. *An example of a client-server network*

Understanding Routing

As data moves between networks, you need to tell it where to go. Moving data through networks is called *routing*. In the following sections, we'll show how to route data packets and how to secure the routing techniques used to move that data along. First, we will explain a packet, and then we will move on to explain the various types of devices that packets will encounter as they traverse the Internet. This includes gateways, routers, and firewalls.

Packets

To understand how routing data works, we first need to explore what a packet is. A *packet* is a general term for a bundle of data, organized in a predetermined way for transmission over computer networks. IP packets consist of two parts, the *header* and the *data*. The *header* marks the beginning of the packet and contains information, such as the size of the payload and the source and destination address. The *data* is the information being carried by this particular packet.

> **NOTE:** Packets are sometimes referred to as *datagrams*. The terms are not interchangeable, however. A datagram is a type of packet, but not all packets are datagrams.

Different protocols use different conventions for distinguishing between different sections of a packet, and for formatting the data. The Ethernet protocol establishes the start of the header and the other data elements by their relative location to the start of the packet. For the purposes of understanding other technologies discussed throughout this chapter, just keep in mind that there are different ways to form a packet based on the protocol that is being used.

A good analogy when thinking about packets is to treat data transmission like moving into a new house. When moving our things, we tend to be efficient. Instead of loading one piece of furniture on to the truck, driving to the new house, unloading it, and then driving back for another piece, we move multiple pieces at a time. We also don't cram everything into one giant box. We load our stuff from one room and put it in a box (or boxes) and label it. The header is the container (or box) for data (our stuff). The application packing up the data writes the name of the data in the header, much like we would write where the stuff in the box would go on a label on the box. This allows the network router (or movers) to know which room each box is destined for and typically which room the stuff came from. The router (or moving truck) will create a list of what was transmitted (moved). Most transfers of data will move more than one packet (box), breaking files into data packets (boxes) to move them more efficiently.

Gateways

A *gateway* is a device that connects two physical or logical networks. Some gateways mediate between networks that use different base protocols, and some relay traffic between two networks using the same protocol. All gateways should have a minimum of two addresses, one on each network to which they're connected.

Routers

A gateway that forwards IP traffic between two networks is referred to as a *router*. Routers forward packets from one network to another. They use routing tables to help guide theose packets to their destination. A *route* is the path that is taken by data traveling from one system or network to another. Routers maintain a table in which they will cache the paths the packets take to get to their destination, which makes communication between devices much quicker than they would be otherwise. The address of each device that the data touches on the path to its destination is a *hop*. Each entry in a routing table specifies thc ncxt hop (or several hops), resulting in reduced lookups and improved performance. Each hop maintains its own routing table unless it is the device that initiated or terminated the connection. These routing tables need to be consistent, or routing loops can develop, which can cause a number of problems. If the path from your system to another forms a loop, your system will be unable to contact the other system. Your system might also cause an inadvertent denial-of-service attack on other systems by re-sending packets along the looped route, taking bandwidth away from legitimate traffic.

One way to view hops is by using the `traceroute` command in Mac OS X. The `traceroute` command will show each hop between your computer and a remote device. The `traceroute` command is followed by the remote hostname. For example, a traceroute for www.apple.com recently resulted in the following output:

```
traceroute to www.apple.com.akadns.net (17.251.200.32), 64 hops max, 52 byte packets
 1  192.168.1.1 (192.168.1.1)  3.501 ms  2.816 ms  2.659 ms
 2  10.67.152.1 (10.67.152.1)  4.271 ms  6.450 ms  6.128 ms
 3  10.1.176.1 (10.1.176.1)  4.670 ms  5.834 ms  5.067 ms
 4  147.225.49.89 (147.225.49.89)  4.686 ms  5.809 ms  5.337 ms
 5  152.161.241.70 (152.161.241.70)  10.346 ms  17.047 ms  10.958 ms
 6  72-254-0-1.client.stsn.net (72.254.0.1)  11.563 ms  12.283 ms  15.622 ms
 7  206.112.96.178 (206.112.96.178)  11.334 ms  10.764 ms  13.055 ms
 8  63.66.208.221 (63.66.208.221)  12.194 ms  14.915 ms  15.028 ms
 9  sc0.ar1.sjc5.web.uu.net (63.66.208.21)  32.809 ms  12.049 ms  10.935 ms
10  0.so-3-0-0.xl2.sjc5.alter.net (152.63.49.58)  10.811 ms  10.897 ms  10.336 ms
11  150.ATM4-0.XR1.SJC2.ALTER.NET (152.63.48.2)  18.823 ms  13.592 ms  14.346 ms
12  0.so-7-0-0.br1.sjc7.alter.net (152.63.48.253)  17.073 ms  16.109 ms  21.148 ms
13  oc192-7-1-0.edge6.sanjose1.level3.net (4.68.63.141)  12.819 ms  13.318 ms
    16.430 ms
14  vlan79.csw2.sanjose1.level3.net (4.68.18.126)  15.149 ms
vlan69.csw1.sanjose1.level3.net (4.68.18.62)  15.668 ms
15  ae-81-81.ebr1. level3.net (4.69.134.201)  15.655 ms ae-61-61 13.229 ms
16  ae-4-4.car2.level3.net (4.69.132.157)  210.512 ms  182.308 ms  41.987 ms
17  ae-11-11.car1.level3.net (4.69.132.149)  15.889 ms  31.446 ms  16.157 ms
18  apple-compu.car1.level3.net (64.158.148.6)  18.413 ms !X *  21.754 ms !X
```

Firewalls

A *firewall* is a device or software that is designed to inspect traffic, and permit, deny, or proxy it. Firewalls can be a dedicated appliance or software running on a host operating system. Firewalls function in a networked environment to prevent specified types of communication, filtering the traffic you want to be able to receive from the traffic you do not want to receive. Mac OS X has a built-in software firewall that you can use to limit incoming traffic. This will allow you to control traffic in a way that keeps attacks at a minimum. In Chapter 11 we discuss the software firewall in more depth.

Many firewalls will help reduce the likelihood of Denial of Service attacks against one of your computers. However, some firewalls are susceptible to these attacks themselves, opening your environment to the threat of not being able to do business. To help with this, most firewalls support the ability to have a fail-over firewall. A fail-over firewall can automatically become the active firewall in situations where the main firewall goes down.

Port Management

Since the introduction of malware and spyware, it is becoming more common to restrict incoming and outgoing access on commonly used (and abused) ports, such as port 25. For example, if you don't need mail services in your environment (perhaps because e-mail is hosted elsewhere), then it is likely that you will want to eliminate outgoing SMTP traffic from passing through your router. If you're not hosting mail internally, you will also want to make sure that all inbound mail-related traffic (SMTP, as well as POP and IMAP) is being denied as well.

As discussed in previous chapters, most savvy network administrators will also restrict incoming access to their networks to all but a select number of ports, and for good reason. Many older protocols, such as FTP, are inherently insecure, or there are weak implementations of these protocols that should not be accessible from the outside. Restricting access is the primary job of most firewalls and is often called *access control*. When looking into configuring the access controls on your firewall, keep in mind that every open port is a security risk, and each one needs to be treated as such. Allow incoming access only for services that are required.

Properly securing your backbone and perimeter will greatly reduce the likelihood of a successful attack. For example, many root kits will attempt to establish an outgoing connection over a certain port to an attacker's computer. If this connection cannot be established, the root kit is less likely to cause harm in your environment. Therefore, it is important to restrict outgoing access as well as incoming access.

> **NOTE:** We discuss root kits in more detail in Chapter 8.

> **TIP:** Keep in mind that port management is a common task and, as an administrator, network management time should be allocated to this vital aspect of network security. Users on a network will frequently ask for certain ports to be opened that are not standard for many environments. Understand that this type of request is common across many networks, and each request should be considered very carefully.

DMZ and Subnets

A *demilitarized zone* (DMZ) is a perimeter network, or a network area that sits outside an organization's internal network. A DMZ is used to hold public-facing servers that need to be accessible to the Internet, and are therefore more likely to face attacks. The purpose of this is to mitigate the damage should one of these hosts be compromised. Important or sensitive information should never be kept in a DMZ. On consumer-grade routers, a DMZ typically refers to an address to which all suspect traffic is forwarded. In home environments, the DMZ is often configured incorrectly. We often find that it is used to forward all traffic to a specific address, rather than researching which ports need to be accessible for each service and only forwarding that traffic to the DMZ. This becomes a big security threat to the computer or network device that has all the traffic forwarded to it.

Whether you choose to use a DMZ is dependent not on the size of your company, but on whether you are using protocols that you think might easily be compromised. For example, FTP is not a secure protocol. Relegating the use of FTP in your environment to a system that lives outside your local network would prevent standard FTP attacks from affecting the entire network infrastructure.

Some administrators might choose to use a second subnet instead of a DMZ to keep certain types of traffic separate from the primary network. Subnetting an IP network allows a single large network to be broken down into what appears (logically) to be several smaller ones. Devices on the same subnet have the same *subnet mask*, a number that determines which part of an address signifies the network range, and which signifies the hosts in that range.

Rather than allowing your users to see one another, you could put them on separate subnets and not allow UDP traffic to pass across the various subnets implemented in your environment. It is even possible to split a network into multiple subnets. Keep in mind, however, that the more complex the subnetting gets, the more difficult it becomes to troubleshoot problems on the network. For example, when a wireless network is introduced into an environment, and a separate wireless subnet is created, wireless users may have difficulty automatically finding printers on the main network. The printers will need to be manually installed using their IP address.

Spoofing

When access controls are configured based on IP addresses versus network security policies, access attacks can occur. *Spoofing*, or the act of masquerading around on a network with a valid IP address that was not legitimately given, is one of these access attacks and is a common way for attackers to establish access. To spoof an IP or MAC address, an attacker need only discover the MAC address or IP address of someone they know can access a network and then change their MAC address to the MAC address that the network is familiar with.

Let's take a command-line look at how to change your MAC address. First run an `ifconfig` command to get your current MAC address. Then, use the `lladdr` option of `ifconfig` to change your MAC address slightly.

```
cedge:/Users/cedge root# ifconfig en0
en0: flags=8863<UP,BROADCAST,SMART,RUNNING,SIMPLEX,MULTICAST> mtu 1500
        ether 00:17:f2:2a:66:12
cedge:/Users/cedge root# sudo ifconfig en0 lladdr 00:17:f2:2a:66:21
cedge:/Users/cedge root# ifconfig en0
en0: flags=8863<UP,BROADCAST,SMART,RUNNING,SIMPLEX,MULTICAST> mtu 1500
        ether 00:17:f2:2a:66:21
```

If any application was blocking traffic from your machine based on its MAC address, the traffic will now be allowed. Once a machine on a network changes its MAC address, other machines will see this change and issue a line similar to the following:

```
kernel: arp: 192.168.55.108 moved from 00:17:f2:2a:66:12 to 00:17:f2:2a:66:21
        on eth0
```

Armed with this information, you can now set up a scanner in your logs to be notified when this line appears and then investigate all changes of MAC addresses. One way to get around this type of attack is by redirecting the access to other sentry machines that are set up to monitor these kinds of spoofing attacks. This is a deceptive active response to fool attackers into thinking attacks are succeeding, allowing an administrator to monitor what the attacker is trying to do. If you are running Snort (discussed further in Chapter 17), then your system should notice the MAC spoof and disable communications from that host automatically, thus defending you against an attack from a spoofed IP address.

Stateful Packet Inspection

Using stateful packet inspection (SPI), a firewall appliance holds the significant attributes of each connection in memory. These attributes, collectively known as the "state of the connection," include such details as the IP addresses and ports involved in the connection and the sequence of packets traversing the connection. The most CPU-intensive checking is performed at the time of the start of the connection. All packets after that (for that session) are processed rapidly because it is simple and fast to determine whether they belong to an existing, prescreened session. Once the session has ended, its entry in the state table is discarded.

Most modern firewalls, including those in some Linksys and Netgear routers found at your local consumer electronics store, will have basic SPI features, as does the Mac OS X Snow Leopard software firewall. Consumer-grade appliances have a limited amount of memory and cannot inspect as many packets as rapidly or as closely as a more advanced device, such as some CheckPoints, SonicWalls, or Ciscos. Typically, SPI on these firewalls will check only the source of the packet against the source defined in the header.

Deep packet inspection (DPI) is a subclass of SPI that examines the data portion of a packet and searches for protocol noncompliance, or some predefined pattern, in order to decide whether the packet is allowed to pass. This is in contrast to the simple packet inspection found in non-stateful firewalls, in which just the header portion of a packet is checked. DPI classifies traffic based on a signature database (as does SPI), and will allow you to redirect, mark, block, rate limit, and of course report based on the classification.

Many DPI devices, rather than simply relying on signature-based detection, can also identify patterns of potentially malicious traffic in the flow of traffic. This allows devices to detect newer attacks rather than react to predefined attacks, providing for a more secure network. If your environment has the budget to acquire a firewall that performs deep packet inspection, you should strongly consider adding one to your network. For the security it provides, it is well worth the investment.

Data Packet Encryption

When two computers on different networks are communicating, they are often sending packets across multiple routers, allowing traffic to be susceptible to a variety of security holes at each stop along the way. Even with good inspection on a firewall, an attacker can still perpetrate a *man-in-the-middle attack*, or an attack where someone spoofs a trusted host while sitting between your server and a user accessing your server. A man-in-the-middle attack is designed to intercept all the traffic between two points, either in order to eavesdrop, or to insert malicious traffic. To keep prying eyes off your data, it is important to implement encryption techniques on your communications, rendering the data unreadable to the interceptor. If your data are passing from your home to your office, for example, you would implement a VPN. If you are taking customer data over web sites, then you might consider using SSL. We discuss using VPN and SSL further in Chapter 15.

Understanding Switches and Hubs

Hubs are dummy devices that connect multiple computers, making them act as a single segment on a network. With hubs, only one device can successfully transmit data at a time. When two computers submit data at the same time, a collision occurs, and a jam signal is sent to all the ports when collisions are detected. This makes one computer able to cause collisions and force an entire network to slow down while packets that were jammed are re-sent by all the computers that attempted to communicate during the jam. Hubs will also allow any computer to see the packets sent by all other computers on the hub.

Switches are more advanced than hubs and provide expandability, allowing more switches, ports, and computers to exist on a network. Switches perform collision detection and isolate traffic between the source of a packet and its destination. Because each computer is not automatically able to see all the traffic from other computers, this is a more secure communications environment. Switches are less likely to become flooded with collisions and offer faster throughput and lower latency.

We advise against the use of hubs as a general rule, unless you have a very explicit reason to use them, because they can act as potential collision centers and cause security breaches. However, hubs do still have limited usefulness in networks. Switches respond to loops, hubs do not. When a cable is plugged into a switch twice, it can cause unwanted network traffic. In areas where many users are plugging in their laptops, a cable can get plugged back into a switch by accident, and some network administrators will use a hub to keep this from occurring. Additionally, protocol analyzers connected to switches do not always receive all the desired packets since the switch separates the ports into different segments. Connecting a protocol analyzer to a hub will allow it to see all the traffic on the network segment. Finally, some cluster environments require each computer to receive all the traffic going to the cluster. In these situations, hubs will most likely be more appropriate than switches.

> **NOTE:** Many managed switches can be configured to act as though they are hubs, so you can get the capabilities you require while maintaining flexibility for more advanced features. However, this can be a security risk and so when convenient you should disable remove configuration on switches.

Stacked switches are switches designed to accommodate multiple switches in a network. When a switch is stackable, it will have dedicated ports for adding more switches that allow speeds of 10 or more gigabits between the switches, using special stacking cables. These are often converted into fiber connections so that latency is optimized over long distances.

Managed Switches

As networks and features of networks have grown, managed switches have become more popular. *Managed switches* can control internal network traffic and are used to split a network into logical segments, giving more granular control over network traffic and providing more advanced error detection. Managed switches also offer more advanced logging features to help network administrators isolate problem areas. Some managed switches are also stacked, although not all of them are capable of stacking.

A standard feature to look for on a managed switch is VLAN support. VLAN, short for *virtual LAN*, describes a network of computers that behave as if they are connected to the same wire, even though they may actually be physically located on different segments of a LAN. They are configured through software rather than hardware, which makes them extremely flexible. One of the biggest advantages of VLANs is their portability. Computers are able to stay on the same VLAN without any hardware reconfiguration when physically moved to another location. This also works the other way; one physical LAN can be split into multiple logical networks by the VLAN software running on switches. This can be useful when implementing a DMZ, as you can isolate your DMZ traffic without actually creating an isolated physical network. Nearly all managed switches have a VLAN feature set.

Newer and more advanced switches also have the capability to perform rogue access point detection, or detection of unwanted access points and routers on a network. Since Apple joined the ranks of operating system vendors that have introduced Internet Sharing as a built-in feature, many networks have been brought to a grinding halt by rogue routers providing IP addresses to networks. Problems with rogue access points have been especially common in networks with large numbers of freelancers who bring their laptops into the office and connect to the wireless network without turning off the Internet Sharing that they were using at home. This establishes an ad-hoc Denial of Service to the rest of the network, because they receive bad DHCP leases with bad TCP/IP settings. This situation can require administrators to comb through every machine on a network to isolate which user has enabled the Internet Sharing features on their computers. Rogue access point detection is also helpful for making sure that random users on networks do not plug in wireless access points or routers they may think are switches. Rogue access points are discussed in further detail in Chapter 12.

Most managed switches also provide some form of MAC address filtering. A *MAC address* is a unique identifier attached to most forms of networking equipment (you can find your Mac's MAC address in the Network pane of System Preferences by clicking on the Advanced button). With MAC filtering, a network administrator can define a destination address so that packets can be received only from a specific port and allow only those same packets to be forwarded to another port. Using MAC address filtering, only users who are connected to port A can access the server connected to port B; packets from other ports, even packets whose destination address is the server on port B, will be dropped. MAC filtering is also referred to as *network access control*, although this could refer to port filtration rather than MAC filtration.

Here are some other features of managed switches:

PoE: Power over Ethernet allows power to be supplied to network devices over an Ethernet cable, rather than over a power adapter.

Spanning tree: This closes loops on networks. If more than one open path between any two ports were to be active at once (a loop), then a *broadcast storm*, or large amount of network traffic, could cause the network to become unstable.

Priority tagging: This specifies ports that are of a higher priority, allowing mission-critical traffic to be differentiated from non-mission-critical traffic.

Link aggregation: This uses multiple network ports in parallel to increase the link speed beyond the limits of any one single cable or port. Link aggregation, also known as *teaming*, is based on the IEEE 802.3ad link aggregation standard.

Flow control: This manages traffic rates between two computers on a switched network. It is not always possible for two computers to communicate at the same speed. Flow control throttles speeds for faster systems by pausing traffic when it is running too fast.

Using managed switches historically meant that large amounts of an IT budget would need to be spent on acquiring them. However, with the increased number of manufacturers now involved in developing managed switches, this is no longer the case. Managed Netgear and D-Link switches (such as the one featured in Figure 10–3) provide many of the advanced features found in Cisco and other top-of-the-line switches for a fraction of the cost. This has made them increasingly popular. Features offered on D-Link and Netgear switches include link aggregation, flow control, network access control, spanning tree, and priority tags.

Figure 10–3. *D-Link 48 port managed switch*

Many administrators of Mac environments are not comfortable deploying managed switches in their environments because they are typically command-line-only configurations, and some of the protocols they use can be incompatible with other devices on the network. To address this concern, Apple has recently begun to align with industry network standards, enabling Mac network administrators to get more comfortable using managed switches to support extended features of Mac hardware products. One example of this is the use of link aggregation (using two network interfaces as one) on Mac servers, which requires a managed switch in order to properly configure this feature.

Restricting Network Services

Network services are the building blocks of many network environments. Connecting to the Internet, DNS, DHCP, and other protocols is the main reason for having a network in the first place. One of the best ways to ensure security for file sharing, web services, and mail services is to limit the access that computers have to them. Some computers may need access to these resources; denying them can be detrimental to the workflow. Others may not need access, and giving them access could be potentially damaging. For example, you might allow local users to your network to access your file server but will probably never want to allow access to the file server for users outside your network.

When architecting a network, each service needs to be handled separately. Analyze which services go in and out of every system in an environment. If protocols will be accessed only from inside the network, such as file sharing and directory service protocols, then they should not be routable. Restricting access to protocols to users outside your network can be handled using the firewall, as mentioned earlier in this chapter. For larger environments, restricting access to services from other computers within your network is often handled using the switches in your environment. Draft up a document, such as the one in Figure 10–4, that lists the servers in your environment, the services they will be providing, and which ports they run on. This can help tremendously when trying to secure all the services needed in a networked environment while maintaining their usability.

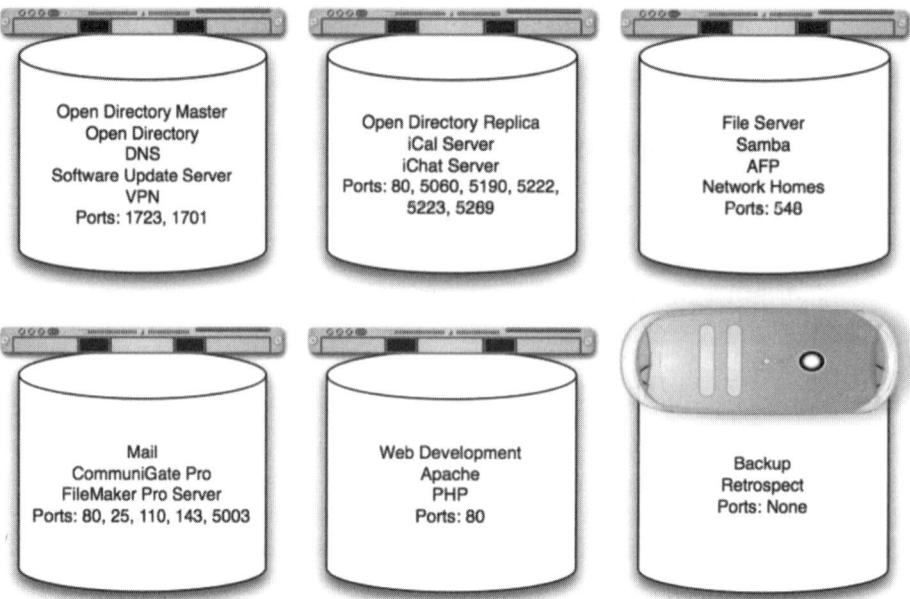

Figure 10–4. *Servers, services, and ports*

For smaller environments, restricting access between computers is usually handled on a per-service basis by using a local firewall running on the computer providing the service. For more information on configuring the software firewall in Mac OS X, see Chapter 11. For firewall configuration for Mac OS X Server, see Chapter 16.

Security Through 802.1x

802.1x is a protocol that Apple added to Mac OS with Leopard. The 802.1x standard can greatly increase the security of a network environment by requiring users to authenticate before they can access the local network for Ethernet or wireless networks. The 802.1x standard can use a third-party authentication authority, such as Open Directory or Active Directory, or you can use pre-shared keys. Authentication to the network rather than just the computer is a fairly new concept for most Mac environments. This level of advanced networking is fairly complex and must be given an appropriate level of planning.

Enabling 802.1x is accomplished by opening System Preferences, clicking the Network pane, choosing the appropriate interface, and then clicking the Advanced button. At this point, you can click the 802.1x tab (Figure 10–5) and select the network to join.

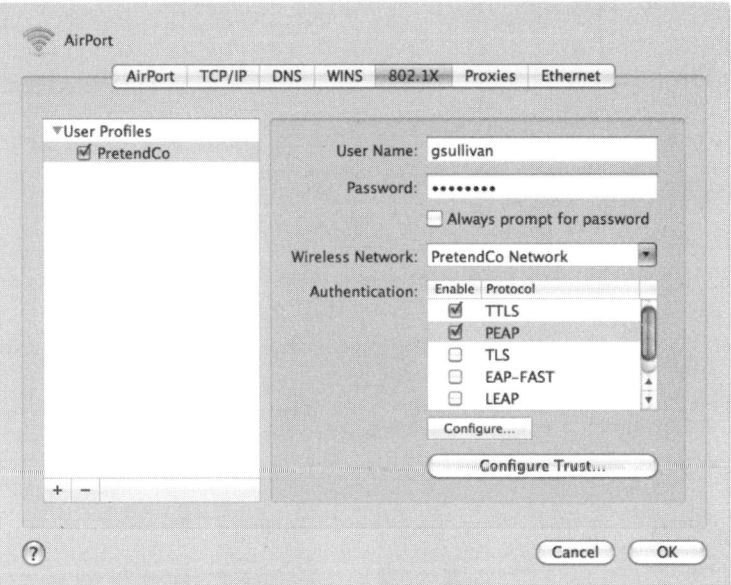

Figure 10-5. *Setting up 802.1x*

Once you have chosen your network, click the authentication protocol you want to use in the Authentication section, and then click Configure. This will allow you to configure settings for the specific protocol to match the settings of your server.

There are some serious vulnerabilities in the 802.1x protocol. 802.1x authenticates only at the beginning of the connection. For example, after authentication is successful and the connection is established, it's possible for an attacker to hijack the authenticated port by getting in between the authenticated computer and the port. This is called a man-in-the-middle attack.

Proxy Servers

One way of filtering traffic on your network is through the use of a *proxy server*. A proxy server allows services to establish network connectivity using one server as a sort of traffic cop. The proxy server is situated between computers and the Internet, and processes requests for external resources on behalf of the users of the network (see Figure 10-6). Using proxy servers, administrators can prevent users from viewing predetermined web sites. In addition to increasing security, proxy servers can increase network performance by allowing multiple users to access data that is saved in the proxy's cache. On the first access of this data, there will be a slight performance loss. Any subsequent attempts to visit the site or access the data will see a performance gain, since the content can be served from the proxy. Therefore, proxy servers accelerate access only to content that is accessed repeatedly.

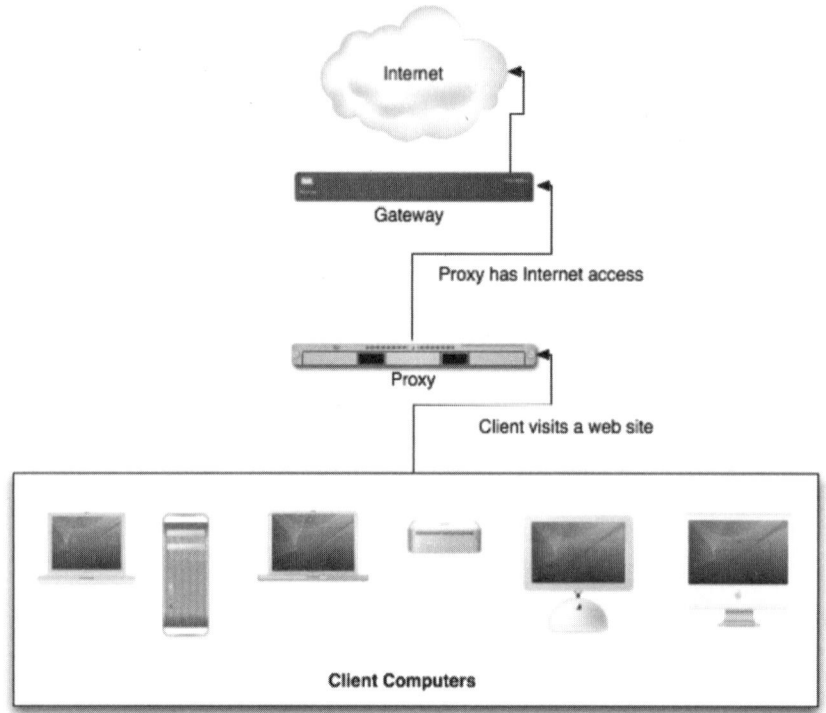

Figure 10-6. *Proxy server network configuration*

Proxies themselves can be exploited as a means to forward malicious HTTP traffic, such as web-based spam e-mail referrals. When setting up a proxy, it is important to take into account security concerns, such as which clients on the network will have access to the proxy. Often proxy servers have a white list (a list of allowed addresses) that can be used to allow access to IP addresses individually or by subnet. This should be configured to allow only those machines on the local area network to access the proxy services.

If external access is required, consider running the proxy on a nonstandard port and requiring authentication, perhaps utilizing an existing directory service, such as Active Directory or Open Directory. This, combined with strong password policies, should help protect against unauthorized access to the proxy. Using proxy servers on desktop computers is discussed in more detail in Chapter 10.

Squid

Squid is an open source product that allows network administrators to easily configure proxy services. It has a robust set of access control options that can be configured to allow or deny access based on user or group access as well as other criteria such as scheduling proxy servers to be enabled at certain periods of time. SquidMan is a utility developed by Tony Gray to provide Mac users with a GUI to assist with installing and configuring a precompiled version of Squid.

To install SquidMan, follow these steps:

1. Download the installer from http://web.me.com/adg/squidman/index.html, and extract the SquidMan .dmg file.

2. Copy SquidMan.app into your Applications folder.

3. Open SquidMan, and enter an administrative password to install the squid components and run the application.

4. At the preferences screen, enter the appropriate settings for the following fields (see Figure 10–7):

    - *HTTP Port*: The port that client computers will use to access the proxy.

    - *Cache Size*: The amount of space used to store data in the cache.

    - *Maximum Object Size*: The size limit for files that are to be cached by the proxy.

    - *Rotate Logs*: When to rotate log files.

    - *Start Squid on Launch After a _ Second Delay*: Enabling this option will automatically start Squid when SquidMan is launched, and enable you to define a delay after launching SquidMan to start the Squid services.

    - *Quit Squid on Logout*: This allows you to determine if you'd like to keep Squid running when the active user logs out of your proxy server.

    - *Show Errors Produced by Squid*: This prompts users with pop-up windows when errors occur. This is helpful if someone is sitting at the desktop of the proxy server when it's running. However, if the desktop of the system is never looked at, then you will probably refer to logs to discover errors.

    - *Disable Initial Squid DNS tests*: This turns off Squid's initial DNS test. This can be useful if SquidMan is configured to start at login (your Internet connection isn't always ready when Squid starts).

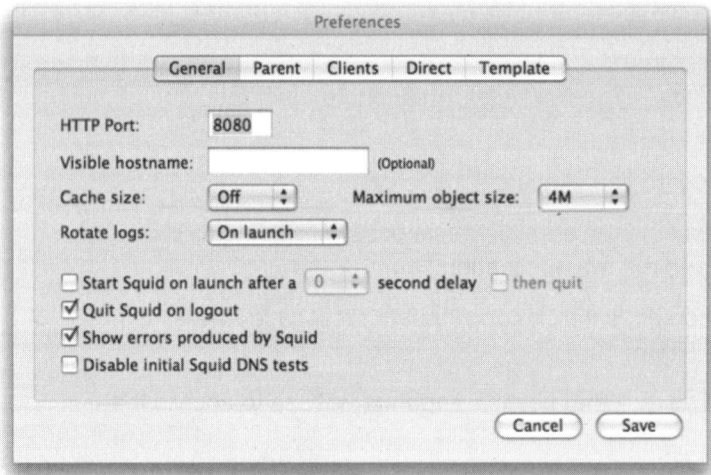

Figure 10–7. *SquidMan preferences: changing ports and hostnames*

5. Click the Parent tab, and use this location to choose whether you will have your Squid server use another Squid server as its proxy server. This can make troubleshooting difficult in proxy environments. Keep the defaults here unless you have multiple Squid servers.

6. Click the Clients tab and enter the appropriate IP addresses in the Provide Proxy Services For field. When entering IP address ranges, you will need to also enter the subnet for the IP range.

7. Use the Direct tab to configure any exclusions to the list of domains that will be proxied by the server. This will be helpful when troubleshooting a parent proxy environment.

8. Click the Template tab, and use this location to edit the Squid configuration file manually. Here, the maximum object size and cache directories can be increased beyond the variables available in the GUI.

9. Once the settings have been configured for SquidMan, use the Start Squid button of the main SquidMan screen to start Squid (see Figure 10–8).

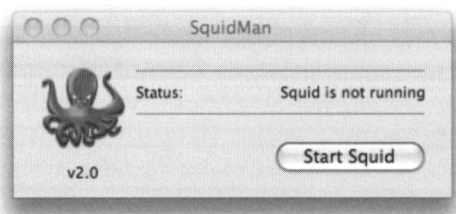

Figure 10–8. *Starting SquidMan*

Once SquidMan is running, you can stop it by clicking the Stop Squid button on the main SquidMan screen. You can get more granular control over the Squid proxy services via command-line administration by editing the settings of the `squid.conf` file located in `/User/<username>/Library/Preferences/squid.conf` once SquidMan is launched for the first time.

> **NOTE:** The help files for SquidMan are very thorough in their explanations of these settings.

Summary

Layers of security breed resilient networks. When securing networks, layer your approach. Start from the center, the computer itself, and move outward, looking at which services should be accessible by which computers. Then, layer the security levels by grouping the computers and building policies to limit access on each of those groups. Determine your firewall policies, both internally and externally. Consider your network's physical layer as you implement security policies based on location within the network. This kind of layered approach gives strength to your network's security blueprint.

Chapter 11

Setting Up the Mac OS X Firewall

Put simply, a firewall is a network traffic moderator. It uses a set of rules to determine what kind of traffic is allowed in and out of your computer or network. The term is a bit ambiguous, because there are many types of firewalls. In Chapter 10, we discussed the importance of using a firewall to act as a gateway into your network, denying and allowing network traffic on a network-wide basis between your computers and the outside world. This is what we refer to as a *hardware appliance firewall*.

For the purposes of this chapter, we will discuss the intricacies of the built-in firewall of Mac OS X, the software in your operating system that determines which traffic your computer will accept. This is referred to as a *software firewall*. The differences between a software firewall and a hardware firewall can be rather significant. For example, a software firewall primarily limits how services from other computers on the same network talk to services on your computer, something hardware appliances typically do not do. A software firewall can also act as a barrier to network traffic of any type that might slip past your firewall appliance. In this respect, a software firewall can act as a powerful second line of defense against malicious attacks.

It is important to note that the firewall built into Mac OS X should only act as the first layer of defense. Inexpensive routers from companies such as Linksys, Netgear, D-Link, Xsense, and hundreds of others offer firewalls that cost less than $100 and have many features that are not configurable in the OS X firewall. In many smaller environments, such as homes and offices with fewer than ten users, these firewall appliances used in conjunction with the Mac OS firewall are more than adequate to protect computers accessing the Internet, because they hide IP addresses from the Internet and expose only the IP address of the router.

Explaining how your software firewall works and how it can be configured requires us to dive into the specific services that your software firewall can blocked and how to teach your computer to allow or deny them. These services are often known as *network services*.

Introducing Network Services

The primary purpose behind most network traffic is for computers to communicate with one another. There are a wide variety of communication paths, or *routes*, that computers take to do this. And there are different purposes, or *roles*, for these varied communication paths. One communication path might have the intent of sending printing commands to a printer, while another might need to send an Internet request to an Internet gateway, or *router*. A network service then communicates with other devices using a structured mechanism for conversing, known as a *protocol*. For firewalls to manage these various protocols, they use rules. A *rule* is a set of parameters that enables the firewall to allow or deny access to a protocol on a computer.

In networking, there are a variety of protocols. Each comes with a default port assigned to it. *Ports* are what computers use to sift through the variety of protocol traffic in order to understand what network service the traffic is destined for. Port numbers fall anywhere between 0 and 65,535, and each protocol is assigned a number so that each type of traffic can be handled differently. When communications between computers occur, applications understand how to connect to each other based on the port number and protocol they use. Rules for applications and network services are then built using port numbers or sets of port numbers. Even though it's possible for thousands of different port numbers to be actively in use at one time, most applications use only a few common ports.

Fortunately, we usually don't have to keep track of port numbers, because the programs we use to access ports (such as Safari for web browsing or Entourage for reading e-mail) usually standardize the use of port numbers. IANA standardizes the port numbers, but they can be customized. For example, if you access a website, you are probably using HTTP, which uses port 80 as its network port. If you send a friend an e-mail, Mail.app is likely using port 25, because it is the default port for outgoing mail traffic. However, if you were to build a web server that runs over port 8080, such as the one built into many inexpensive routing or firewall devices, you would need to specify that web traffic moves through that port.

> **NOTE:** When working with firewalls, you will often need to know about port numbers in order to allow or block certain types of traffic. If you want to allow incoming access for the Web, for example, which would turn your computer into a web server, you would open port 80 on your computer. It's good practice to frequently reference port number tables in order to remember which ports typically work with various protocols. Apple publishes a list of commonly used ports at http://docs.info.apple.com/article.html?artnum=106439. Mac OS X also has a file, /etc/services, that lists the port numbers and the protocols that use them.

To demonstrate the way the network process structure works, let's look at an essential service of the Mac OS, the Apple Filing Protocol (AFP). AFP is a network communications service that allows the sharing of files between computers. It allows one machine to talk to other machines running AppleFileServer in order for files to move back and forth. AppleFileServer runs on the computer, sharing files as a process. That process listens on port 548. Another computer requests traffic over port 548, and when the host computer is listening, it responds, and a communication link between the two computers is established. And this all happens in a matter of milliseconds.

Many processes are easy to identify. Processes that listen for traffic can also be running as hidden processes or as a different user. mDNS (called Bonjour or Rendezvous in Mac OS X 10.3 and later and Rendezvous in 10.2 and earlier) is the protocol that allows other computers to discover information about your machine. mDNS (the process is known as the *mDNS responder*) runs over port 5353 as the root user, a user hidden by default. This means that if you were to log in as any registered user on a machine besides the root user and open the My Processes section of Activity Monitor, you would not find any processes running the mDNS protocol, because root processes are hidden. If you were to change the filter from My Processes to All Processes, you would find the mDNS responder, which is the actual process that is typically referred to as Bonjour.

Now that we've discussed what a network service is and how it talks to your computer, we'll move on to looking one of two components of the software firewall in Mac OS X. The *Application Layer Firewall* (or ALF) component of the software firewall will allow or deny an application from establishing communication over the network, not based on its ports but based on the application itself. Rather than open and close ports on your computer, an ALF grants access based on whether the application itself has access, not through the configuration of ports.

The second component of the software firewall is the command line ipfw tool (described in detail later in this chapter), which opens and closes ports. The combination of the two provides a maximum of security if you so choose to use them (and is a serious annoyance if they are configured incorrectly).

Controlling Services

To get started controlling the application layer firewall, you will first need to define the services on your computer that need filtration. For ease of use, Apple has included the most common in the Sharing System Preferences pane. To get there, open System Preferences, and go to the Sharing pane (see Figure 11–1). If the padlock icon in the bottom left-hand corner of the screen is in the locked position, click it to be able to configure settings for the Sharing preferences. To enable a service, select the box that corresponds to each service; after you've checked the box, wait for it to start. This is the quickest and easiest way to enable a service.

> **NOTE:** If you enable services for the strict purpose of testing, we recommend that you then disable them when you are finished with your testing.

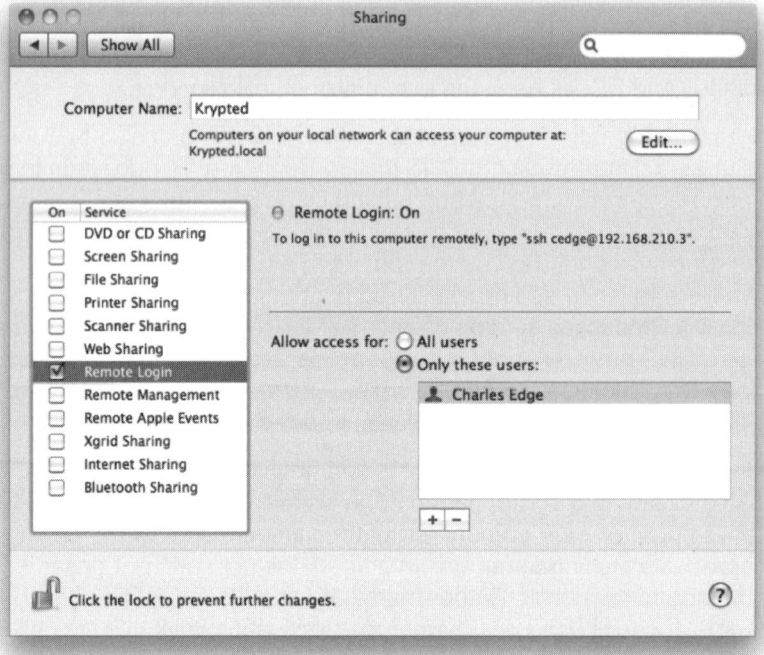

Figure 11-1. *Sharing system preferences*

To disable a service, open Sharing in System Preferences, highlight the service you want to disable on the Sharing pane, and click the Stop button. You can actually watch services appear and disappear in Activity Monitor as you start and stop them and review the resources (in terms of memory and processor utilization) that the services are using. This allows you to learn more about services as you go.

Services are accessible from any computer once they are started (we'll discuss fixing that later in this chapter). Because the firewall works based on applications, Apple lists commonly used services by name rather than by port number. For example, you will see File Sharing on the Services pane versus port 548. By adding File Sharing and some of the other more common Apple-centric ports by default, Apple has made basic service management tasks simple to perform. This allows you to quickly enable or disable outgoing and incoming traffic for the ports you will most commonly need to access.

For another computer to connect to yours, you'll need to know your IP address or the computer name that corresponds to your IP address, and the user will need to know which address to use. To find the IP address of your machine, look at the bottom portion of the Sharing pane (Figure 11-1) where the computer name is also displayed. Usually when you connect to resources on another computer, you can browse to them using various programs, such as the Finder or Bonjour Browser, and you will see the computer referenced by name. This makes things easier for users wanting to connect to your computer from your local network. However, you might need the IP address when connecting over the Internet or when the name does not appear on its own.

Anytime you are configuring the firewall on a Mac, you must first determine which services to enable and which to disable. Remember to run only those services that are required to receive *necessary* communications from other computers. Unless a service is absolutely required, do not enable it. Because they have direct access to your machine, each service running on your computer represents another possible vulnerability whereby an attacker, bot, bug, or other malware might crawl into your system and wreak havoc. Table 11–1 indicates when the default services included with OS X should be run and the potential pitfalls enabling them could bring.

Table 11–1. *When to Enable a Service*

Services	When to Enable	Dangers
Personal File Sharing (AFP port 548)	Enable when you want other Mac users to have access to files on your computer.	If you have weak passwords (or no password), then others could gain access into your file system. There have also been a few exploits specifically targeting AFP that have been released.
Windows Sharing (SMB)	Enable when you want Windows users to have access to files hosted by your computer.	If you have weak passwords (or no password), then others could gain access into your file system. Additionally there are a number of vulnerabilities in the CVE database for Samba.
Personal Web Sharing (WWW port 80)	Enable when you want to run your system as a web server.	Poorly written web code and Apache configuration could lead to vulnerabilities on your system.
Remote Login (SSH port 22)	Enable when you want a command-line or Secure Shell (SSH) interface into your system.	Systems with SSH exposed to the Internet are prone to brute-force attacks, where an attacker attempts repeatedly to guess your password. This will show up in your logs, waste your bandwidth, and, if you have weak passwords, give an attacker full control over your computer. Additionally, while strong passwords do mitigate the chance of success they do not obviate it.
FTP Access (FTP port 21)	Enable when you want to turn your system into an FTP server.	FTP has not changed in 30+ years. Need we say more?
Apple Remote Desktop (VNC port 5900)	Enable when you want to allow remote control over the desktop of your computer.	Weak passwords and poor configuration could give an attacker access to everything on your computer.
Remote Apple Events (SNMP ports 161–162)	Enable when you want to turn on SNMP monitoring so other systems can review vital statistics about your system.	Others could gain too much information about your system if SNMP is not configured appropriately.

Services	When to Enable	Dangers
Printer Sharing (port 1179)	Enable when you want other users to access your printers.	There are very few access controls for printing services, but CUPS does allow for extremely granular control over the printer sharing aspect of Mac OS X.
XGrid (port 4111)	Enable when your system is a grid node of an XGrid deployment.	Your computer could be abused as a grid client, reducing your performance and arbitrary code execution could be leveraged given the level of access that the Xgrid service has.

Configuring the Firewall

Once you have enough information to understand what services you are trying to control by configuring the firewall, you're ready to move on to the nuts and bolts of working with those services and/or the firewall itself. First things first: let's turn the Application Layer Firewall on.

Working with the Firewall in Leopard and Snow Leopard

Out of the box, the firewall in any version of Mac OS X is turned off by default. In Mac OS X client (as opposed to Mac OS X Server) it can be enabled using the Firewall tab of the Security system preferences (see Figure 11–2). Make sure the padlock icon at the bottom of the screen is unlocked in order for you to make changes to the System Preference pane. To enable the firewall, click on the Start button.

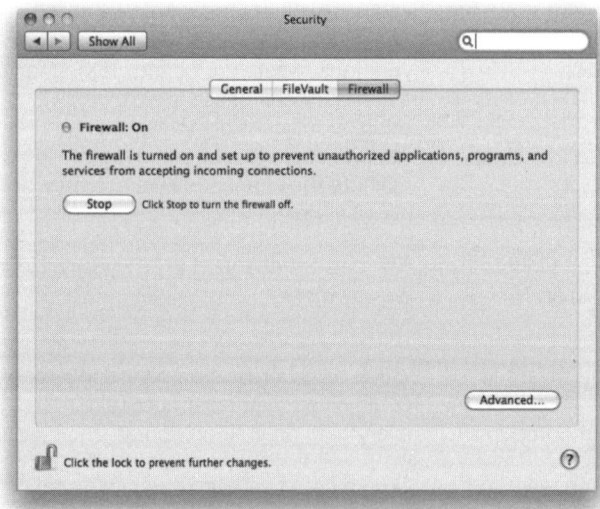

Figure 11–2. *The Firewall tab in the System Preferences Security pane*

Enabling the firewall allows incoming connections only to certain Apple services by default, such as Personal File Sharing or Web Services. If you are using the firewall in Mac OS X, then you cannot disable these from the Firewall System Preference and must configure them from the Sharing System Preference pane instead (unless you use the command line tool ipfw, as we discuss later in the chapter). You can see this in Figure 11–3, which shows the default settings that were enabled by enabling the firewall. As you can see in the figure, SSH is allowed, because it is a sharing service that is enabled. You cannot remove any sharing services that show up here. But if you disable them in the Sharing System Preferences, they will no longer appear in the firewall.

> **NOTE:** The Firewall and Internet tabs are not located in the same place in OS X Server. These options are configured using Server Admin on Mac OS X Server, as we discuss later in Chapter 16.

To enable third-party services or applications to accept or make communications requests, you must add them based on the application rather than the port. This gives each you access to open its required ports on the firewall.

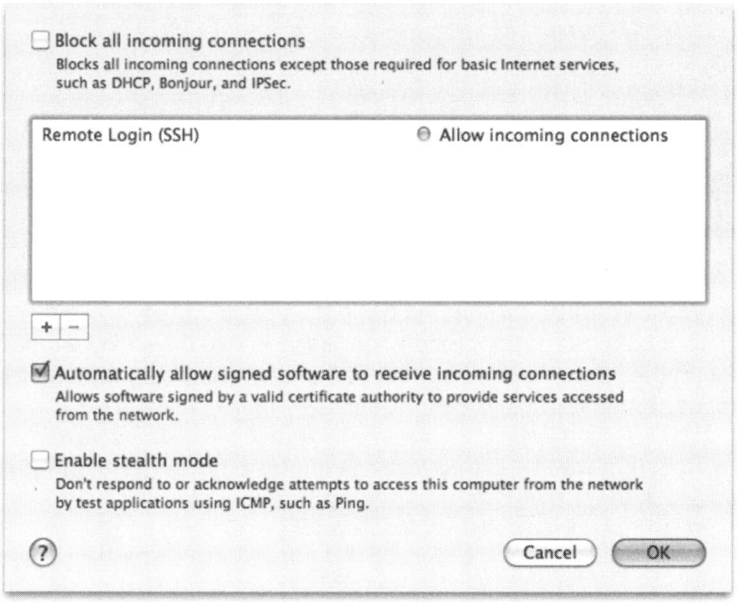

Figure 11–3. *Configuring the Firewall*

To enable other services, click on the plus (+) sign and then browse to the application. For example, in Figure 11–4 we will choose Cyberduck, a popular FTP and SFTP client for Mac OS X. Once you click on the application, click on the Add button to add it to the list.

NOTE: The Application Layer Firewall in Mac OS X is built on a chain of trust methodology. You are trusting the application, therefore the firewall trusts the application. This means that the most critical aspect of working with the firewall is only adding trusted applications that come from trusted sources, such as a trusted application vendor.

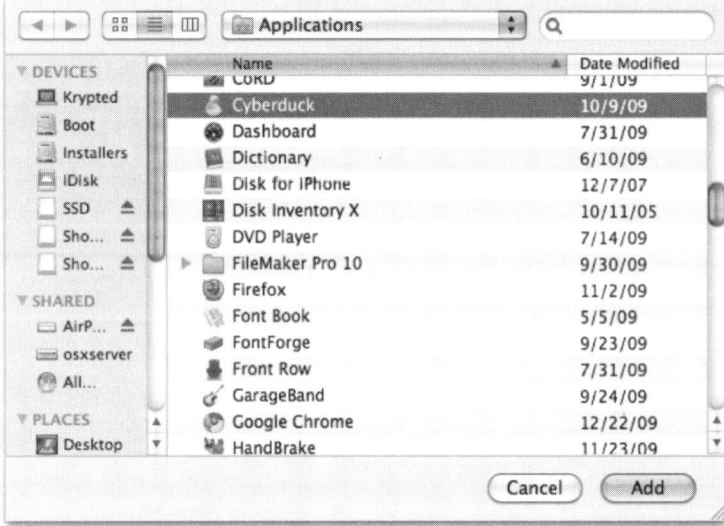

Figure 11–4. *Selecting the Cyberduck application*

Once you've added your application, connections will be allowed, which you can see by clicking on "Allow incoming connections." Notice the options in Figure 11–5; you also have the "Block incoming connections" option. Since connections can be added ad-hoc (which we are about to cover) the "Block incoming connections" option will suppress the request to allow you to add a connection ad-hoc.

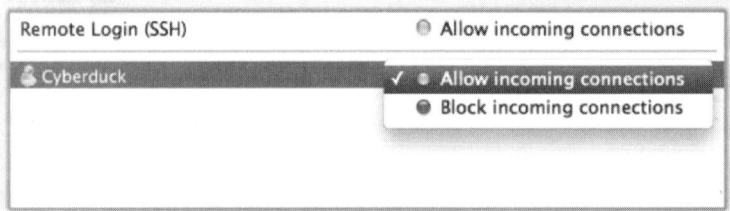

Figure 11–5. *Configuring the Firewall to allow incoming connections for Cyberduck*

To add an application ad-hoc, simply attempt to establish a connection to your computer from that application. For example, open Cyberduck (assuming it is not in your list already) and you will see a dialog box asking if you want to Allow or Deny access for the application, as can be seen in Figure 11–6. Clicking Allow will add it with the Allow incoming network connections settings or clicking on the Deny button will Deny incoming network connections.

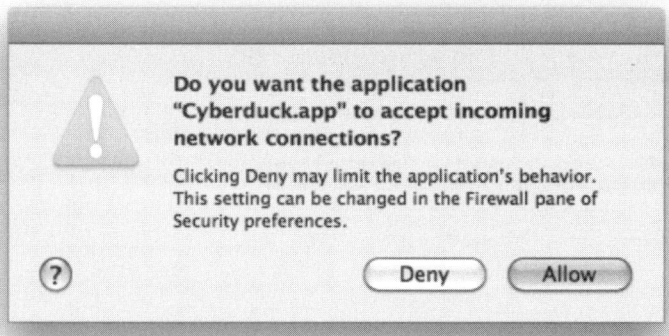

Figure 11-6. *Accepting an application ad-hoc*

Once you have configured which applications can and cannot communicate with computers outside of your system, it's time to configure the Advanced settings on the Security pane's Firewall button.

> **NOTE:** If you encounter services that cannot function once you have enabled the firewall, you can quickly determine whether the firewall is the problem. Try disabling the firewall to see whether it is blocking those services (click the Stop button on the Firewall tab of the Sharing pane). If the problem persists, then the firewall is not the culprit. If this resolves the issue, then the firewall is most likely the problem.

Setting Advanced Features

There are also a few more advanced features. These include blocking all incoming connections, automatically allowing signed software to create connections and enabling stealth mode. From the Security System Preferences pane, click on the Firewall tab and then on Advanced… to access these options.

Blocking Incoming Connections

The "Block all incoming connections" option will disable all non-essential incoming connections on the computer. Because they are required, DHCP, Bonjour registration, and other services that will lead to instability will be left enabled. However, all sharing services will be disabled, as will any third-party applications that have been allowed. To disable incoming connections, check the "Block all incoming connections" box in the Advanced options in the Firewall System Preference pane.

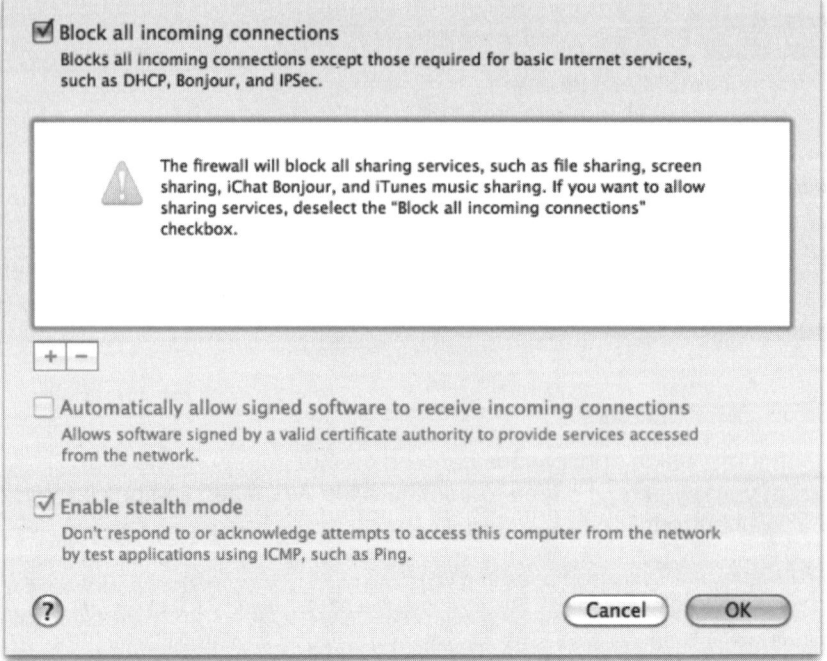

Figure 11–7. *The "Block all incoming connections" option in the Firewall pane*

Notice in Figure 11–7 that once this feature has been enabled, you cannot configure any other features of the firewall in Mac OS X. Once enabled, sharing services will be disabled, and you'll be unable to configure any of the other options as well.

Allowing Signed Software to Receive Incoming Connections

Perhaps one of the most dangerous options in the Firewall is to allow all signed applications access to receive incoming connections. This option, shown in Figure 11–7, will rely on application signatures, which is good, but will allow all signed applications to communicate, which is bad. An application is considered signed if the application bundle has a signature, a designated requirement, and if the signature matches the requirement. The signature is then used when the application is opened to verify that it has not been altered since it was signed and to detect that it is the same application if it is a new version of the same application.

To determine if an application has a signature, browse to the application in question and then Ctrl-click (or right-click if you have a multi-button mouse) on it and then click on Show Contents. From here, open the CodeSignature folder and check that there is a CodeResources file (see Figure 11–8). If so, then there is a signature. But who signed the app? And when was it signed? In some cases, this method of verifying the signature will not work as intended and so the codesign command, covered in more detail in Chapter 6, can be used as well.

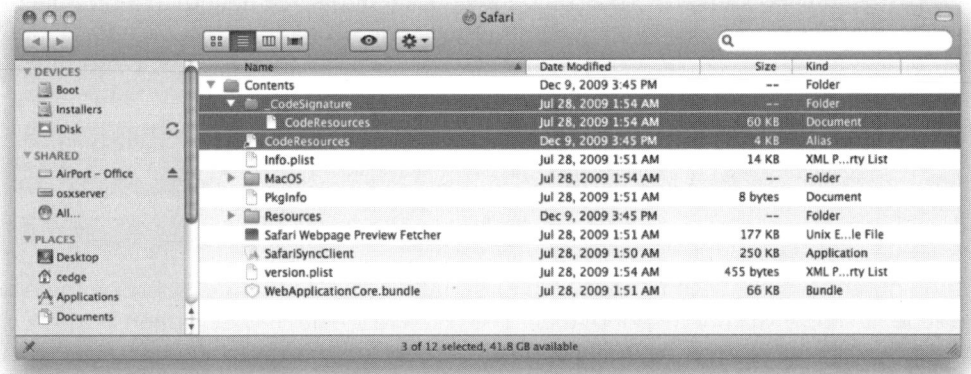

Figure 11–8. *Looking inside the Safari bundle*

> **NOTE:** All applications built for the iPhone must be signed, and someday we hope to see this replicated in Mac OS X as well!

To check the signature of the application and obtain more granular information about it, Apple has provided the `codesign` application. While this tool is covered more granularly in Chapter 6, a good example of its use would be to obtain very verbose output of the Safari application with the following command:

```
codesign -vvv Safari.app
```

The output would simply indicate that the Safari.app checks clean against the tests performed:

```
/Applications/Safari.app: valid on disk
/Applications/Safari.app: satisfies its Designated Requirement
```

Going Stealthy

When Computer A sends a request to Computer B, Computer B determines how to respond. Responses contain either the data requested or a rejection to the request, which is sent back to the requesting computer. If a process is running and traffic is allowed, then Computer A will get a message from Computer B allowing it to connect. If a process is not running or a firewall rule is active that prohibits Computer A from connecting to a given port on Computer B, then Computer A will get a deny message from Computer B. This process occurs before a web page is loaded or before a password is requested.

This seemingly innocuous process is the basis for much of the process by which computers communicate, and can also be used to expose rather important details about your system. By analyzing the patterns in delivery times and the actual content of responses to requests for traffic, it is possible to determine the operating system you are running, the patches you have installed on your operating system, and in many cases the type of hardware that is in your system. Armed with this information, a hacker can easily attack a system. So, how does one safeguard against this? One employs the use of Stealth mode.

> **NOTE:** Computers with "Block all incoming connections" enabled automatically run in Stealth mode.

If a computer does not wish to appear to exist, rather than sending a response to deny a message, it simply will not respond at all. The "Enable stealth mode" option in Mac OS X tells the system not to reply to traffic that is not specifically allowed. By not responding to requests, your system will make it more difficult for other computers to fingerprint the machine and locate the system on a network. By making it more difficult to *enumerate*, or discover, the essential details of, a system's operating system, you make the system more secure. If you are running a firewall on a Mac, you should definitely be running stealth mode with it.

Stealth mode causes the system to not reply to response requests, or *echo requests*. However, this doesn't make it completely impossible to locate a system on a network. It is still possible to get the system time information or *ARP requests* (which show details about the network settings on your computer) on a machine that is running stealth mode. One reason for this is that stealth mode simply tells the computer not to respond to network requests that aren't running. However, because Apple built zero-configuration networking into the operating system, there are a large number of services that are running and easily discoverable, making it easy to enumerate the Mac OS. One way to help mitigate this discovery is to use custom ipfw rules, which we discuss in further detail later in the chapter.

Testing the Firewall

Once you have closed the ports and configured your firewall to your liking, you will want to test impact of your security change and verify that the services you have denied are no longer accessible. Performing a port scan is the best way to test the configuration. A port scan will check whether a service is available to other systems. Apple has included a port scanner in Network Utility, which is located at /Applications/Utilities (see Figure 11-9). Port scanning is explored in more depth in Chapter 10.

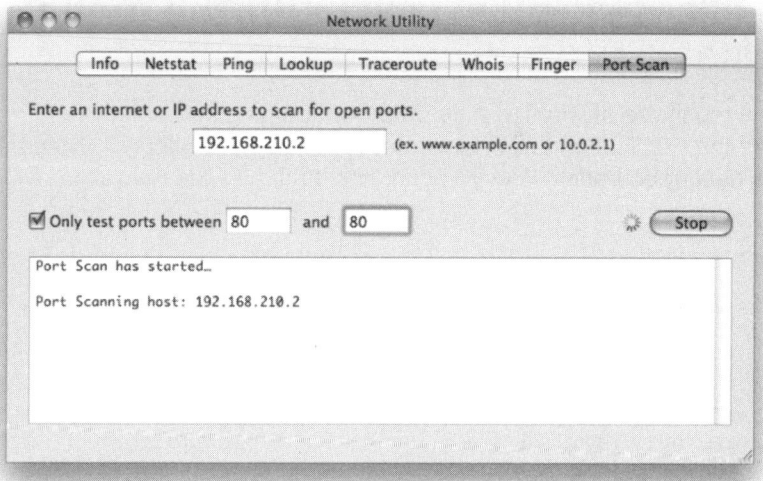

Figure 11–9. *Port scanning with Network Utility*

> **NOTE:** The ability to run a port scan on versions of OS X older than Tiger is disabled unless the BSD subsystem is installed. The BSD subsystem is installed by default; if it is explicitly not installed, and the system is then upgraded to newer versions of OS X, in most cases the BSD subsystem will not be installed.

Network Utility, although robust, can tend to run rather slowly. For a quicker, dirtier port scan, there is a hidden command-line scanning utility, called `stroke`, that will allow you to use the port scanner included with Mac OS X much more quickly to scan ranges of ports. The `stroke` command is just the command-line version of the port scanner in Network Utility, separate from the GUI, causing it to run much faster. It is located in the /Applications/Utilities/Network Utility.app/Contents/Resources folder. To invoke the `stroke` command, you will need to use the Terminal application to access it. For example, if you wanted to scan ports 25 (SMTP) to 80 (HTTP) of a mail server to see what services are listening on what port, using the `stroke` command, you would type the following:

stroke mail.mydomain.com 25 80

This command would result in something much similar to what Network Utility would display, only it's quicker because it's coming from the command line:

```
Port Scanning host: 208.57.132.195
        Open TCP Port:      25
        Open TCP Port:      53
        Open TCP Port:      80
```

Configuring the Application Layer Firewall from the Command Line

Mac OS X 10.5 has a multitude of ways to stop data from coming into or leaving a system. To configure the Application Layer Firewall you will use the Security System Preference pane (as described earlier). But you can also configure the firewall from the command line.

Stopping and starting Application Layer Firewall is easy enough, using launchd. To stop:

```
launchctl unload /System/Library/LaunchAgents/com.apple.alf.useragent.plist
launchctl unload /System/Library/LaunchDaemons/com.apple.alf.agent.plist
```

To start:

```
launchctl load /System/Library/LaunchDaemons/com.apple.alf.agent.plist
launchctl load /System/Library/LaunchAgents/com.apple.alf.useragent.plist
```

These will start and stop the firewall daemon (aptly named firewall) located in the /usr/libexec/ApplicationFirewall directory. As you can imagine, the settings for Application Layer Firewall can be configured from the command line as well. The `socketfilterfw` command, in this same directory, is the command that actually allows you to manage ALF.

When an application is allowed to open or accept a network socket, it's known as a trusted application, and ALF keeps a list of all of the trusted applications. You can view trusted applications using `socketfilterfw` with the -l option. The output can be difficult to read and can be constrained by using grep for TRUSTEDAPPS as follows (assuming that the /usr/libexec/ApplicationFirewall is your current working directory):

```
./socketfilterfw -l | grep TRUSTEDAPPS
```

You can also use the command line to add a trusted application using the -t option followed by the path and then the application to be trusted. For example, to add FileMaker to the list of trusted apps, you'd want to use something similar to the following, pointing to the binary, not the app bundle:

```
./socketfilterfw -t
"/Applications/FileMaker Pro 9/FileMaker Pro.app/Contents/MacOS/FileMaker Pro"
```

> **NOTE:** You can also use the codesign command to sign applications, verify signatures and enable debugging, using the -s, -v options and -d options respectively.

Finally, there are a number of global preferences for the firewall that can be configured using the /usr/libexec/ApplicationFirewall/com.apple.alf.plist preferences file. The com.apple.alf.plist file there is a bit temperamental. Changes there simply don't seem to have the desired response. Therefore, stick with the one in the /Library/Preferences directory. Some keys in this file that might be of interest include globalstate (0 disables the firewall, 1 configures for specific services and 2 is for essential services like the GUI), stealthenabled, and loggingenabled.

Using Mac OS X to Protect Other Computers

Mac OS X provides users with the ability to share an Internet or network connection with other computers. Internet Sharing is a handy utility that Apple included in its operating system that allows you to use your computer as a router in much the same way that a firewall appliance is used, as discussed in Chapter 10. Sharing an Internet connection can be extremely useful in a pinch, however, it should be disabled when not in use.

Enabling Internet Sharing

The controls for enabling Internet Sharing are located on the Internet tab of the Sharing pane (see Figure 11–10). This pane allows you to choose the port connection to share from, which is similar to how you would configure your WAN, or outside Internet connection on a firewall appliance. You can also choose which network adapter you'd like to use to share the connection. This option is similar to the LAN, or internal network accessing clients, option on firewall appliances.

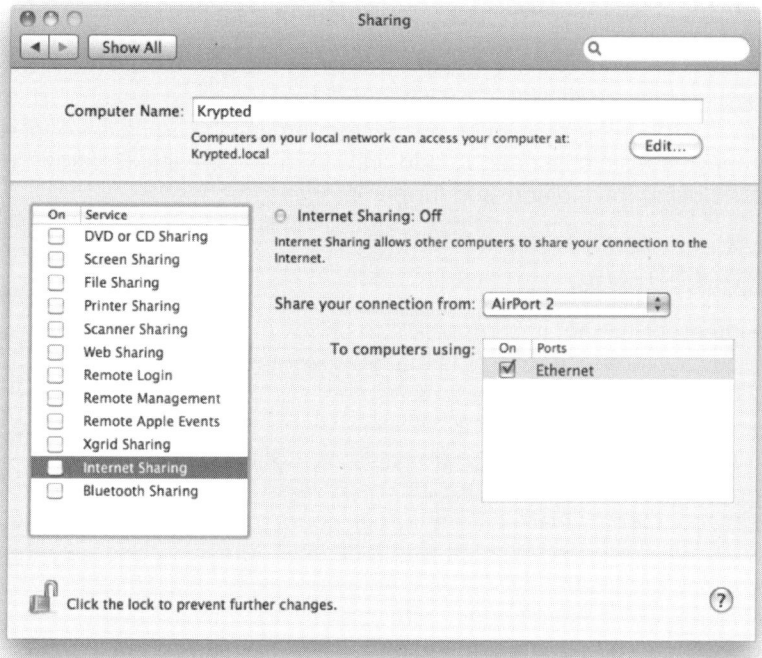

Figure 11–10. *Internet Sharing settings*

Once you have set your sharing settings and started the Internet Sharing service, you'll need to assign IP address information for client computers in order for them to access the Internet. If they are set to use Dynamic Host Control Protocol (DHCP), a protocol used specifically for handing out IP addresses, the Internet router (which could be your computer or an AirPort using Internet Sharing) will provide dynamic IP addresses to them. Or you can assign static IP addresses to them. To use a static IP address, you'll need to know the network settings on your computer or router and configure the other computers in the same way. At this point, any system that can connect to your computer's IP address can access the Internet, provided it has the correct information and is patched or wirelessly connected to your computer.

Configuring Clients

The first network you'll establish using Internet Sharing on your system will use the IP address of 192.168.2.1. This will allow all client systems that are connected to the network to connect to the Internet. To connect to the Internet, client computers will need an IP address that falls between 192.168.2.2 and 192.168.2.254. The subnet mask that would be used in this setup is 255.255.255.0. All subsequent subnets and networks would use the same subnet mask as the first.

IP and gateway settings do change when establishing multiple networks. The second network uses the IP address 10.0.2.1, and computers using the IP addresses from 10.0.2.2 10.0.2.254 can communicate with it. A third adapter would use 192.168.3.1, and clients would communicate using 192.168.3.2 to 192.168.3.254.

Clients connected to each network will use the IP address of the adapter as their Default Gateway or Router setting (the name of this option varies per operating system). This routes all traffic bound for the Internet through the system on which you have enabled Internet Sharing. In many cases, you'll need to add firewall rules for each IP range, which can only be done using ipfw, discussed further later in this chapter.

Dangers of Internet Sharing

When implementing Internet Sharing, it is important to check the configuration to make sure it is set up correctly. One reason for this is that your computer, when running Internet Sharing, will by default give IP addresses to other computers using DHCP. If you set it up improperly, you can cause entire networks that are not protected sufficiently against rogue DHCP servers to go down. Rogue DHCP servers can be difficult to track down in environments that use inexpensive switches. It's also fairly common in creative environments where different freelancers move in and out of the company on a daily basis (a common situation with Mac environments). Because the first interface that provides connections to other computers issues 192.168.2 IP addresses, any time your client systems begin getting an IP address that starts with 192.168.2, you should look for a Mac running Internet Sharing. This is often the place to look if you are the network administrator of a network and you notice that many of your computers are getting bad dynamic IP information.

Also, connecting to a network and sharing a connection using the same adapter for both your Internet connection and your client computers can cause serious network problems. In a cable modem or DSL environment, you'll more than likely cause your service to be turned off. If your service does not get cut off, congratulations, you've successfully bridged your network to the network of your Internet service provider. This can cause any computer on their network, of which there are likely tens or hundreds of thousands, to have the ability to access any computer on your network. This is only a risk if you have two Ethernet cards, patch the cables incorrectly *and* if you are sharing an Ethernet connection.

If we wanted to share a network connection and had only one network interface, such as an Ethernet card, our best way to accomplish this would be to install a second Ethernet card into the system to share the connection. Sharing a network connection over an AirPort card is risky, and you'll need to address some security concerns. The most important concern is the fact that the security of the network is based on wireless protocols which, by their very nature, are seldom properly secured. Traffic sent over a wireless network is easily interceptable, potentially exposing passwords and other private information. We will discuss this further in Chapter 12.

Working from the Command Line

Although it is possible to adequately configure the firewall through the Mac OS X Sharing System Preference or through third-party applications, sometimes you'll want to get even more granular. For example, you might want to perform a more advanced security lockdown such as denying outgoing traffic for certain ports while continuing to allow incoming traffic on those same ports. Or you might want to disable communications to and from certain IP addresses rather than across the board. These and other specific tasks, such as bandwidth throttling, can be accomplished only by using the command line. They cannot be accomplished with the GUI. Before we delve into the specific commands, we need to discuss some of the ways to get more granular with controlling your firewall and why it is important to maintain this control.

Getting More Granular Firewall Control

A *network adapter* is a physical connection that your computer makes to a network. Network adapters include your Ethernet card (or cards if you have a MacPro), your AirPort interface (whether it is built into your computer or a card that you have added), your FireWire interface, modems, and any other item that allows your computer to access other computers.

Because of the nature of complex networking, sometimes you'll want to assign differing rule sets to different interfaces or different IP addresses within different interfaces. For example, you might want to put multiple e-mail domains on separate IP addresses within the same network interface. There are definite benefits to this. The configuration of multiple IP addresses can bring a more fault-tolerant network connection to the server, it can provide other features with the mail server, and it could be used to run various services over the same port on the same system. However, these configurations can be difficult to set up using the graphical tools built into the OS, because each instance of a network interface must be configured separately. By default, all firewall rules created on the Sharing pane are applied to all network interfaces. To make these configuration changes possible, you will need to use the command line to configure the firewall.

Configuring multiple IP addresses on a Mac is a fairly straightforward process. Each network interface is not limited to using one IP address. Adding an IP address to a network interface is fairly simple. You can do this by opening the Network system preferences pane, clicking the + icon, choosing the appropriate adapter, and clicking the Add button. This creates a second listing for the duplicated network interface and allows you to give it an IP address. If you have multiple IP addresses, you will notice that although network requests can be sent to multiple interfaces on the system, they will always reply from the one that is the primary interface. An example of a system using multiple IP addresses for the same interface, in Figure 11–11, shows that the instance of the AirPort occurs twice: once under the heading of AirPort 3 and once under the heading of AirPort 2.

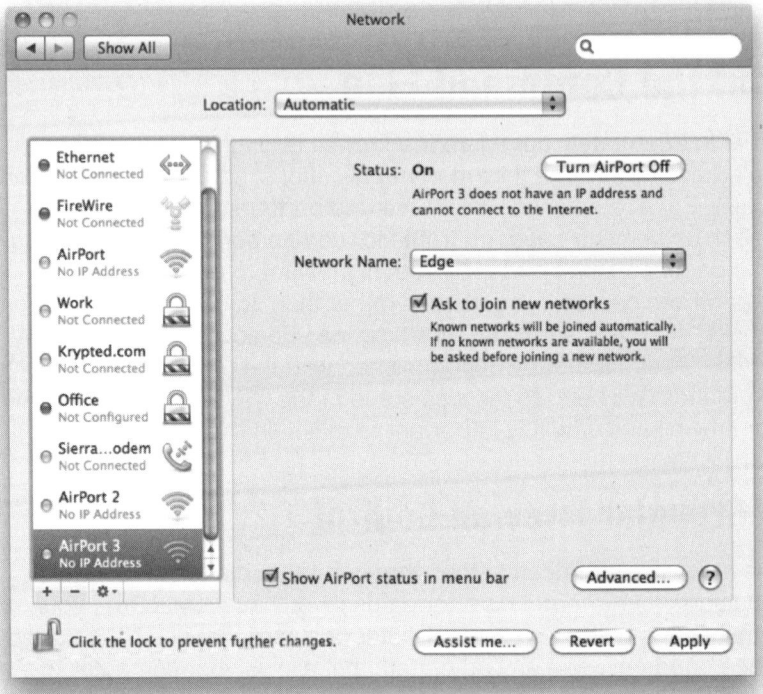

Figure 11-11. *Adding another IP address*

As mentioned previously, a really important security measure to take with your network is to lock down certain types of outgoing traffic on specific ports. For example, in an educational environment, a system administrator may want to lock down most types of outgoing Internet traffic. Remote control applications, instant messaging applications, and file-sharing peer-to-peer software all tend to be unnecessary on client computers in a classroom environment. Because these programs make requests for outgoing traffic, they will need their ports locked down for them to be properly secured. In the workplace, you might want to block streaming Internet music stations to help conserve precious bandwidth, or you might want to restrict staff from using a file-sharing protocol to keep them from taking creative assets out of your environment. All of this must be configured using the command line.

Some outgoing network traffic blocking can be configured using a firewall device at the edge of your network, but not all. Even if it is possible at the firewall-device level, it's wise to impose a rule at both the software level and the hardware level to circumvent a breach at one of your layers of defense. This layered, or tiered, approach to security helps keep your network as secure as possible. But little of this would be possible without `ipfw`. Another reason to use `ipfw` to configure your firewall is to block outgoing traffic for certain ports, a feature not available otherwise.

> **NOTE:** Later in this chapter we will discuss blocking outgoing traffic, but it is important to point out that you can block outgoing traffic only by using either the command line or a third-party application. You can block incoming traffic by using the built-in firewall in System Preferences.

Using ipfw

The firewall located on the Sharing pane in Tiger is based on the open source program `ipfw`. Ipfw is short for Internet Protocol Firewall and can also be used with Leopard and Snow Leopard. The `ipfw` program has the ability to configure the port-based firewall in OS X, different from the application layer firewall in that rather than relying on application signatures it monolithically blocks specified ports. However, there is a rather steep learning curve when configuring the firewall with the `ipfw` interface for the first time, especially if you aren't very experienced with BSD. But learning curves are good. They offer you a chance to know more about the firewall on your system, what it is doing, and the key factors you should consider to make your network more secure. You also have the opportunity to get to know more about the inner workings of your system and how the different pieces to the security puzzle fit together.

Because `ipfw` works at the kernel level, or innermost level, of the operating system, it has particular security requirements and requires that you run it from a superuser account. This is accomplished by using the `sudo` command to issue commands and create rules for it. Applications such as LimeWire or Samba (the Windows file-sharing component of Mac OS X) cannot override rules enforced by `ipfw` because of the secure nature of the command. The official syntax for the base `ipfw` toolkit is as follows:

```
ipfw [-cq] add rule
    ipfw [-acdefnNStT] {list | show} [rule | first-last ...]
    ipfw [-f | -q] flush
    ipfw [-q] {delete | zero | resetlog} [set] [number ...]
    ipfw enable {firewall | one_pass | debug | verbose | dyn_keepalive}
    ipfw disable {firewall | one_pass | debug | verbose | dyn_keepalive}
```

Inspecting ipfw Rules

To understand how to make the firewall perform many of its more complex features, you first need to understand what the firewall is doing and how it interacts with rules and the rule set. An `ipfw` rule is a line of code that informs your firewall about what is acceptable to allow and what to do when a pattern that you indicate is encountered. The `ipfw` rule set is the combination of all the `ipfw` rules that need to be invoked to provide the proper configuration for the policy item. Ipfw applies this rule set as criteria for whether network traffic that is being scanned is acceptable to enter the network. This can include which rules to log, what to do when a pattern matches a rule, and how much bandwidth is possible on a rule (limiting bandwidth is possible using dummynet).

Rules in an `ipfw` rule set are processed based on their numerical priority. Each rule requires a unique five-digit number in the first column of the rule with a maximum value of 65535 that tells `ipfw` what priority to assign it in a rule set. They are then processed in order from highest to lowest. This is an example of an `ipfw` rule:

```
01000 allow log all from any to any via en0
```

> **NOTE:** The rule number of this rule is 01000. Multiple rules can share the same number, but this is typically discouraged because it can make troubleshooting difficult.

This particular example rule allows all traffic into or out of the computer from any source over the en0 network interface and logs the activity (more about logging later). The en0 signifies the particular network interface our computer is using for the rule. To find out what naming conventions a computer uses for its network interfaces, reference Network Utility, located at `/Applications/Utilities`, to list the various network interface names. Network Utility shows each network interface, and when you click an interface, it shows detailed information about the interface on the screen.

You can get a detailed list of all the rules that are applied to your system by running the `ipfw show` command. When you run this command, you will see something like this:

```
00001       0      0 allow udp from any 626 to any dst-port 626
12301   11552 669920 allow tcp from any to any out
12302       0      0 allow tcp from any to any dst-port 22
12302       0      0 allow udp from any to any dst-port 22
12308       4    336 deny icmp from any to any icmptypes 8
12309       4    336 deny icmp from any to any icmptypes 0
12311       0      0 allow tcp from any to any dst-port 497
12311   20649 462537 allow udp from any to any dst-port 497
65535    4270 469852 allow ip from any to any
```

> **NOTE:** Notice that each service on the Sharing pane corresponds to a line in the `ipfw show` command.

The first column of the `ipfw show` output contains the rule's unique number (keep in mind that rule numbers should be unique). The second column shows the number of packets that matched each rule. The third column shows the number of bytes processed by that rule. The rest of the data indicates (in this order) whether the rule allows or denies traffic, the type of traffic it is moderating, the target of the traffic, the source of the traffic, and the port the traffic is using. What is of particular importance is the second column of numbers that shows you the amount of packets matching a rule. This allows you to see how often a rule is being processed and can help you determine whether you should block traffic on another device interface if the system is running slowly on this one.

To add a new rule to the current rule set, type `ipfw add` and then the rule you want to add. For example, the following command would add a rule to our firewall that limits outgoing traffic on port 80, effectively removing our ability to open or serve web sites (a common use for `ipfw`) on our local computer:

```
ipfw add 500 deny tcp from any to any dst-port 80
```

After invoking this rule, if we attempted to open a web browser, we would see an error. The add statement tells `ipfw` to add that rule to the current `ipfw` rule set using the unique number provided by `ipfw`.

To delete a rule from the current rule set, type `ipfw delete` followed by the unique number of the rule you want to remove. To delete the rule that is now blocking us from being able to access web sites, we would type the following:

```
ipfw delete 500
```

> **NOTE:** The first rule entered by a user (so it doesn't conflict with any autogenerated rules) should be 500. Rules can be numbered all the way up to 65,534. If you want to allow traffic to be processed only on a specific network adapter, then use the network interface ID being controlled, and append via `<network interface>` to the end of the line. For example, you would use the following code to allow any traffic to pass through your primary Ethernet interface: ipfw allow ip from any to any via en0

A WORD ABOUT LOGGING

Logging is a tricky thing. Too many logs, and you have too much data to make heads or tails of anything. Too little data, and your logs aren't comprehensive enough. When using `ipfw`, you can set logging options per rule. This allows you to prioritize which rules you consider important enough to receive logs about. To enable logging, add the word `log` following your `allow` or `deny` variable. In the following rule, we will log any attempts to access the network components of the popular game World of Warcraft III:

```
ipfw allow log tcp from any to any dst-port 6112-6119
```

ipfwloggerd

Once you are finished customizing your `ipfw` rule set, you can start looking into reviewing the logs that you set up to receive from your firewall. These can be pretty lengthy because many systems receive a lot of traffic. You can tell `ipfw` to log every packet that comes into your system or leaves your system by adding log to each rule.

Logging high loads of traffic can be far too much of a workload for `ipfw` to handle on its own, but many administrators require it for security tracking purposes. Because `ipfw` sometimes cannot handle the immense logging load, a daemon was developed to unload the logging of `ipfw` events to another process. Ipfwloggerd is the process that manages logging `ipfw` events. Logs containing information about traffic that is dropped are stored at /var/log/system.log and can be viewed using the Console application located at /Applications/Utilities.

For a more thorough discussion of reviewing logs and the `ipfw` log, see Chapter 5.

/etc/ipfilter/ipfw.conf

Up to this point, we've discussed creating rules and checking the logs for attempts to access resources that match the rules. But none of the rules that have been created will still be active on the next restart. When using `ipfw` interactively, any rule changes that are made to the `ipfw` rule set are not saved on the next reboot. Experimenting with firewall rules can cause harsh problems on systems if done without taking precautions. So, it is a good idea to avoid applying rules permanently until you are savvy enough to remove them if you get into trouble.

When your computer is booted up and `ipfw` first starts, it processes the `ipfw.conf` file. To make these changes persistent, you need to update this .conf file. But, before we jump into that, let's discuss how to get yourself out of a jam if you make a mistake. In the `ipfw.conf` file, there is a significant amount of commented-out text that tells you the proper syntax to use in the file. This is a way for you to undo what you've done. To exclude or comment text out from /etc/ipfilter/ipfw.conf, you need to add # in front of the rule. Adding # in front of a rule tells the system not to process the rule when booting.

> **NOTE:** If you do not see a /etc folder on the root of your boot volume, then cd to the /private folder, and then look for the /etc folder in that directory.

Anytime you change your `ipfw.conf` file, you should back it up first. You can and probably should keep multiple versioned backups as you edit the `ipfw.conf` file. Once you update the `ipfw.conf` file and save it, you will need to restart `ipfw` for the changes to take effect. Don't forget to scan blocked ports to verify your changes were applied and are correct after restarting the firewall.

Using Dummynet

On a drive down from San Francisco to Los Angeles, one of the authors of this book was very safely speeding down the 101 freeway. While coming through Santa Barbara, a police officer sped up behind him, sirens blazing. Prepared for the worst, he slowed down, expecting to get pulled over. To the author's pleasant surprise, she raced passed his car heading toward the traffic ahead of him. As he came around the corner into a wall of fog, he noticed that what she was actually doing was slowing the pace of traffic down to prevent everyone from crashing into what he later learned was a 13-car pile-up. He immediately made the connection: this is what can happen with DoS, or Denial of Service, attacks.

A variety of attacks take place against systems by flooding the computer with traffic and causing them to crash. These attacks are typically referred to as DoS attacks and can often be protected against by limiting the bandwidth that is available for a specified port; in effect, slowing the traffic down before it crashes into itself. Network traffic can accidentally attack itself by simply using too much bandwidth when connecting to a computer. Limiting bandwidth, often referred to as *throttling* or *traffic shaping*, is a good way to keep from overloading a system and crashing into a pile-up of network traffic.

Dummynet is a built-in Mac OS X tool that can be used to throttle traffic on a network. It allows the administrator to limit bandwidth for certain ports or IP address groups on the network. This is more than a basic Boolean, or true/false, argument indicating that traffic can or cannot be allowed. Dummynet works in conjunction with `ipfw` to limit the throughput of traffic that matches certain criteria when `ipfw` rules are created. It is not run as a command but is instead called by using pipes and queues, which we will discuss next.

> **NOTE:** Like `ipfw`, dummynet is a kernel-level facility.

Creating Pipes

To use dummynet, you start by creating a pipe or a set of pipes for traffic to flow through. A pipe is created by inserting a `pipe` command into an `ipfw` command, while using a unique numerical identifier to access it in the `ipfw` rule. The official syntax for the `ipfw` pipes is:

```
ipfw {pipe | queue} number config config-options
```

Each pipe has a maximum amount of throughput that can flow through it. The following creates pipe 1 that allows for 752KB worth of traffic to travel through the pipe per second:

```
ipfw pipe 1 config bw 752KByte/s
```

The previous command creates a pipe that limits traffic coming through the pipe and caps it at half a T1 worth of traffic. That is all it does. If you want to attach services to it, you need to augment the command with more specific criteria.

Let's say you want to create a rule that enforces a pipe to a specific port range. In the following example, we will limit AFP traffic to half of our T1 by binding pipe 1 to port 548.

```
ipfw add 1 pipe 1 src-port 548
```

> **NOTE:** The maximum number of pipes, by default, is 16. This is primarily because the `net.inet.ip.dummynet.max_chain_len` variable, which controls the maximum number of pipes, is set to 16. You can change this using sysctl. If you need more than 16 pipes, then you may have stability issues with high-traffic loads.

The final task with bandwidth throttling will be to limit the amount of throughput that each individual connection can take. In this case, you will use something known as *address masking*. When you use masking, you are telling the system to limit a specific IP address or set of IP addresses to a specified pipe size rather than applying a pipe to a port. To configure a pipe that limits each AFP connection (port 548) to 75Mbps, you would add the following series of lines to the system:

```
ipfw add pipe 1 ip from any to any src-port 548
ipfw pipe 1 config mask src-ip 0x0000ffff bw 75Mbits/s
```

> **NOTE:** As with other `ipfw` rules, your pipes must be added to your `ipfw.conf` file in order to be persistent after restarts.

Pipe Masks

Pipes can allow multiple queues per traffic flow. This allows you to cap the bandwidth of each server and not just the aggregate bandwidth of all traffic moving through the pipe. This allows an administrator to manually create a pipe for each server when using Mac OS X as a gateway device (router).

Masks are used to define which hosts belong to a pipe. Masks can be specified as follows:

`dst-ip`: IP packets sent using the pipe for which they're bound.

`src-ip`: Mask for the specified source.

`dst-port`: Mask for the specified destination port.

`src-port`: Mask for the specified source ports.

`proto`: Mask for the specified protocol.

`all`: Mask for any computer.

For example, if you have a network behind a firewall and all your systems have a desired 500Kbit/s bandwidth maximum, all the traffic can be sent through a pipe. The cap of the pipe will then be applied to the aggregate traffic from all the hosts and not applied to each pipe individually. If the traffic for each host is sent into a separate queue and applied the bandwidth limit separately, you could use the following rule:

```
pipe 20 config mask src-ip 0x000000ff bw 500Kbit/s queue 100Kbytes
pipe 21 config mask dst-ip 0x000000ff bw 500Kbit/s queue 100Kbytes
add 10101 add pipe 20 all from 10.0.0.0/16 to any out via <IP of server>
add 10102 add pipe 21 all from 10.0.0.0/16 to any in via <IP of server>
```

> **NOTE:** Pipe masks get very complicated. We are looking to help you get started with using them, but mastering pipe masks is beyond the scope of this book. Refer to the manual page for `ipfw` in order to gain a mastery of them.

Queues

Sometimes you may want to assign priority to certain protocols. For example, you may be surfing the Internet from your home office computer and notice that the Internet is running very slowly. You have already designated certain pipes to allow certain bandwidth capacities. However, you would rather have Internet traffic take priority over other protocols on your network. This is different from throttling in `ipfw` rules. You have already told each service that it can take only a certain amount of resources. At this point you want to control which service will receive priority when two services compete for those resources.

A *queue* is one way to prioritize traffic that runs over a certain pipe. Queues have weights (similar to priorities) assigned to them using a range of 1 to 100. A weight can take up a certain percentage of a pipe. If you have two queues with weights of 20 and 80, they will take up 20 and 80% of a pipe, respectively. However, if you specify weights that do not equal 100, the pipe will assume you are splitting the weight between the two and divvy the weight up proportionately. For example, if you have two queues with weights of 10 and 40, it will compute that they will take up 20 and 80%of the pipe, respectively. By allowing traffic shaping in such a highly configurable manner, it is possible to have many different groupings, or *queues*, of systems that can receive various proportions of throughput to a pipe.

For example, a creative workgroup environment accessing a computer with File Sharing enabled will need some throttling to prevent the computer from being overloaded with requests. We know that the system will choke if it receives more than 800Mb worth of connections, so we will build a pipe allowing only 800Mb at a time. Of the connections we have coming into that pipe, we will build four queues. These will receive weights proportional to the bandwidth we want them to have.

In our example, we'll consider a typical creative workgroup. Queue 1 contains our creative users who are accessing the server using AFP (548). Queue 2 has our executive producers who are accessing the server through HTTP (80). Queue 3 contains our external users that access the server over FTP (21), and queue 4 has our backup system that uses Retrospect (497). The following represents a series of commands to build the appropriate queues for pipe 1 using what would typically be proportional weights:

```
ipfw pipe 1 config bw 800Mbit/s
ipfw queue 1 config pipe 1 weight 90
ipfw queue 2 config pipe 1 weight 80
ipfw queue 3 config pipe 1 weight 30
ipfw queue 4 config pipe 1 weight 10
ipfw add 40 queue 1 from any to any dst-port 548
ipfw add 41 queue 2 from any to any dst-port 80
ipfw add 42 queue 3 from any to any dst-port 20-21
ipfw add 43 queue 4 from any to any dst-port 497
```

In the previous rule set, we first created a pipe with an 800Mb limit. Then we created four queues with varying weights to create the various pipes for traffic to move through. From there we added four firewall rules (40 through 43) and assigned a destination port to each individual queue, allowing traffic from different ports to travel on their respective pipes. We could have also replaced the any statements on a per-rule basis to limit which IP addresses or ranges of IP addresses for which each queue is processed. For example, if you wanted to limit Retrospect traffic coming from one bandwidth-hogging computer (192.168.55.89) but not for the other computers, then you would be able to use the following in place of the last line of the previous code:

```
ipfw add 43 queue 4 from 192.168.55.89 to any dst-port 497
```

Now our creative group is functioning with traffic shaping based on their prioritized needs for accessing data.

Summary

ALF can be used to limit access that specific applications have in accessing network resources. In this chapter we spent a good amount of time looking at ALF. We first looked at configuring ALF from the System Preferences and then from the command line. We then switched into looking at a different firewall, which controls network access at a port level, meaning that all configurations per port are made for all applications. Given that there are no built-in graphical controls for ipfw, we only looked at configuring it from the command line; however, there are a number of third-party solutions that will allow you to configure ipfw without going to the command line.

All of these changes are made on wireless and wired clients alike. Next, in Chapter 12, we will focus on those changes that you can make to your wireless configuration and wireless environment.

Chapter 12

Securing a Wireless Network

At the Black Hat conference in August 2006, David Maynor and Jon "Johnny Cache" Ellch shocked the Mac community by demonstrating to the world something that hackers had known for a long time: the Mac could be hacked, easily. Maynor and Ellch, two security professionals with long-time careers in the security industry, were able to release what is known as a *proof-of-concept attack* by exploiting the wireless Atheros drivers built into the Mac operating system. Using a script called `setup.sh`, which turned a Mac computer (with its wireless card turned on) into an access point, an attacker could gain control of an unsuspecting Mac user's laptop. Another hacker script, called `bad_seed`, could then be run from the host computer to exploit the vulnerability in the target computer's wireless driver; this would give an attacker access to a Terminal session on the target computer running `root` (which is a "superuser" that is allowed full control of the computer). The exploit was not released, but it did provide proof that the Mac community was a long way away from an operating system immune to wireless attacks. The concept used in the wireless exploit was not specific to Apple computers, but pointed instead to general flaws in wireless networking protocols as a whole.

In this chapter, we'll cover securing Apple AirPort-based wireless networks. We'll begin with an introduction to wireless networking in general and then move into securing an Apple AirPort base station. Later in the chapter, to help show the importance of wireless security, we will showcase some common wireless hacking tools. We'll illustrate just how easy it is to listen in on wireless traffic, emphasizing why security measures are so important.

Wireless Network Essentials

From a basic security perspective, wireless networks can be rather challenging. Most amateur wireless setups are usually left unsecured, exposing user credentials, e-mails, and other data submitted over the network to the world, causing unnecessary security risks to sensitive information. It is all too easy to plug in an open wireless device on a wired network, causing a breach in the network that can then be exploited by someone tapping in from an outside location, such as a parking lot or nearby coffee shop. These and other security threats make it important to practice good security when configuring wireless networks.

To properly secure a wireless network, it is key to first have a fundamental understanding of what a wireless network is. A wireless network is different from an Ethernet network or a local area network (LAN), although the topologies often follow many of the same standards covered in Chapter 10. In fact, a wireless network is often referred to as a wireless LAN (wLAN).

Logging in to a wireless network is like connecting to a hub with all the other users of that network. But rather than traveling across copper wires to interconnect devices like LAN networks, wireless networks use channelized, low-powered radio waves running on the same frequencies as microwave ovens and cordless telephones. The 2.4GHz band is pretty crowded these days, now that the Bluetooth technology also runs on this frequency. This can often place a large quantity of traffic on these channels, causing data to get lost or fragmented in transit.

The speed and reliability of a wireless network depends on the hardware and proximity of the devices. Ranges between wireless devices are typically limited to a few hundred feet. The greater the distance, the greater the chance that packets will be intercepted.

> **NOTE:** A key element to focus on when studying wireless security is what happens with data that is not properly delivered between wireless devices.

Wireless networks that need to encompass a large area will be composed of multiple wireless devices, because of the short-range capacity of wireless connectivity. Wireless access points (WAPs) are the devices used to distribute the wireless signal across this network. They accomplish this using a *radio*, the device within the WAP that talks to the client computer's wireless card, creating a wireless signal. WAPs will often connect directly into a wired network, piggybacking on the wired network via an Ethernet connection, to distribute connectivity to the wireless network. This connection is known as a *backhaul*.

Wireless networks use the IEEE 802.11 protocol, which differs from other wireless protocols in how it processes the wireless signal and the frequency used for connectivity.

There are four flavors of 802.11 used in wireless networking as it applies to Macs. Each of the four primarily distributed wireless protocols runs at a different speed. The most common flavors are 802.11b running at 11 megabits per second, 802.11g running at 54 megabits per second, 802.11n running at 108 megabits per second, and 802.11a, which uses the 5GHz band for communications.

> **NOTE:** 802.1x is a highly secure wireless protocol typically found in larger network infrastructures. If your network can leverage this technology, check out our section on integrating 802.1x into your environment in Chapter 10.

Introducing the Apple AirPort

Over the years, Apple has released a variety of products in its family of WAPs, typically referred to as Apple AirPorts (see Table 12–1).

Table 12–1. *Types of Apple AirPorts*

Product	Description
AirPort (graphite)	The original gray AirPort. This AirPort ran at 802.11b.
AirPort Extreme (snow)	This AirPort ran at 802.11g and included a pair of Ethernet interfaces (one LAN and one WAN) and a USB port for printer sharing across a network.
AirPort Express	This is the first device Apple released with the ability to communicate with audio equipment. The AirPort Express has only one network connection and is limited to ten users, making it perfect for a home or small office.
AirPort Extreme (N)	This square white AirPort is the latest and greatest. It incorporates the newest 802.11 protocol, 802.11n, and also facilitates file sharing for smaller networks.

The AirPort supports a variety of encryption protocols that can be used to secure the wireless network. Encryption protocols that are specific to wireless networking include the following:

WPA2: Also known as 802.11i, WPA2 uses the AES block cipher to make cracking keys difficult. Unless you have a RADIUS server, WPA2 is the best form of encryption to use on an AirPort with Apple clients.

WPA2 Enterprise: Similar to WPA2 in supported encryption standards, WPA2 Enterprise also adds support for usernames, which can be obtained using a RADIUS server, such as FreeRadius, Mac OS X 10.5 or 10.6 Server, and Microsoft Windows Active Directory servers.

WEP: This is the weakest of the security features supported by Apple AirPort. Windows computers need to use the hex equivalent to log into the network. This can be found using the Equivalent Network Password option in the Edit menu of the AirPort Utility or AirPort Admin Utility.

The Apple AirPort devices were designed to be easy to use. In many environments, the Apple AirPort will work right out of the box. However convenient this may be, the default settings are widely known, so an AirPort left with the default settings running represents a considerable security risk for any network.

> **TIP:** AirPorts do not always need an Ethernet cable connection to become part of the network. If there are other AirPorts on the network, it is possible to use the wireless network of an existing AirPort network as the network connection that the AirPort will use. This is what is known as a wireless distribution system (WDS) cloud. A WDS network can allow you to extend a wireless network for great distances, and create a wireless network that goes far beyond the 300-foot limitation documented by Apple.

Configuring Older AirPorts

The first generation of Apple AirPorts, the AirPort (graphite), the AirPort Extreme (snow), and the AirPort Express, shipped with the AirPort Admin Utility. To configure an AirPort using the AirPort Admin Utility, open the application from /Applications/Utilities, and select the AirPort to configure from the list of AirPorts the computer can detect (see Figure 12–1).

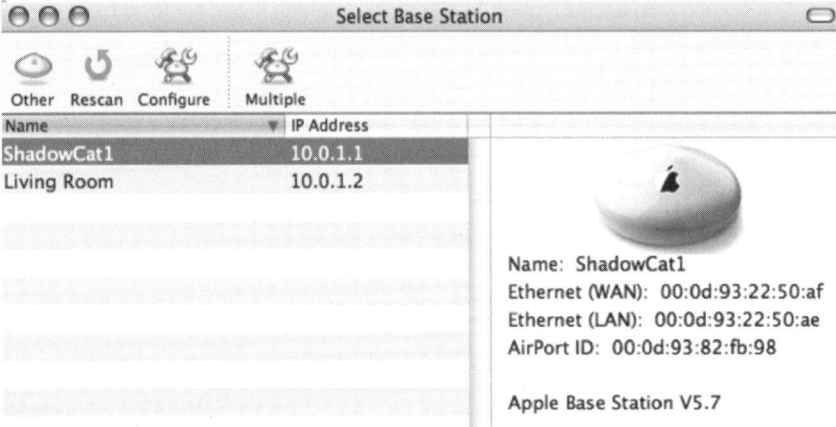

Figure 12–1. *The AirPort Admin Utility*

To add basic security using the AirPort Admin Utility, start by entering the appropriate contact information in the fields supplied (see Figure 12–2).

Figure 12–2. *Basic settings of an Apple AirPort*

The most important setting to change on the older AirPorts is the password to configure the device. The default password for an AirPort base station is *public*, and it is fairly common for users to leave the password set to this. You should always change this by clicking the Change Password button and entering a new one.

To set the form of encryption on an Apple AirPort using the AirPort Admin Utility, click the Wireless Options button. On the next screen (shown in Figure 12–3), select the form of security you want using the Wireless Security option. Then enter the password and click OK.

> **NOTE:** If you are changing the form of encryption on a network with WDS enabled, you will likely break the WDS network and need to set it up again. The WDS protocol requires all AirPorts to use the same security settings.

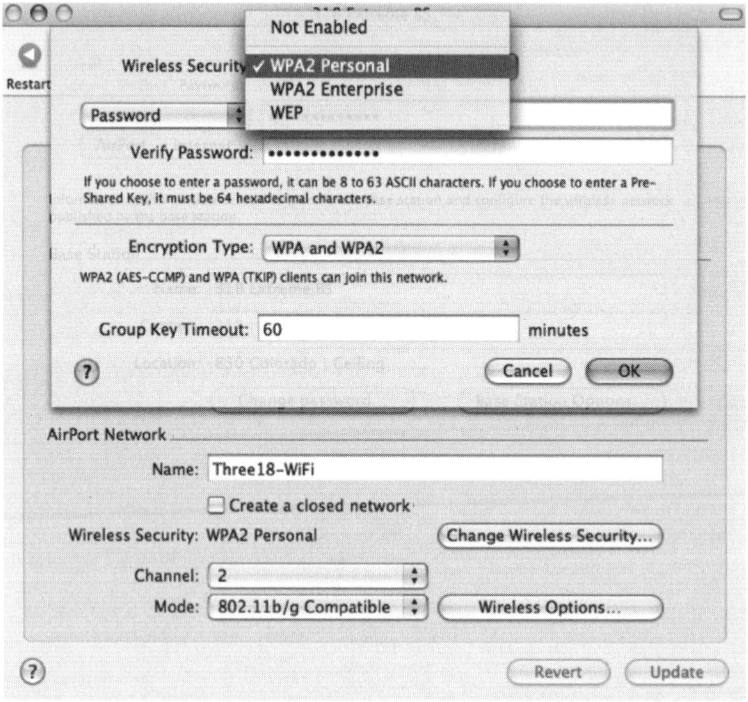

Figure 12-3. *Choosing a wireless protocol*

AirPort Utility

In the winter of 2007, Apple released the AirPort Utility, which shipped concurrently with the AirPort Extreme (N). The AirPort Utility, an upgraded version of the AirPort Admin Utility, has built-in controls for disk sharing and a more user-friendly, wizard-like approach to configuring AirPorts of all types, including older AirPorts. The new AirPorts greatly increased the ease of configuration from the older AirPorts. Not only were printer and disk sharing introduced, but the ability to run dual 2.4 and 5GHz networks on the same device became possible.

Configuring the Current AirPorts

When you start the AirPort Utility, you're immediately able to browse all the AirPorts on the network at once in a list on the left side of the screen. This list includes all AirPorts that are visible over the Ethernet interface, as well as AirPorts on the wireless network. You can choose to have the AirPort configured with the wizard by clicking Continue, or to be configured manually by clicking Manual Setup. Clicking Manual Setup opens the screen shown in Figure 12–4.

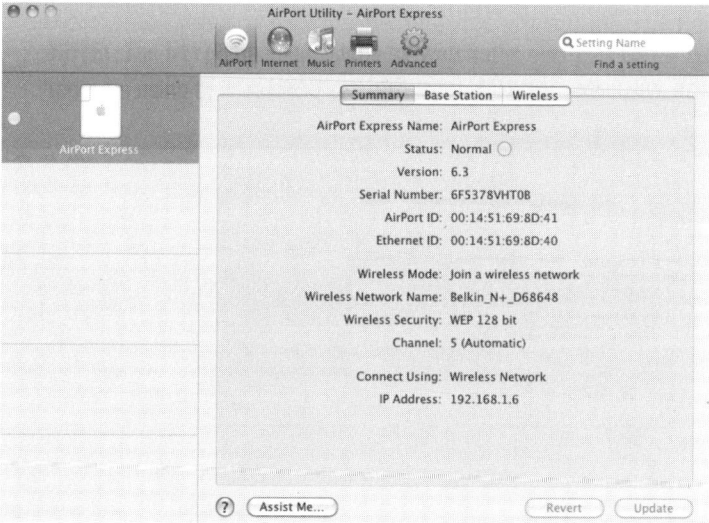

Figure 12-4. *Airport Utility Summary screen*

Once you have logged into the appropriate AirPort, click the AirPort icon in the toolbar, and then click the Base Station tab. On the Base Station tab, you will be able to reset the password to administer the AirPort, rename the base station, and add a network time server so the base station's time is always up to date (see Figure 12-5). As mentioned before, the administrator password should be changed immediately. This section also allows the administrator to set the time on the AirPort automatically by clicking Set Time Automatically. This is important for making sense of system logs, and can play a critical role in dealing with encryption keys.

Once you have set an administrative password, click the Wireless tab.

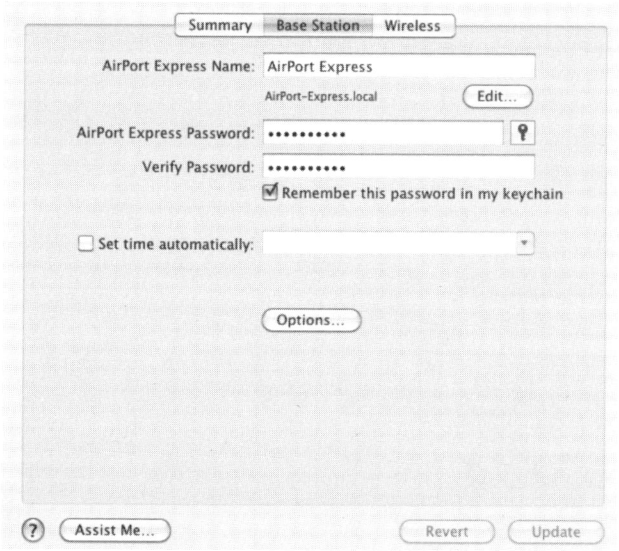

Figure 12-5. *Base station configuration*

CHAPTER 12: Securing a Wireless Network

From here, the first priority is to configure the wireless encryption type by selecting the encryption type from the Wireless Security drop-down list and entering the password that should be used to join the wireless network (see Figure 12–6).

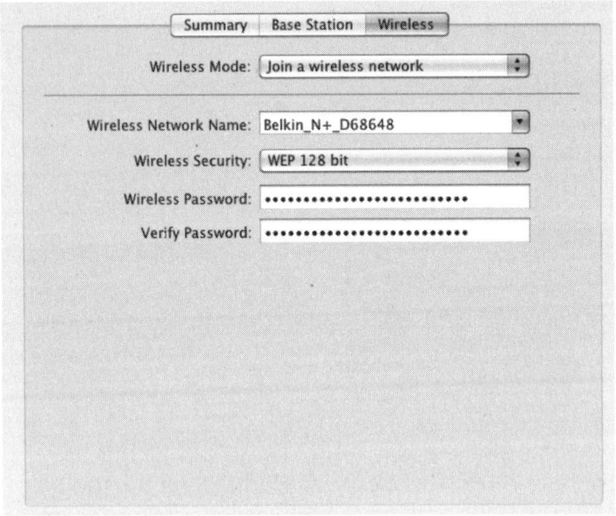

Figure 12–6. *Wireless Configuration*

Once the wireless network security is configured, if you are not configuring an AirPort Extreme and the AirPort receives an Internet connection from a DSL modem or some other publicly accessible source, it is a good idea to enable the basic firewall feature of the AirPort, also known as NAT. To enable NAT, click the Internet icon on the AirPort Admin Utility's toolbar, and then click the Internet Connection tab (see Figure 12–7). Selecting "Share a public IP address" enables NAT on the AirPort, making it act like a router/firewall. (For more about NAT, see Chapter 10.)

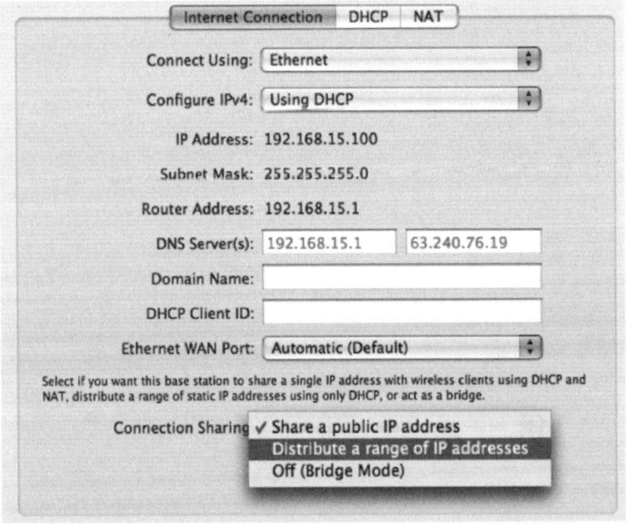

Figure 12–7. *Enabling routing on a base station*

Once router/firewall services are configured on the AirPort, it might be desirable to direct traffic to a local computer on the network. For example, if there is a web server on the network, web traffic may need to be directed to it. Or if one user wants access to files hosted on another computer on the network, traffic may need to be guided toward that computer. This is accomplished via port forwarding. To enable port forwards on the AirPort, click Internet in the AirPort Utility, then click the NAT tab, and check the Enable NAT Port Mapping Protocol box (as shown in Figure 12–8).

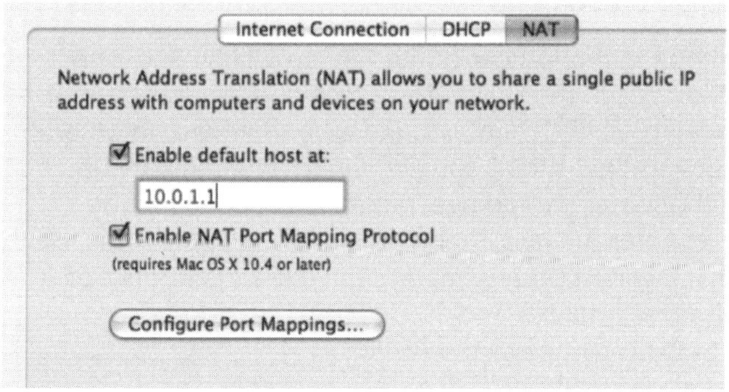

Figure 12–8. *NAT settings*

Once NAT is enabled, you need to specify the port (or ports) that are to be forwarded. You can do this by clicking the Configure Port Mappings button on the NAT tab. This opens a dialog box (shown in Figure 12–9) that asks for the public and private port numbers that the forwarded port should point to as well as the IP address to which traffic should forward.

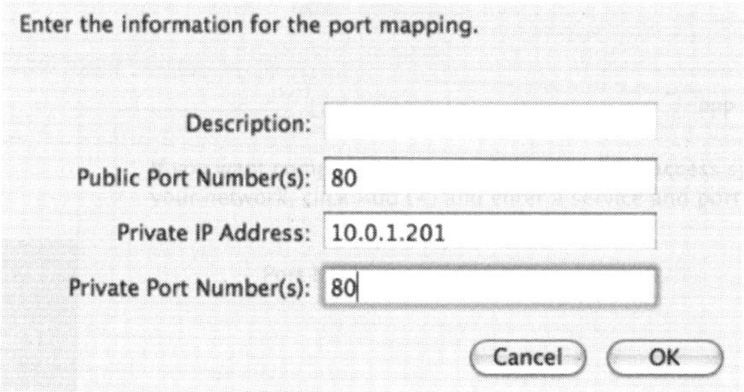

Figure 12–9. *Port mappings*

Using public and private ports allows the administrator to have more control over the network by redirecting traffic to different ports. If, for example, incoming traffic comes in on port 80 but, for heightened security, should point to port 81 on the server, then you'd enter **80** in the Public Port Number field and **81** in the Private Port Number field.

Limiting the DHCP Scope

If the AirPort is acting as a routing device and there are multiple computers for which the AirPort is directing traffic, then you should use the built-in DHCP feature on the AirPort.

The DHCP feature will configure the AirPort to hand out IP addresses to client computers on the network. A good way to secure the network is to limit the number of IP addresses assigned to networked computers. Limiting the number of assignable IP addresses to the exact number of computers on the network is a good way to ensure that only certain computers are able to use the address. Not allowing an unlimited number of computers to join the network limits the threat of unknown systems compromising your environment (although not as much as limiting access based on MAC address would as we will discuss later on).

To enable DHCP, click the Internet icon in the toolbar of the AirPort Utility, and select the DHCP tab (see Figure 12–10). Next, click the DHCP Range field, and select the IP address scheme to use. When choosing an IP scheme, make sure there are no other IP schemes already in place on the network that might conflict. Once an IP scheme is selected, enter the first IP address the router should use in the DHCP scope in the DHCP Beginning Address field. Then enter the last IP address in the scope in the DHCP Ending Address field. For example, if five computers need to have IPs distributed to them, then you'd use 10.0.1.2 as the first address and 10.0.1.6 as the last address. Clicking the Update button commits the changes to the AirPort.

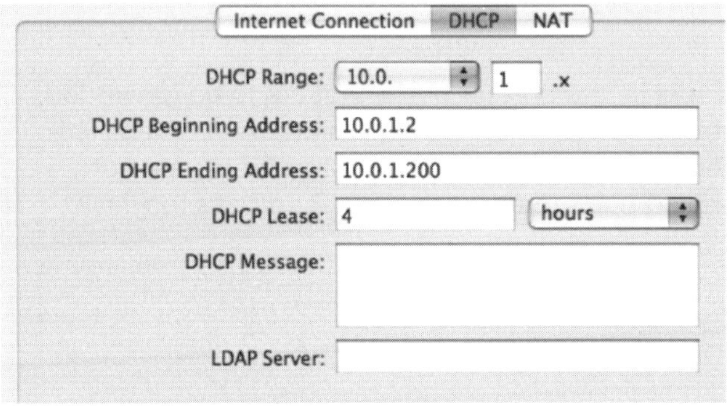

Figure 12–10. *DHCP settings*

Hardware Filtering

The AirPort can also restrict computers that are allowed to log in to it based on the MAC address of each client computer. The MAC address is a unique address on a network adapter (either wireless or wired) that is stamped by the vendor during assembly and is unique to the card. There should never be two cards with the same address. By using the actual hardware address of a computer to decide whether the computer can log in to the wireless network, a second layer of security is added to the wireless network (encrypted passwords providing the first layer, as discussed earlier).

To filter by MAC address, it is important to find the AirPort ID (the MAC address on a Mac) of each computer. This is located on the Network pane of System Preferences on the client computer. Clicking the Network tab, then clicking on the AirPort tab, and then clicking on the Advanced tab at the bottom opens a list of various protocols that the

Mac will use to communicate on the network. At the bottom of this pane, you'll see your computer's AirPort ID (see Figure 12–11).

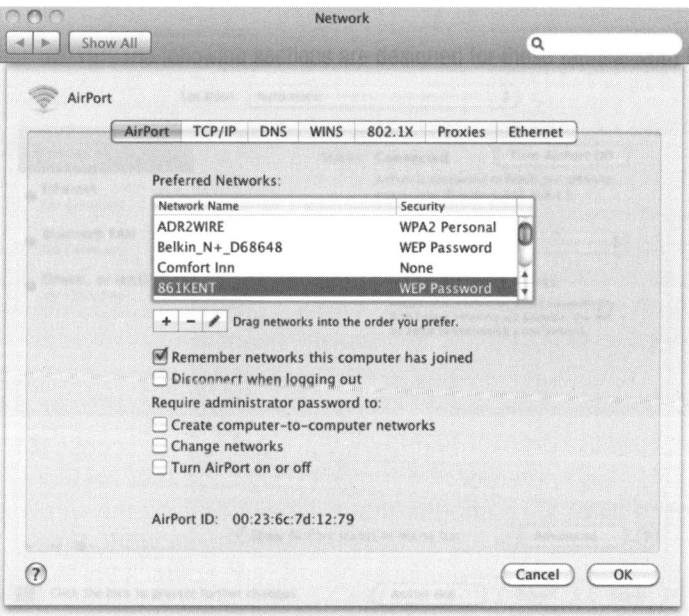

Figure 12–11. *Identifying your MAC address*

> **NOTE:** We suggest writing down all the AirPort IDs on your network before beginning this process, and adding them during the initial setup of the AirPort.
>
> Once the AirPort IDs have been assembled, enable MAC filtration on the AirPort by opening the AirPort Utility and clicking the AirPort icon in the toolbar. Then select the Access Control tab, and set the MAC Address Access Control feature to Local (see Figure 12–12). This can only be done on AirPorts other than Airport Express AirPorts.

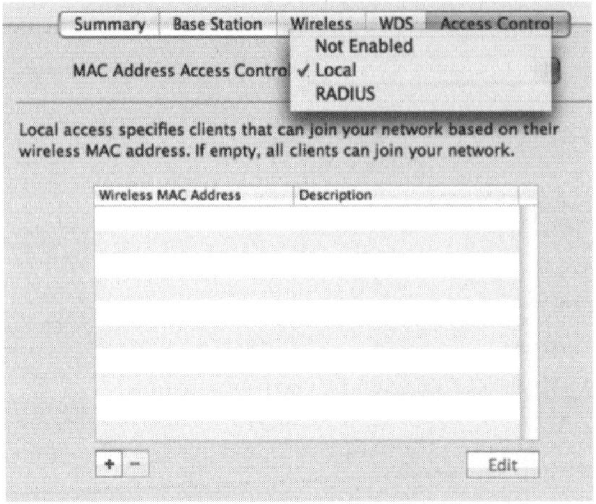

CHAPTER 12: Securing a Wireless Network

Figure 12-12. *MAC address access controls*

Before clicking Update, make sure to add the computers you want to give access to on the wireless network. To add a computer, click the plus (+) sign at the bottom of the screen. Now type the AirPort ID of the computer that will be accessing the wireless network. If you want to limit which machines can access the wireless network, then you can click the plus (+) sign. As you can see in Figure 12-13, this opens a screen that enables you to enter the MAC address of the AirPort card (or other wireless adapter). If you are using MAC addresses, only the systems listed will be able to join the wireless network.

> **CAUTION:** If the computer configuring the MAC filtering is not configured, it will not be able to tap back into the wireless network and will need to use a wired computer for access once you click Update.

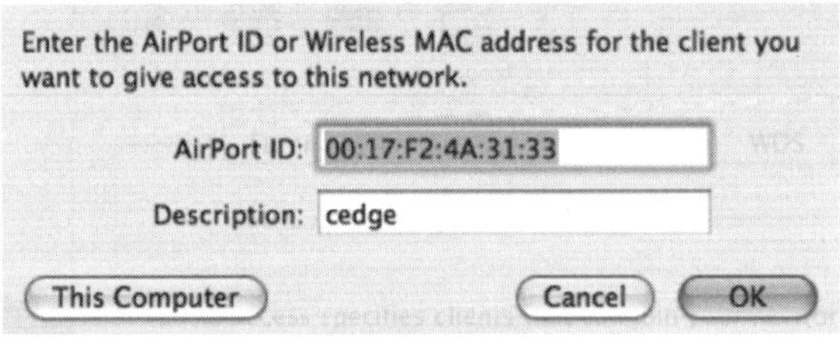

Figure 12-13. *Using the MAC address*

AirPort Logging

The AirPort does not keep logs for an indefinite amount of time. For longer log retention, an OS X Server should be configured with the syslog service option to keep AirPort logs long-term. Syslog is a built-in configurable service of OS X Server. To enable the syslog function of OS X Server, click the Advanced button in the toolbar of the AirPort Utility. Then, click the Logging & SNMP tab (see Figure 12-14), and enter the IP address for the syslog OS X Server. Choose the level of alerts that are sent to the server using the Syslog Level drop-down list.

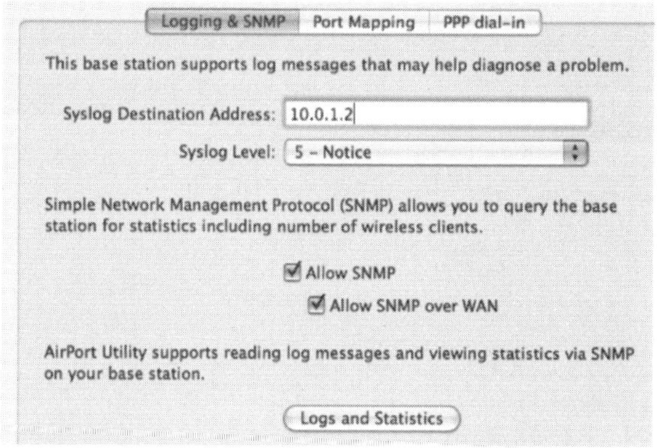

Figure 12-14. *Enabling logging*

> **NOTE:** If a syslog server is not available, you can still click the "Logs and Statistics" button to review logs. However, the AirPort will erase these log files the next time it loses power or is reset.

Hiding a Wireless Network

Another good way to protect an Apple wireless network is to hide the SSID of the network, (also known as SSID suppression), which will cause the wireless network not to appear in the list of available networks for users. If fewer people can discover a wireless network, it is less likely to be hijacked and abused. This isn't to say that hiding the SSID makes the network completely undiscoverable. Later in this chapter, we will discuss tools such as KisMAC and iStumbler that will allow those who "wardrive" to see networks even when the SSID has been suppressed. SSID suppression is a good mechanism for security, but only when used in conjunction with other security measures.

To suppress the SSID for your Apple AirPort, click the Wireless tab for your AirPort, and then click the Wireless Options button. This opens a screen similar to Figure 12-15, from which you can select to "Create a Closed Network." An AirPort environment with the SSID suppressed is synonymous with a closed network in Apple terminology.

> **NOTE:** *Wardriving* is the act of searching for wireless networks in a moving vehicle using a computer or a PDA to detect and access wireless networks.

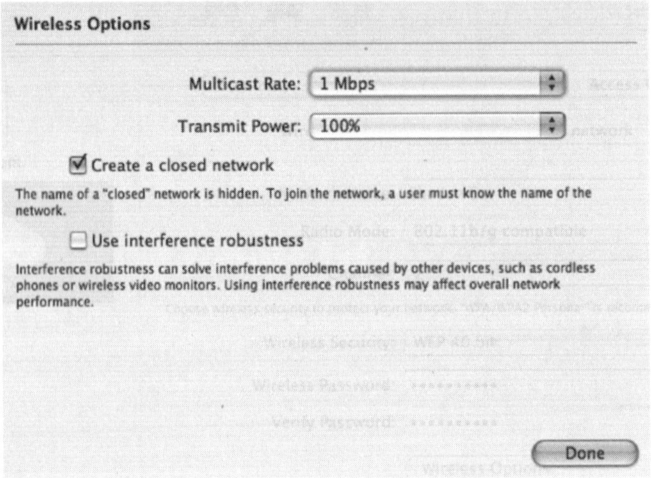

Figure 12-15. *Creating a closed network*

Base Station Features in the AirPort Utility

Every Apple computer comes with a utility to manage Apple AirPorts. This means that every Mac on your network has the ability to configure your AirPorts, which can be dangerous. Now imagine if every Apple computer on the Internet were able to configure your AirPort. If you select "Allow configuration over Ethernet WAN port" (see Figure 12-16), this is exactly what you are allowing. Do not use this feature unless you really must use it. If it is absolutely necessary to allow administration over the Ethernet, make sure to put an administrative password on the AirPort and give the password only to those who absolutely need it.

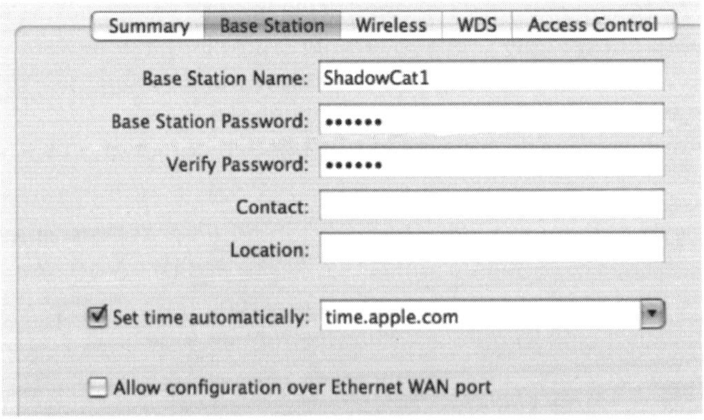

Figure 12-16. *Allowing configuration over the Ethernet WAN port*

The AirPort Express

From a security perspective, the Apple AirPort Express closely resembles the Apple AirPort. However, there are certain features, such as NAT enabling and Access Control, that cannot be configured on the AirPort Express. One extra security precaution to consider on the AirPort Express is its port dedicated for playing audio. iTunes has a field that can be used to log into an AirPort Express and play audio to the device.

To reliably secure the AirPort Express features for playing audio, log into the AirPort Express and click the Music Icon in the toolbar. This opens a screen that allows you to disable AirTunes, which you should do if you are not using this feature. If you are using AirTunes, then create a speaker password using the AirTunes option in AirPort Setup (shown in Figure 12–17), which will then be required by anyone using the AirPort Express to listen to music.

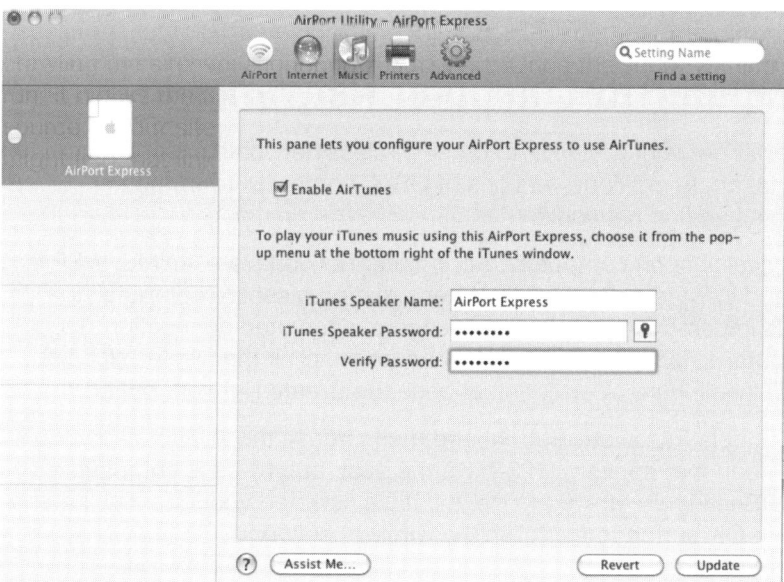

Figure 12–17. *Securely Configuring AirTunes*

Wireless Security on Client Computers

As mentioned, David Maynor clearly demonstrated that Apple client computers are not immune to wireless attacks. When using a public wireless network, it is often best to make sure you are using a secure means of authenticating and transmitting data. For example, when traveling, we always use a VPN to connect to our office network and access resources. This extra layer of authentication keeps the data away from prying eyes that may be watching these public networks.

> **NOTE:** When your AirPort connection is not in use, make sure to turn off the AirPort. Anytime you are not using the wireless, try to keep it turned off. To disable it, just click the AirPort icon at the top of your screen, and click Turn AirPort Off (see Figure 12–18).

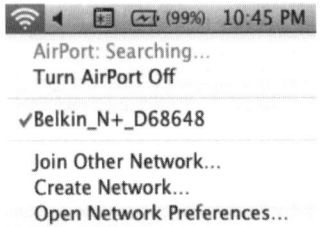

Figure 12–18. *Airport options*

Securing Computer-to-Computer Networks

A *computer-to-computer network* is similar to other wireless networks except it does not have a central base station. In previous versions of OS X, computer-to-computer networks were known as *ad hoc networks*.

The security features available on computer-to-computer networks are limited. WEP is disabled by default, and WPA is not available. When creating a secure computer-to-computer network it is imperative to implement a secure, encrypted connection. To create a secure computer-to-computer network connection, click the wireless icon at the top of your screen (see Figure 12–18), and choose the Create Network option.

From there, click the Enable Password Button, and then choose the level of encryption from the drop-down menu that appears (128-bit is the best, but 40-bit is compatible with older machines). (See Figure 12–19.) Once you have selected your channel, enter a password and click the OK button to establish the wireless network.

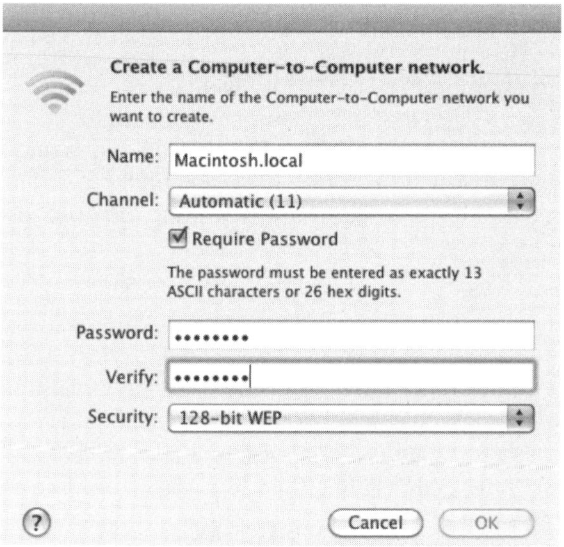

Figure 12-19. *Creating computer-to-computer networks*

Wireless Topologies

A wireless network's placement within a network can greatly impact the security level of the network. Many wireless networks, for ease of use, will want to have NAT disabled, allowing AppleTalk and Bonjour connections into devices on the wired network. For larger networks where security is paramount, network administrators should strongly consider putting an Apple AirPort in a demilitarized zone (DMZ). A DMZ sits outside the corporate firewall and can have a completely different set of rules for how network traffic is managed.

The default configuration of an Apple AirPort has NAT enabled. This removes the ability of the wireless clients to communicate over broadcast networks with upstream networks. However, clients can still communicate by IP address with upstream networks. Therefore, this is not actually a DMZ but instead a subnetwork of your main network. Communications are still possible and less controllable.

The preferred location of AirPorts and wireless access points is in a DMZ. It is important to note that placing the wireless access point in a network above rather than below (in terms of the network architecture) will render your NAT wireless clients unable to communicate directly with your corporate network. They will need to establish a VPN tunnel to talk to the network. With this setup, traffic can be most effectively encrypted.

This network topology is often employed in larger companies, and in the future we expect more and more wireless protocols to be developed around it.

Wireless Hacking Tools

Several tools can be used when looking to enumerate or crack into wireless networks. Many of these have graphical user interfaces (GUIs) that allow less-savvy users to perform very complicated tasks, such as mapping out WEP keys for physical areas and cracking wireless networks with relative ease, even if they don't have any background in hacking. We'll spend some time covering these tools so you'll know what to look out for when securing your wireless network.

KisMAC

KisMAC is a free network scanning utility that was not intended to be a hacking utility. But it can definitely be used to detect and crack wireless networks. When scanning, KisMAC shows networks in four colors, based on their level of encryption. Green is open, yellow is unknown, red is WEP, and blue is WPA (see Figure 12–20).

KisMAC
KisMAC 0.21a
Packets
15 sec
6 packets/sec
Smarte Carte Office
2WIRE628
LAX_WPA
swissport
6 packets/sec
Stop Scan

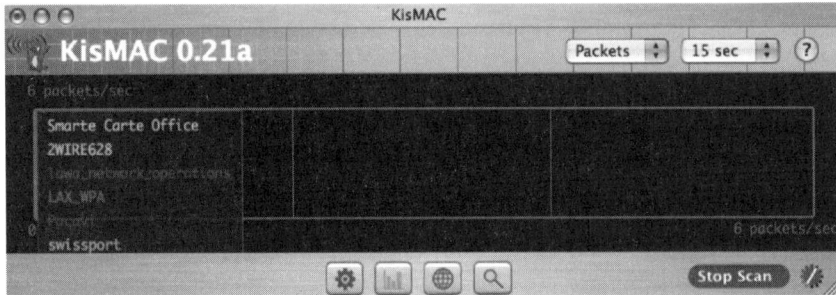

Figure 12–20. *KisMAC*

Figure 12–21 lists all of the wireless networks that are visible by KisMAC scanners. KisMAC will show the signal strength and type of encryption for each of the networks, making it very easy to find AirPorts that are close to you as well as isolating networks with weak signal strengths.

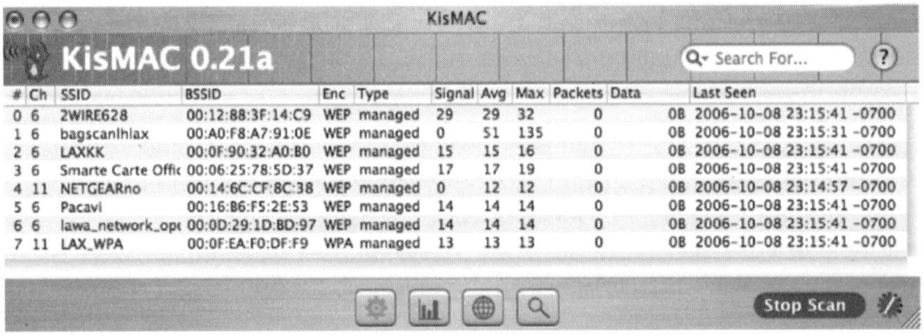

KisMAC
KisMAC 0.21a
Search For...
Ch SSID BSSID Enc Type Signal Avg Max Packets Data Last Seen
0 6 2WIRE628 00:12:88:3F:14:C9 WEP managed 29 29 32 0 0B 2006-10-08 23:15:41 -0700
1 6 bagscanlhlax 00:A0:F8:A7:91:0E WEP managed 0 51 135 0 0B 2006-10-08 23:15:31 -0700
2 6 LAXKK 00:0F:90:32:A0:B0 WEP managed 15 15 16 0 0B 2006-10-08 23:15:41 -0700
3 6 Smarte Carte Offic 00:06:25:78:5D:37 WEP managed 17 17 19 0 0B 2006-10-08 23:15:41 -0700
4 11 NETGEARno 00:14:6C:CF:8C:38 WEP managed 0 12 12 0 0B 2006-10-08 23:14:57 -0700
5 6 Pacavi 00:16:B6:F5:2E:53 WEP managed 14 14 14 0 0B 2006-10-08 23:15:41 -0700
6 6 lawa_network_ope 00:0D:29:1D:BD:97 WEP managed 14 14 14 0 0B 2006-10-08 23:15:41 -0700
7 11 LAX_WPA 00:0F:EA:F0:DF:F9 WPA managed 13 13 13 0 0B 2006-10-08 23:15:41 -0700
Stop Scan

Figure 12–21. *KisMAC base stations*

It is also possible to see detailed information about the wireless networks that KisMAC accesses. Other programs can give the same information, such as Mac Stumbler and iStumbler, but the more advanced cracking and wireless scanning features found in KisMAC make it a more compelling application for the hacker to use.

Cracking wireless networks with KisMAC is possible only if a second wireless network interface is installed on the machine. The second network interface runs in a passive monitoring mode, while the first active network interface sends out probe requests and waits for answers. Be aware that this is no longer the bleeding edge of hacking technology, but it is still very effective in testing out the "hackability" of your network.

Packet reinjection is a WEP cracking technique used to crack wireless networks. With this attack, KisMAC will try to send captured packets of data in order to cause another computer to respond. If the computer responds, KisMAC will send these packets repeatedly. If KisMAC detects any answers, then it will go into injection mode. Injection mode generates a lot of traffic, causing more easily captured pieces of data to be generated. Wireless networks with WEP can be broken within an hour, sometimes only ten minutes, maybe even five.

Many wireless access points offer a key generation process using an easy-to-remember passphrase. Unfortunately, many wireless manufacturers implemented a very dangerous algorithm, called the Newsham 21-bit attack, for the generation of 40-bit WEP keys. This algorithm generates keys with an effective strength of only 21 bits. KisMAC is able to *brute-force*, or attempt all possible combinations until the correct password combination is found (see Figure 12–22), finding these keys quickly. Wireless access points from Linksys, D-Link, Belkin, and Netgear are confirmed to be vulnerable to the Newsham 21-bit attack.

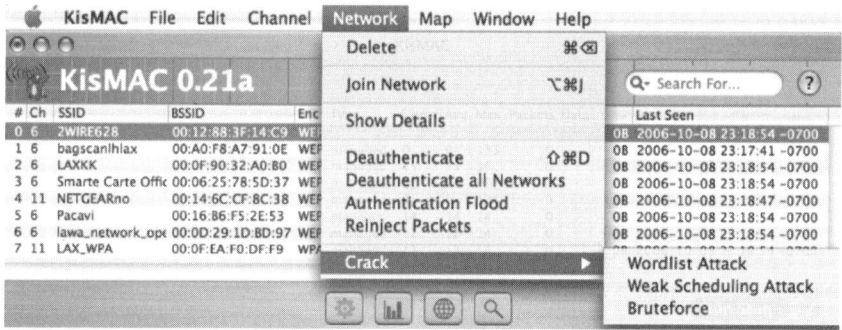

Figure 12–22. *Cracking into base stations*

Most network interfaces that are available are PCMCIA cards, which is an interface that MacBook and MacBook Pro users cannot use because of the lack of a PCMCIA interface on the machines. The Netgear MA-111 USB adapter is a good alternative for Mac users. However, make sure to check the KisMAC site before purchasing a card, and make sure it is still supported or that there aren't other interfaces that might be more readily available to purchase for the Mac.

Detecting Rogue Access Points

If a rogue access point is suspected on the network, it is possible to use KisMAC to quickly locate the WAP. If you have a GPS unit, the Map menu provides users with the ability to set their current position on a map and then follow the wireless signal to the rogue access point's source using signal strength readings.

To set up a map, you will need to import an image and switch to the Map tab. You should now see a map. Click the Set Waypoint 1 entry in the Map menu and click a position in the map for which you know the geographical position. KisMAC will now ask you for this position. If you have a GPS device attached to your computer, your current position is set as the default coordinates.

Now use the Set Waypoint 1 entry to set up a second waypoint. After you have set up these two points, KisMAC can use the image as a map (see Figure 9-22). Networks are automatically displayed. You can also show your current position by clicking the Current Position entry in the Map menu.

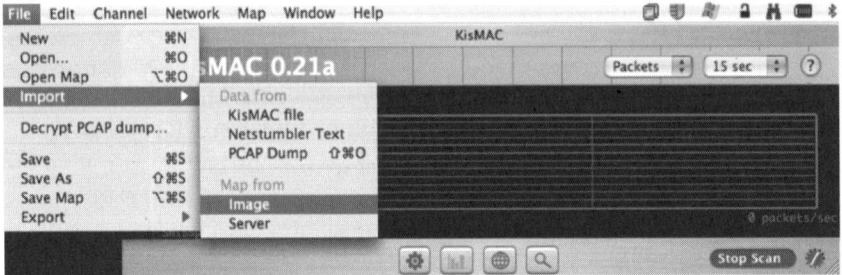

Figure 12-23. *Setting up a map for KisMAC*

iStumbler and Mac Stumbler

iStumbler is a good discovery tool for Mac OS X that is available under a BSD-style open source license and allows users to find AirPort networks, Bluetooth devices, and Bonjour services. You can download iStumbler from www.iStumbler.net. After downloading, open the application and it will automatically scan the wireless networks that are accessible to the computer running it. The default graph (see Figure 12-24) will show the wireless network name, the type of security employed on the wireless network, the signal, the vendor of the WAPs, the wireless channel, and the Mac address of the wireless base stations.

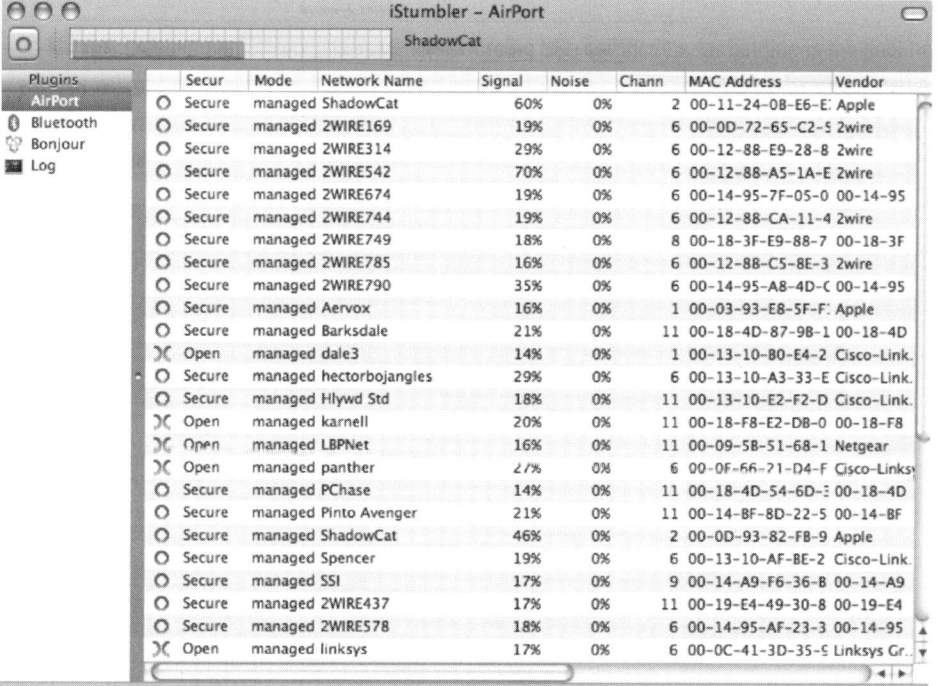

Figure 12–24. *iStumbler*

It will also compute a graph that displays a history of the wireless network's signal strength. You can view this in a stand-alone window by selecting Monitor from the AirPort menu. The monitors can be used to help in troubleshooting wireless signal issues by finding overlapping SSIDs, finding rogue access points, and helping determine what channel to use in a physical location highly saturated with wireless access points.

Another nice feature of iStumbler is the ability to view details about wireless networks using the AirPort Inspector. The Inspector includes details such as the noise level and the average signal level of the network. The advanced information that can be obtained using AirPort Inspector (see Figure 12–25) is accessible in the Edit menu. iStumbler provides you with a lot more information than we can cover in this chapter. However, suffice it to say that this level of detail can be handy if you are troubleshooting an issue on the phone with a vendor or looking to hack into your wireless network to test the security of your environment.

Figure 12-25. *AirPort Inspector Base station details*

MacStumbler

MacStumbler displays various bits of information about 802.11b and 802.11g wireless access points. Designed to be a tool to find access points while traveling, MacStumbler can also be used for wardriving and coordinating with a GPS unit while traveling to help map access points. MacStumbler requires an Apple AirPort Card and, unlike KisMAC, does not support PCMCIA and USB wireless devices. MacStumbler does not generate as much useful information as iStumbler but is worth mentioning because of its popularity as a tool for discovering unsecured wireless networks.

Ettercap

Ettercap is a tool used to perpetrate "man-in-the-middle" attacks on a LAN. Features include sniffing network traffic, network analysis, and content filtering. It can also be used to intercept packets, to perform ARP spoofing, and to perform character injection. It will perform password collection for a variety of protocols including Telnet, FTP, POP, SSH, ICQ, SMB, MySQL, HTTP, IMAP, MSN Messenger, and Yahoo Messenger. Ettercap can perform OS fingerprinting, kill network connections, and check for other poisoners. It can also do all of this on wired networks.

You can download Ettercap from http://ettercap.sourceforge.net.

EtherPeek

EtherPeek is closed source software available from WildPackets.com that is used on Ethernet networks. It can perform traffic monitoring and packet capture. It will also capture traffic, set triggers, view packets in real time, and deliver updates on packet statistics in real time.

There are three versions of EtherPeek, available from WildPackets.com:

EtherPeek VX: EtherPeek VX, WildPackets' Expert VoIP Network Analyzer, is the application that is used for diagnosing VoIP deployment and Ethernet network issues within enterprises.

EtherPeek NX: This provides network analysis with tools to troubleshoot, diagnose, and configure networks.

EtherPeek SE: WildPackets' Ethernet Protocol Analyzer is an intuitive, powerful network and protocol analyzer for Ethernet networks. It gives visual access to the Ethernet network through real-time views of the LAN and can perform baseline analyses of the Ethernet network. It also has triggers that can be tripped to deliver notifications when settings are activated.

> **NOTE:** EtherPeek is not sold for the Mac platform. To use it as a means to secure a Mac environment, it will need to run from a Windows computer.

Cracking WEP Keys

To drive home why it is so important to practice good security with your wireless environment, let's look at cracking a few types of wireless security protocols. Let's start with a WEP key. There are three steps we will need to go through in order to crack a WEP key. First, we need to locate the AirPort using a tool such as KisMAC.

Second, we need to generate a minimum of 400,000 WEP initialization vectors (random bits of data used to decrypt wireless traffic). We will capture the traffic using Aireplay to generate the required initialization vectors. Aireplay is available at http://www.wirelessdefence.org/Contents/Aircrack_aireplay.htm. Once captured, Airodump will be used to save the captured initialization vectors into a file.

Run the Airodump command, as shown in the following example:

`./airodump <wireless interface> <outputfilename> <MACfiler>`

> **NOTE:** Aireplay and Airodump are free to download and use.

Make sure your output filename ends with the file extension `.cap`. The MAC filter would be used when you have more than one access point or AirPort on the same channel within range of the system you are launching the attack from. In this case you would use the MAC address of the access point you are targeting. With Airodump still running, open another Terminal session, and run Aireplay with the following command:

`./aireplay -b <maca ddress of wireless access point> -x 512 <wifiport>`

> **NOTE:** The b in the previous line of code is the `bssid` (MAC address of the access point), and the x is the `nbpps` (number of packets per second).

This will catch an initialization vector packet and replay it against the AirPort to get enough raw data to allow you to crack the WEP password. You can tell when you have enough initialization vectors by watching the IV column in Airodump. The more traffic running through the AirPort, the faster packets will be caught (if the AirPort is not being used, the AirPort might take a long time to crack). Once you have reached 400,000, use the Ctrl+C shortcut to exit Aireplay and Airodump. This will save the file you specified in Airodump and stop Aireplay from re-sending the IV packet out to the AP.

Once you have your initialization vectors in a file, you can analyze the packets to recover the actual WEP key using Aircrack to analyze the file and recover the WEP key. Aircrack is a set of tools used for auditing wireless networks by allowing you to crack WEP and WPA keys:

`./aircrack -n 128 <outputfilenamefromairodump>`

> **NOTE:** n is the "nbits" or WEP key length (listed in KisMAC).

If the attack that you have just launched was executed correctly, then you will get the key in red text followed by "KEY FOUND."

Cracking WPA-PSK

Of the wireless encryption protocols, WPA is one of the hardest to hack. Let's explore a way to do it. For this we will use two open source security tools, Airforge and Aircrack.

Once a target network using a WPA access point has been identified, using a tool such as KisMAC, you can begin to launch the attack using Airforge to create a deauthentication packet (assuming the current working directory contains the `airforge` binary).

`./airforge <MACaddressofap> <MACofclient> filename.cap`

What Airforge will do is cause a user connected to the WAP to become deauthenticated from the network. Once disconnected, the deauthenticated user's system will attempt to reauthenticate, and the SSID will be sent over the air in plain text. You will typically want to set the packet length to 26, -u 0, -v (to specify sub), -w0, -x1 (number of packets), -r (to redirect to file), and eth0 (adapter to inject to).

While you're running this, you'll want to open Ethereal (or another packet capturing application) and start catching packets. After you are done packet catching (after about 5,000 to 10,000 packets), you will want to sort by EAP over LAN (EAPOL). After filtering by EAPOL, analyze the remainder of the packets for the password. Once you find the four-way packets, save the packets. Then you will be able to use a tool called `cowpatty` or Brutal Gift to run a dictionary attack on the saved packets, and after some time you will be able to crack the WPA password.

> **NOTE:** It is possible to further secure WPA by using WPA2 enterprise security.

General Safeguards Against Cracking Wireless Networks

Encryption should always be implemented on wireless networks. It is one of the best safeguards against allowing users to crack your WEP keys.

Determining the strength of encryption is always a trade-off between security and speed. The more encrypted, the slower the network will be. But increased levels of encryption mean increased time to crack. Most wardrivers will not bother with heavily encrypted networks, moving on to less well-protected environments. Keep in mind that the encryption strength is not only determined by the number of bits that the encryption is using but also by the complexity of the passphrase being used. More complex passwords are harder to crack using a dictionary attack. Corporate environments concerned about wireless security will use WPA2 Enterprise, which goes beyond simple WEP keys by employing a RADIUS server (included in Mac OS X 10.5.*x* Server) on the network. This allows the administrator to use a server that can lock accounts if someone is attempting to break into them using password policies and the other account management security measures described in Chapter 16.

> **NOTE:** WPA2 requires a RADIUS server, which can only be configured on Mac OS X Server.

Having good signal strength helps keep packets from becoming orphaned. Because orphaned packets make cracking wireless networks easier, maintaining good signal strength is another good way to keep wireless networks protected.

Summary

Securing your network is a must in today's global environment. But because of the damage that can be done on a local area network and the quantity of people now able to perpetrate such damage, it is also now critical to act locally as well with regard to network security. And this starts with the wireless network.

In this chapter we looked at some of the techniques used to both secure and break into a wireless network. Password protection, MAC address filtration, and NAT firewalls are good security techniques. They should not be the only security measures used for securing wireless networks, but they are good first steps toward securing wireless networks. While breaking into any networks should be reserved to labs and securing your own networks, our main goal in looking at these practices was to portray how easily some of these security mechanisms are to bypass and the damage that can be done once they have been circumvented.

Now that we are finished looking at wireless networks, in Chapter 13 we will look at one of the most critical of services on the inside of your network, file sharing.

Part **IV**

Sharing

Chapter 13

File Services

Configuring file-sharing security can be one of the more challenging aspects of working with shared computer data in a networked environment. The challenge is twofold—how do you keep files accessible to those who need them while simultaneously keeping them inaccessible to those who don't? Sharing files over a network is also an inherently dangerous activity. Other computers' users can access files on your system without physically gaining access to your computer; thus, if configured incorrectly, the wrong data can easily get into the wrong hands, which can prove to be catastrophic. However, in most environments, it is crucial that multiple computers have access to data on a single computer. So, how do we manage this file-sharing conundrum?

In Chapter 3 we discussed how to apply security settings to users and groups. In this chapter, we will discuss these security settings as they apply to sharing files. We'll explore the security differences between file sharing between Macs on a peer-to-peer network versus a central file-sharing networked system, and we'll look at how to strengthen these file-sharing policies in a networked Mac environment using the native tools within Mac OS X (Apple Filing Protocol when file sharing with other Macs, and Samba to connect a Windows-based machine to a Mac.). We'll also look at third-party software, DAVE and FTP.

The Risks in File Sharing

Giving others access to files on your computer can be risky on many levels. First, you risk someone obtaining access to the system who shouldn't. For example, when a file is remotely deleted from your system, the file does not go to the trash, you do not get alerted about the deletion, and anyone who knows the right password typically can delete files. If the wrong folders on a system are shared, you can also give someone the ability to delete critical files, whether intentionally or not. For all of these reasons, and with the risks of confidential data being accessed over file-sharing protocols, you need to properly lock down the security of any file sharing on your systems.

In Chapter 3, we discussed creating a limited Sharing Only account. This was added into Mac OS X Leopard for this very reason, and when creating accounts solely to give access to files, we recommend using this account type versus any other.

Peer-to-Peer vs. Client-Server Environments

Before we discuss how to configure file-sharing permissions correctly, it's important to examine the differences between peer-to-peer and client-server file-sharing environments.

It is common in a networked Mac environment to have a handful of computers, each with file sharing enabled, with users trading files back and forth between each other without a central repository for the files. This type of environment is known as *peer-to-peer networking* (P2P). Security in a P2P environment is generally straightforward and tends to be rather loose. Anyone with access to the computer usually has access to files on that machine.

> **NOTE:** Peer-to-peer in this context is not the same as it is when using an application like LimeWire to access files hosted anonymously on the Internet. In this context, peer-to-peer is strictly meant to indicate sharing files over network connections in small environments.

As environments mature and grow larger, the distributed file sharing of P2P will give way to centralized file servers in what is typically described as a *client-server*, or *two-tier*, environment. Client-server environments offer a single and centralized location for users to access files that are needed by multiple users. In a client-server environment, backup and security begin to play a much more critical role, because files are now accessible by multiple users who have access to that repository. File permissions become critical to maintaining security. The permissions and backup strategies are easier to deal with in client-server environments for two reasons. First, because client-server environments have dedicated servers to handle many of the tasks that clients will handle in P2P environments. Second, because in a client-server environment, most data is stored on a server.

There are some inherent challenges to migrating from a P2P to a server-based file-sharing environment. Some users might have a hard time moving away from their old method of sharing files. The proper permission controls are often not set up correctly on the centralized data, if they are set up at all. Client machines might continue to share files after the transition simply because they weren't configured to not share them. This can lead to security issues that can be disastrous if not managed appropriately.

File Security Fundamentals

Before we dive into how to properly secure file services, let's discuss some fundamentals of file security in Mac OS X. This will include the LKDC, POSIX and ACLs (covered more fully in Chapter 4).

LKDC

Because Apple is concerned about protecting peer-to-peer environments just as much as client-server environments, it has equipped every copy of Mac OS X with a Kerberos Local Key Distribution Center (LKDC). The LKDC, based on a Kerbeross authentication scheme, (Kerberos is discussed in Chapter 16) secures AFP, CIFS (Samba), and VNC services (VNC is covered more in Chapter 15). The LKDC implementation helps to secure communications, because it requires the nodes communicating with one another to prove their identity prior to communicating. Once a system has initiated communications, keys are used instead of passwords when authenticating users and services. This keeps passwords from being sent over the network, helping to keep them secure.

By forcing the same identity requirements that are common in client-server environments, the LKDC protects against eavesdropping and replaying sessions (where traffic is captured and replayed to get around security mechanisms). And tho LKDC is implemented by default in every Mac, meaning there is nothing to do to set it up! The LKDC is dedicated to providing and protecting authentication. But how does the system determine what you are authorized to access? It starts with POSIX.

Using POSIX Permissions

Mac OS X is a SUS-compliant operating system. POSIX is a standardized feature set developed to make operating systems compatible with Unix-based operating systems. POSIX permission levels are divided into three categories: read (users can access the file), write (users can write data to it), and execute (users can run the file, such as an application). When viewing these permissions from the terminal command ls, read is indicated by an r, write is indicated by a w, and execute is indicated by an x.

> **NOTE:** For more information on changing permissions from the command line, see Chapter 4.

When you look at the permission designations for files, you'll see they are displayed in the order of *owner*, *group*, and (if needed) *everyone*. The owner is the user that owns a file, can set permissions on the file, and is listed in the text following the permissions of the file. The group of a file is listed next. The everyone designation is given to every user accessing a file who is not listed in either the owner or the group designation. The everyone designation is also known as a guest user of that file.

> **NOTE:** When looking at file permissions, you might find that an admin or wheel group is listed in a file's permissions. These are part of the built-in users and groups that a system defaults with upon installation of the operating system. We'll discuss these in more depth in Chapter 4.

The output of the permissions for a file will use the following syntax:

```
(permissions) (owner) (group) (everyone) (file size) (last modified)
```

The ls command followed by the -al option can show you the permissions, as indicated in the following example:

```
cedge:/Users cedge$ ls -al
total 16
drwxrwxrwx    8 root       admin       272 Dec 24 22:07 .
drwxrwxr-t   35 root       admin      1292 Apr 13 20:27 ..
-rwxrwxrwx    1 cedge      admin      6148 Oct 23 13:55 .DS_Store
-rwxrwxrwx    1 root       wheel         0 Jul  1  2006 .localized
drwxrwxrwx   16 318admin   318admin    544 May 26  2006 318admin
drwxrwxrwt   10 root       wheel       340 Oct 23 13:14 Shared
drwxrwxrwx   38 cedge      cedge      1292 Apr 13 15:40 cedge
drwxrwxrwx   12 postgres   postgres    408 Dec 24 22:22 postgres
```

NOTE: The d in front of the permissions in the previous example indicates that the item is a directory rather than a file.

Getting More out of Permissions with Access Control Lists

Traditionally, Mac OS X has been limited to the standard POSIX permission model of read, write, and execute. This system has served Unix-based operating systems well for many years now; however, it is starting to show its age. The main concern is that it isn't very flexible, and several special modes, such as the *sticky bit* (a setting that indicates that only the owner can delete a file from the respective folder), have been added over time.

For more complicated permission structures, access control lists (*ACLs*) provide you with the most granular control available over permissions for files and folders. An ACL is a list of permissions attached to files and folders. These replace POSIX permissions in the traditional sense of Mac OS X security. ACLs give the Mac an equal set of permissions that is found in Microsoft Windows. ACL information is stored in the extended attributes of the Mac OS Extended file system (HFS+).

It's easiest to understand the ACLs if we break down how they work and are applied. These are the two key system properties that allow ACLs to function:

- The generated unique identifier (GUID) is a value that is used many times in Mac OS X because it can be guaranteed to be unique across computer systems. Your user account has both a traditional Unix-style UID and a new GUID.

- An access control entry (*ACE*) is the individual rule that determines what access is given to any particular user or group.

NOTE: An ACL is a list of ACEs that can be attached to a directory or file, providing permissions similar to those used in Microsoft Windows.

The following are the possible permissions that can be applied to files and folders with the new ACL model. This is a huge jump from the read-write-execute model we are used to on Mac OS X. Here are the permissions:

- Change Permissions
- Change Owner
- Read Attributes
- Read Extended Attributes
- List Folder Contents
- Traverse Folder
- Read Permissions
- Write Attributes
- Create Files
- Create Folder
- Delete
- Delete Subfolders and Files

NOTE: When defining ACLs, you should typically do so at a group level. Reserve user-level ACEs for special cases such as deny rules for problematic users. For more on defining the users and groups that make up ACEs, see Chapter 4.

Sharing Protocols: Which One Is for You?

Computers can connect in various ways in order to talk to one another. The way in which computers communicate is known as a *protocol*. When configuring global settings for a file-sharing environment, you must consider that computers connecting to each other will more than likely use different protocols to do communicate. For example, one protocol, Apple Filing Protocol (AFP), will typically be used when connecting two Macs, and an entirely different protocol, Samba (SMB), will be used to connect a Windows-based machine to a Mac. However, one fact remains constant among these protocols: permissions must be set when accessing resources from one computer to another.

Apple Filing Protocol

AFP is a presentation-layer network protocol that is the primary protocol for providing file services for Mac computers. AFP is rarely used outside the Mac platform, so little security attention has been paid to it as a protocol from security researchers. However, you should take certain steps to ensure the security of the files and data that use AFP to communicate.

To configure AFP sharing, you must first enable AFP on the computer. To enable AFP in OS X, open your System Preferences, and click the Sharing preference pane (see Figure 13–1). Select the File Sharing check box. The File Sharing indicator button will turn green.

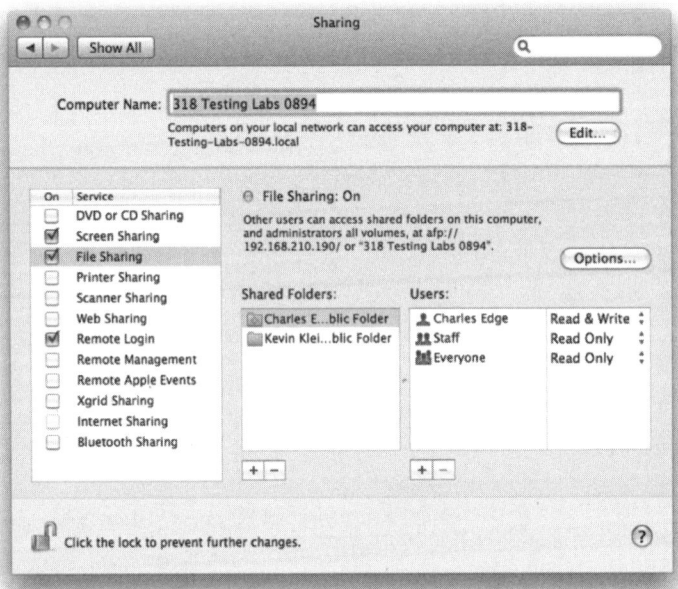

Figure 13–1. *Enabling file sharing*

> **NOTE:** Configuring AFP is different and much more feature-rich in Mac OS X Server than in the Mac OS X client. For more information on this portion of AFP configuration, please see Chapter 16.

Now that you've enabled file sharing, you will want to limit access to files and folders. To do so, review the shared folders in the Shared Folders list. Here you can stop sharing any folders that should not be shared by clicking the minus (–) sign in order to "unshared" them. Once you have verified that everything in the list should be there, you can now create new shared folders. To do so, click the plus (+) sign, which will open a window that allows you to browse your folders (see Figure 13–2). In this window, find the folder you want to share, and click the Add button.

Figure 13-2. *Browsing to a folder*

Once you have shared a folder, you can move on to setting sharing permissions. To do so, first review the list of users and groups (for more information on configuring users and groups, see Chapter 3) in the Users list. Click any of the users and groups that should not have access to the data in the Shared Folders list, and click the minus (–) sign (while those users or groups are highlighted) to deny access. After you have removed users who should not have access to the folder, click the plus (+) sign to add users who should have access. At this point, you will see a window with all of your users. Any users who already have access to the directory will be disabled. Find the users you want to grant access to, select them, and click the Select button to add them to the Users list.

Setting Sharing Options

Click Options to select which protocols you will use. On this screen, simply select the check box for each protocol to enable it, as you can see in Figure 13-3. For the purposes of this discussion, we have selected SMB. Here you can also configure which users will have access to the SMB service.

Samba

Only enable SMB, as well as any of these services if you actually need them. When adding users to this list, you will be asked to enter a password (see Figure 13-4). The reason for this is that the respective user's password file must be modified to allow for an older style of password, which is used by the Samba Windows file-sharing engine.

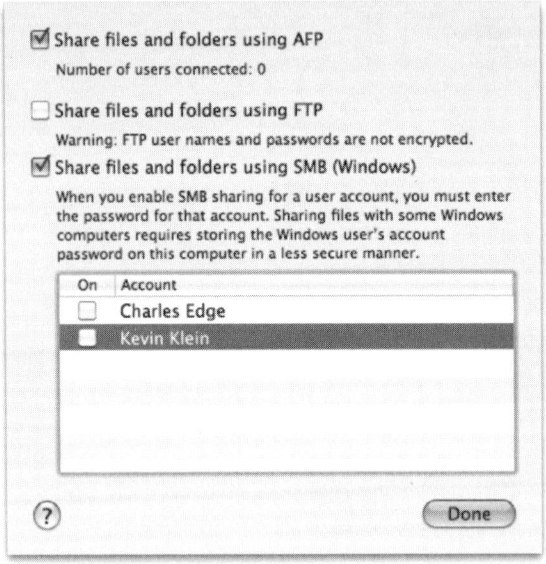

Figure 13-3. *Defining an SMB/Windows user*

It's important to note that you are decreasing the overall security of your system by using the SMB service. Apple does not enable the storage of these weak passwords by default because dictionary attacking these older LAN Manager (LM MD4) passwords has been fairly simple. Any attacker who has gained root access to your system could view this weak password "hash" in your password file and potentially recover your login password. This might seem counterintuitive to worry about security concerns for someone with root access, but remember that even the root account cannot view a user's encrypted keychain file without knowing that user's password. Therefore, in this instance, if an attacker has gained complete control of the system, they could be able to decrypt files that are based on the user's login password, such as keychains or file vaulted home folders.

> **NOTE:** If you use the same password for all services, then compromising this password could lead to compromising the password for all of your services that use that same password.

Once you are satisfied that your files and folders have an appropriate level of permissions assigned to them, it's time to turn to other protocols that computers will be using to access resources on your Mac. First on the list is the Samba protocol.

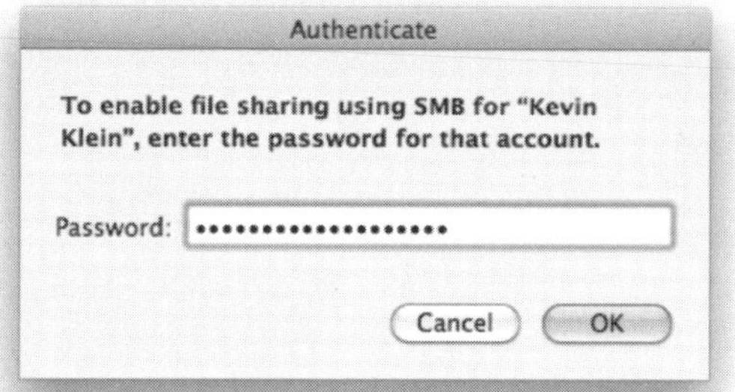

Figure 13–4. *Providing the password for a Windows user*

Once you have enabled a Windows user, then you will be able to connect to the system using SMB. To test this from a Mac, click the Go menu from the Finder, and select the "Connect to a Server" option. In the "Connect to Server" window (as shown in Figure 13–5), type **smb://** followed by the IP address of the computer to which you are connecting. When you click Connect, you will be asked to enter the password and will be given a list of share points that have access through SMB. Make sure the user you are logged in as has access only to the locations that you want the user to be able to access.

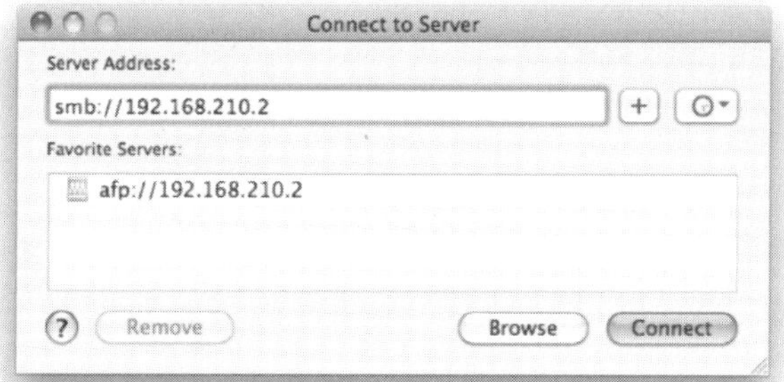

Figure 13–5. *Connecting to an SMB share point*

The SMB.conf File

From System Preferences, you may want to only share certain directories over Samba. By default, all shares are shared by any protocol enabled. Therefore, to only provide the least amount of privileges and access to any directory while still achieving your objectives, you will want to disable shares where possible. The SMB.conf file is a good place to look to see which SMB directories are being shared. The following is the basic/default `smb.conf` file for the Windows service:

```
Apress-MacBook-cedge:/private/etc cedge$ cat smb.conf
 [global]
  guest account = unknown
```

```
    encrypt passwords = yes
    auth methods = guest opendirectory
    passdb backend = opendirectorysam guest
    printer admin = @admin, @staff
    server string = 318 Administrator?s iBook G4
    unix charset = UTF-8-MAC
    display charset = UTF-8-MAC
    dos charset = 437
    client ntlmv2 auth = no
    os level = 8
    defer sharing violations = no
    vfs objects = darwin_acls
    brlm = yes
    workgroup = Workgroup
; Using the Computer Name to compute the NetBIOS name.
netbios name = 318-Administrat
    use spnego = yes
[homes]
    comment = User Home Directories
    browseable = no
    read only = no

;[public]
;   path = /tmp
;   public = yes
;   only guest = yes
;   writable = yes
;   printable = no

[printers]
   path = /tmp
   printable = yes
```

Review each section of the previous file. Make sure that any file shares (denoted between two [ ] symbols) have been planned and that the permissions are appropriate. Try to always disable guest access by changing the `public` variable to no. Try to always set the `read only` variable to yes, thus making many shares read-only. Also try to not make shares browseable unless otherwise required.

Using Apple AirPort to Share Files

The File Sharing feature of Mac OS X provides the most granular approach to a workgroup-oriented file-sharing scenario that you can get without upgrading to Mac OS X Server. There will be instances, however, when users may want to configure the File Sharing feature to run off an AirPort base station. The Apple AirPort N (the square one) has the capacity to share files using a portable hard drive connected over USB to the AirPort device. To share files using the Apple AirPort, plug an external hard drive into the AirPort, and open the AirPort Utility in the /Applications/Utilities folder, authenticate, click on the Manual Setup button and then click on the Disks icon in the AirPort Utility application toolbar.

From here, you will see a window similar to that shown in Figure 13–6. This window will list the disks attached to your AirPort along with their names and capacities. It will also list the users attached to the AirPort and allow you to disconnect any users you would prefer to not use the disk.

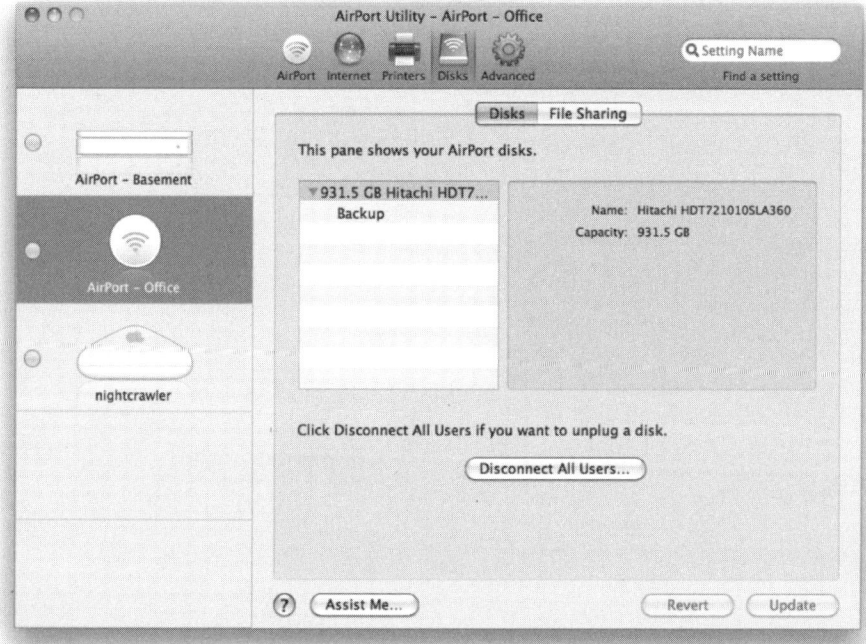

Figure 13-6. *AirPort disk sharing overview*

Once you have verified that the disks you want to use are plugged into the AirPort N, then you will need to enable file sharing on the AirPort. To do so, click the Disks toolbar icon in the AirPort Utility. Then click the File Sharing tab, and select the Enable File Sharing box. You can now configure the type of permissions to be used for the disks you need to share. The most secure setting to use for the Secure Shared Disks option is With Accounts, which allows you to create accounts for use with the disks attached to the AirPort. For security purposes, the Guest Access field should always be set to Not Allowed, as you can see in Figure 13-7, unless you absolutely need to allow guests to access the data.

NOTE: It is common to refer to a wireless access point, such as an Apple AirPort's shared disk, or a hard drive connected to a network as *network-attached storage* (NAS).

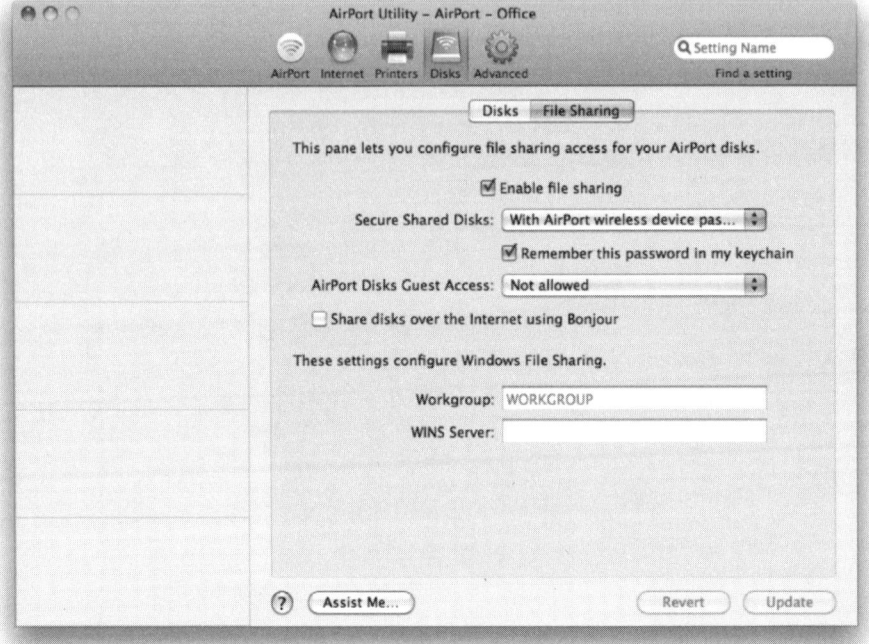

Figure 13-7. *Configuring file sharing on the AirPort*

Once you have set your base station to use accounts for shared storage, you can also configure the Workgroup setting, which allows the Windows systems on your network to browse the AirPort and access the shared media. The WINS Server option allows you to assign a WINS server that can be run on OS X Server, Windows NT Server, Windows 2000 Server, Windows 2003 Server, Samba on Unix or Linux, and Windows 2008 Server. These settings have little usefulness for your file sharing if you are not using Windows machines in your environment. In other words, if there are no Windows machines around, do not enable them.

Once you have configured the sharing settings for the AirPort, click on Configure Accounts… to take you to the Accounts tab, where you can set up the users who can access the data on the disks attached to your AirPort base station. In the Accounts window, click the plus (+) sign to add accounts that can access the drive (see Figure 13-8). This opens the Account Setup Assistant. The Account Setup Assistant allows you to enter a simple name and password, along with what level of access the user has to the media attached to the AirPort base station. The levels of access include Not Allowed, Read Only, and Read and Write (see Figure 13-9). These are similar to what is allowed in Mac OS X but with fewer features.

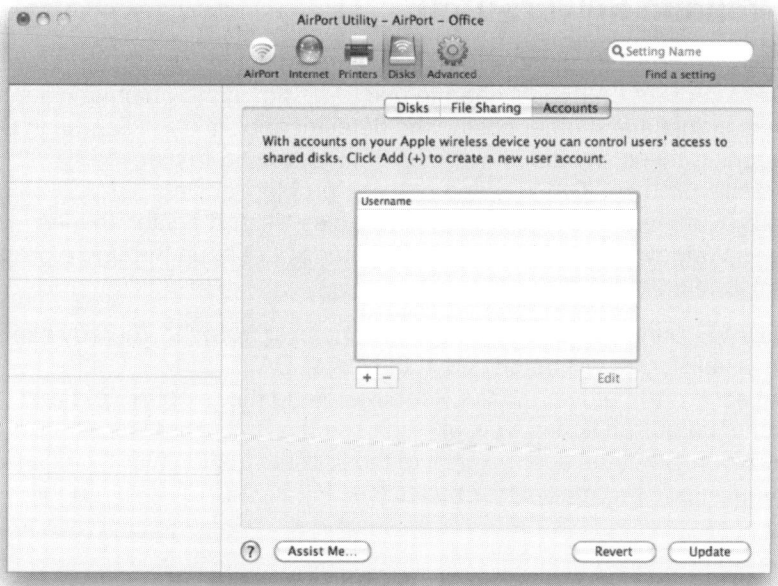

Figure 13–8. *Adding accounts to AirPort disk sharing*

> **CAUTION:** There is little protection for these accounts; the usernames and passwords do not benefit from policies, the users and passwords are not shared between various systems, and there is no adaptive firewall as with OS X or OS X Server to protect the device whatsoever.

Figure 13–9. *AirPort disk sharing Account Setup Overlay*

Third-Party Problem Solver: DAVE

From time to time, file and application incompatibilities will arise that cannot be solved by enabling the Samba protocol. Or you'll need to use SMB signing to communicate with Windows servers In these and other cases, the default capabilities of Samba in OS X are often not enough. In these situations, we recommend turning to third-party applications to solve this problem. DAVE is one of these problem solvers. DAVE, distributed by Thursby Software (www.thursby.com), enables file and printer sharing compatibility between Windows and Mac operating systems. Let's run through a proper installation and configuration of DAVE.

To get started with DAVE, purchase and download the installer from the Thursby site. When you open the installer, you will be placed in the Install DAVE screen. Click Continue on the first screen to be taken to the Read Me. Read the supplied text and then click on the Continue button again. You will then see the Software License Agreement. Here, click on Continue again, agree to the licensing, and enter the license information. Once you've entered the license codes (see Figure 13–10), click on the Continue button.

NOTE: Before installing DAVE, disable Samba on the Sharing preference pane in System Preferences. DAVE cannot be installed if Samba is currently enabled.

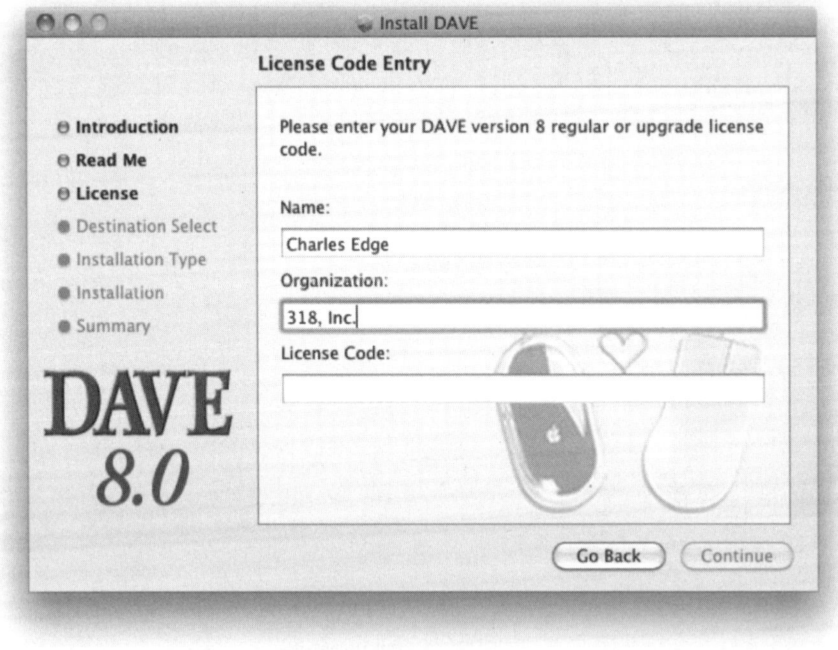

Figure 13–10. *Entering the license codes*

At the Destination Select screen, select the drive you would like to install DAVE on and click on the Continue button. At the Installation Type screen, select the volume to install DAVE on or simply click on the Install button to install DAVE in the /Applications folder. When you click on the Install button, the installer will install DAVE and when it's done, click on the Close button to complete the process.

Once the installation is complete, the DAVE Setup Assistant will start. The first screen that you'll see will ask you to read the introduction. Once you've done so, click on the Continue button.

DAVE will ask whether you have a Windows server in your environment (see Figure 13–11). If you are going to be using DAVE to communicate with an Active Directory controller, you'll need to check the Use Windows Server box on this screen and click Continue. Otherwise, leave this box unchecked and click Continue.

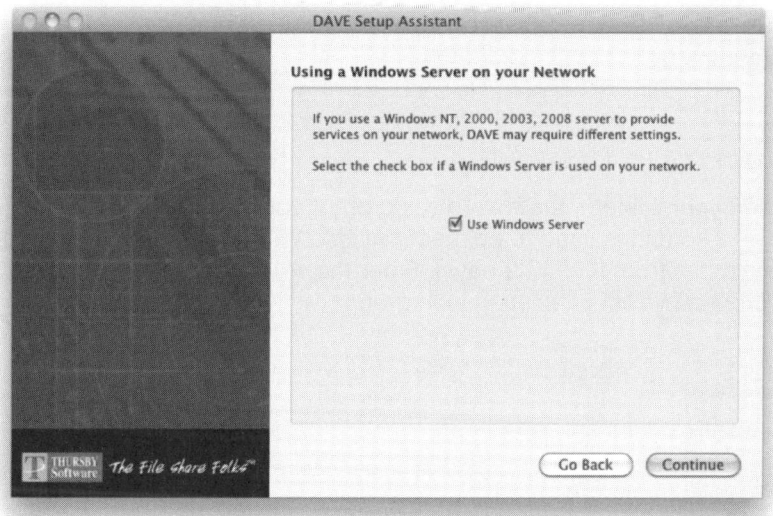

Figure 13–11. *Configuring DAVE to use an existing Windows network*

Next, enter your computer name (see Figure 13–12). This is the name that will be broadcast to other Windows systems when they browse to see your computer on the network. It should be a unique name that no other computer on the network shares. This is also known in Microsoft Windows networking terminology as the *NetBIOS name*.

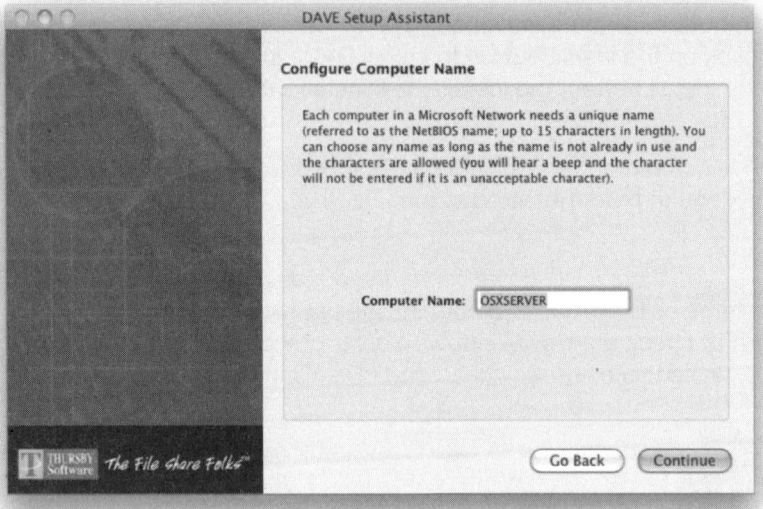

Figure 13-12. *Configuring the SMB Setup name in DAVE*

Once you have named your system, the wizard will prompt you for the workgroup to join (see Figure 13–13). This setting is used to connect multiple Windows systems in a group (much like AppleTalk zones from the OS 9 days). Enter the workgroup name, or select the name from the drop-down list of existing workgroups.

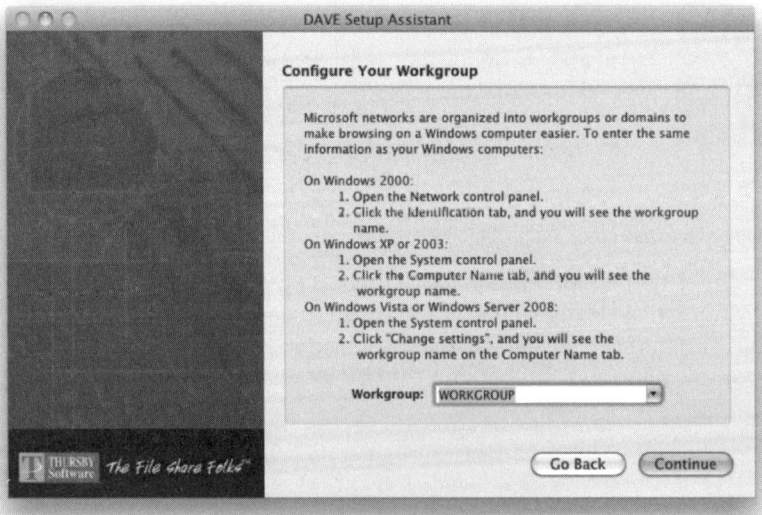

Figure 13-13. *Configuring the SMB workgroup for DAVE*

On the next screen, enter a friendly description of the computer (this setting has little ramification on the network or on network security but is helpful), as you can see in

Figure 13–14. Once you have entered a brief description of the computer, click the Continue button. This will trigger the CIFS daemon of DAVE to be restarted, prompting you to enter an administrative username and password. Once the CIFS daemon and the Directory Services daemon are restarted, click Continue.

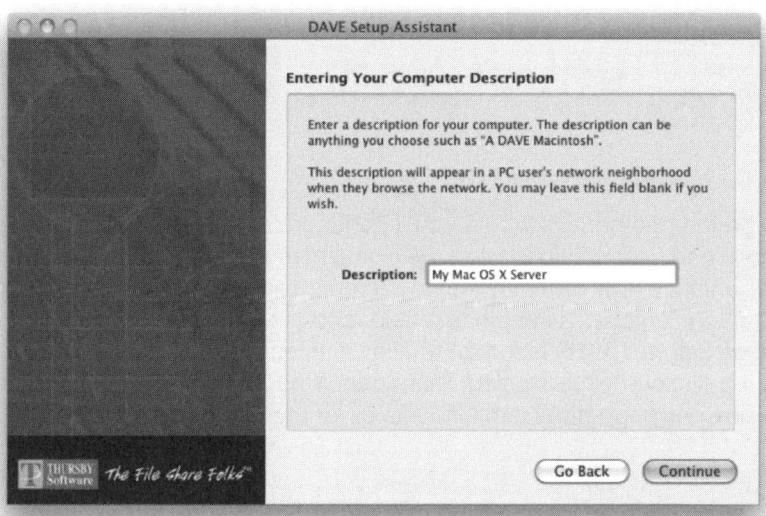

Figure 13-14. *Providing DAVE with a description*

On the next screen, you'll be asked if you'll be using DAVE to share data through Samba, which will in turn allow you to share data using the Samba protocol to other systems on the network. If you will be sharing data to Windows computers, use the Open DAVE Sharing button and click the Continue button twice. You can then click on the Quit button, which will finish the installation process. Open your Mac OS X System Preferences, and you will notice three new preference panes: DAVE Login, DAVE Network, and DAVE Sharing. The DAVE Login preference pane will allow you to configure your system to log into a Microsoft domain environment. The Log In button allows you to join a domain provided you have the credentials for an account with the appropriate levels of access. Change Password (see Figure 13–15) allows you to change your password for the domain you have joined. The Change Password feature is not one that is native to Mac OS X for Windows-based domains, and thus enables a greater level of account-based security to be applied for user accounts.

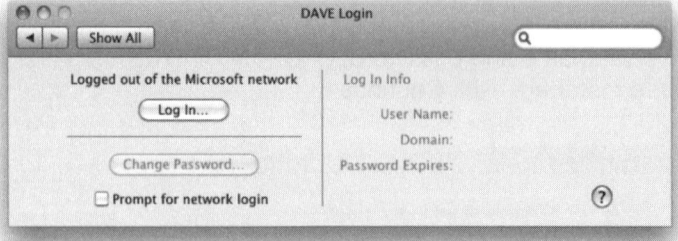

Figure 13-15. *Logging into a Windows network with DAVE*

The DAVE Network preference pane is where you'll configure how your system is perceived by Windows and Samba systems in the domain environment. This includes the computer name, which is how other Windows systems see your computer (using NetBIOS); the description, which is a simple text field; and the workgroup. The workgroup setting (see Figure 13–16) is meant to allow systems of a like type to see each other, making it a discovery mechanism. Although Windows computers can see the computers in their workgroup, they can also see computers in other workgroups.

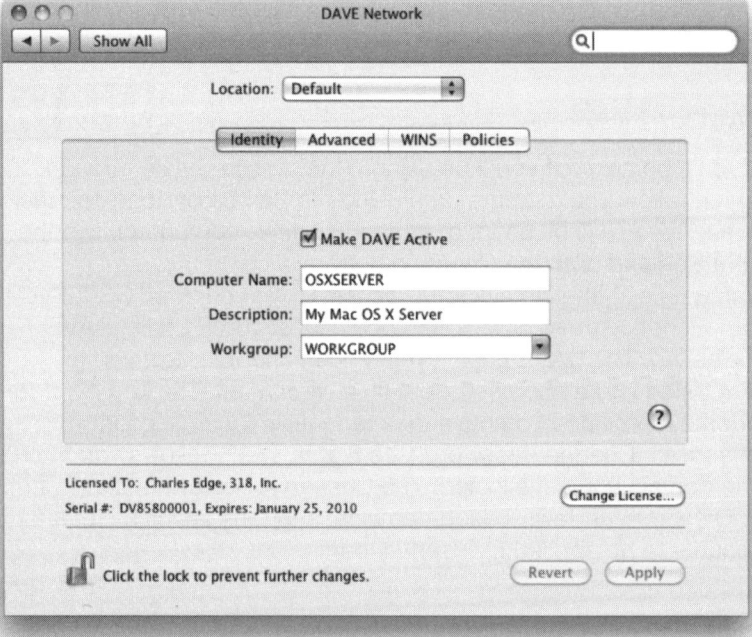

Figure 13-16. *Changing SMB settings with DAVE*

By clicking the Policies tab of the DAVE Network preference pane, you will be able to configure signing and the acceptable authentication levels for the Samba sharing. A *man-in-the-middle* attack is when an attacker is able to read or modify communications between two parties. Digital signing for SMB, or *SMB signing*, allows you to protect against man-in-the-middle attacks by placing a digital signature in each packet. If the packet is then intercepted in transit, the digital signature will be altered, and the parties will drop the connection. However, digital signing only mitigates the threat of data being modified while in transit. A man in the middle attack that does not alter data can go undetected. SMB signing is one of the best ways to protect SMB traffic. Many corporate security policies require SMB signing for communications over SMB to their file servers, a default option for Windows domain controllers since Windows 2003.

SMB authentication primarily occurs over LANMAN, NTLMv1, and NTLMv2. LANMAN used a weak (by modern standards) authentication protocol known as LM Hash. NTLMv1 was a great step forward and represented the introduction of a challenge-response protocol. With NTLMv1, the server authenticates the client by sending a random number, known as the *challenge*. The client uses the challenge and a password, or *ticket*, known by both the client and the server. The client identity then is configured using the result of combining the two. The server verifies that the client has calculated the correct result and verifies the identity of the client. NTLMv2 is also a challenge-response protocol, but with more steps involved to enhance the security of the challenge-response process. Of these, NTLMv2 is by far the most secure; however, it has been replaced in many situations by Kerberos.

If Kerberos is available, then the DAVE client will always use it. The Policies screen of the DAVE Network preference pane (shown in Figure 13–17) allows you to set the minimum acceptable security level. The LAN Manager Authentication Level setting should be set to the highest possible, eliminating all other protocols from the options available to DAVE for authentication. If you are in an environment that supports NTLMv2, then you should be using NTLMv2 response only. Otherwise, the order of security for these options, from most secure to least secure, is as follows:

- Send NTLMv2 Response Only
- Send NTLM Response Only
- Send LM & NTLM Responses
- Send LM & NTLM

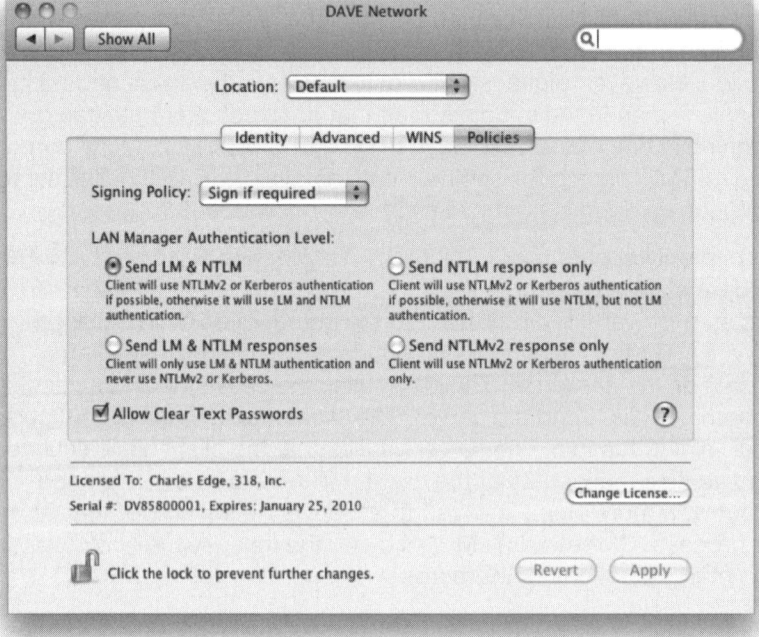

Figure 13-17. *Configuring authentication levels*

DAVE is a great tool to allow the Mac to thrive in a more corporate Microsoft-based environment. There are also some nice file-sharing features in DAVE, which make it a must in testing if you are performing file sharing in a Windows-based environment. If the features make it worth obtaining a third-party package, then look into volume licensing it.

FTP

FTP is a very old protocol, much older than SMB and AFP. FTP is most commonly used to transfer files over the Internet. However, FTP does not encrypt data, and should not be used as a sharing protocol unless absolutely required (and if you think it's absolutely required, we urge you to continue to research other means because there usually is a better way). To enable FTP, click the Sharing preference pane, and click the Options button. Select the Share Files and Folders Using FTP box (see Figure 13-18).

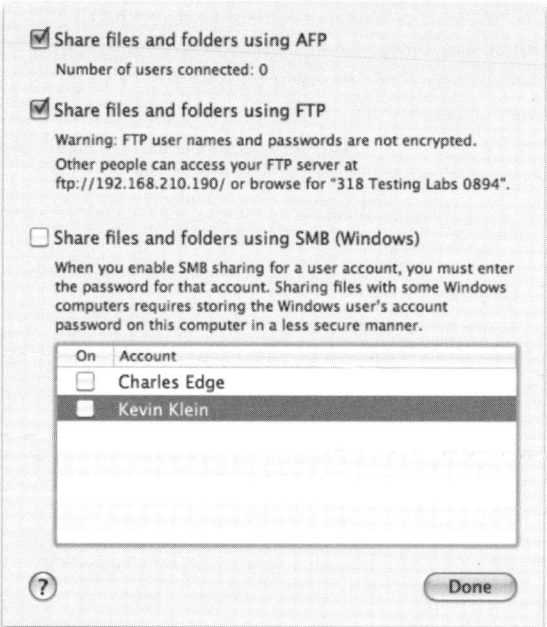

Figure 13–18. *Enabling FTP sharing*

Once you have enabled FTP sharing, you can connect to the FTP share by clicking Go and then "Connect to Server" in the Finder. From here, you can enter **ftp://*ipaddress*** in the Server Address field (as shown in Figure 13–19). Once you have entered the address, click Connect.

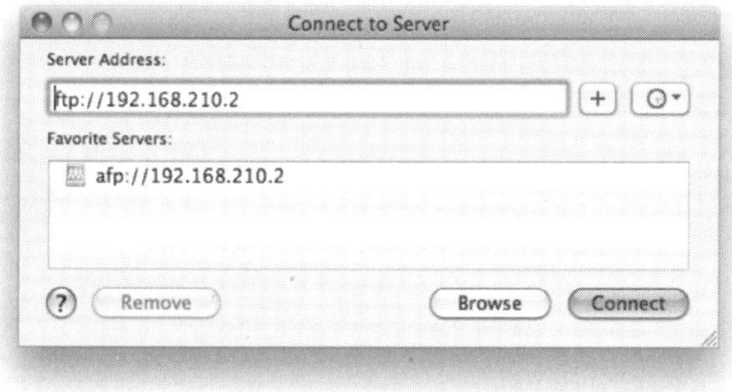

Figure 13–19. *Connecting over FTP*

Attempting to edit data in files via FTP will result in frustration. When folders are accessed by FTP using the Finder, the files are mounted as read-only to your user account and cannot be modified. If you need to write to this folder, then you will want to connect to it using an FTP client such as Fetch or Transmit.

FTP security is a bit thin. FTP bounce attacks allow users to establish a connection between FTP servers and an arbitrary port on another system while connected to the server. This connection can then be used to bypass access controls that would otherwise apply. FTP traffic is also unencrypted, which can lead to the exposure of passwords. There is also a mode for FTP known as PASV, which allows FTP to work with firewalls. PASV sessions can become hijacked by other users using a PASV theft attack. In short, there are a lot of other solutions to FTP, such as web-based browsing through Rumpus or WebDAV, that can be used. Consider replacing FTP with one of them in order to eliminate the use of FTP in your environment.

Permission Models

In larger environments, system administrators have been grappling with various methods to handle file permissions for a good while now. Over the years, the Mac administrative community has developed a few different methodologies as standard practices for managing permissions. In this section, we'll touch on these permissions methodologies, or models, to give you a better understanding about the ways that file-sharing permissions policies can be implemented on Mac networks.

Discretionary access control (DAC) allows data owners to administer file permissions themselves. In a DAC model, administrators often spend less time assigning permissions (which often means spending more time restoring accidentally deleted files). Discretionary access control systems permit users to entirely determine the access granted to their resources, which means they can (through accident or malice) give access to unauthorized users. The owner of any resource has access to control the privileges to that resource. There are often no security checks ensuring malicious code is not distributed or that the owner of a file or folder is well trained enough to be assigning permissions in the first place. This is the default model and, unfortunately, the most common model for controlling permissions. However, in addition to time spent on restoring deleted files, DAC is also limited in that security breaches can be caused when users who do not understand the appropriate access levels for files within their organization assign permissions that cause security breaches.

Mandatory access control (MAC) is a model that can augment or even replace DAC for file permissions. MAC's most important feature involves denying users full control over the access to resources that they create. The system security policy (as set by the administrator) entirely determines the access rights granted, and a user cannot grant less restrictive access to their resources than the administrator specifies.

MAC has the goal of defining an architecture that requires the evaluation of all security-related information and making decisions based on what is done with data and the various data types in use in your organization. MAC is a strict hierarchical model usually associated with governments. All objects are given security labels known as *sensitivity labels*, and are classified accordingly. All users are then given specific security clearances as to what they are allowed to access. A common term when working with MAC is *lattice*, which describes the upper and lower bounds of a user's access permission. In other words, a user's access differs at different levels.

Role-based access control (RBAC) involves limiting access to files based on the responsibilities of a user. When using a role-based security model for access controls, each role in an organization is created for various job functions. The permissions to perform certain operations are assigned to specific roles. Users are then assigned particular roles, and through those role assignments they acquire the permissions to perform particular system functions. Role-based access requires that an organization review the various positions and build access levels for resources based on those roles.

As an organization looks to scale, it should define roles based on potential future hires. As organizations grow, they are more likely to build out new organizational charts that contain current and future positions within the organization. This often represents a good building block for developing roles, which become users or groups in the directory structure. Security groups can then be used within any document management system or enterprise resource planning (ERP) solution that an organization might decide to deploy. This is the most common permissions model being used today because it accommodates growth within an organization while being careful to limit permissions definitively.

Summary

Throughout this chapter we have discussed securing your file shares. While many of the security mechanisms that have been put in place by Apple will help, such as the LKDC and various encryption protocols, but they will not be effective if your password is not secure. They can also be easily circumvented if you do not have good password policies, such as requiring a password to be changed at certain intervals (see Chapter 16 for more on password policies). Therefore, the most important aspect of securing your files over file shares is to practice good password security.

In Chapter 14, we will turn our attention to perhaps the most popular way to access data today, web servers.

Chapter 14

Web Site Security

In the trenches, we hear it all the time: "My web site is hosted on a Mac. How could it be hacked?" or "My web site is too small. Why would anyone want to hack it?" Although it's true that infiltrating and grabbing personal or business information from your web server might be significant, there are other reasons to break into a web server. For example, hackers want to exploit and control the largest amount of servers in the shortest amount of time, creating zombie systems to do their bidding. Unix-based systems (such as those running Mac OS X) are more capable in many ways than their Windows-based counterparts. Because of this, they are often targeted by botnet creators for use as command-and-control nodes. Also, web servers (running on any platform) are often used as a platform for distributing malware.

An obscure niche web site is not safe just because it isn't a household name like Amazon or Facebook. We've seen time and time again that, although obscurity may seem like a safe haven, in today's modern security landscape it's not enough to fall off a hacker's radar because the main threat is often automated attacks against essentially anonymous web servers. This chapter is devoted to exploring the ways in which you can further secure your Mac OS X web server from intruders. First we'll discuss how to set up web services on a Mac.

Securing Your Web Server

Enabling Web Sharing on a Mac is as simple as a few mouse clicks. However, making it secure is another story altogether.

To enable the Apache 2.2 web server, the default web server in OS X Leopard, open System Preferences, and click the Sharing preference pane. Then, select the Web Sharing box (see Figure 14–1). That's it. You've just configured web services in OS X. But what exactly is the web server in OS X?

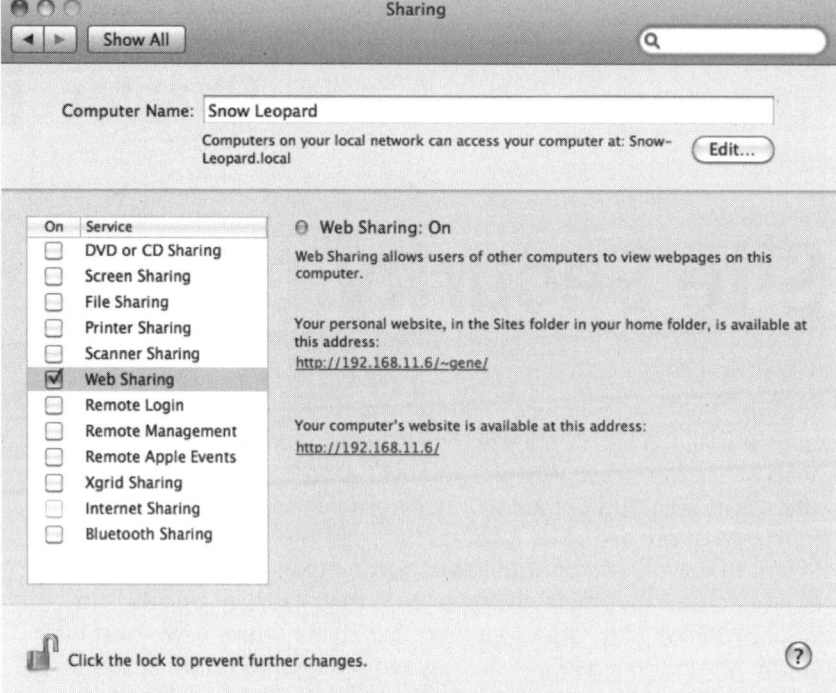

Figure 14-1. *Turning on Web Sharing in OS X System Preferences*

The Apache web server in Mac OS X Server is a powerful open-source web server capable of running on anything from a small web appliance to large computing clusters. Apache is the most widely used web server on the Internet, and is used for small and big sites alike, from small web sites run out of people's homes to large corporate sites with hundreds of servers that process web requests from thousands of users every secondMac OS X Server provides more configuration options with Server Admin, but it is possible to perform the same tasks from the configuration files that you can when enabling Web Sharing. OS X and OS X Server use the same version of Apache.

Web Sharing allows Mac OS X users to host web sites on their computers. As you can see, it's fairly easy to enable, right in the Sharing preference pane. However, administrators cannot properly secure Apache using only the options available in the Sharing preference pane. To do this, you need to dig deeper. Let's examine how you accomplish this.

Introducing the httpd Daemon

Once the web services are turned on, if you open Activity Monitor, and look for the httpd service (short for *HTTP daemon*) under your processes, you will not find it. Why is that? As you can see in Figure 14-2, the web httpd runs as the root user, giving it a high level of access. It is possible to modify the start-up scripts for httpd and have it run as a dedicated Apache user. This can help to mitigate the risk of further damage being done if someone were to exploit the web server.

> **NOTE:** The httpd daemon listens for web traffic over port 80 (by default) and processes those requests using the Hypertext Transport Protocol (HTTP).

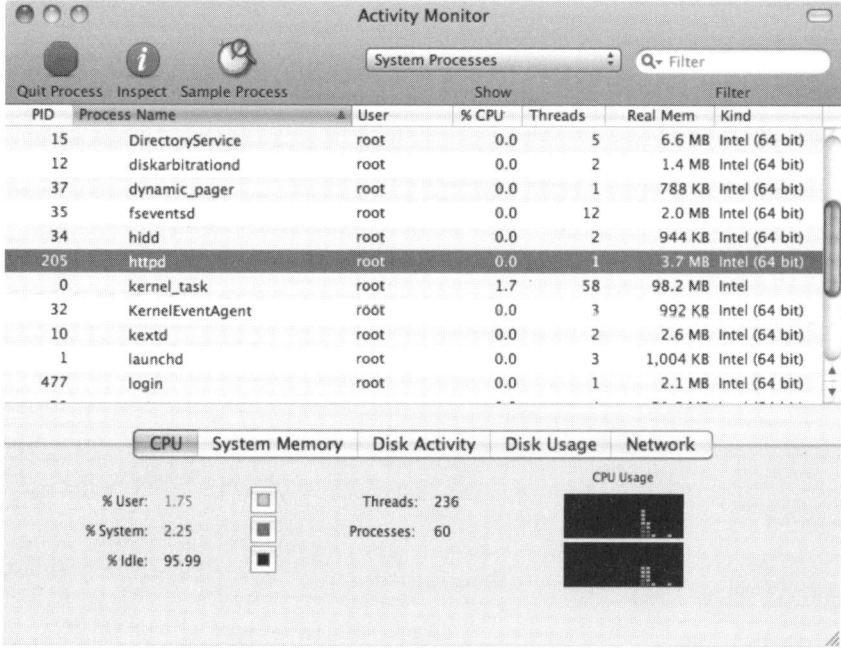

Figure 14-2. *The httpd process in Activity Monitor*

Removing the Default Files

One of the first steps you should take to secure the Mac OS X web server is to replace the default web site files. The files are stored in the /Library/WebServer/Documents folder and have no other purpose except as a test site to determine whether the web server is working properly. If your system is visible to the Internet via a publicly-routable IP address, your site will be crawled by search engines such as Google and Bing unless you specifically disallow it. Leaving the default files in place will tell potential attackers that you're not taking an in-depth approach to security, and that you're a target worthy of further consideration.

Changing the Location of Logs

Changing the location of where logs are written can give a hacker one less place to look for pertinent information about your web site. Writing logs to a separate location can also help centralize them, which can come in handy when you need to quickly troubleshoot intrusion attempts. It can also take some of the headache out of developing scripts that grab information from these logs, such as the number of visitors to the site. These logs can be written to a local server or to a different destination entirely. The default location of your logs is /private/var/log/apache2/. To change this, open the httpd.conf file in /private/etc/apache2/, scroll down to the CustomLog variable, and change the path using the complete path of the file to which you want to write your logs.

Restricting Apache Access

As discussed in Chapter 11, by using the Mac OS X firewall, it is possible to limit access to various ports in OS X using the ipfw command. If you host a web site that should be accessible only to computers on the internal network, you need to configure your firewall to restrict access to the web server, allowing only local systems to access it. If necessary, you can add rules to allow access to computers outside of your network as well.

For instance, if you have a web server that should only be accessible to your Accounting department, you could assign static IP addresses to those users (or reserve addresses for them on your DHCP server), and then restrict access to Apache's ports to only those addresses.

> **NOTE:** If you restrict access to your internal site based on IP addressing, make sure that as new IP schemes are added to your network environment, these changes are accounted for in later revisions of your ipfw tables.

Run on a Nonstandard Port

One way to avoid unwanted traffic is to run Apache on a port other than port 80. If your web site is Internet facing, you can then redirect incoming traffic on port 80 to a different system on your network. This is not entirely foolproof, however, because some visitors who have outgoing traffic limited by their own firewalls may have trouble getting to your web site if it runs over a different port. Also, you may make it difficult for users to find the right port on which to access services, leading to possible frustration for legitimate users. To customize the port on which the web server runs, open the httpd.conf file from the /private/etc/apache2/ folder. From here, scroll down until you see the Listen variable. Edit the number for the listener to reflect the port you want the web server to run on, and save your changes. When you restart apache (or the computer), it will be running on the new port.

> **NOTE:** If you are using a Mac as a dedicated web server, you should disable any ports that are not being used. Port 80 (unless it has been redirected) and port 443 are the two ports you'll need open for web access. See Chapter 11 (for OS X Client) or Chapter 16 (for OS X Server) for more details about disabling ports.

Use a Proxy Server

Web servers do not have to run on the frontline right behind your firewall. It is possible to use the IP address of another server to masquerade as your web server, filtering out unwanted visitors and then relaying the legitimate traffic back and forth between your LAN and the Internet. For more about securing Proxy Servers, see Chapter 10.

Disable CGI

The Common Gateway Interface (CGI) and server-side includes are both methods for allowing apache to call other applications. CGI is typically used to process data entered in a form on a web site. Server-side includes are used for including dynamic information in documents sent to clients, such as the current date, the last modification date of the file, and the size or last modification of other files. As with other options within Apache, these should be enabled only if required. To disable them, use -Includes or -ExecCGI in your options line. These options can be used on a per-directory basis using Apache directives in the `httpd.conf` file.

Web designers will often place CGI files in locations that are not secure or attempt to assign them rights that are insecure and give wrong permissions to users who access these files and scripts. Restricting the allowed locations of executable scripts allows administrators to keep all CGI scripts in a central location to ensure proper security for these scripts. This also limits the damage that can be done by scripts that may be uploaded to a web directory and executed by someone with improper permissions.

Many administrators are already familiar with using a dedicated directory for running CGI scripts or includes. The industry standard is to use the `CGI-BIN` directory on web servers. In Mac OS X, this folder is called the `CGI-Executables` directory by default. To maintain standards, you will notice the following line in the `httpd.conf` file:

```
ScriptAliasMatch ^/cgi-bin/((?!(?i:webobjects)).*$) "/Library/WebServer/CGI-
Executables/$1"
```

This line allows references to directories called `cgi-bin` to point to the `CGI-Executables` directory. The default permissions on this directory allow only the "everyone" group to execute the contents of the directory. By using `ls -al` on this directory, you can see the appropriate permissions for files Apple already has there.

Disable Unnecessary Services in Apache

The immense popularity of Apache is due in part to the large number of modules that have been developed for it. However, when used improperly, these modules can represent a security risk. To reduce the risk associated with running a web server, all modules not required should be disabled by placing a # at the beginning of the `LoadModule` line in httpd.conf.

To learn which modules are required, look to the manual pages at apache.org to get a better idea of what they are, or simply disable them one by one to see which modules will break the site if disabled. All the lines in httpd.conf that begin with LoadModule (and do not have a # in front of the line) will load a module.

One example of a module that can be easily disabled without impacting the performance of the web server is bonjour_module, a module used to allow your web server to be discovered through Bonjour. Because most users will be visiting your site using a domain name, it is not important for the server to work with Bonjour. To disable bonjour_module, place # at the beginning of the line so that it reads as follows:

#LoadModule bonjour_module   libexec/apache2/mod_bonjour.so

Now restart the web server, and the bonjour_module will no longer be running.

> **NOTE:** Mac OS X runs Apache 2.2. You can review any module on the Apache vulnerabilities site at http://httpd.apache.org/security/vulnerabilities_22.html to review whether it is safe to run. Keep in mind that this site only lists known, patched vulnerabilities, and new vulnerabilities, or *Zero Day Explits*, are discovered all the time.

PHP and Security

PHP, (which stands for "PHP:Hypertext Preprocessor") is a programming language that allows web developers to easily create dynamic content. PHP is most often used for developing web-based software applications. Not all web sites use or need PHP. For web servers with sites that do not need PHP, you can leave the module disabled. But if you need to enable it because you are developing PHP code for the site, then you can do so by removing the commenting from the line in the httpd.conf file that loads the PHP module. Find the following line and remove the # from the beginning of the line:

#LoadModule php5_module   libexec/httpd/libphp5.so

It should look like:

LoadModule php5_module   libexec/httpd/libphp5.so

> **NOTE:** Perl, a scripting language, discussed later in the chapter, can be enabled by adding a similar line or disabled by adding a # character in front of the same line:
>
> LoadModule perl_module   libexec/httpd/libperl.so

Securing PHP

If PHP is required to make your web site function, there are ways in which it can be further secured. Once you've decided to enable PHP, you should get to know every setting of the PHP configuration file. With Snow Leopard, Apple has included a PHP configuration file, located at /private/etc/php.ini.default. Before enabling PHP, this file should be renamed to `php.ini`. PHP, much like Apache, is configured using Directives, which control the operation specific features of PHP.

> **NOTE:** The following sections are designed for those familiar with the inner workings of PHP.

The `register_globals` directive is one of the most insecure parts of PHP, and most security auditors recommend that system administrators set this option to off. This directive is disabled by default in Snow Leopard, but it can still be enabled if necessary. Relying on this directive was, at one point, quite common, and many administrators had no idea that it even existed. If they did, they assumed it was at the core of how PHP works. When enabled, `register_globals` will inject your scripts with all sorts of variables, such as request variables from HTML forms. Coupled with the fact that PHP doesn't require variable initialization, this means that the PHP code that relies on this directive will be much less secure.

> **NOTE:** You should also be careful to review how you use `cgi-redirect` and other features of PHP. For a full review of PHP security, refer to *Pro PHP Security* by Chris Snyder and Michael Southwell (Apress, 2005).

Tightening PHP with Input Validation

Form data can be an entryway into a web site's inner workings. Any information can be entered into a form, and remote code could be executed through the forms (provided you have not disabled the ability to execute any code that is sourced from outside the system), allowing a potential hacker to infiltrate your machine through a form on your web site. The following code will remove all data from a variable except letters and numbers using regular expressions in PHP. This is a good way to eliminate the possibility of arbitrary data being entered into a form.

```
<?php
$string = "This is some text and numbers 12345 and symbols !£$%^&";
$new_string = ereg_replace("[^A-Za-z0-9]", "", $string);
echo $new_string
?>
```

Allowing users to input file names should be done only on secured pages such as those using a .htaccess file or realm for security, discussed later in this chapter. Allowing users to specify file names can be dangerous, opening your site up to injection attacks and directory traversal attacks. Directory traversal attacks allow attackers to access directories that should be restricted, and execute commands that are located outside the web server's root directory. If you do use these types of scripts, do not allow two periods (..) in your file names. You can also use `basename`, a PHP function that returns the filename part of a path. This will help you to keep from putting path information in your scripts.

Some PHP directives are important in securing PHP code validating input. For example, you can use the `open_basedir` directive in the php.ini file to limit paths that files can be opened from. You can put all user files into a directory set in the `include_path` and restrict use outside of your `include_path`.

While input validation is strongly recommended as a security precaution, it must be performed within the code for the forms within the site. Therefore, systems administrators can often only request or require the practice of validating each field, rather than building in the input validation themselves. How scripts react to submitted data becomes another source of concern for many sites.

Taming Scripts

Writing scripts can be risky if you don't consider security issues when creating them. Insecure scripts can leave gateways for others to take over your web server. This could mean defacing your web site, but it could also extend to controlling the operating system. Once the operating system has become compromised by a wayward script, the only dependable way to restore integrity to that web server is to reload it from scratch (something we like to refer to as "nuke and pave"). There is no magic bullet that can properly secure scripts, which is why they are so risky to implement in the first place. Practicing good scripting techniques is the best way to secure a script. Additionally, you should consider a mixture of editing `httpd.conf`, using `mod_security`, and using `dosevasive`. These (and other) script-hardening techniques are covered in more detail in the book *Hardening Apache* by Tony Mobily (Apress, 2004).

Many of the scripts contained in this book (and anywhere else in the world) are not, in and of themselves, secure. They should be treated with some degree of caution. The same is true for scripts that you find on the web or elsewhere. These scripts, even those from reliable sources, can and often do contain security holes. Before deploying scripts that you find on the Internet, always perform your own security checks on them.

Securing Your Perl Scripts

> **NOTE:** This section is intended for scripting professionals.

Perl is an extremely powerful language built into every Mac OS X system. One of Perl's strengths is its flexibility in dealing with its variables. Variables can contain almost anything, including file paths. Storing file paths in variables can be an issue if a visitor to a site can change that variable. The visitor can be tricked into running and showing the output of arbitrary commands, showing the wrong files, or showing the contents of directories. To avoid this problem, always specify a redirection statement such as using the > character before a variable. You should also include a space between the redirection statement and the variable that contains a file name. Newer versions of Perl improved the open function to avoid this problem by introducing the three-argument call to use when opening a file.

> **NOTE:** If your Perl code will run only on newer versions of Perl, always use the three-argument version.

In Perl, backticks (`` ` ``) allow the Perl exec function to run external programs. Although easy to use, backticks can result in security problems from their use in environments that involve user input.

The following is a simplistic method for validating user input based on the HTTP_REFERER variable, which contains data about the address of the webpage that is sending direction requests to a server. This variable can be faked by visitors, but it is meant to be used as the first line of defense and can thwart a number of attacks. You should always check the HTTP_REFERER header to ensure that data is originating in the proper place. Generally, a user should not be sending data directly to a script. If a user is trying to do so, this is more than likely evidence of malicious activity.

```perl
#!/usr/bin/perl
$referer=$ENV{'HTTP_REFERER'};
print "Content-type:text/html\n\n";
if ($referer =~ m#^http://www.apress.com/#){
    print "insert processes and code in place of this line";
} else {
    print "The server has encountered an error.  Please go back and try again.";
}
```

The following code shows a way of capturing and printing information about a visitor to a page. This data could also be compromised by being passed to another variable and captured with a form. Obviously, the security implications for these variables are substantial. Validating the remote address is a good way to add a layer of protection to scripts against the possibility of man-in-the-middle attacks:

```php
<?php
echo "<p>IP Address: " . $_SERVER['REMOTE_ADDR'] . "</p>";
echo "<p>Referrer: " . $_SERVER['HTTP_REFERER'] . "</p>";
echo "<p>Browser: " . $_SERVER['HTTP_USER_AGENT'] . "</p>";
?>
```

Another method for protecting Perl scripts is to restrict the script from using any data coming from outside the script. This can include visitor input and environment variables. Alterations to script data are thought of as tainted data. One way to instruct Perl to restrict the use of tainted data is to use the -T switch at the end of the first line of your script. This will cause Perl to issue warnings when you try to do something potentially dangerous. You can still use tainted data, but you must first sanitize it. The safest way to do this is to check your input against a list of valid characters and strip away anything else. If you wrote your script using the CGI.pm library, something like the following will sanitize incoming data:

```perl
use HTML::Entities ();
use CGI qw/:standard/;
$ok_chars = 'a-zA-Z0-9 ,-';
foreach $param_name ( param() ) {
    $_ = HTML::Entities::decode( param($param_name) );
```

```
    $_ =~ s/[^$ok_chars]//go;
    param($param_name,$_);
}
```

Be mindful that using this code will not guarantee security in situations where you're protecting your Perl scripts with the -T switch. If you use the Perl command line to test syntax, you can still do so by using `perl -cT scriptname.pl`.

Securing robots.txt

If you have a web site, you can assume that search engines will find it and index the text and code of your site, adding it into their extensive catalog of sites for users to search. Many administrators do not want their sites to appear in search engines for a variety of reasons. The `robots.txt` file is a simple text file script at the root of your web host that tells a robot whether it has access to a certain file or directory. It is designed for companies that want to keep their data from being scanned by bots, preventing search engines from scanning or crawling their web site. It's flexible, in that different rules can be specified based on the robot's user agent. A sample `robots.txt` is as follows:

```
User-agent: *
Disallow: /secret-files/
```

This simple file tells all robots not to enter the `/secret-files` folder.

A more complex `robots.txt` or `robots(AllowRoot).txt` file looks like this:

```
User-agent: *
Disallow:    /_vti_bin/
Disallow:    /clienthelp/
Disallow:    /exchweb/
Disallow:    /remote/
Disallow:    /tsweb/
Disallow:    /aspnet_client/
Disallow:    /images/
Disallow:    /_private/
Disallow:    /_vti_cnf/
Disallow:    /_vti_log/
Disallow:    /_vti_pvt/
Disallow:    /_vti_script/
Disallow:    /_vti_txt/

Allow All traffic:
User-agent: *
Disallow: /
```

Blocking Hosts Based on robots.txt

This is all well and good, and most robots, such as those of Google and Yahoo, respect your rules. But what happens when a robot blatantly ignores your rules? The simple answer is, it does whatever it wants. Because it's up to the robot to obey or ignore the rules, any disreputable robot can download your entire site.

The solution is to proactively block wayward robots. There are a few different ways to do this, such as blocking known bad robot user agents and blocking IPs. Blocking certain user agents is easy, but it's also easy for the robot to spoof its user agent, so you'll find that you have to continuously update your list of bad user agents. Blocking IP addresses is effective too, but you'll also need to consistently update your blocked IP list. The best solution involves a combination of techniques that, once implemented, requires little or no maintenance and lays a trap for bad robots.

First, put a hidden link into the main page of your site. This hidden link is a zero-by-zero-pixel image that links to a script within `/secret-files/`.

```
<a href="/secret-files/robot.cgi"><img border="0" width="0" length="0" src="images/spacer.gif"></a>
```

Because this image isn't viewable in a browser, the only way it's ever likely to be accessed is if a robot is crawling your site. Because your `robots.txt` file is blocking access to that folder, the only time this script will actually get called is if a robot is crawling the site while ignoring `robots.txt`. Once the script within `/secret-files/` is run, it blocks the user's IP. Of course, it's possible that an inquisitive user viewing the source of your site (using the View Source option available in most modern browsers) might find that link, follow it, and find herself blocked. When you're devising methods of blocking bad traffic, you should always consider the potential for collateral damage.

> **TIP:** Typically, sites have more than one entry point, so it's a good idea to place this hidden link in more than one page. If you take advantage of server-side includes (SSIs), then placing it inside the `header.html` or `footer.html` file offers excellent protection.

The following are the contents of the `robot.cgi` script (big thanks to Erin Scott for whipping this up):

```perl
#!/usr/bin/perl -w
$htaccess = "/path/to/web/root/.htaccess";      # needs to be the full path
open (HTACCESS, ">> $htaccess") or die $!;
print HTACCESS "deny from $ENV{REMOTE_ADDR}\n";
close (HTACCESS);
```

Another benefit to this script is that it stops robots from crawling your site *before* they download anything more than your front page.

If you have other domains that are using Apache's `mod_rewrite` module in the root of your web folder, they will also be inaccessible by the bad robot's IP address. Ninety-nine percent of the time, this is preferable.

Protecting Directories

You can provide access to directories based on passwords in a variety of manners, including using Kerberos, `mod_auth`, `ldap`, or the `.htaccess` file. Using an `.htaccess` file is common when dealing with web hosting environments and when creating files using scripts to control access to directories and files.

An .htaccess file is a simple ASCII text file that allows administrators to personalize error pages, password-protect directories, and redirect traffic. The .htaccess file can be stored in your main site directory, or in any subdirectory that you want to protect. You can use a regular text editor, such as TextEdit, TextMate, vi, or pico, to create and edit an .htaccess file. Not all web hosts will support .htaccess files, so you should consult your hosting administrator if you are in a shared hosting environment. .htaccess files will also not be available if you are running Apache on Windows.

> **TIP:** Before editing the .htaccess file, keep a backup of the original .htaccess file and web site configuration handy in case you have any problems with the file.

Although the .htaccess file can be stored in the main site directory, or any of the subdirectories, the commands in the .htaccess file will directly affect the containing directory, as well as any subdirectories contained therein. If it is stored at the root of your site, it will affect the whole site. If it is stored in a subdirectory, it will affect only the files in that subdirectory. Each file in a directory is affected by the closest .htaccess file available, whether that is in the same folder as the file, or the directories above it. The same is true for .htgroup and .htpasswd files.

There are many ways to create a .htaccess file. You can use the `touch` shell command to create the file and then edit it with a text editor. You can also create the file within a text editor and use an FTP program to upload the file into the proper directory. When you are uploading a .htaccess file, make sure the file transfer typs is set to ASCII mode to avoid any initial errors when working with the file.

The permissions on an .htaccess, .htgroup, or .htpasswd file should typically be 644 (`rw- r-- r--`). This will give the group and user read-only access to this file. For more information on reading permissions, refer to Chapter 4.

> **NOTE:** Commands in the .htaccess file are meant to be on one line only. Be sure that your text editor has line wrap turned off.

Customizing Error Codes

The .htaccess file gives you the ability to redirect visitors to a different page if they try to access an invalid location. You can use a custom error page for any type of error that corresponds with its unique error number. One of the most common, and frustrating, error codes is the dreaded error 404, Page Not Found.

The layout for this command in the .htaccess file is as follows:

`ErrorDocument errornumber /path/to/filename.html`

If you create a page called 404.html that you would like to use as your 404 error page, the command is as follows:

`ErrorDocument 404 /404.html`

If you want to keep all the error pages in a separate directory, just include the directory name in the file path like this:

`ErrorDocument 404 /errorpages/404.html`

Table 11-1 lists the most commonly used error codes.

Table 11-1. *Common Web Site Error Codes*

Code	Name	Description
400	Bad Request	Typically a generic error.
401	Authorization Required	Invalid access to a protected area without authorization.
403	Forbidden	You do not have permissions to access the file.
404	Not Found	The page could not be found.
500	Internal Server Error	Internal server errors in any scripts you have running.

By customizing your error code pages, you will also be increasing the overall security of your server. Most servers use the same error pages that the server came with. This has led to people attempting to use Google to search for all the web pages that have a certain string of text in them in order to obtain a list of all the web servers running a certain version of software, ultimately looking for servers that will have a specific exploit. Customizing error codes will help you stay away from these kinds of Internet searches and the exploits that the results target.

Using .htaccess to Control Access to a Directory

Password protection is one of the most commonly used features of `.htaccess` files. It is also a bit more difficult to set up than customized error codes, but it's far more versatile in its ability to control access to directories.

First, create a new file called `.htpasswd`. Create and save this file in the same fashion as the `.htaccess` file. Include the username and password information in it, in the following format:

```
username:password
username:password
charles:mypassword
```

As you can see, the username and a password, separated by a colon, are on individual lines and there should not be any spaces at the end of each line.

> **NOTE:** The username fields remain in English, but the password fields should to be encrypted to keep them secure. You can accomplish this with the `htpasswd` command.

Once the .htpasswd file is created, the file must be uploaded (in ASCII format) and stored above your Web root or public_html folder. You might want to ask your web host exactly what path you should use. Remember that the .htaccess file will affect the current directory, plus any subdirectories contained in it. Be sure you are placing the file in the right folder. Sometimes one directory section needs protection; other times, the whole site needs it.

Next, you will need to add coding to the .htaccess file for the directory you want to protect:

```
AuthUserFile /home/pathto/.htpasswd
AuthType Basic
AuthName "My Secret Place"


<LIMIT GET POST>
require valid-user
</LIMIT>
```

Let's explore what this code means, starting with the first line:

- AuthUserFile /home/pathto/.htpasswd allows the browser to find the right path to your .htpasswd file. The rest of the command after AuthUserFile specifies the path leading to the actual file name.
- AuthType Basic defines the type of encryption to be used. There are multiple methods of encryption, but Basic is the most commonly used. However, it shouldn't be used for any systems that host high-traffic or high-security environments.
- AuthName "My Secret Place" defines how your protected directory is referred to in the pop-up message box when the visitor hits the protected area. This name is yours to choose. The users see only what is inside the quotes.

This last part of the script tells the browser to check credentials that the visitor enters into the box against the information in your .htpasswd file:

```
<LIMIT GET POST>
require valid-user
</LIMIT>
```

When visitors try to access a page within a protected directory, they will get a dialog box asking for a username and password. If they enter bad information, they will be directed to an error page.

If you would rather password-protect a specific file than a folder, you can use this file name in your .htaccess file, where the AuthUserFile variable defines the specific file or web page for which you want to control access:

```
<files "filename.cgi">
AuthUserFile /home/pathto/.htpasswd
AuthType Basic
AuthName "Secret Place"
require valid-user
</files>
```

Finally, you can and should protect your .htaccess file from being viewed by visitors using this code in the .htaccess file:

```
<files ".htaccess">
order allow,deny
deny from all
</files>
```

> **NOTE:** If you are using Mac OS X Server then see Chapter 16 for how to build realms using Server Admin.

Tightening Security with TLS

Transport Layer Security (TLS) began appearing on commerce servers on the Web in the mid-to-late 90s as a means to securely submit confidential financial data over the Web. TLS is based on a protocol called SSL, and is itself often called SSL. This high-level open source security protocol is now an industry standard and is used with various mail protocols, instant messaging protocols, and web sites. TLS is based on RSA Data Security's public-key cryptography algorithms and is denoted by the letter *S* in the https part of a web site's URL. By default, HTTP over TLS operates over port 443, although this can be customized.

OpenSSL is the package that provides the SSL service for Mac OS X and Mac OS X Server. The current version of OpenSSL that is running on a system can be found by using the interactive command-line OpenSSL tool. To do this, use the following command:

```
openssl version
```

The `openssl` command then responds with an output equaling the following, showing the exact version of OpenSSL being run on the system:

```
OpenSSL 0.9.8k 25 Mar 2009
```

OpenSSL uses asymmetric key pairs to encrypt a session key, which is in turn used to encrypt traffic between the server and the client. The server's public key is stored in an X.509 certificate.

Implementing Digital Certificates

Sensitive data that is transported back and forth from the web server to the web browser needs to be secured. All too often, this data is sent across the Internet unencrypted and exposed to anyone who has the ability to intercept it. Digital certificates, such as those used to secure SSL and TLS connections, were invented to cut down on this kind of information hijacking. When a digital certificate is used, an encrypted "handshake" is initiated with the server and browser. These certificates can be created using open-source tools such as OpenSSL, or they can be purchased from companies such as VeriSign or Thawte, which offer many different configuration options for the certificate.

There are two ways to implement certificates. The first, and the least expensive route, is to use a self-signed certificate. This option uses the built-in SSL feature of your server to create the certificate (more on this in Chapter 16). The second option is to purchase a certificate from a trusted authority, such as Thawte or VeriSign. The key difference between the two options is that when using a certificate provided by a trusted authority, there is a chain of trust that assures your users that your site is, indeed, your site. When using a self-signed certificate, your users will be warned that the certificate can't be verified, and they will have to choose to accept the certificate.

When considering whether or not to use SSL to protect your web site, it is important to consider whether you will have users interacting with your site in such a way that they want their privacy to be protected. For example, if you have a very small web site that only provides data for users, but does not have any forms or ways for users to actually enter data into your site, then you probably do not need to implement SSL on your web server. The certificate and infrastructure that is required for the use of SSL would simply not be worth the expense.

Protecting the Privacy of Your Information

It is important to protect the privacy of your information. Remarkably, it can be rather easy to discover personal information about a web site's owner. If you were interested in discovering the owner of a site's domain, you could perform a WHOIS lookup for the domain to discover more information about the site's owners including their name, e-mail address, and possibly even the phone number and physical address. If you were crafty enough, this information could then be used for social engineering purposes. Many domain registrars, such as Network Solutions, even provide information about domain names by using a WHOIS button on their front pages. But it's not just Network Solutions that will provide this information; almost every domain registration web site will give the inquisitor access to a WHOIS database to look up information about a site as long as the owner has not asked for that information to be shielded. The WHOIS database is even accessible via the Network Utility in Mac OS X (see Figure 14–3).

Once you know the IP address of a server, it is also possible to query ARIN within the Network Utility to discover more information about the owner of the IP address block (see Figure 14–4). Established in December 1997, ARIN is a nonprofit that allocates IP addresses and develops policies used to govern how they are used.

So, how can you protect your web site registrar from displaying this potentially sensitive information? To protect this information, many registrars offer an add-on service that allows you to hide your information from others, thus repelling a variety of spam and the discovery of other information. There are also proxy services that will register domains on your behalf and obscure identifying information from attackers.

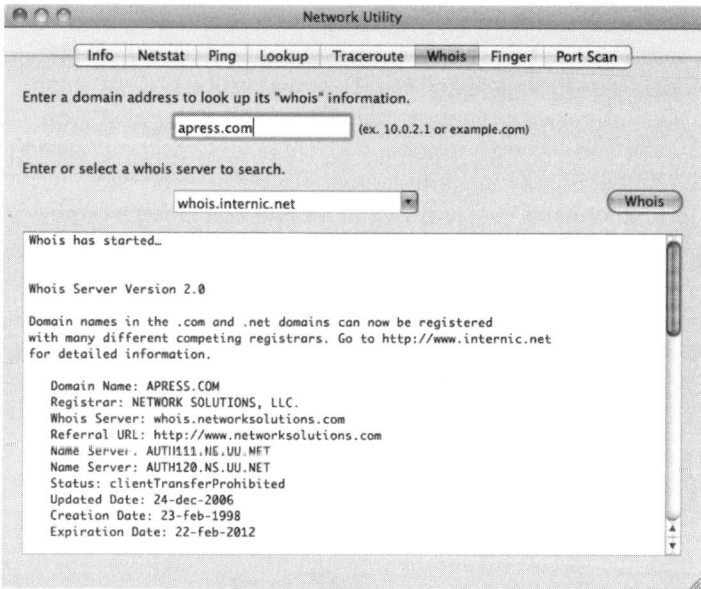

Figure 14-3. *Network Utility Whois tab*

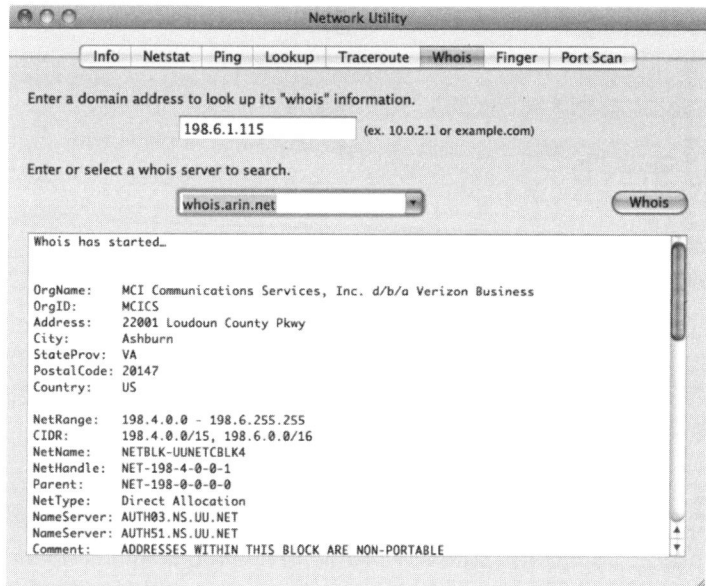

Figure 14-4. *Network Utility Whois tab*

Protecting from Google?

Google is one of the greatest hacking tools ever created, so it is important to understand what an attacker might use Google to do. Google offers attackers the ability to mine information about a web site without leaving any traces. When you run a search on

Google, there are multiple ways to view the results. One option is to view the cached version of a site (see Figure 14–5). The Cached button loads the destination page using a cached copy of the web site located on Google's servers. This means you are not writing to the target web server's log files from your own computer. This gives savvy would-be attackers the ability to have Google show them information about a server without leaving a trace. An attacker would then gather as much information about a site as possible before launching the attack. To help prevent this, know what information Google has cached for your site, and if you feel it necessary, disable the Googlebot from scanning your site. Both of these functions, as well as many others, can be performed with Google's Tools for Webmasters, at https://google.com/webmasters/tools/ siteoverview.

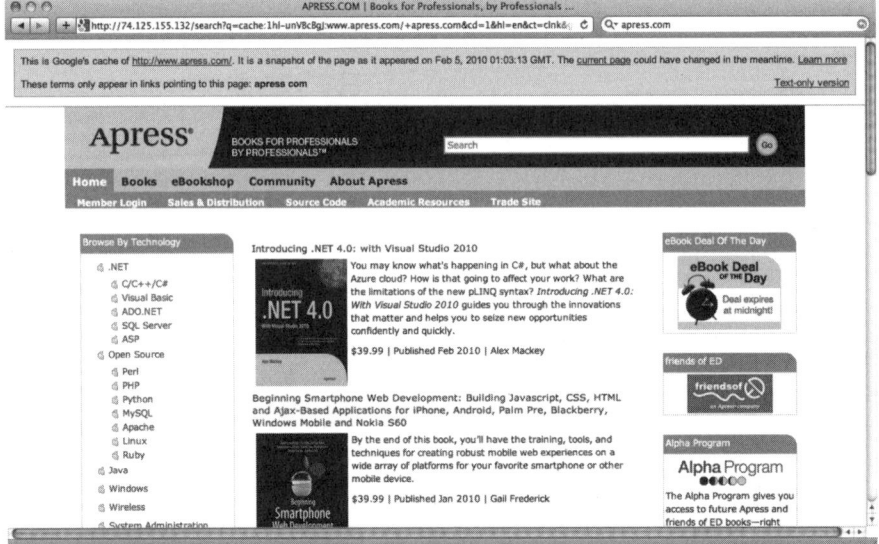

Figure 14–5. *Google's cached version of Apress.com*

There is an argument that can be made that information that should not be made public should not be put on your organization's web site. Placing information in a public forum is not always intentional; therefore, you can contact Google to have them remove a site from searches and flush their cached pages of that site should you need to do so.

Enumerating a Web Server

What other information is available about your web site? Apache communications occur by transferring text data over port 80. As is true with many ports, it is possible to use the text-based communications application `telnet` to connect to port 80 and talk to the server without using a web browser. The command `telnet <IP Address> <port 80>` would result in a prompt that would enable you to send data to a web server and request a response. For example, the following command:

```
telnet www.318.com 80 <RET>
HEAD /HTTP/1.0 <RET>
```

responds with the following lines:

```
<!DOCTYPE HTML PUBLIC "-//IETF//DTD HTML 2.0//EN">
<html><head>
<title>400 Bad Request</title>
</head><body>
<h1>Bad Request</h1>
<p>Your browser sent a request that this server could not understand.<br /></p>
<hr>
<address>Apache/2.2.13 (Unix) PHP/5.3.0 Server at 318.com Port 80</address>
</body></html>
Connection closed by foreign host.
```

As shown in the previous example, when using the Telnet command to get information about Apache, look for the Apache banner to get information on the version number, local server IP address, and any information about the server that might not otherwise be available.

Securing Files on Your Web Server

File security plays an integral part in web security. If your server allows too lenient of permission to files such as scripts, then you are opening yourself up to a wide range of attacks. This includes HTML files and CGI scripts.

Files located in standard web directories are typically assigned permissions of 744 (again, for more information on permissions, see Chapter 4), which gives the everyone user (unauthenticated web visitors are assigned to the everyone group) read-only access for HTML files. One exception to this would be files that have to be rewritten and updated by a script. In that case, apply the 766 permission level to both the directory and the file, but only after making sure that there is a very good reason for this to be the case. By allowing write access to files in your web root, you might be opening yourself up to tampering. Permissions for files that are added to the server are controlled by the mask of the application that uploads the files. In some cases, these are the default permissions of FTP, Apache, a CMS package such as Drupal, or maybe just the umask variable of your system.

CGI applications for different web sites that run on the same server all run with the same permissions, and in Mac OS X they all run as the same user account by default. CGI applications can be dangerous, especially when they have the wrong permissions applied to them, because they can possibly be edited and then run with arbitrary code. The proper permission for executable scripts is typically 755. However, developers will sometimes use unusual permissions—such as 606, which give write access to only the owner (probably root) and everybody, which is the user running the Apache process—according to what they are attempting to accomplish. If you do not have a specific reason to use something other than 755, it's a good idea to stick with this permission level.

Disabling Directory Listings

To make sharing files to the Web easy, Apache will, by default, serve all files that it can access to any user who tries to access it. Any files within a path to a web site or any files available using symbolic links within the web site code are accessible through Apache. This makes limiting access to files available to the Apache user an important aspect of web server security.

One way to mitigate this issue is to deny access to the file system and allow access only to the document root using the `httpd.conf` file. By adding the following code to the `httpd.conf` file, any access other than that granted by this line would be denied:

```
<Directory />
    Order Deny,Allow
    Deny from all
</Directory>
<Directory /Library/WebServer/Documents>
    Order Allow,Deny
    Allow from All
</Directory>
```

This uses the `Directory` option in Apache to limit access but still does not offer protection against following symbolic links located in directories that point to files within the directory structure. To do this, you would use what is known as an *options directive* to further limit access to files within the directory structure. Options directives are specified with a + sign or a minus (–) sign in front of the option to enable and disable access, respectively. `FollowSymLinks` is the option directive to control the ability to follow symbolic links. Use the following syntax to implement it:

```
<Directory /Library/WebServer/Documents>
    Order Allow,Deny
    Allow from All
    Options -FollowSymLinks
</Directory>
```

In many cases, symbolic links are required for code to properly execute. In this case, you can use the `SymLinksIfOwnerMatch` directive. This would allow symbolic links to function only if the owner of the link is the same as the owner of the file to which the symbolic link points. Here's an example of enabling `SymLinksIfOwnerMatch`:

```
<Directory /Library/WebServer/Documents>
    Order Allow,Deny
    Allow from All
    Options -FollowSymLinks  +SymLinksIfOwnerMatch

</Directory>
```

> **TIP:** It is important to always provide the lowest level of permissions possible to users accessing the web server. This can help toward the goal of creating the securest possible site while still allowing for full functionality.

Uploading Files Securely

FTP is a protocol that is used by web developers to upload files to web servers. FTP is a very unsecure protocol that transmits usernames and passwords in plain text. Because it has been around just about as long as the Internet, it's difficult to force webmasters and hosts to use something else. So if people really must use FTP, configure sftp, a part of OpenSSH. For more information on SSH, see Chapter 15.

> **NOTE:** Never allow a database administrator to access a web site's database through a firewall. Database administrators should be accessing their code through a secure VPN tunnel and not by its IP address.

Code Injection Attacks

Some attacks are the result of a web application's inability to process data that falls outside the boundary of what's expected. These attacks are generally the result of design decisions made by the developers of your web application. However, as an administrator, you can keep an eye on your web applications (and your developers) by knowing what to look for.

SQL Injection

SQL Injection vulnerabilities are very common in web applications that use an SQL database, and they are easily exploitable. The vulnerability exists when user input is not filtered for escape characters, allowing a user to enter SQL statements into a form field. For example, on an authentication page with a username and password field, suppose the user entered this in the password field:

```
a' or 1=1
```

When the SQL statement is built, the password condition would be Password='a' or 1=1, which is always going to evaluate to true. An attacker could enter any valid username and be authenticated successfully.

This is an example of a very simple attack, but much more complex exploits exist that can result in data theft, changes to the content of your database, or damage to your database.

Cross Site Scripting

Cross-site scripting (XSS) attacks on popular web sites have been widely publicized recently. Cross-site scripting attacks allow a web application to gather data from a user's session on a different site. SSL and other methods of protecting sites do not help with XSS attacks. Data can be gathered in the form of a link with malicious code that is embedded in the body of an e-mail or directly linked from another site. The attacker can then put the malicious portion of the link into the site in another encoding method to make the request less suspicious. Once the data is collected by a web application, it generates a page for the user that contains the malicious data originally sent to it. This data appears as valid content.

Many of the most popular content management systems and forums let users submit HTML and JavaScript-embedded posts. If a user logs into a site and reads a message posted by another user that contains malicious JavaScript, then it might be possible for the attacker to hijack the session using information from the bulletin board post. Attackers can also inject foreign code into a vulnerable application in order to steal data, hijack accounts, or distribute malware. This kind of attack is called an XSS *hole*. If an XSS hole is found on a web site and the site uses cookies, then it might be possible to steal them. One example of a web application that has been attacked with XSS holes is MediaWiki, the software behind Wikipedia. The developers of MediaWiki have fixed more than 20 XSS holes.

XSS vulnerabilities can allow malicious code insertion, which, in turn, might allow malicious code execution. If an attacker exploits a browser flaw, they might be able to execute commands on the client computer. Command execution is possible only on the client computer. And although command execution is not usually possible on a Mac, having a Windows system attacked by malicious code on your web server is definitely not a desirable result either.

Protecting from Code Injection Attacks

The easiest way to protect yourself as a web site user is to follow links only from the main web site you are visiting. If you visit one web site and it links to another one, visit their main site and use their search engine to find the page you would otherwise have been visiting. This eliminates the possibility of encountering most XSS attacks. Another way to protect yourself from XSS attacks is to turn off JavaScript in your browser settings, as explained in Chapter 7.

As a web site administrator, properly filtering user input will help you avoid many code injection vulnerabilities. If your web site has forms, do not trust the input as valid. Certain characters can allow unintended results. Convert < and > to < and >. You should also filter out (and) by translating them to (and). You should convert # and & to # (#) and & (&). You should remove ' and " from input completely.

Summary

By including Apache in Mac OS X, Apple has given you, the administrator, the most stable, capable Web Server on the Internet. If you plan to make use of it, you'll need to take care that you take an active approach to keeping your website and your users' data secure. It's important to remember that the Internet is made up of many skilled and knowledgeable individuals who are very well versed in all of Apache's capabilities and vulnerabilities. If you're dealing with sensitive data, you should use SSL or TLS, and you should disable any modules you're not using, and you should always validate any input coming from the Internet. Don't count on obscurity or "being on a Mac" to keep your web sites secure.

There are a number of resources available to help you secure web sites. Some of the steps are included in this chapter. Additionally, securing the code of a site is critical, as it can provide a back door into the server that hosts the site. While we got you started looking at the possible pathways into exploiting your systems through your website's code, there is an entire field surrounding site security. If you will be administering sites (especially publicly accessible ones) then we strongly recommend using this chapter as a springboard for learning more about the possible vulnerabilities to your site and how to secure them.

Chapter 15

Remote Connectivity

As a security expert, consider this all-too-real scenario: a passenger sits in the airport, working on his computer, waiting for the plane to start boarding. While sitting there, surfing on the wireless airport network, he notices that almost every laptop in sight is a Mac. On a hunch, he opens Bonjour Browser to discover that many of these laptops have various remote management tools (the Apple Remote Desktop client or Screen Sharing, based on VNC), SSH, Telnet, or Timbuktu enabled. He also notices that many of these computers are not password-protected, and are therefore easily controllable by anyone with the gall to tap into the computer. Within 10 minutes, nearly all the laptop lids are closed with their owners suspiciously looking around, attempting to determine which passenger was entertaining them with the "joke of the day" on their display.

On a serious note, this is possibly the best-case scenario for these unsuspecting Mac owners in the airport. With Screen Sharing, Apple Remote Desktop (ARD), Timbuktu, SSH, and many of the other remote access options improperly secured on these machines, it would be possible to cause much more damage than simply sending a humorous message to their desktops. Deleting files, capturing passwords, reconfiguring operating system preferences, and issuing damaging commands from a shell are all possible. It would also be very easy to simply submit a program that would run in the background and provide access to anyone attempting to control it, using what is called a *root kit*. (Root kits are explained in further detail in Chapter 8.)

More often than not, communication over public networks is not properly secured. When sitting in an airport, coffee shop, hotel, or any other publicly available network, it is important not only to password-protect the means of communicating, but also to encrypt the traffic you are sending over the network. Sending information in an unprotected manner across a public network can be painfully embarrassing, not to mention expensive. This chapter will focus on securely configuring and using the most common remote management applications (both built-in and third party) in the Mac community.

Remote Management Applications

Apple has created a number of remote management programs that are included with Mac OS X. In this section we will cover the two that are available graphically: Apple Remote Desktop and Screen Sharing. We will also cover Back to My Mac, which uses Screen Sharing to establish connectivity between two systems via the MobileMe service.

Apple Remote Desktop

Apple Remote Desktop (ARD) allows administrators to remotely control and administer Mac OS X systems, either from within your company's network or from outside of it. ARD can be used to send shell commands to workstations, transfer files to client systems, and install software remotely on computers. ARD also allows for very extensive reporting of user history, application usage, and software versions.

Screen Sharing

Mac OS X 10.5 introduced a feature called *Screen Sharing*. Screen Sharing allows you to control a remote system and send and receive clipboard contents, simply by clicking on an icon in the sidebar of a Finder window. Screen Sharing is also built into iChat, allowing for very easy remote management from an Instant Messaging session. Screen Sharing provides only very limited capability compared to ARD, but it can be very useful for remote support or emergency server management.

> **NOTE:** Although opening the Screen Sharing application is most easily done from the sidebar of a Finder window, you can also open the application from the /System/Library/CoreServices folder. This means that you do not have to see a client, but can connect over an IP address; this is handy for connecting to remote locations where the computers will not appear in your sidebar for Mac OS X.

Both Screen Sharing and Remote Desktop use the Virtual Network Computing (VNC) protocol to observe and control remote systems. The VNC system (and Screen Sharing) by itself does not provide for the same level of control as ARD. For example, you cannot send Unix commands over VNC or set up tiered access to VNC. ARD is easy to set up, and its customizable security features make the operating environment much more secure than VNC alone. Apple has expanded beyond the capabilities of VNC in its development of ARD, and has added a lot of new features while maintaining backward compatibility with clients such as Chicken of the VNC, UltraVNC, and RealVNC. If you do not have the ARD client installed, then you can still use VNC to access another computer remotely using Screen Sharing, but although this is equally as secure (it uses Kerberos to protect passwords by default), Screen Sharing has less configurable options than the Remote Desktop component of Apple Remote Desktop.

Because VNC is a multiplatform remote connectivity protocol that allows you to remotely view and control Mac, Windows, or Linux systems, the Mac can be managed by any platform and likewise manage any platform, provided the client has a VNC server running. Other operating systems can connect using a standard VNC client, allowing you to quickly tap into another computer, no matter what kind of machine you're connecting from. This is obviously a dangerous aspect of VNC, as an attacker can compromise your system by remotely accessing it if the VNC client is not secured properly. If you do not want to allow other systems to connect to yours, then we recommend disabling this feature entirely (it is not enabled by default). If you would, however, like to allow other systems to be able to connect to yours, there is a way to set this up securely. Let's walk through setting up screen sharing in a secure manner.

Enabling Screen Sharing

To enable Screen Sharing, open the Sharing preference pane. Then click either the Screen Sharing or Remote Management check box (see Figure 15-1). Checking Screen Sharing will allow for only remote control and observation. We'll discuss remote management shortly. Once you have started the Screen Sharing service you will be able to click on the "Allow access for" section, and set it to "Only these users."

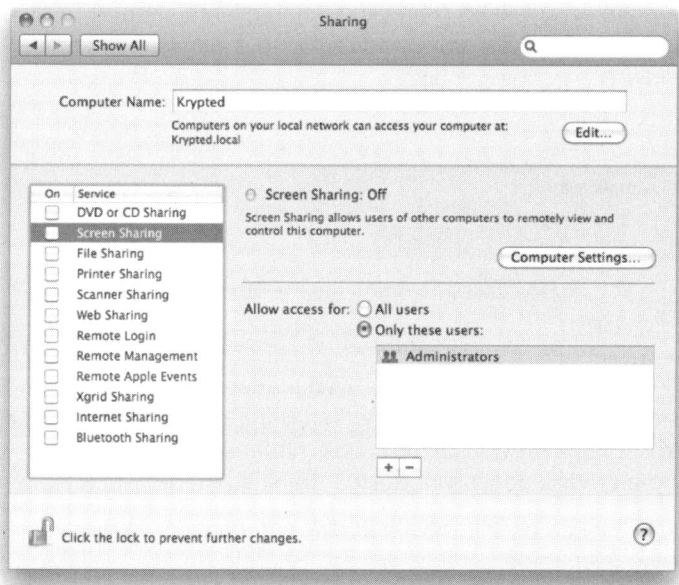

Figure 15-1. *Setting up Screen Sharing*

One of the most critical aspects of securing Screen Sharing is limiting which users are allowed to connect to your system remotely. The "Allow access for" section is where you would configure which users (from the Accounts pane in System Preferences) have access to share any of these services by clicking the plus (+) button. Select the user from the list in the dialog box (see Figure 15-2) that you would like to grant access to this preference, and then click the Select button.

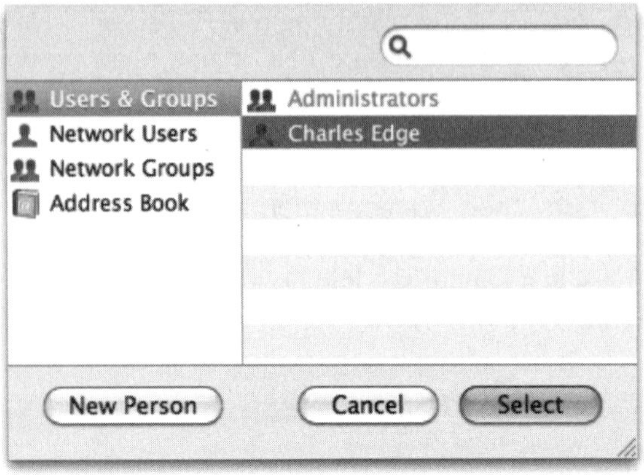

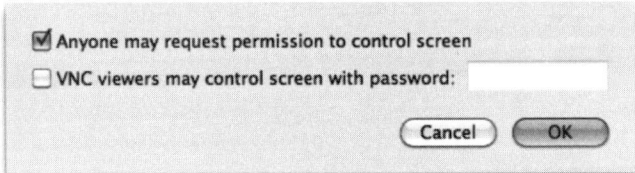

Figure 15–2. *Selecting users*

Once you have added the users to whom you would like to grant VNC client access, click the Computer Settings button in the Sharing preference pane, and verify that the "Anyone may request permission to control screen" is unchecked (see Figure 15–3). Leaving this option enabled means you will be prompted when clients attempt to gain access. In many cases, it is preferable to be prompted because it allows users to be informed when a remote connection is being made.

Figure 15–3. *Screen sharing computer settings*

If you know that users without ARD (such as Windows workstations or those using Chicken of the VNC) will need to control the machine with a different VNC client, click the "VNC viewers may control screen with password" box. Otherwise, leave it unchecked, because allowing any VNC access increases the susceptibility of a system.

To control your computer, VNC clients on the local network can connect to it via IP address or Bonjour. As a Bonjour-enabled service, Screen Sharing is also available via Wide-Area Bonjour, courtesy of .Mac.

Implementing Back to My Mac

If you have a current .Mac account and you are using Mac OS X 10.5 or later, the Back to My Mac feature of .Mac allows you to connect to any computer that has your .Mac username and password entered in the .Mac pane of System Preferences. This eliminates the need to forward ports on your router, because it accesses the remote system using the .Mac system preference. Leopard's built-in Screen Sharing feature is used to allow both Back to My Mac and VNC to connect to your computer. You can stop or start Back to My Mac using the Back to My Mac tab in the .Mac preference pane (see Figure 15–4).

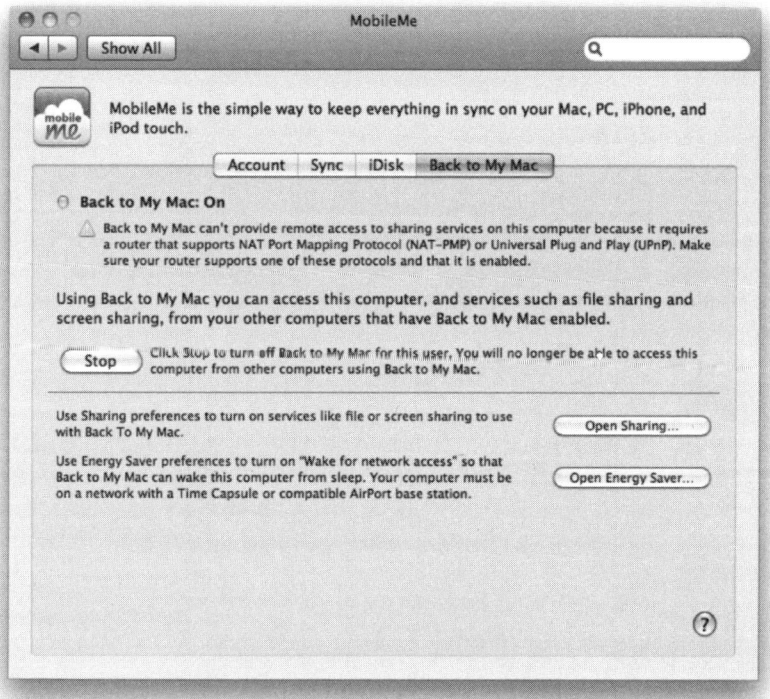

Figure 15–4. *Back to My Mac in the .Mac preference pane*

Configuring Remote Management

Screen Sharing is great for home use, but ARD is far superior for larger environments with more requirements. If you only need remote control, then Screen Sharing will typically suffice. If you have large numbers of systems to manage, or you need the ability to remotely install software or send Unix commands, then Remote Management is likely going to be of more use to you. In the Sharing preference pane, the management features are referred to as Remote Management, and can be controlled granularly on a per-task basis. The Remote Desktop application, used to control Macs using ARD, is licensed separately. If you enable Remote Management, Screen Sharing will automatically be disabled. Remote Management includes the VNC access managed by Screen Sharing.

Enabling Remote Management

To enable Remote Management, click the Remote Management service in the Sharing preference pane (see Figure 15–5). From here, you should set the "Allow access for" option to "Only these users" and add the users who will have access privileges as you did for Screen Sharing in the previous section.

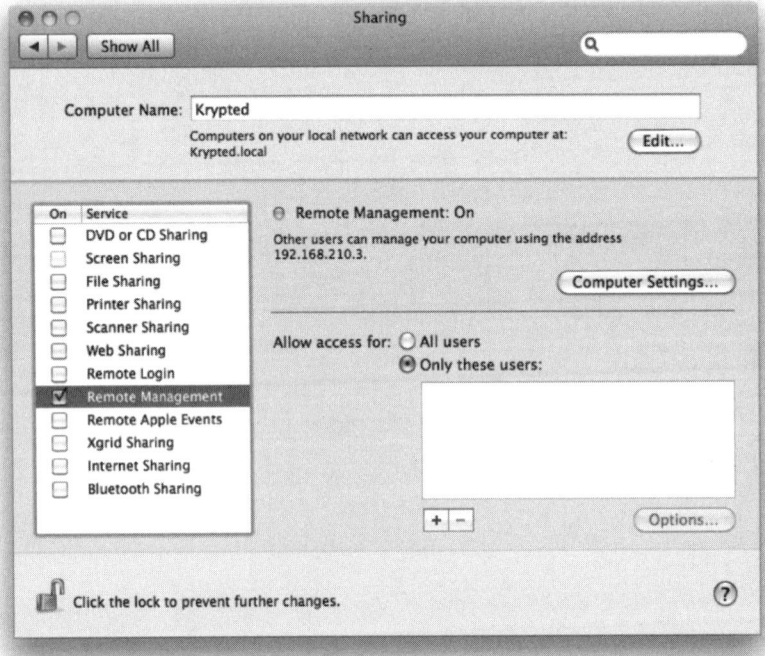

Figure 15–5. *Setting up Remote Management*

In the Sharing preference pane, you can also select what level of access other users have to your system. The Remote Management panel also lets you select what level of access a user should be given by clicking the Options button. Check the boxes (see Figure 15–6) for the appropriate level of access you want to grant. Remember that for every user, only the minimum required level of access should be given. For example, if you want the ARD to be used to build reports on a machine only, then you would click the Generate reports box and nothing else.

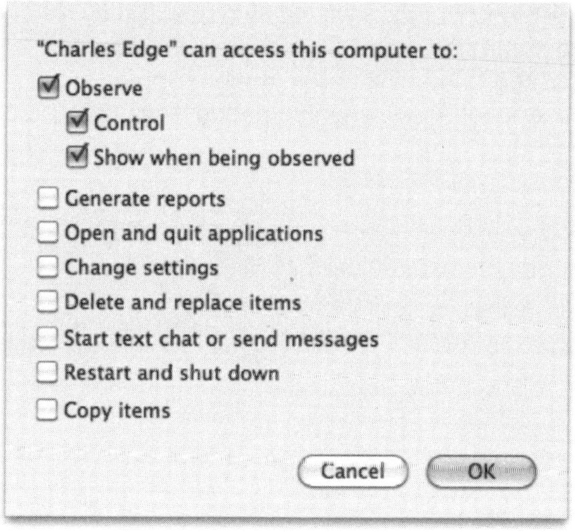

Figure 15-6. *Remote Management options*

Here are descriptions of the settings that can be enabled:

Observe: Remote users can see the activity on their computer, but cannot take control of a session.

Control: Remote users can see the activity on their computer and can take control of the mouse and keyboard. Keep in mind that, if they can take control of an administrative user, they have the capability to elevate their own privileges.

Show When Being Observed: Users being observed will see an icon in the toolbar indicating that their computer is being controlled.

Generate Reports: Remote users can view software, hardware, and other information about your system.

Open and Quit Applications: ARD can be used to open and quit applications without using the remote control function.

Change Settings: Application and System Preferences Settings can be changed without using menu options from within the Remote Desktop application.

Send Text Messages: The ARD text message feature can be used to send instant messages to the remote user.

Restart and Shut Down: ARD can be used to shut down the system and reboot it without controlling the screen.

Copy items: ARD can be used to copy data to the computer.

Once you have granted access to those users and configured management access for those who absolutely must have remote access management capabilities, click the Computer Settings button, and check the "Show remote management status in menu bar box" (see Figure 15–7). This allows the user to see the Remote Desktop icon in the upper right-hand corner of the screen. The Menu Bar icon will notify a user if they're being observed or their computer is being controlled, and will also allow the user to interact with an administrator via the "Message to administrator" option. Some environments, however, prefer that their users not know when someone is watching what they're doing. If this is the case, don't check the box.

> **NOTE:** You can also enable VNC clients to access the system in this screen, but keep in mind that VNC viewers will have a lower encryption protocol than ARD users. Once you are satisfied with your settings, click the OK button to return to the Sharing preference pane.

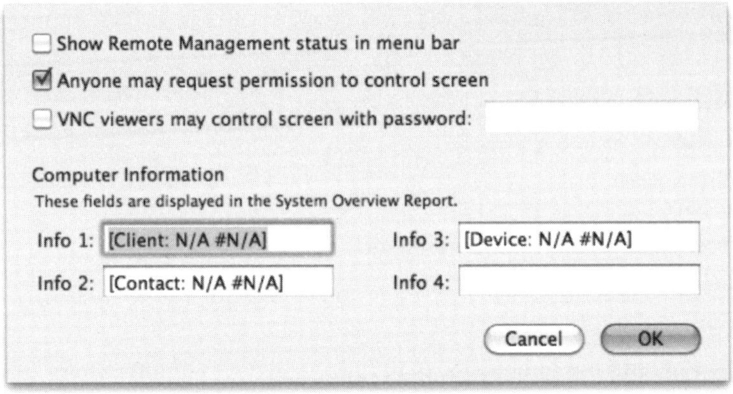

Figure 15-7. Remote Management computer settings

Using Timbuktu Pro

Netopia's Timbuktu Pro was the dominant remote administration application for a long time, and is still widely used in many Mac and mixed platform environments. Although the utilization of this application has dropped drastically since the rise of VNC, Microsoft's RDC and Apple's Remote Desktop, Timbuktu Pro still has a strong following, and Netopia is still developing for it. The choice of whether to use Timbuktu Pro over ARD is often an emotional one rather than one based on feature set and price comparisons. Many of the features that most administrators are looking for are mirrored in Screen Sharing or Apple Remote Desktop, but Timbuktu Pro has better cross-platform capabilities. In a heterogeneous environment, this may make it a better choice than ARD.

Installing Timbuktu Pro

Installation of Timbuktu Pro is as simple as copying the Timbuktu Pro folder from the install disk to your Applications folder and launching the application. On the first launch, you will need to agree to the License Agreement and enter an Activation Key.

Adding New Users

Setting up and establishing appropriate access for new users is the first and most important security step to take after installing Timbuktu. To set up a new user, click Define Users in the Setup menu of Timbuktu and click Add. From there, enter the name and password of the user you are adding. If the account is not connected to a directory service or set to use local OS X accounts, then set the Type menu to Timbuktu user. Enter a password, and then give the user the minimum permissions they need by checking the appropriate boxes for access (Figure 15–8). Unless you are using a modem to dial into the computer (which, in this day and age of high-speed Internet access, is highly unlikely), uncheck the "Let user dial into your computer" box, and click the Save button.

Figure 15–8. *Timbuktu User setup screen*

It is more secure to use accounts hosted in other directory service databases, which can be configured by changing the Type drop-down to Open Directory or Computer User. The Open Directory option type allows the administrator to set policies using the Open Directory services schema within OS X Server, essentially delegating security of the account to the directory services system. An added benefit to using an Open Directory-based user account is that all your computers will use the same username and password, which can help keep security management centralized and simple. It is far easier to routinely change the passwords on 100 computers by using an Open Directory account rather than trying to visit 100 desktops to push out a password change. This is more than likely not the case in smaller environments, however, so we will stick to the Timbuktu User type.

Testing the New Account

Once you have set your account up, test it by moving to another system and attempting to log in to the system that was just configured. At this point, you can use the Registered User or Registered User (Secure) option (see Figure 15–9). Clearly, we recommend using the secure version of login. If you click Add to Keychain to save the password in the keychain, keep in mind that this could potentially cause a security breach if the computer with stored passwords is compromised.

Figure 15–9. *Connecting to a Timbuktu client system*

Use the password rules built into the Timbuktu Preferences (choose Preferences from the Setup menu) to establish a minimum set of good password criteria (see Figure 15–10). These options include the following:

Allow Users to Save Passwords in Connection Documents: We typically disable this option because it allows users to save passwords, which is a security concern.

New Passwords May Match User's 3 Previous Passwords: Disable this option because it allows the password to stay the same when it should routinely be changed as a best practice.

Allow Common Passwords: Disable this option, because it allows users to use passwords that are routinely used in dictionary attacks.

Minimum Number of Characters in Password: Eight is fairly standard.

Number of Days until Password Expires: This should be enabled and set to the number of days before a password needs to be changed and should also be set in accordance with your company's password policy.

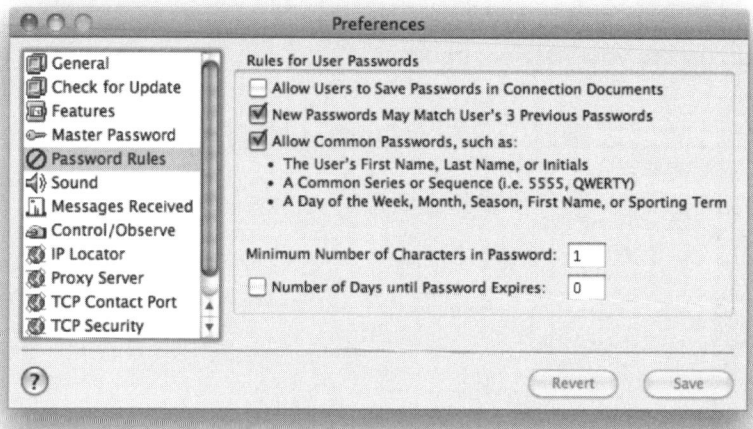

Figure 15-10. *Configuring the Timbuktu password rules*

The Master Password feature of Timbuktu allows administrators to set a password that locks users from changing any of the settings for Timbuktu's preferences. The Master Password feature should be enabled if you would rather not have remote users changing their Timbuktu settings on the computer. Use the Master Password preference pane (see Figure 15-11) to set the features that require entering the master password to enable it; all of these options should be checked.

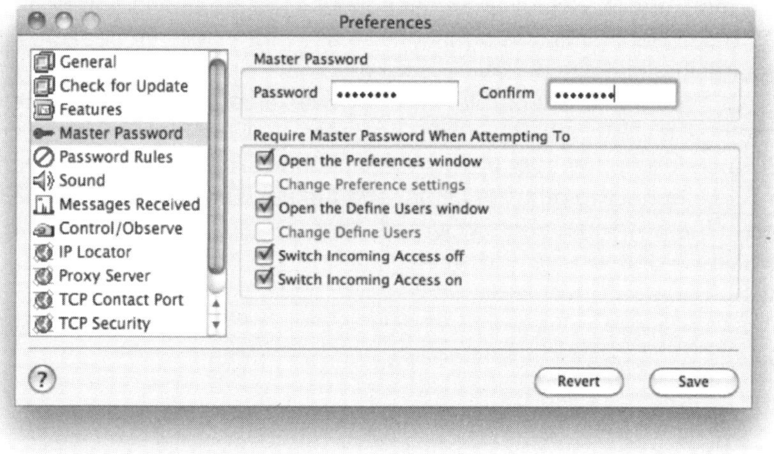

Figure 15-11. *Configuring the Timbuktu master password*

To configure maximum security options for Timbuktu, open the TCP Security preference, which is also located in Preferences in the Setup menu (see Figure 15-12). Within this preference, you can prevent your system from being browse-able through Bonjour by unchecking the Register with Bonjour option. We highly recommend that you restrict all incoming connections to be SSH-enabled by selecting the Only Accept Secure (SSH) Incoming Connections option. Also, Respond to TCP/IP Scanner should be disabled to help obfuscate your network traffic.

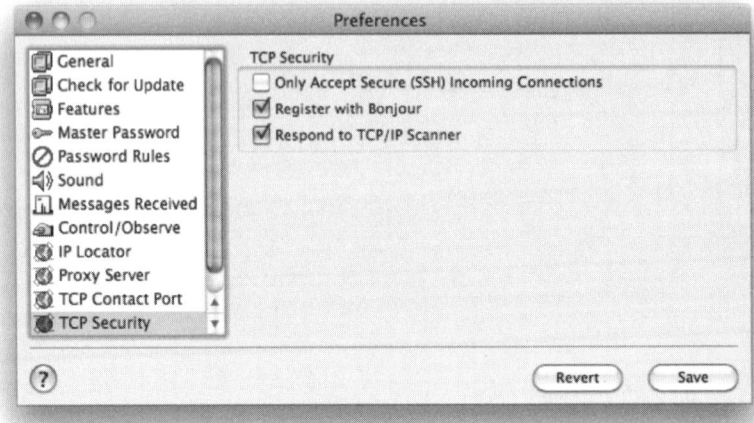

Figure 15-12. *Configuring Timbuktu services*

Using Secure Shell

Telnet was once the primary method for remotely connecting to client systems with command line over remote shells. However, Telnet connections are unencrypted, and therefore insecure forms of transmitting information. As use of the Internet became more widespread, the security implications of having login credentials and user data transmitted in cleartext became unacceptable, and SSH was created. SSH is a better version of this technology, giving an administrator a remote shell (or Terminal access) to send commands to a user computer over a secure connection. These commands can be used to transfer files, connect to other systems, and run any Terminal commands. SSH should be used in those environments where opening a variety of ports to allow remote ARD connectivity is undesirable and where GUI level access is not needed to remotely manage the computer.

Enabling SSH

To enable incoming SSH access to your system, click the Sharing preference pane, and click Remote Login service (see Figure 15–13). From here, click "Only these users," and click the plus (+) button to add users who will be allowed to remotely access the computer using SSH. Checking the box turns the Remote Login indicator light green. You can now use SSH to access the system remotely.

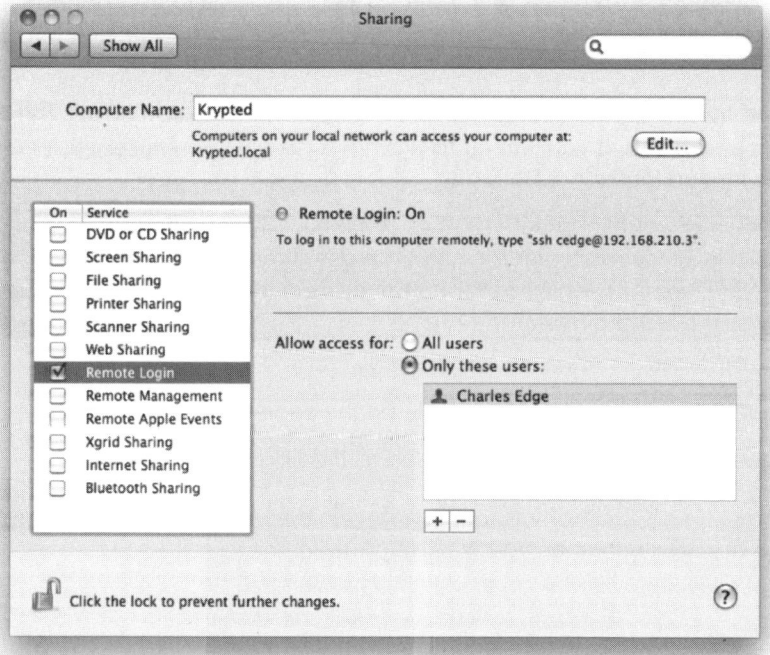

Figure 15-13. *Using the Remote Login feature to enable SSH access*

Further Securing SSH

SSH is a secure protocol, but you can make SSH even more secure with the command line by using public/private key pairs, which make it unnecessary for your password to go over the wire at all. Your private keys should be secured with a passphrase, to keep your private key safe if your system is compromised. You can store your passphrase in your keychain, but this can prove to be just as dangerous as having no passphrase at all if your system is compromised. Therefore make sure that a passphrase is set and required for every access of your keys.

Connecting to an SSH host will request authentication from the client. If you have a key set, your SSH client will generate a temporary key based on your private key. It will then send this key to the server, and the server will compare it to the public keys that it has. If your public key can unlock the temporary key, you are authenticated and allowed access. If the keys fail, then SSH drops back to password-based authentication and will prompt for a password.

Let's see how this works:

> **NOTE:** For the purposes of this example, we assume you haven't generated an SSH key yet.

First you need to make a key pair. To do this, you will use DSA as the key type to ensure that you will be connecting via the more secure SSH2 protocol:

```
ssh-keygen -t dsa
```

You will be prompted for a filename; press Return to accept the default. You will then be prompted for a key passphrase. If you want it to prompt for a passphrase, enter it now; otherwise, for unchallenged logins, hit Return to set it to blank.

Now you will have your new public-private key set in ~/.ssh. The private key is named id_dsa, and the public is id_dsa.pub. For the server to use the key, you must copy your public key to it. If keys have not been used for authentication up to this point, you can simply copy the key to the remote host and rename it:

```
scp ~/.ssh/id_dsa.pub user@host:~/.ssh/authorized_keys
```

This will create or replace your authorized keys file on the server.

If you have authorized keys already, you should add to the file like so:

```
cat ~/.ssh/id_dsa.pub | ssh user@host 'cat - >> ~/.ssh/authorized_keys'
```

Now try logging into the SSH server as you would normally:

```
ssh host.domain.com -l username
```

If you specified a passphrase, you will be asked for it; otherwise, it will automatically grant you access.

> **TIP:** If you are using single sign-on with a Mac OS X Server, then authentication will be handled by Kerberos instead and won't need to implement key-based login.

When using keypairs without passphrases, it is imperative that the private key not fall into the wrong hands. If a compromised passphrase is suspected, the key should be removed from the authorized_keys file of any computer on which it has been installed, and a new keypair should be generated immediately.

Using a VPN

A virtual private network (VPN) is a private communications tunnel, established within a public network, between two points, one inside a home or corporate network and one outside of it. Safe communication through this tunnel is possible through encrypted network traffic.

Connecting to Your Office VPN

Many companies will have VPN's in place for uses to remotely connect to the office. When you use the VPN to connect to your office, then you are using a public network (in other words, the Internet) to establish a private network (a VPN tunnel). Once you have a private network, then you will more than likely be able to access many of the resources just as you would if you were in the office, albeit a little slower because you are not actually working from the LAN. Let's run through a basic VPN client setup to connect to your office's LAN.

If you are going to set up a VPN client, then you first need to obtain configuration settings from your network administrator. First, you need to know what VPN protocol your network is using. The two main types of VPNs are PPTP and L2TP over IPSec. Once you know the type of VPN you are connecting to, then you will need to know the address of the VPN server. This is often an IP address or a DNS name.

To start, open the Network preference pane, and click the plus sign to open the Select the Interface screen. At the Select the Interface screen, choose VPN as the interface, and then choose appropriate VPN type (PPTP or L2TP) for your environment. Once you have entered this information, click the Create button (see Figure 15–14).

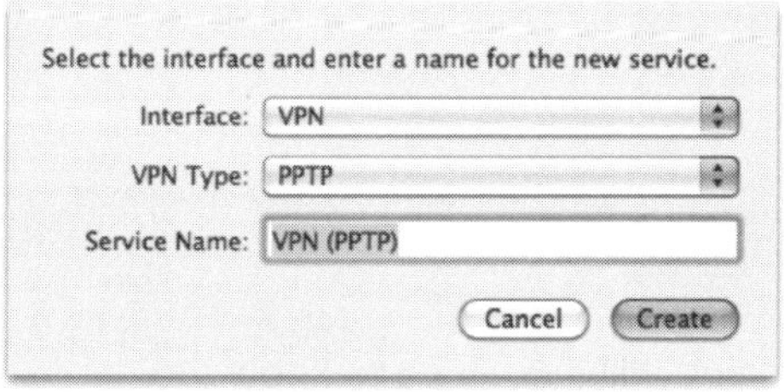

Figure 15–14. *Adding a VPN connection*

Setting Up L2TP

If you are given a choice of PPTP or L2TP, then you should use L2TP, because it is more secure. If you will be connecting to an L2TP-based VPN, then you will have a few more configurable options available to you, and you'll need to know more information about the technical nature of network you are connecting to. In addition to some form of user authentication, L2TP also requires machine-based authentication, such as a *shared secret*, a term that can be used to refer to a password. The authentication can also be an SSL certificate (see Figure 15–15), which can be imported or manually added using the Keychain Utility.

Figure 15–15. L2TP user and machine authentication types

Setting Up PPTP

If you are connecting to a PPTP-based VPN, then you will also need to know the username and password to connect with this connection. Once you have this information, you will be able to configure the VPN.

Once you have a connection created and you have obtained the correct address, account, and password, then you can complete the setup. To do so, open the Network preference pane, and click the PPTP connection you created earlier. Then enter the username in the Account Name field (see Figure 15–16) and the address of the VPN server in the Server Address field.

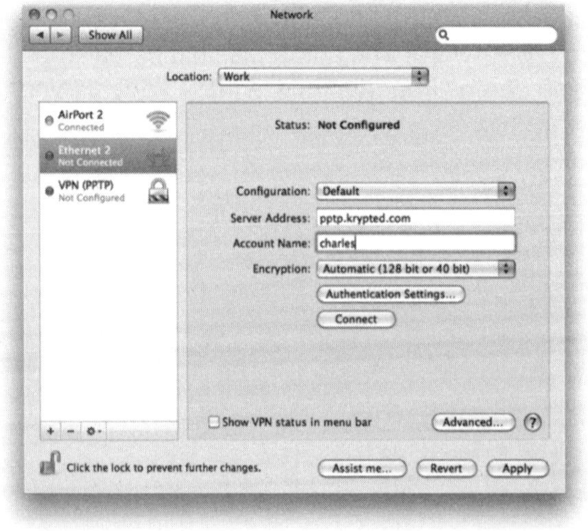

Figure 15–16. Configuring a VPN connection in System Preferences

If you have an authentication method other than the simple password authentication required to establish a connection, click the Advanced button. At the User Authentication screen (see Figure 15–17), select your authentication type and click OK. Once you are finished configuring all the required settings, click Apply in the Network preference pane, and test your connection by clicking the Connect button.

> **TIP:** To make connecting easier, select the Show VPN Status check box in Connection Settings. This will put an icon in the menu bar that allows you to quickly connect to any of the VPN connections you have setup.

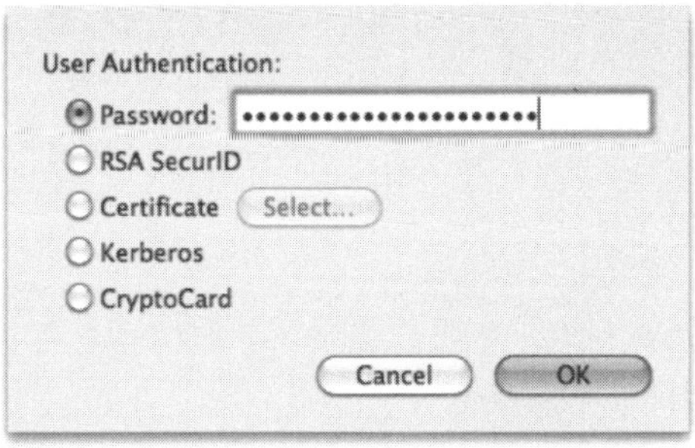

Figure 15–17. *PPTP user authentication types*

Connecting to a Cisco VPN

One of the latest features introduced in Mac OS X 10.6 is the ability to connect to a Cisco-based VPN without any third party software. This is made possible by the new Cisco feature in the VPN type option available in the Network System Preferences pane. To configure the Cisco IPSec VPN Client, first open the Network System Preference pane. Then click on the plus icon below the list of network services. Here, you will choose the Cisco IPSec option, as you can see in Figure 15–18, and assign the new service a name using the Name: field.

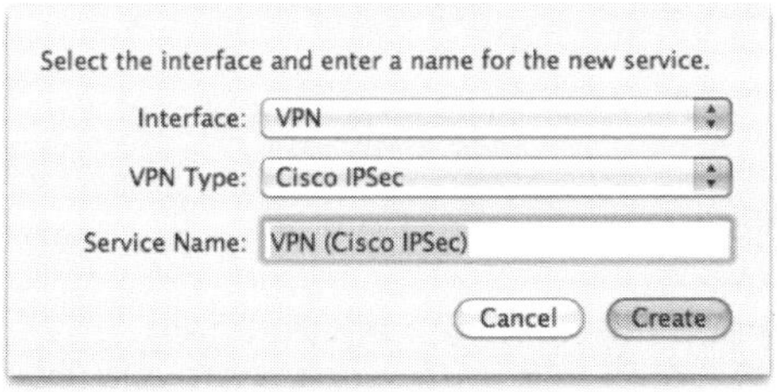

Figure 15–18. *Setting up the Cisco VPN client*

You will then see a screen with the settings to connect to the IPSec VPN client, as you shown in Figure 15–19. Here, provide the name or IP address of the server that you will be connecting to in the Server Address field. You will also need to provide a username and password to connect to the VPN.

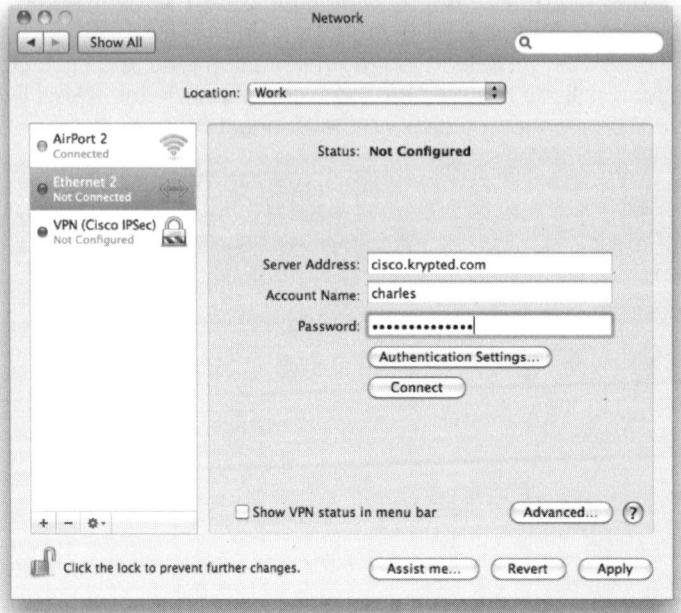

Figure 15-19. *Configuring the Cisco VPN client settings*

If you need to provide a shared secret then click on the Authentication Settings button and provide it in the Shared Secret field. Or, if your environment uses an SSL certificate, click on the radio button for Certificate and then click on the Select button. You can then select the certificate. See Figure 15-20.

Figure 15-20. *Configuring the Cisco VPN Authentication Settings*

Finally, many environments will use or require a group name. If your environment requires a group name, enter it into the Group Name field and click on OK. You will then be able to test your new Cisco IPSec VPN client by clicking on the Connect button. If you are able to establish a connection then the setup process is complete!

PPP + SSH = VPN

Whenever possible, you should use a VPN to tunnel all traffic between remote users and internal services. There is a PPTP VPN daemon available to Mac users running Mac OS X Server (which we cover more in Chapter 13), but unfortunately it is not available out of the box to standard Mac OS X client systems. However, there is a way around this by using an alternative solution: PPP and SSH can be combined to form a VPN link.

> **NOTE:** If you have a VPN server in your office or a Mac OS X Server, the following procedure is not necessary. This method is only for building a VPN between two Mac OS X client systems and not for connecting between a Mac OS X client and a Mac OS X Server

This PPH + SSH method works by creating a PPP link between two systems over an SSH connection. The server machine initiates an SSH connection to the client. The client machine is the machine that is connected to the main network. This is the same box that would run the actual VPN server, but in this situation it is the client of the PPP link. This is also the easiest method of establishing a VPN connection because it allows the remote machine to build and tear down the VPN connection every time a connection is made. Once it has authenticated the connection, the client machine launches pppd, with output going to the inbound SSH session. On the server machine, pppd is launched to respond to the client's pppd. The two daemons sync up and begin passing packets, which are in turn encrypted by SSH. It is not the quickest connection possible, but it does the trick.

Setting Up the VPN account

To create this VPN, you'll first need to create an account in the Account pane of System Preferences on the client machine (for the purposes of discussion, we will refer to the client machine in this example as cedge.318.com) for our server machine to log into. The account being created should be a new account and should not be used for any other purpose than for the VPN, mainly because you'll be modifying some of the account settings that may cause a normal user to become unusable for any other purpose. In this example, we will use the account named cedge.

The next step is to set up the VPN account with the ability to launch the PPP daemon. To do this, edit the sudoers file. Open the Terminal, and navigate to the file /etc/sudoers. You'll want to add the VPN Cmnd_Alias and VPN user privileges to make your sudoers file look like this one:

```
# Cmnd alias specification
Cmnd_Alias VPN=/usr/sbin/pppd, /sbin/route

# Defaults specification

# User privilege specification
root     ALL=(ALL) ALL
%admin   ALL=(ALL) ALL
vpn      ALL=NOPASSWD: VPN
```

> **NOTE:** For more information on the `sudoers` file, see Chapter 3.

Setting Up SSH

The server machine is the machine you are using remotely. This machine will initialize the SSH connection and then respond to the PPP daemon launching on the client. In this example, the server machine is `cedge.318.com`. To log in to the client machine to launch pppd, you first need to generate a key, using SSH key authentication, and then copy the public portion of the key to the VPN account's home directory on the client machine. You don't need to use a password on the key, but of course it's always a good idea to do so.

First establish an SSH key. To do this, use the `ssh-keygen` command. The following iteration of this command will build a key using the RSA encryption method:

```
sudo ssh-keygen -t rsa
```

The command will result in the following lines. At each colon (:), type the password you will be using:

```
Generating public/private rsa key pair.
Enter passphrase (empty for no passphrase):
Enter same passphrase again:
Your identification has been saved in /var/root/.ssh/id_rsa.
Your public key has been saved in /var/root/.ssh/id_rsa.pub.
The key fingerprint is:
a2:3b:11:1d:dd:aa:bd:00:ff:aa:aa:ff:00:ab:ab:11 cedge@cedgetestcomputer
```

Now enter the following command to copy the key pairs to the second computer:

```
sudo scp /var/root/.ssh/id_rsa.pub vpn@cedgecomputer.com:~
RSA key fingerprint is a2:3b:11:1d:dd:aa:bd:00:ff:aa:aa:ff:00:ab:ab:11
cedge@cedgetestcomputer
```

Type yes at the verify prompt, and press the Enter key, as shown here. Once this is complete, type the password, and your preshared key setup will be complete.

```
Are you sure you want to continue connecting (yes/no)? yes
Warning: Permanently added cedge@66.4.4.2' (RSA) to the list of known hosts.
cedge@cedgetestcomputer password:
id_rsa.pub 100% |*************************************************************|
```

Once you've copied the public key to the client system, you'll want to connect to it and finish setting up the VPN account. First `ssh` into the client machine and then attempt to connect to the server machine from the client to exchange host keys, as shown here:

```
ssh cedge@cedgetestcomputer
cedge@cedgetestcomputer password:
```

Next, you'll want to confirm, adding the server to your client's known hosts:

```
ssh cedge@cedgetestcomputer
The authenticity of host 'cedge (66.4.4.2)' can't be established.
RSA key fingerprint is aa:aa:ff:11:11:11:aa:aa:aa:00:00:00:00:aa:aa:aa.
```

```
Are you sure you want to continue connecting (yes/no)? yes
```

Verify that there is a file in the VPN account's `~/.ssh` folder called `known_hosts`. Next, move the generated public key to the file called `authorized_keys` in the `~/.ssh` folder.

```
mv ~/apress.pub ~/.ssh/authorized_keys
```

Finally, configure the PPP daemon to launch passively upon login. The following commands will perform this task:

```
echo "sudo /usr/sbin/pppd passive; logout" > ~/.login
```

To verify that your client machine is set up properly, use the following command from the server machine:

```
sudo ssh cedge@cedgetestcomputer
```

At this point, your server machine should have connected to the client machine, authenticated via the SSH key, and begun to see the garbled output of the PPP daemon. If this is all working properly, then your client machine is ready to go. However, you're not completely out of the woods just yet. To finish configuring the server machine, you'll need to issue a few more commands.

Setting Up PPP

As you saw earlier, when you `ssh` to the client machine, the PPP daemon will launch and start filling your screen with data garbage. To get the two machines to connect, you need to have the PPP daemon on the server machine launch to respond to the client's PPP daemon. The problem is that you can't launch pppd very well if there's a constant garbage stream that the client machine is outputting. You'll need to use a tool called `pty-redir` to get around this. This little program will execute a passed command on a separate TTY.

First download `pty-redir` (from `http://www.shinythings.com/pty-redir/`), and use the following set of commands to install it:

```
make
sudo mkdir /usr/local/bin
sudo cp pty-redir /usr/local/bin
```

These commands will put the `pty-redir` binary in your `/usr/local/bin` directory. To test it, use the following command:

```
sudo /usr/local/bin/pty-redir /usr/bin/ssh cedge@cedgetestcomputer.318.com.
```

You should see a result along the lines of `/dev/ttyp4`. This output tells you which TTY was allocated for your command and where its output is going. In this case, the client machine's PPP daemon is sending its connection information to the redirected TTY. To complete the link, launch pppd on the server machine and have it use the redirected port. This is accomplished with the following command (replace `/dev/ttyp4` with the output of `pty-redir`):

```
sudo /usr/sbin/pppd /dev/ttyp4 local noauth proxyarp persist 192.168.10.1:10.0.0.55.
```

This will tell the server machine's PPP daemon to use the redirected TTY and use the IP address of 10.0.1.1 for the other end of the PPP link. The client machine's IP would be 10.0.0.55. If everything is working up to this point, you should be able to ping 10.0.0.55 and get a response from the client machine. This verifies that your connection is up and running.

Configuring Routing

Now that the tunnel is up, you can use a static route to point to the client machine's network. You will then be able to pass traffic to other hosts on the client's network through the encrypted PPP tunnel securely. If the network you are trying to access is 10.0.0.0/24, you would use the following command to create a route for traffic directed at specific IP addresses:

```
sudo /sbin/route add -net 10.0.0.0/24 10.0.0.55
```

Depending on the client machine's routing setup, you might be able to have the server machine pass all Internet traffic through the client machine. This is a good way to help secure traffic if you're using a wireless access point in a public place. You can bring up the VPN connection and then change your default route with the following command:

```
sudo /sbin/route add -net 0.0.0.0 10.0.0.55
```

This will route all of your Internet traffic through the VPN link, securing your wireless traffic. Remember, it might likely take a hit in performance, slowing things down a bit, as your traffic will be encrypted, passed through the tunnel, decrypted, passed out of the client machine, and then passed out onto the Internet. Performance slowdowns are an expected result.

Disconnecting

The process to disconnect is fairly simple. On the server, use `ps ax | grep pppd` to search for the PPP daemon's process ID. Then use the `sudo kill <Process ID>` command to stop the daemon. The server machine's PPP daemon will bring down the link. This allows the client machine's PPP daemon to quit. Upon quitting, the client machine will log the VPN user out of the connection. At this point, the PPP connection will have stopped, both daemons will have quit, and your SSH connection should be disconnected.

Summary

Remote access is invaluable to administrators, whether you're managing a small office or a large corporate network. If you take care to configure VPN tunnels and remote management properly, you can securely connect to your LAN and administer your systems without making those same tools an avenue for attacks.

Chapter 16

Server Security

It may look similar, but Mac OS X Server has some very different functionality from Mac OS X Client. The differences lie in the fact that Mac OS X Server, like most other servers, is used to share data. That data is shared across a variety of protocols, according to the type of data being shared. Therefore, it naturally follows that you will need to take additional precautions to properly secure Mac OS X Server and on a per-service basis. In this chapter, we'll primarily focus on the services that are specific to Mac OS X Server and how to secure them, paying attention to where the best practices differ from Mac OS X Client.

A number of services are included with Mac OS X Server. We will focus on security as it pertains to the most heavily used services: directory services, file sharing, web server services, wireless services, user account management, Internet security, and the iChat Server. We'll start with common security themes that persist across each service. Because many of the other services are dependent on directory services, we'll then move on to securing Open Directory, an innovation in Mac OS X Server that distinguishes it from Mac OS X Client. Finally, we'll take a look at each service and the special security precautions that should be taken with each.

Limiting Access to Services

A key aspect of Mac OS X Server is its ability to determine which users can access specific services, as well as its ability to delegate management control over each service to the appropriate users. The granularity of control in Mac OS X Server is much finer than that in Mac OS X Client. When securing AFP, for example, you can control which share points each user can access per protocol, including NFS. And you can create a support user who has the capability of starting and stopping the service while removing their ability to access the data shared by that service. Or, if you'd rather not make a configuration change that restricts a specific user from mounting a share point, you can also set a control that denies access to certain services, or protocols, for specific users.

> **NOTE:** Tomcat and other Java services are exceptions to the rule, and need to be configured within the service's security settings rather than in Server Admin.

Service access control lists (SACLs) allow administrators to limit access to services for certain users. To configure SACLs, open Server Admin, and click the name of the server. Then click Settings in the toolbar and click the Access tab. Uncheck the "Use same settings for all services" box. Next, click each service you want to limit access to, and then select "Allow only users and groups below," as shown in Figure 16–1. Then, click the plus (+) sign, and drag the users over to grant them access to the list.

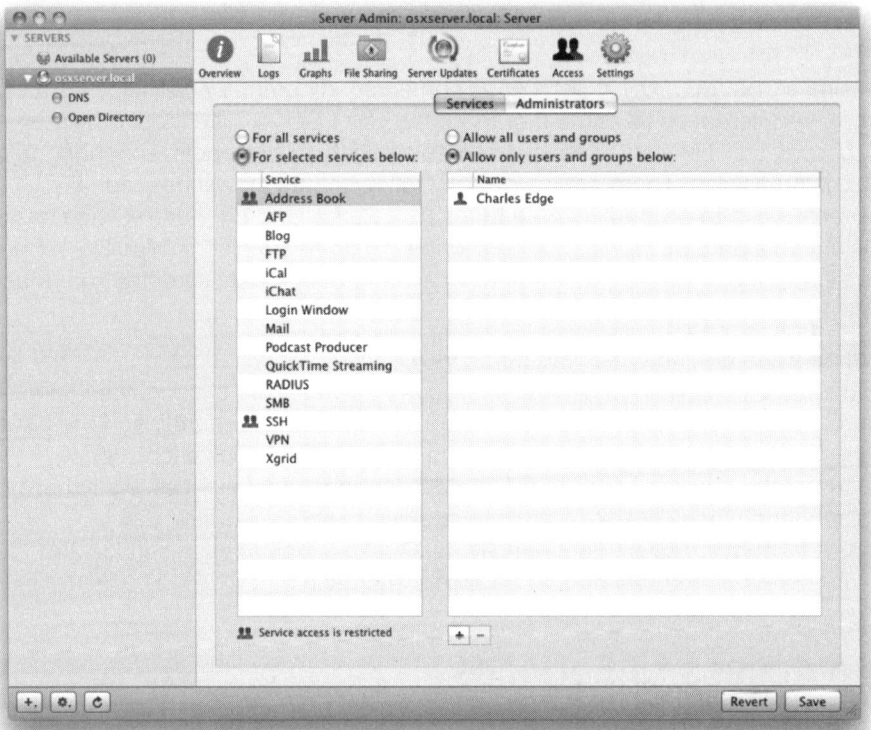

Figure 16–1. *Configuring SACLs*

> **TIP:** Using SACLs can be helpful with services such as VPN that do not have their own granular user controls within the service.

You can also use the Administrators sub-tab to configure users and groups that have been granted privileges to administer and monitor specific services. These users would then be able to change configuration settings for defined services, as well as have the ability to start and stop them.

The Root User

Unlike Mac OS X Client, Max OS X Server enables the root user by virtue of the first administrative password that is provided at first boot. By default, the Server Assistant uses the local administrative user's password (such as *admin* or *mycompany admin*) that was entered in the setup screens for the password of the root user. Keep in mind that any subsequent password changes to that first administrative account are not replicated when you change its password. In practice, this often leads to a stale password for root if left enabled; in other words, the password does not have any policies applied to it, and can provide an entry point for a potential hack. This is one strong argument for leaving the root user disabled on Mac OS X Server and enabling it only when it's needed. To disable the root user, use the following command:

```
dsenableroot -d
```

> **NOTE:** One caveat to disabling the root user is that you will not be able to promote an Open Directory system to a replica. The root user does not need to be active during standard replication intervals, but will need to be enabled during replica setup. Disabling the root user will result in an error during the setup of the replica.

Foundations of a Directory Service

One of the most substantial aspects of Mac OS X Server and its impact on a Mac OS X-based network is the ability to run directory services. Open Directory, Apple's native directory service technology, is built on open standards such as OpenLDAP, SASL, and Kerberos. Open Directory gives administrators the ability to centralize usernames and passwords for an environment, which increases security. But a directory service also allows for the ability to deploy policies to workstations over the network in a somewhat automated fashion. Using directory services, it becomes possible to lock down client computers with the security settings you want, to enforce password policies to keep users from having simple passwords, and to limit the frequency that passwords are required on the network, also greatly increasing the overall security of your environment.

While we will focus on Open Directory throughout most of our discussions about directory services, it is worth noting that every Mac OS X computer ships running a local directory service. This includes many of the components found in Mac OS X Server, which allows for optimal security among Mac computers without a server. The local directory service can also be used to deploy *managed preferences*, or policies, without the use of a centralized server.

Defining LDAP

A *directory service* organizes information such as users, groups, and computers. The directory service is the interface to the directory and provides access to the data that is contained in that directory. In addition to Open Directory, popular directory services include OpenLDAP, Active Directory, and eDirectory. The one item that nearly all directory service implementations share is the Lightweight Directory Access Protocol (LDAP). LDAP provides access to a centralized data structure commonly used to track information such as usernames, computers, printers, and other items on a network by performing fast queries of the database. LDAP is a popular protocol and allows for a wide variety of uses.

Apple's Open Directory technology runs LDAP on a Berkley Database (bdb), which is made accessible via OpenLDAP for storing user account information. Slapd is the process behind Apple's implementation of the OpenLDAP server. Slapd hosts access to the Berkeley Database where user account information, such as the user ID, is stored. When broken down to their bare components, these accounts are merely sets of *attributes*. Attributes are fields for a given object that constitute the makeup of a standard user, such as a username, a unique ID, a home directory path, and a password slot. Think of it this way: if you were to print out all of your attributes then the data set would resemble a spreadsheet.

> **NOTE:** When directory services are enabled on the first server of an organization, that server is considered the Open Directory *Master*.

Kerberos

Kerberos is a highly secure computer network authentication protocol developed at MIT that allows individuals, communicating over an insecure network, to prove their identity to one another in a secure manner.

Kerberos helps prevent eavesdropping to discover passwords or replay attacks (resending packets to obtain similar results from the original transmission) and ensures the integrity of the data. It provides mutual authentication much like a client-server model, where both the user and the service verify each other's identity. Let's dive into how Kerberos authenticates its users.

> **NOTE:** In Greek mythology, Kerberos was the hound guarding Hades—a monstrous three-headed dog with a snake for a tail and innumerable snake heads on his back.

Kerberos Deconstructed

In Mac OS X Server, Apple has modified Kerberos to handle communication with the Apple PasswordServer, which is responsible for building and replicating the user Kerberos database. PasswordServer keeps the passwords encrypted internally on the server, but Kerberos allows computers from the outside to communicate securely with the server. (We'll discuss PasswordServer a bit later.)

Kerberos is divided into three components: the Kerberos key distribution server, the Kerberized service, and the Kerberos client. This trio communicates with a Kerberos network known as a *realm*. Kerberos guards your passwords and enables single sign-on to configured servers. Kerberos does this by identifying each user and server with a *principal*. A principal is then assigned a time-sensitive *ticket* or (TGT) to submit credentials over the network rather than sending passwords, establishing a session. Kerberos relies on a series of challenges and session keys that then allow a user or server a TGT assigned to the user's principal. The TGT contains the time stamp used by the key distribution server to verify its authenticity.

> **NOTE:** Apple's implementation of the MIT Kerberos key distribution server (KDC) is krb5kdc.

The TGT is issued as an authentication token to gain access to additional service tickets during the TGT's lifetime. This can be illustrated by logging in at the loginwindow as an Open Directory or Active Directory user, which authenticates you to the directory server and provides a TGT placed in a shared *credentials cache*. Other services such as file sharing will then provide single sign-on based on the TGT.

> **NOTE:** Clients who are using Open Directory for authentication (known as *binding*) will be automatically configured to use Kerberos using special entries provided and updated by the LDAP server. You can manually initialize the configuration by using the `kerberosautoconfig` command, but this is typically not required.

One of the most critical aspects of Kerberos configuration is time synchronization. If a client or server is more than five minutes apart from its Kerberos KDC server, then authentication will fail. This value is normally best synchronized using the Network Time Protocol (NTP). To enable the NTP service on the Mac OS X Server, configure the server as your Open Directory master (explained a bit later in the section "Configuring and Managing Open Directory"), and enable the NTP check box in the General settings of the Server Admin application. The NTP setting can then be pushed out to client machines using scripts or applications. The NTP client setting can also be configured manually in the Date & Time pane of System Preferences.

> **TIP:** You can also manually initiate time synchronization using the command line with the following command: `sudo ntd -q`.

Another important consideration for Kerberos is DNS. Prior to setting up an Open Directory master or replica, make sure that the server's DNS is accurate in both forward and reverse DNS resolution. To do so, run the changeip command with the -checkhostname option, as follows:

```
changeip -checkhostname
```

Kerberos is frequently called the "keys to the kingdom," on an OS X Server. An improperly configured Open Directory service can give way to those keys. If a Kerberos system is deployed on an OS X Server, it's important to make sure the services on your Open Directory servers are properly patched and securely locked down. Let's discuss the proper ways to do just that.

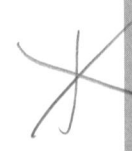

NOTE: Typically, a secure Kerberos environment consists of a standalone system that doesn't run any other services and is used as a KDC. However, in Mac OS X Server the Open Directory Master already runs other services, such as passwordserver and LDAP. Therefore, for a fully secure environment we recommend running your Open Directory master on a dedicated host that isn't running any other services other than the Open Directory master service.

Configuring and Managing Open Directory

Because directory services give such a boost to the security of larger environments, we will spend the first part of this section discussing how to set up and bind to Open Directory. Once you have a solid Open Directory environment, we will then show you how to secure Open Directory, more than it is secured in the stock implementation of Mac OS X Server, by disabling anonymous binding and implementing LDAP ACLs. Anonymous binding allows unauthenticated users to be able to enumerate your directory structure, whereas LDAP ACLs control what is visible to unauthenticated users and specified groups for authenticated users of the directory.

To start setting up Open Directory, open Server Admin, and click the name of the server. Then click Settings. In the toolbar, select the Services tab. On the Services tab (see Figure 16–2), check the Open Directory box, and click the Save button to see Open Directory added to the list of services available on the server.

In the list of services, click on Open Directory, and then click on the Save button. You will then see that the Open Directory service is running as a stand-alone server by clicking on the Open Directory service, which will then be populated in the SERVERS list (see Figure 16–3).

CHAPTER 16: Server Security 429

Figure 16–2. *Adding the Open Directory service*

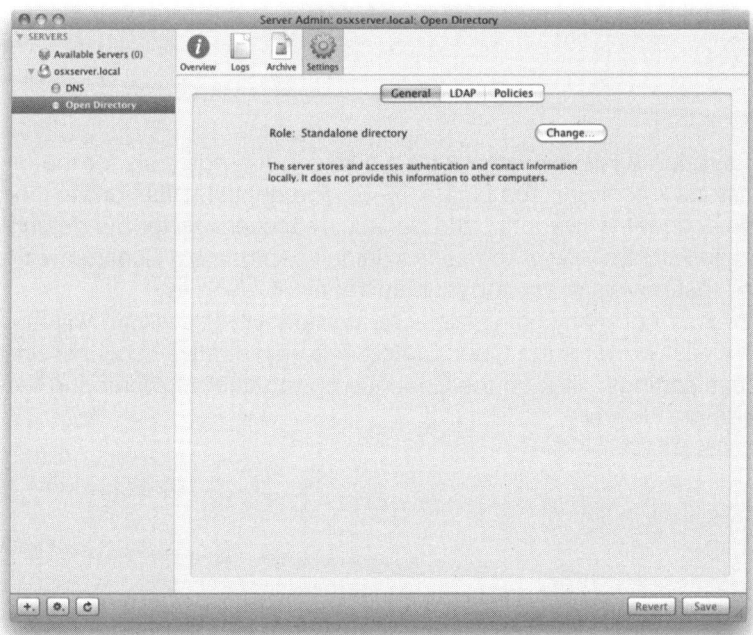

Figure 16–3. *Promoting the server*

Click on the Change button and the Service Configuration Assistant will open. You will then be stepped through a wizard asking for details about the configuration in order to promote the server to an Open Directory master. Because this is the first system in the directory domain, click on Open Directory Master, and then click on the Continue button (see Figure 16–4).

> **NOTE:** As an Open Directory master, the system will run the LDAP database, run as a Kerberos KDC, run the PasswordServer, and be responsible for processing user and workstation policies.

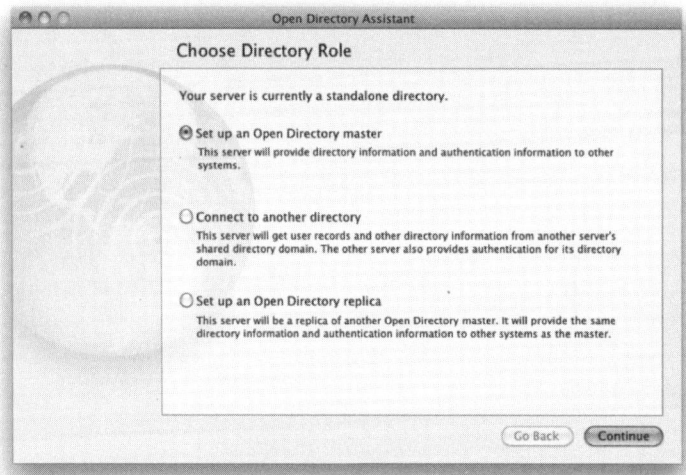

Figure 16–4. *Choosing a role*

Next, the Server Configuration Assistant will ask for a new set of credentials for the Open Directory administrative account (see Figure 16–5). The default value for the Open Directory administrative account is *diradmin*, and because attackers go for the default login information first, you will rarely want to use the default usernames. Change this value to something else that makes sense for your environment, such as *[company]admin* (where your company name replaces [company]). The wizard will then prompt you to provide a password for the Open Directory administrative account. Once you're finished with these settings, click on the Continue button to start promoting the system to an Open Directory master.

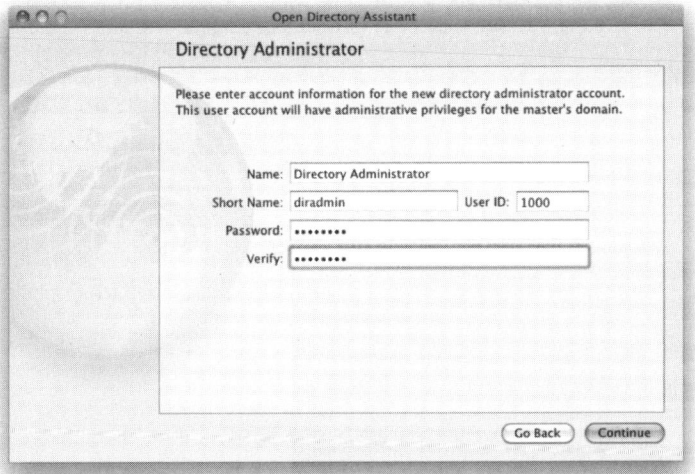

Figure 16-5. *Configuring the credentials*

When this wizard is complete, you will see the server role set to an Open Directory Master. Let's move on to configuring some basic security settings for LDAP.

Securing LDAP: Enabling SSL

You can use SSL to secure the user's communication within your Open Directory environment. At this point, you may have already purchased an SSL certificate and installed it onto your server, or you may have chosen to use the default certificate Apple includes with Mac OS X Server during your testing. If you choose to purchase a certificate, you can follow the steps in the "SSL Certs for Web Servers" section to implement it.

To enable the SSL Certificate setting for your server, click the LDAP tab of the Open Directory settings in Server Admin. Using the Secure Sockets Layer (SSL) section, check the Enable SSL box (see Figure 16-6), and choose an appropriate certificate from the drop-down menu.

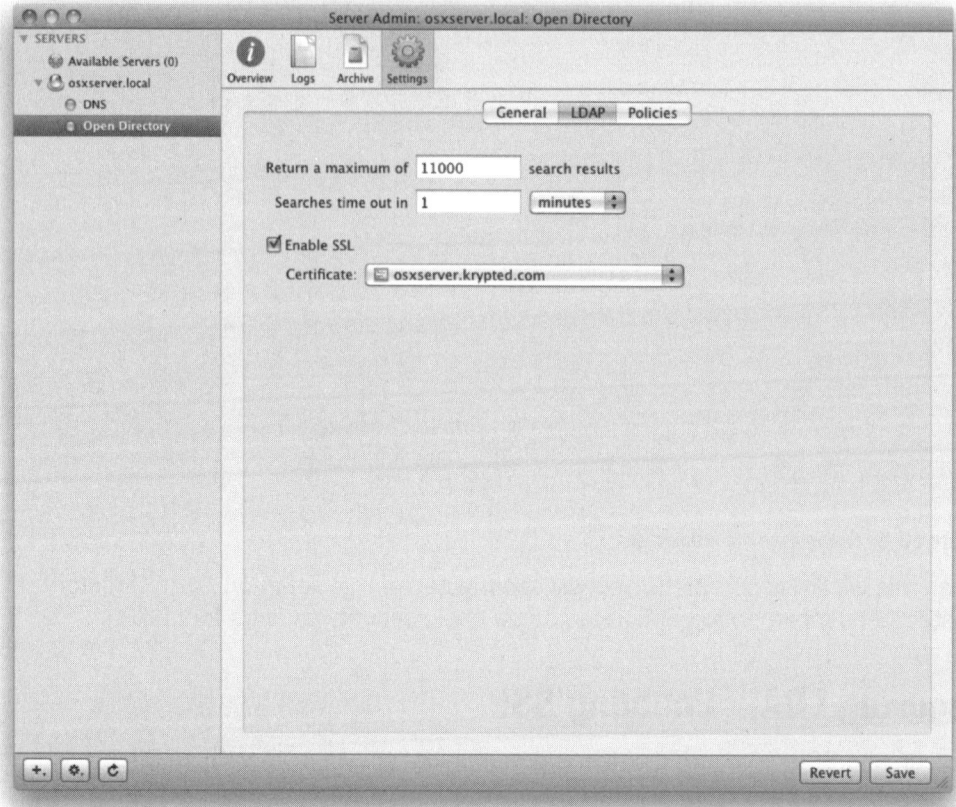

Figure 16–6. *Choosing an SSL certificate*

Once you have selected an SSL certificate, click the Save button to save the changes.

Securing Open Directory Accounts by Enabling Password Policies

Password policies include server-side rules that limit the age and strength of passwords that can be used in your environment. Some password policies are available only globally (network-wide), while others are available on a per-user (or per-account) basis. To see global policies, open Server Admin, and click Open Directory. To edit password policies, click the Policies tab (see Figure 16–7), and then click the Passwords sub-tab.

NOTE: Global password policies are overridden by user password policies, and do not apply to administrative users.

Two types of global password policies exist: Disable Login controls when accounts are able to log in, and Passwords Must controls various requirements for a password to be allowed. We strongly recommend using as many of these as possible, because they provide a substantial amount of Open Directory security. However, keep in mind that the harder a password is for a user to remember, the more likely they are to write it down, so a certain amount of balance between complexity and ease of remembrance should be practiced here.

Let's briefly discuss each:

- *Disable Login Passwords*: Allows logins to be disabled when the following criteria are met (per policy choice in Server Admin):

    - *On specific date*: Disables the account on a set date. Disabling accounts that could still be active can be an administrative burdon, but it can be helpful for environments with a large number of temporary or freelance users.

    - *After using it for*: Disables new accounts after they have been active for a determined number of days.

    - *After inactive for*: Disables new accounts after they are dormant for a definable number of days. For most environments, a number between 7 and 30 is a suitable amount of inactivity for an account before it should be considered dead. This option helps for environments where the sheer number of accounts makes it difficult to keep track of account activity.

    - *After user makes ___ failed attempts*: Disables accounts after a definable number of failed attempts have occurred. For most environments, a number between 3 and 10 is a suitable number of failed attempts.

- *Passwords Must*: Allows password policies to be made, including the following:

    - *Differ from account name*: This option keeps the password from being identical to the username.

    - *Contain at least a letter*: This option forces an account to have at least one character from the alphabet (*a* to *z*) in the password. This enforces a policy that avoids passwords such as 1234.

    - *Contain both uppercase and lowercase letters*: This option requires at least one letter be uppercase and at least one letter be lowercase. Passwords are case sensitive.

    - *Contain at least a number*: This option forces a password to have a number in it. An example of an allowable password would be 1paSsworD1. Passwords should typically have at least one lowercase letter, at least one uppercase letter, and at least one numeric character.

- *Be reset on first login*: This is a good option for new accounts or accounts that have had their passwords reset. This will keep administrators from knowing their users' passwords (a policy that protects the administrator as well as the user). This will provide a certain level of comfort to users that the administrator is not snooping through their personal data. If you need access to an account, then you should be forced to reset a password to obtain it.

- *Contain at least*: This option allows you to define the minimum length of a password in characters. The minimum length of a password is something debatable in any environment. For many, eight is a good number, but this is not as much a technical decision as it is a management decision.

- *Differ from last*: This option allows you to force users to change their passwords to something different every time they change their password for as many times as you specify. Some administrator's think 3 is enough, others say 18 is better. This is a decision that should be made on a management level in many cases.

- *Be reset every*: This option allows you to force your users to change passwords at specific times and to define the number of days, weeks, or months that can transpire before a new password must be set. Passwords should also be changed as often as management will allow.

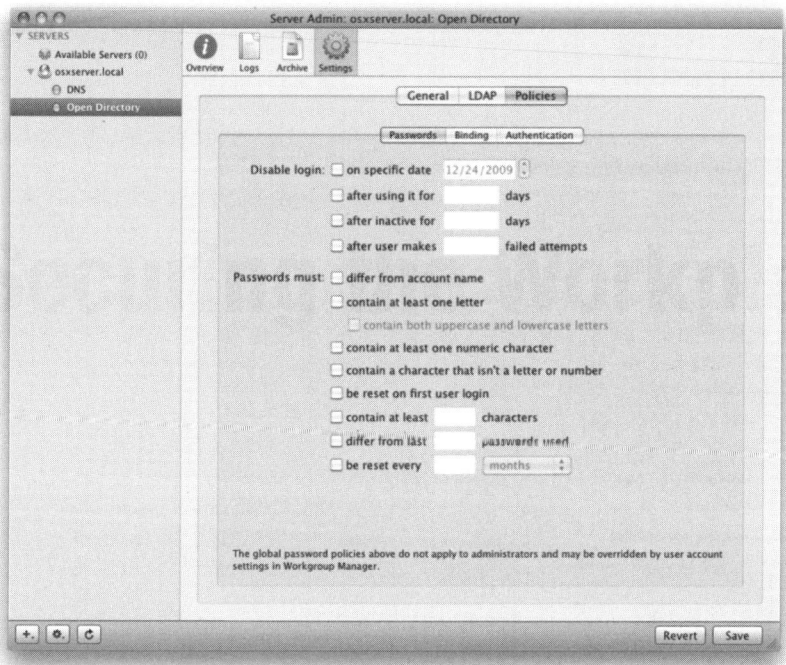

Figure 16-7. *Configuring global password policies*

Securing Open Directory Using Binding Policies

Once you have set up Open Directory, to effectively secure client systems and communications between clients and the server, you'll want to secure the actual Open Directory services. The next step after using SSL to secure transport communications is to move on to securing the communications between clients and the server by using binding policies.

On the Binding sub-tab of the Open Directory Policy tab (see Figure 16-8), you will find the option to Enable Authenticated Directory Binding. This option is used to give Mac OS X clients a directory administrator's username and password to create a computer record in the Open Directory database, and then enforce a rule that only Mac OS X computers with computer records will be allowed to bind to the directory service. This standard computer record is then associated with a Kerberos principal, though you won't see a difference in the graphical interface. With the Kerberos principal, the client and server can then verify the integrity of their communication with one another.

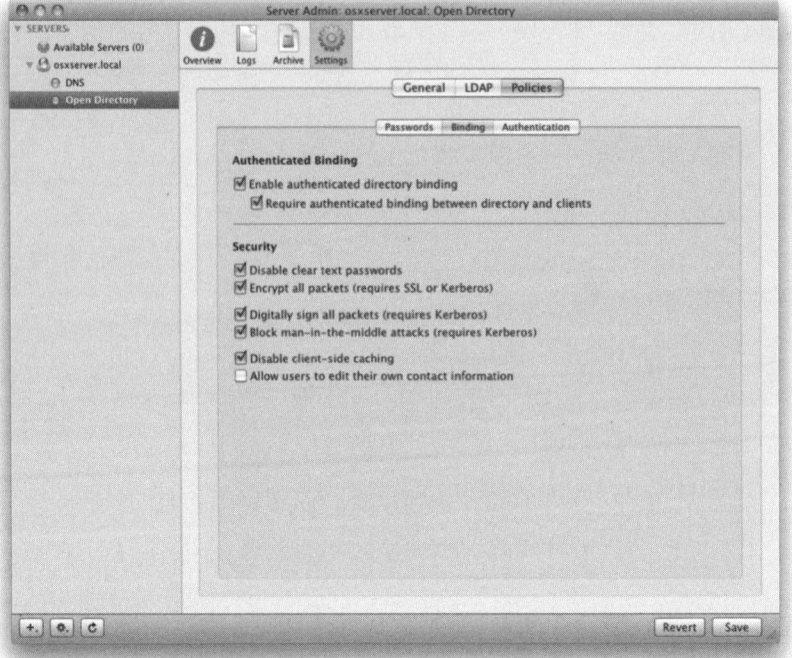

Figure 16-8. *Binding policies*

Once you have enabled authenticated directory binding, the next step is to force Mac OS X workstations into authenticated, or trusted, binding by selecting the Require Authenticated Binding Between Directory and Clients option. This will require a Mac OS X client to actually bind to the domain rather than just query it for login settings (adding the directory services entry into the search path), which is how an unauthenticated, or untrusted bind, works.

Binding to Open Directory increases the security of the network by forcing all clients who log into the server to be bound to the server. Binding options can also enforce more stringent security requirements by forcing client systems to follow certain rules in how they communicate with the server, whether they are Mac OS X clients or an LDAP client from a different operating system. The options listed in the Security field enforce communication policies and include the following:

Disable clear text passwords: This forces clients to encrypt data communications to the server.

Digitally sign all packets: This places checksums on digital communications.

Encrypt all packets: This forces clients to use SSL or Kerberos.

Block man-in-the-middle attacks: This option checks to see whether the signatures match the session keys.

Disable client-side caching: By default, OS X clients cache LDAP information. This option disables this kind of caching in the event that you suspect a client system has been compromised.

Allow users to edit their own contact information: If you are not using the Address Book integration with the server, you should disable this option. Users should be allowed to edit their own information in a self-updating address book environment only. When disabled, this option will edit the LDAP-based ACLs, which we will discuss later in this chapter.

> **TIP:** Once you have enforced the appropriate binding policies, keep a detailed account of what has been enforced, because the client setup will require the policies you are using to be mirrored in the client configuration.

Securing Authentication with PasswordServer

In Open Directory on Mac OS X Server 10.5 and later, the password is stored, by default, in the password database. This is a very secure approach to handling passwords, as they are stored in an encrypted form and somewhat disconnected from LDAP itself. In previous versions of Open Directory, the password could be stored in an encrypted form in the LDAP database. This had the potential to allow any user to cache an encrypted version of the password offline and attempt to crack it with various password-cracking tools. But in Mac OS X 10.5 and later, the location of the password in the password database is referenced in the LDAP database so that passwords cannot be cached and then decrypted at a later date. The password slot is a location in the database of the PasswordServer. By listing the password slot (or slot ID) rather than the password itself, the password is never exposed to end users, and therefore more secure than if it were stored within LDAP.

The PasswordServer is used for standard authentication for many services such as the Apple File Protocol. It is based on the Simple Authentication and Security Layer (SASL) standard originally created for the Cyrus e-mail system, but ported into Mac OS X for use with Open Directory. It allows various protocols within Mac OS X Server to communicate with Open Directory while keeping the passwords themselves well encrypted and somewhat obfuscated.

In addition to handling standard password requirements, the PasswordServer can also limit the types of passwords that can be used, and has the ability to enforce rules on passwords. These rules include enforcing the quality of passwords that can be used, the frequency of required password resets, and how passwords can be used by various services in Mac OS X.

PasswordServer handles password exchanges of the following authentication types:

LAN Manager, NTLMv1, and NTLMv2: Mostly used for the Windows File Sharing engine known as SMB. Apple added SASL support for the more modern NTLMv2 password format in version 10.4 of Mac OS X.

DHX: Diffe-Hellman exchange, used extensively for communications of proprietary protocols, such as the Apple File Protocol, and services such as those serving directory service clients (i.e., the Workgroup Manager application).

MS-CHAPv2: Microsoft Challenge Access Protocol, typically used for the Apple Point-to-Point Tunneling Protocol (PPTP) Virtual Private Network (VPN) server.

WEBDAV-Digest: Used for authenticating user sections of a web site, known as *realms*, when connecting with a standard web browser or Web Distributed Authoring and Versioning (WebDAV) client such as the Mac OS X Finder's Connect to Server dialog box.

APOP: Authenticated Post Office Protocol, a legacy option held over from the standard.

Cyrus SASL libraries: Used for IMAP.

You can enable and disable authentication methods via the Server Admin's Open Directory service on the Authentication sub-tab of the Policy tab, as shown in Figure 16–9.

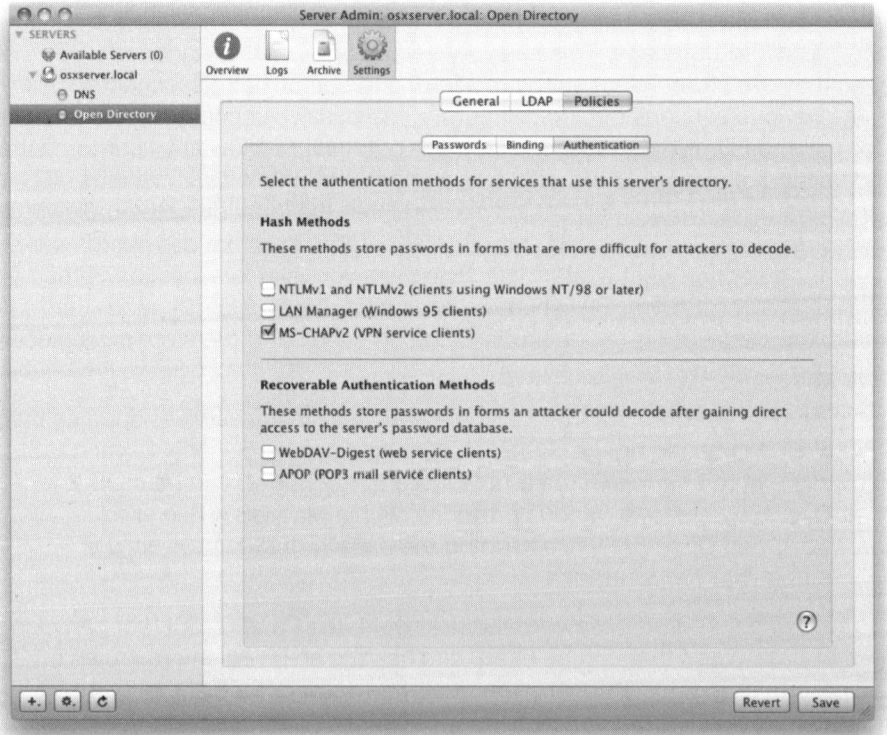

Figure 16–9. *Password authentication methods*

Disable any authentication methods that are not required in your environment. For example, in the likely event that you do not support Windows 95 clients in your environment, you can prudently disable the option for LAN Manager. If you do not have

VPN enabled, then disable the option for MS-CHAP. If you are not using POP3, then disable the option for APOP. By disabling the authentication methods that are not being used, you will increase the security of your environment, as leaving these methods open can reduce the strength of password protection in your network.

Many other methods are not listed in the GUI, and it is a good idea to go through them and disable the ones you do not need. To configure authentication methods with the command line, use the `slapconfig` command:

```
slapconfig -getauthmechanisms
```

```
"SMB-LAN-MANAGER" Enabled Hash
"CRAM-MD5" Enabled Hash
"NTLM" Disabled Hash
"APOP" Disabled Plain
"TWOWAYRANDOM" Disabled Plain
"MS-CHAPv2" Enabled Hash
"PPS" Enabled Hash
"DHX" Enabled Hash
"OTP" Enabled Hash
"SMB-NTLMv2" Enabled Hash
"WEBDAV-DIGEST" Disabled Plain
"SMB-NT" Enabled Hash
"DIGEST-MD5" Enabled Hash
"GSSAPI" Enabled Hash
"KERBEROS_V4" Disabled Hash
"CRYPT" Disabled Hash
```

NOTE: The command `slapconfig` is useful for server setup and management scripts, and can be automated using scripts that run on a schedule such as `crontab` or `launchd`.

To disable authentication methods you do not need, you can use the -setauthenticationmethods argument on the `slapconfig` command. This will allow you to turn off each method you are not using.

```
slapconfig -setauthmechanisms APOP off
slapconfig -setauthmechanisms WEBDAV-DIGEST off
```

NOTE: In previous versions of Mac OS X Server, this functionality was covered by the NeST commands rather than `slapconfig`. These commands no longer function in Mac OS X Server 10.6.

Securing LDAP by Preventing Anonymous Binding

In the previous section, we discussed the Require Clients to Bind to Directory option, but it is important to note that it affects only automatically configured clients. When this option is enabled, no changes are made to the running LDAP process (slapd). This option enables a preference key in the Open Directory client configuration container cn=config. This preference key will be enforced on Mac OS X clients that read this record (but not on most flavors of Linux or Unix). You can view this client configuration record using `dscl`:

`dscl /LDAPv3/127.0.0.1/ -read Config/macosxodpolicy`

When the setting is enabled, you will see the Binding Required key set to `true` when you review the output of `dscl`. However, because only Mac OS X clients read this configuration, they are the only LDAP clients that are actually "required" to bind. In other words, you are not restricting access to your LDAP server; you are in fact requiring binding only for clients that use the Max OS X LDAP plug-in. A standard LDAP browser from a rogue machine can anonymously bind even with this option enabled. If you wish to restrict access to only authenticated users, you must add the `bind_anon` option to the top of the OpenLDAP configuration file stored at `/private/etc/openldap/slapd.conf`.

> **NOTE:** Be aware that configuring slapd to refuse anonymous connections means all clients will be required to bind. This includes the Open Directory master, which is automatically configured with the local host value 127.0.0.1 upon its promotion to an Open Directory master. You will need to update this and all other entries before clients will be able to access the database.

Once connected, test that your binding is working by running the following command:

`dscl localhost list /LDAPv3/127.0.0.1/Users.`

The above dscl command should output a list of all users in your Open Directory domain. If it doesn't then return to Directory Access, and make sure your binding username and password are correct. Once you have verified that your server can access your authenticated LDAP server, you can disable anonymous binding. To do so, edit the slapd configuration using your favorite text editor:

`sudo nano /private/etc/openldap/slapd.conf`

Add the following `disallow bind_anon` near the top of the file:

```
#
# See slapd.conf(5) for details on configuration options.
#
# This file should NOT be world readable.
#
disallow bind_anon
```

Next, save the configuration file, and restart the LDAP service by sending it a HUP signal using the following command:

`sudo killall -HUP slapd`

> **NOTE:** Disabling anonymous binding while forcing SSL certificates for binding is the goal here. This will provide a highly secure solution, and the binding process can easily be automated to help alleviate the added administrative burden that distributing SSL certificates and performing an authenticated bind will incur.

Securely Binding Clients to Open Directory

Once you have securely configured Open Directory on your servers, you can then bind the individual client workstations and non-directory services servers to Open Directory. At this point, all of the password policies are enforced, and many of the services' communications will be Kerberized. So, *why bind clients*? If client workstations are not bound, then workstation policies will not be enforced. This includes pushing out Software Update Server settings, mobility and network home folder settings, and any of the managed preferences you may have defined (or will define). Also, usernames and passwords for workstations would not be centralized, which is a key to effectively managing and securing larger numbers of systems as is required in most enterprise environments.

To bind client workstations, you will need to be logged in as an administrator and use the Directory Utility on the client workstation. This is achieved in different ways on different versions of Mac OS X. In Leopard, the Directory Utility is found in the Utilities folder and it's called Directory Utility. In Snow Leopard, the application has been removed from the Utility folder entirely and moved to /System/Library/CoreServices. To bind the client workstation in Snow Leopard, you can also navigate to the Accounts System Preference pane in System Preferences, click on Login Options, and then click on Join, located next to Network Account Server. Then, enter the IP address of the Open Directory server (see Figure 16–10). From here, you can launch Directory Utility, if necessary, to add the client machine to a server other than an Open Directory or Active Directory. Here, you can also graphically configure some of the more granular directory services settings and configure third-party directory services plug-ins that you may have installed (such as Centrify or Likewise).

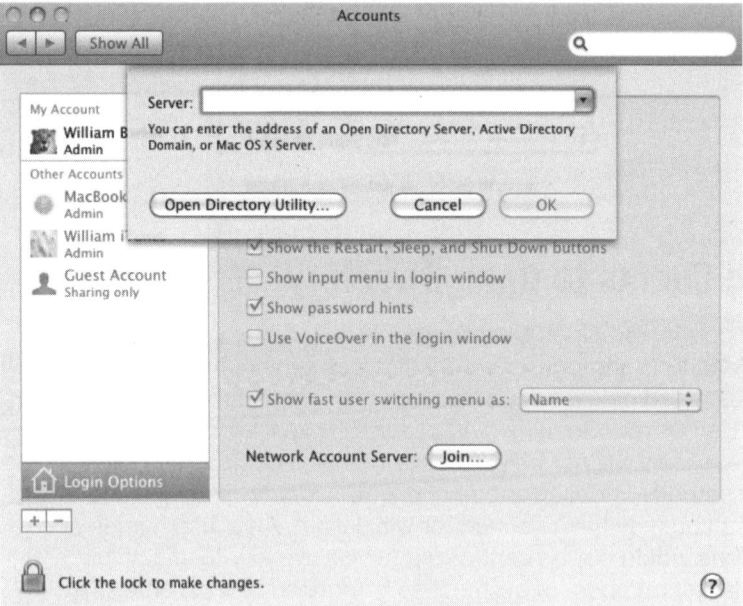

Figure 16–10. *Binding to Open Directory in Snow Leopard*

In Leopard, open Directory Utility within Utilities, click the plus (+) sign, and choose Open Directory from the Add a New Directory of Type drop-down menu (see Figure 16–11). (In Tiger, you will need to click LDAPv3 on the Services tab, and click the Configure button.) Next, type in the IP address of the Open Directory server, and click OK.

Figure 16–11. *Binding to Open Directory in Leopard*

If you are implementing an SSL certificate, check the Encrypt Using SSL box here. This is easiest if you first copy the self-signed certificate to the local client or user's keychain before binding the local client. We will explain setting up SSL certificates later in this chapter.

Once you have added the server, you will want to apply the same security settings that you applied when securing the Open Directory master under the binding policies. To do this, click the Services icon in the Directory Utility toolbar, and click the Open Directory Master server (named ODM in Figure 16–12). Once you click the appropriate server, click Edit to change the client settings.

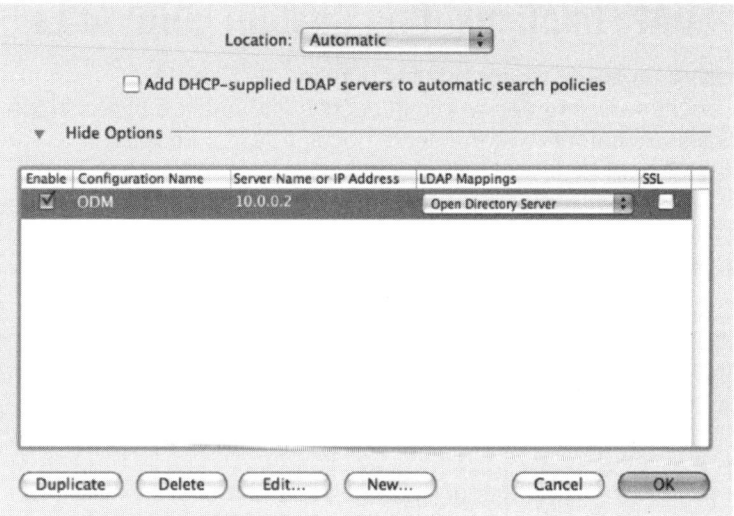

Figure 16-12. *Choosing a directory service to configure in Leopard*

Here you can choose the appropriate items that correspond with the setup of your Open Directory master using the Security Policy section of the screen (see Figure 16–13). Previously, in the Securing Open Directory Using Binding Policies section of this chapter, we discussed the settings on the server side, so you will want to match these as closely as possible on the client side.

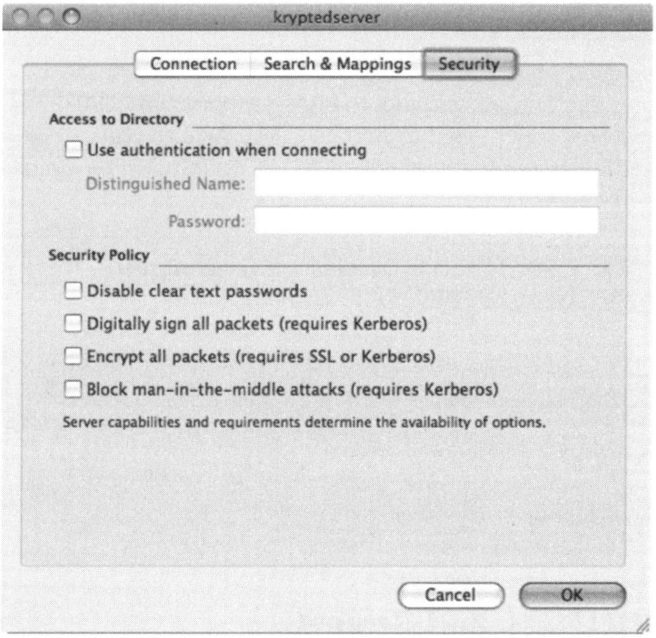

Figure 16-13. *Configuring service security in Leopard*

Further Securing LDAP: Implementing Custom LDAP ACLs

An access control list for LDAP is a way to manage security for the OpenLDAP database. This is secure, because it enforces who can access and change things in the LDAP database. ACL policies are enforced at the server level. If ACLs are not configured, you can use LDAP data to access information about network layouts, users, and other information without authentication. One example of this methodology is to use the "Force Clients to Bind" option in the Open Directory policy settings in Server Admin. For most of these configurations, however, you will need to jump into the command line to create these ACLs.

> **NOTE:** You can use `ldapsearch` from the command line to search LDAP databases without authenticating.

To restrict bound users from viewing attributes of other users, add the following to your /etc/openldap/slapd.conf:

```
Access to dn=".*,dc=your dcname,dc=.com" attr=userPassword
    by self write
    by * auth
Access to dn=".*,dc=your dcname,dc=.com"
    by * read
```

To fully disable anonymous reads, use this series of commands:

```
Access to dn=".*,dc=your dcname,dc=.com"
    by dn"uid=nssldap,ou=people,dc=dcname,dc=com" read
    by * none
```

To restrict access to an LDAP database and allow users to change their own LDAP information in the shared address book, you'll need to add an LDAP ACL to your `slapd.conf` file. To do this, add the following series of lines (we will go into further detail on LDAP ACLs later in this chapter):

```
access to
attrs=mail,sn,givenName,telephoneNumber,mobile,facsimileTelephoneNumber,street,
    postalAddress,postOfficeBox,postalCode,password
by self write
```

> **TIP:** A number of different LDAP ACLs are configured in Mac OS X 10.6 Server out of the box. When you are configuring the access controls, these may conflict with the ACLs already on your network. In short, it can get very confusing very fast. For more assistance with configuring this type of policy see the book *LDAP System Administration* from O'Reilly Press.

Creating Open Directory Users and Groups

Now that you have Open Directory set up securely, you might want to start building out the users and groups for your server. Later you can log into client systems using these accounts, but for now you'll need to set up accounts securely so they can log into the server and access services. You can create users and groups in the LDAP database in Mac OS X Server by using the Workgroup Manager application in /Applications/Server.

To create your first user, open Workgroup Manager from the Open Directory master, and select the LDAPv3/127.0.0.1 directory (see Figure 16–14). Then click the New User button in the toolbar, and give the user a name and password.

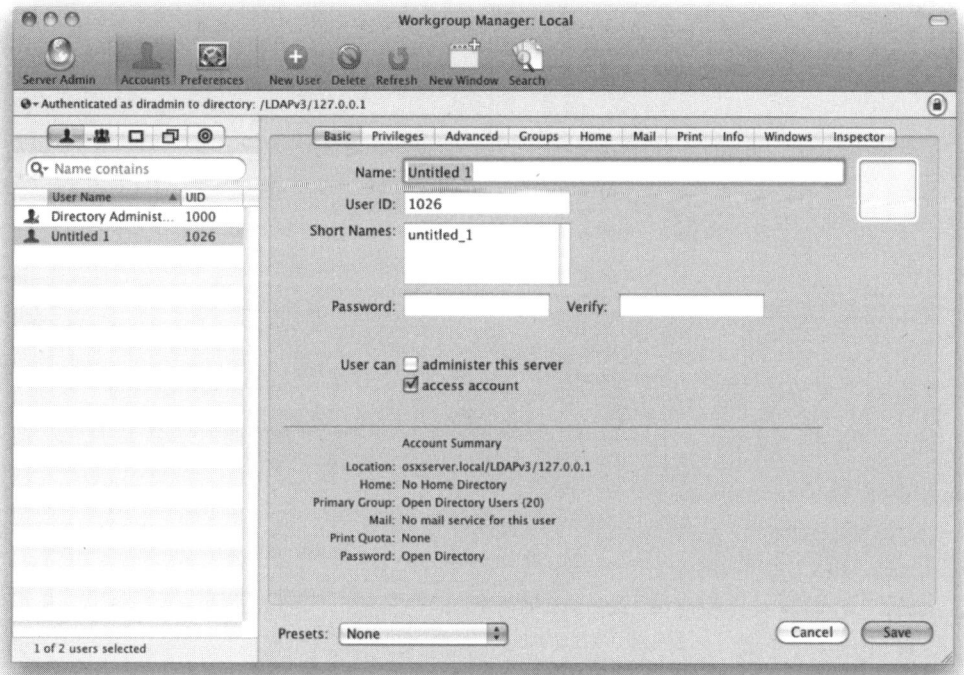

Figure 16–14. *Creating a user with Workgroup Manager*

Next, click the Privileges tab (see Figure 16–15), set Login Shell to None (which removes the new user's ability to open Terminal on the server), and uncheck the "Allow simultaneous login on managed computers" box (which will allow each user to log into only one machine concurrently). Scroll through each additional tab looking for any other settings you feel need to be set. Once you are satisfied with the user settings, click the Save button to create the user account.

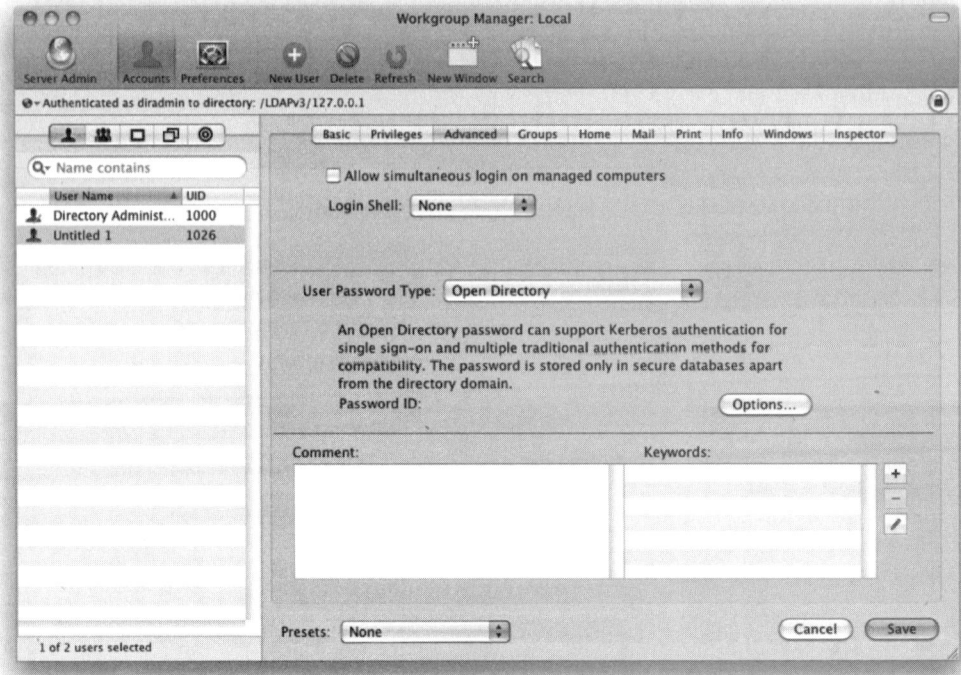

Figure 16–15. *Setting user privileges*

> **TIP:** Near the bottom of the screen you will see the Presets option. This allows you to create a template for user accounts that can be used to deploy multiple accounts once you have determined all of the appropriate settings for your environment.

To create a new group, click the Groups tab in Workgroup Manager and then click the New Group button in the Workgroup Manager toolbar. Here, provide a name for the group and any comments you have regarding the group. Click the Members tab and drag any users who should be in the group into the list of users. Then, click the Options button to configure user policies. At the Policies screen, you will be able to configure a limited set of policies similar to those available in the global policies, as you can see in Figure 16–16. These policies will mirror some of those available globally that were configured earlier in this chapter.

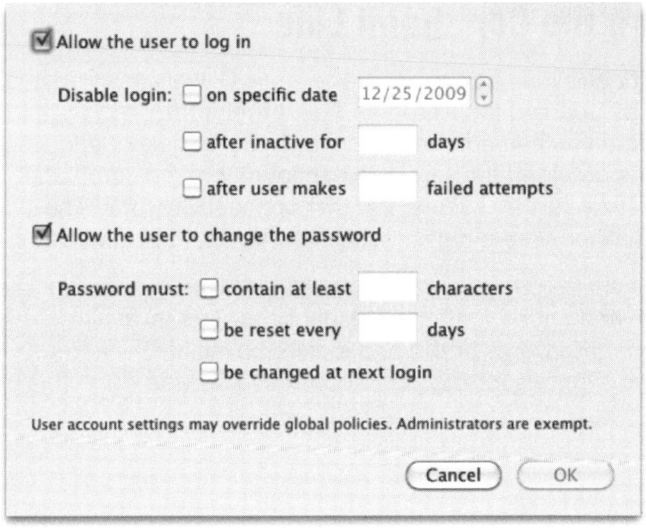

Figure 16–16. *User policies*

Click OK when you are satisfied with your password policies, and then click Save (see Figure 16–17) when you are satisfied with all of the settings for the newly created account.

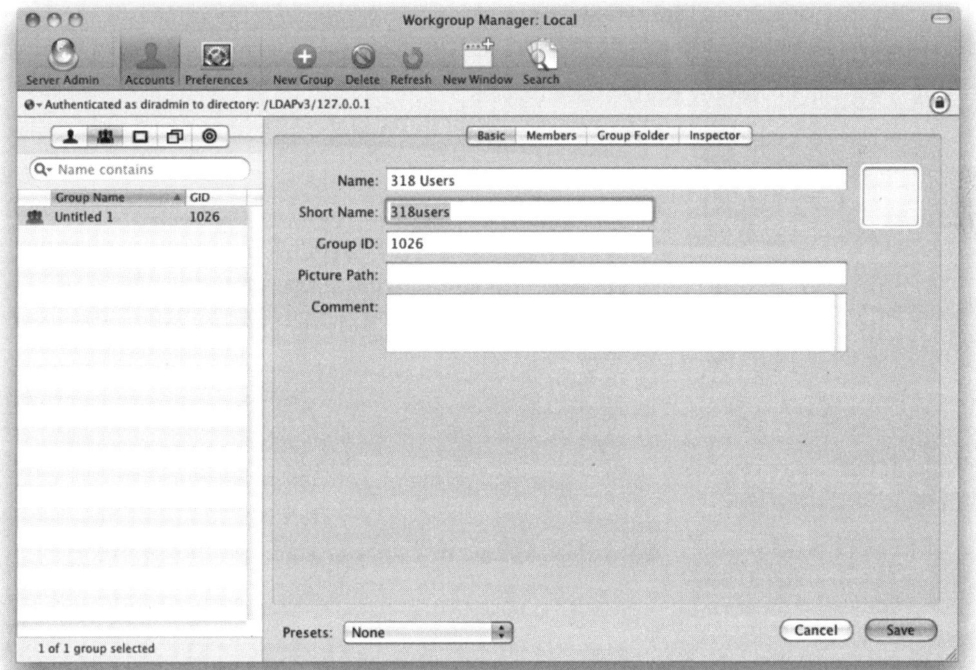

Figure 16–17. *Creating a group with Workgroup Manager*

Securing Kerberos from the Command Line

Kerberos is a powerful application, and the options you have in the GUI are fairly limited. These settings can be accessed by opening the Kerberos Agent tool from /System/Library/CoreServices. Here you can add and remove Kerberos tickets and view existing tickets. While a GUI tool is provided for Kerberos configuration, the command line gives you far more options to help further secure and test connectivity for it. The command-line tools available to further secure Kerberos include `kinit`, `klist`, `kdestroy`, and many others.

- `kinit` is used to establish and cache Kerberos connections. This is useful when troubleshooting Kerberos errors and looking to initiate Kerberos communications. Options for the `kinit` command include the following:
    - `-F`: Makes tickets nonforwardable
    - `-f`: Makes tickets forwardable
    - `-P`: Makes tickets nonproxyable
    - `-v`: Forces validation
    - `-R`: Renews tickets
- `klist` lists tickets. This is useful when looking to list all of the Kerberos service principals that a user is authorized to access. Options for `klist` include the following:
    - `-4`: Lists only Kerberos 4 tickets
    - `-5`: Lists only Kerberos 5 tickets
    - `-A`: Lists all tickets
    - `-s`: Runs silently
- `kdestroy`: Removes tickets from the cache. This is useful in troubleshooting Kerberos/KDC issues. The following is the option:
    - `-a`: Destroys all tickets

> **NOTE:** As is true with Windows, a RAM-based ticket cache is used instead of a file-based ticket cache, much like most versions of Kerberos for Unix and Linux variants.

Some command-line applications available for the Kerberos server include the following:

- `kdcsetup` creates the first admin account.
- `kerberosautoconfig` creates the keytab files.

Managed Preferences

The ability to manage preferences is one of the most powerful aspects of directory services. In previous sections, we showed you how to set up Open Directory to have a centralized repository of usernames and passwords. You can further secure the server itself (and any other servers in our environment) using Kerberos and password policies. We have also shown you how to secure Open Directory accounts by enabling password policies and restricting the types of communications with the server. Now, we'll cover enforcing policies, known as *managed preferences*, on client systems and user accounts. Although much of what we will discuss demonstrates how to perform these tasks on Mac OS X Server in a distributed management environment, keep in mind that you can perform much of the same tasks using Workgroup Manager on a local computer as the managed preferences framework is similar in Mac OS X as it is in Mac OS X Server.

To access and configure policies in Mac OS X Server, first open Workgroup Manager, click Preferences, and change to the directory service for Open Directory (or leave /Local if you will be configuring local managed preferences). Then, click a computer, user, or group on the left column, and click the type of policy in the right column (see Figure 16–18).

Each policy has options for First or Always. The First option pushes managed preferences out to end users the first time they log in. The Always option pushes managed preferences out to end users every time they log in.

These policies include the following:

Applications: Chooses the applications that users can access or denies access to specified applications.

Classic: Controls users' ability to use Classic applications and controls how they are handled.

Dock: Controls what icons are in the Dock, where the Dock is located, and whether autohide can be configured.

Finder: Controls whether Simple Finder is used and what settings for the Finder are used. Simple Finder disables items on the finder such as keystrokes. Other more granular settings include the ability to configure whether the computer shows mounted disks on the desktop, where new Finder windows place users in directory trees, and whether to confirm when emptying the trash.

Internet: Controls mail server, mail account type, and home page settings.

Login: Sets login items, adds share points to login items, installs scripts to run for computers, controls login items preference pane settings for computers, and controls Fast User Switching settings.

Media: Controls whether users can access CDs, DVDs, and removable storage.

Mobility: Sets up roaming profile settings for OS X clients and selects which folders sync with the server during intervals specified by the administrator. This is useful when configuring backup systems (backing up is covered further in Chapter 18).

Network: Configures the proxy settings for all client machine network interface cards (NICs).

Printers: Pushes out printers to client machines as well as controls which printers the users can view.

Software Update: Pushes out software update server settings to client machines.

System Preferences: Controls which System Preferences users can access.

Universal Access: Controls settings for users with special needs.

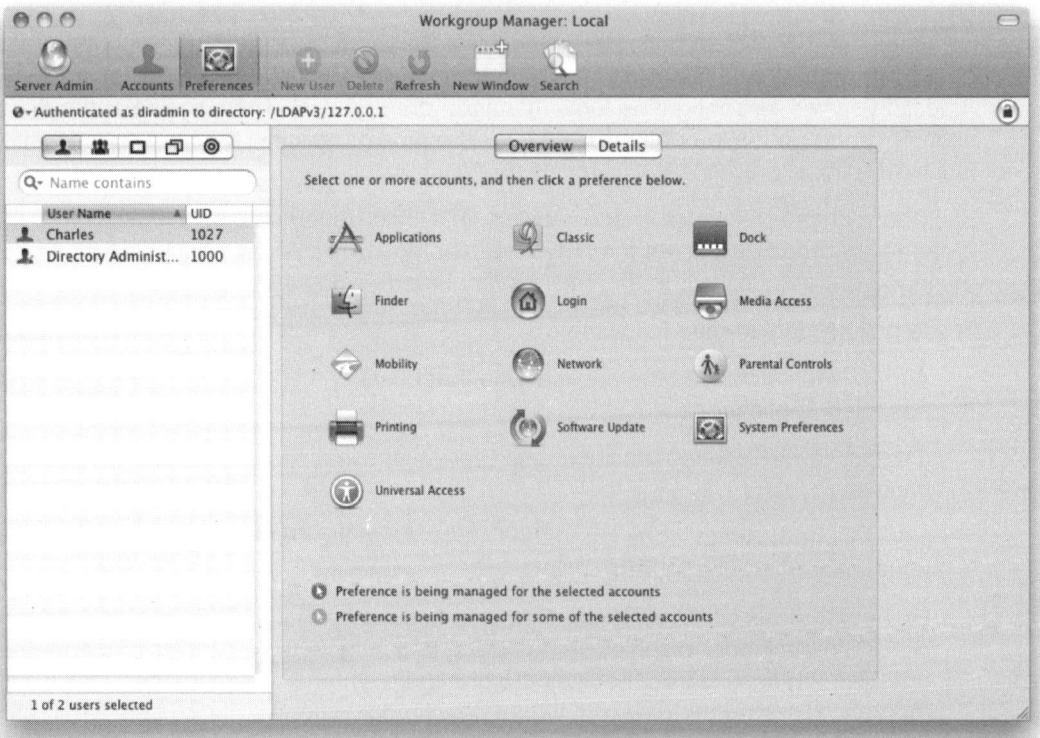

Figure 16-18. *Policies*

Managed preferences are stored in managed preference manifests (MCX). MCX enforces managed preferences by caching to local workstations. If you are using a third-party LDAP structure, then you can use MCX files to push out managed settings, even if you do not use Open Directory (although Open Directory makes it easier by providing administrators with an easy-to-use GUI for controlling policies). You can also customize managed preferences to build managed settings for applications or settings that are not provided in the GUI for Server Admin.

The features available in an MCX include access to removable hard drives, how the drives appear to users, login items, and Finder settings. They are standard configuration files that are mostly configured by the GUI in the Computer Policies section under Settings in Workgroup Manager. However, administrators can go far deeper with granular control by creating custom managed preferences. A custom-managed preference can then be pushed to client systems and will enforce custom policies for third-party software or settings that Apple didn't include in the default policies (such as items available to the `defaults` command).

Once managed preferences have been configured, you can view them in a couple of different ways. The first is using the dscl command along with the -mcxread option. The MCX extensions to dscl also allow you to use the -mcxset option to manually configure managed preferences and the -mcxedit option to edit them. You can also import and export managed preferences using the -mcximport and -mcxexport options, respectively. The MCX extensions can be leveraged in both Mac OS X client and Mac OS X Server.

If you would prefer a graphical equivalent, then Workgroup Manager can be run on a Mac OS X client. When running in this capacity, you can connect to the local directory service and configure preferences as you would in an Open Directory environment. The preferences are then enforced for the local machine and any users or groups that preferences are configured for. However, preferences configured for the local database are not shared to other computers or accounts running on other computers.

Securing Managed Preferences

In the upgrade from Tiger to Leopard and then from Leopard to Snow Leopard, new policies were added along the way, and features for some of the existing policies were expanded upon with each iteration. These include the following, which have an impact on the security of the client systems:

Applications: There are now more features in managed features for applications. The most important one is a more advanced limiting of user access to applications. You can now allow or disallow user access to applications by selecting the user individually or by selecting a folder full of applications. This means that you can allow access to applications located in the `/Applications` folder, but disallow all applications located in the `/Applications/Utilities` folder. There are also controls now for allowing specific widgets as well as the ability to disable the Front Row application, an unnecessary application in most corporate environments. This limiting of user access functionality is a fix that has been overdue for a while. The original application launch restrictions were based solely on a bundle identifier key within applications. A would-be attacker could easily change this key. In fact, because of the launch restrictions configurable only at the application level and not in the kernel of the operating system, even Apple's own software would allow you to bypass these limitations by configuring an application to launch when clicking an assigned mouse button. This is no longer the case in Snow Leopard.

Finder: There are new options to limit users from performing tasks when in the Finder such as ejecting a disk, connecting to servers, rebooting, and burning optical media such as CDs or DVDs.

Login: There is a more fine-tuned control of the login process. You can now control the list of users displayed to a user at the login screen, including mobile accounts and network users. You can also show/hide the Restart button, disable automatic logon, enable Fast User Switching, set the local computer record name to the name of the computer on the server, enable guest access, control the inactive time to log out users, and configure computer-based ACLs. In previous operating systems, when you disabled the Restart, Shutdown, and Sleep buttons at the login window, users could still access this functionality using special commands at the username prompt such as >shutdown or >restart. This workaround has been disabled in Leopard.

Mobility: Mobility now allows administrators to set an expiry for a user's home folder on the system they are logging into. This allows administrators to keep local desktop systems from getting polluted with hundreds of home folders without using custom scripts to do so. Administrators can also now force accounts on local systems to use FileVault with Mobility accounts to keep data on local systems as secure as possible and set quotas for user home directories. Finally, it is also now possible to control the path that the user home folder points to on local desktops.

Network: Administrators can now disable Internet Sharing, AirPort, and Bluetooth for client computers.

Parental Controls: Administrators can hide profanity in the dictionary, control access to web sites, set the amount of time per day that a computer is allowed to be used, and set times when login is not allowed in this new managed preference.

Printing: Users can be forced to put their username, date, and/or MAC address in a page that is sent with each print job.

System Preferences: Users can be allowed or denied access to each system preference.

You can enforce these managed preferences on systems that use Active Directory by modifying the LDAP schema in Active Directory. Once the schema has been modified, you will be able to use Workgroup Manager to configure managed preferences as you do with Mac OS X Server. Third-party applications, such as Thursby's ADmitMac, will store this managed preference data outside of Active Directory, allowing you to manage your Mac OS X clients without modifying your Active Directory infrastructure (which most Active Directory administrators are not going to want to do). Other third-party directory clients, such as Centrify's DirectControl or Likewise, rely primarily on custom code for preference management.

> **NOTE:** Most Active Directory administrators are generally hesitant to modify the LDAP schema, because schema extensions cannot be undone in Active Directory.

Providing Directory Services for Windows Clients

Open Directory is not Mac OS X client exclusive. Mac OS X Server, running as a primary domain controller (PDC), can be configured to provide a centralized database of usernames and passwords and provide remedial managed preferences for Windows clients. This PDC feature is available only in Mac OS X Server when it is running as an Open Directory master. A backup domain controller (BDC) should be used in this environment for fault tolerance. The BDC must be run on an Open Directory replica and provides some form of high availability for the Windows domain structure.

Although Windows systems can authenticate through the PDC, you will not have the same level of granular control in an Open Directory-based environment with Windows clients that you have in an Active Directory based environment. But there are some powerful things that can be done. For example, you can push out home folders for roaming profiles and login scripts using LDAP attributes that are built into Workgroup Manager (graphically) using the Windows tab. You can also push out basic preferences in much the same way that NT 4.0 did.

To enable an Open Directory server as a PDC, open Server Admin from an Open Directory master and click on the SMB service. Then click Settings, and choose Primary Domain Controller as the role (see Figure 16–19). Once the role has been set, enter a computer name and a workgroup name. Optionally, you can enable WINS registration on the Advanced tab. Legacy Windows systems need legacy authentication methods such as LAN Manager authentication. Therefore, you will need to determine whether your server will be supporting older clients such as Windows 95 or third-party appliances requiring this authentication type. Disable WINS registration if legacy clients will not be accessing the server.

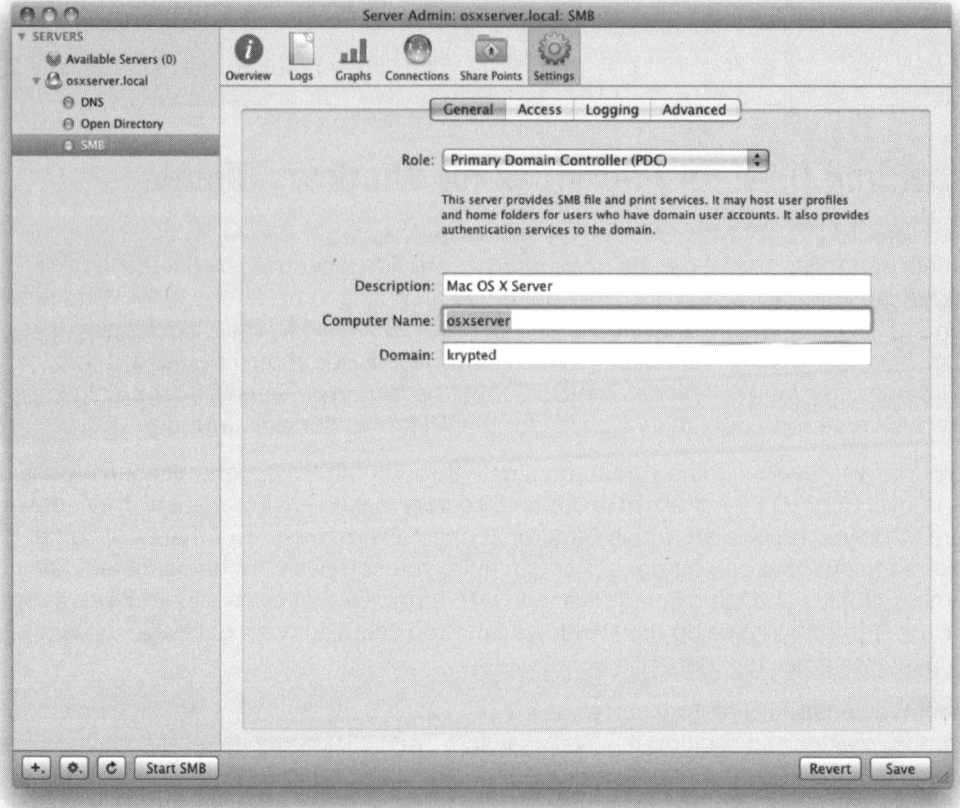

Figure 16-19. *Creating a Windows PDC*

Active Directory Integration

The Apple Active Directory service plug-in (AD-Plug-in) is an extension that Apple added to its DirectoryService API to enable Mac OS X Client or Mac OS X Server to bind to Active Directory, making interconnectivity between Apple's Open Directory and Microsoft's Active Directory easier. It also supports Kerberos autoconfiguration for clients bound into Active Directory using DNS entries known as *service* (SRV) records. The Active Directory plug-in is configured using the Directory Access application within Mac OS X Server or by using the dsconfigad command line tool.

When you use the Active Directory plug-in to bind to Active Directory, you can set up Open Directory to connect to an Active Directory domain controller and have items accessible to Open Directory from Active Directory. Because you are connecting to an existing Active Directory service, you will more than likely have all the policies for binding and passwords in place in your current directory services environment. This architecture is known as a *dual-directory* environment.

> **NOTE:** Much of the Active Directory integration configuration is available in the GUI for 10.6 through 10.4 and in the command line for 10.3. Some of the more granular settings such as packet signing, namespace configuration and machine password intervals will require using `dsconfigad`, although they can be configured during or following the actual binding process.

Using the AD-Plugin

When binding to Active Directory, you will need to know the forest (top-level directory structure) and domain name to which you are trying to bind. All Windows Active Directory setups include at least one domain and one forest. A *forest* is the top level of any Active Directory infrastructure, and a *domain* is a logical segmentation of a forest. In a basic Active Directory setup (and most Active Directory environments are a basic setup), you will have only one domain in a forest and will often simply use the same name for the domain and the forest.

You would bind to Active Directory in much the same way that you would bind to Open Directory. Simply open the Accounts System Preference pane, click on Login Options and then click on the Join... button. At the dialog, provide the domain name in the Server: field (see Figure 16–20). When you tab out of the field, the domain information will be filled into the dialog and you will be able to click on the Bind button to complete the binding process.

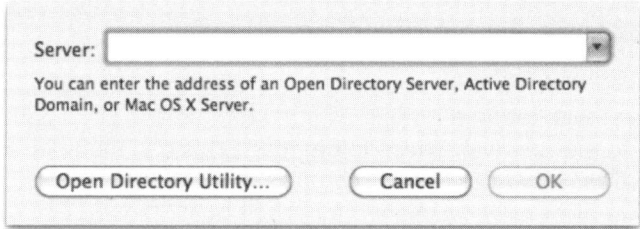

Figure 16–20. *Binding to Active Directory Using the Accounts System Preference pane*

You can also use Directory Utility, commonly needed for more granular configuration options, such as configuring network home directory options and delegating administration over local systems for Active Directory accounts. To configure the OS X machine to use Active Directory, open Directory Utility, click the lock to authenticate, and enter the local administrator's username and password. Then click the plus (+) button, enter the domain name of the Active Directory domain, enter the desired computer name (see Figure 16–21), and click Bind. Provided that the Active Directory environment is set up properly, you will now have a Mac OS X Client or Server that is bound into Active Directory.

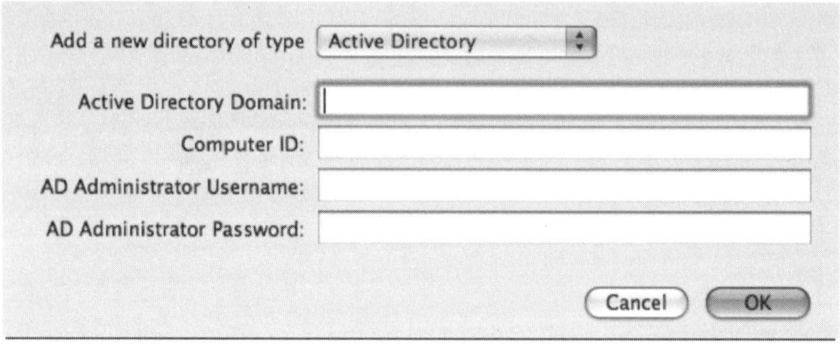

Figure 16–21. *Binding to Active Directory using Directory Utility*

> **NOTE:** If you need to do an advanced setup, the name of the domain needs to match the name of the forest when the domain is a member of a similarly named forest. With a Windows server, when you create the first domain controller and give that domain a name, the forest will also take on that same name. Which is not to say that you cannot have different domains in the same forest; you can, in which case you would leave the forest the same but change the name of the domain. Remember that all domains belong to a forest, and multiple domains can belong to a single forest.

Setting Up Network Homes with Active Directory Clients

A universal naming convention (UNC) is used for mapping drives within the Windows operating system, resulting in drives with lettered mappings (for example, the UNC path of \\server\share can be mapped to the S: drive). These folder mappings can then be used to provide synchronized profiles, known as *roaming profiles*, for Windows clients. The Use UNC Path from Active Directory to Derive Network Home Location option in Directory Utility will allow you to use the Active Directory profile location as a UNC path for network home folders, the Mac OS X equivalent to roaming profiles.

By default, a home directory is not created in this scenario; however, in a Windows environment, many organizations enable this home directory in order to ensure that the users' data is stored on the server for the centralization of sharing, permissions, and auditing, as well as the decentralization of end user, or *edge*, backups. The option offered here will allow you to keep that structure in the Apple environment as well, preserving the Active Directory–planned file and folder structure for profiles to be preserved across platforms.

The "Network protocol to be used" option allows you to then choose one of two protocols from the drop-down menu: SMB or AFP. If you are using Windows servers, then you will likely select SMB, although if you have a solution such as Extreme Z-IP from GroupLogic then you may be running AFP off of your Windows servers. This option determines how a home directory is mounted on the desktop. Server Message Block

(SMB) is the default protocol used by Windows to communicate with other Windows computers when accessing shared resources (including printers, files, and serial ports). The SMB option here will allow Apple workstations to communicate with the Windows server using the native protocol that Windows uses to communicate with its files and directories. Unix variants can communicate in the same manner using Samba.

Using the AD-Plugin from the Command Line

It may become necessary to bind a Mac to Active Directory using the Active Directory plug-in from the command line. Perhaps you need to force the binding, you want to use a setting not available in the GUI, or you want to use the Active Directory plug-in in a server script. In these circumstances, you will need to turn to the command line. You'll find the command dsconfigad to be very handy in performing these tasks. dsconfigad does not require root privileges to run for all of its options to be enabled and it can be used from the command line to force certain aspects of directory services to work even when the GUI will not bind clients as needed. These include the following:

- -enableSSO enables Kerberos authentication for services, such as AFP, by generating Kerberos principals (commonly used with the magic triangle, described in the next section).
- -ggid maps group ID information.
- -mobile automates the enabling of mobile accounts.
- -preferred enables the use of a preferred server.
- -localhome places the home folder on the local system rather than using a server shared home.
- -f forces the command to run (which is useful when forcing an unbind).
- -packetsign enables packet signing when communicating with domain controllers.
- -namespace enables the use of multiple domains within a forest.
- -packetencrypt enables encryption of data being transmitted between Active Directory and the client system.
- -passinterval configures the number of days between each iteration of the machine password within Active Directory.

These options become very helpful when scripting server bindings, as they allow for easy mass deployment and for the scripting of specific options to be pushed out to clients for binding. A script can also be told to run on the first access of an imaged system. This type of programmatic interfacing between Active Directory and Mac OS X clients and servers is one of the primary focuses of the Enterprise Mac Admin title, also from Apress.

Integrating Open Directory with Active Directory: Dual Directory

Setting up a *dual directory* involves the administrator building an Open Directory infrastructure, binding it to an Active Directory infrastructure and binding managed clients to both Active Directory and Open Directory. It is a common way in the Mac OS X Server community to get Mac management policies and still use centralized Active Directory-based directory services. This seemingly awkward setup results in Active Directory handling password authentication and Open Directory handling policy management, giving administrators a fairly simplistic way to manage their Mac systems, even within the confines of Active Directory. It is also possible to extend the Active Directory schema to include managed client preferences that can be used to provide the managed preferences covered earlier in this chapter on Mac workstations.

> **NOTE:** You can also use augmented records to provide attributes for clients that are missing in your primary directory service, which requires much of the same infrastructure but has less of a clear integration roadmap. We will continue to focus on the dual directory environment rather than digging deeper into augmented records.

To set up a magic triangle, bind the server into Active Directory, as described in previous sections of this chapter. Then, promote your first server to an Open Directory master (also covered earlier). When you perform the promotion though, provided that you have already bound to Open Directory, you will have an option to leave the Active Directory binding and supplement the promotion with that existing Active Directory binding. Once the Open Directory server is a master and has been bound into Active Directory, it is possible to re-enable single sign-on functionality. To do this, run the following command:

```
dsconfigad -EnableSSO
```

Finally, bind Mac clients into both directory structures (using the same steps for both Open Directory and Active Directory that were mentioned previously). Active Directory will now process user credentials, and Open Directory will now process system policies for the Mac clients.

> **NOTE:** This is a rather quick explanation on setting up a dual directory environment. You may run into errors or problems along the way with DNS, Active Directory, Open Directory, or server communications. If this is the case, check the extensive community forums at http://www.AFP548.com to see whether others have experienced the same issues (more than likely they have) and published fixes for them. Also, see Chapter 3 of *The Enterprise Mac Admin's Guide* from Apress for additional information.

Web Server Security in Mac OS X Server

Chapter 14 discusses web server security for Mac OS X Client. Apache is very similar in Mac OS X Server as it is in Mac OS X Client. But there are differences in how the web server operates in Mac OS X Client versus Mac OS X Server. In this section, we will cover the differences between the two and discuss how to configure secure settings for the web server in Mac OS X Server.

Using Realms

As we discussed in Chapter 14, using `htaccess` files is the traditional way to password-protect a folder in Apache. However, `htaccess` can get rather complicated and, if not configured correctly, could cause more security headaches than solved. Instead, if you have Mac OS X Server, then try using realms for limiting access to specified directories. In Mac OS X Server, when discussing the web server, a *realm* is a password-protected folder that uses a username and password in Mac OS X to share files. Realms use WebDAV, a protocol designed with this exact purpose in mind, and a protocol which Apple has integrated with Kerberos in Mac OS X Server. With WebDAV you will be using a password from your directory service rather than one stored in an `htaccess` or `passwd` file (this is more secure because it is often easy to find a password in unencrypted text rather than in the highly encrypted PasswordServer).

To use realms, first create a site using a subdirectory you would like to password protect. Create the users who will need to access the directory in Workgroup Manager and optionally a group containing those users. Next, open Server Admin, and click on the Web Service. Then click Sites in the Server Admin toolbar, click the appropriate site that the realm will be built for, and click the Realms tab. If you have not used realms before, the list of realms will likely be empty (as shown in Figure 16–22).

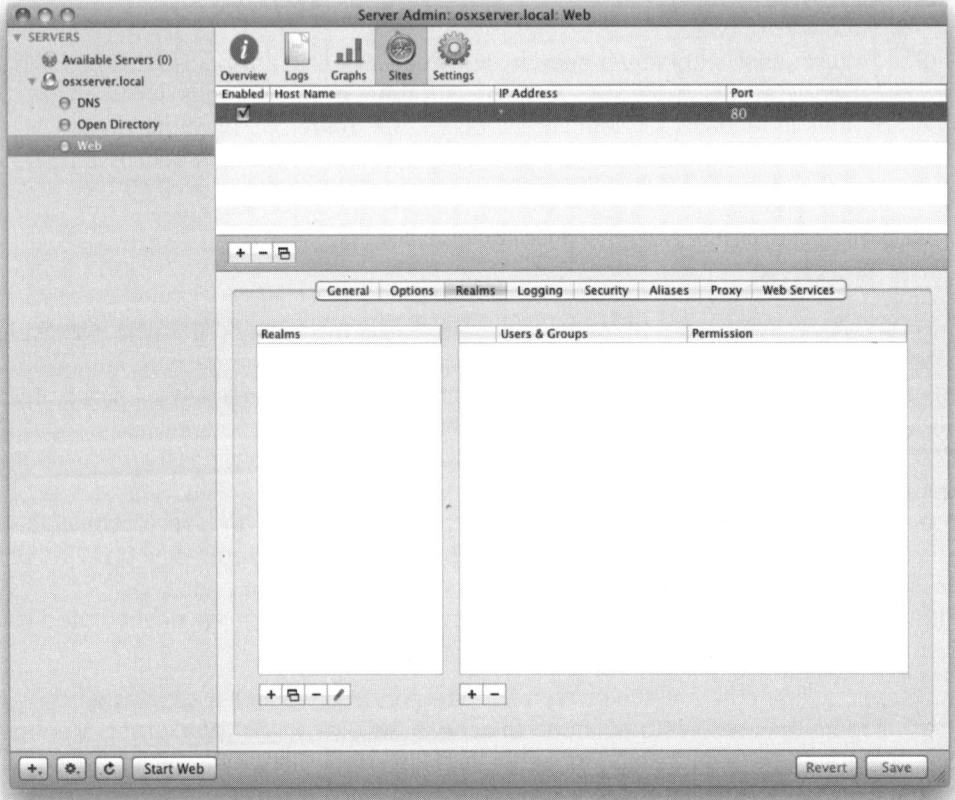

Figure 16–22. *Navigating to realms*

Click the plus (+) sign, and enter the name of the realm in the resultant screen (see Figure 16–23). Also enter the folder to access, and choose an authentication type (we suggest Kerberos). When you are satisfied with your settings, click OK.

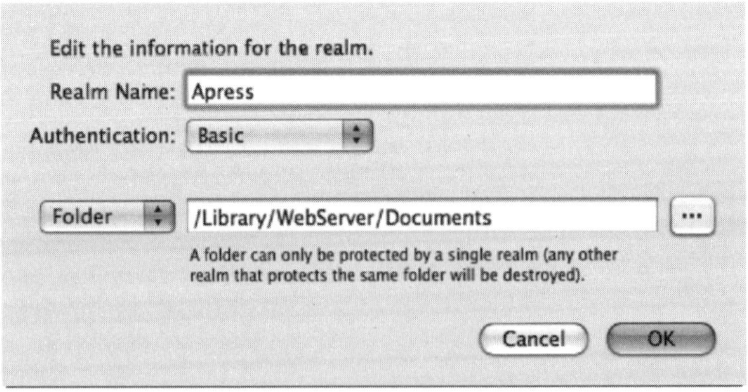

Figure 16–23. *Creating a realm*

Now, click the plus (+) sign (see Figure 16–24) to open the Users & Groups list, and drag the users or groups that require access to the realm to the Users & Groups panel. Under Groups, drag the groups, and set the value in the Permission column for each of the objects in the Users & Groups list.

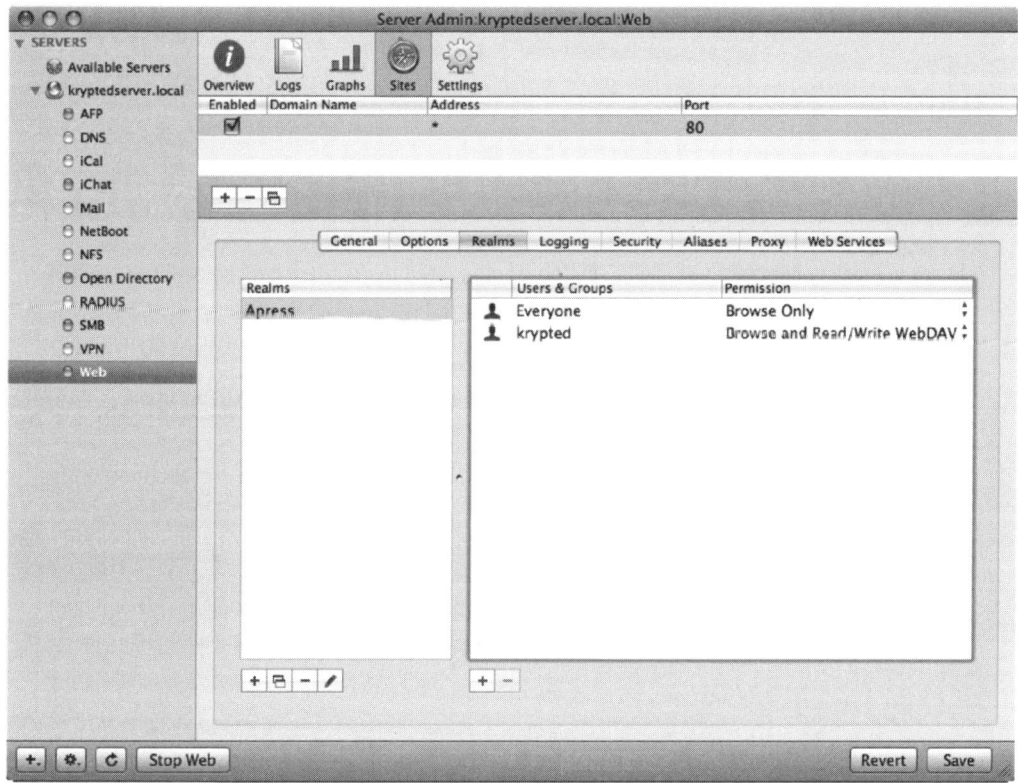

Figure 16–24. *Assigning permissions to a realm*

Once you are satisfied that the users and groups have the appropriate permissions, you will be able to log into the site using Kerberos or the protocol you set earlier.

SSL Certs on Web Servers

If you are doing any form of e-commerce, you should be using an SSL certificate (in fact we think that you should be using SSL for every service that has an option to do so). Many would argue that if you are trading any information with a client computer, such as a web form for submitting a support request, you should also be using SSL to encrypt the traffic. To enable HTTPS Access (SSL) on the web server, you will first need to create and install an SSL certificate (we will discuss implementing SSL on OS X Server later in the chapter). Then from Server Admin, you will click the web service and click the plus (+) sign to add a new site.

On the General tab (see Figure 16–25), enter the appropriate domain name in the Domain Name field, and enter **443** (the default port for SSL) in the Port field.

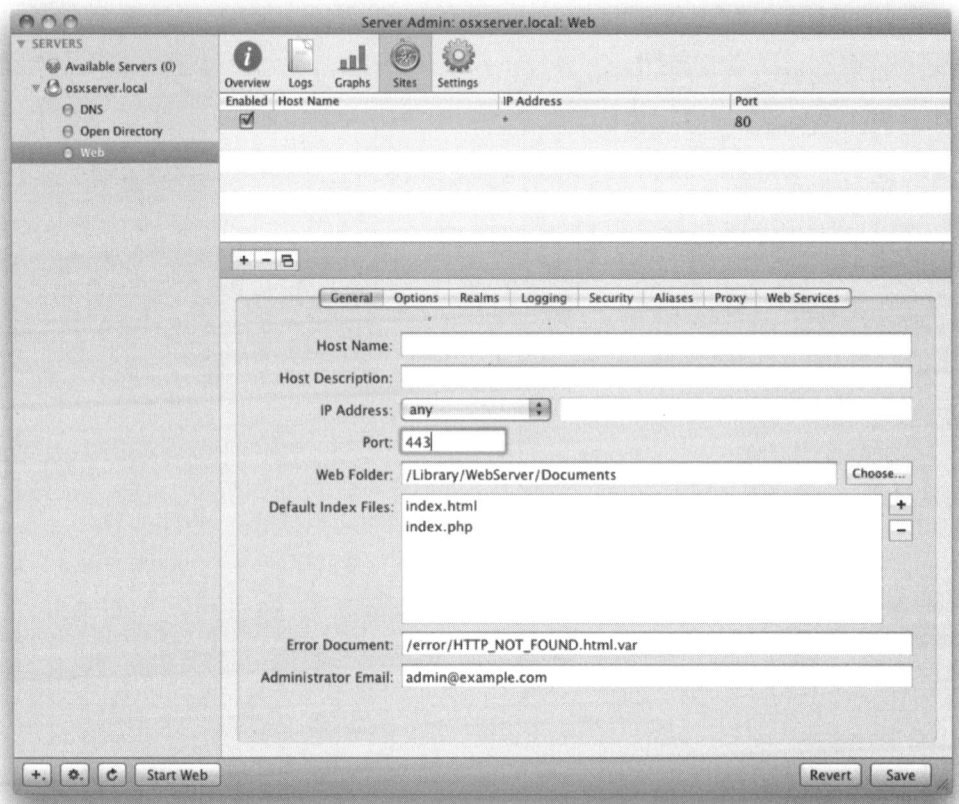

Figure 16–25. *Creating a site on port 443*

To assign the appropriate certificate, click on the Security tab (see Figure 16–26), and check the box to enable SSL. Next, select the appropriate SSL certificate, and click Save to complete the setup.

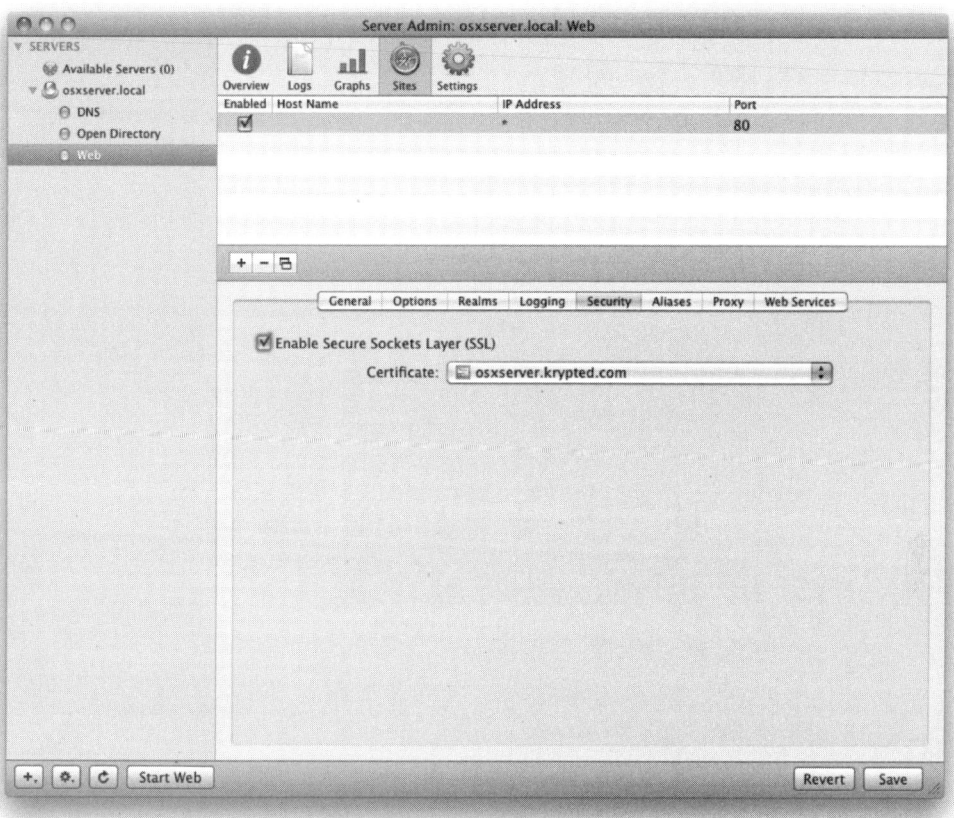

Figure 16-26. *Choosing the certificate*

File Sharing Security in OS X Server

File Sharing is more mature in Mac OS X Server than in Mac OS X Client, and thus has a more unified security context across services. For example, to view all the shared folders on a system, first open Server Admin, and click the name of the server in the Servers list. From here, click the File Sharing button in the Server Admin toolbar, and you will see a list of the logical volumes that your server can see along with a handy disk space image showing how full the various volumes are (see Figure 16-27). At this point, you can click share points to see which folders are currently being shared over SMB, AFP, NFS, or FTP. If you click Volumes and then click Browse, you will be able to configure new folders as share points that you would like others to be able to access. To do this, browse to the folder to be shared, and then click the Share button in the upper-right corner below the toolbar.

Figure 16–27. *Viewing shared folders*

In the File Sharing admin screen, you will see three tabs along the bottom: Share Point, Permissions, and Quotas (if quotas are enabled). From here, click Share Point, and review the options:

- Enable AutoMount provides options to set up an Open Directory link to the volume.

- Enable Spotlight Searching allows the volume to be searchable using Spotlight.

- Enable as TimeMachine Backup Destination means client computers can back up using Time Machine.

- Protocol Options opens the screen that allows SMB, AFP, NFS, and FTP settings to be configured (and looks similar to the screen in previous versions of Workgroup Manager).

> **NOTE:** From a security perspective, you should enable only the file sharing protocols that are necessary on a per-share basis.

Once you have configured the options for each share point, click on the Permissions tab to configure who can access the data shared by the share point. The Users & Groups floating window will appear when you click on the plus (+) sign. ACLs are listed above POSIX permissions, indicating their prioritization; when you drag a user or group into the Server Admin window from the floating users and group window, a blue line will appear indicating that dropping the object into the screen will apply it. Each user and group can then have custom permissions, roughly mirroring custom permissions available on Microsoft Windows servers.

Keeping a server secure also means not allowing users to fill up hard drive space on these shared volumes, which can not only reject other user's ability to save files on the server, but also cause the server to become unstable or even unresponsive. This often means implementing quotas on the volumes. To implement quotas, click the Quotas tab, and notice that when you enable quotas, you cannot drag users and groups into this window. Only users with home folders on the volume can be configured for quotas using Server Admin. Make sure to issue warnings to your users. They might not be accustomed to the idea of quotas and it may take some time for users to get used to them.

A Word About File Size

One of the challenges of life as a Mac OS X Server administrator is that Mac users (typically artists and designers) generally work with large files. In the most extreme cases, single files can be in the hundreds of gigabytes. Mac users accustomed to files normally 100MB in size are less likely to notice that they are sending files to each other that are too big for emailing. So, limit files, but make sure to communicate what's appropriate with the users in order to reduce support calls. Explain when to use FTP or file sharing and when not to use it.

Securing NFS

NFS (network file system) is a file system used for sharing files on a network. One great feature of NFS is that it provides home folders to large numbers of computers by using the auto-mount feature combined with the NFSHomeDirectory attribute in LDAP. The settings for NFS in Server Admin are minimal at best. NFS trusts the client, which is one reason that it has such a high number of security flaws. However, Mac OS X Server 10.5 and later, provide Kerberized NFS, making it slightly more appealing than on some competing platforms.

NFS has two global service options in Server Admin: the number of server daemons and the option to use TCP or UDP (or both) for serving up your data, neither of which is very security policy-friendly. But notice that you cannot stop or start the NFS daemon from Server Admin. There are only two services like this: Open Directory and NFS. If you have

NFS enabled for any share point, then you're stuck running the NFS daemon; if not, the daemon will not start. If you don't have an export on any share points, then you can't run it, so in order to stop the NFS daemon, verify that no shares are using NFS.

Workgroup Manager settings give the administrator per-export (share point) configuration capability. This is where each export would be secured independently, which is very different from securing AFP shares, for example. When you set up an export, you will have the option to export the directory listing to Client (certain IPs), World (everyone), or Subnet (all IPs in the specified subnet), which can be seen in Figure 16–28. These options are included to mitigate the risks associated with running NFS (such as man-in-the-middle attacks). Once you have chosen who can access this data, you can determine how to handle data access. Each export has the ability to map the root user to nobody (the root user receives permission as guest), map all users to nobody (all users act as the guest permission set), and can be set to read-only (useful for backups or remote sync operations) as well as for mounted shares such as /Network/Applications or /Network/Library, directories where clients should never need access to write to them.

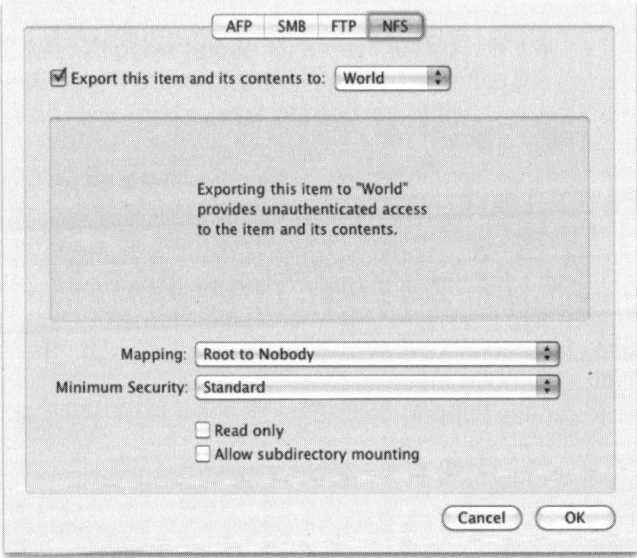

Figure 16–28. *NFS Export Options*

AFP

The AFP service in Mac OS X Server is similar to that in Mac OS X Client. However, it has a myriad of other features that can be used to further secure the server that increase performance for the AFP service. As we covered AFP in OS X Client in Chapter 13, we will be picking up where Chapter 13 left off by investigating unique aspects of the AFP service in Mac OS X Server.

AFP Authentication Options

One feature that is unique to the Apple File Protocol engine in Mac OS X Server is its ability to authenticate any user account with the password for any administrative account. This is called *AFP masquerading*. AFP masquerading will allow any administrative account on a system to potentially compromise all users' AFP access. Password policies don't apply to administrative accounts. If an administrative password is compromised, then the administrator can access all files as though they were any user. If one admin user had the password *Charles*, then all accounts on the system would be able to authenticate with a password of Charles.

Although this may be helpful in verifying a host operating system's interpretation of access permissions, it should always be disabled when not in use. It does not require a restart of the service or server for the setting to be disabled. AFP masquerading also reduces the administrator's ability to practice the delicate art of non-repudiation, or proof of identity of the responsible party for an action found in one's logs.

To define access methods for AFP in Mac OS X Server, open Server Admin, click on Settings, and click AFP. Then click the Access tab, and uncheck the Enable Administrator to "Masquerade as any user" box (see Figure 16–29). You will also want to limit the number of users to AFP to something that is reasonable in order to keep the AFP server from crashing (AFP can only typically handle approximately 350 clients mounting from the volume). To do so, change the Client Connections in the Access screen.

NOTE: Guest access is disabled by default for AFP but can be enabled by new administrators. To verify that it is disabled, use the Access screen to verify that the box Enable Guest Access is unchecked.

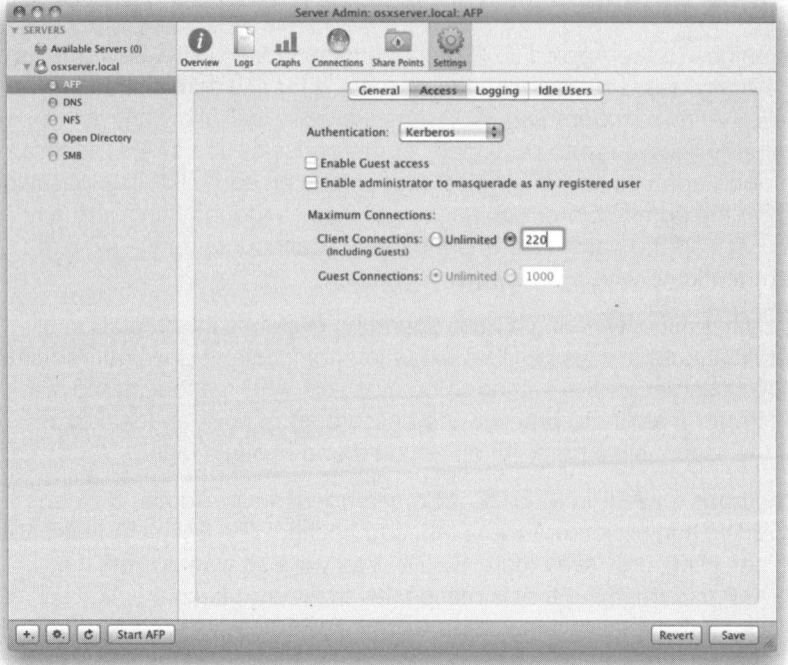

Figure 16-29. *Disabling the "masquerade as any user" option*

Kerberized AFP

Kerberos authentication, as mentioned earlier, is a superior authentication method to the standard Diffe-Hellman exchange (DHX) authentication scheme. Kerberos authentication can be required for the AFP server, but it is worth noting a few gotcha's with this configuration:

- When Kerberos authentication is required, only clients with a properly configured edu.mit.Kerberos file can authenticate with the service. This can disable access for any client that is not bound into the Open Directory network.

- Clients must not have a time skew longer than five minutes. This should be configured on the client by using a network timeserver.

- Users within the local authentication database will not be able to authenticate to the AFP server because their passwords are not authenticated using *Open Directory*. This may prevent the first user created on the system from being able to authenticate because they are created in the local authentication database.

Forcing Kerberos authentication requires AFP clients to use Kerberos to connect to the server, a good way to increase the security of your AFP environment. To force Kerberos authentication, set the authentication type to Kerberos on the Access tab of the AFP Service in Server Admin. Users that are not in the Open Directory database will not be able to authenticate via Kerberos. This means that those clients with local accounts that do not have proper Kerberos configurations files in /Library/Preferences/edu.mit.kerberos will not be able to authenticate to the AFP server once this setting is enabled.

AFP Logging

By default, Mac OS X Server does not log all events. From a security perspective, if there is a compromised server, then you will want as many logs as possible to pull data from, in order to reconstruct the events that transpired on your server.

To maximize logging, open Server Admin, and click the AFP service. Then click the Logging tab, and choose what you want the AFP service to log (Figure 16–30). We recommend checking all the boxes, but if you have a large quantity of AFP traffic, this could prove cumbersome to your log files. If so, reduce the scope by lowering the logging level incrementally until you have a workable solution.

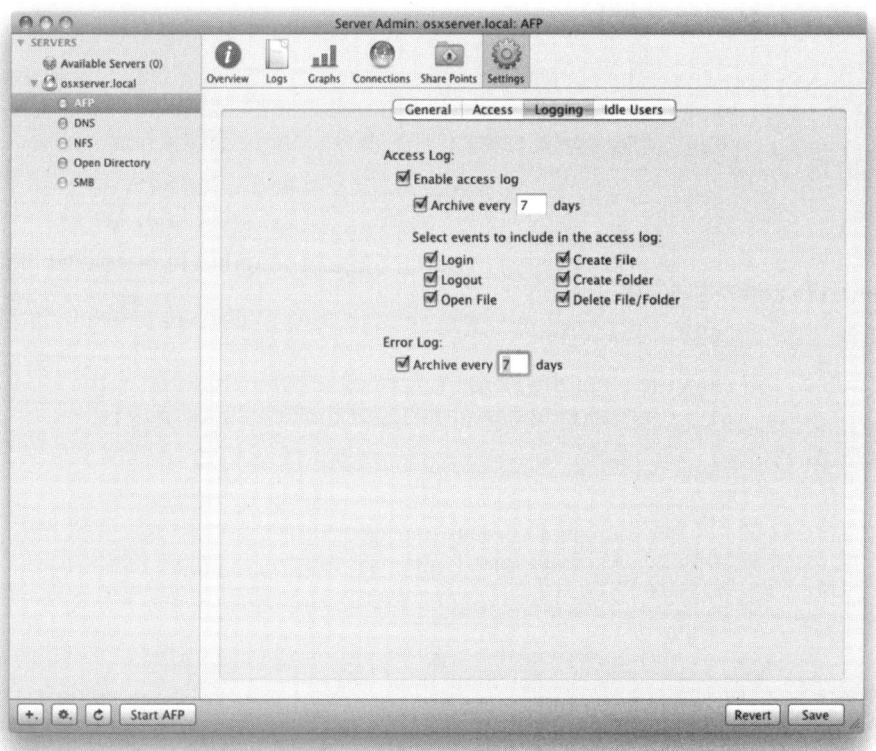

Figure 16–30. *Maximizing AFP Logs*

> **NOTE:** You will not see the path to files and folders in the logs. Even if logging is maximized, these seemingly important elements will still not appear.

SMB

Mac OS X Server and Windows integration often go hand in hand. Samba, Unix, and Mac OS X's Windows file service, is the primary means with which this is often done. Samba has the capability of authenticating via Kerberos when used with an Active Directory domain controller. This is accomplished by the following additions to the /etc/smb.conf file:

```
security = ads
realm = apress.com
use spnego = yes
```

The Simple and Protected GSSAPI Negotiation Mechanism (SPNEGO) allows for the Samba engine to negotiate a Kerberos connection with an Active Directory server. This means a Windows client can use a principal from a Windows Active Directory Kerberos realm to authenticate to the Samba file share point on Mac OS X Server.

The Samba process also runs the NetBIOS server in Mac OS X Server. Often overlooked is the NetBIOS name command option, which should match the hostname of the server, to support correctly formatted Kerberos tickets. This is analogous to the name chosen when binding to Active Directory via the Directory Utility.

```
netbios name = seldon
```

These additions can be facilitated by using the `dsconfigad` command to enable single sign-on using the command:

```
dsconfig -enableSSO
```

Once completed, you can verify that the Kerberos principals were created in the local keytab by using the `ktlist` command and searching for the key name of `cifs`:

```
klist -kt | grep cifs
```

```
2 01/14/09 14:41:56 cifs/seldon.krypted.com@KRYPTED.COM
2 01/14/09 14:41:56 cifs/seldon.krypted.com@KRYPTED.COM
2 01/14/09 14:41:56 cifs/seldon.krypted.com@KRYPTED.COM
```

> **NOTE:** Three keys are listed due to the variations of encryption used when creating Kerberos principals: these keys are stored in /etc/krb.keytab and must be kept secure (by default they are readable only by root and should remain that way). An attacker could use them to authenticate to the service without knowing the password of a given user.

FTP

Apple's built-in FTP server supports Kerberos authentication and can be used with third-party software to allow for better authentication security. By default, FTP transmits the session username and password via clear text. When using the Apple FTP server with a third-party client such as Fetch.app, the FTP client software can negotiate a GSSAPI connection using Kerberos. This allows the client to authenticate with a Kerberos ticket rather than a password. Although this does allow for better security during the authentication exchange, it does not prevent an attacker from watching the session data. Apple's current built-in FTP server does not support transport layer security such as SSL, while the OpenSSH suite does have a more secure protocol known as SFTP, which supports both Kerberos authentication and session layer security. Unfortunately, it cannot be easily configured via the graphic interface, and as a result, users effectively are not jailed (or trapped, the good kind) within a specific directory such as their home folder or linked share points. FTP on Mac OS X Server is a highly insecure transport protocol. If it must be used, it's advisable to use SFTP or a third-party tool, such as Rumpus.

> **NOTE:** A chroot command is a technique under *nix whereby a process is permanently restricted to an isolated subset of the filesystem. Because there are insecurities within FTP and use in Mac OS X, chroot can be used to further secure FTP. One easy way to obtain this functionality without a lot of command-line configuration is to use Rumpus, a web-enabled FTP application.

Wireless Security on OS X Server Using RADIUS

By default, when you connect to an AirPort based network you will only need to provide a password. According to how the network was configured, this password can be either pretty weak or pretty strong, but despite the strength of the encryption or the strength of the password, it has no policies that will lock the password out after incorrect attempts. Remote Authentication Dial In User Service (RADIUS) can help take the security of your wireless network to the next level by tying the password of your wireless environment into that of your Open Directory environment. In this section, we'll look at leveraging RADIUS to configure an AirPort environment to use Open Directory.

> **NOTE:** Before you begin this walk-through of implementing RADIUS on your server, make sure the server is running Open Directory and that the forward and reverse DNS information for the server is correct.

The first step to using RADIUS is to enable it. To do this, open Server Admin, click the name of the server in the Servers list, and click the Services tab. Find RADIUS in the list of services below each server, and place a check mark in the box to the left of it. Click Save, and you should see RADIUS in the Servers list.

Now that RADIUS has been enabled, let's select a certificate. For the purpose of this walk-through, we're going to use the default certificate that comes with OS X Server. Click RADIUS under the Servers list, and then click the Settings button. Click the RADIUS Certificate drop-down menu, and select the Default certificate as you can see in Figure 16–31. Click the Edit Allowed Users button to go to the SACL screen in Server Admin.

Back at the RADIUS screen in Server Admin, click on the Start RADIUS button in the bottom-left corner of the screen. RADIUS is now ready to accept authentication. The next step is to configure an AirPort device to work with RADIUS. To do this, click the Base Stations button in the toolbar at the top of the screen. Now click Browse, and select the first base station of your wireless environment from the list of found base stations. Enter the password for the AirPort device, and click Save. Wait for the AirPort device to complete its restart.

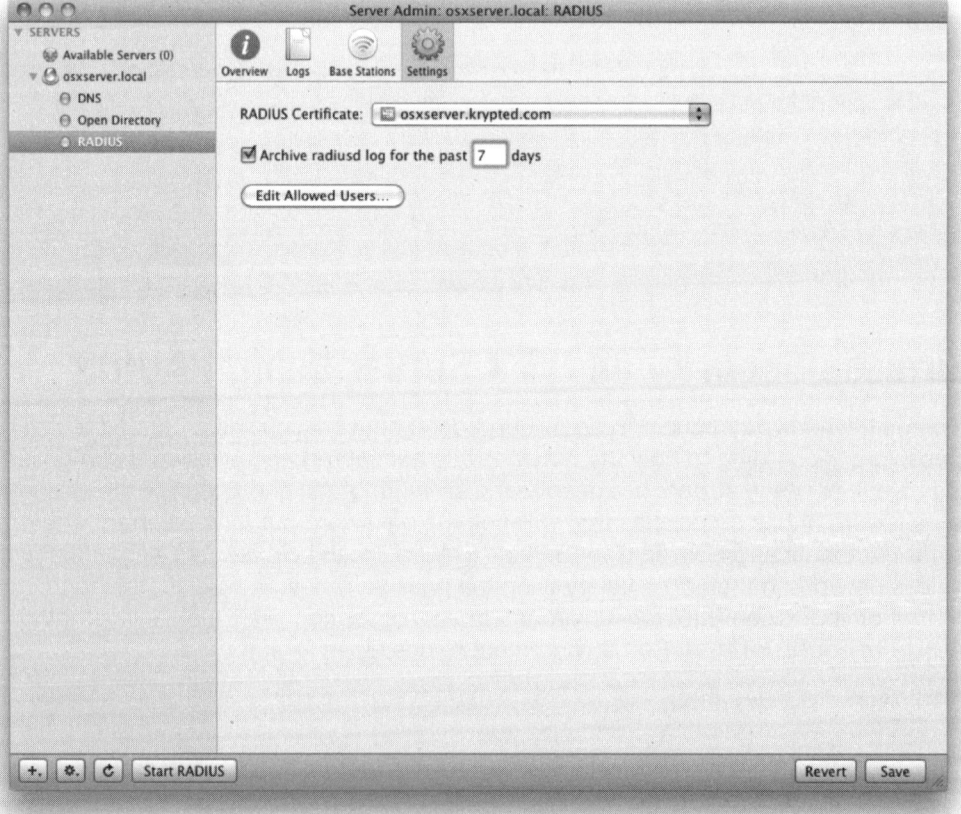

Figure 16–31. *Enabling RADIUS*

To log in from a client, select the name of the wireless network from the wireless networks list, and enter the username and password to the environment. The first time you do this, you will get a second dialog box asking you to enter the 802.1x username and password. Enter the same username and password, and click OK. If you click the Use this Password Once check box, then this password will not be saved for future use.

> **NOTE:** Chapter 10 covers 802.1x in more depth.

That's all there is to it. This setup may be a little more complicated than WPA personal or WEP 128, but it's far more secure and should be considered for any AirPort environment that has an OS X Server. Although the default certificate will work for clients, things are often easier from a deployment and interoperability perspective if you purchase a certificate from a Certificate Authority (CA) such as Thawte.

DNS Best Practices

Over the years, DNS has had a variety of weaknesses. A common reason for these vulnerabilities is improper security configurations of DNS servers. But most recently there have been attacks against even the best-defended servers. Some of these attacks seem fairly innocuous, such as the act of gaining useless information about an environment, while other attacks have been known to forward data through the DNS responder to arbitrarily execute commands. We suggest keeping public-facing DNS on a server outside your environment (with your registrar perhaps) so that other servers can find your domain for mail and web services while not exposing your environment to hacks.

A good number of other services require DNS to function properly, such as Open Directory, Mail Server, and some Apache modules. If the DNS service is overloaded, other services on other servers that use that DNS service will have problems, and also potentially crash. Therefore, we suggest you maintain a separate internal DNS infrastructure that is not accessible from outside your network. It is also strongly suggested that you customize the resources that the DNS service has available to it using sandbox, a means of separating different running services on your server (more on sandbox in Chapter 6).

> **NOTE:** To ease administration woes, Apple and Microsoft both suggest naming your internal domain something other than what you use for your public presence. Although this may cause more administrative burden, maintaining separate domain names does generally increase the security of your server environment.

> **TIP:** As with all services, you should maximize logging for DNS. To do so, open Server Admin, and click DNS. Then click Settings, and click Logging. Then set your Log Level for the service to Debug.

SSL

Implementing an SSL certificate on your server to encrypt traffic on Mac OS X Server is an essential security precaution to take if you are going to enable most any service (especially for mail, web and collaborative services). If you want to purchase a certificate rather than use a self-signed certificate (including the one installed by default), open the Keychain Access tool from /System/Library/Core Services and then from the Keychain Access menu, click on Certificate and then click Request Signed Certificate from a CA, which you can see in Figure 16–32. This will give you a text string that is then pasted into a CGI form with Thawte (or the CA that is issuing the SSL Certificate).

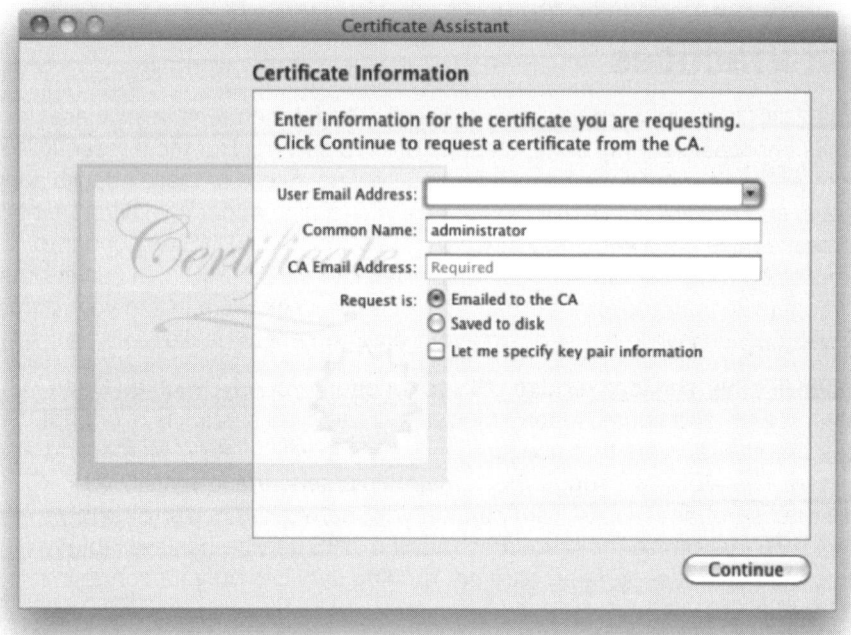

Figure 16–32. *Certificate information*

Once your certificate has been approved, paste the code obtained from the certificate authority into Server Admin on this screen, and your certificate will be active. Keep in mind that most certificates are based on server names, so make sure that it's spelled correctly.

Once your certificate is active, you will be able to use SSL when connecting to Open Directory. To do this, click Open Directory from Server Admin, and click the Protocols tab. From here, check the Enable SSL Certificates box, and choose the appropriate certificate. Once complete, click Save. Now you are ready to authenticate from an SSL-enabled client.

To use SSL on the client, follow these steps:

1. Import the certificate using Keychain Access (not required if the certificate is from a CA).
2. Open Directory Access from the /Applications/Utilities folder.
3. Click LDAPv3, and select your Open Directory environment.
4. Check the Encrypt Using SSL box.
5. Use DSCL to test whether you can query the Open Directory database.

To generate a self-signed certificate, you can use the Certificate Assistant or the command-line CA utilities that ship with Mac OS X's OpenSSL implementation. An easy-to-launch link to the Certificate Assistant is available from the Keychain Access application in the Utilities folder. However, you may choose to purchase and implement a third-party certificate, which can be far easier to distribute across your environment, as you typically won't need to install and manually trust it on every client.

Reimporting Certificates

If you need to re-import your certificate, you will need to convert it to a PEM certificate by running the command:

```
openssl x509 -in your.domain.com.cer -inform DER -out
    server.krypted.com.crt -outform PEM
```

Open the resulting .crt file in a text editor and copy the contents. Then, from Server Admin, choose Add Signed or Renewed Certificate from Certificate Authority, and paste the contents in from the previous step. Next your certificate should show that it has been signed by your CA (if you are using serveradmin on the same machine as your certificate server, then the certificate should be trusted as well).

SSH

Mac OS X Leopard Server ships with the ssh service automatically enabled. This service, by default, will allow connections on port 22 by any authenticated user known to the server. This has many security implications, such as the ability for standard accounts to run services on ports 1024 and higher. This means that by default any user of your server has the ability to start a proxy or traffic redirector (such as the Internet relay chat client Bouncer) without admin authorization.

Firewall safeguards should prevent remote access to those services, but even in a full firewall lock down, if port 22 is open, there are still many vectors that an attacker with user credentials could use to cause mischief and mayhem, so disable ssh unless you plan to use it. If you use it, make sure to secure it as described in Chapter 15. An example of this type of exploit of ssh would be the ability for users to send large quantities of spam e-mail through the default mail (postfix) system. Spammers controlling compromised systems often use this technique to send large quantities of unsolicited e-mail.

If you are not using ssh to manage servers, disable ssh in Server Admin by clicking the server name, then clicking Settings, and then clicking General. In this screen, uncheck the SSH box, and click Save (Figure 16–33). You can then configure service access controls in Server Admin by clicking on Access in the Server Admin toolbar and then selecting who has access to login through SSH.

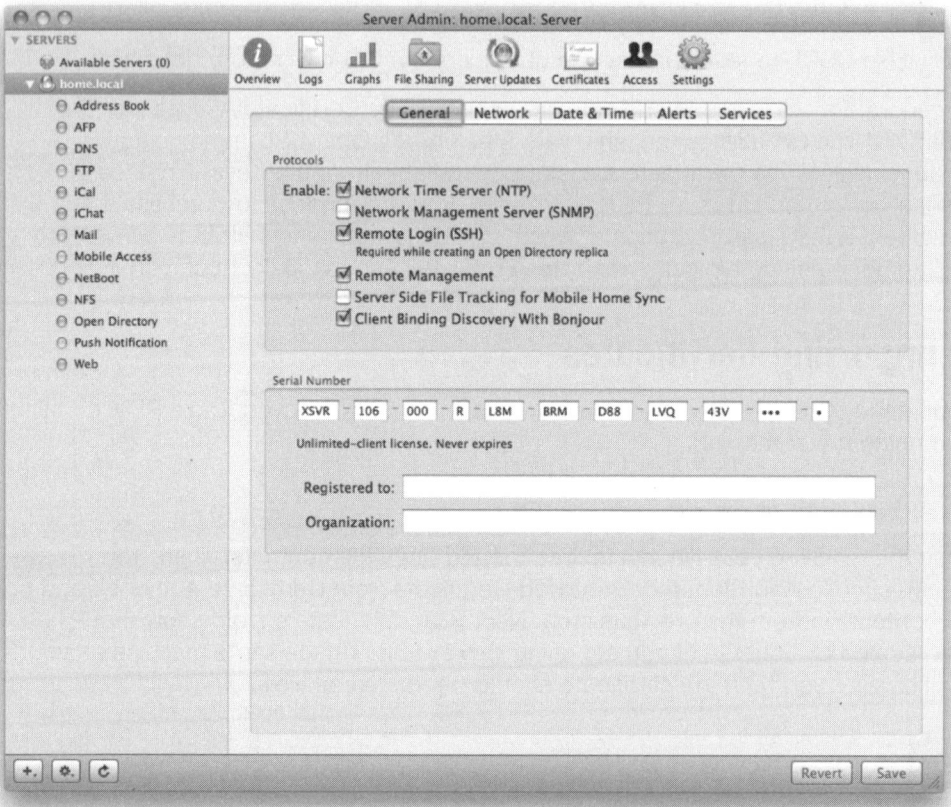

Figure 16-33. *Disable SSH*

> **NOTE:** As mentioned in the SACLs section earlier in this chapter, you cannot create an Open Directory replica when SSH is disabled. Once the replica is created, then SSH can be disabled, but for the replica creation process, it will need to be enabled.

You can also increase security of the SSH daemon by limiting older encryption protocol versions that have known exploits and by restricting access to certain groups. You can do this by editing /etc/sshd_config to include the following lines:

```
Protocol 2
PermitRootLogin no
```

Then type the following:

```
sudo dseditgroup -o edit -a <USERNAME> -t user com.apple.access_ssh sudo
    killall -HUP sshd
```

Server Admin from the Command Line

Mac OS X Server is a strange beast. On the surface, it's the greatest gift known to sysadmins, granting admins the ability to perform all kinds of complicated configurations quickly through a nice GUI. It can also dismay many of us who know where Unix-specifics live in the operating system and would prefer to configure things there. So, where are all those settings that override so many of the default Unix configuration files? `serveradmin` is the command that gives access to much of what you see in Server Admin as well as what you don't see graphically.

To see all the services you can configure and view, use the command `serveradmin list`. Or use the `serveradmin settings vpn` command and check the settings applied to the firewall service. `serveradmin` use starts out with viewing data on a specific service. For example, type `sudo serveradmin fullstatus vpn` to see a full status on the settings and use of the VPN service. Then use the command `serveradmin start vpn`, followed by a `serveradmin stop vpn`. Stopping and starting services on a server using the command line is incredibly helpful as you can actually issue these commands over an SSH session rather than needing to use a remote management utility such as ARD (Apple Remote Desktop) to connect. This can become invaluable when a bad firewall rule locks you, the admin, out of the Server Admin tool. Just issue a `serveradmin stop ipfilter` command, and you're right back in!

You can also configure settings that aren't available in the GUI. For example, we'll use VPN to customize where we put our logs.

First, type `sudo serveradmin settings vpn`. Now, look for the following entry:

`vpn:Servers:com.apple.ppp.pptp:PPP:Logfile = "/var/log/ppp/vpnd.log"`

To change this setting, type the following:

`Serveradmin settings vpn:Servers:com.apple.ppp.pptp:PPP:Logfile = "/var/log/ppp/pptpvpnd.log"`

Now the PPTP logs will be stored in a separate location than the logs for the rest of the VPN service. This can be done only using the `serveradmin` command and not with a configuration file. Nifty, huh?

To see all of the useful things that can be done with the `serveradmin` command, we suggest running a `man` command on `serveradmin`.

iChat Server

Instant messaging is making great strides in becoming one of the cornerstones of modern corporate communication, and it doesn't show any signs of slowing down. With its heavy presence in the modern workplace, it has become very common for business-related communications to be sent over IM. However, because of its humble insecure consumer upbringings, these communications are often not encrypted at all. Many modern packet sniffers have plug-ins or filters specifically designed for tracking session data such as connection passwords and chat transcripts. Because of IM's prevalence and its potential for eavesdropping, securing your IM communication by way of an encrypted chat server should be a top priority.

The Mac OS X iChat Server uses the XMPP protocol with an available option to enable SSL. You can use the default SSL certificate created when your Mac OS X Server was first configured, or you can choose to import your own. If you opt not to purchase a SSL certificate from one of the public CAs, make sure to generate your own certificates for distribution to your clients, as covered in the previous section on SSL.

Customizing the welcome message to new users of your iChat Server is a fairly simple task, and from a security context it allows an administrator to push out an acceptable use policy for their iChat environment. For this, we'll cover the Jabber configuration because Jabber is the open source package on which iChat Server is built.

When you first set up Jabber, the /etc/jabber directory will be created. Inside this folder is a file called jabber.xml. Open the jabber.xml file, and look for the welcome tag. Then, any data between "welcome" and "/welcome" will be the information that is shown in a welcome screen when a new user signs onto the iChat Server.

> **TIP:** Before you edit the /etc/jabber/jabber.xml file, make sure to back it up.

For this example, we will have all new users receive a message that says "Welcome to the 318 iChat Server."

To do this, delete or comment out the information between the existing welcome tags, and add the following information:

```
<welcome> <subject>to our iChat Server</subject> <body> Welcome to the 318
    iChat Server</body> </welcome>
```

Save the jabber.xml file, and you've now customized the welcome message for your iChat Server.

Securing the Mail Server

The mail server in Mac OS X Server has a few settings designed specifically for security. In Chapter 7 we discussed using the SpamAssassin and ClamAV features to limit mail that SpamAssassin and ClamAV identify as potentially sent from a spammer or system that has been infected with viruses. But what if your server is hijacked and set up as an open relay used to send spam? An *open relay* is a server that allows any user to relay mail through it. To verify your system isn't being used as an open relay, open Server Admin and click on the Mail service in the SERVERS list. From here, click on the Relay tab and remove any addresses that are not in your local network from the Accept SMTP Relays from These Hosts and Networks field, as you can see in Figure 16–34.

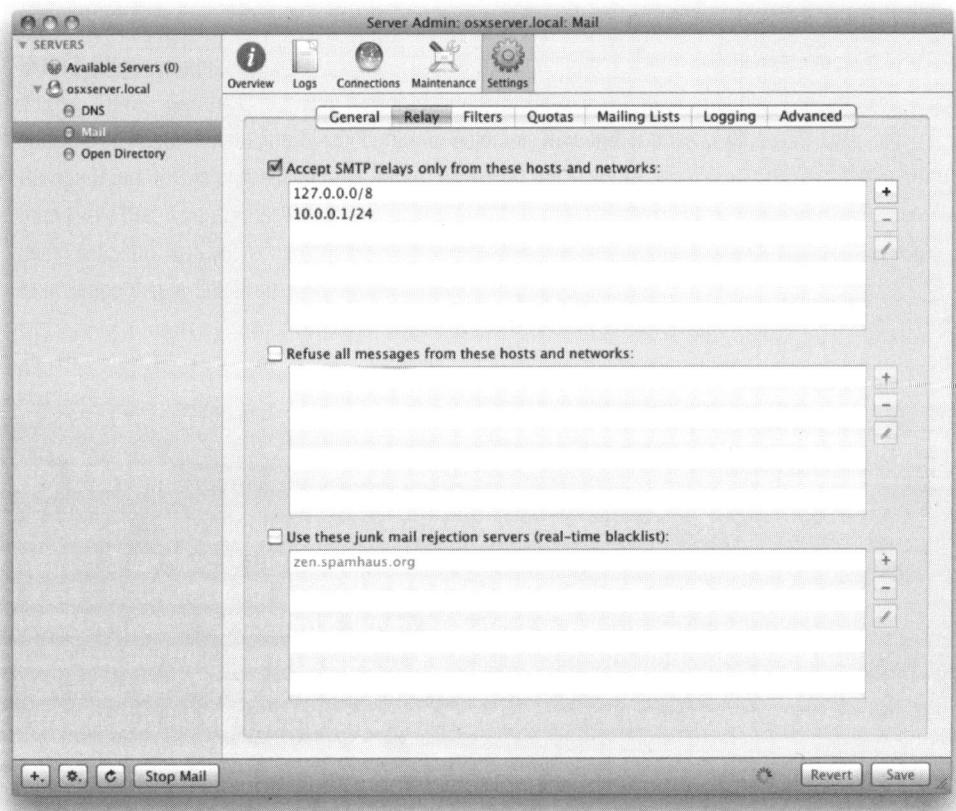

Figure 16-34. *Removing SMTP Relays*

Limiting the Protocols on Your Server

To reduce the footprint of mail services, you should also limit the number of protocols in use on your server. To do so, click the Settings tab for the Mail service in Server Admin, and verify you are using only the services you need (see Figure 16–35). For example, many environments will use only POP or IMAP. If you aren't using one of the two protocols, then disable the other.

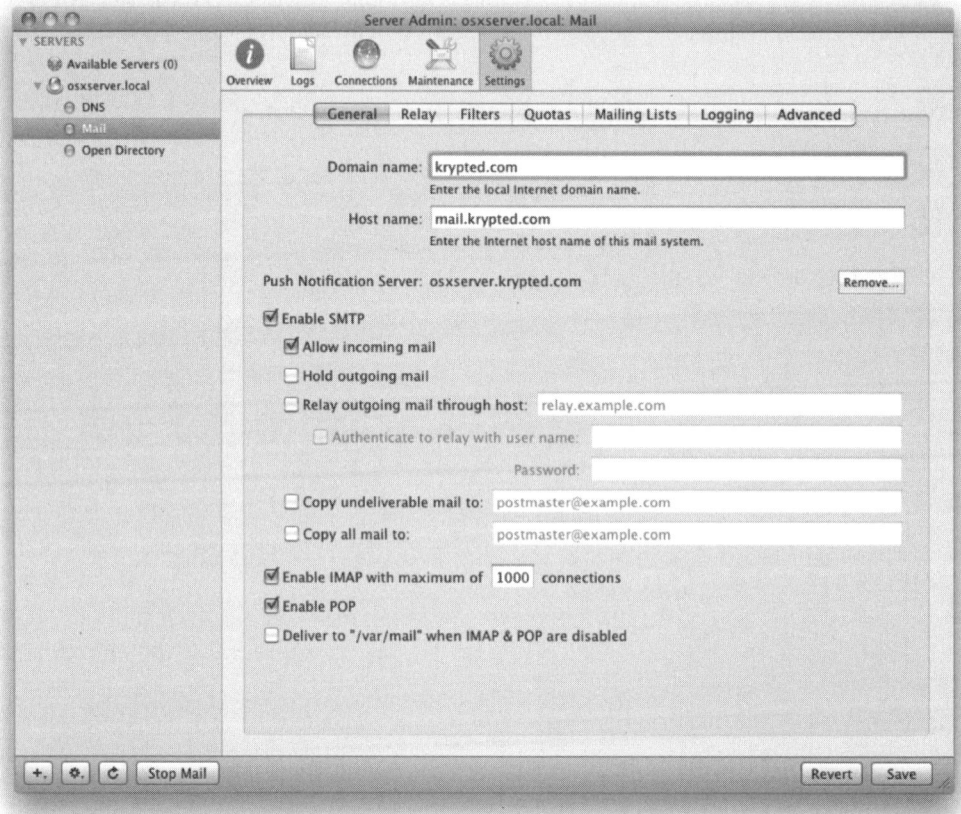

Figure 16-35. *Limiting the protocols on the Mail server*

Proxying Services

The final service that we will discuss in this chapter is the proxy service that can be leveraged to protect incoming traffic, which Apple refers to as Mobile Access. A Mobile Access server represents a dedicated server that sits outside of your firewall and is provided exclusive access to the IP addresses inside your environment that serve calendars, address books and mail. This server helps to keep your actual server protected by not exposing it directly to any traffic coming in over the Internet.

To setup your Mobile Access server, first connect your server to a location outside of your firewall, such as a DMZ (demilitarized zone) of your environment or a collocation facility. Then, enable the Mobile Access service in Server Admin. Once enabled, click on the Mobile Access service and check the box for each service that you are enabling, as you can see in Figure 16-36. Use the Advanced button to configure which ports will be used to transfer data between the Mac OS X Server acting as the Mobile Access service and the Mac OS X Server that is actually hosting each of the services.

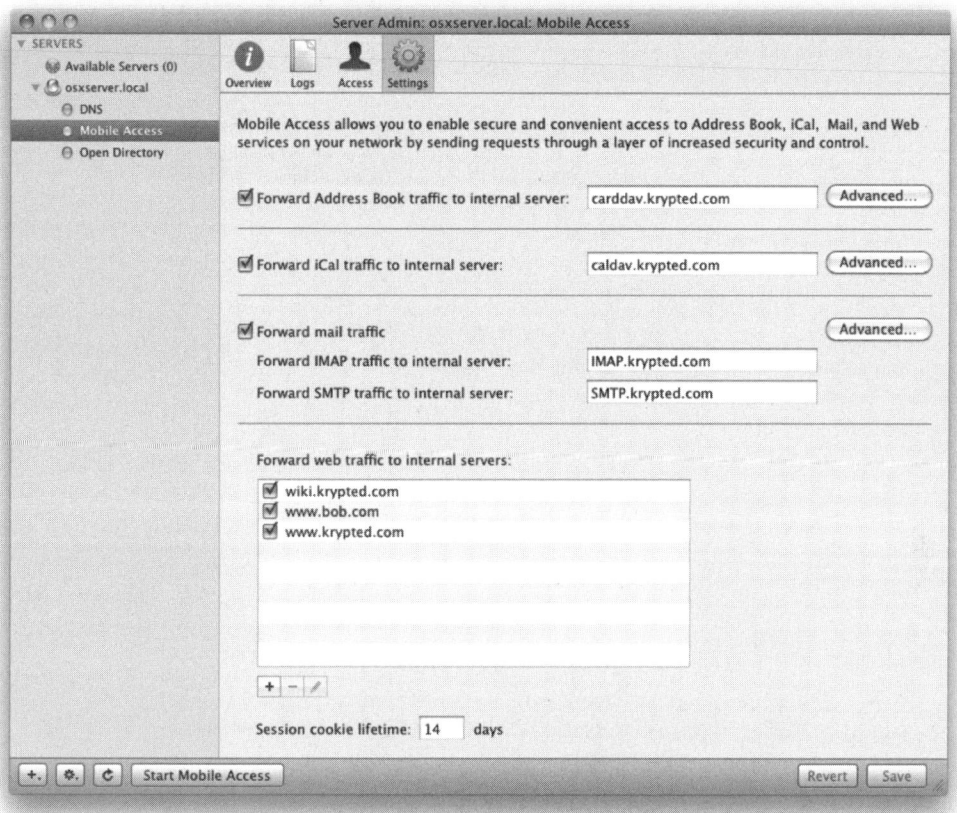

Figure 16–36. *Configuring the Mobile Access Service*

Summary

In a Mac client-server environment, you're only as secure as a properly configured server. With the knowledge of how to securely configuring file-sharing services, directory services, the root user, Kerberos, realms, mail services and the myriad other capabilities of your OS X Server, you have yet another weapon in your arsenal to defend your networked environment against attacks. Now, let's turn to the next line of defense: network intrusion detection and prevention.

Part V

Securing the Workplace

Chapter 17

Network Scanning, Intrusion Detection, and Intrusion Prevention Tools

Would your network withstand an attack? How easy would it be for someone to break into your network, find anything they want on your Mac, and steal enough information to masquerade as you on the Internet? To answer this question, you'd need to take a good hard look at your network and audit for intrusion vulnerabilities. Imagine having to catalog all the programs, files, and services that run on your Mac, cross-referencing each program and file extension on the Internet, one at a time, against all the known exploits. This auditing process would take a considerable amount of time. Unfortunately, hackers have easy access to a wide variety of auditing tools, and already have a good idea of which exploits to look for. Thankfully, the very same auditing software can help you expedite the process of keeping them out.

This is not to say you shouldn't be mindful of open ports, listening services, and the daily activities of a computer when analyzing security on a machine. You should be. Keep in mind, however, that each item that represents a security risk will need to be handled separately. The more time you can save in the actual audit of a computer, the quicker you will be able to secure the items that are flagged as a security threat. In this chapter, we'll cover the types of scans that hackers and auditors are likely to employ and how to use auditing software to counteract them.

Scanning Techniques

White-box testing is a methodology used when the auditor has full knowledge of the target environment. If you know all the relevant network information about the environment, such as the IP address of each system and what types of computers and network appliances exist, then you do not have to perform any discovery and can move straight into attempting to exploit systems or document threats.

Black-box testing assumes that the person auditing the network knows nothing about the environment. Because security information about an environment can be difficult to obtain, black-box testing should be conducted to assess security threats in the environment. If you're new to the environment, the first step in black-box testing is to understand what kind of information an attacker might be able to obtain. Once you have a full understanding of an environment, the techniques then become similar to those used in white-box testing. For the discovery portion of black-box testing, you can use a variety of techniques, which generally fall into two categories: active or passive scanning.

Active scanning involves targeted probing of a network or a specific host, trying to ferret out vulnerabilities. Many attackers will avoid active scanning, because it will often leave traces in the target system's logs, making their activities easier to trace. Active scanning methods include using a port scanner to find open ports, testing web applications for weak passwords or insecure code, or sending web links to users in the hope that they will visit a web site that will log their IP address and information that might identify potential attack vectors.

Passive scanning uses less intrusive means of observation, so as not to leave indications that a scan is taking place. Passive scanning requires much more patience, because the techniques are rather investigative in nature. Searching newspapers and job boards for specific technologies will give indications of what technologies are being used. Requests for assistance on a vendor's support page or a mailing list will tell an attacker not only what technologies are in use, but what problems the users are having, and potentially very detailed information about what solutions are being implemented. You may also be able to gather information about the staff responsible for the network. When looking for information that could be used against an organization, the search must be comprehensive, often including chat rooms, the whois database, newsgroups, web sites, mailing list archives, and the target user or company's web site. A company web site can even give an attacker usernames, e-mail addresses, and the location of CGI scripts on web servers. Sometimes there will even be passwords discovered, or at least hints as to password policies. To help reduce the amount of information about your organization that is on the Web, consider routinely using Google to search for information that is available about your organization. There are a number of advanced Google search operators that make it easier to narrow your search. For example, A search for `site:mysite.com filetype:doc` will return all indexed Word Documents on your site.

Fingerprinting

Fingerprinting is the practice of gathering as much information as possible about your systems or network and using that information to positively identify the hardware and software in use. The goal is to get as much information as possible about a network or host's security, including its remote access capabilities, vulnerable services, and open ports. Successfully attacking a system depends on having this information. Tools that can be used in fingerprinting include general-purpose tools such as host, dig and traceroute, and specialized tools like nmap and Ethereal.

The easiest and safest way to go about finding information about a company is to use publicly available information. This includes researching and collecting phone numbers, addresses, press releases, SEC filings, and other seemingly innocuous information. Company blogs are wonderful mediums for discussing technology, but they can also be a great resource from which to extract information about a company's infrastructure. Many companies post a great deal of information about themselves on their web site, including information about the systems they have deployed, the revisions of services running on these systems, and the security solutions used to protect these services. A lot of this information can be very useful to hackers.

Let's fingerprint the site `apress.com` to find out as much as we can about our publisher. We can hopefully assume that, as a publisher of books on network security, they maintain good security practices.

According to whois, the domain was registered in 1998. The administrative contact email address tnguyen@apress.com. We can glean from this that the format for apress.com e-mail address is first initial + last name. The current registrar for the domain is Network Solutions, and the technical contact address is customerservice@networksolutions.com. The authoritative DNS servers for the domain are owned by UUNet, which is a part of Verizon's network. See Figure 17-1.

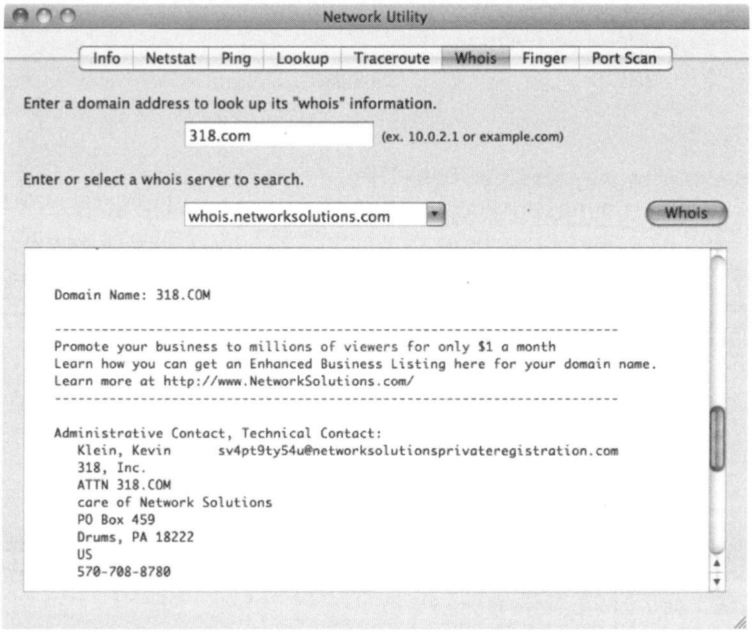

Figure 17-1. *Using Network Utility to perform a whois lookup*

Next, let's find the IP address of www.apress.com. The host command performs both forward and reverse DNS lookups. Running it on www.apress.com returns the IP address 66.211.109.45. Running host on the IP address returns NXDOMAIN, which means there's no reverse DNS mapping for that address. Running whois on the IP address reveals that the address belongs to Evocative, Inc, a colocation and managed services provider in

Northern California. A perusal of Evocative's web site reveals that this web server is probably running Linux.

A cornerstone of fingerprinting is port scanning. Apple has provided a built-in port scanner with OS X, under the Port Scan tab of the Network Utility application (located in the /Applications/Utilities folder) Later in this chapter we will review nmap, a far more capable port-scanning utility. For now, open Network Utility, and click the Port Scan tab. Then, type www.apress.com in the search box, and let's see what services are running on that computer by clicking the Scan button. The most common and important services use the lower-numbered ports, so we'll limit our scan to only ports between 1 and 1000. Our results are as follows:

```
Port Scan has started…

Port Scanning host: 66.211.109.45

        Open TCP Port:          21              ftp
        Open TCP Port:          22              ssh
        Open TCP Port:          25              smtp
        Open TCP Port:          80              http
        Open TCP Port:          110             pop3
        Open TCP Port:          111             rpcbind
        Open TCP Port:          119             nntp
        Open TCP Port:          143             imap
        Open TCP Port:          443             https
        Open TCP Port:          688             unknown

Port Scan has completed…
```

From this scan, we can see that www.apress.com has HTML and e-mail ports open, so it is either running or pretending to run mail services as well as web services. It's accepting RPC requests, and also has port 688 open, which is assigned for use by the ApplianceWare Management Protocol. ApplianceWare is a provider of Network Attached Storage solutions, and RPC is used for Network File System connections. We can now begin looking for potential exploits for these services.

Enumeration

Network enumeration is the process of identifying domain names and their associated networks. Enumeration involves querying whois databases and performing DNS lookups. Whois databases often hold names and contact information for people involved in managing a domain, and the date a domain was registered. The information gathered from these inquiries can be used to facilitate *Social engineering* attacks. Social engineering is the art of convincing network users to divulge private information (information they should not be giving out) about the network, such as IP addresses, usernames, and even passwords. In some cases, a lucky (or skillful) attacker only needs to ask a user nicely for their password.

> **NOTE:** DNS zone transfers are used to pass DNS information between DNS servers. Many environments are mistakenly configured to allow untrusted hosts to perform a DNS zone transfer, which means that any machine masquerading as a DNS server can request a zone transfer in order to obtain DNS information. You can find a wide variety of tools on the Internet that can be used to perform DNS interrogation. For more information on DNS security, see Chapter 16.

Vulnerability and Port Scanning

Scanning can be performed on a single host or a whole network. Scanning with a vulnerability scanner allows you to rapidly review your computer and the computers on your network for known security holes such as outdated software. You can then move on to penetration testing, which typically starts by going a step beyond scanning and into using automated tools that attempt to exploit vulnerabilities.

Be very careful when trying to access any open ports you may find. Brute-forcing an FTP or a web server can land you in a pile of trouble. As a rule of thumb, if attempting to access a service requires a password, you probably shouldn't be there. In fact, in some jurisdictions, accessing a resource without permission is illegal, even when it is configured to allow anonymous access. However, if you access something important and the system doesn't ask you for a password, then this is a problem that should be resolved immediately.

nmap

Nmap is a network exploration tool that can be installed on Mac OS X from `nmap.org`. It is one of the most valuable tools for a security engineer or penetration tester (someone who attempts to break into a system in order to test its security). It is, as its name suggests, a network mapping tool. With nmap, you can probe an entire network and discover which services are listening on each specific port on every workstation, server, and router accessible. Nmap can also perform operating system fingerprinting. By comparing different fingerprints, nmap gives users an educated guess as to the operating system a target machine is running.

Nmap is very flexible, and offers a lot of options or flags that let you perform a wide variety of scans. For example, you can perform a `TCP connect()` scan (which initiates a full connection to the host) or a SYN scan (also known as a *half connection*). You can test firewall rules and distinguish whether you are scanning a firewall or a packet filter. You can also throw out decoys to make your real address harder to trace. Table 14-1 describes the nmap options for the actual binary command. The proper usage of nmap includes the following:

```
nmap [Scan Type] [Options] <target(s)>
```

Table 14-1. *Common Scanning Options*

Option	Description
-sO	Scan for supported IP protocols rather than open ports.
-sS	TCP SYN stealth port scan (default if running as root).
-sT	TCP `connect()` port scan (default for nonroot users).
-sU	UDP port scan.
-sP	Ping scan (find any reachable machines).
--interactive	Interactive mode (then press H for help).
-sR/	RPC scan (use with other scan types).
-O	Use TCP/IP fingerprinting to guess remote operating system.
-p <range>	Define ports to scan. Example range: 1-80, 8010, 8080, 10000.
-F	Scans only ports listed in `nmap-services` to speed up scans.
-v	Verbose. Its use is recommended. Use twice for greater effect.
-PN	Don't ping hosts before scanning (needed to scan www.microsoft.com and others).
-D decoy_host1, decoy2[,...]	Hide scan using decoys.
-6	Scans via IPv6 rather than IPv4.
-T <timing>	General timing policy. Settings are Paranoid, Sneaky, Polite, Normal, Aggressive, Insane.
-n/-R	Do not use DNS resolution/always resolve (the default is to sometimes resolve).
-oN/-oX/-oG <logfile>	Output normal/XML/grepable scan logs to <logfile>.
-iL<inputfile>	Get targets from file; use - for stdin.
-S <your_IP>/-e <devicename>	Specify source address or network interface.

Here's an example:

```
nmap -v -sS -O www.318.com 10.0.0.0/16 '10.0.*.*'
```

The stealthiest and most widely used nmap-scanning method is SYN scanning, also known as *half open* or *stealth scanning*. There are a couple of downsides to using this method. Unfortunately, most intrusion detection systems (described more later in this chapter) can detect these packets, and some firewalls and packet filtration mechanisms will drop SYN packets, which make it harder to get an accurate list of what ports on the host are open.

With a SYN/stealth scan, you do not actually make a full connection with the host. It will send a SYN packet and request a connection. The host being scanned then responds with a SYN/ACK packet informing you about whether the port is open and responding. As soon as you receive the SYN/ACK packet from the remote host, nmap sends one RST packet terminating the connection. It does not make a full connection or three-way handshake (full connection), which is why SYN/stealth scanning is called a *half open scan*.

Running a SYN/Stealth Scan

Here is what an nmap SYN/stealth scan would typically look like. First, we initialize the scan with the following Terminal command, assuming we are scanning a system with the IP address of 192.168.11.5:

```
nmap -sS 192.168.11.5
```

This command results in the following output:

```
Starting Nmap 5.21 ( http://nmap.org ) at 2010-02-29 20:15 PST
Nmap scan report for 192.168.11.5
Host is up (0.018s latency).
Not shown: 985 closed ports
PORT       STATE    SERVICE
22/tcp     open     ssh
88/tcp     open     kerberos-sec
139/tcp    open     netbios-ssn
445/tcp    open     microsoft-ds
515/tcp    filtered printer
631/tcp    open     ipp
777/tcp    filtered unknown
1063/tcp   filtered unknown
3306/tcp   open     mysql
3689/tcp   open     rendezvous
5100/tcp   filtered admd
5900/tcp   open     vnc
12000/tcp  filtered cce4x
60443/tcp  filtered unknown
MAC Address: 00:0D:93:83:F3:B0 (Apple Computer)

Nmap done: 1 IP address (1 host up) scanned in 5.99 seconds
```

> **NOTE:** A filtered port, such as the port 515 in the previous scan, usually indicates the machine is running a firewall.

Here is a log of a stealth SYN scan from an intrusion detection system called snort (we will discuss intrusion detection systems, including snort, later in the chapter):

```
[**] [111:13:1] spp_stream4: STEALTH ACTIVITY (SYN FIN scan) detection [**]
09/21-19:18:03 10.0.0.4:80 -> 10.0.0.8:88
TCP TTL:255 TOS:0x0 ID:2304 IpLen:20 DgmLen:42
******SF Seq: 0x90AB763  Ack: 0x0  Win: 0x1000  TcpLen: 20
9-21 19:18:04 10.0.0.4:80 -> 192.168.0.8:88 SYN ******S*
```

As you can see by the warning message, snort has built a rule set that is able to identify nmap's SYN/stealth scanning sequence.

Other nmap Scans

Nmap scans can be limited to specific criteria. For example, if you wanted to scan only UDP ports 1 through 80 on a server using the IP address 10.0.0.4, you would use the following command:

```
nmap -sU -p 1-80 10.0.0.4
```

If you only wanted to find out what addresses actually have machines responding, you can skip the actual port scan and simply send a ping. This is commonly called a *ping sweep*. For the whole 10.0.0.1-254 network, you would use this command:

```
nmap -sP 10.0.0.0/16
```

Using the -O flag, nmap can also identify many operating systems, based on how the target responds to a large number of tests. The results of a scan are compared against a large database of known OS fingerprints. Nmap can often identify an operating system even when very few services are running.

Scanning a network for vulnerabilities is only one piece of the network intrusion pie. We must now make steps to secure the weaknesses that our scans have uncovered. So that we aren't overlooking anything, we should first look for intrusion instances that may have already been attempted and then implement measures to prevent future attempts.

Intrusion Detection and Prevention

In information security, *intrusion detection* is the practice of detecting attempts (successful as well as unsuccessful) to compromise a network resource. Intrusion detection does not usually involve the prevention of intrusions; however, we will discuss some preventive measures that can work in tandem with intrusion detection. With any intrusion detection solution, it is important that it somehow alerts you to potential intrusions so that you can determine whether your security was actually compromised, allowing you to act swiftly in order to limit the damage. Once you've mitigated the damage, you can examine what the attack vector was, investigate whether it was done maliciously, and then take measures to prevent future intrusions based on this information.

Host Intrusion Detection System

The purpose of a host intrusion detection system is to monitor and analyze a system in such a way that an administrator can determine whether a change has occurred on a system. Most host-based intrusion detection systems focus on checking for changes to configuration files or folders containing binary files (applications).

Tripwire

Tripwire is an intrusion detection system that is used to track changes to the files on a computer. Tripwire can scan for files on computers by creating a checksum of the files and folders on a system, and then comparing that against a checksum created at installation time. This enables a fast scan of a variety of files and folders on a computer. Regular Tripwire scans will alert system administrators of changes to the file system that shouldn't be made.

Some folders we recommend scanning regularly include the following:

```
/dev
/opt
/usr
/usr/sbin
/bin
/mach.kern
/Library/Preferences
/Library/FileSystems
/etc
/System/Library/Extensions
/System/Library/CoreServices
```

Tripwire Installation

The simplest method of installing Tripwire is to first install MacPorts or Fink. Both of these are package management tools that allow for easy installation of software from a large repository of open source projects. Tripwire is available through both of these tools, and the source is also available from Sourceforge.

To install Tripwire from MacPorts, you would use the port command.

`sudo port install tripwire`

After installation is finished, run the tripwire configuration script. This will create the necessary configuration files and passphrases, and then sign the configuration files with those passphrases.

`sudo /opt/local/etc/tripwire/twsetup.sh`

When that's finished, you need to define the baseline state of the computer.

`sudo tripwire --init`

To update your Tripwire database after making system changes, run this command:

`sudo tripwire -m u -r /opt/var/db/tripwire/report/day-month-year-initials.twr`

To update your Tripwire config, change the /opt/local/etc/twcfg.txt file, and run this command:

```
sudo twadmin -m F -S /opt/local/etc/tripwire /site.key /opt/local/etc/tripwire/twcfg.txt
```

To enforce a new policy, edit the /opt/local/etc/tripwire/twpol.txt file, and run this command:

```
sudo twadmin -m p > /opt/local/etc/tripwire/twpol.txt
```

To view Tripwire reports, run this command:

```
sudo twprint -m r -r /opt/local/var/db/tripwire/report/*.twr
```

> **NOTE:** A .twr file is a Tripwire report file.

To scan for changes that have been made to the system, run this command:

```
sudo tripwire -m c
```

To e-mail these changes to the e-mail address listed in the config file, if you have identified an e-mail address, run the following command:

```
sudo tripwire -m c -M
```

Bear in mind that Tripwire will not be able to restore any modified files that it finds. This is another reason that proper backups are important.

Network Intrusion Detection

Host-based intrusion detection scans the system for changes. But it is also possible to use a network intrusion detection system (NIDS), which can scan the network interface of systems to identify traffic patterns based on signatures of known exploits. One example of a popular NIDS application is snort.

Snort from the Command Line

Snort is an open source network intrusion detection and prevention system that is capable of packet logging and real-time traffic analysis. Proprietary solutions that include integrated hardware and support services are sold by Sourcefire, and there are hundreds of additional rule sets and downloads available to extend the snort platform.

Snort can perform protocol analysis along with content matching, and it is often used to help detect attacks and probes. But it's mainly used as a means of finding existing threats to your network infrastructure. Some of the attacks that snort can detect include buffer overflows, stealthy port scans (such as those stemming from nmap), specific CGI attacks, SMB probes, and OS fingerprinting techniques. Snort can also be used for intrusion prevention by dropping attacks as they are taking place or augmenting your firewall to block future attempts from flagged IP addresses. SnortSnarf, sguil, OSSIM, and the Basic Analysis and Security Engine (BASE) help administrators effectively analyze the mountains of data generated by snort.

> **NOTE:** Snort patches that can be configured to work with antivirus scanning within ClamAV are available from Emerging Threats (www.emergingthreats.net). Any potential threats are isolated into signatures. These signatures are network traffic patterns that are then recorded. When future traffic comes through the network interface that matches these signatures, snort will perform the action that it is configured to perform (more on configuring these later in this section).

The easiest way to install snort is to use MacPorts.

```
sudo port install snort
```

Once it's installed, snort can immediately be run in sniffer mode or packet logger mode, both of which will give you a real-time view of the traffic on your network. Create a folder in your home directory called snortlogs, and then run the following command:

```
sudo snort -dev -l ~/snortlogs
```

This will run snort in logger mode. All the traffic that snort can see will be captured to file in snortlogs for later review.

In order to run snort in NIDS mode, you will need to install rules that snort can match traffic against. To install rules, you need to make a place for snort settings files, rules, and logs:

```
sudo mkdir -p /opt/local/etc/snort/rules
sudo mkdir /var/log/snort
```

Go to the snort rules page at http://www.snort.org/snort-rules/, download the latest snort rules package, and unzip it. In order to download rules, you'll need to register as a user with snort.org. Once you've unzipped the rules:

```
cd <snort-rules-download-dir>/rules
sudo mkdir /opt/local/etc/snort/rules
sudo cp rules/* /opt/local/etc/snort/rules
sudo cp etc/* /opt/local/etc/snort/etc
```

Copy the default snort.conf.dist sample file to snort.conf. Keep the original as a failsafe:

```
cd /opt/local/etc/snort
sudo cp snort.conf.dist snort.conf
```

Now it's time to fire up snort and test it. If you have installed snort, then the first thing you will want to do is run the following command to initialize snort:

```
sudo snort -c /opt/local/etc/snort/snort.conf
```

After the initialization information is displayed, you will see live packet capture information on the Terminal screen if you are connected to a network. Now kill the snort foreground process by pressing Ctrl+C to take a look at the summary information. You should be ready to roll if you see packet captures that resemble Figure 14-3.

> **NOTE:** For official snort training, see www.sourcefire.com/services/education/.

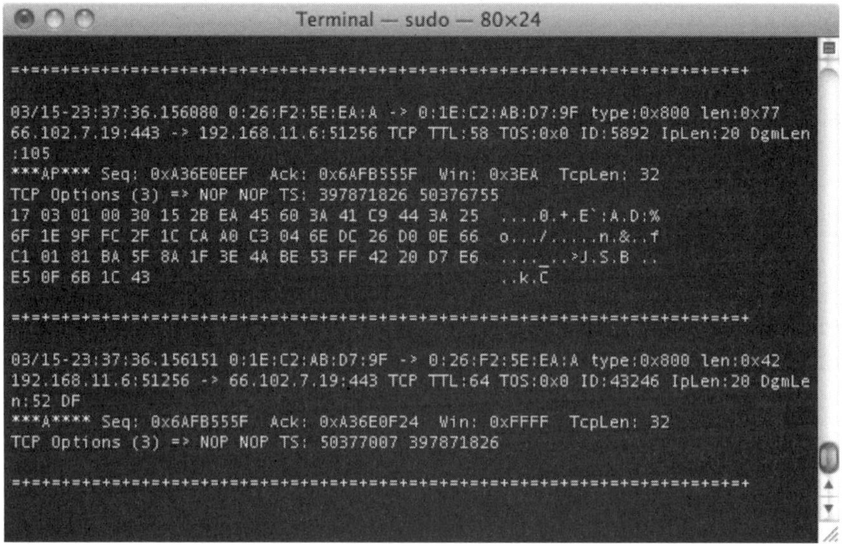

Figure 17–2. *Packet capture*

> **NOTE:** snort has no mechanism to update rules automatically. To keep snort updated, you should add a script to your weekly or monthly periodic tasks that will download the current rules.

Honeypots

A *honeypot* is a trap set by a network administrator to detect, deflect, or even attract attempts at unauthorized use of the network. Generally, it consists of a computer, data repository, or network resource that appears to be part of a network, containing information valuable to attackers, but is actually isolated and monitored by the network admins.

Honeypots are valuable surveillance and early-warning tools. Honeypots should have no production value, and should not see any legitimate traffic or activity. They should in no way be connected to actual production networks, and should not be running any production services. Whatever they capture can then be assumed to be malicious or unauthorized. For example, honeypots designed to thwart spam by masquerading as zombie systems can categorize the material they trap 100% accurately: it is all illicit. A honeypot needs no spam-recognition capability and no filter to separate ordinary e-mail from spam. Ordinary e-mail should never come to a honeypot.

Web traffic can be reviewed in the same manner. Create a script to put a file in a web directory that tells bots not to search the folder. If a bot then searches the folder, you can update the firewall configuration on that server to block future traffic from the IP address of the originating bot. This is a rudimentary form of a honeypot. MacPorts includes a port of honeyd, a small daemon that creates virtual hosts that appear to be running arbitrary services.

Honeypots can take on other forms, such as files or data records or even unused IP address space (for example, a file that is watched with verbose logging called payroll.xls). A collection of honeypots is known as a *honeynet*.

Security Auditing on the Mac

Several products on the market allow for vulnerability scanning and security auditing on the Mac. Some of them are freeware, and some of them are not. SAINT, Nessus, and Metasploit are our favorites for this critical piece of the security puzzle. Only Nessus and Metasploit are free products.

Nessus

Nessus is a comprehensive vulnerability scanner and analyzer, which is estimated to be used by more than 75,000 organizations. The core of Nessus is *nessusd*, the Nessus daemon, which performs the actual scanning. nessusd provides a web-based management interface.

Nessus begins by performing a port scan with its own internal port scanner (or it can optionally use nmap) to determine which ports are open on the target and then tries various exploits on the open ports. The vulnerability tests, available as a large body of plug-ins, are written in Nessus Attack Scripting Language (NASL), a scripting language optimized for custom network interaction.

Optionally, the results of the scan can be reported in various formats, such as plain text, XML, HTML, and LaTeX. The results can also be saved in a knowledge base for reference against future vulnerability scans. Scanning can be automated through the use of a command-line client by using the nessus command located in the /Library/Nessus/run/bin folder.

If the user chooses to do so (by disabling the option safe checks), some of Nessus's vulnerability tests may try to cause vulnerable services or operating systems to crash. This lets a user test the resistance of a device before putting it in production.

Nessus provides additional functionality beyond testing for known network vulnerabilities. For instance, it can use Windows credentials to examine patch levels on computers running the Windows operating system and can perform password auditing.

Installing Nessus

To install Nessus, go to the Tenable Network Security web site at www.nessus.org, and download the Nessus installer. You'll also need to register for a subscription. All of the audits performed by Nessus are coded as plug-ins. In order to download plug-ins, you'll need to register for either the HomeFeed or the ProfessionalFeed. The HomeFeed is free, but can only be used by home users. If you're planning on using Nessus for professional or government use, you'll need to purchase the ProfessionalFeed. When you register for a feed, an activation code will be emailed to you.

> **NOTE:** An older version of nessus that does not require a registration key is available via MacPorts.

During the install, it gives you the option to choose whether you want the server to start when the system boots or whether you want to start it manually. If the system is a dedicated Nessus server, then you will want the Nessus daemon to launch at boot. Otherwise, it's better to launch manually as needed, especially if Nessus is installed on a laptop (it can be a sizeable resource hog).

After installation, launch the Nessus Server Manager application, enter your activation code and click Register. Once your copy of Nessus is registered, you'll be able to start the Nessus Server (see Figure 17-3).

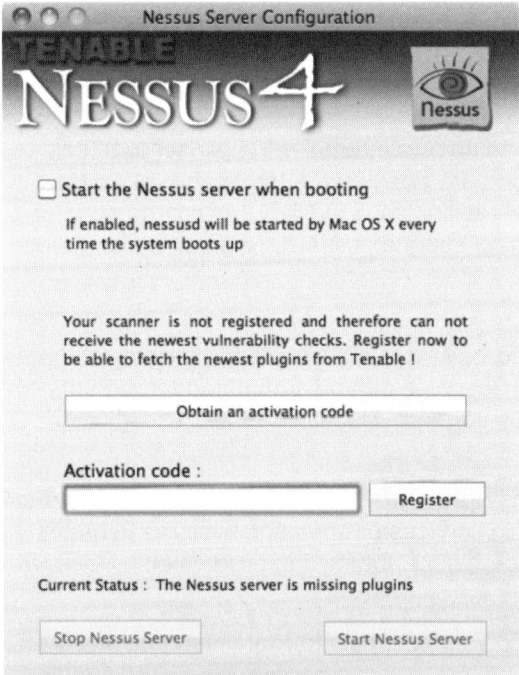

Figure 17-3. *Starting the Nessus server*

Before you can log into Nessus, you'll have to create a user. In the Nessus Server Manager, click on Manage Users, and add a user. Now, open a web browser and go to http://localhost:8834 (double-click on the Nessus Client.url that was installed with the

Server Manager). Log into the client with the user account you just created, and you will see the Reports view. Because we haven't scanned anything yet, there aren't any reports to view.

In order to scan a target, you'll need to define a *policy*. A scanning policy defines options like types of scan and range of ports to use, and also which plug-ins to use. Each plug-in typically corresponds to a specific vulnerability. Enabling fewer plug-ins will speed up scans, since the scanner will not take the time to perform disabled probes. For example, if you're scanning a Mac OS X Server system, you can probably disable the Cisco plug-in family.

> **NOTE:** Care should be taken with disabling plug-ins. If you disable a scan for a vulnerability that actually exists on one of your systems you could inadvertently leave an exploitable vulnerability on your system.

To define a policy, click on Policies, and then click Add. Under General, give your policy a name and select your scanning options. The Credentials tab lets you enter user credentials for the system to be scanned. Nessus will use those credentials to check for vulnerabilities that can be exploited by valid users. The Plug-ins tab is where you can enable or disable the plug-ins, and the Preferences tab lets you configure some options for enabled plugins. See Figure 17–4.

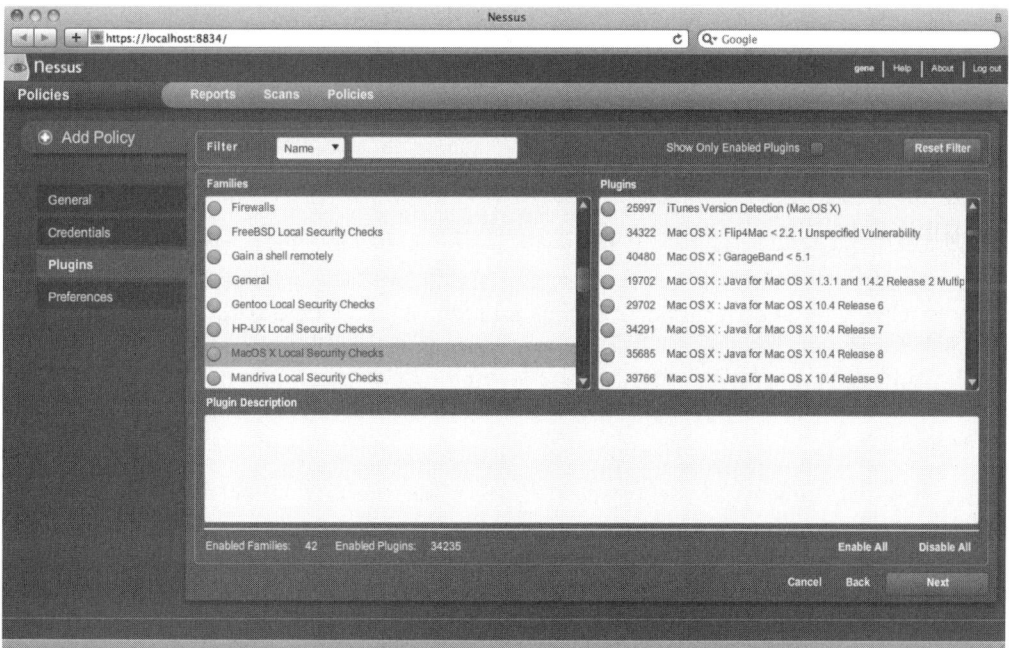

Figure 17–4. *Defining a policy*

Once you have defined a policy, you can create a scan and select your targets. There are multiple options for defining a target (see Figure 17-5). These options can give security auditors a more granular approach to scanning. You can scan a single host, and range of IP addresses, a subnet with CIDR notation, or a fully-qualified domain name. You can also import a text file containing a list of hosts defined in the same fashion.

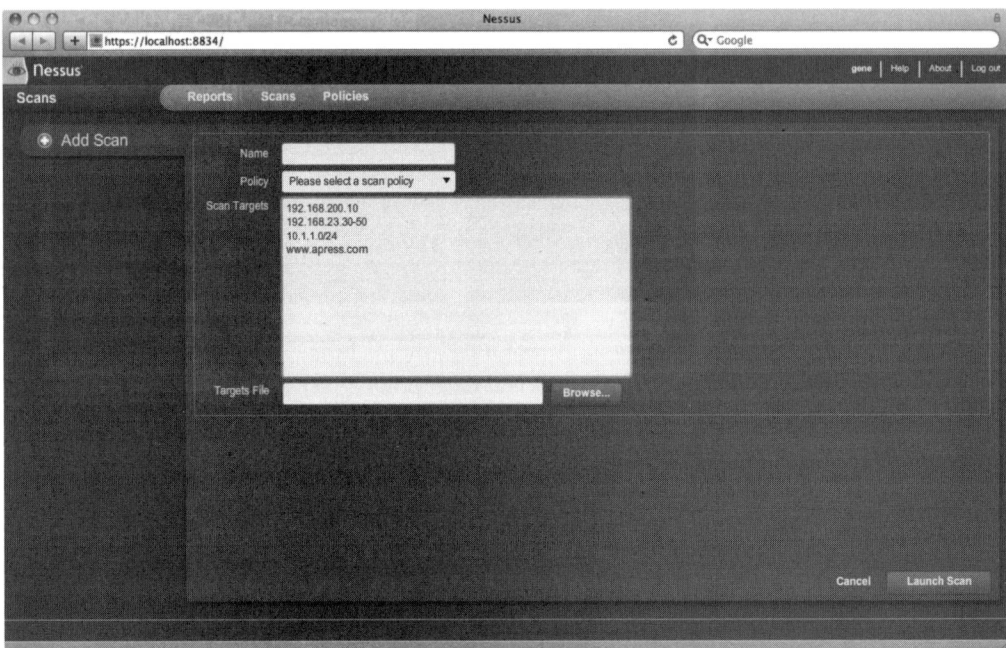

Figure 17-5. *Defining your targets*

Running a Scan

Once you have selected the appropriate plug-ins and options, it is time to scan your systems. Give your scan a name, and click Launch Scan. Once the scan is finished, you can click the Report tab to view the vulnerabilities available for your system (see Figure 17-6). Clicking on a scanned host will show you the open ports and running services. Clicking on a service will show you more details about the vulnerability as well as possible exploits.

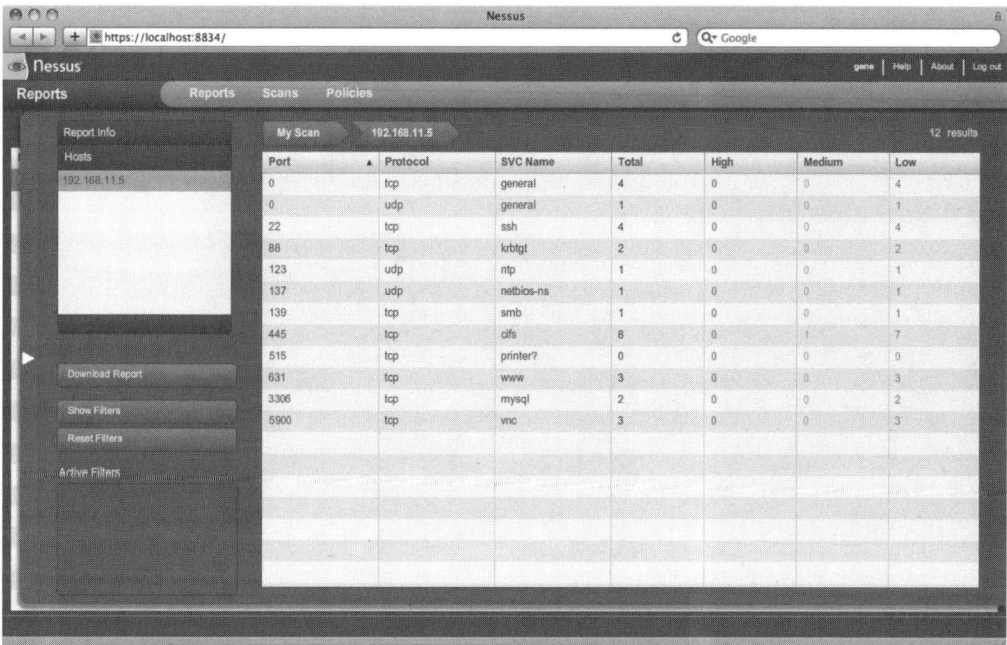

Figure 17–6. *Reviewing the Nessus report*

You can export Nessus reports into HTML to make reviewing and saving them easy. There are companies that specialize in running automated scans of servers on behalf of institutions, such as credit card processors and insurance companies. These companies often simply rebrand a Nessus scan by replacing the images in the HTML exports. To export a scan, click the Export button in your report.

Metasploit

Metasploit is a free, open source framework that can be used to launch automated exploits to target known vulnerabilities. The Metasploit framework makes it easy for administrators to use these exploits to discover how vulnerable their network is.

You can download the latest version of Metasploit at www.metasploit.com. Download the Unix Tar format, uncompress it, and copy the msf3 folder to the location where you'd like it to reside. For this example, we'll copy it to the /Applications folder and rename the folder to Metasploit. Open Terminal and cd into the /Applications/Metasploit folder. From within the Metasploit folder, run the command ./msfconsole, which puts you at the msf > prompt, as shown in Figure 17–7.

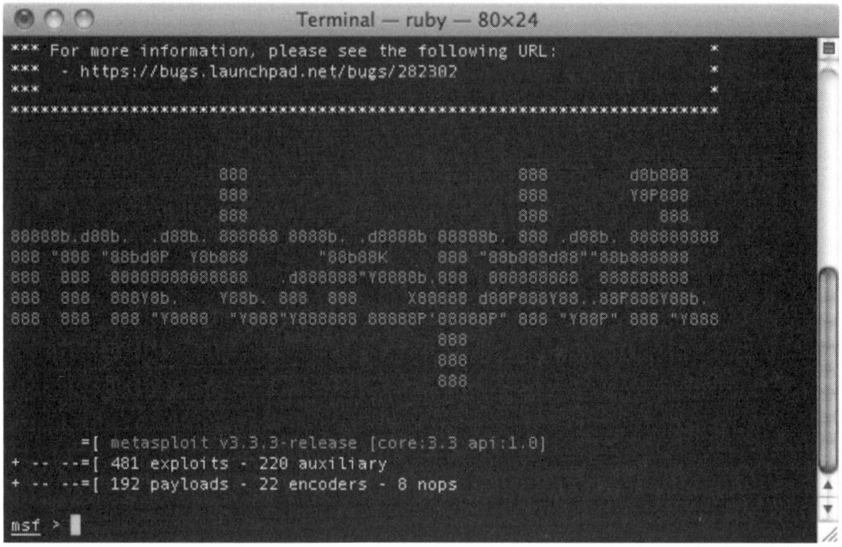

Figure 17–7. *Metasploit opening screen*

At the `msf>` prompt, you have a variety of commands that can be run. To access more detailed information for each command, see the help section of Metasploit. Commands include the following:

`cd`: Changes the working directory (much like the bash shell).

`exit` and `quit`: Exits the `msf` console.

`info`: Obtains detailed information about the exploit or payload that you are running.

`reload`: Reloads the exploits and payloads you have chosen.

`save`: Saves your configuration to `~/.msf3/config`.

`setg`: Sets the global variables of Metasploit, including logging, nops, debug level, and alternate exit.

`show`: Shows the exploits, payloads, encoders, and nops available to the `msfconsole` (for example, `show exploits` or `show payloads`).

`unsetg`: Clears the environmental variables set using the `setg` command.

`version`: Shows the version of the `msfconsole` being used.

`use`: Sets the exploit to be used.

Once you have set an exploit, you can type `show payloads` to see the available payloads for the exploit you will be running. You will also need to set an rhost and an lhost before launching an exploit. The rhost is the target, and the lhost is the IP address that Metasploit will tell packets used in the exploit to return to. To set an rhost, you use the `set rhost` command followed by the IP address of the target system, as shown here with a target of 10.10.10.2:

```
set rhost 10.10.10.2
```

To set an lhost of 10.10.10.203, you would use the following command:

```
set lhost 10.10.10.203
```

Once you have set your IP addresses, it is time to set the *exploit*, the vulnerability you'll by trying to take advantage of. One you've chosen an exploit, you'll need to choose a *payload*, which is the action that will be taken if the exploit succeeds. There are a wide variety of exploits and payloads available for Mac OS X. Once you've chosen an exploit, the `show payloads` command will show you what payloads are available with the current exploit.

You'll need to consider your target system carefully when choosing exploits and payloads. Each exploit and payload has a specific list of available targets, which are operating system or software versions that are vulnerable to this weakness. To see which targets are available for the payload that you have chosen, type **show targets**. This will open a screen of targets that can be used to exploit a system. Next, type **set** followed by the target number you select, for example, **set target 0**.

Once the payload, exploit, target, and hosts have been set, it is time to launch your first exploit. Enter the command `show options` to review your settings, and make sure everything is set as intended. If it is, run the `exploit` command to run your chosen exploit.

SAINT

SAINT, or Security Administrator's Integrated Network Tool, is a vulnerability scanner much like Nessus. SAINT prepares reports detailing the extent and seriousness of these weaknesses and provides links to fixes and recommended security procedures for these vulnerabilities. SAINT is licensed based on the number of hosts you'd like to scan.

Installation

Download the installer from www.saintcorporation.com, uncompress it, and move it to the folder in which you'd like SAINT installed. The SAINT installer launches Terminal and guides you through the installation process, which will create a saint-x.x (x.x being the current version of SAINT) folder in place of the installer. You will also have the option to create a launcher in the Applications folder.

The SAINT launcher will start up Terminal and prompt you to authenticate, and then open the SAINT interface in your default web browser. To use SAINT, the user needs to know only the IP ranges of the machines to scan. SAINT provides six levels of scanning intensity, allowing for long and involved scans or quick checks. Scan results can be viewed in real time, and all scan data is conveniently saved into an internal database that is stored between sessions. Scans can even be scheduled for a specific date, or at regular intervals, and through the use of OS X's cron daemon, the scans will run in the background with no user interaction required.

SAINT's scan covers a staggering number of vulnerabilities, ranging from warnings about open shares or writable directories to more critical problems such as services with known buffer overflows. SAINT's comprehensive scan uses the Common Vulnerabilities and Exposures (http://cve.mitre.org/) database to provide detailed information and updates on each vulnerability. SAINT releases updates regularly to keep SAINT's scanning abilities up to speed.

SAINT's reports are professional and comprehensive. SAINT supports six types of reports with varying detail, allowing for everything from a quick overview to detailed technical summaries. For more information on vulnerabilities, SAINT provides automated links to Common Vulnerabilities and Exposures (CVE) bulletins. CVE is a standardized list of vulnerabilities that many different security vendors reference.

Summary

If you want to keep your network and your systems secure, you should be mindful of the methods that potential intruders use and be aware of the attack vectors they will try to use. Take the time to understand the methods that attackers use and apply their techniques to your network, and you'll be better prepared to defend yourself from them.

Chapter 18

Backup and Fault Tolerance

"Stop hackers dead in their tracks by securing your systems and network." That has been our mantra up to this point. However, there is another piece in the security pie that often goes unexamined. Any conversation about security on a system or network must go beyond discussing the prevention of unauthorized access and into backup, because the capacity to recover data minimizes the potential impact of an attack. Securing the data on these systems with a reliable data backup scheme is a crucial element in any security framework.

As digital assets become increasingly valuable, organizations are becoming more and more reliant on their data. Many companies have invested large amounts of labor in building their company data. If they were to suffer a catastrophic loss of data (for some this could mean as little as 30%), due to the number of hours it would take to re-create that data, it would prove impossible to rebuild, and would simply cause them to go out of business. Therefore, backing up data is very important in any security footprint and critical in any organization.

When developing a backup schematic, you should answer some important questions that start with the following(there are more but this is a good start):

- What is the source data to be backed up?
- To what destination device is the data to be backed up?
- How far back in time will the backups need to go?

As we move through this chapter, we will examine how backups are performed for a variety of software packages. We will start by discussing the most simplistic backup topology and work our way up to more complicated backup schemas, including fault-tolerant solutions. This will allow you to see the increasing complexity and weigh it against your needs to eventually choose which is best for you. Once you have a backup solution that you trust, you should continue to refer to this chapter, because as your needs increase, so will the complexity of your backup topology. Backing up a computer is nothing more than a waste of time and equipment, right up until the time when it becomes critical to restore the data. Readers should get into the habit of testing their restoration process (and should document it if it's at all difficult) so that when the time comes, they know they can rely on their backups.

Time Machine

Time Machine is an application introduced in Mac OS X Leopard that allows you to back up your computer to a second hard drive at set regular intervals. Time Machine is a straightforward application that is simple to configure. However, it is a new feature of OS X and is fairly limited in its granularity and flexibility. The good thing is that Time Machine is installed by default on every new Mac, so you don't need to purchase any additional software. To set up disk-based backups using Time Machine, open the Time Machine Preference pane (see Figure 18–1).

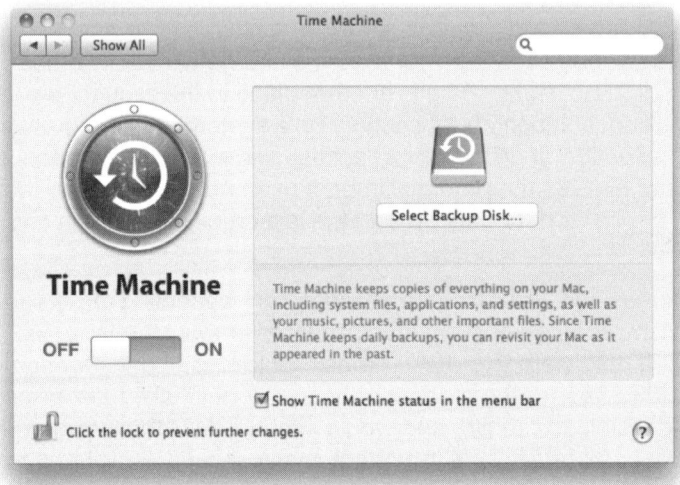

Figure 18–1. *Time Machine preference pane*

Next, select the target device for your backups. This is where the data that is backed up on your computers is stored. To do so, click on the Select Backup Disk... button and then select the device you want to backup to. Once you are satisfied with your selection click the Choose Backup Disk button (see Figure 18–2).

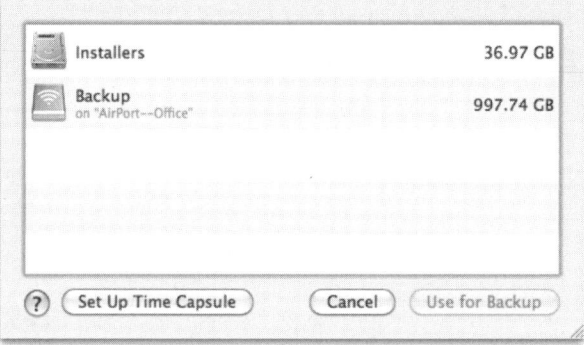

Figure 18-2. *Choosing the backup device*

Once you have selected the target disk, the screen will change to reflect the critical statistics of your backup operations (see Figure 18–3). Here you will see the volume you are backing up to, how much available free space is on that volume, the date and time of both the oldest and most recent backups, and when the next backup is scheduled. For many smaller backup environments, this information is the most crucial to track.

NOTE: Knowing which volume you are backing up to means that you know where additional copies of your data are. Sure this increases availability, but the backed up file now needs the same protection from theft and tampering that you applied to the "master" version. This is an important (and to many people, surprising) point: adding security countermeasures doesn't make a system more secure, it makes it differently secure. You have to consider risks affecting those countermeasures, which wasn't the case before they were deployed.

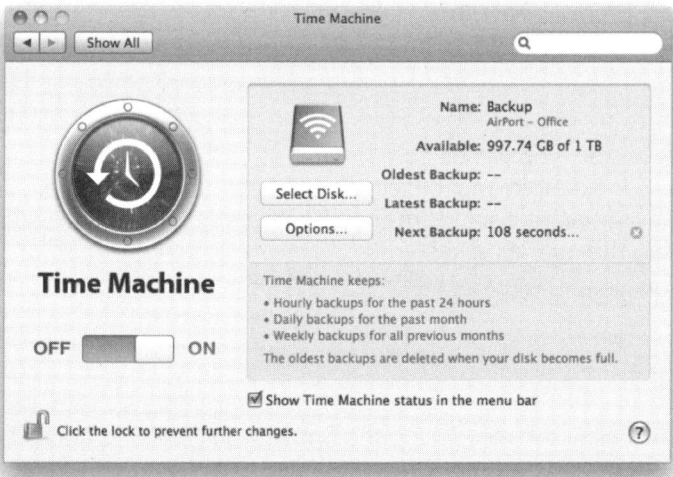

Figure 18-3. *Time Machine configured*

On this screen, you can also click the Select Disk button at any time to change the destination of your backups. This will allow you to fill up a disk and then move to the next disk in your backup scheme. Multiple disks can give you a deep historical backup set of your data, which is crucial if collecting multiple versions of files is important to your backup strategy.

NOTE: Unfortunately the Time Machine workflow doesn't really support recovery from multiple disks, so different versions of files will end up strewn across the disks with no central catalogue to tie them together.

You can also set what data on your computer will not be backed up. By default, Time Machine will back up all the data on your computer's hard drive. To limit what is backed up, click the Options button, and you will be presented with the "Exclude these items from backup" window (Figure 18–4). Here you can specify which items are to be excluded from the backup sets.

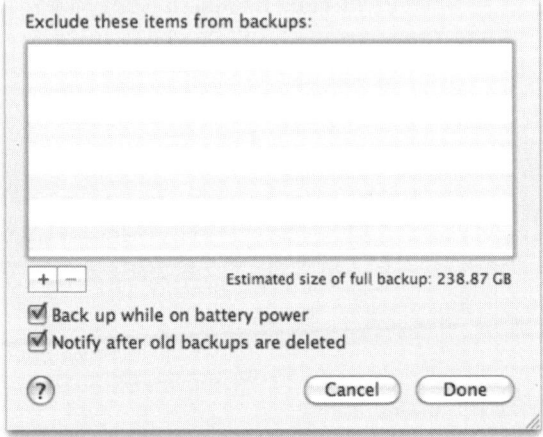

Figure 18–4. *Time Machine device exclusions*

Next, if you click the plus (+) button, you will be able to browse to folders that are not worth the space to back up. For example, most users do not need to back up the following directories unless they plan to do a "bare-metal" restore (a restore from a hard drive crash without reinstalling the operating system):

- /Applications
- /Library
- /System

Invisible items (which are accessible by unchecking the Show Invisible Items check box) include the following:

- /.TemporaryItems

- /.Spotlight-V100
- /.Trashes
- /bin
- /opt
- /private
- /sbin
- /var
- /Network

> **NOTE:** To view the files that are not backed up by default, check the information listed in the file /System/Library/CoreServices/backupd.bundle/Resources/StdExclusions.plist.

Which data are backed up is really dictated by your personal backup strategy. Some feel comfortable backing up the whole machine. For others, just backing up the /Users folder is sufficient because that is where the bulk of the irreplaceable data is stored.

> **NOTE:** If you have been following along with the other chapters, you will now have a heavily modified OS configuration. Having a strategy to replace your chosen configuration and application set is a fundamental aspect of reactive security, and backing the whole lot up with Time Machine is one way to achieve that.

Once you have selected all the items you are going to exclude, click the Exclude button (Figure 18–5), and the initial setup of your backup system will be complete. Time Machine will then run an incremental backup (backups of any files that have changed since the last backup) once an hour, every hour. According to how much data you have, the data can fill up your backup drive rather quickly, because every change to a file, big or small, will cause it to be copied to the Time Machine destination again. For this reason, we suggest Entourage databases not be backed up in Windows Exchange or IMAP environments where a database is backed up elsewhere, as is the case with many corporate environments. We also suggest reviewing the larger files on your systems and deciding whether you need to back them up. If they are changed often, then you will more than likely want to back them up, but educating yourself about the files that you are backing up can often be an eye-opener for you. Virtual machines are a good example. Choose whether to back up the virtual disk file (which is many gigabytes big and frequently changes), or run an incremental backup of the VM's filesystem from within the VM. Also, you should strongly consider investing in a rather large hard drive, 500GB at the minimum, but we often see 2TB drives as a good size for backups if you want historical backups of your data. If malware infected your system three hours ago and your only recovery option is a backup from one hour ago, then you can only recover to an infected configuration.

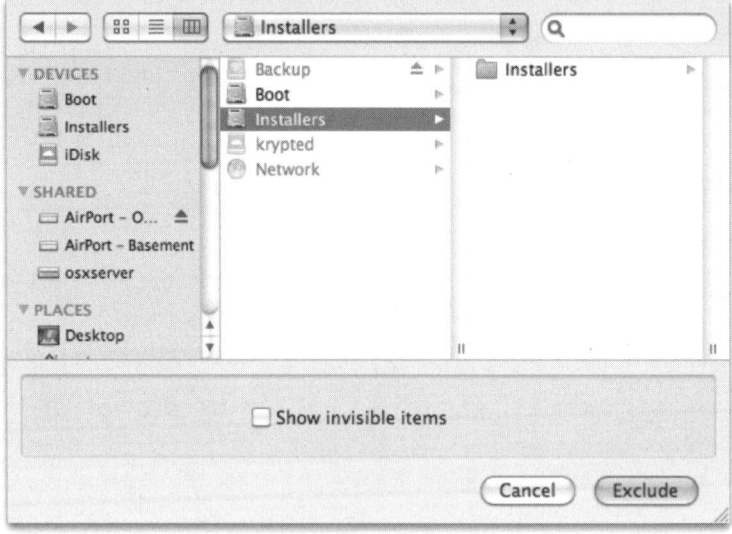

Figure 18–5. *Excluding Directories with Time Machine*

You can also disable Time Machine backups altogether. To do so, click the Time Machine preference pane, and use the slider to move the backup status to the Off position (see Figure 18–6).

Figure 18–6. *Turning Time Machine on or off*

Restoring Files from Time Machine

To restore files from Time Machine backups, open Time Machine from the /Applications folder. When the Time Machine restoration utility opens, use the timeline on the right side of the screen to select the restore point you are going to restore to (see Figure 18–7). Next, browse to the file or folder you want to restore, and click the Restore button.

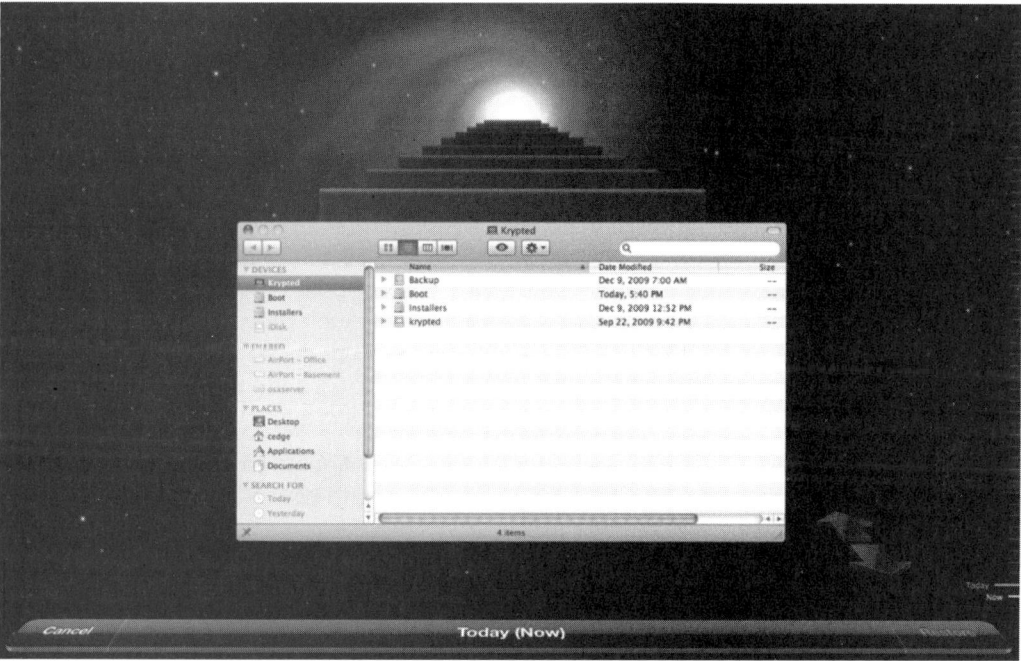

Figure 18–7. *Time Machine Restore screen*

You can also see the files that were backed up and restore files by browsing to the `Backups.backupdb` directory located on your target drive. Inside this directory, you will see a folder containing your computer's name. If you are backing up multiple computers to a single device, you will see multiple computer names in this directory. If you open these folders, you will see the date on which a backup was run and the files that were backed up at the time.

> **NOTE:** Backing up multiple systems to the same device is putting all of your eggs in the same basket. Hard drives are cheap, but your data probably isn't.

Using a Network Volume for Time Machine

Time Machine is capable of performing backups over the network. These backups can be saved to a disk attached to an AirPort device using AirPort disk sharing, an AFP volume hosted by a Mac OS X Server, or any other volumes to which your computer has access. To allow backups over a network volume, make sure the network volume is mounted, and simply select the network volume from the Change Disk menu option in the Time Machine configuration page, as mentioned earlier.

Apple officially supports using Time Capsule and Mac OS X Server share points with the Time Machine checkbox enabled for network backups only. However, if you want to use an unsupported network disk type for your Time Machine archives, such as a different type of server or a NAS appliance, running the following command on workstations will allow you to do so:

```
defaults write com.apple.systempreferences TMShowUnsupportedNetworkVolumes 1
```

SuperDuper

One of the easiest-to-use and most versatile third-party backup programs available for the Mac platform is SuperDuper, an application developed by David Nanian and available from www.shirt-pocket.com/SuperDuper. SuperDuper is more flexible than Time Machine and has more features. If you're willing to plunk down $30 for the software, you'll be given the extra ability to write custom backup scripts, schedule backups, and use sandboxing (a highly useful utility that backs the system up to a separate volume that can be used to boot the machine if it crashes).

After you've downloaded and installed SuperDuper, a configuration window opens that allows you to configure what data should be backed up and where it should be backed up to (see Figure 18–8).

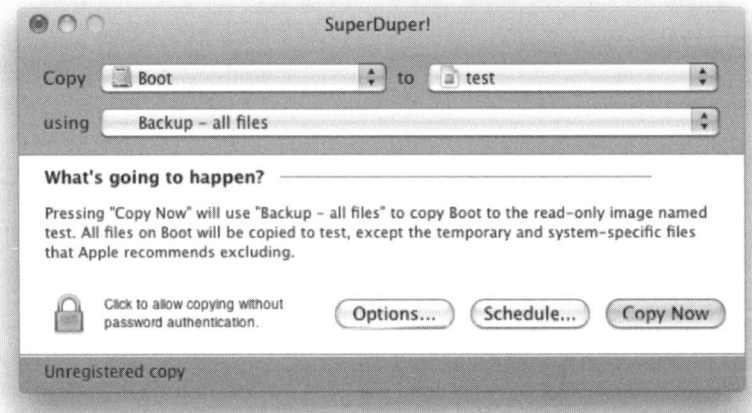

Figure 18–8. *The SuperDuper configuration window*

Using the default options will back up the entire hard drive. However, you may choose to back up only the /Users folder if you're not concerned with having to rebuild the operating system if the machine crashes, or if you don't fear an attack that might threaten the integrity of the operating system (see Figure 18–9).

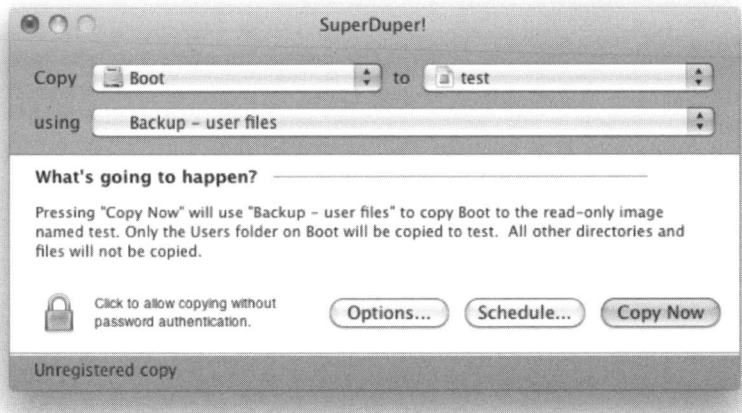

Figure 18-9. *Backing up all files with SuperDuper*

You can use SuperDuper to back up your computer to an image file. You can also store multiple image files on one hard drive for historical backups, or back up multiple computers to one drive. To make this organized and clean, you can also back up multiple computers to one drive by partitioning the drive that the backups will reside on and dedicating a partition to each user's backup.

Backing Up to MobileMe

Another easy way to back up your Mac is by using a MobileMe (formerly called .Mac) account. Because MobileMe has become an integral part of the Mac operating system, it's highly likely that if you own a Mac, you either own a MobileMe account or at a minimum know what one is. Apple sells MobileMe accounts to give Mac users space on Apple servers to access their files, websites, and e-mail from remote locations, and with BackToMyMac, MobileMe can also now be used to access your computer from another Mac OS X computer. The MobileMe accounts can also be a great way to back up and store a small amount of critical data in an offsite location.

If you haven't set your computer to log into MobileMe, then you will need to do that before you can back up, or *sync*, any of your data to Apple's servers. To configure your computer to work with a MobileMe account, go to the sign-in screen in the MobileMe Preference pane, as shown in Figure 18-10. In this screen, enter your MobileMe username and password, and click the Sign In button. If you don't yet have a MobileMe account, you can click the Learn More button to obtain one.

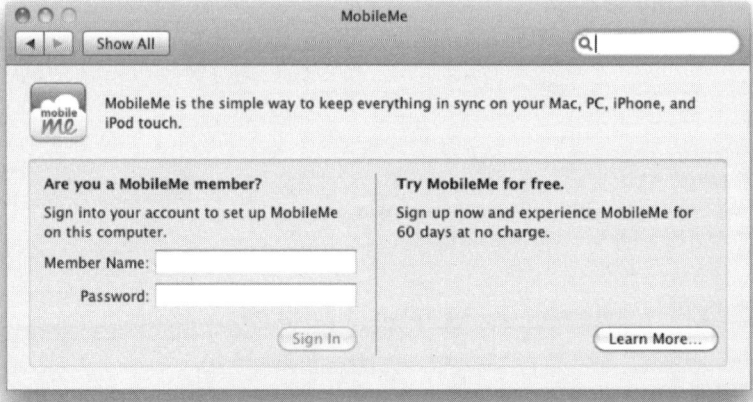

Figure 18–10. *MobileMe sign-in screen*

As you can see in Figure 18–11, once you are logged in you can see the amount of storage that you have available on your iDisk, which is typically ample for backing up the types of data that MobileMe is best used for.

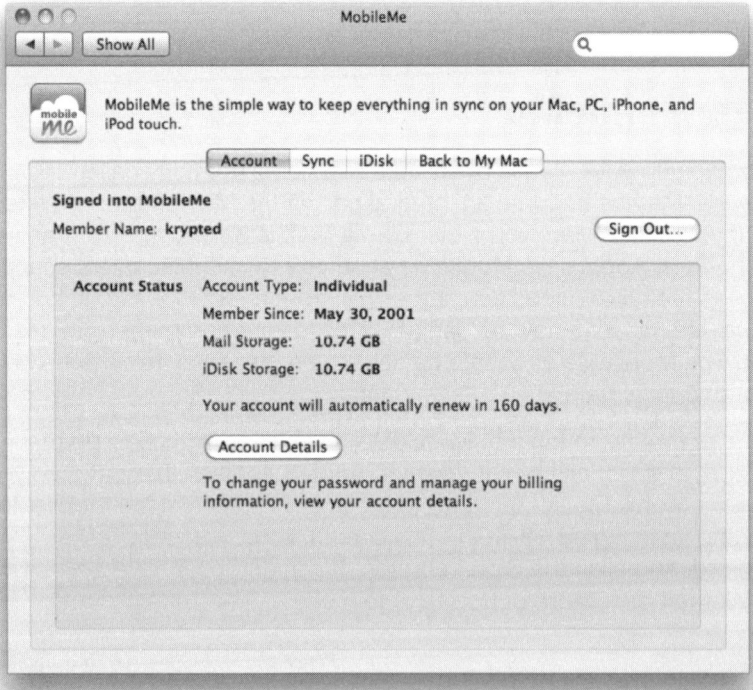

Figure 18–11. *MobileMe Account Overview*

Once you have configured your computer to talk to your MobileMe account, you can then configure it to sync information with the account. Using the Sync tab of the MobileMe System Preference pane, you will be given a list of preconfigured locations where your Mac thinks you may have pertinent data to sync, as shown in Figure 18–12. Items such as Dashboard Widgets Dock Items and Preferences are probably not necessary to back up, because they are easily re-created (additional drive space on a MobileMe is a bit pricey, so discretion is necessary).

Figure 18–12. *MobileMe sync preferences*

Once you are satisfied with what you are going to sync, you will need to instruct the system as to when this information should be synchronized. Click the Synchronize with MobileMe drop-down box next to Manually to display the various options for scheduling (see Figure 18–13). Here you will be able to tell the system to sync Automatically (when changes are made), Every Hour, Every Day, or Every Week. As faulty humans, we tend to forget to manually sync data, so we recommend that you have it sync automatically.

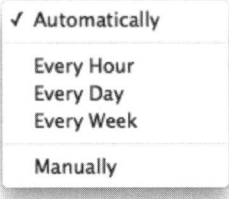

Figure 18–13. *Manually syncing the MobileMe account*

Once you have set the time interval to sync, click the Advanced button. This will show you the computers that you have authenticated to synchronize with your MobileMe account. You can remove a system from the list using the Unregister button, clear out what is currently stored on the MobileMe servers by using the Reset Sync Data button, or just check the last time that any systems were synchronized (see Figure 18–14).

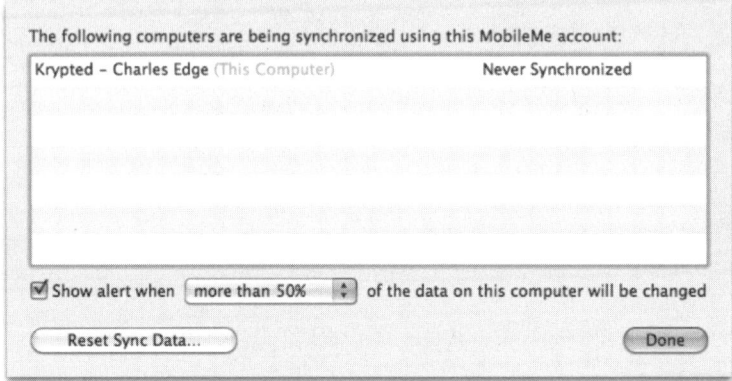

Figure 18–14. *Computers synchronized with MobileMe*

Conversely, backing up your iDisk data to your computer allows you to access your iDisk data locally. This can be useful if the MobileMe connection is lost, and you're finding that it takes an unusually long amount of time for Apple to restore it. This can also be useful if you want to work on data that is stored on your iDisk while your computer is offline. To set up iDisk to synchronize with your computer, click the MobileMe System Preference pane and click the iDisk tab (as shown in Figure 18–15). Then click the Start button in the iDisk Sync Sharing section of the screen. You can (and probably should) set the Update option to Automatically.

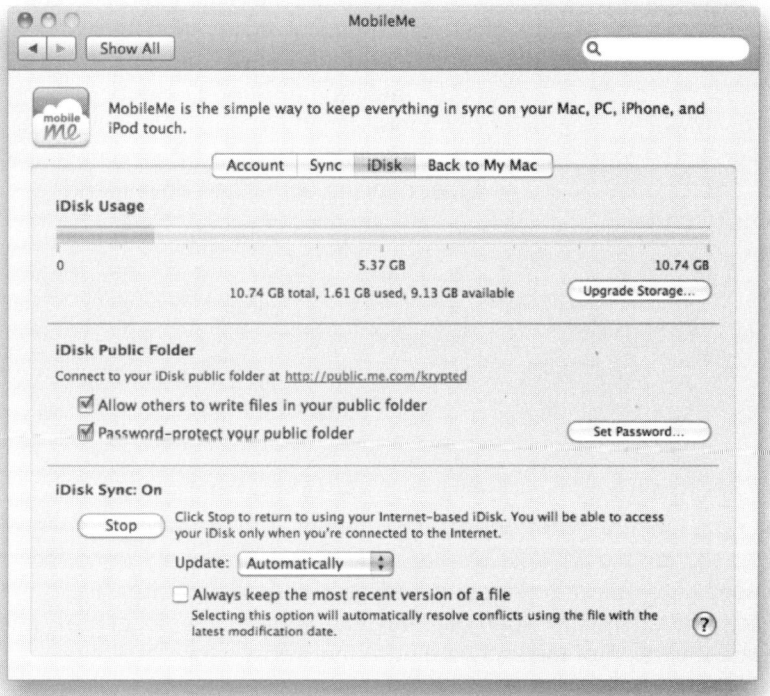

Figure 18-15. *Backing up with iDisk*

Unless you are looking to distribute files from it, it would be wise to change the permissions that others have to access your iDisk public folder. You don't want this information falling into the hands of random intruders. To restrict access to your public folder, select the check box to password-protect your public folder, click the Set Password button, and then enter the password you want users to use to access your data if you do plan on sharing files. You should also select the Read Only option to let other users only read your iDisk content, and not edit it, from the iDisk.

> **NOTE:** You may want to obtain more storage with your .Mac account. The Upgrade Storage feature on the iDisk tab (shown in Figure 18-15) will allow you to do so. Apple routinely increases the levels of disk space provided, and your disk quota will automatically be upgraded to the level you purchased.

Retrospect

We initially discussed Time Machine to explain how to simply back up your Mac. For those who require a slightly more capable solution (albeit slightly different), we reviewed how to use SuperDuper. Then we explored using the MobileMe Sync feature to create an offsite copy of your most critical data. Now we'll move on to covering how to use a more powerful application altogether, called Retrospect, from EMC Insignia. At its most basic usage, Retrospect can perform any of the features that SuperDuper or Time Machine can perform. However, the power of a more advanced application such as Retrospect can also go far beyond this, backing up client computers on a network, moving data between computers based on type, backing up to tape drives, and performing many other features.

> **NOTE:** There was a time when backing up a system meant writing data to a tape using a Unix `tar` command. Backups needed to be scripted from the ground up using shell scripts. Assigning different values to blocks and troubleshooting `tar` issues were standard daily routines. Many of these tasks have been automated with current software. (That's not to say that backups don't still require troubleshooting, mind you.)

The first step to getting a functional Retrospect deployment is to purchase and install the application. To do so, you would first download the latest version of Retrospect from the EMC Insignia website at www.retrospect.com/supportupdates/updates. Even if you purchase the software in a retail outlet such as the Apple Store in your local area, it is still best to use the latest version of the software from the website for installation.

Once downloaded, the disk image will mount. Here you will see a collection of directories and the Install Retrospect Engine package. Retrospect 8 introduces the ability to run your backups on a dedicated computer and to manage those backups from any system that is running the Management Console; this means that the Management Console can run on your laptop or on your backup server. For the purpose of this example setup, we're going to run the Management Console on the same system as the Retrospect Engine (what the Management Console manages). To put the Management Console on your system, simply drag the folder from the disk image to the Applications alias in the disk image as you can see in Figure 18–16.

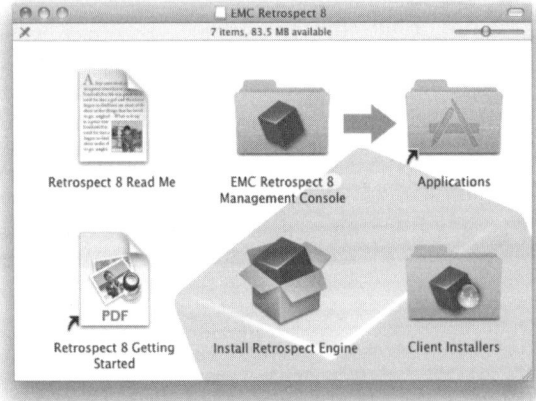

Figure 18–16. *The Retrospect Disk Image*

Once the copy is complete, double-click on the Install Retrospect Engine. This will bring up the Welcome to the Retrospect Installer screen. Click on the Continue button, agree to the Software License Agreement, and then click on the Continue button again. Next, you'll be presented with the Standard Install screen. Here, you can click on the Change Install Location… button to select a different drive to perform the installation on, as you can see in Figure 18–17.

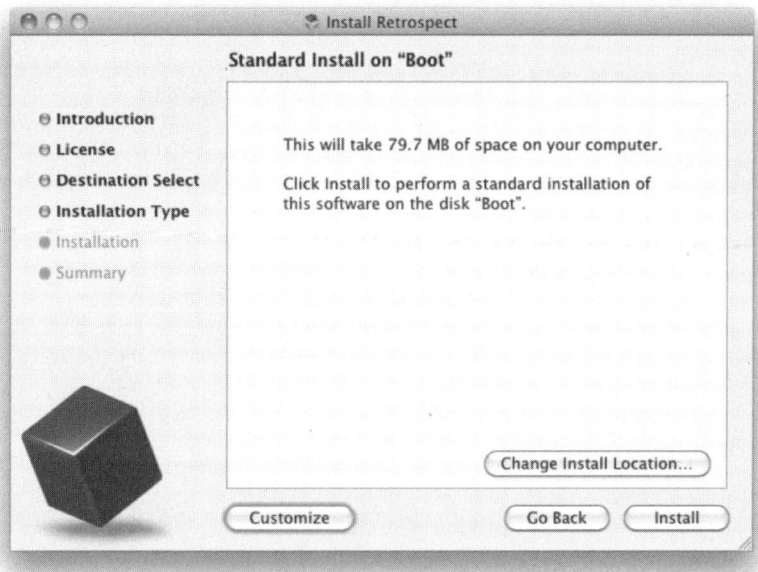

Figure 18–17. *Performing a standard installation*

Click on the Install button and the installation will complete. Provided that the installation is successful you will then click on the Close button to proceed with configuration of your first backup.

Configuring a Backup

Once you have installed Retrospect, you'll want to connect to your Retrospect Backup server. To do so, go into your /Applications directory and you will find the EMC Retrospect 8 directory. Within this directory will be the Retrospect application. Double-click on it to bring up the main Retrospect window, which you can see in Figure 18–18.

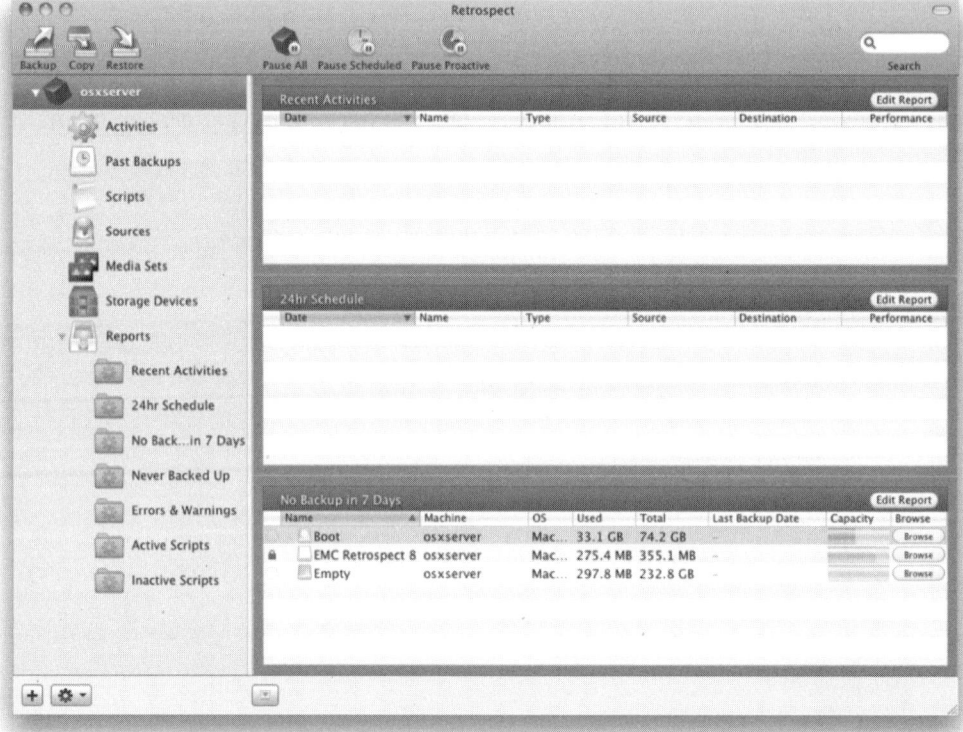

Figure 18–18. *Retrospect*

The quickest and easiest way to get backing up right away is to use the Backup, Copy, or Restore buttons in the Retrospect application toolbar. The Backup option will back up files and folders into files (essentially disk images), disks, network shares or tape media. The Copy function will copy data, uncompressed, to another location. The Restore option will allow you to restore data that was backed up using a Backup operation.

> **NOTE:** Retrospect provides more customization options once a job is created.

Let's go ahead and click on the Backup option in the Retrospect toolbar, which will bring up the Backup Assistant. At the Getting Started screen, simply click on the Continue button to bring up the Select Sources screen. Here you'll be able to choose which volumes on your system will be backed up and what files to back up. For the purpose of this example, we're going to backup all of the files on the server, but keep in mind that you have a plethora of options you can bring to the table with specific files and folders that you would like to skip. For example, you can skip certain folders, certain file types (such as MP3 or AAC files) and even skip directories based on the color codes of objects that have been labeled from the finder. Go ahead and select the backup drive (see Figure 18–19) and then click on the Continue button.

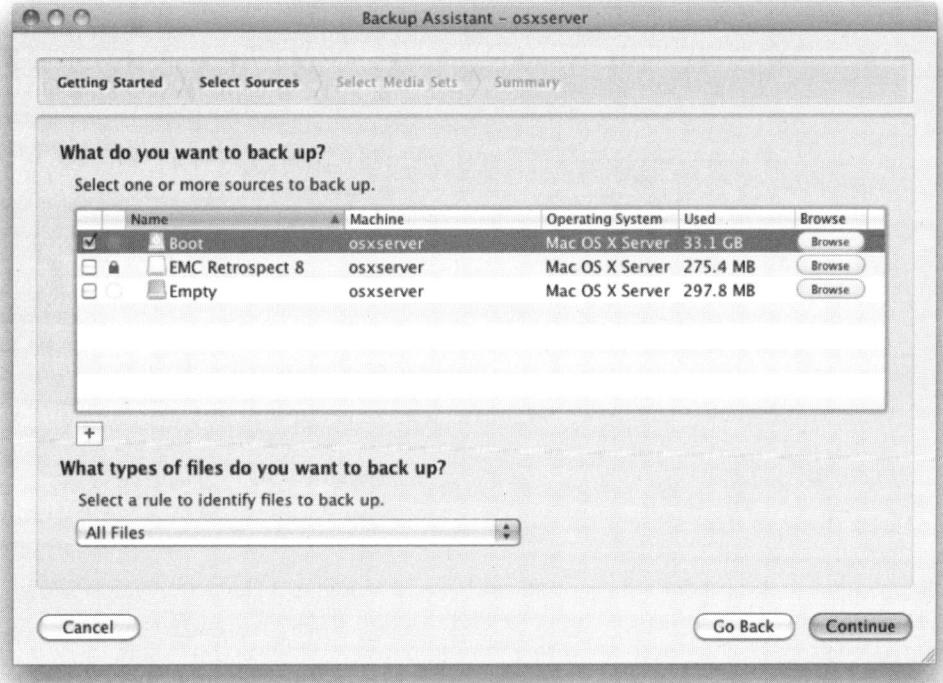

Figure 18–19. *Selecting sources in Retrospect's backup assistant*

The next screen will allow you to select a media set; however, if there are no media sets on the system yet, you will immediately see the Media Set creation screen. Here, you can provide the specifics to the target of your backup. Remember that backups can have a variety of destination types in Retrospect. Here, in the Media Set Type, you will have the option to select those from a list of Tape, Tape WORM, Disk, Optical, and File. Of these, the most common will be Tape, Disk (which assumes control of an entire volume), and File, which creates a disk image (or an encrypted disk image) as a backup destination. In the Media Set Name provide a name for the device (weekly offsite, Set A, daily recycle, and so on) as seen in Figure 18–20. Then choose a location for the Catalog files using the Catalog Location field.

> **TIP:** Don't forget to back up the catalog location as this will be needed during restores (although it can be rebuilt if needed, but it's not exactly a zippy process)!

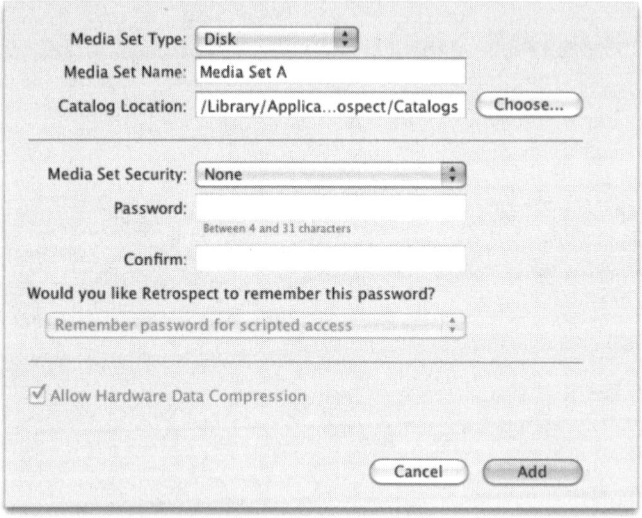

Figure 18-20. *Creating a Media Set*

Another option in the media set creation process is Media Set Security, which allows you to assign various encryption levels to your backup destinations. When using encryption with backups, there are a few things to keep in mind. The first is the password: DO NOT FORGET THE PASSWORD! Next, consider speed: each level of encryption will slow the backup process down. Finally, keep in mind that there are a number of full disk encryption products (including those by Check Point and PGP) that, if backing up to a disk, can do a great job encrypting data without the need to perform the encryption in the operating system. By using full disk encryption rather than the encryption engine from within Retrospect you can get great protection at a fraction of the performance cost.

Once you are satisfied with the choices for your media set, click on the Add button. You will then see the Add a new member screen. Figure 18-21 shows the "Add a new member" screen for a disk-based set. If you are using a tape-based set, then you will be able to add tapes as members and if you are using a file based set then you will be able to add files sourced in multiple locations as members. Backup sets in Retrospect are very useful, because they represent a logical consolidation of media. This means that you can leverage multiple locations for a resultant set of storage that logically appears in Retrospect as a single repository. This virtualization of the destination storage layer allows you to have a massive amount of storage on relatively inexpensive mediums.

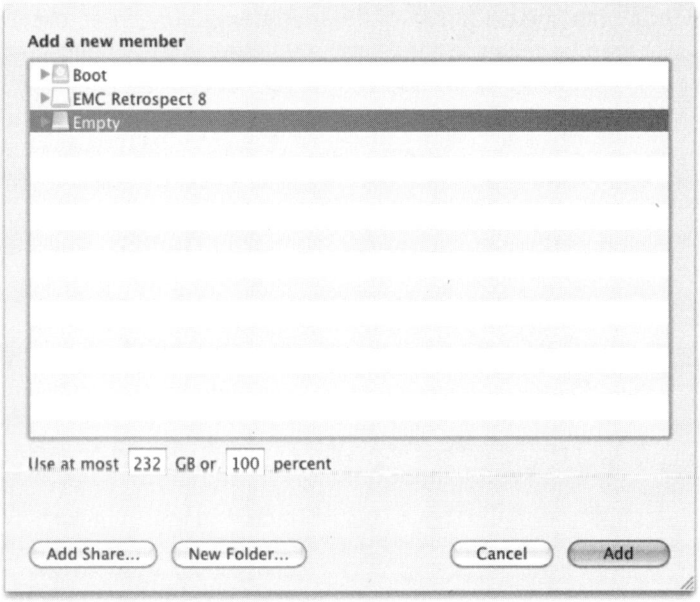

Figure 18–21. *Add a Member in Retrospect*

Once you have chosen the members of your set, click on Add and the assistant will take you to the screen where you can choose the set that you will back up to. Here, you can use the plus sign (+) to add more sets or the Add Member button to add members to an existing set, which you can see in Figure 18–22. By adding multiple sets you can have a rotation of media, as you might do if one set of media were to always remain offsite as an offsite backup component in your backup scheme.

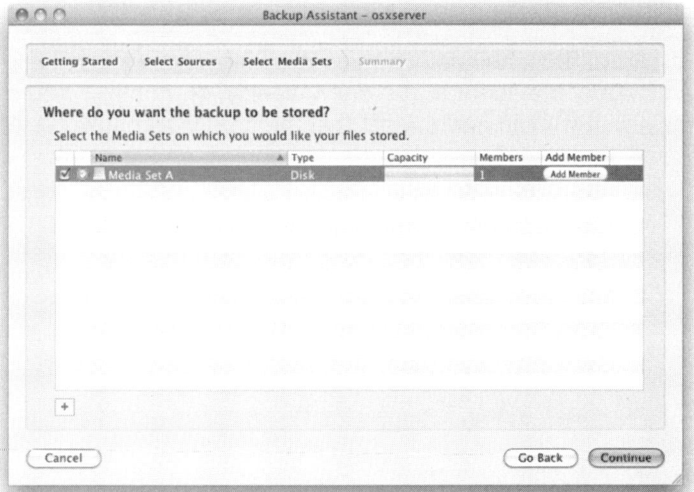

Figure 18–22. *Retrospect's Select Media Sets screen*

Once you have created all of your sets and added all of the members to each set, click on the Continue button. You will then be taken to the Summary screen. As you can see in Figure 18-23 you can start the backup script immediately if you so choose.

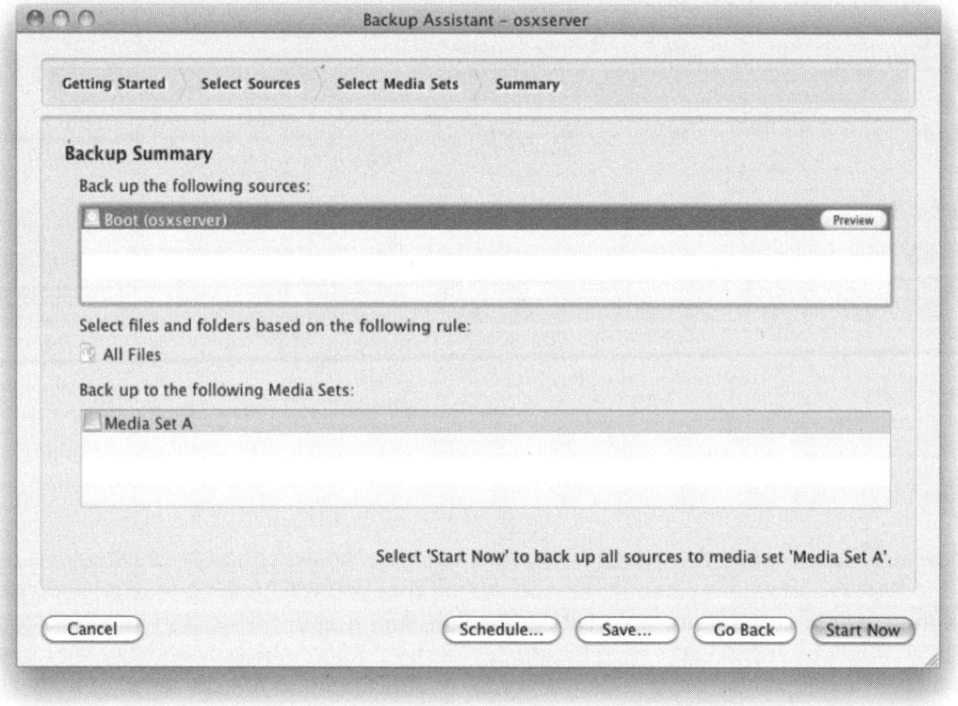

Figure 18-23. *The Backup Assistant summary screen*

Alternatively, you can also click on the Schedule… button to configure the script to run automatically. Here, you can instruct the script to run daily, weekly, or monthly. You can also choose the time that the script will run and the set that the script will back up to. As Figure 18-24 shows, there are a number of options in the schedules, and strategies behind the use of each one. For example, when automating the weekly rotation of backup drives or tapes you can use the Every field to select that a scheduled instance of a script run every two weeks. You can then create another scheduled instance of the same script for the other weeks. Each would have a different set, which would allow for the routine swapping out of drives.

Figure 18-24. *Scheduling a script in Retrospect*

Once you have scheduled your backups then it's time to consider *utility* scripts or *grooming* scripts to keep your backups running lean and mean.

Grooming Scripts

Retrospect backup scripts use snapshots. So as an example, if you were to do a backup without a recycle 20 times, then you have 20 snapshots. If you changed a 1GB file every day, then you'd have 20GB occupied by that one file. Now let's say that you groom away 10 of those backups by setting a grooming policy of 10. You'd now only have 10GB used by that file. So any file not required for the 10 last backups will be removed from the disk based backup set when the next grooming script runs. Any time you have sets that grow and you don't want to recycle them, you're going to want to use some kind of grooming script. And why wouldn't you want to recycle them? For the simple reason that, right after the recycle event, you'd have a potential point of failure where you wouldn't have a copy of your data. You're mitigating risk by having multiple sets with the same data.

One of the things consistent about Retrospect for Windows over the years is the ability to groom a backup set. Grooming is essentially taking the old data that doesn't need to be in the set and removing it, providing there's still a copy of the file still resident on the source. In the Scripts section you can add a Utility Script. In this case, we'll select Groom. You then check the box for each set you'd like to groom using this script and set a schedule. See Figure 18–25.

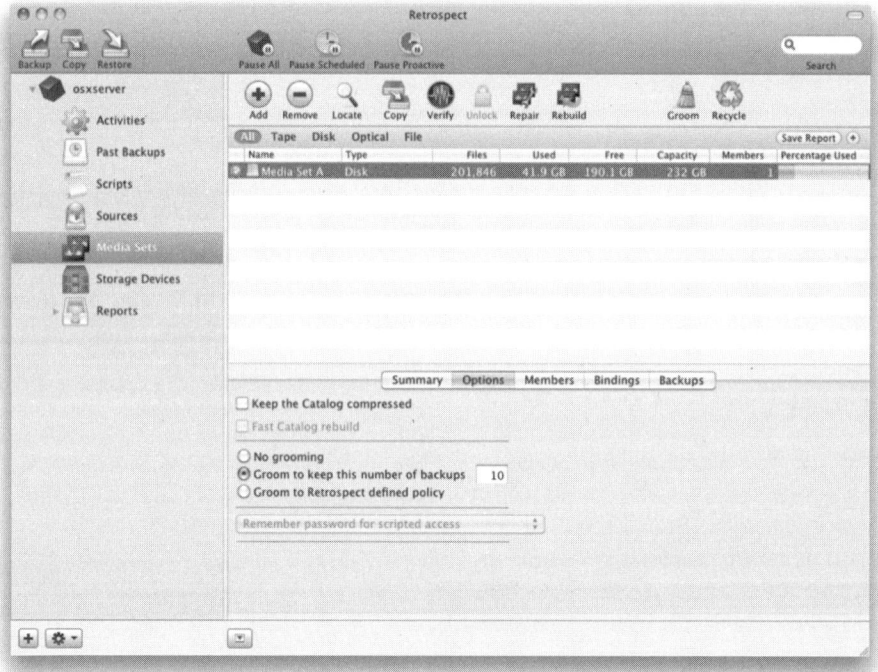

Figure 18–25. *Configuring Retrospect 8 grooming scripts*

Next, you'll want to go into your sets and configure a grooming policy. To do so, click on Media Sets and then click on the set you'd like to set a grooming policy for and then click on the Options set tab. Here (as you'll notice in Figure 18–25), you'll see an option for No grooming (the default) or the number of backups to keep.

By telling Retrospect to retain Retrospect 6 or 7 backups for a given set, you are eliminating the need to do an occasional recycle script, unless you'd like to continue to use the same script architecture you used in previous versions. You can also tell a given set to use the global grooming policy. Overall grooming is a requirement for modern backup software. If you haven't updated from previous versions of Retrospect, then his feature alone will cut down considerably on complexity and annoyance for many organizations that has plagued Mac admins over the past few years.

While grooming is nice, we'd be lying if we said it didn't have its drawbacks. Keep in mind that it has a history of causing corrupt catalog files in the Windows version of the software, an issue not as prevalent in the Mac OS X version of the software. So make sure to backup your catalog files. Also, be very careful stopping grooming scripts when they're running. This can cause corruption, and cause your catalogs to require a rebuild.

Also, if you've been doing file-based sets, then grooming scripts are not for you. Retrospect grooms disk-based sets, not file-based sets. Finally, don't groom across disks. Use grooming on sets that only take up one disk.

> **NOTE:** iWork 08 applications (Keynote, Numbers, Pages) and iLife 08 components including iPhoto, iTunes, Garage Band have a slight issue with Retrospect: their data files are not considered documents using the Documents Selector. Now in the case of iPhoto, iTunes, and Garage Band, this is probably a good thing. However, for Keynote, Numbers, and Pages, it's more than likely that if you're using these then you will want Retrospect to back them up. So if you are using selectors and you are using the Documents selector then checkGrooming Scripts out this Knowledgebase article from EMC/Dantz:
> http://kb.dantz.com/display/2n/articleDirect/index.asp?aid=9632&r=0.2114527

Utility Scripts

In Retrospect, utility scripts are scripts that manage backups. One great utility script in Retrospect 8 for Mac is the ability to copy a media set or a backup. This allows you to skip a step in a number of offsite rotation scripts or disk-to-disk-to-tape scenarios. This is especially useful, for example, when acquiring a recently groomed set of disk-based backups and sending them to tape in order to send them off to an offsite storage facility like Iron Mountain. To setup a copy in this fashion, simply open Retrospect and then click on the plus (+) sign in the lower left-hand corner of the window. At the new script dialog box, click on Copy Media Set. Then click on the Sources and Destinations tabs and select the source and target media sets. Finally, click on the Options tab and choose the options you want. These options include (see Figure 18–26):

- Copy Backups: Enables the copy of the backup set.
- Media Verification: Compares the source and target to verify they are the same.
- Data Compression: Enables compression in the software (disable when using tapes).
- Recycle Source Media Set after Successful Copy: Good option for disk to disk to tape environments where the source is a disk-based staging area.
- Don't Add Duplicate Files to the Media Set: Performs minimal de-duplication.
- Eject Tapes and Discs When Script is Complete: Eject the target media when the script has completed.

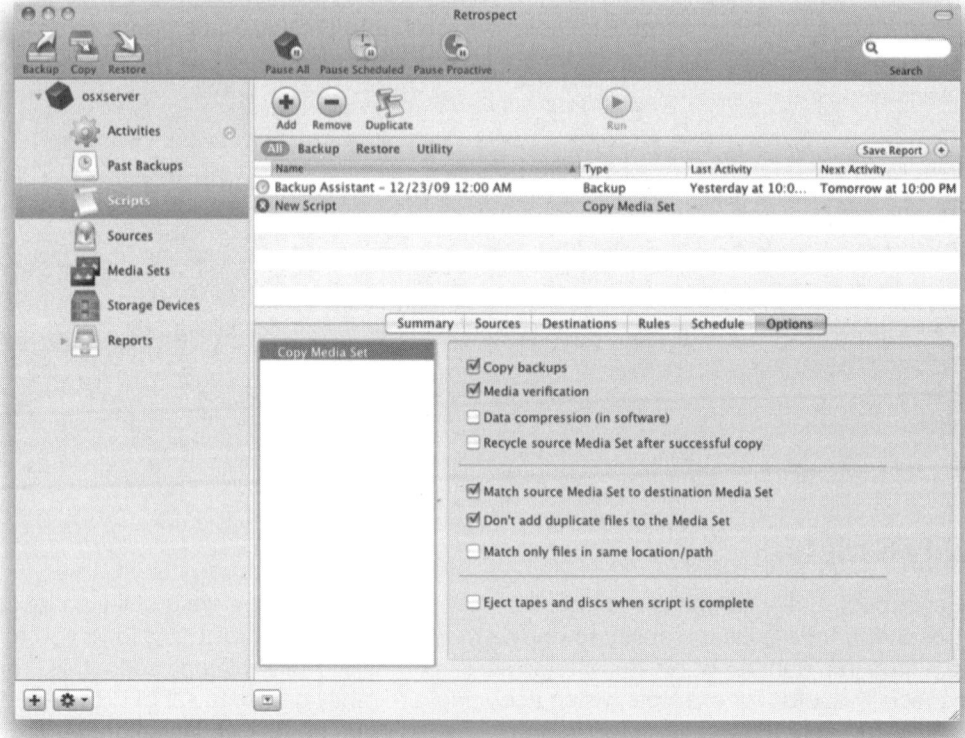

Figure 18-26. *Retrospect 8 for Mac Copy Media Set*

> **NOTE:** Media verification is the process whereby Retrospect reviews the source and destination to ensure the integrity of the data. You can also configure selectors. Selectors allow you to limit what will be backed up based on file type, labels, and other attributes.

Checking Your Retrospect Backups

Once you have configured and started your backups, then it is critical to review their performance. There are typically too many moving pieces to blindly trust that the backups are running as they should and actually backing up all your data in a restorable format.

Many organizations perform checks on their backups daily, weekly, or biweekly. Often, they will also perform a test restore monthly or quarterly. To keep staff (or yourself) from missing critical steps in the backup checking process, it is wise to use a checklist to make sure you don't miss a step in the process. A quick and easy checklist should include the following:

All backups executed successfully:

[ ] Yes

[ ] No

    If not, please identify cause(s):

        [ ] Destination full

        [ ] Source unavailable

        [ ] Error with backup software

        [ ] Operating system error

        [ ] Other: _____

Corrective action(s): _____

Free space for future backup(s): _____

Every environment will require a different level of need for how often to check backups. Some organizations choose to check their backups on a daily basis, while others will check weekly. No matter what, it is important to check the logs and make sure your systems are being backed up rather than trust that the software has you covered.

In addition to checking that the backups are occurring on schedule, it is also important to occasionally perform a restore just to make sure that the backups are not corrupt or incomplete. Some people choose to restore a folder or a randomly selected file, while others choose to restore an entire volume and check the contents to see whether all the required data has in fact been backed up as it should be. This is strongly suggested, especially if you are backing up to tape or to compressed disk images.

In Retrospect, you can check your backups by opening Retrospect and clicking on Past Backups. As you can see in Figure 18–27) you will then see a list of each backup instance that has been run. You can then perform a cursory scan for the number of files and the color indicating the status (green means success, anything else means "sorry buddy").

Figure 18-27. *Retrospect reports options*

Using Tape Libraries

Retrospect is a great application and fairly simple to use when backing up to a single tape drive with only a few tapes involved in your sets. There are other products that are designed from the ground up with tape libraries in mind. BRU by the Tolis Group, NetVault by Bakbone, PresStor by Archiware, and Time Navigator by Atempo are the primary applications currently used to provide more industrial-strength backups. They are used primarily to back up Xserve RAIDs and other larger volumes ranging from 2TB to 150TB.

A tape library will typically consist of one or more tape drives and a *hand* (also referred to as a *robot*) that is used to move tapes within the library, placing them in the tape drives Many libraries will also come outfitted with a bar-code scanner in order to quickly find assets within the library. Many tape libraries come with a dedicated slot that is meant to be used for housing a cleaning tape.

> **TIP:** Routinely cleaning your drives when they get dirty is critical to ensure that the drives will perform as needed.

Many of these applications will also allow you to "stage" your data onto disk. By staging data to a disk, it is possible to restore data more quickly. Your backups are also compartmentalized because they are being written to a much more efficient storage medium. For example, this could be a FireWire disk or a RAID. The name that many of these programs call this compartmentalization is different, and many vendors will consider it an add-on that requires an additional charge to use it, but when you begin backing up a large amount of data, you will find it to be a lifesaver and well worth the money.

Backup vs. Fault Tolerance

Data backup frameworks don't need to stop at redundant copies of data. Backup and downtime discussions go hand in hand. How long would it take to get a system back online if a primary server with important data went down? How crucial would this be to the organization's operation?

Fault tolerance goes a step beyond the conversation of backing up your data and into the conversation of what you would do if any component of the whole network environment failed. For example, if you are running a mail server and your primary Internet connection goes down, then what is the contingency plan? What if you were to lose the hard drive on the server because of hardware failure? What if the logic board on the server dies? Some organizations go so far as to have a duplicate of every device in their environment. For most, though, it is a matter of analyzing what you can live without in the event of a failure because some fault-tolerant solutions do not have an appropriately high return on investment in case of a failure.

If downtime is a critical factor in keeping a data structure alive, you should consider implementing a failover or *fault-tolerant* solution. In fact, the cost of providing fault tolerance could actually mitigate the cost of downtime in cases where downtime can cause loss of productivity. When configuring Mac OS X Server (or Mac OS X Client as a server) hosting various services, you may choose to provide a fault-tolerant solution when high availability is required.

Fault-Tolerant Scenarios

Fault tolerance comes in two types. The first is *active-passive*. In an active-passive topology, you would maintain a host spare of the service you are load balancing, which is passive (or dormant) until the primary server crashes. The OS X service that maintains this fault-tolerant scenario is *failoverd*.

As with most failover services, once the primary server comes back online, you must manually tell the backup server to stop processing requests (backups) and reactivate the primary host. Failoverd is not meant to be a load balancer. You do not receive any additional benefits other than maintaining a backup server that you would flip to if the primary were to go down. Typically, the backup server will be a less expensive version of the primary server. For example, a cluster node might be a backup to an Xserve.

The second type of fault-tolerant solution is called *active-active*. In an active-active topology, multiple active servers are used. In this scenario, you will often also engage in load balancing those servers. This gives you the ability to provide increased bandwidth to mission-critical services. The complexity introduced in this scenario is that the data store must be either synchronized with the primary server or shared between the servers, as is the case with using multiple servers as bridgehead servers using an Xsan to reshare data. Data in an active-passive topology must be synchronized between the servers, but not as frequently as in active-active environments.

Round-Robin DNS

While active-passive topology traffic reroutes data using the failover daemon (failoverd), in an active-active topology, traffic must be routed between multiple servers on a constant basis. There are two methods predominantly used for doing this. The first is using *round-robin DNS*. Round-robin DNS controls the order in which a load-balanced service forwards traffic across multiple servers. The administrator fills the domain records with multiple address records using the same host name but points to one or more IP addresses that serve the same service. As the DNS request is looking for your DNS server, the web server responds to the client with the next address from the list.

The most basic round-robin DNS setup shapes traffic based on the assumption that each server can handle the same load, which is considered an *equal cost path*. A typical list of A record addresses in your zone file might look like the following if you have three servers:

```
afp   IN   A      10.0.0.7
afp   IN   A      10.0.0.8
afp   IN   A      10.0.0.9
```

You can tell one server to handle more traffic than the others, as is the case with *unequal cost paths*, or paths that send more traffic to one server than the others. You can do this by listing the same server multiple times in the listing of A records for a given address. For example, if you have one server at 10.0.0.4 that is much faster than the others in a six-node cluster of web servers, you might direct traffic using the following entries in a zone file:

```
afp   IN   A      10.0.0.4
afp   IN   A      10.0.0.4
afp   IN   A      10.0.0.5
afp   IN   A      10.0.0.6
afp   IN   A      10.0.0.7
afp   IN   A      10.0.0.8
```

You can use the `rrset-order` command to define how round-robin requests are forwarded. The default `rrset` order is cyclic. There are three different options for record handling:

- Cyclic records are returned in numerical order.
- Fixed records are returned in the same order that they are listed in the file.
- Random records are returned in a random order.

When using round-robin DNS, the traffic is shaped in a static manner and cannot adapt to changes in the servers, such as performance counters and current user load.

Load-Balancing Devices

A *load balancer* can provide many features. Among them is the ability to shape traffic based on multiple factors (IP addresses, port, amount of traffic), automatically failing over to another server when one server becomes unresponsive, and providing a single address for systems to use when requesting a service. The load balancer in most configurations will probably not handle synchronizing data but will perform almost everything else that will be required when architecting this type of solution. Load balancers include Coyote Point Equalizers, F5s/Dell BigIPs, Barracuda Load Balancers, and Cisco Load Directors.

The cost of deploying a solution using round-robin DNS is typically very low compared to the cost of purchasing a load balancer. However, the load balancer will become a more scalable solution over the long run. In cluster environments, the load balancer can become a single point of failure. To build a completely fault-tolerant environment, implement a backup load balancer to automatically go live if there is a problem with the main load balancer. It may seem redundant, but even load balancers can and will fail.

Cold Sites

When discussing redundancy, it is important to explore the physical redundancy of the actual location where your equipment resides. Secondary locations are important for situations where there is a need to be back up and running quickly in the event of a communications error with your primary location. The secondary location, or *cold site*, often consists of a set of servers that are slightly below the speed of your primary site, that are shut down (or offline), and that contain a fairly recent copy of the data stored in your hot site.

Planning is everything when dealing with a secondary location. Much like an evacuation procedure at an office, in the event of a failure at your primary site, a procedure should be written and followed to activate the cold site. These processes often resemble a series of steps that enable you to be online providing the assets that you need quickly and efficiently. An example of this might include a complex flowchart, or it might be as easy as a simple checklist outlining what steps to take.

We cannot stress enough the importance of documenting and testing these mission-critical business processes before you begin to rely on them.

Hot Sites

For locations that require even more redundancy and cannot suffer a performance loss should the primary site go down, a redundant site, or *hot site*, should be implemented. With a hot redundant site, practically a one-to-one ratio of your equipment in the primary location would be available in the secondary site. A hot site is critical for large web sites, such as Amazon.com and Expedia.com, which would lose millions of dollars an hour if users were unable to check the status of accounts, book travel, or purchase MP3s because of an outage.

The goal of any hot site is not to quickly be up and running with a subpar system, as it is with a cold site, but instead to be instantly up and running with an equally powerful system. Many hot sites begin as a redundant location used only in an emergency and often end up running in tandem with various systems in the primary site, allowing any of the systems in the primary site to fail over to the secondary. This can lead to increased throughput capacity for server farms, which might otherwise be sitting idle.

Backing up Services

Finally, it's worth mentioning that each service running on Mac OS X and Mac OS X Server *can* require a special type of backup. These often involve stopping a service and then running a backup, given that some of the data cannot be backed up while the service is running. Many of these services, if provided by Apple, will be fairly straightforward to back up. For example, the comic in Figure 18–28 shows the process for backing up Apple's Final Cut Server, a popular solution for storing video assets in Mac OS X.

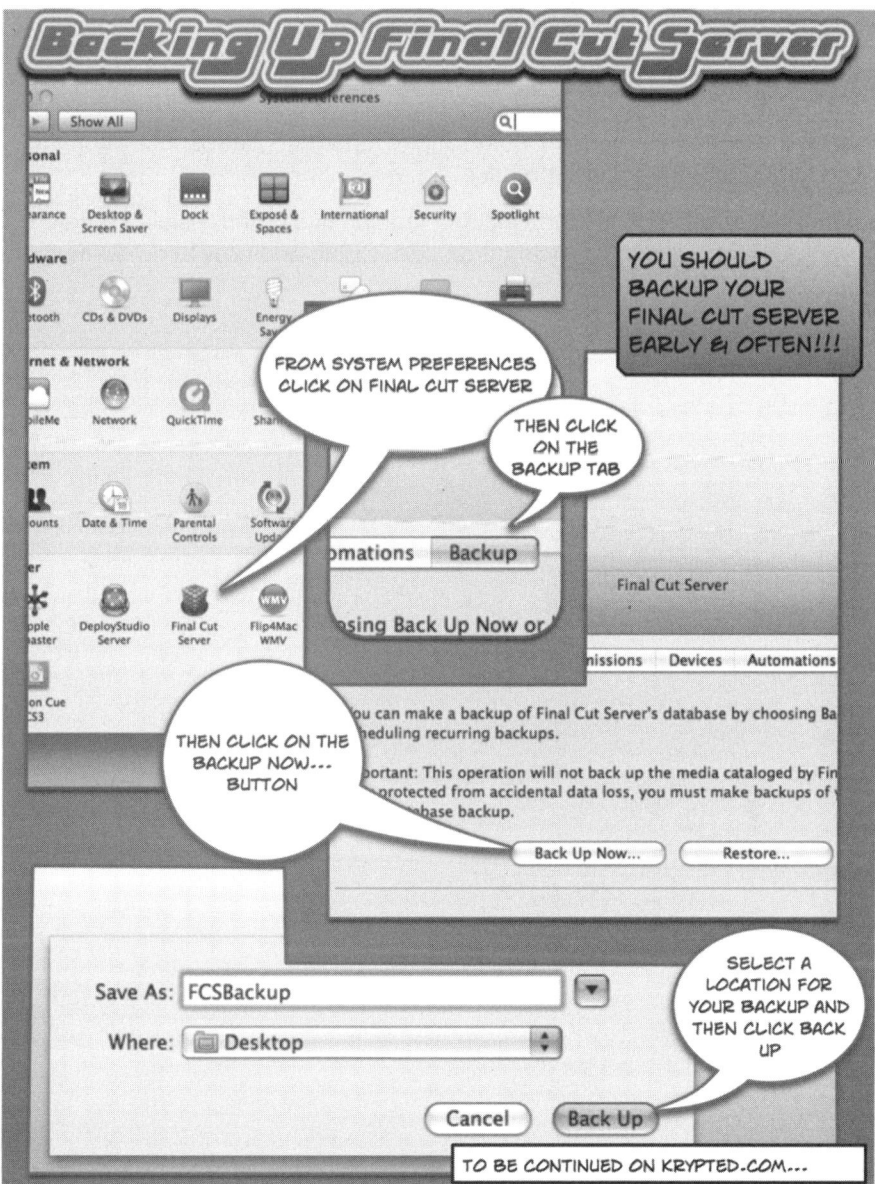

Figure 18–28. *Backing up Final Cut Server*

Summary

Whether due to an intrusion, due to a hardware failure, or due to accidental deletion of data (we are our own worse security risks), chances are that at some point you will loose data. In this chapter we looked at backing up Mac OS X so that if you lose data (or have data that is compromised), you will be able to restore that data.

In this chapter, we started out by looking at some backup and storage theory. We then moved on to using Apple's Time Machine, which is built into Mac OS X. Because Time Machine isn't for everyone, we then looked at SuperDuper and Retrospect. Along the way we looked at bringing theory into practice.

Another item that many will look to following an intrusion is data forensics. Therefore, in Chapter 19, we'll look at building an incident response plan and how to do some basic forensics steps in Mac OS X.

Chapter 19

Forensics

You never can be completely prepared for a security breach. Even if you take every precaution and follow every security measure, it can still happen. Practicing good security measures can only mitigate risks, not obviate them. You can reduce the impact and likelihood of an attack, but you cannot remove the fact that an attack can still happen.

Thievery is one of the unpleasant realities of our world today. And data theft as a result of a break-in or security breach is one of the hardest hurdles to overcome. Some companies don't survive it. Others take years to recover from the damage. Fortunately, a field has developed over the years in which investigations of computer crimes are conducted to find the perpetrators of these crimes and bring them to justice. And a conversation about security would not be complete without a discussion surrounding the field of *computer forensics*.

Computer forensics is the scientific investigation of digital assets in order to provide evidence of a crime to a court of law. Forensics is also useful even if you never plan to pursue legal action. The term (and techniques) also allow one to react to a security incident. This can mean discovering the cause of an incident and altering your policies and practices to keep it from happening again. A variety of fairly mature forensic tools can be used to sleuth out the scene of a computer crime. In this chapter, we'll discuss key elements of computer forensics and explore some of the tools used to perform these investigations on (or for) Mac OS X.

This chapter is by no means meant to be a comprehensive discussion of the computer forensics field. There are many books and courses dedicated to forensics, and you can find a number of resources on the Web for guidance. If forensics fascinates you, we encourage you to join online computer forensics groups such as Computer Forensics World (www.computerforensicsworld.com) or the Yahoo Mac Forensics group (http://tech.groups.yahoo.com/group/macos_forensics/) to learn more about computer crime investigation and how it relates to Mac OS X.

Incident Response

The first part of any discussion about forensics should involve being proactive in developing an incident response plan. Incident response involves answering these basic questions: How will I, as a home user or IT administrator, deal with a break-in involving data theft? If someone broke into my file server tomorrow, copied all the data, and then reformatted my data volume, what would I do immediately following the break-in? Hopefully, after reading this chapter you will have an incident response plan ready, and some inexpensive digital forensics tools at your disposal.

It is important to be as proactive as you can, and one of the best steps you can take is to create a step-by-step plan to handle a violation of your security policy. What immediate action is taken after the break-in is considered the incident response. The incident response plan is your blueprint to how you are going to handle a breach in data security. Much like keeping the phone numbers of the various medical and law enforcement agencies near the phone in case of emergency, the incident response plan should be developed and communicated to all persons involved in your IT security policies.

If you are an IT administrator in a large environment, then the incident response plan will include procedures that match your business. Incident response time should also go hand in hand with any service-level agreements you may have with an IT support company (if you outsource your IT resources) to make sure there is an adequate response to the crime. The impact of the incident response depends on how quickly and efficiently steps are taken to remedy the situation.

We've all seen crime dramas on television where the investigator wears gloves when handling evidence at the scene of a crime. Their bare fingerprints can damage, or *taint*, the evidence. The same is true when mounting a drive. Any data that is written to it is like taking the gloves off; it can damage the evidence. By mounting a drive, you write a small amount of data to the drive. Therefore, you should always disable *disk arbitration*, or the ability of your system to automatically mount a drive, unless you are using a write blocker.

> **NOTE:** If any data is modified, then you will risk compromising the integrity of all collected data. This is akin to the appearance of tampering with evidence that are all too common in courtroom dramas on television.

Disk arbitration is a background process, or daemon, that handles mounting drives as they are attached to the system. You can also disable the disk arbitration daemon to tell the system not to mount drives as they're attached to the system. To do so, move the file `/System/Library/LaunchDaemons/com.apple.diskarbitrationd.plist` to another directory, such as the desktop. Once the file is renamed, reboot the system. When the system comes back online, it will no longer automatically mount volumes. To mount a drive, you will be required to use the `mount` command, a forensic software tool, or Disk Utility; and when mounting the drive you can flag it as read-only.

Write blocking, or the halting of writing data to a drive, is key to establishing a *chain of custody* of the data, or history of all interactions with the data. You can purchase a dedicated write-blocking device, or *write blocker*, to stop data from being written to the drive. These devices allow the system to communicate to a drive, but will stop any data from actually being written to it. When your USB, SATA, eSATA, or other type of drive is plugged into the write blocker, you will be presented with a read-only volume. Some good write blockers can be found at Digital Intelligence's website. WeibeTech also makes a good USB device for write blocking on the Mac.

If forensics is not something you plan to do often and purchasing multiple write blockers to accommodate the various drives seems cost prohibitive, there is another route you can go with software. BlackBag Technologies and Faronics both make products that do this. BlackBag's SoftBlock is write-blocking software for the Mac that provides GUI control over the mounting and management of devices at the kernel level of Mac OS X. When you plug a device into your computer, SoftBlock identifies them, and then allows you to select whether to mount it as read-only or read-write. It gives you control over how each hard drive mounts. Faronics DeviceFilter is similar in concept, except all devices are controlled from one central management console. Both are built on the same concept.

MacForensicsLab

AccessData's Forensics Toolkit (FTK) and Guidance Software's EnCase are two of the predominantly used packages for digital forensics in law enforcement today. However, they are not natively installable on the Mac platform; therefore, we will concentrate on SubRosaSoft's MacForensicsLab, which is native to the Mac platform and has many of the same features as other non-Mac native apps. It is the best Mac-native solution for forensics on the market today.

> **NOTE:** MacForensicsLab can run on Windows and Linux as well. However, it is only available to private forensics investigators and law enforcement officers who can provide bona fide credentials.

MacForensicsLab automates many aspects of the acquisition (performing forensically sound clones of data), analysis (reviewing the data to tell a compelling story), auditing, and reporting of digital forensics. The techniques we will be describing here should lay the framework for any forensics software you may choose to use, because these techniques are standard techniques used in the digital forensics field.

Installing MacForensicsLab

In this section, we'll show you how to set up and use MacForensicsLab to write block your system. When you first run the MacForensicsLab software, you will be asked to install some files on the system that will run the application. Click on Install to do so, and you'll be presented with a Preferences screen. In the Preferences toolbar, you will first see the Database icon. By default, the database will be disabled.

This database is where you will set up the case database where all the information on each of your cases will reside. A *case* is each investigation that you will perform, and consists of multiple volumes of data. This could consist of one system that you're investigating, or a number of systems that have related information. The database for this example will reside in a local file; however, if there are multiple users, we would likely choose to use a MySQL or REAL SQL database server to store our data. To set up the local file during the initial install process, click the Local File option below the Database toolbar item (see Figure 19–1), and then click on Create (or Select to browse to an existing case database).

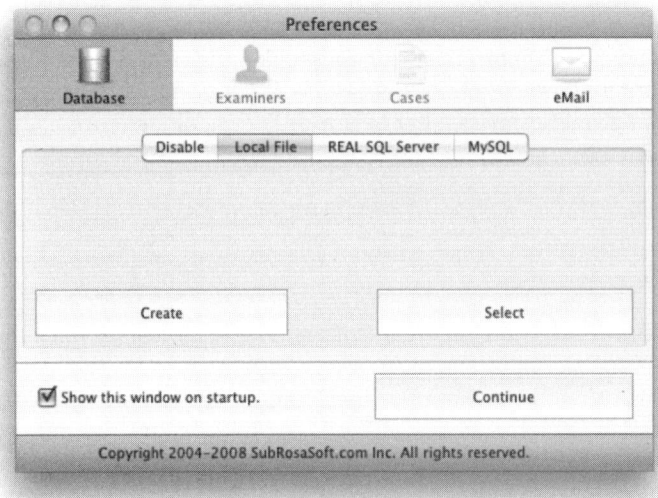

Figure 19–1. *Using a local file as a database*

NOTE: You can use MacForensicsLab without using a database, but it will not track your actions, which is important to protecting your chain of evidence.

Next, click Create (twice), and indicate where the file should be located. Once you have browsed to the appropriate location (see Figure 19–2), then click the Save button. This will take you back to the Preferences screen.

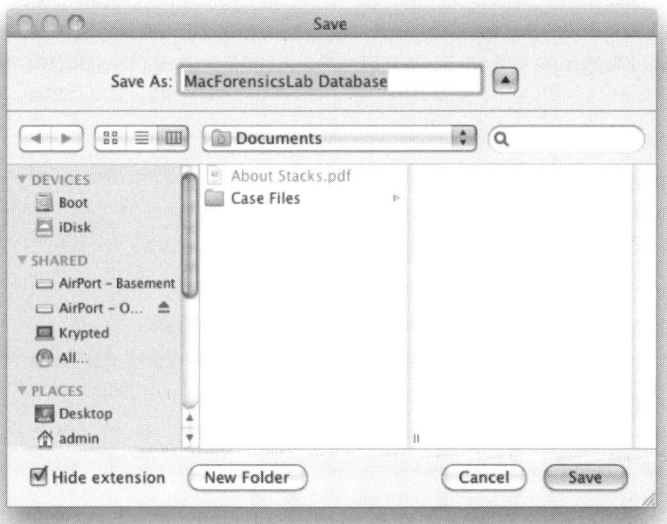

Figure 19–2. *Creating a database*

Once you have created your database, you will want to set up the *examiners*, which are the users who will be investigating the case. To add an examiner, click the Examiners icon in the Preferences toolbar and then click on the plus (+) sign (see Figure 19–3).

Figure 19–3. *The Examiners screen*

From here, a default user will be added (see Figure 19–4). If it is just one person, you can simply edit the default user. Add their user's name, e-mail address, phone number, and agency. You can also add an image to the user, which can later be used by reports from this screen. When you are satisfied with the information for the user, click the Save button.

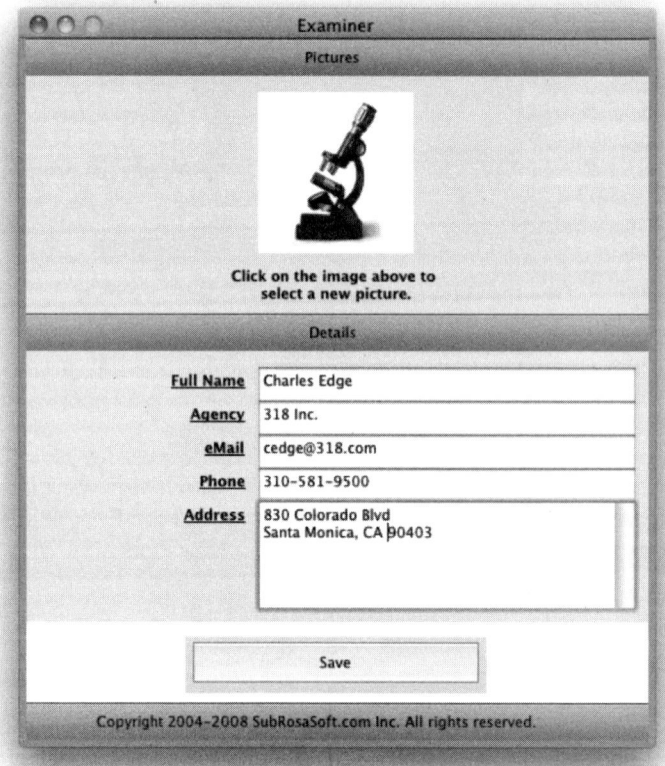

Figure 19-4. *Creating an examiner*

Once you are satisfied with the examiners you have created, you will want to set up your first case. Click the Cases button in the toolbar, and click the plus (+) sign to create a case for the investigation you will be conducting (see Figure 19–5).

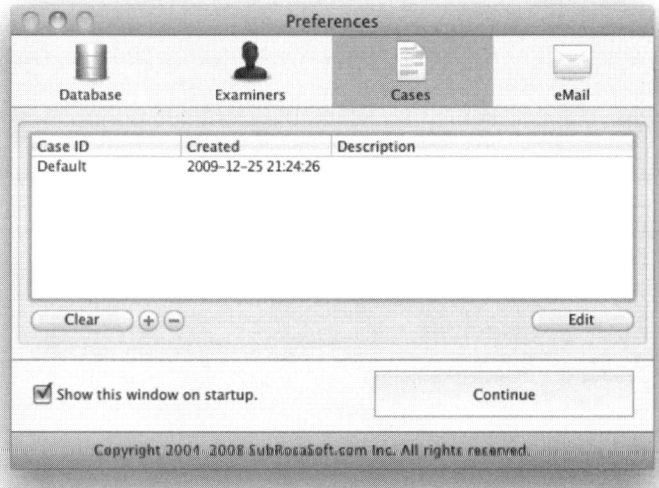

Figure 19–5. *The Cases screen*

For this test case, we'll call the investigation "whereswaldo." At the new screen, enter **whereswaldo** and any pertinent description of the case (see Figure 19–6).

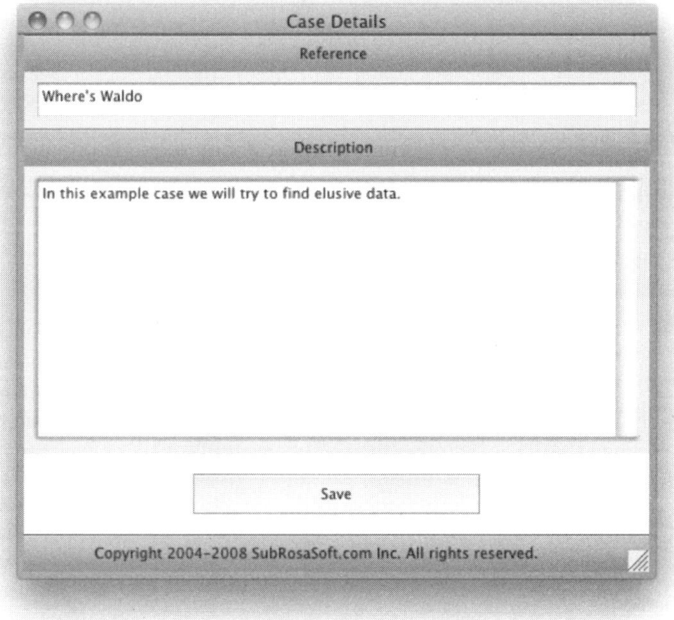

Figure 19–6. *Case details*

Once you have set up the case, click the eMail button in the toolbar. Here you can set up e-mail updates to alert you as to the progress of the software. E-mail updates can be extremely helpful, especially when examining large hard drives, as they can take hours to examine during the acquisition process. Here, enter the required information needed to send e-mail updates through your mail server, and click the Continue button (see Figure 19–7).

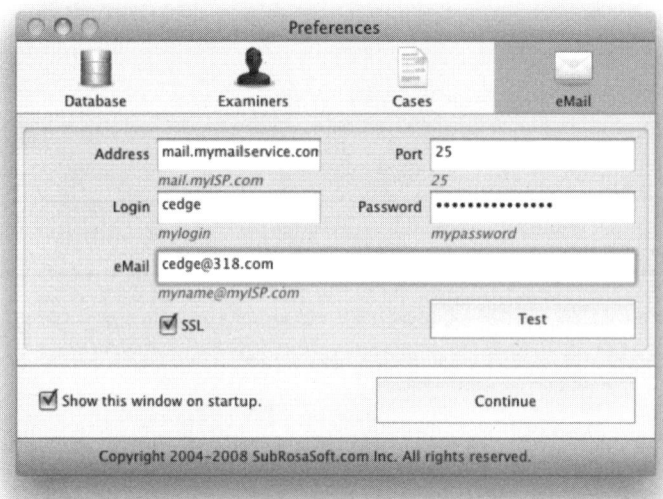

Figure 19–7. *E-mail setup*

Using MacForensicsLab

Once you have completed the setup process, it is time to start investigating the evidence. Before you can investigate the workstation, you need to create an image of the unaltered evidence in order to keep it from being tampered with, or even appearing to have been tampered with (and that evidence was possibly planted). When you open the software for the first time (by clicking on that Continue button referenced earlier), you will be prompted to disable disk arbitration, as shown in Figure 19–8. You should always disable disk arbitration unless you are using a hardware write blocker, as described in the "Incident Response" section of this chapter. If you disable disk arbitration at the operating-system level rather than in the software, then you can click on Ignore here; otherwise, click on Disable to disable disk arbitration.

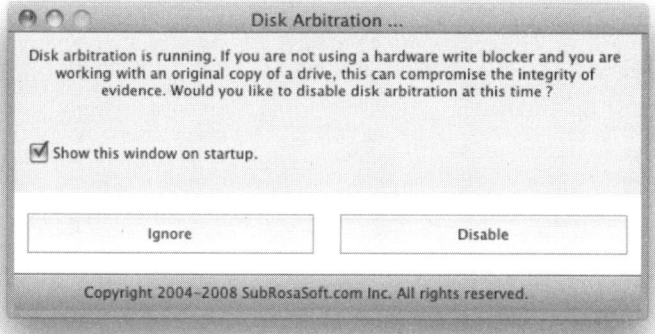

Figure 19–8. *Disk arbitration setup*

After setting up the disk arbitration status, you will be taken to the main screen. From here, you can select a drive and see the statistics for the volume (see Figure 19–9). This information will be stored in the database and tagged accordingly.

Each section of the screen shows a different aspect of the analysis process (again, see Figure 19–9). Devices are displayed on the Device screen. A device can have multiple volumes, or at times no volume. The file screen shows critical information on the volume that is selected on the Device screen. The toolbar along the bottom of the screen lists many of the actions you can perform, given the status of the drive. These options include the following:

Acquire: Creates a forensic image of the system.

Search: Searches a volume for a narrow selection of data.

Analyze: Analyzes files in their raw format, sector-by-sector or byte-by-byte.

Salvage: Retrieves deleted files.

Browse: Browses a file system.

Audit: Performs an automated review of assets.

Figure 19-9. *The main MacForensicsLab screen*

Image Acquisition

At this point, you can move forward with acquiring your first drive image. When acquiring an image, it is important to keep in mind what type of image you will be acquiring. If you are building an image of a live system, as is often the case with a server or a system that has not been turned off yet and is running MacForensicsLab from the DVD, you will typically want to perform what is known as a *smeared image*. Images that are created from live media and not frozen in time are referred to as a *smear*. If you were to use a smeared image and the case were to go to court, then you would need to defend the choice in court, as possible changes in the data set can be challenged as possible points of tampering.

A different option is to create a *golden master*, or a second unaltered copy of the data in case the original physical media the data is captured from becomes compromised. Most forensics investigators today will maintain a golden master at all times; however, if you are imaging a system solely for the purpose of sending it to someone else for analyzing, then you probably will keep only the original media.

MacForensicsLab also has the ability to split an image into segments. This is a nice option if you plan on providing a copy of your image on optical media such as CD or DVD to another party.

A *checksum* is a computed value based on the contents of a block of data at the its destination. The receiving system computes a new checksum based on the data and compares it with the one sent with the packet. The Packet Size feature of MacForensicsLab allows you to assign a size for each block of data that will be checksummed.

To acquire an image, click on the volume or disk you want to acquire, and set the options for the imaging process (see Figure 19–10). Once you are satisfied with all your choices, click the Acquire button to move to the next screen.

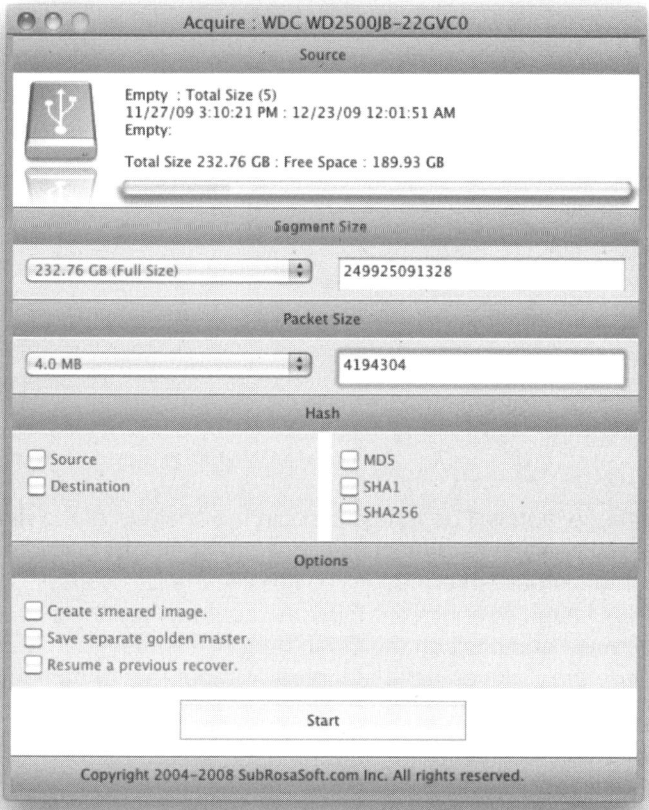

Figure 19–10. *Acquire image screen*

Once you click the Start button, the system will ask you where you want to save your image. At the Save dialog box (see Figure 19–11), browse to the location to store the image, and click the Acquire button.

> **NOTE:** Before you start imaging, verify that there is enough hard drive space on the target volume.

Figure 19-11. *Saving the database*

Analysis

Once you have acquired the image, you will be ready to begin the analysis of the data. Many forensics professionals will analyze data manually, looking for files throughout the system that they know will contain crucial information. To browse the file system manually, select the Attach Disk Image option in the File menu of MacForensics Lab. Then browse to the acquired image and click on the Open button. You can then browse the disk image as though it were the disk you have mounted, without fear of damaging the originating evidence.

You can also use the Browse option located at the bottom of the screen to bring up a filtered list of the files on the system. Clicking this Browse button allows you to select exactly which types of files you want to see. See Figure 19-12.

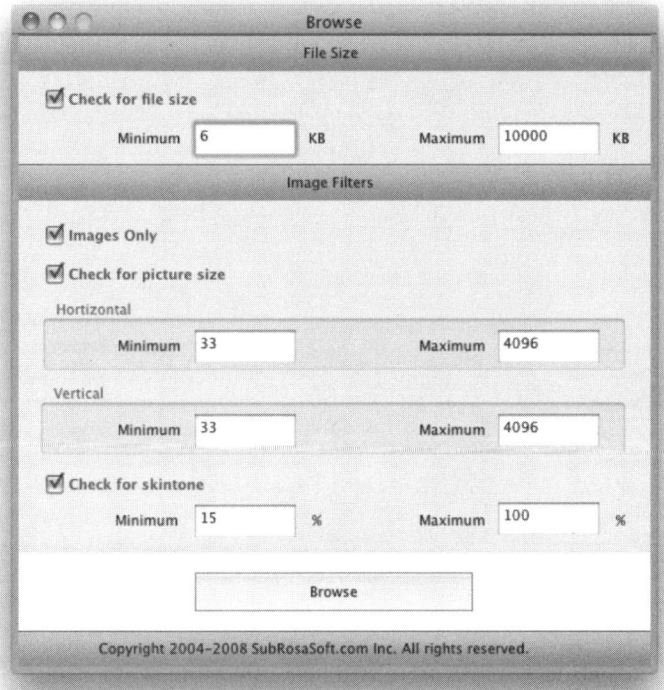

Figure 19–12. Browsing drive contents

> **TIP:** Once you've enabled the ability to browse a directory, Spotlight searching can help to isolate data that is otherwise difficult to find! Make sure that your image has been checksummed prior to indexing with Spotlight though, as it could damage the integrity of your data otherwise.

You can now simply browse to a file and double-click it. This will open the Analyze screen for that file (see Figure 19–13). The Hex Content tab of this screen will show you the raw data that makes up the file. The Native tab will show you how the file should look to the system (for example an image file will appear on the Native tab as the image).

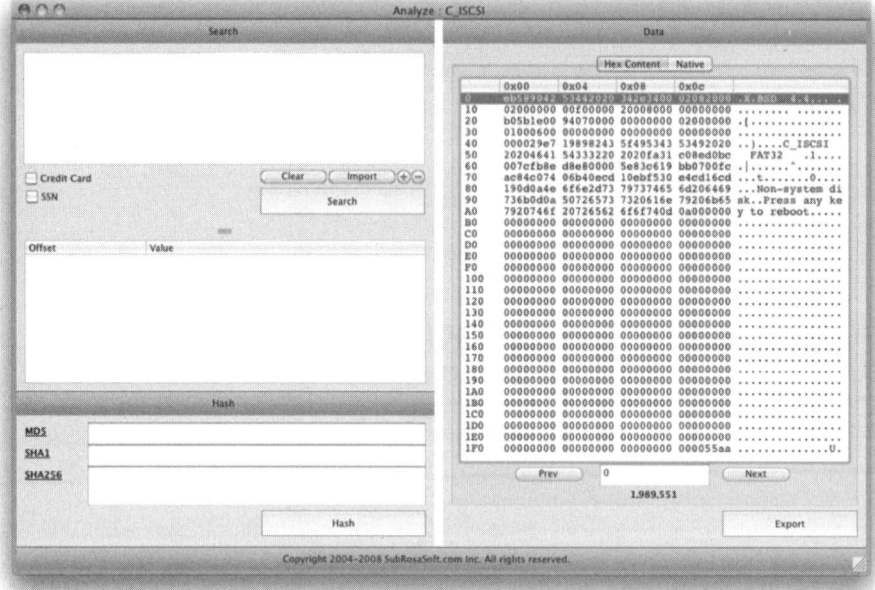

Figure 19–13. *The Analyze screen*

Another way to conduct analysis is to search for files and then view them. This can be especially helpful if you are looking for all the files on a disk that are of a certain type, such as images. For example, if you wanted to search a drive for all the Adobe EPS or PSD files, you would click Search on the MacForensicsLab toolbar. This opens the Search window (see Figure 19–14). From the Search window, you can use the Filters section to add the file extensions for the application file types you are looking for. In this case, you would enter **.eps** and **.psd** to look for these Adobe files.

In addition to finding files with certain names, you can search for files by content. This will search the contents of all files and display any with the contents that are indicated. You can also use the Credit Card and SSN check boxes to have the system search for credit card numbers and Social Security numbers.

The options on the right side of the Search window deal with how you want to manage the search results. The Browse Results check box will allow you to see a listing of all files found that match your search criteria. The Bookmark check box will bookmark all files discovered by the search in the Active Cases bookmarks. The Hash option allows you to establish a chain of custody of some form on all files discovered by calculating a hash value for them and adding them into the case database. This is because it provides some confidence that you're looking at the same data as the person who generated the hash.

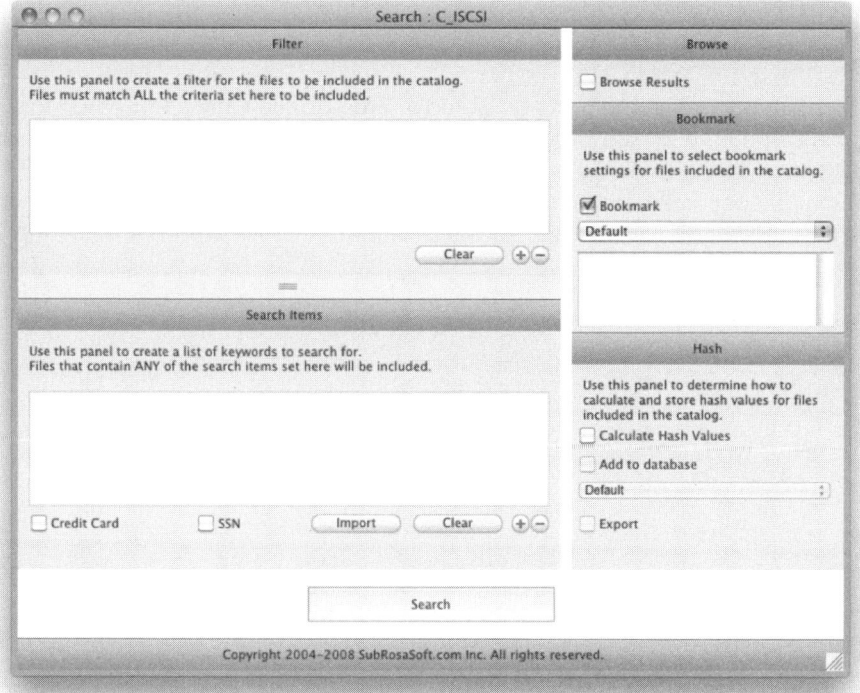

Figure 19–14. *The Search window*

Once you are satisfied with your search criteria, click the Search button toward the bottom of the screen, and wait for the search to complete.

Salvage

If you do not find the file you are looking for using the Search feature, the Salvage feature of MacForensicsLab can be another place to find what you need. The Salvage feature will look through free space and attempt to find any files that have been deleted, even if the trash has been emptied. This feature is not very effective if a Secure Empty Trash operation has been performed, but it can be quite effective for finding files not emptied from a Secure Trash Empty command. From the main MacForensicsLab screen, click a drive, and select the Salvage button. This opens the Salvage screen (see Figure 19–15).

> **NOTE:** While Secure Empty Trash will reduce the likelihood that a file can be recovered, a number of other factors can as well. For example, writing data to the disk (by creating new files)

will often overwrite the free space that a deleted file inhabits. Additionally, as users of Data Rescue X will painfully note, recovered files are often missing things, such as file names.

You can select two options in the Salvage window: Free Space Only and Search for Embedded Files. The Free Space Only check box will limit the search to free space on the hard drive, or to space that was possibly marked as free when a Secure Empty Trash operation has occurred, but has not yet been overwritten by files. The Search for Embedded Files check box will attempt to search within other files for files matching your search criteria.

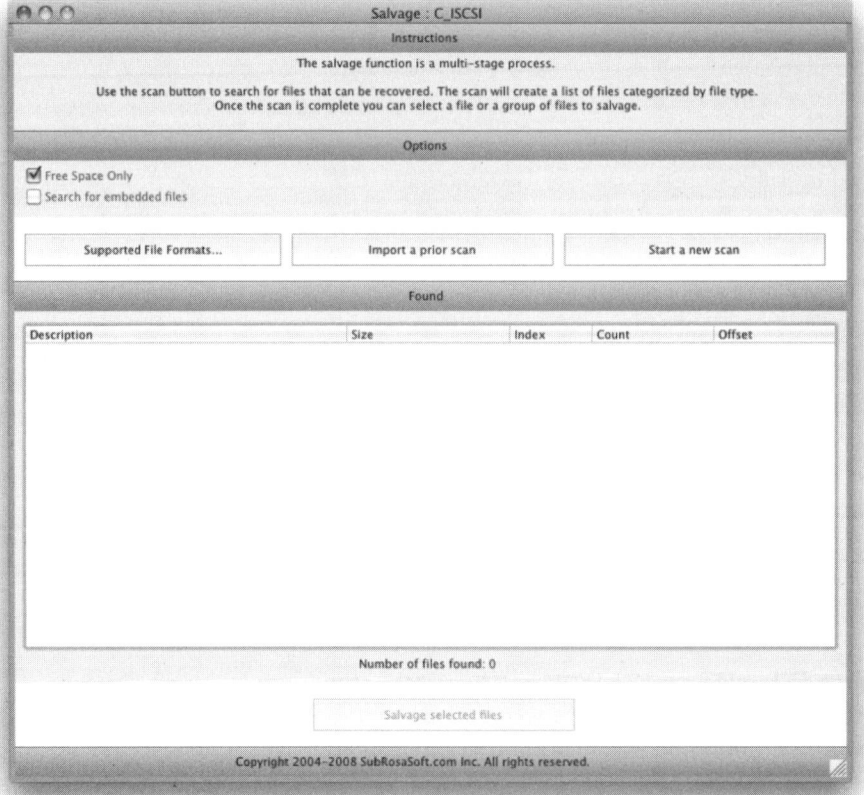

Figure 19-15. *The Salvage window*

To define the types of files you want the Salvage operation to find, click the Supported File Formats button. This opens the File Types to Include window (see Figure 19-16). From here, hold down the Command key and select all the file types you want to find. To continue with the example from the Search section, we'll look for all Adobe files. Next, click Continue and then click the Salvage selected files button from the Salvage window.

Figure 19–16. *The File Types to Include screen*

Once the Salvage operation is complete, you will see a listing of all salvaged files in the Found screen. In many cases, salvaged files will lose their names but not their contents in this process.

Other applications can perform salvage operations, such as FileSalvage (also by SubRosaSoft), MacDataRecovery, and, our favorite, Data Rescue II from ProSoft. Although these tools are helpful, it is important to keep as much information logged about the case in the MacForensicsLab case notes as possible. Whenever possible, it is preferable to use a forensics tool before using any nonforensics tools to keep all the actions logged, preventing future allegations of evidence tampering.

Performing an Audit

Another aspect of reviewing a drive, and one of the most powerful and timesaving features of MacForensicsLab, is the Audit feature. Clicking the Audit button on the MacForensicsLab screen opens a listing of all the users who have home folders on the drive you are auditing. When you click the Audit button (see Figure 19–17), you will see information that the system has found on that particular user. The information includes folders, preferences, address book entries, cookies, Safari bookmarks, Safari history, iChat sessions, e-mails, and e-mail attachments.

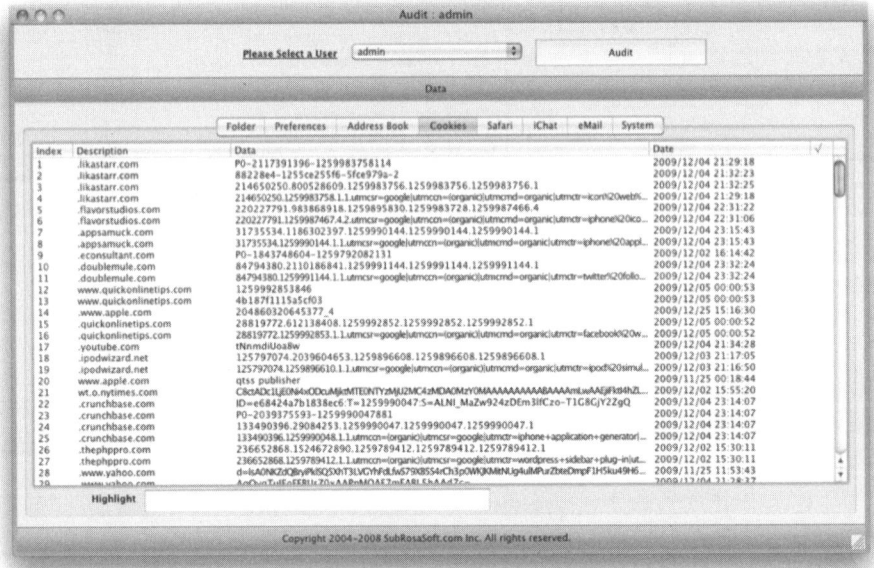

Figure 19–17. *Audit screen: cookies*

The audit feature is not foolproof, but it does provide a quick review of some of the most critical aspects of an investigation without having to know details of the structure of user folders and where old copies of information can be stored.

Reviewing the Case

Once you have found the information you are looking for and think you have compiled the evidence you are looking to compile, then it is a good idea to have someone else review the case for any omissions or errors. One effective way to review a case is to use the chronology of events as recorded on the drive to verify that all the actions taken have the correct checksums. These time records are crucial for the case to stand up in a court of law, and they can rule out any possibility that evidence was contaminated by foreign files or overwrites.

To view the chronology of a case, click Window and then click Database. At the database screen you will see a Chronology tab. If you click the Chronology tab, you will be able to trace each step an auditor took on a case, click by click (see Figure 19–18).

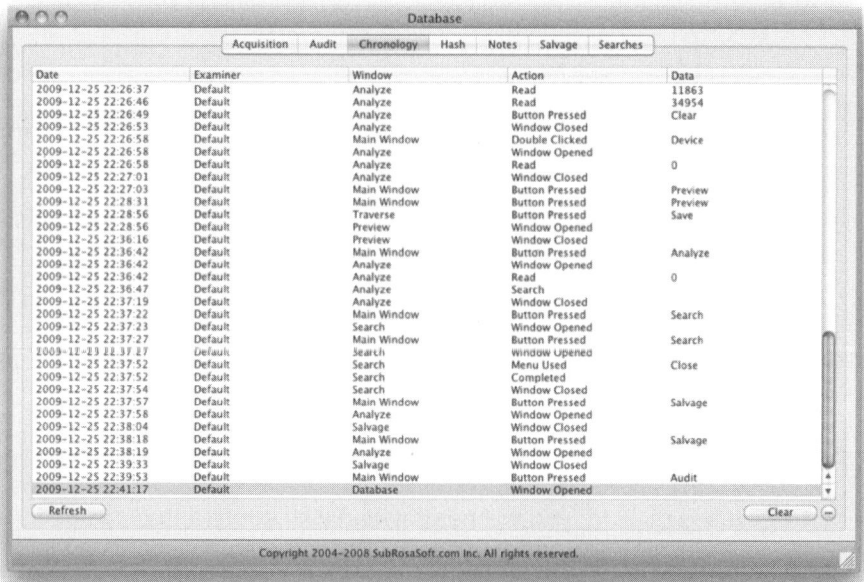

Figure 19–18. *Reviewing chronology*

Reporting

Once you are comfortable that the work will stand up under scrutiny, then you can move on to building a report. You can use the report to give an overview of the case details to another person within your organization for review. You can access the reporting mechanism of MacForensicsLab using the Write Report option under the File menu. When the Report screen opens, you can select which type of information to include in the report (see Figure 19–19) by clicking the appropriate check boxes. Once you are satisfied with the report contents, click the Start button to run the report.

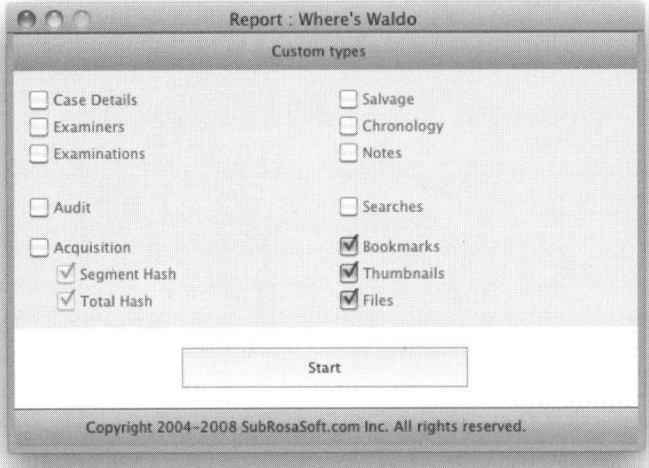

Figure 19–19. Report settings

When the report is finished running, you will be provided with content that can be used to present evidence to another party and eventually, if need be, to be used in a trial.

Other GUI Tools for Forensic Analysis

MacLockPick is a tool from SubRosaSoft that is only sold to law enforcement personally. MacLockPick allows an investigator to grab contacts, logs, and other data from a sleeping system in a covert manner. MacLockPick takes advantage of the fact that the default state of the Apple Keychain is open, and it uses the settings files of commonly used programs to keep track of contacts, Internet histories, passwords, and logs.

A database of the tracked information is placed on the MacLockPick flash drive. This database can then be read by the log readers in Microsoft Windows, Linux, or Apple Mac OS X computers. MacLockPick also includes a log reader for accessing the data from other platforms. MacLockPick functions in a forensically safe manner and will never write to the disk or device being investigated.

MacQuisition is a tool also developed by BlackBag Technologies. MacQuisition was designed to make the process of acquiring a forensic image simple. MacQuisition is a bootable Mac OS X DVD used to boot a suspect computer and acquire a forensic image, saving it either to a locally mounted external drive or to a network storage location.

MacQuisition doesn't provide tools for analyzing an image. It does, however, provide a simple method for acquiring that image. This can be a far better fit than a more complicated package, such as MacForensicsLab for first responders who simply need to acquire the image and do not need to perform any further processing of those images.

Forensically Acquiring Disk Images

It is not uncommon for digital malfeasants to store data in disk images. In order to forensically acquire these, you might find yourself leveraging what is known in the industry as a *shadow mount*. A shadow mount allows you to mount a read-only file system (from a .dmg) as a read-write structure without altering the original image, similar to how NetBoot works. This is useful for a variety of instances, most of all, for forensics.

Let's say you're performing forensics on a machine, and you find that the volume you're inspecting was dismounted dirty. In order for Mac OS X to perform a consistency check on the file system, the volume needs to be mounted as read-write. If you shadow mount the volume, the file system will be mounted read-write, but it will leave your original image intact writing all the changes to the shadow file. In the following example, we will mount a disk image called badguy.dmg that is stored on /Volumes/Images with a shadow mount at /Shadow. First, let's mount it without a shadow mount, using the following command:

```
hdiutil mount /Volumes/Images/badguy.dmg
```

> **NOTE:** This is an example of various techniques for mounting disk images. Do not use the above command on live data, as it will attempt to clean the file system. If the data should be tracked as part of an actual investigation, then proceed on with the subsequent examples.

Now, we're going to add the -shadow option and follow it with the location of the shadow mount:

```
hdiutil mount /Volumes/Images/badguy.dmg -shadow /Shadow
```

You can now write data into the image or remove data from the image and then unmount it:

```
hdiutil unmount /Volumes/Images/badguy.dmg
```

Remounting the image should give you an image that did not save any of the previous changes. While forensics is one place for this type of technology, there are others, such as the NetBoot environment, where you don't want users writing data anywhere except for a userland space. Another place for this is the default EC2 environment, where users will be working on virtual machines all day long, but will only write changes back in if they save a copy of the machine into a local space, such as their S3 account. It also makes for a nice way to store images (and images containing packages) during the imaging process for a number of environments.

Tools for Safari

SFT (Safari Forensic Tools) is a collection of command line tools that can be used to analyze information from Safari. The tools include parsers for Safari history, downloads, cookies, bookmarks, icon caches, and other information. They're easy to use and can aid you in learning a bit more about what kind of information you leave behind on your own system. To download SFT visit http://jafat.sourceforge.net/files.html.

Command-Line Tools for Forensic Analysis

A wide variety of command-line tools are included with Leopard that can be used with forensic investigations and primarily the acquisition of forensic images.

You can use the `mount` command to mount connected disks to a forensic system. To mount a system as read-only for inspection, you can use the `mount -r` command. Once the disk is mounted, you will typically want to use `dd` on the drive.

The `dd` command is a method for creating disk images that can be used for acquiring a forensic disk image. The `dd` command is preferred over Disk Utility, because it can create a disk image without being required to actually mount a drive, which, as discussed, can potentially contaminate the drive for future use as evidence. The `dd` command can also split disk images into segments, allowing you to burn the image to optical media or place it onto hard drives to present evidence to another party for their own forensic investigation.

Once the disk has been imaged, you can move on to building a hash of the drive using the `openssl` command. Be aware, though, that unless you know exactly what you are doing with the command-line tools, you run the risk of contaminating your evidence. This is one instance where the danger of breaking your chain of custody may outweigh the cost of purchasing a package like MacForensicsLab.

Summary

In this chapter we took a cursory look at the delicate art of forensics. We also looked heavily at using MacForensicsLab to perform the acquisition and analysis of a drive, but we wouldn't want to take anything away from many of the other solutions out there. They are almost all fantastic. What software cannot do is actually parse through every single file and folder and return all of the relevant data. This could be because a date is stored in some kind of encoded format, or because it's in an image. Manual analysis of the acquired data will net a far more accurate account of events if done so in the hands of a well-trained forensics analyst.

Use this chapter as a reference to perform front-line forensics analysis or as a reference for porting existing forensics skills from Windows to Mac OS X. However, if you have an in-depth investigation that you would like to perform consult a professional in that field.

Appendix A

Xsan Security

Xsan is Apple's implementation of a *Clustered File System*. This means that the file system can be accessed by multiple machines concurrently. *Fibre Channel* is an extension of the SCSI protocol and can be accessed through fiber optic cabling. Using Xsan, multiple Macs can simultaneously access shared storage provided over a Fibre Channel network. This allows multiple users to access data striped across a large number of physical drives (let's just say six Promise VTrak RAIDs' worth) as though they are one volume. Each client can access data at speeds of up to 4Gbps. Xsan is commonly used high-definition video and multiuser high-bandwidth creative environments, and it is also found in web and file-sharing farms.

Xsan is based on the StorNext File System, made by Quantum. Apple and Quantum both claim interoperability between StorNext and Xsan, which means that by combining the two, it's possibly for Macs, Windows, and many Unix variants (including Solaris, AIX, Linux and IRIX) can share communicate and share storage in a fast Fibre Channel environment. When looking to secure Xsan, you may find that there are specific features of StorNext that you want to use. Because Xsan is based on StorNext, many of the features of StorNext are built into the Xsan but might not be available through Xsan Admin. To begin unlocking some of the hidden features of Xsan, you will need to dip into the command line.

Xsan stores most of its data in /Library/Filesystems/Xsan. Configuration files are stored in the Config directory, and binaries are in the `bin` directory. The files in `Config` contain information about the structure of the SAN and any volumes on the SAN. The `Config` directory should not be world-writable, because if it is altered or deleted, the entire SAN volume could be deleted with it.

The commands to control and configure Xsan are cvlabel, cvadmin, cvfsck, and cvcp. These commands are analogous to some Unix commands (and are similarly named), but they are quite specific to Xsan. Be wary of using a Unix commands in place of the Xsan-specific command. As an example, you should never, ever run `fsck` on an Xsan volume.

Metadata

In an Xsan, your Metadata is the information about where on the physical disks your files are found, how many pieces they're in, how to assemble those pieces when a client requests a file, and which clients have those files locked for writing. Metadata should be stored on a dedicated Fibre Channel LUN (logical unit number, which each logical segmentation of a target storage device has to uniquely identify it within the target storage). It is very important that it live on a mirrored RAID set, to lessen the risk of it being lost.

Xsan storage is broken down into three parts:

LUN: "Logical Unit Number". A logical grouping of drives into a single entity. Usually a RAID set, but it could be a single drive.

Storage pool: A group of LUNs. Each client can write to multiple LUNs through a single storage pool.

Volumes: The logical volume presented to the client. It appears as a single local drive.

Metadata is then managed by a metadata controller, which determines where data will go on the SAN and keeps track of where each slice of the data resides (similar to a file allocation table). Each volume should have two metadata controllers, a primary and a secondary. While you can have multiple metadata controllers, only one is ever active (per volume) at a given time.

Each SAN client requires full access to all LUNs in order to write data. The metadata is simply a pointer that tells the SAN where to write data. If any of the LUNs that make up a storage pool cannot be seen over the Fibre Channel network by a metadata controller or a client, the storage pool reports "STRIPE GROUP DOWN," and your Xsan volume will go down. For example, if you were to unplug the cable for one target, you would likely bring an entire Xsan environment down. Therefore, physical security becomes very important with Xsan environments.

> **NOTE:** If you are just using Xsan as a back-end file system for a number of bridgehead file servers then you can restrict access to the LUNs to only the WWNNs of the metadata controllers and file servers.

The root user of any workstation that is connected through Fibre Channel to an Xsan environment can write directly to any accessible LUNs by writing data into /dev/<LUN>. A common path might be /dev/rdisk4. The association between and device ID and a LUN can be found in the Xsan labels for each LUN. If you write enough arbitrary data into the metadata LUN, then you will cause a volume to become inaccessible. This can be dangerous, because once the Xsan environment is restarted, it will read an invalid amount of data about itself, and therefore be unable to mount the volume. This is a denial of service attack and a tampering attack on the SAN that can be initiated by any client system that has a valid admin/root account. This is very dangerous, and there is no workaround for it, other than restricting access to administrative or root accounts on SAN clients.

Fibre Channel

With Fibre Channel, you can *cascade* two switches by *bonding* (sometimes referred to as *stacking*) their backplanes with a 10GB to 20GB connection. Most environments use bonding in order to achieve very fast speeds between switches. From a security perspective, one nice feature of a stacked environment is that you can apply access controls across multiple switches.

Affinities

Storage pools can be assigned an *affinity*. When data is moved to the affinity, space is allocated from a specific storage pool rather than in a round-robin fashion across all the storage pools. Affinity data can be restricted to specific LUNs. Access to affinities can be limited to certain groups. Data that requires a higher level of integrity can then be given an affinity or volatile data that requires speed (such as a capture scratch) can be given the fastest possible storage (ie – SAS drives running on a RAID 0-based LUN).

You can use Xsan Admin to assign an affinity to a folder at the top level of a volume. However, to assign an affinity to a nested folder, use the `cvmkdir` command. For example:

```
sudo /Library/Filesystems/Xsan/bin/cvmkdir -k <affinity-name> <path-to-folder>
```

Permissions

Xsan volumes appear, to the client, as local storage. Therefore, when a file or folder is created on a volume, POSIX permissions will be assigned it based on the umask of the client user. Ownership of the files and folders will be tracked by the UID on the local system of the user who created them. A common practice in Xsan environments is to change the default umask of the client systems to 002, which will grant read and write access to owner and group, and read-only for all others. Managing permissions using only local user accounts and POSIX permissions can be very difficult. Many administrators will use Open Directory to manage users and groups, and Access Control Lists (ACLs) to manage permissions on files.

ACLs greatly simplify permissions management, and they are even more valuable when other operating systems are accessing your volume. Windows and Linux clients treat ownership and permissions differently than Macs if they are tapping in through NFS, AFP and /or SMB. When ACLs are in use, new files added to the SAN volume will have the same permissions, no matter how the specific services are configured.

To enable an ACL, open Server Admin, click on Sharing and browse to the root of a volume. Click Sharing, and then Volumes, and then List. Next, click the root of an Xsan volume, and then click on the Permissions tab. Check the box for Enable ACLs on selected volume. Next, configure the permissions that should be in the ACL box, and then click the Save button.

Data that is written to the Xsan volume will now have the permissions of the folder above it, provided the ACEs are set to inherit permissions (see Chapter 4). ACL entries can easily be added using Server Admin. This can be much easier than using the default umask.

Quotas

Quotas are also an important part of Xsan. A *quota* is the amount of space a user can utilize on the SAN. As an administrator, you can set hard and soft quotas for every user on the Xsan. A *soft quota* lets the user continue to save files when they pass their quota, but they will be warned that they are over their limit. When they reach the *hard quota*, they will not be able to save any more data until the administrator of the SAN gives them more space, or they delete some files. When users near their quotas, they will be alerted.

Other SAN Solutions

Xsan is a fast and fairly straightforward SAN product. It does not provide any capability for backup or snapshots, it is not as fault tolerant as it could be, and it is a little too latent for certain applications (such as Pro Tools by Digidesign).

Other providers of SAN solutions include EMC, NetApp, and LeftHand Networks (a division of HP). These products can be made to work with the Mac OS X platform, although many do not work without using third-party software. For example, Studio Network Solutions' Ellipse allows Mac OS X clients to mount LUNs from EMC targets. However, most of these solutions do not offer a clustered file system for the Mac. Most allow Macs to connect by acting as NAS bridgeheads. Other solutions will allow an HFS+ volume to be mounted read-only on many clients, but only one client will have read/write access at a time. This means it is not a true clustered file system.

Vmirror by Vicom Systems gives you the ability to mirror LUNs. This provides redundancy to protect against the loss of a RAID. If a RAID array is lost in an Xsan environment, the whole SAN will be lost. Vmirror can stop this from happening.

Cloverleaf by Cloverleaf Communications gives the ability to snapshot Xsan and has some other benefits such as more granular control over virtualization and the ability to combine the presentation of various forms of storage to a wide variety of devices.

Appendix B

InfoSec Acceptable Use Policy

> **Note:** Created by the SANS Institute. Feel free to modify or use for your organization. If you have a policy to contribute, please send e-mail to stephen@sans.edu.

1.0 Overview

InfoSec's intentions for publishing an Acceptable Use Policy are not to impose restrictions that are contrary to <Company Name>. established culture of openness, trust and integrity. InfoSec is committed to protecting <Company Name>'s employees, partners and the company from illegal or damaging actions by individuals, either knowingly or unknowingly.

Internet/Intranet/Extranet-related systems, including but not limited to computer equipment, software, operating systems, storage media, network accounts providing electronic mail, WWW browsing, and FTP, are the property of <Company Name>. These systems are to be used for business purposes in serving the interests of the company, and of our clients and customers in the course of normal operations. Please review Human Resources policies for further details.

Effective security is a team effort involving the participation and support of every <Company Name> employee and affiliate who deals with information and/or information systems. It is the responsibility of every computer user to know these guidelines, and to conduct their activities accordingly.

2.0 Purpose

The purpose of this policy is to outline the acceptable use of computer equipment at <Company Name>.

These rules are in place to protect the employee and <Company Name>. Inappropriate use exposes <Company Name> to risks including virus attacks, compromise of network systems and services, and legal issues.

3.0 Scope

This policy applies to employees, contractors, consultants, temporaries, and other workers at <Company Name>, including all personnel affiliated with third parties. This policy applies to all equipment that is owned or leased by <Company Name>.

4.0 Policy

4.1 General Use and Ownership

1. While <Company Name>'s network administration desires to provide a reasonable level of privacy, users should be aware that the data they create on the corporate systems remains the property of <Company Name>. Because of the need to protect <Company Name>'s network, management cannot guarantee the confidentiality of information stored on any network device belonging to <Company Name>.

2. Employees are responsible for exercising good judgment regarding the reasonableness of personal use. Individual departments are responsible for creating guidelines concerning personal use of Internet/Intranet/Extranet systems. In the absence of such policies, employees should be guided by departmental policies on personal use, and if there is any uncertainty, employees should consult their supervisor or manager.

3. InfoSec recommends that any information that users consider sensitive or vulnerable be encrypted. For guidelines on information classification, see InfoSec's Information Sensitivity Policy. For guidelines on encrypting email and documents, go to InfoSec's Awareness Initiative.

4. For security and network maintenance purposes, authorized individuals within <Company Name> may monitor equipment, systems and network traffic at any time, per InfoSec's Audit Policy.

5. <Company Name> reserves the right to audit networks and systems on a periodic basis to ensure compliance with this policy.

4.2 Security and Proprietary Information

1. The user interface for information contained on Internet/Intranet/Extranet-related systems should be classified as either confidential or not confidential, as defined by corporate confidentiality guidelines, details of which can be found in Human Resources policies. Examples of confidential information include but are not limited to: company private, corporate strategies, competitor sensitive, trade secrets, specifications, customer lists, and research data. Employees should take all necessary steps to prevent unauthorized access to this information.

2. Keep passwords secure and do not share accounts. Authorized users are responsible for the security of their passwords and accounts. System level passwords should be changed quarterly, user level passwords should be changed every six months.

3. All PCs, laptops and workstations should be secured with a password-protected screensaver with the automatic activation feature set at 10 minutes or less, or by logging-off (control-alt-delete for Win2K users) when the host will be unattended.

4. Use encryption of information in compliance with InfoSec's Acceptable Encryption Use policy.

5. Because information contained on portable computers is especially vulnerable, special care should be exercised. Protect laptops in accordance with the "Laptop Security Tips".

6. Postings by employees from a <Company Name> email address to newsgroups should contain a disclaimer stating that the opinions expressed are strictly their own and not necessarily those of <Company Name>, unless posting is in the course of business duties.

7. All hosts used by the employee that are connected to the <Company Name> Internet/Intranet/Extranet, whether owned by the employee or <Company Name>, shall be continually executing approved virus-scanning software with a current virus database. Unless overridden by departmental or group policy.

8. Employees must use extreme caution when opening e-mail attachments received from unknown senders, which may contain viruses, e-mail bombs, or Trojan horse code.

4.3 Unacceptable Use

The following activities are, in general, prohibited. Employees may be exempted from these restrictions during the course of their legitimate job responsibilities (e.g., systems administration staff may have a need to disable the network access of a host if that host is disrupting production services). Under no circumstances is an employee of <Company Name> authorized to engage in any activity that is illegal under local, state, federal or international law while utilizing <Company Name>-owned resources.

The lists below are by no means exhaustive, but attempt to provide a framework for activities, which fall into the category of unacceptable use.

System and Network Activities

The following activities are strictly prohibited, with no exceptions:

1. Violations of the rights of any person or company protected by copyright, trade secret, patent or other intellectual property, or similar laws or regulations, including, but not limited to, the installation or distribution of "pirated" or other software products that are not appropriately licensed for use by <Company Name>.

2. Unauthorized copying of copyrighted material including, but not limited to, digitization and distribution of photographs from magazines, books or other copyrighted sources, copyrighted music, and the installation of any copyrighted software for which <Company Name> or the end user does not have an active license is strictly prohibited.

3. Exporting software, technical information, encryption software or technology, in violation of international or regional export control laws, is illegal. The appropriate management should be consulted prior to export of any material that is in question.

4. Introduction of malicious programs into the network or server (e.g., viruses, worms, Trojan horses, e-mail bombs, etc.).

5. Revealing your account password to others or allowing use of your account by others. This includes family and other household members when work is being done at home.

6. Using a <Company Name> computing asset to actively engage in procuring or transmitting material that is in violation of sexual harassment or hostile workplace laws in the user's local jurisdiction.

7. Making fraudulent offers of products, items, or services originating from any <Company Name> account.

8. Making statements about warranty, expressly or implied, unless it is a part of normal job duties.

9. Effecting security breaches or disruptions of network communication. Security breaches include, but are not limited to, accessing data of which the employee is not an intended recipient or logging into a server or account that the employee is not expressly authorized to access, unless these duties are within the scope of regular duties. For purposes of this section, "disruption" includes, but is not limited to, network sniffing, pinged floods, packet spoofing, denial of service, and forged routing information for malicious purposes.

10. Port scanning or security scanning is expressly prohibited unless prior notification to InfoSec is made.

11. Executing any form of network monitoring which will intercept data not intended for the employee's host, unless this activity is a part of the employee's normal job/duty.

12. Circumventing user authentication or security of any host, network or account.

13. Interfering with or denying service to any user other than the employee's host (for example, denial of service attack).

14. Using any program/script/command, or sending messages of any kind, with the intent to interfere with, or disable, a user's terminal session, via any means, locally or via the Internet/Intranet/Extranet.

15. Providing information about, or lists of, <Company Name> employees to parties outside <Company Name>.

Email and Communications Activities

1. Sending unsolicited email messages, including the sending of "junk mail" or other advertising material to individuals who did not specifically request such material (email spam).

2. Any form of harassment via email, telephone or paging, whether through language, frequency, or size of messages.

3. Unauthorized use, or forging, of email header information.

4. Solicitation of email for any other email address, other than that of the poster's account, with the intent to harass or to collect replies.

5. Creating or forwarding "chain letters", "Ponzi" or other "pyramid" schemes of any type.

6. Use of unsolicited email originating from within <Company Name>'s networks of other Internet/Intranet/Extranet service providers on behalf of, or to advertise, any service hosted by <Company Name> or connected via <Company Name>'s network.

7. Posting the same or similar non-business-related messages to large numbers of Usenet newsgroups (newsgroup spam).

4.4 Blogging

1. Blogging by employees, whether using <Company Name>'s property and systems or personal computer systems, is also subject to the terms and restrictions set forth in this Policy. Limited and occasional use of <Company Name>'s systems to engage in blogging is acceptable, provided that it is done in a professional and responsible manner, does not otherwise violate <Company Name>'s policy, is not detrimental to <Company Name>'s best interests, and does not interfere with an employee's regular work duties. Blogging from <Company Name>'s systems is also subject to monitoring.

2. Company Name>'s Confidential Information policy also applies to blogging. As such, Employees are prohibited from revealing any <Company> confidential or proprietary information, trade secrets or any other material covered by <Company>'s Confidential Information policy when engaged in blogging.

3. Employees shall not engage in any blogging that may harm or tarnish the image, reputation and/or goodwill of <Company Name> and/or any of its employees. Employees are also prohibited from making any discriminatory, disparaging, defamatory or harassing comments when blogging or otherwise engaging in any conduct prohibited by <Company Name>'s Non-Discrimination and Anti-Harassment policy.

4. Employees may also not attribute personal statements, opinions or beliefs to <Company Name> when engaged in blogging. If an employee is expressing his or her beliefs and/or opinions in blogs, the employee may not, expressly or implicitly, represent themselves as an employee or representative of <Company Name>. Employees assume any and all risk associated with blogging.

5. Apart from following all laws pertaining to the handling and disclosure of copyrighted or export controlled materials, <Company Name>'s trademarks, logos and any other <Company Name> intellectual property may also not be used in connection with any blogging activity

5.0 Enforcement

Any employee found to have violated this policy may be subject to disciplinary action, up to and including termination of employment.

6.0 Definitions

Term Definition

Blogging Writing a blog. A blog (short for weblog) is a personal online journal that is frequently updated and intended for general public consumption.

Spam Unauthorized and/or unsolicited electronic mass mailings.

7.0 Revision History

Appendix C

CDSA

If you are a developer of Mac OS X-based software then there are a few very basic principals that we can impart relating to the security model used when developing software for the Apple platform. While depth is something most developers look for, this is a theory and not a specific technology.

Apple has designed its security around the Common Data Security Architecture (CDSA) model, developed by Intel. CDSA is a set of layered security services and a cryptographic framework that provide an interoperable, cross-platform infrastructure for creating security-enabled applications for client-server environments. CDSA covers the essential components to equip applications with security services that provide cryptography, certificate management, trust policy management, and key recovery.

CDSA is defined by a horizontal, four-layer architecture:

- It includes applications such as Mail, Safari, iChat, Disk Utility, Keychain Access, and other applications developed by Apple. For example, 3rd party applications from Tweetie to 1Password take part in the CDSA model, leveraging Keychain services to custom CSSM cryptographic store modules respectively.

- It includes layered services and middleware including the *Application Programming Interfaces (API)s* used by the applications previously listed. An API is a set of definitions that determines how one piece of computer software communicates with another. It is a method of achieving abstraction, usually (but not necessarily) between lower-level and higher-level software. These APIs include interfaces for keychains, file signing, SSL, and certificate management.

- The Common Security Services Manager (CSSM) infrastructure's Cryptographic Services Manager has functions to create and verify digital signatures, generate cryptographic keys, and create cryptographic hashes.

- Security service provider modules, also known as *add-in modules*, are third-party and nonapplication items built using the APIs in the second layer of the CDSA. This allows for extensibility to the framework.

The CDSA is an open source framework, allowing it to closely parallel many of Apple's other initiatives for security and development. It receives peer review from a larger audience than just Apple users; security and development experts contribute to reviewing the CDSA fundamentals. CDSA allows Apple and the community of third-party developers to architect software in a secure manner while still supporting the network features required for the modern applications of today and tomorrow. For more information on the CDSA model, see the Intel CDSA site at http://www.intel.com/ial/security.

Appendix D

Introduction to Cryptography

The word cryptography is derived from the Greek words *kryptos*, meaning "hidden," and *grafein*, which means "to write." Throughout history, *cryptography* has been used to hide messages that might otherwise be intercepted in traditional means of communication. This is accomplished by concealing the contents of the message from all except those who have the key to unlock it. In modern times, cryptographic techniques are used to protect e-mail messages, information transmitted over the internet, credit card information, and data on corporate networks.

A wide variety of cryptographic techniques are used with computers. They are typically provided for one of two reasons: to protect data while at rest on a computer or to protect data as it is being transferred between two computers or across networks.

Most cryptographic techniques for submitting data over the Internet rely heavily on the exchange of keys. Some techniques include:

- *Symmetric-key cryptography* refers to encryption methods where both senders and receivers of data share the same key and data is encrypted and decrypted with algorithms based on those keys. The modern study of symmetric-key ciphers revolves around block ciphers and stream ciphers and how these ciphers are applied.

- *Block ciphers* take a block of plain text and a key and then output a block of cipher text of the same size. DES and AES are block ciphers. AES, also called Rijndael, is a designated cryptographic standard by the U.S. government. AES always uses a key size of 128, 192, or 256 bits as well as a block length of 128 bits. DES is no longer an approved method of encryption as an exhaustive key search attack on a block of DES-encrypted data would take a modern Mac OS X computer a few minutes to decipher. Triple-DES, its variant, remains popular. Triple-DES uses three 56-bit DES keys and is used across a wide range of applications from ATM encryption to e-mail privacy and secure remote access. Many other block ciphers have been designed and released, with considerable variation in quality.

- *Stream ciphers* create an arbitrarily long stream of key material, which is combined with plain text bit-by-bit or character-by-character, somewhat like the one-time pad (or an encryption cipher that is only used once) encryption technique. In a stream cipher, the output stream is based on an internal state, which changes as the cipher operates. That state's change is controlled by the key and, in some stream ciphers, by the plain-text stream as well. When the state doesn't depend on the plain input, two messages encrypted with the same key can be combined to gain information about the plain-text. RC4 is an example of a well-known stream cipher.

- *Cryptographic hash functions* do not use keys but take data and output a short, fixed-length hash in a one-way function. For good hashing algorithms, collisions (two plain texts that produce the same hash) are extremely difficult to find, although they do exist. Collisions must exist, as there are infinite possible inputs to a hash function but only a finite range of outputs.

- *Symmetric-key cryptosystems* typically use the same key for encryption and decryption. A disadvantage of symmetric ciphers is that a complicated key management system is necessary to use them securely. Each distinct pair of communicating parties must share a different key. The number of keys required increases with the number of network members. This requires very complex key management schemes in large networks. It is also difficult to establish a secret key exchange between two communicating parties when a secure channel doesn't already exist between them.

NOTE: If you don't already have a secure channel, it's *impossible* to establish a shared but secret key. DHX gets around this by creating a transient secure channel.

Whitfield Diffie and Martin Hellman are considered by some to be pioneers of *public-key cryptography*. They proposed the notion of public-key (also called *asymmetric-key*) cryptography, with the Diffie-Hellman key exchange protocol, in which two different but mathematically related keys are used: a public key and a private key. A public key system is constructed so that calculation of the private key is computationally infeasible from knowledge of the public key, even though they are necessarily related. Instead, both keys are generated secretly, as an interrelated pair. In public-key cryptosystems, the public key may be freely distributed, while its paired private key must remain secret. The public key is used for encryption, while the private or secret key is used for decryption.

Who actually invented the first public-key cryptography systems is still up for debate. Ronald Rivest, Adi Shamir, and Len Adleman invented RSA, another public-key system. Later, it was widely held that asymmetric cryptography had been invented by James H. Ellis at GCHQ, a British intelligence organization, even though the Diffie-Hellman and RSA algorithms had been previously demonstrated. In the end, Diffie-Hellman and RSA, were shown to be the first public examples of high quality public-key cryptosystems and are among the most widely used.

In addition to encryption, public-key cryptography can be used to implement digital signature schemes. *Digital signatures* are somewhat like ordinary signatures; they are easy for a user to produce but difficult for anyone else to forge. Digital signatures can also be permanently tied to the content of the message being signed because they cannot be "moved" from one document to another; any attempt would be detectable. In digital signature schemes, there are two algorithms: one for signing, in which a secret key is used to process the message (or a hash of the message or both), and one for verification, in which the matching public key is used with the message to check the validity of the signature. RSA and DSA are two of the most popular digital signature schemes. Digital signatures are central to the operation of public-key infrastructures and to many network security schemes (SSL/TLS, many VPNs, and so on). Digital signatures provide users with the ability to verify the integrity of the message, thus allowing for nonrepudiation of the communication.

Public-key algorithms are most often based on the computational complexity of "hard" problems, often from number theory. The hardness of RSA is related to the integer factorization problem, while Diffie-Hellman and DSA are related to the suitability of an algorithm as the basis of a public-key cryptosystem depends on the difficulty of deriving the private key from the public key. Ideally it would be at least as hard as guessing the private key at random.. More recently, *elliptic-curve cryptography* has developed in which security is based on number theoretic problems involving elliptic curves. Because of the complexity of the underlying problems, most public-key algorithms involve operations such as modular multiplication and exponentiation, which are much more computationally expensive than the techniques used in most block ciphers, especially with typical key sizes, which are frequently exclusive-OR (XOR) operations.. As a result, public-key cryptosystems are commonly "hybrid" systems, in which a fast symmetric-key encryption algorithm is used for the message itself, while the relevant symmetric key is sent with the message, but encrypted using a public-key algorithm. Or, relating back to the introduction of Diffie-Hellman Exchange earlier, two parties use asymmetric encryption to agree on a shared session key. Subsequent communication is symmetrically encrypted using that key. Hybrid signature schemes are also often used, in which a cryptographic hash function is computed, and only the resulting hash is digitally signed.

Cryptography continues to move forward in an almost exponential manner. Although much of the cryptographic data in use today stems from the research done in the 1970s and earlier, new advances and refinements occur all the time. New techniques are emerging today that will change the shape of cryptography 10 to 20 years from now, making the keys, hashes, and algorithms we use today look like child's play. As data grows and computers get faster, though, it is important to have a basic understanding of some of the cryptographic standards you will run into on a regular basis.

Index

■Symbols and Numerics

\# character, Unix files, 69
\#MREGS column, top command, 37
\#PRTS column, top command, 37
% character
    referencing groups, 72
    Unix files, 70
% CPU column, Activity Monitor, 34
%MEM column, ps command, 36
* wildcard, sudoers file, 73
\+ character
    indicating ACEs exist, 96
- (file) type, POSIX, 83
/ character, sudoers file, 73
? wildcard, sudoers file, 73
[!...] wildcard, sudoers file, 73
[...] wildcard, sudoers file, 73
_ (underscore) character
    accounts beginning with, 65
35-Pass Erase option, 22
400/401/402/403 error codes, 389
500 error code, 389
7-Pass Erase option, 22
802.11a/802.11n protocols, 326
802.11b/802.11g protocols, 326, 346
802.11i protocol, AirPort, 327
802.1x protocol, 292–293, 326

■A

a option
    mount command, 75
    ps command, 35
about:config page, Firefox, 195
access control
    controlling directory access, 388–391
    controlling search engine access, 386
    controlling use of Finder, 56
    discretionary access controls (DAC), 156, 374
    enabling MAC filtration, 335
    firewalls, 285
    granular control of managed settings in Leopard, 63
    limiting access to services, 423–424
    limiting access to web sites, 58–59
    MAC address access controls, 336
    mandatory access control (MAC), 157, 374
    network access control, 290
    password reset utility, 11
    restricting access with sudoers, 69–74
    restricting Apache access, 380
    restricting network services, 291–292
    restricting user access to applications, 57
    role-based access control (RBAC), 374
    sandbox access control, 157
    securing mount points, 74–75
    service access control lists (SACLs), 424
    setting time limits for access, 61–62
    setting up parental controls, 56–62
access control entries *see* ACEs
access control lists *see* ACLs
Access Control tab, Keychain Access, 238, 239
access levels, POSIX, 80, 82–84
access rights, ACEs controlling, 80
access rights, ACLs *see under* ACLs
access.log file, 134
accessibility
    file system permissions, 79
    keychain securing sensitive data, 234
Account tab, MobileMe, 514
account types, Mac OS X, 51–53
    administrative user, 51
    group accounts, 53
    guest accounts, 53

root users, 53
standard user, 51
accounts
 beginning with underscore (_), 65
 disabling superuser account, 55, 56
 enabling superuser account, 54–55
 external accounts, 68
 hidden service users and groups, 65
 local administrative accounts, 68
 Mac OS X security, 4–6
 sharing accounts, 52–53
Accounts preference pane, 4–8
 Advanced Options, 64
 Automatic login option, 6
 Change Password button, 5
 encrypting user data, FileVault, 258, 259
 Login Options button, 6
  removing administrative access, 8
 securely binding clients to Open Directory, 441, 442
 setting passwords, 4, 5
 setting up group accounts, 53–54
 setting up sharing accounts, 52
 setting up VPN account, 419
Accounts tab, AirPort, 364
ACEs (access control entries), 91–94
 ACL access rights, 91–93
 administration category, 91
 avoiding ACEs for specific users, 96
 conflicting access privileges, 97
 creating inherited ACEs with chmod, 106
 defining custom privilege sets, 99, 100
 indicating ACEs exist, 96
 inheritance category, 93
 Mac OS X, 80
 mapping ACE permissions, 99
 permissions with ACLs, 356
 propagating permissions, 100
 read-permissions category, 92
 removing, 107
 write-permissions category, 92–93
ACLs (access control lists), 80, 91–97
 access rights
  Append/Add Directories, 93
  Apply to All Descendants, 93
  Apply to Child Files, 93
  Apply to Child Folders, 93
  Apply to this folder, 93
  Change Ownership, 91
  Change Permissions, 91
  Delete, 93
  Delete Child, 93
  Execute/Search, 92
  Read access, 92
  Read Attribute, 92
  Read Ext Attribute, 92
  Read Permissions, 92
  Write Attributes, 92
  Write Ext Attributes, 92
  Write/Add Files, 92
 conflicting ACEs, 97
 Discretionary Access Controls, 156
 Finder managing permissions, 103
 implementing custom LDAP ACLs, 444
 inheret_only flag, 93
 managing from command line, 106
 managing on OS X server, 97–103
 managing permissions with chmod, 105–106
 mtree support for, 110
 NFS shares, 94
 permissions, 356–357
 propagating ACLs, 101
 protocol support and effective permissions, 94–95
 removing, 107
 using ACLs, 95–97
Acquire image screen, MacForensicsLab, 546–548
actions
 mandatory access control (MAC), 157
Active Directory
 AD-Plugin, 454, 455–456, 457
 binding to, 455, 456
 configuring OS X machine to use, 455
 DAVE communicating with AD controller, 367
 domain, 455, 456
 enforcing managed preferences on systems using AD service, 452
 forest, 455, 456
 integrating Open Directory with, 454–458
  dual directory, 458
 setting up network homes with AD clients, 456–457
 using profile location as UNC path, 456
Active Processes option, Activity Monitor, 33
active scanning, 486
active-active fault-tolerant solution, 532
 round-robin DNS, 532–533
active-passive fault-tolerant solution, 531

Activity Monitor utility, 31–35
    % CPU column, 34
    analyzing processes, 50, 51
    Kind column, 35
    Process ID (PID), 33, 34
    Process Name column, 34
    RAM used, 35
    Real Memory column, 35
    Show options, 31, 32
    SUID applications, 75
    Task Manager, Windows, 131
    Threads column, 34
    User column, 34
    virtual memory, 35
actors
    mandatory access control (MAC), 157
ad hoc networks, securing, 340
add command, ipfw, 319
add directories privilege, ACEs, 93
add file privilege, ACEs, 92
Add new member screen, Retrospect, 522, 523
add_file privilege, 92
add-in modules, CDSA, 572
address masking, 322
admin user, Mac OS X, 81
administration category, ACEs, 91
Administration tab, CUPS, 19, 20
administrative users, 8, 51
    local administrative accounts, 68
    removing administrative access, 8
    sudo command, 69
    when to log in as, 8
AD-Plugin, 454, 455–456
    using from command line, 457
Advanced Options, Accounts preference pane, 64
Advanced tab, Firefox security, 190
adware, 228
AES (Advanced Encryption Standard)
    block ciphers, 573
    encrypted disk images, 244
        hdiutil command, 253
    Encryption field, Disk Utility, 246
affinities
    storage pools, Xsan, 561
AFP (Apple Filing Protocol), 300, 357–359
    configuring AFP sharing, 358
    file sharing security, OS X Server, 466–470
        AFP authentication options, 467–468

AFP logging, 469–470
    Kerberos authentication, 468–469
    limiting access to files/folders, 358
    port number, 301
AFP masquerading, 467
    disabling, 468
agentpass option, hdiutil command, 255
agents
    LaunchAgents service, 44
Aircrack, 348
Aireplay, 347
Airforge, 349
Airodump command, 348
AirPort, 327–328
    changing default password, 329
    choosing wireless protocol, 330
    configuring, 330–333
        older versions, 328–330
        port mappings, 333
        wireless encryption type, 332
    creating closed network, 337, 338
    dangers of Internet Sharing, 315
    directing web traffic, 333
    disabling, 340
    DMZ (demilitarized zone), 341
    enabling firewall, 332–333
    enabling MAC filtration, 335
    encryption protocols, 327
    hardware filtering, 334–336
    limiting DHCP scope, 333–334
    logging, 336–337
    network adapters, 315
    redirecting traffic to different ports, 333
    setting encryption, 329
    sharing files with, 362–366
    SSID suppression, 337
    types of, 327
    wireless hacking tools, 342–347
AirPort (graphite), 327
    configuring, 328
AirPort Admin Utility (for older versions)
    adding security using, 328
    changing default password, 329
    choosing wireless protocol, 330
    configuring older versions, 328–330
    setting encryption, 329
AirPort Express, 327, 339
    configuring, 328
AirPort Extreme (N), 327
    AirPort Utility, 330–334
AirPort Extreme (snow), 327

configuring, 328
AirPort ID
    identifying MAC address, 335
AirPort Inspector, 345
    Base station details, 346
AirPort networks
    finding, 344
    wireless AirPort network, 279
AirPort Utility, 330–334
    Accounts tab, 364
    Base Station tab, 331, 338
    DHCP tab, 333–334
    Disks tab, 363
    Internet Connection tab, 332
    Logging & SNMP tab, 336
    NAT tab, 333
    Wireless tab, 331, 332
AirTunes, 339
ALF (Application Layer Firewall), 301, 306
    configuring from command line, 312
    launchd starting/stopping ALF, 312
    socketfilterfw managing, 312
algorithms, public-key, 575
aliases, adding, 64
aliases, sudoers file, 72
    Cmnd_Alias, 73
    granting resource access to, 73
    Host_Alias, 73
    Runas_Alias, 73
    User_Alias, 72
all mask, pipes, 322
All Processes option, Activity Monitor, 32, 34
allow command, ipfw, 319
Allow option
    accessing applications, 306, 307
    Location directive, CUPS, 19
Always option, managed preferences
    configuring policies, 449
always_set_home flag, sudoers file, 71
Analyze screen, MacForensicsLab, 548–551
anonymous binding, 428
    securing LDAP by preventing, 439–441
antispam tools, Mac OS X Server, 210–211
antivirus software, 218–228
    best practices for combating malware, 227
    ClamXav, 221–226
    Mac OS X, 219
    McAfee VirusScan, 220
    Norton AntiVirus, 220–221
    problems with, 220
    Sophos Anti-Virus for Mac OS X, 226–227
    virus definitions, 220
    virus files to test system, 228
    zero-day exploits, 221
Apache web server, 378
    enabling, 377
    restricting access, 380
    securing by disabling unnecessary services in, 382
APIs (Application Programming Interfaces)
    Common Data Security Architecture, 571
APOP (Authenticated POP)
    options for securing mail password, 198
Append/Add Directories access right, 93
appfirewall.log file, 120–121
Apple Active Directory service *see* Active Directory
Apple AirPort *see* AirPort
Apple Filing Protocol *see* AFP
Apple Keychain, 556
Apple Mail *see* Mail
Apple Partition Map, Disk Utility, 250
Apple PasswordServer *see* PasswordServer
Apple Remote Desktop *see* ARD
Apple updates
    Software Update preference pane, 14
AppleScript
    script malware attacks, 217
application authentication, 141–143
application bundle, 30
application identification
    see also identification
    application authentication, 141, 143
    bundle identifier, 142
    creator codes, 141, 142
application integrity, 143–144
application layer, 278
    moving packets, 279
    securing, 278
Application Layer Firewall *see* ALF
Application Programming Interfaces *see* APIs
application signing, 139–156
    application authentication, 141–143
    application integrity, 143–144
    signature enforcement in OS X, 144–152
    keychain access, 145–146
    signing/verifying applications, 153–156
application-level encryption, 278

applications, 29
    allowing/denying access to, 306
    Common Data Security Architecture, 571
    enabling third-party applications, 305
    restricting user access to, 57
    signing and verifying, 153–156
    SUID applications, 75–76
    trusted applications, 145, 312
    validating authenticity of, 46
Applications policy
    managed preferences, 449, 451
Apply to All Descendants access right, 93
Apply to Child Files access right, 93
Apply to Child Folders access right, 93
Apply to this folder access right, 93
architecture
    Common Data Security Architecture, 571–572
archiving logs *see* rotating logs
ARD (Apple Remote Desktop), 402
    pushing sudoers file to other users, 74
    when to enable and dangers, 303
ARIN, 393
ARP requests, stealth mode, 310
ASL (Apple System Logger) database
    viewing log files using Console, 115
aslmanager, 115
asymmetric-key cryptography, 574
attach verb, hdiutil command, 251, 252
attacks
    code injection, 398–399
    cross-site scripting (XSS), 398–399
    Distributed Denial of Service (DDoS), 215
    Denial of Service (DoS), 215, 321
    dictionary, 349
    directory traversal, 384
    man-in-the-middle, 288
    Newsham 21-bit, 343
    PASV theft, 374
    proof-of-concept, 325
    social engineering, 488
    SQL Injection, 398
attributes, 426
    augmented records, 458
    Read Attribute access right, 92
    Read Ext Attribute access right, 92
    Write Attributes access right, 92
    Write Ext Attributes access right, 92
Attributes tab, Keychain Access, 237, 238
Audit screen, MacForensicsLab, 554
auditing

mtree file system permissions, 109–111
augmented records, 458
authenticate flag, sudoers file, 71
Authenticated Binding field options
    securing Open Directory, 435–436
Authenticated POP (APOP), 438
    options for securing mail password, 198
authentication, 49, 50
    802.1x protocol, 292, 293
    application authentication, 141–143
    authenticating protocols, 197
    Cisco VPN client, 418
    file sharing security, AFP, 467–468
        Kerberized AFP, 468–469
    Kerberos, 426
    L2TP-based VPN, 415
    pluggable authentication modules, 50
    passwordless authentication, 172, 174
    securing with PasswordServer, 437–439
    SMB authentication, 371
    SSH (Secure Shell), 413
authentication authority
    Kerberosv5, 65
    ShadowHash, 65, 66
authentication methods
    enabling/disabling, 438, 439
authentication settings, Mail, 199
authentication_authority key, .plist, 65
authenticity
    validating applications/services, 46
authorization, 49
    401 error code, 389
auto-lock settings
    managing multiple keychains, 241
Automatic login option
    Accounts preference pane, 6
    disabling automatic login, 9
Automator
    application bundles, 31
    creating new services, 40
    Mac OS X, 217
    script malware attacks, 217

B

Back to My Mac feature, 404–405
Back to My Mac tab, MobileMe, 405
backdoors, 143, 214, 216
    RavMonE.exe, 216
backhaul, 326
backticks (`)

securing Perl scripts, 385
Backup Assistant, Retrospect, 520–525
    encryption for backup destinations, 522
    selecting sources to backup, 520, 521
    specifying backup destination, 521, 522
backup domain controller (BDC), 453
backup.sb profile, 177
backups
    creating offsite copy of critical data, 513–517
    effect of volumes changing, 248
    MobileMe, 513–517
    need for, 505
    redundancy, cold sites, 533
    redundancy, hot sites, 534
    Retrospect, 517–529
    security of, 507
    services, 534–535
    sparse bundles, 248–250
    SuperDuper, 512–513
    tape libraries, 530–531
    Time Machine, 506–512
    virtual machines, 509
backups vs. fault tolerance, 531–533
    fault-tolerant solutions, 531–532
    load-balancing devices, 533
    round-robin DNS, 532–533
BAND SIZE
    sparse-band-size key, diskutil, 257
bandwidth limiting, 321, 322
Base Station tab, AirPort, 331, 338
base.sb profile
    using Sandbox to secure user shells, 167–170
basename function
    securing PHP, 384
BDC (backup domain controller), 453
beta versions of software, 213
BIND, 177–178
BIND DNS server, 177
binding
    securely binding clients to Open Directory, 441–443
    securing LDAP by preventing anonymous binding, 439–441
    to Active Directory, 455
binding policies
    securing Open Directory using, 435–437
bit-flag system
    modes (access levels), POSIX, 83, 84
BitTorrent sites, 280

black-box testing, 486
block ciphers, 573
Block incoming connections
    Cyberduck, 306
    firewall settings, 149, 307–308
blogging
    InfoSec acceptable use policy, 568, 569
blued daemon, 30
Bluetooth preference pane
    Discoverable option, 16
    System Preferences, 16–18
Bluetooth security, 16–18
Bluetooth Sharing service, 39
Bluetooth-PDA-Sync, 18
bonding, 561
Bonjour
    configuring Timbuktu security, 412
bonjour_module
    disabling unnecessary services in Apache, 382
boot loader, 267
bots
    controlling search engine access, 386
    disabling Googlebot, 394
broadcast storm, 290
browser security *see* web browser security
Brutal Gift tool, 349
brute force
    attempting to guess passwords by, 120
    KisMAC, 343
bsd.sb sandbox profiles
    accessing low-level functions, 165
bssid, 348
bundle identifier, 142
bundles
    application bundle, 30
    Safari bundle, 309
    sparse bundles, 248–250

C

caching
    dscacheutil command, 67
    securing Open Directory, 437
Carbon
    launching non-Mach-O Carbon-based application, 160
Carbon Copy Cloner *see* CCC
Cases screen, MacForensicsLab, 542, 543
cases, computer forensics, 540
cases, MacForensicsLab

reviewing case, 554–555
Casper Suite
    pushing sudoers file to other users, 74
CCC (Carbon Copy Cloner), 172–174
    rsync, 172, 173, 174
    scp, 172, 173
    ssh, 172
cd command, Metasploit, 502
CD/DVD with ISO data option, 250
CDSA (Common Data Security Architecture), 571–572
Certificate Assistant
    Keychain Access application, 475
certificates
    adding, Entourage, 200
    creating self-signed signing certificate, 154
    digital certificate, 153
    guarantee of legitimacy, 149
    self-signed certificates, 392
    signing and verifying applications, 154
    SSL certificates, OS X security, 474–475
    trusted authorities, 392
    user changing password on disk images, 254
    viewing certificates for contacts, 201
Certificates screen, Entourage, 200, 201
CGI (Common Gateway Interface)
    disabling, 381
    securing files on web server, 396
CGI-BIN directory, 381
CGI-Executables directory, 381
cgi-redirect, securing PHP, 383
CGPSA, using with CommuniGate Pro, 211
chain of custody of data, forensics, 538
challenge, NTLMv1, 371
Change Ownership access right, 91
Change Password button
    Accounts preference pane, 5
Change Permissions access right, 91
Change Settings setting, Remote Management, 407
characters
    filtering user input, 399
Check Point, 267–269
checksum, MacForensicsLab, 546
chflags command, 105
chgrp command, 104
child files/folders
    Apply to Child Files/Folders access rights, 93

child processes, 30
chmod command
    ACL group names containing spaces, 106
    creating inherited ACEs with, 106
    managing ACLs using, 97
    managing permissions, 104–107
    suid/sguid bits, 87
chown permission, 91, 104–107
chpass verb, hdiutil command, 254
Chronology tab, MacForensicsLab, 555
chroot command, 471
CIFS daemon
    configuring SMB workgroup for DAVE, 369
ciphers
    block ciphers, 573
    steam ciphers, 574
Cisco VPN client
    authentication, 418
    configuring, 418
    connecting to, 417–418
ClamAV antispam tool, 478
    Mac OS X Server, 210
ClamXav antivirus software, 221–226
    Folder Sentry feature, 225, 226
    schedule scan preferences, 225
    Snow Leopard, 221
    virus scanner, 224
Classic policy
    managed preferences, 449
Clear Recent History option, Firefox, 191
client IP addresses
    enabling Internet Sharing, 314
client management
    Managed Client OS X (MCX), 149–152
    parental controls, 152
client security *see* firewalls
client-server networks, 282, 354
client-side caching
    securing Open Directory, 437
clients
    providing directory services for Windows clients, 453–454
    securely binding clients to Open Directory, 441–443
    wireless security on client computers, 339–340
Clients tab, SquidMan utility, 296
clipboard (pboard) process, 43
Cloverleaf, 562

clustered file systems, Xsan, 559
CMD column, ps command, 35
Cmnd Alias, sudoers file, 70, 73
    combining PPP and SSH as VPN link, 419
    syntax of sudoers file, 74
code injection attacks, 398–399
    cross-site scripting (XSS), 398–399
    protecting web site from, 399
    SQL Injection, 398
Code Red worm, 216
code signing, 144, 153
codesign tool, 155, 309
cold sites, backups, 533
com.apple.pboard process, 43
command line commands
    viewing output one screen at a time, 36
command-line logs, 123
Common Data Security Architecture (CDSA), 571–572
Common Gateway Interface *see* CGI
Common Security Services Manager (CSSM), 571
Common Unix Printing System *see* CUPS
communication
    limiting via iChat and Mail, 59–61
communication paths, roles, 300
CommuniGate Pro, 211–212
computer forensics, 537
    see also MacForensicsLab
    cases, 540
    chain of custody of data, 538
    checksum, 546
    command-line tools, 558
    creating image of unaltered evidence, 544
    disabling disk arbitration, 538
    forensically acquiring disk images, 557
    incident response, 538–539
    MacForensicsLab, 539–556
    other GUI tools for, 556
    Safari Forensic Tools (SFT), 557
    smeared images, 546
    tainting evidence, 538
    write blocking, 538
Computer Forensics World, 537
computer programs, 29
computer-to-computer networks, securing, 340–341
confidentiality *see* data confidentiality
connections

automatically allowing signed software to create, 149, 308–309
Block incoming connections, Cyberduck, 306
blocking all incoming connections, 149, 307–308
connecting over FTP, 373
finding IP addresses, 302
half connection, 489
remote connectivity, 402–408
TCP connect scan, 489
Console Messages screen
    viewing log files, 115
Console utility, 115–118
    copy data from log files, 117
    Database Searches section, 117
    Event Viewer, Windows, 130
    marking log files, 116–117
    searching log files, 117–118
    viewing log files, 115–116, 125
        large log files, 117
contacts
    securing Open Directory, 437
    viewing certificates for, 201
Content tab, Firefox, 194, 195
Control setting, Remote Management, 407
controlling access *see* access control
cookies, 186
    Only from sites I visit option, Safari, 187
    Show Cookies button, Safari, 186
copy issues, troubleshooting, 43
Copy items setting, Remote Management, 407
copyrighted material
    InfoSec acceptable use policy, 566
    peer-to-peer networks, 281
cowpatty tool, 349
CPU column, Activity Monitor, 34
cracking WEP keys, 347–348
cracking wireless networks
    safeguards against, 349–350
cracking WPA-PSK, 348–349
CrashReporter, 124
create verb, hdiutil command, 253
creator codes
    application identification, 141, 142
credentials
    configuring Open Directory, 430, 431
    Nessus, 499
crontab
    hard links security issues, 107

cross-site scripting (XSS) attacks, 398–399
cryptographic hash functions, 574
cryptography, 573–576
    asymmetric-key cryptography, 574
    block ciphers, 573
    Diffie-Hellman key exchange protocol, 574
    elliptic-curve cryptography, 575
    public-key cryptography, 574, 575
    stream ciphers, 574
    symmetric-key cryptography, 573, 574
CSSM (Common Security Services Manager), 571
cu.modem.log, 129
CUPS (Common Unix Printing System), 18
CUPS web interface, 19
    Administration tab, 19, 20
    Allow option, Location directive, 19
    Require User option, Limit directive, 20
cupsd daemon, 30
cut issues, troubleshooting, 43
Cyberduck, 305, 306
    allowing/denying access to, 306
    Block incoming connections option, 306

D

d (directory) type, POSIX, 83, 356
d option, mount command, 75
DAC (discretionary access control), 156
    bypassing DAC model, 157
    permission models, 374
daemons, 30
    BIND, 177
    bypassing DAC model, 157
    DirectoryService, 68
    diskarbitrationd, 43
    httpd, 378–379
    ipfwloggerd, 320
    launchd, 33, 34
    LaunchDaemons service, 44
    nessusd, 497
    pppd, 419
    sandboxing, 159
    services, 38
    slapd, 426
    stopping, 43–44
    turning on or off, 38
    verifying not running, 44
    viewing running on Mac, 38–39
daily.out log file, 126–127

Data Compression option, Retrospect, 527
data confidentiality, 233
    disk images as encrypted data stores, 243–257
    file system permissions, 79
    FileVault encrypting user data, 257–265
    full disk encryption, 266–272
    keychain securing sensitive data, 234–243
data packet encryption, 288
data theft, forensics, 537, 538
data transmission, packets, 283
data, IP packets, 283
database administrators
    accessing web site database through firewall, 398
Database Searches section, Console, 117
Database toolbar item
    installing MacForensicsLab, 540
database, MacForensicsLab, 541
datagrams, 283
DAVE, 366–372
    client using Kerberos, 371
    communicating with Active Directory controller, 367
    configuring SMB Setup name in, 368
    configuring SMB workgroup for, 368
    installing, 367
    providing description for, 369
    sharing data through Samba, 369
DAVE Login preference pane, 369
DAVE Network preference pane, 370
    Identity tab, 370
    LAN Manager Authentication Level setting, 371
    Policies tab, 370, 371, 372
dd command, forensics, 558
DDoS (Distributed Denial of Service) attacks, 215
declarations, sandbox profiles, 161, 162
    restriction declarations, 162
decryption *see* encryption
deep packet inspection (DPI), 288
default (out of the box) security settings, 3
default web site files, replacing, 379
Delete access right, ACEs, 93
Delete Child access right, ACEs, 93
delete command, ipfw, 319
delete privilege, 93
Denial of Service attacks *see* DoS
deny command, ipfw, 319

Deny option, access to applications, 306, 307
descendants
    Apply to All Descendants access right, 93
DES-encrypted data, block ciphers, 573
Desktop Database
    application identification, 141, 142
desktop solutions for securing e-mail, 207
Destinations tab, Retrospect, 527
detach verb, hdiutil command, 253
df command, 75
DHCP scope, AirPort, 333–334
dictionaries
    Hide Profanity in Dictionary option, 57
dictionary attacks
    safeguards against cracking wireless networks, 349
Diffe-Hellman exchange (DHX), 438, 574
digital certificates
    implementing, web site security, 392
    signing and verifying applications, 153
digital signatures, 575
    man-in-the-middle attack, 371
Direct tab, SquidMan utility, 296
directives, securing PHP, 383, 384
directories
    controlling directory access, 388–391
    dual-directory environment, 454
    execute mode, POSIX permissions, 82, 83
    making invisible, 105
    securing directory listings, 396–397
    sticky bit preventing deletion, 87
    write mode, POSIX permissions, 82
Directory Access application
    Active Directory integration, 454
directory nodes
    creating second local directory node, 68
directory services
    configuring in Leopard, 443
    ds prefixed commands, 66–67
    Kerberos, 426–428
    LDAP, 425–426
    local directory services, 65–69, 425
    Mac OS X Server security, 425–428
    managed preferences, 449–453
    Open Directory, 425, 428–458
    popular directory services, 426
    providing for Windows clients, 453–454
Directory Services database

POSIX permission groups, 81
directory traversal attacks, 384
directory type, POSIX, 83
Directory Utility
    binding to Active Directory using, 456
    configuring OS X to use Active Directory, 455
    disabling superuser account, 55
    enabling superuser account, 54
    root account, 69
    securely binding clients to Open Directory, 441, 442
directory_inherit permission, 93
DirectoryService daemon, 68
Disable automatic login option, 9
Disable Location Services option, 10
Disable Login Passwords options, 433
Disable remote control infrared receiver option, 10
Disable Root User option, 55
discoverable devices, 16
Discoverable option, Bluetooth, 16
discretionary access control see DAC
disk arbitration, 538
    disabling, MacForensicsLab, 544
disk images
    as encrypted data stores, 243–257
        agentpass option, hdiutil, 255
        attach verb, hdiutil, 251
        chpass verb, hdiutil, 254
        create verb, hdiutil, 253
        creating encrypted disk images, 245–251
        creating sparse image, 253
        data confidentiality, 251
        detach verb, hdiutil, 253
        Disk Utility options, 246–250
        effect of volumes changing on backups, 248
        encryption option, hdiutil, 253
        format option, hdiutil, 256
        hdiutil command, 251–257
        interfacing from command line, 251–257
        mounting disk images, 251, 252
        mountpoint option, hdiutil, 252
        nobrowse option, hdiutil, 252
        owners option, hdiutil, 252
        preventing volume showing in user's devices list, 252
        recover option, hdiutil, 255

securing data on mounted volume, 252
sparse bundles, 248–250
stdinpass option, hdiutil, 253, 255
type option, hdiutil, 253, 255, 256
volumes changing, 248
encrypted disk images, 24–25
    creating, 245–251
file extension denoting, 244
forensically acquiring disk images, 557
mounting, 244
    attach verb, hdiutil command, 251
    automating for backups, 252
    in Finder, 250
user changing password on, 254
Disk Utility application
    controlling mounting/unmounting of disks, 75
    creating encrypted disk images, 245
        Encryption field, 246
        Format (file system) field, 250
        Image Format field, 246–248
        options, 246–250
        Partitions field, 250
    encrypted disk images, 24
    restricting disk access, 74
    securely erasing disks, 21
Disk Utility logs, rotating, 121
diskarbitrationd process, 43
    disabling, 75
DiskRecording.log file, 122
disks
    controlling mounting/unmounting of, 75
    full disk encryption, 266–272
    restricting access using mount points, 74, 75
    securely erasing, 21–23
    showing mounted disks, 75
    showing volumes mounted on system, 75
Disks tab, AirPort Utility, 363
diskutil command
    controlling mounting/unmounting of disks, 75
    image formats used with, 256
    sparse-band-size key, 257
DiskUtility.log file
    reviewing command-line logs, 123
    reviewing user-specific logs, 121
Distributed Denial of Service (DDoS) attacks, 215

dmg file extension, 244
DMZ (demilitarized zone), 286
    AirPort, 341
    managed switches, 290
DNS, 277
    BIND DNS server, 177
    Kerberos, 427
    Mac OS X Server security, 473
    masquerading as DNS server, 489
    reverse-domain notation, 142
    round-robin DNS, 532–533
DNS zone transfers, 489
Dock policy, managed preferences, 449
domain names, identifying, 488
domains
    Active Directory, 455, 456
    naming internal, 473
    reverse-domain notation, 142
    Safe Domains tab, Entourage, 205, 206
DoS (Denial of Service) attacks, 215, 321
    firewalls, 285
    InfoSec acceptable use policy, 567
    security through obscurity, 279
dosevasive, script security, 384
DPI (deep packet inspection), 288
drives
    mapping within Windows, 456
    mount command, 75
    not automatically registering/mounting, 75
drones, 215
drop-box folder
    hard link security issues, 107
    POSIX example, 90
dscacheutil command, 67
dscl command, 67, 440
    viewing managed preferences, 451
dsconfigad command
    Active Directory integration, 454, 455
    file sharing security, Samba, 470
    using AD-Plugin from command line, 457
dseditgroup command, 67
dsenableroot command, 55, 67
dserr command, 67
dsexport command, 67
dsimport command, 67
dsmemberutil command, 67
dsperfmonitor command, 67
dst-ip mask, pipes, 322
dst-port mask, pipes, 322
dual-directory environment, 454

dual directory, setting up, 458
Duh worm, iPhone, 144
dummynet, 321–324
    creating pipes, 321–322
    pipe masks, 322–323
    queues, 323–324
DVD or CD Sharing service, 38
DVD/CD Master option, Disk Utility, 246
Dynamic Host Control Protocol (DHCP)
    enabling Internet Sharing, 313

E

echo requests
    stealth mode, 310
edu.mit.Kerberos file
    file sharing security, AFP, 468
Effective Permissions tool, Server Admin, 102, 103
EFI (extensible firmware interface), 268
Eicar.org
    virus files to test system, 228
Elk Cloner, 216
elliptic-curve cryptography, 575
e-mail
    Junk E-mail Found alert, 206
    macro viruses attaching to, 217
    spam, 206
        protecting against, 184
    SSL protection, 185
    using strong passwords, 184
e-mail alerts, MacForensicsLab, 544
e-mail attachments
    best practices for combating malware, 227
    script malware attacks, 217
e-mail headers, 202
e-mail hoaxes
    socially engineered malware, 218
e-mail security, 196–202
    see also mail protocols
    antispam tools, Mac OS X Server, 210–211
    blocking access to mail being sent over port 25, 200
    CommuniGate Pro, 211–212
    desktop solutions, 207
    Entourage, 199–202
    establishing mail provider protocol support, 197
    GPGMail, 207
    Kerio MailServer, 208–210
    Keychain Access utility, 197
    Mail port settings for SSL, 197
    mail server-based solutions for spam and viruses, 207–212
    options for securing mail password, 198
    PGP Desktop, 207
    SSL, 196–199
    verifying authenticity of server, 197
    viewing certificates for contacts, 201
Enable Junk Mail Filtering checkbox, 203
Enable Root User option, 54
Enable stealth mode, 149
enableSSO option, dsconfigad command, 457
EnCase, 539
encrypted disk images, 24–25
    creating, 245–251
        Disk Utility options, 246–250
    disk images as encrypted data stores, 243–257
    interfacing from command line, 251–257
        hdiutil command, 251–257
    user changing password on disk images, 254
encrypted keychains, 25–26
encryption, 233–272
    AirPort encryption protocols, 327
    AirPort, setting for older versions of, 329
    application-level encryption, 278
    Check Point, 267–269
    configuring Entourage to use SSL, 199
    cryptography, 573–576
    data packet encryption, 288
    disk images as encrypted data stores, 243–257
    extensible firmware interface (EFI), 268
    encrypting beyond home directory, 13
    FileVault, 11
        encrypting user data, 257–265
    Firefox security, 190
    FTP, 374
    full disk encryption (FDE), 13, 266–272
    GPG tools, 207
    InfoSec acceptable use policy, 565
    keychain securing sensitive data, 234–243
    password security, 184
    PGP Desktop, 207
    PGP Encryption, 269–270
    public-key-encryption, 174

safeguards against cracking wireless networks, 349
SecureDoc, 271–272
symmetric-key cryptography, 573, 574
TrueCrypt, 270–271
Encryption field, Disk Utility, 246
encryption option, hdiutil command, 253
encryption, AirPort, 332
Entourage
adding certificates, 200
advanced receiving options, 199
advanced sending options, 200
Certificates screen, 200, 201
configuring to use SSL, 199
e-mail security, 199–202
filtering spam with, 204–205
programming with, 202
security preferences, 201, 202
using white listing in, 205–206
viewing certificates for contacts, 201
enumerating web servers, 395–396
enumeration, 488
env_editor flag, sudoers file, 71
equal cost path, round-robin DNS, 532
Erase tab, Disk Utility, 21, 22
error codes, 389
error keyword
items to lookout for in log files, 129
errors
dserr command, 67
escaping characters, sudoers file, 73
etc/authorization file, 50
etc/ipfilter/ipfw.conf, 320
etc/services file
port utilization for services, 278
etc/smb.conf file
file sharing security, Samba, 470
Ethereal, 349
Ethernet card, network adapters, 315
Ethernet network, 279
Power over Ethernet (PoE), 290
Ethernet protocol, 283
EtherPeek, 347
Ettercap, 347
Event Viewer, Windows, 130–131
accountability for reviewing logs, 134
EventID.net, 131
everyone, POSIX permissions, 355
evidence, computer forensics
creating image of unaltered evidence, 544

risk of tainting evidence, 538
Examiners screen, MacForensicsLab, 541
examiners, MacForensicsLab, 542
execute mode, POSIX permissions, 82, 83
alpha/decimal/binary formats, 84
file sharing, 355
execute permission, files, 92
Execute/Search access right, ACEs, 92
exit command, Metasploit, 502
exploits, Metasploit, 503
exporting directory services data, 67
Exposé application
assigning key or hot corner, 10
extended attributes
Read Ext Attribute access right, 92
Write Ext Attributes access right, 92
Extended file system (HFS+)
permissions with ACLs, 356
external accounts, 68

F

f option, dsconfigad command, 457
f option, mount command, 75
failed keyword
items to lookout for in log files, 129
failover see fault-tolerant solutions
false positives, spam filtering, 203, 204, 207
Fast User Switching, 8
fault tolerance see backups vs. fault tolerance
fault-tolerant solutions, 531–532
active-active, 532
active-passive, 531
FDE see full disk encryption
Fibre Channel, 559, 561
Xsan metadata, 560
file permissions see permissions
file security, Mac OS X, 354–357
LKDC, 355
POSIX permissions, 355–356
file security, web server, 396–398
file sharing
AirPort, 362–366
Apple Filing Protocol (AFP), 357–359
limiting access to files/folders, 358
client-server networks, 354
configuring AFP sharing, 358
DAVE, 366–372
FTP, 372–374
peer-to-peer (P2P) networks, 354

permission models, 374–375
permissions with ACLs, 356–357
risks of, 353
Samba (SMB), 359–362
Sharing Only account, 353
viewing shared folders, 464
file sharing security, OS X Server, 463–471
  AFP, 466–470
  FTP, 471
  NFS, 465–466
  Samba (SMB), 470
File Sharing service, 39
File Sharing tab, Server Admin
  managing ACLs, 97, 98
  modifying POSIX permissions, 98
file size, 465
file system access, sandbox profiles, 164
file system, Disk Utility, 250
file systems
  clustered file systems, 559
  mount command options, 75
  mtree auditing permissions, 109–111
file type, POSIX, 83
File Types to Include screen, MacForensicsLab, 553
file_inherit permission, 93
files, making invisible, 105
FileVault, 11, 12
  changing settings, 13
  enabling FileVault for users, 260–262
  encrypting beyond home directory, 13
  encrypting user data, 257–265
  full disk encryption, 266, 267
  limitations of sparse images, 264–266
  master password, 263–264
  reclaiming space, 264–266
  setting master password, 13
  setting up before other users, 12
FileVault tab
  Security preference pane, 12–13
FileVaultMaster keychain, 263, 264
file-write* provisions, sandbox, 164
Filter box, Console Toolbar, 117
filtered port, 491
filtering
  Apple Mail for spam, 203–204
  characters from user input, 399
  hardware, AirPort, 334–336
  spam with Entourage, 204–205
Final Cut Server, backing up, 535
Finder
  controlling use of, 56
  finding log files, 118
  full disk encryption, 266
  managing permissions, 103–104
  modifying .DS_Store files, 248
  mounting disk images in, 250
  Sharing & Permissions window, 104
  sparse bundles viewed from, 249
Finder drop-box folder
  POSIX example, 90
Finder policy
  managed preferences, 449, 452
Finder Services menu, Snow Leopard, 40
fingerprinting, 486–488
  IP addresses, 487
  Network Utility performing whois lookup, 487
  nmap, 489
  port scanning, 488
  tools for, 486
Firefox
  indicating allowed application is not signed, 151
  Mac OS X standards and, 196
  Master Password dialog box, 193
  privacy, 190–192
  security
    about:config page, 195
    Advanced tab, 190
    Content tab, 194, 195
    encryption, 190
    Java, 195
    JavaScript, 194
    pop-up windows, 194
    Privacy icon, 190, 191
    saving passwords, 192 194
    Security tab, 193
  viewing saved passwords, 194
  web browser security, 189–196
Firewall tab, Security preferences, 13–14, 147, 304–310
firewalls, 285, 299
  accessing web site database through firewall, 398
  advanced settings, 148–149
  Application Layer Firewall (ALF), 301, 306, 312
  allowing/denying access to applications, 306
  allowing signed software to create connections, 308–309

appfirewall.log file, 120–121
blocking all incoming connections, 307–308
command line configuration, 315–324
    dummynet, 321–324
    ipfw, 317–320
configuring, 303, 304–307
controlling services, 301–304
disabling, 305
enabling, 13, 305
    AirPort, 332–333
    stealth mode, 309–310
    third-party services/applications, 305
hardware appliance firewall, 299
ipfw firewall, 147
launchd starting/stopping ALF, 312
Mac OS X protecting other computers, 313–315
network adapters, 315
network services, 300–301
OS X application firewall, 147–149
outgoing network traffic blocking, 317
removing sharing services, 305
rules, 300
setting advanced firewall features, 307–310
socketfilterfw managing ALF, 312
software firewall, 299, 301
ssh security, 475
testing, 310–311
troubleshooting problems, 307
working in Leopard and Snow Leopard, 304–307
FireWire interface, network adapters, 315
First option, configuring policies, 449
flags, sudoers file, 70–71
Flash
    disabling pop-ups in Safari, 186
flow control, 291
Folder Sentry feature, ClamXav, 225, 226
folders
    Apply to this folder access right, 93
    permissions with ACLs, 356–357
    viewing shared folders, 464
FollowSymLinks directive, 397
Force Quit option, 41, 42
forensics *see* computer forensics
Forensics Toolkit (FTK), 539
forest, Active Directory, 455, 456
forgotten passwords
    password reset options, 11

Format (file system) field, Disk Utility, 250
format option
    diskutil command, 256
    hdiutil command, 256
fqdn flag, sudoers file, 71
FTP, 372–374
    connecting over, 373
    DMZ (demilitarized zone), 286
    enabling FTP sharing, 372, 373
    encryption, 374
    file sharing security, OS X Server, 471
    PASV mode, 374
    security, 373
    sftp, 397
FTP Access service
    when to enable and dangers, 303
Full Control permission, ACE
    mapping permissions to rights, 99
full disk encryption (FDE), 13, 266–272
    Check Point, 267–269
    PGP Encryption, 269–270
    SecureDoc, 271–272
    TrueCrypt, 270–271
fully qualified hostnames
    flags defining privileges in sudoers file, 71

G

gateways, 283
General tab
    Security preference pane, 9–11
    SquidMan utility, 295–296
Generate Reports setting, Remote Management, 407
generated unique identifier (GUID)
    permissions with ACLs, 356
generateduid key, 65
ggid option, dsconfigad command, 457
gid keyword, mtree, 109
global password policies
    securing Open Directory accounts, 432–435
gnam keyword, mtree, 109
golden master, MacForensicsLab, 546
Google
    protecting privacy of information, 394–395
Googlebot, disabling, 394
GPG tools, 207
GPGMail, 207

grooming scripts, Retrospect, 525–527
group accounts, 53
    storage of, 65
groups
    adding users to, 53–54
    creating, 53
        Open Directory groups, 446–447
    defining group of computers, 73
    dseditgroup command, 67
    POSIX permissions, 104, 355
GSSAPI (Kerberos Version 5)
    options for securing mail password, 198
guest accounts, 53
    hidden service users and groups, 65
GUID partition map
    Partitions field, Disk Utility, 250

H

hacking tools *see* wireless hacking tools
half scan, 491
hard links
    drop-box folder, 107
    security issues, 107–108
hard quotas, 562
hardening security, 49
hardware appliance firewall, 299
hardware filtering, AirPort, 334–336
hash directory, 66
hash files
    ntlm hash type, 66
    ShadowHash authentication, 65, 66
hash functions, cryptographic, 574
Hash Methods options
    Open Directory authentication, 437, 438
hdiutil command, disk images, 251–257
    agentpass option, 255
    attach verb, 251, 252
    chpass verb, 254
    create verb, 253
    creating sparse image, 253
    detach verb, 253
    encryption option, 253
    format option, 256
    mountpoint option, 252
    nobrowse option, 252
    owners option, 252
    recover option, 255
    stdinpass option, 253, 255
    type option, 253, 255, 256
header, IP packets, 283

Hex Content tab, MacForensicsLab, 549
HFS+ (Extended file system)
    permissions with ACLs, 356
hidden links
    blocking hosts based on robots.txt, 387
hidden processes, 301
hidden service users and groups, 65
Hide Profanity in Dictionary option, 57
hiding wireless network, 337–338
history
    Clear Recent History option, 191
history command
    accountability for reviewing logs, 134
history files
    rotating logs, 123
    reviewing command-line logs, 123
home folders
    file sharing security, NFS, 465
HOME variable
    flags defining privileges in sudoers file, 71
HomeDirectory attribute
    enabling FileVault for users, 261
honeypots, 496–497
hops
    moving packets, 278, 284
host intrusion detection, 493–494
Host_Alias, sudoers file, 70, 73
    syntax of sudoers file, 74
hosts
    blocking based on robots.txt, 387–388
hot corners
    Exposé application assigning, 10
hot sites, backups, 534
htaccess file, 388–391
    controlling directory access, 388, 389–391
    customizing error codes, 389
    password protecting Apache folder, 459
htgroup file, 388
htpasswd file, 388
    controlling directory access, 390–391
HTTP
    network protocols, 278
    port 80, 278
    port for HTTP over TLS, 391
HTTP_REFERER variable
    securing Perl scripts, 385
httpd (HTTP daemon) service, 378–379
https, SSL protection, 185
hubs, 288, 289

I

I state, ps command, 36
IANA, port numbers, 300
iChat
    limiting communication via, 59–61
iChat server, security, 477–478
id command, 67
id_dsa/id_dsa.pub keys, SSH, 414
identification, 49
    see also application identification
    authentication, 50
Identity tab, DAVE Network pane, 370
identity theft, 183, 233
iDisk data, backing up, 516
iDisk tab, MobileMe, 516, 517
IEEE 802.11 protocol, 326
ifconfig command
    changing MAC address, 287
iKee worm, iPhone, 144
image acquisition, MacForensicsLab, 546–548
Image Format field, Disk Utility
    encrypted disk images, 25, 246–248
        DVD/CD Master option, 246
        Read/Write disk image option, 246
        Sparse bundle disk image option, 247
        sparse bundles, 248–250
        Sparse disk image option, 247
images
    disk images as encrypted data stores, 243–257
    Load images automatically option, Firefox, 195
IMAP
    configuring Entourage to use SSL, 199
    e-mail security, 197
        using SSL, 196
    network protocols, 278
importing directory services data, 67
Inactive Processes option, Activity Monitor, 33
incident response plan
    reviewing logs, 134–135
incident response, forensics, 538–539
include_path, securing PHP, 384
incorrect keyword
    items to lookout for in log files, 129
infiltration, networks, 277
info command, Metasploit, 502
InfoSec
    acceptable use policy, 563–569
infrared remote controls, 10
inheret_only flag, 93
inheritance
    creating inherited ACEs with chmod, 106
    directory_inherit permission, 93
    file_inherit permission, 93
    limit_inherit permission, 93
    Make Inherited Entries Explicit, 101
    only_inherit permission, 93
    propagating ACLs, 101
    propagating permissions, 100
inheritance category, ACEs, 93
inheritance, POSIX, 84–86
injection attacks
    code injection, 398–399
    cross-site scripting (XSS), 398–399
    SQL Injection, 398
input validation
    PHP, 383–384
    securing Perl scripts, 385
install.log file, 114
insults flag, sudoers file, 71
integrity
    application integrity, 143–144
    file system permissions, 79
Intel CDSA site, 572
Internet Connection tab, AirPort, 332
Internet policy, managed preferences, 449
Internet Protocol Firewall see ipfw
Internet Sharing, 313
    dangers of, 314–315
    enabling, 313–314
    rogue access points, 290
    settings, 313
Internet Sharing service, 39
Internet tab, OS X, 305
Internet tab, Sharing preferences, 313
intrusion detection, 492–497
    host intrusion detection, 493–494
    network intrusion detection, 494–497
intrusion potential see network scanning
invisible items, Time Machine, 508
IP (Internet Protocol) see TCP/IP
IP addresses
    blocking hosts based on robots.txt, 387
    client IP addresses, 314
    configuring multiple IP addresses, 316
    connecting names with, 277
    enabling Internet Sharing, 314
    finding, 302

fingerprinting, 487
llmltIng DHCP scope, 334
moving packets, 278
restricting Apache access, 380
security through obscurity, 279
spoofing, 287
IP packets, 283
IP traffic, four-layer model, 278
IPC (inter-process communication)
Mach IPC, 163
ipfw (Internet Protocol Firewall), 317–320
commands, 318, 319
creating pipes, dummynet, 321–322
disabling firewalls, 305
etc/ipfilter/ipfw.conf, 320
ipfw rules, 318–319
outgoing network traffic blocking, 317
restricting Apache access, 380
setting logging options per rule, 319
shareware GUI tools for firewall, 147
software firewall, 301
syntax for ipfw toolkit, 317
ipfw.conf file, 320
ipfwloggerd, 320
iPhone
jail-breaking, 144
malware, 144
signing/verifying applications, 153
Ipkts field, daily.out file, 126, 127
IPSec VPN client
connecting to Cisco VPN, 417
ISP (Internet service provider)
blocking access to mail being sent over port 25, 200
establishing mail provider protocol support, 197
iStumbler, 344–346
iTunes port, AirPort Express, 339

J

Jabber, 478
jail-breaking, iPhone, 144
Java plug-ins
web browser attacks on Mac, 187
Java, Firefox security, 195
JavaScript, Firefox security, 194
Junk E-mail Found alert, 206
junk mail *see* spam

K

kdcsetup command, 448
kdestroy command, 448
Kerberized POP, 198
Kerberos, 426–428
components, 427
creating keytab files, 448
DAVE client, 371
establishing/caching Kerberos connections, 448
file sharing security, AFP, 468–469
listing tickets, 448
options for securing mail password, 198
realms, 427
removing tickets from cache, 448
securing from command line, 448
Kerberos Version 4, 198
Kerberos Version 5 (GSSAPI), 198
kerberosautoconfig command, 427, 448
Kerberosv5 authentication authority, 65
Kerio MailServer
configuring spam filter, 208–210
kernel_task process, 33, 34
kernels
memory manager for OS X kernel, 34
key authentication
securely automating remote rsync, 175
keychain
securing sensitive data, 234–243
keychain access
signature enforcement in OS X, 145–146
Keychain Access utility
Access Control tab, 238, 239
Attributes tab, 237, 238
Certificate Assistant, 475
creating secure notes and passwords, 237–240
managing multiple keychains, 240, 241, 243
options, 25, 26
resetting password, 235
signing and verifying applications, 154
SSL certificates, 197
OS X security, 474
Keychain Minder application, 235, 236
keychain passwords, 25
keychains
encrypted keychains, 25–26
FileVaultMaster keychain, 263, 264
global keychain, 237
login keychain, 234–237

creating secure notes and
passwords, 237–240
resetting password, 235–236
managing multiple keychains, 240–243
System keychain, 237
keys
cracking WEP keys, 347–348
establishing SSH key, 420
Exposé application assigning, 10
generateduid key, 65
symmetric-key cryptography, 573, 574
keywords
items to lookout for in log files, 129
kill command, 4, 42
killall command, 42
Kind column, Activity Monitor, 35
kinit command, 448
KisMAC, 342–344
rogue access points, 343
klist command, 448
kSBXProfileNoWrite profile
seatbelt framework, 179, 180
ktlist command
file sharing security, Samba, 470

L

l (symbolic link) type, POSIX, 83
L2TP-based VPN, 415
setting up, 415–416
LAN Manager, 437
Authentication Level setting, DAVE Network preferences, 371
LANMAN, SMB authentication, 371
Latest Threats web site, 221
lattice, MAC, 374
LaunchAgents service, 44
launchctl command
stopping daemons, 43
launchd daemon, 33, 34
GUI tools for managing, 44–45
logging data, 122
starting/stopping ALF, 312
types of launchd services, 44
LaunchDaemons service, 44
launchd-user.conf file
applying new umask value, 86
layers, link/physical, 279
layers, protocols, 277
application layer, 278
four-layer model, 278

transport layer, 278
LDAP (Lightweight Directory Access Protocol), 425–426
enforcing managed preferences on systems, 452, 453
LDAP, securing
enabling SSL, 431–432
implementing custom LDAP ACLs, 444
preventing anonymous binding, 439–441
ldapsearch command, 444
legacy Windows systems
enabling Open Directory server as PDC, 453
Leopard
account types, 51, 53
binding clients to Open Directory, 441, 442
choosing directory service to configure in, 443
configuring security service in, 443
granular control of managed settings, 63
ipfw program, 317
mandatory access control (MAC), 157
parental controls, 56, 58
quarantine function, Launch Services, 219
sandbox, 156, 158
seatbelt access control, 157
working with firewalls in, 304–307
library logs, 124
Library/Logs folder
reviewing library logs, 124
reviewing user-specific logs, 121
Lightweight Directory Access Protocol *see* LDAP
Limit directive, CUPS, 20
limit_inherit permission, 93
Lingon tool, 44–45
link aggregation, 291
link keyword, mtree, 110
link layer, 279
links, hidden, 387
list permission, folders, 92
listeners, ports, 278
LKDC, 355
lladdr option, ifconfig, 287
Load images automatically option, Firefox, 195
load verb, launchd, 312
load-balancing devices, 533
loaders

virus replication, 143
local administrative accounts, 68
local directory services, 65–69, 425
    creating second local directory node, 68
    ds prefixed commands, 66–67
    ShadowHash authentication, 66
localhome option, dsconfigad command, 457
Location directive, CUPS, 19
location services
    Disable Location Services option, 10
locked-down process, sandbox, 162
log files
    AirPort logging, 336–337
    appfirewall.log, 120–121
    archiving, 125
    brute force password attempts, 120
    changing location, 379
    command-line logs, 123
    copying data from, 117
    daily.out log file, 126–127
    DiskRecording.log, 122
    DiskUtility.log, 121
    finding, 118–121
    flags defining privileges in sudoers file, 71
    identifying who ran programs, 120
    information in, 113–115
    items to lookout for in, 129
    launchd daemon logging data, 122
    library logs, 124
    Library/Logs folder, 121
    maintenance logs, 124–129
    marking, 116–117
    monthly.out log file, 129
    newsyslog, 125
    periodic.conf file, 125
    reviewing, 133–135
        accountability, 133–134
        incident response plan, 134–135
    sandbox declarations, 161
    searching, 117–118
    secure.log, 119–120, 125
    system.log, 125
    user-specific logs, 121–122
    value and importance of, 113
    viewing, 115–116
        large log files, 117
    weekly.out log file, 128
    Windows methods to log events, 130–133

Log out option, Security preferences, 10
log_host/log_year flags, sudoers file, 71
logging
    file sharing security, AFP, 469–470
    ipfwloggerd, 320
    setting options per ipfw rule, 319
Logging & SNMP tab, AirPort, 336
logic bombs, 214, 215
logical unit number (LUN), 560
login accounting
    monthly.out log file, 129
Login Items tab, Accounts pane, 45, 46
login keychains, 234–237
    creating secure notes and passwords, 237–240
    encrypting user data, FileVault, 258
    Keychain Minder application, 235, 236
    managing multiple keychains, 240–243
    resetting password, 235–236
    security risks, 237
login options
    changing what runs at login, 45–46
    disabling automatic login option, 9
    keychain passwords, 25
    Mac OS X security, 6–8
    Remote Login service, 39
Login Options, Accounts preferences, 6
    enabling root user, 6
    removing administrative access, 8
    Show Password Hints option, 7
Login policy, managed preferences, 449, 452
logins
    DAVE Login preference pane, 369
    Disable Login Passwords options, 433
logout option, 10
logs see log files
Logs tab, parental controls, 62
Logs window, Console, 116
logsentry, 130
LUN (logical unit number)
    Xsan, 560

M

Mac
    as carriers of malware, 216
    Back to My Mac feature, 404–405
    classifying malware, 213–216
    macro viruses, 216
    security auditing, 497–504

simultaneous access to shared storage, 559
threat of malware on Mac, 216–217
web browser attacks on, 187
MAC (mandatory access control), 157, 374
MAC address, 290, 334
    changing, 287
    filtering, 290, 334–336
    identifying, 335
    spoofing, 287
MAC filtration, enabling, 335
Mac OS
    application bundles, 31
    file permissions, 80–81
    hard links security issues, 108
    POSIX permissions, 80
    viewing daemons running on, 38–39
    viewing processes running on, 31–40
        Activity Monitor, 31–35
        ps command, 35–36
        top command, 36–38
    viewing services available, 39–40
Mac OS X, 50
    account types, 51–53
    access control entries (ACEs), 80, 91–94
    access control lists (ACLs), 80, 91–97
    antivirus software, 219
    application firewall, 147–149
    authorization, 49
    Automator, 217
    default umask value, 85
    discovery tool for, 344
    file security, 354–357
        LKDC, 355
        POSIX permissions, 355–356
    Firefox and Mac OS X standards, 196
    firewall, 299
    hard links security issues, 107–108
    Mach microkernel, 163
    maintenance scripts, 125
    Managed Client OS X (MCX), 149–152
    managing ACLs on server, 97–103
    memory manager for kernel, 34
    not automatically registering/mounting drives, 75
    out of the box user/group, 81
    password reset utility, 11
    permissions problems, 81
    POSIX permissions, 81–91
    protecting other computers, 313–315
    sandbox profiles, 159
    Server Admin console, 211
    services, 30
    signature enforcement in, 144–152
    Sophos Anti-Virus for, 226–227
    stopping processes, 41
    suid/sguid bits, 87
Mac OS X Client security *see* firewalls
Mac OS X security
    see also security
    accounts, 4–6
    Bluetooth security, 16–18
    customizing system preferences, 4
    encrypted disk images, 24–25
    encrypted keychains, 25–26
    list of best practices, 27
    login options, 6–8
    out of the box default settings, 3
    printer security, 18–20
    root account, 69
    Secure Empty Trash feature, 23–24
    securely erasing disks, 21–23
    security preferences, 9–14
    Software Update preference pane, 14–16
    using strong passwords, 4
Mac OS X Server
    antispam tools, 210–211
    ClamAV antispam tool, 210
    SpamAssassin tool, 210
Mac OS X Server security, 423
    see also security
    directory services, 425–428
    DNS, 473
    file sharing, 463–471
    iChat server, 477–478
    Kerberos, 426–428
    LDAP, 425–426
    limiting access to services, 423–424
    Open Directory, 428–458
    proxy service, 480–481
    root user, 425
    Secure Shell (SSH), 475–477
    securing Mail server, 478–480
    server admin from command line, 477
    SSL certificates, 474–475
    web server security, 459–462
    wireless security using RADIUS, 471–473
MacForensicsLab, 539–556
    see also computer forensics
    Acquire feature, 546–548

Analyze screen, 548–551
Audit screen, 554
browsing drive contents, 549
case details, 543
Cases screen, 542, 543
checksum, 546
creating image of unaltered evidence, 544
Database toolbar item, 540
database, creating, 541
disabling disk arbitration, 544
Examiners screen, 541
examiners, creating, 542
File Types to Include screen, 553
Free Space Only check box, 552
golden master, 546
image acquisition, 546–548
main screen, 545–546
Packet Size feature, 547
reviewing case, 554–555
Salvage screen, 551–553
Search for Embedded Files check box, 552
Search window, 550, 551
Secure Empty Trash operation, 551
setting up, 539–544
setting up e-mail alerts, 544
smeared images, 546
Write Report option, 555–556
Mach IPC, 163
Mach-O
launching non-Mach-O Carbon-based application, 160
MacLockPick, 556
MacOSXServerUpdCombo10.6.2.dmg, 244
MacQuisition, 556
macro viruses, 215, 216
preventing infection of Mac by, 217
macros, 215
Macs *see* Mac
MacScan, 229
MacStumbler, 346
magic triangle, setting up, 458
Mail
authentication settings, 199
filtering Apple Mail for spam, 203–204
limiting communication via, 59–61
port settings for SSL, 197
mail protocols
authenticating protocols, 197
e-mail security, 196
establishing mail provider support for, 197
IMAP, 196, 197
POP, 196, 197
SMTP, 196
Mail server, securing, 478–480
mail servers
Kerio MailServer, 208–210
limiting protocols on, 479
solutions for spam and viruses, 207–212
mail_xyz flags, sudoers file, 71
Mail.app
e-mail security, 196
maintenance logs, 124–129
daily.out log file, 126–127
monthly.out log file, 129
weekly.out log file, 128
maintenance scripts
Mac OS X, 125
running with Yasu, 127–128
Make Inherited Entries Explicit option
propagating ACLs, 101, 102
malware, 213
adware, 228
antivirus software, 218–228
backdoors, 214, 216
best practices for combating, 227–228
classifying threats, 213–216
configuring firewalls, 303
iPhone, 144
logic bombs, 214, 215
macro viruses, 215, 216
Macs as carriers of, 216
retrovirus, 215, 216
rootkits, 216, 230–231
script malware attacks, 217–218
socially engineered malware, 218
spyware, 228–229
threat of malware on Mac, 216–217
Trojan horses, 214, 215
virus files to test system, 228
virus replication, 143
viruses, 213, 215
worms, 214, 215
zombies, 215, 216
Managed Client OS X *see* MCX
managed preferences, 449–453
Applications policy, 449, 451
Classic policy, 449
Dock policy, 449

enforcing on systems using Active Directory, 452
enhanced security for, 451–453
Finder policy, 449, 452
Internet policy, 449
Login policy, 449, 452
MCX files, 450
Media policy, 449
Mobility policy, 450, 452
Network policy, 450, 452
Parental Controls policy, 452
Printing policy, 450, 452
Software Update policy, 450
System Preferences policy, 450, 452
Universal Access policy, 450
viewing, 451
managed switches, 289–291
administrator concerns, 291
MAC address filtering, 290
manufacturer features, 291
rogue access points, 290
VLAN (virtual LAN) support, 289
mandatory access control *see* MAC
man-in-the-middle attacks, 288
802.1x protocol, 293
digital signing for SMB, 371
Ettercap, 347
file sharing security, NFS, 466
securing Open Directory, 436
securing Perl scripts, 385
mapping drives within Windows, 456
masks
pipe masks, 322–323
Master Boot Record (MBR) partition map, 250
master password
FileVault, 263–264
Set Master Password button, 12
Master Password dialog box, Firefox, 193
Master Password feature, Timbuktu Pro, 411
master password, Firefox
saving passwords, 192–194
setting master password, 193
Use master password option, 192
McAfee VirusScan, 220
MCX (Managed Client OS X), 149–152
configuring application white listing, 150
enabling FileVault for users, 261, 262
managed preferences, files, 450
restricting applications with, 150
Workgroup Manager tool, 149–152
mcxxyz options, dscl command, 451
MD5 (Message Digest 5), 198
md5digest keyword, mtree, 109
mDNS, 301
Media policy, managed preferences, 449
Media Set creation screen, Retrospect, 521, 522
Media Verification option, Retrospect, 527
media verification, Retrospect, 528
Melissa worm, 216
MEM column, ps command, 36
memory management, OS X kernel, 34
Message Digest 5 (MD5), 198
metadata, Xsan, 560–561
Metasploit, 501–503
commands, 502
exploits, 503
payloads, 503
targets, 503
Microsoft Challenge Access Protocol (MS-CHAPv2), 438
Microsoft event IDs, Event Viewer, 131
Microsoft Office for Windows
macro viruses attacking, 217
Mobile Access server, 480
Mobile Accounts
external accounts, 68
mobile option, dsconfigad command, 457
MobileMe
Account tab, 514
Back to My Mac tab, 405
creating offsite copy of critical data, 513–517
iDisk tab, 516, 517
managing multiple keychains, 241
manually syncing, 516
sign-in screen, 514
Sync tab, 515
syncronizing data, 515–516
Mobility policy
managed preferences, 450, 452
mod_rewrite module
blocking hosts based on robots.txt, 388
mod_security, scripts, 384
mode keyword, mtree, 109
modes (access levels), POSIX, 82–84
bit-flag system, 83, 84
execute mode, 82, 83
read mode, 82, 83
write mode, 82

modules
    disabling unnecessary services in Apache, 382
    reviewing safety of, 382
monthly.out log file, 129
mount command, 75, 538
    forensics, 558
    options, 75
mount points
    securing, 74–75
mounting disk image
    attach verb, hdiutil command, 251
    automating for backups, 252
    POSIX permissions, 252
mountpoint option, hdiutil command
    interfacing with disk images, 252
MREGS column, top command, 37
mtree
    auditing file system permissions, 109–111
    flags, 110
    keywords, 109
MTU field, daily.out file, 126
multiple keychains, managing, 240–243
multiuser operating systems
    Mac OS X and Firefox, 196
    Mac OS X security, 4, 50
My Processes option, Activity Monitor, 32
MyDoom worm, 216

N

namespace option, dsconfigad, 457
NAT (Network Address Translation), 279
    enabling firewall, AirPort, 332
    network structure impacting security level, 341
NAT tab, AirPort Utility
    configuring port mappings, 333
    directing web traffic, 333
Native tab, MacForensicsLab, 549
nbits, 348
Nessus, 497–501
    defining policy, 499
    defining targets, 500
    reviewing report, 501
    running scan, 500
    scanning policy, 499
    starting Nessus server, 498
Nessus Attack Scripting Language (NSAL), 497

nessusd daemon, 497
NeST commands, 439
NetBIOS name, 367
    file sharing security, Samba, 470
Netgear MA-111 USB adapter, 343
NetNanny
    limiting access to web sites, 58
network access control, 290
network adapters, 315
Network Address Translation see NAT
network administrators
    configuring Safari security preferences, 189
network authentication
    Kerberos, 426
network backups
    Time Machine, 511–512
network enumeration, 488
Network field, daily.out file, 126
network file system see NFS
network homes, setting up
    Active Directory clients, 456–457
network intrusion detection, 494–497
    honeypots, 496–497
    snort, from command line, 494–496
network layers, moving packets, 278
Network policy
    managed preferences, 450, 452
Network preference pane
    configuring multiple IP addresses, 316
    configuring PPTP-based VPN, 416
network protocols
    AFP, 357–359
    Samba (SMB), 359–362
network scanning
    active scanning, 486
    black-box testing, 486
    enumeration, 488
    fingerprinting, 486–488
    half scan, 491
    KisMAC, 342
    nmap, 489–491
    other nmap scans, 492
    passive scanning, 486
    port scanning, 488
    scanning options, 490
    scanning techniques, 485–492
    stealth scanning, 491
    SYN scan, 489
    SYN/stealth scan, 491–492
    TCP connect scan, 489

vulnerability scanning, 489–492
white-box testing, 485
network security
see also security
802.1x protocol, 292–293
creating closed network, AirPort, 337, 338
hardware filtering, 334–336
InfoSec acceptable use policy, 567
security through obscurity, 279
network services, 300–301
Apple Filing Protocol (AFP), 300
configuring firewalls, 303
controlling services, 301–304
disabling, 302
enabling, 301
listing by name not port numbers, 302
restricting network services, 291–292
when to enable and dangers, 303
Network Time Protocol (NTP), 427
network traffic
outgoing, 300, 302, 315, 316, 317, 319
queues, 323
routes, 300
throttling, 321
Network Utility
naming conventions for network interfaces, 318
testing firewalls, 310–311
whois lookup, 487
Whois tab, 393, 394
network volume
Time Machine backups, 511–512
networks, 277
client-server networks, 282, 354
communication over public networks, 401
data packet encryption, 288
DAVE Network preferences, 370
deep packet inspection, 288
DMZ (demilitarized zone), 286
gateways, 283
hubs, 288, 289
Mac OS X protecting other computers, 313–315
managed switches, 289–291
peer-to-peer (P2P), 280–282, 354
protocols, 300
proxy servers, 293–294
proxy services, Squid configuring, 295–297

routers, 284
routing, 283–285
securing computer-to-computer networks, 340–341
securing, incoming ports, 278
stateful packet inspection (SPI), 287–288
spoofing, 287
subnets, 286
switches, 289
types of, 280–282
virtual private network (VPN), 414–422
wireless networks, 325–327
Newsham 21-bit attack, 343
newsyslog, 125
NFS (network file system)
file sharing security, OS X Server, 465 466
NFS shares, 94
NFSHomeDirectory attribute, 261, 465
Nimda worm, 216
nmap, 489–491
other nmap scans, 492
nobrowse option, hdiutil, 252
Nointernet sandbox profile, 160
Nonet sandbox profile, 160
NOPASSWD tag, sudoers file, 74
normal.dot file
macro viruses attacking, 217
Norton AntiVirus, 220–221
notes, secure
login keychain creating, 239–240
Nowrite sandbox profile, 160
NSUmask, 77, 86
NTLM
options for securing mail password, 198
NTLM hash
managing multiple keychains, 242
ntlm hash type, 66
NTLMv1/NTLMv2
Open Directory authentication, 437
SMB authentication, 371
NTP (Network Time Protocol), 427

O

o flag, mount command, 75
Observe setting, Remote Management, 407
OD *see* Open Directory
ODSAgent service, 38
one-time passwords, 50
online accounts

using strong passwords, 184
only_inherit permission, 93
Open and Quit Applications setting, Remote Management, 407
Open Directory, 425, 428–458
    Active Directory integration, 454–458
        binding Mac clients into both directory structures, 458
        dual directory, 458
        setting up network homes with AD clients, 456–457
        using AD-Plugin, 455–456, 457
    configuring, 430–431
    creating groups, 446–447
    creating users, 444–446
    enabling Open Directory server as PDC, 453
    granular control of user access, 63
    Kerberos, 428
    LDAP, 426
        enabling SSL, 431–432
        implementing custom LDAP ACLs, 444
        preventing anonymous binding, 439–441
    Mac OS X Server security, 428–458
    managed preferences, 449–453
    promoting to replica, 425
    providing directory services for Windows clients, 453–454
    securely binding clients to, 441–443
    securing accounts by enabling password policies, 432–435
    securing authentication with PasswordServer, 437–439
    securing Kerberos from command line, 448
    securing using binding policies, 435–437
    setting up, 428–429
    SSL certificates, OS X security, 474
Open Directory master, 426, 427, 428, 430, 431, 440, 442, 443, 445
open relay, 478
open_basedir directive, PHP, 384
OpenLDAP, 426
openssl command, forensics, 558
OpenSSL tool, 391
Opkts field, daily.out file, 127
options directive
    securing directory listings, 397
Options tab, Retrospect, 526, 527

orphaned packets, wireless networks, 350
OS X *see* Mac OS X
OS X Server security *see* Mac OS X Server security
OSX.Leap.A worm, 214, 221
Other User Processes option, Activity Monitor, 33
owner, POSIX permissions, 104, 355
owners option, hdiutil command, 252
ownership
    Change Ownership access right, 91
    multiuser operating systems, 50

P

P2P networks *see* peer-to-peer
packet reinjection, 343
Packet Size feature, MacForensicsLab, 547
packetencrypt option, dsconfigad, 457
packets, 278, 283
    data, 283
    data packet encryption, 288
    datagrams, 283
    deep packet inspection, 288
    Ethernet protocol, 283
    header, 283
    interception on wireless networks, 326
    IP packets, 283
    MAC address filtering, 290
    moving, 278
    orphaned packets, 350
    securing Open Directory, 436
    stateful packet inspection, 287–288
packetsign option, dsconfigad, 457
PAMs (pluggable authentication modules), 50
parent process, 30
Parent tab, SquidMan utility, 296
parental controls
    restricting application access, 152
    setting up, 56–62
Parental Controls policy, 452
Parental Controls preference pane
    controlling use of Finder, 56
    copying Parental Controls settings, 62–63
    enabling Parental Controls feature, 56
    limiting access to web sites, 58–59
    limiting communication via iChat and Mail, 59–61
    Logs tab, 62

Index   **603**

restricting access to applications, 57
setting time limits for access, 61–62
setting up parental controls, 56
Partitions field, Disk Utility, 250
passinterval option, dsconfigad, 457
passive scanning, 486
passphrases, securing SSH, 413, 414
PASSWD tag, sudoers file, 74
Password
  options for securing mail password, 198
Password Assistant
  setting passwords, 5, 6
  using strong passwords, 4
password policies
  securing Open Directory accounts by enabling, 432–435
password protection, realms, 459, 460
Password quality meter
  Master Password dialog, Firefox, 194
password reset utility, 11
password-based authentication, SSH, 413
passwordless authentication
  Carbon Copy Cloner (CCC), 172
  public-key-encryption, 174
  securely automating remote rsync, 174
passwordless ssh authentication, 174
passwords
  bad password attempts
    accountability for reviewing logs, 134
    brute force guessing, 120
  controlling directory access, 390
  DAVE Login preference pane, 369
  Disable automatic login option, 9
  Disable Login Passwords options, 433
  encrypted keychains, 25
  encryption as security for, 184
  Firefox, saving passwords in, 192–194
  InfoSec acceptable use policy, 565
  keychain passwords, 25
  login keychain creating, 237–239
  options for securing mail password, 198
  Require password option, 9
    unlocking System Preferences, 10
  securing Open Directory, 433, 436
  self-service password reset, 11
  Set Master Password button, 12
  setting, 4
  ShadowHash authentication, 65
  Show Password Hints option, 7
  SSL protection, 185
  usability and user security, 50

use of special characters in, 184
user changing password on disk images, 254
using same password for all services, 360
using strong passwords, 4, 184
Passwords Must options
  securing Open Directory accounts, 433
passwords, Firefox
  viewing saved passwords, 194
PasswordServer, 426
  securing authentication with, 437–439
paste issues, troubleshooting, 43
pasteboard (pboard) process, 43
PASV mode, FTP, 374
PASV theft attack, 374
patches
  Software Update preference pane, 14
path_info flag, sudoers file, 71
payload, worms, 214
payloads, Metasploit, 503
pboard process, 43
PCMCIA cards, 343
PDA
  Bluetooth-PDA-Sync, 18
PDC (primary domain controller), 453
  creating Windows PDC, 454
peer-to-peer (P2P) networks, 280–282, 354
  copyrighted material, 281
penetration testing, 489
performance
  browser plug-in issues with, 187
Performance counters, Windows, 132, 133
performance monitors
  dsperfmonitor command, 67
periodic command, 125
periodic scripts, 125
  accountability for reviewing logs, 134
  daily.out log file, 126–127
  monthly.out log file, 129
  running with Yasu, 127–128
  weekly.out log file, 128
periodic.conf file, 125
Perl
  enabling/disabling, 382
  web site security, 385–386
permission models
  file sharing, 374–375
permissions
  403 error code, 389

access control lists (ACLs), 91–97, 356–357
   managing on OS X server, 97–103
access rights, ACL, 91–93
   see also under ACLs
   administering, 97–103
   alpha/decimal/binary formats, 84
   chown and chmod managing, 104–107
   creating files with, 77–78
   determining default on new files, 85
   directory_inherit permission, 93
   Effective Permissions tool, 102, 103
   file system permissions, 79
   file_inherit permission, 93
   Finder managing, 103–104
   htaccess/htgroup/htpasswd files, 388
   indicating ACEs exist, 96
   limit_inherit permission, 93
   Mac OS, 80–81
   mapping ACE permissions, 99
   mtree auditing file system permissions, 109–111
   only_inherit permission, 93
   POSIX permissions, 81–91, 355–356
   problem with 644 permission, 85
   propagating, 100
   readextattr permission, 92
   securing files on web server, 396
   Show Effective Permissions Inspector, 102
   Xsan, 561
Personal File/Web Sharing
   when to enable and dangers, 303
PGP Desktop
   desktop solutions for securing e-mail, 207
PGP Encryption, 269–270
phishing
   spear phishing, 184
PHP, enabling/disabling, 382
PHP:Hypertext Preprocessor (PHP)
   input validation, 383–384
   securing PHP, 383
   web site security, 382–384
physical layer, 279
PID (Process ID), 33
   Activity Monitor, 34
   kernel_task process, 33
   launchd daemon, 33
   other processes, 34
   ps command, 35

pipe masks, 322–323
pipes
   creating, dummynet, 321–322
   queues, 323, 324
PKE (Public Key Encryption)
   user changing password on disk images, 254
pkg packages, 249
PKI (Public Key Infrastructure)
   signing and verifying applications, 153
plausible deniability, 271
plist files *see* property list (.plist) files
pluggable authentication modules (PAMs), 50
plug-ins
   AD-Plug-in, 454, 455–456
   browser performance issues, 187
   disabling plug-ins, 499
   web browser attacks on Mac, 187
   web browser security, 188
PoE (Power over Ethernet), 290
policies
   configuring, 449
   creating Open Directory users/groups, 446, 447
   defining policy, Nessus, 499
   managed preferences, 449–453
   scanning policy, Nessus, 499
   securing Open Directory accounts, 432–435
   securing Open Directory services, 435–437
Policies tab, DAVE Network pane, 370, 371, 372
POP
   configuring Entourage to use SSL, 199
   e-mail security, 196, 197
   Kerberized POP, 198
   network protocols, 278
POP3
   Authenticated POP, 198
pop-ups, Firefox security, 194
pop-ups, Safari security, 185
   Block Pop-Up Windows option, 186
   disabling Flash pop-ups, 186
port 1179, 304
port 161, 303
port 162, 303
port 21, 303
port 22, 303, 475
port 25, 300

blocking access to mail, 200
   port management, 285
port 4111, 304
port 443
   e-mail security using SSL, 196
   HTTP over TLS, 391
   web site security, 381, 462
port 5353
   mDNS responder, 301
port 548, 303
   Apple Filing Protocol (AFP), 301
port 5900, 303
port 80, 278, 300, 303
   httpd daemon listening, 379
   redirecting traffic, 333, 380
   telnet application connecting to, 395
port 8080, 300
port forwarding, AirPort, 333
port management, 285–286
port mappings, AirPort, 333
port numbers, 300
   listing services by name not, 302
   moving packets, 278
port scanning
   fingerprinting, 488
   InfoSec acceptable use policy, 567
   stroke utility, 311
   testing firewalls, 310, 311
ports, 278
   commonly used ports, 300
   e-mail security using SSL, 196
   filtered port, 491
   iTunes, AirPort Express, 339
   link aggregation, 291
   listeners, 278
   listing services by name not port numbers, 302
   MAC address filtering, 290
   Mail port settings for SSL, 197
   opening and closing, 301
   priority tagging, 290
   protocol traffic, 300
   redirecting traffic to different ports, 333
   redirecting traffic to nonstandard ports, 380
   running on nonstandard port, 380
   securing networks, 278
   spanning tree, 290
   utilization for services, 278
POSIX permissions, 80, 81–91, 355–356
   access levels, 80

alpha/decimal/binary formats, 84
changing group using chgrp, 104
changing ownership using chown, 104
Discretionary Access Controls, 156
education example, 88–90
execute mode, 82, 83
Finder managing permissions, 103
inheritance, 84–86
managing permissions with chmod, 105–106
modes (access levels), 82–84
   bit-flag system, 83, 84
modifying with Server Admin, 98
mounted/encrypted disk images, 252
mounting disk image in Finder, 250
read mode, 82, 83
sticky bit, 87, 356
suid/sguid bits, 87–88
write mode, 82
Power over Ethernet (PoE), 290
PPP
   combining with SSH as VPN link, 419, 422
   setting up, 421–422
pppd daemon, 419, 420, 421
PPTP (Point-to-Point Tunneling Protocol), 438
PPTP-based VPN, 415
   setting up, 416–417
preferences, managed, 449–453
preferred option, dsconfigad, 457
prefs.js file
   Mac OS X and Firefox, 196
pre-shared key authentication, 175
primary domain controller *see* PDC
principal, Kerberos, 427
Print & Fax preference pane, 18
printer security, 18–20
   Limit directive, CUPS, 20
   Location directive, CUPS, 19
Printer Sharing service, 39
   when to enable and dangers, 304
printers, 18
Printing policy, 450, 452
priority tagging, 290
privacy
   Firefox, 190–192
      Clear Recent History option, 191
      clearing private data, 191
   information, web site security, 392–396

protecting information from Google, 394–395
Safari, 188–189
Privacy icon, Firefox security, 190, 191
private key
    signing and verifying applications, 153
    user changing password on disk images, 254
private/var/log directory
    finding log files, 118
privilege blocks
    sandbox profiles, 167, 168
privilege-escalation vulnerability, 166
privileges
    add_file privilege, 92
    defining custom privilege sets, 99, 100
    delete privilege, 93
    readattr privilege, 92
    readsecurity privilege, 92
    Show options, Activity Monitor, 31
    writesecurity privilege, 91
Process Name column, Activity Monitor, 34
processes, 30
    Activity Monitor analyzing, 50, 51
    All Processes options, 32
    diskarbitrationd process, 43
    hidden processes, 301
    kernel_task, 33, 34
    launchd daemon, 33
    pboard process, 43
    RAM used, 35
    Show options, Activity Monitor, 31, 33
    stopping, 41–42
    stopping daemons, 43–44
    stopping wrong process, 41
    viewing daemons running on Mac, 38–39
    viewing processes running on Mac, 31–40
        Activity Monitor, 31–35
        ps command, 35–36
        top command, 36–38
processor services, 39
profanity
    Hide Profanity in Dictionary option, 57
profiles
    backup.sb profile, 177
    base.sb profile, 167–170
    kSBXProfileNoWrite profile, 179, 180
    Mac OS X and Firefox, 196
    Sandbox profiles, 158–178
    shell.sb profile, 170–171

programs, 29
proof-of-concept attack, 325
Propagate Permissions option
    propagating permissions, 100
property list (.plist) files
    authentication_authority key, 65
    editing, 77, 78
    Mac OS X and Firefox, 196
    managing data from, 66
    storage of user/group accounts, 65
Property List Editor, 77, 78
proto mask, pipes, 322
protocol support, ACLs, 94
protocols, 357
    see also mail protocols
    802.1x protocol, 292–293
    AFP, 357–359
    AirPort encryption, 327
    DNS, 277
    Ethernet, 283
    FTP, 372–374
    HTTP, 278
    IMAP, 278
    ipfw, 317
    Kerberos, 426–428
    L2TP, 415
    layers, 277
    LDAP, 425–426
    limiting protocols on server, 479
    network services, 300
    networks, 300
    POP, 278
    POP3, 198
    PPTP, 416
    Samba (SMB), 359–362
    SMTP, 278
    TCP/IP, 277–279
    UDP, 277
    VPN, 415
    WEP, 327
    WPA2, 327
    WPA2 Enterprise, 327
provider services, 39
proxy servers, 293–294
    securing web servers, 381
    Squid, configuring proxy servers, 295–297
    SquidMan utility, 296
proxy service
    Mac OS X Server security, 480–481
PRTS column, top command, 37

ps command
    %MEM column, 35–36
    a option, 35
    action before using, 31
    CMD column, 35
    Process ID (PID), 35
    RAM used, 36
    STAT (state) column, 36
    TIME column, 35
    TTY column, 35
    u option, 35
    viewing output one screen at a time, 36
    x option, 35
pty-redir tool, 421
public key, 153, 172, 174
Public Key Infrastructure (PKI), 153
public/private key pairs, SSH, 413
public-key algorithms, 575
public-key cryptography, 574, 575
public-key-encryption, 174
pure-computation sandbox profile, 160

Q

queues, dummynet, 323–324
Quicklook
    generation of proxies, 248
quit command, Metasploit, 502
Quit option, stopping processes, 41
quotas
    file sharing security, OS X Server, 465
    Xsan, 562

R

r (read) permission, POSIX, 83
    alpha/decimal/binary formats, 84
r option, mount command, 75
R state, ps command, 36
RADIUS (Remote Authentication Dial In User Service)
    wireless security on OS X Server using, 471–473
RADIUS server
    safeguards against cracking wireless networks, 349
radmind, 74
RAIDs
    restricting access using mount points, 74
RAM
    Activity Monitor utility, 35
    ps command, 36
RavMonE.exe, 216
RBAC (role-based access control), 374
Read & Write permission, ACE, 99
Read access right, ACEs, 92
Read Attribute access right, 92
Read Ext Attribute access right, 92
read mode, POSIX permissions, 82, 83
    alpha/decimal/binary formats, 84
    file sharing, 355
Read Only permission, ACE, 99
read permission, files, 92
Read Permissions access right, 92
readattr privilege, 92
    making files/directories invisible, 105
readextattr permission, 92
Read/Write disk image option, Disk Utility, 246
read-permissions category, ACEs, 92
readsecurity privilege, 92
Real Memory column, Activity Monitor, 35
realms, 438
    Kerberos, 427, 470
    web server security, OS X, 459–461
receiving options, Entourage, 199
reclaiming space, FileVault, 264–266
recover option, hdiutil, 255
Recoverable Authentication Methods options, 438
redirection statement, Perl scripts, 385
redundancy
    cold sites, 533
    hot sites, 534
register_globals directive, PHP, 383
reload command, Metasploit, 502
Remote Apple Events service, 303
Remote Authentication Dial In User Service
    see RADIUS
remote automation
    securely automating remote rsync, 174–177
remote connectivity
    Back to My Mac feature, 404–405
    combining PPP and SSH as VPN link, 419–422
    configuring Remote Management, 405–408
    remote management applications, 402–408
    Screen Sharing application, 402–404

Secure Shell (SSH), 412–414
Timbuktu Pro, 408–412
virtual private network (VPN), 414–422
Remote Login service, 39
    SSH, 412, 413
    when to enable and dangers, 303
remote management applications, 402–408
Remote Management service, 39
    computer settings, 407–408
    configuring, 405–408
    disabling Screen Sharing, 405
    options, 406–407
    setting up, 406
replication
    disabling SSH, 476
    promoting Open Directory to replica, 425
    viruses, 143
reports, MacForensicsLab, 555–556
reports options, Retrospect, 530
Require Authenticated Binding Between Directory and Clients option, 436
Require password options, Security preferences, 9, 10
Require User option
    Limit directive, CUPS, 20
requiretty flag, sudoers file, 71
Reset Safari window, 188, 189
resetting passwords, 11
Restart and Shut Down setting, Remote Management, 407
restoring files, Time Machine, 510–511
restricting access *see* access control
restriction declarations, sandbox, 162
Retrospect, 517–529
    Add new member screen, 522, 523
    adding destinations, 522
    Backup Assistant, 520–525
    checking backups, 528–530
    configuring backup, 519–525
    copying media set or backup, 527, 528
    Data Compression option, 527
    Destinations tab, 527
    download and installation, 518–519
    encryption for backup destinations, 522
    grooming scripts, 525–527
    Media Set creation screen, 521, 522
    media verification, 527, 528
    Options tab, 526, 527
    reports options, 530
    retrovirus attacks on, 215
    Schedule tab, 524, 525
    scheduling scripts, 524, 525
    Select Media Sets screen, 523
    selecting sources to backup, 520, 521
    Sources tab, 527
    specifying backup destination, 521, 522
    Summary screen, 524
    utility scripts, 527–528
Retrospect Backup server
    configuring Retrospect, 519
retrovirus, 215, 216
reverse-domain notation, 142
rights, ACL access, 91–93
roaming profiles
    mapping drives within Windows, 456
robots.txt
    blocking hosts based on, 387–388
    securing, 386–388
rogue access points
    KisMAC, 343
    managed switches, 290
role-based access control (RBAC), 374
roles
    communication paths, 300
    configuring Open Directory, 430
root account
    dsenableroot command, 67
    enabling root user, 6, 69
    enabling unnecessarily, 4
    leaving disabled for security, 56
    Mac OS X security, 4, 69
    using SMB service, 360
root kits, 285
    remote connectivity, 401
    SH.Renepo.B, 230
root privilege
    SUID applications, 75–76
root user, 53
    bypassing DAC model, 157
    disabling superuser account, 55, 56
    enabling superuser account, 54–55
    Mac OS X Server security, 425
root_sudo flag, 71
Rootkit Hunter, 230–231
rootkits, 216, 230–231
rootpw flag, sudoers file, 71
rotating logs
    cu.modem.log, 129
    Disk Utility logs, 121
    history files, 123
    maintenance scripts, 125
    monthly.out log file, 129

newsyslog.conf, 125
system.log file, 127
round-robin DNS, 532–533
routers, 284
    DMZ (demilitarized zone), 286
    Mac OS X firewall, 299
routes
    data transmission, 284
    network traffic, 300
routing, 283–285
    combining PPP and SSH as VPN link, 422
    enabling on base station, AirPort, 332
    firewalls, 285
    gateways, 283
    packets, 283
routing tables, 284
RPRVT column, top command, 37
rrset-order command
    round-robin DNS, 532
RSA encryption method
    establishing SSH key, 420
RSHRD column, top command, 37
rsync
    Carbon Copy Cloner (CCC), 172, 173, 174
    securely automating remote rsync, 174–177
rules, firewalls, 300
Rumpus
    limiting sftp access, 167
    logging, 118, 119
Runas_Alias, sudoers file, 70, 73, 74
runaspw flag, sudoers file, 71

■S

S state, ps command, 36
S/MIME Certificates, 241
SACLs (service access control lists), 424
    disabling SSH, 476
Safari
    installation of unwanted software, 188
    privacy, 188–189
    Reset Safari option, 188, 189
    Security preference tab, 185
        Show Cookies button, 186
    security preferences, 187
        network administrators configuring, 189
        setting, 186–188
    web browser security, 185–189
        disabling Flash pop-ups, 186
        pop-ups, 185, 186
Safari bundle, 309
Safari Forensic Tools (SFT), 557
Safari Toolkit, 189
Safe Domains tab, Entourage, 205, 206
safe lists
    using white listing in Entourage, 205
SAINT, 503–504
salvage operations
    other applications performing, 553
Salvage screen, MacForensicsLab, 551–553
Samba, 359–362
    see also SMB
    file sharing security, OS X Server, 470
    providing password for Windows user, 361
    smb.conf file, 361–362
samba directory
    accountability for reviewing logs, 134
SAN solution providers, 562
sandbox, 156–180
    granular control of managed settings in Leopard, 63
    restriction declarations, 162
    seatbelt framework, 178–180
Sandbox profiles, 158–178
    accessing low-level functions, 165
    anatomy of, 161–165
    Apple OS X support for, 160
    backup.sb profile, 177
    base.sb profile, 167–170
    BIND, 177–178
    Carbon Copy Cloner (CCC), 172–174
    conflicting access provisions, 161
    declarations, 161, 162
    file system access, 164
    file-write* provisions, 164
    inline comments (;), 161
    kSBXProfileNoWrite profile, 179, 180
    locked-down process, 162
    logs, 161
    Mac OS X, 159
    Mach IPC, 163
    Nointernet, 160
    Nonet, 160
    Nowrite, 160
    privilege blocks, 167, 168
    pure-computation, 160
    sbshell script, 171

securely automating remote rsync, 174–177
shell.sb profile, 170–171
specifying path to, 159
System Private Interface, 160
using Sandbox to secure user shells, 166–171
write-tmp-only, 160
sandbox_init function, 178, 180
save command, Metasploit, 502
Sawmill, 130
sbshell script, 171
scanning *see* network scanning
scanning policy, Nessus, 499
schedule scan preferences, ClamXav, 225
Schedule tab, Retrospect, 524, 525
Scheduled Check tab, Software Update preferences, 15
scheduling scripts, Retrospect, 524, 525
scp
    Carbon Copy Cloner (CCC), 172, 173
Screen Sharing application, 402–404
    computer settings, 404
    opening, 402
    selecting users, 403, 404
    setting up, 403
    VNC and, 402
Screen Sharing service, 38
scripting languages, 29
scripts, 29, 217
    sbshell script, 171
    script malware attacks, 217–218
        Automator, 217
    web site security, 384–386
SCSI protocol, Fibre Channel, 559
search engines
    robots.txt denying access to, 386
search permission, folders, 92
Search window, MacForensicsLab, 550, 551
searching
    Execute/Search access right, 92
seatbelt
    framework, 178
    Snow Leopard, 157
Secure Empty Trash feature, 23–24
Secure Erase Options window, 23
secure notes
    login keychain creating, 239–240
Secure Shell *see* SSH
Secure Sockets Layer *see* SSL
secure.log file, 119–120, 125

SecureDoc, 271–272
securely erasing disks, 21–23
security
    see also Mac OS X security; Mac OS X Server security; network security; web browser security; web server security; web site security
    802.1x protocol, 292–293
    Activity Monitor analyzing processes, 50
    application signing, 139–156
    authentication, 49
    authorization, 49
    backups, 507
    Bluetooth security, 16–18
    CDSA, 571–572
    computer forensics, 537
    dangers of Internet Sharing, 315
    e-mail security, 196–202
    enabling root account, 4
    encrypted disk images, 24–25
    encrypted keychains, 25–26
    file security, Mac OS X, 354–357
    file system permissions, 79
    FTP, 373
    hard links, 107–108
    hardening, 49
    iChat server, 477–478
    identification, 49
    identity theft, 183
    InfoSec acceptable use policy, 564
    intrusion detection, 492–497
    keychain securing sensitive data, 234–243
    leaving root account disabled, 56
    list of best practices, 27
    Mail server, 478–480
    Open Directory, 428–458
    physical layer, 279
    printer security, 18–20
    readsecurity privilege, 92
    Sandbox, 156–180
    Secure Empty Trash feature, 23–24
    securely erasing disks, 21–23
    securing web servers, 377–382
    sharing services, 20
    through obscurity, 279
    usability and user security, 50
    using SMB service, 360
    wireless networks, 325–327
    writesecurity privilege, 91
    Xsan, 559–562

security auditing on Mac, 497–504
    Metasploit, 501–503
    Nessus, 497–501
    SAINT, 503–504
Security field options
    securing Open Directory, 436–437
security patches
    Software Update preference pane, 14
Security preference pane, 9–14
    Disable automatic login option, 9
    Disable Location Services option, 10
    Disable remote control infrared receiver option, 10
    enabling FileVault for users, 260
    FileVault tab, 12–13
    Firewall tab, 13–14, 147
        Automatically allow signed software to receive connections option, 307, 308–309
        Enable stealth mode option, 309–310
        setting advanced firewall features, 307–310
        working with firewalls in Snow Leopard, 304
    General tab, 9–11
    Log out option, 10
    Require password option, 9
    Require password to unlock System Preferences option, 10
    Set Master Password button, 12
    Use secure virtual memory option, 10
security preferences, 9–14
    Entourage, 201, 202
    Firefox
        about:config page, 195
        Content tab, 194, 195
        Security tab, 192, 193
    Safari, 185, 187
        network administrators configuring, 189
        setting security preferences, 186–188
        Show Cookies button, 186
security threats see malware
Select Media Sets screen, Retrospect, 523
Select the Interface screen, VPN, 415
Selected Processes option, Activity Monitor, 33
self-service password reset, 11
self-signed certificates, 392
Send Text Messages setting, Remote Management, 407

sending options, Entourage, 200
sensitive data
    keychain securing, 234–243
    mtree auditing file system permissions, 109–111
sensitivity labels, MAC, 374
Sentry feature, ClamXav, 225, 226
Sentry Tools, 130
Server Admin application
    defining custom privilege sets, 99, 100
    Effective Permissions tool, 102, 103
    File Sharing tab, 98
    Make Inherited Entries Explicit, 101
    managing ACLs on OS X server, 97–103
    propagating permissions, 100
    Show Effective Permissions Inspector, 102
Server Admin console, Mac OS X, 211
Server Message Block see SMB
server security see Mac OS X Server security
serveradmin command, Mac OS X Server security, 477
servers
    500 error code, 389
    limiting protocols on server, 479
    mail server-based solutions for spam and viruses, 207–212
    proxy servers, 293–294
        Squid, configuring proxy servers, 295–297
    securing web servers, 377–382
SERVERS list
    setting up Open Directory, 428
server-side includes see SSIs
service (SRV) records, 454
service access control lists see SACLs
services, 30
    see also network services
    Active Directory, 454–458
    backups, 534–535
    configuring firewalls, 303
    controlling, 301–304
    creating, 40
    daemons, 38
    disabling unnecessary services in Apache, 382
    enabling third-party services, 305
    Finder Services menu, 40
    limiting access to services, 423–424
    listing by name not port numbers, 302

Open Directory, 428–458
port utilization, 278
processor services, 39
provider services, 39
sharing, 20–21
types of launchd services, 44
validating authenticity of, 46
viewing services available, 39–40
Services tab, Server Admin
setting up Open Directory, 428–429
Set Master Password button, Security preferences, 12
set_home/set_logname flags, sudoers file, 71
setg command, Metasploit, 502
setgid bit, 88
setuid bit, 87, 88
SFT (Safari Forensic Tools), 557
sftp, 397
limiting access, 166
SGID (group SUIDs), 76
sguid bit, 87–88
SH.Renepo.B, 230
SHA-1 hash
managing multiple keychains, 242
sha1digest keyword, mtree, 109
shadow mount
forensically acquiring disk images, 557
ShadowHash authentication, 65, 66
Shared Folders window, 20
shared folders, viewing, 464
Sharing & Permissions window, Finder, 104
sharing accounts, 52–53
Sharing Only account, 52, 353
Sharing preference pane, 20–21
configuring AFP sharing, 358
configuring settings for, 301, 302
disabling firewalls, 305
disabling network services, 302
enabling Apache 2.2 web server, 378
enabling Apache web server, 377
enabling FTP sharing, 372
enabling Internet Sharing, 313
enabling network services, 301
finding IP addresses, 302
turning daemons on or off in, 38
viewing daemons running on Mac, 38
Sharing tab, Print & Fax preferences, 18
shell scripts
script malware attacks, 217
shell.sb profile, 170–171

shells
reviewing command-line logs, 123
using Sandbox to secure user shells, 166–171
show command, ipfw, 318, 319
show command, Metasploit, 502
Show Effective Permissions Inspector, 102
Show options, Activity Monitor, 31, 32
Show Password Hints option, Login Options screen, 7
Show When Being Observed setting, Remote Management, 407
signature enforcement in OS X, 144–152
indicating application not signed, 151
keychain access, 145–146
Managed Client OS X (MCX), 149–152
OS X application firewall, 147–149
parental controls, 152
signed software
allowing to create connections, 308
signing, 153–156
application signing, 139–156
code signing, 144, 153
codesign tool, 155
indicating application not signed, 151
Keychain Access utility, 154
Public Key Infrastructure (PKI), 153
Simple Authentication and Security Layer (SASL) standard, 437
Single Unix Standard, version 3 (SUS3), 85
size keyword, mtree, 109
slapconfig command
Open Directory authentication, 439
slapd, 426
configuring to refuse anonymous connections, 440
SMB (Server Message Block), 457
see also Samba
configuring SMB Setup name in DAVE, 368
configuring SMB workgroup for DAVE, 368
defining SMB/Windows user, 360
sharing data through using DAVE, 369
SMB authentication, 371
SMB signing
man-in-the-middle attack, 371
smb.conf file, 361–362
smeared images, forensics, 546
SMTP

blocking access to mail being sent over port 25, 200
configuring Entourage to use SSL, 200
e-mail security, 196
network protocols, 278
options for securing mail password, 198
SMTP Relays, 479
SMTP traffic, port management, 285
snort, from command line, 494–496
Snow Leopard
    802.1x protocol, 292
    account types, 51, 53
    Finder Services menu, 40
    ipfw program, 317
    Kerberosv5 authentication authority, 65
    parental controls, 58
    running ClamXav on, 221
    signature matching malware, 219
    securely binding clients to Open Directory, 441, 442
    services available, 39
    working with firewalls in, 304–307
social engineering, 488
social engineering attacks, 488
socially engineered malware, 218
socketfilterfw command
    managing ALF, 312
soft quotas, 562
software
    antivirus software, 218–228
    Safari and installation of unwanted software, 188
    vulnerability of, 167
software firewall, 299
    Application Layer Firewall (ALF), 301
    ipfw tool, 301
Software Update policy, 450
Software Update preference pane, 14–16
    Scheduled Check tab, 15
software updates, testing, 15
Sophos Anti-Virus for Mac OS X, 226–227
Sources tab, Retrospect, 527
spam, 202, 206
    antispam tools, 210–211
    CommuniGate Pro, 211–212
    false positives, 203, 204, 207
    filtering Apple Mail for, 203–204
    filtering with Entourage, 204–205
    InfoSec acceptable use policy, 567, 569
    Kerio MailServer, 208–210
    mail server-based solutions for, 207–212
    outsourcing spam and virus filtering, 212
    proxy servers, 294
    using mail server-based solutions for, 211–212
    using strong passwords, 184
    using white listing in Entourage, 205–206
    X-Spam-Status, 203
SpamAssassin tool, 478
    Mac OS X Server, 210
spanning tree, 290
Sparse bundle disk image option, Disk Utility, 247
sparse bundles, 248–250
    additional command line properties, 256
    downside of, 250
    encrypting user data, FileVault, 258
    viewed from Finder, 249
Sparse disk image option, Disk Utility, 25, 247
sparse image, creating
    diskutil command, 256
    hdiutil command, 253, 255, 256
sparse images
    limitations of, FileVault, 264–266
sparse-band-size key, diskutil, 257
SPARSEBUNDLE image format, diskutil, 256
spear phishing, 184
special characters
    filtering user input, 399
SPI (stateful packet inspection), 287–288
Splunk, 130
spoofing, 287
Spotlight
    changes to volumes, 248
spyware, 228–229
    MacScan, 229
SQL Injection attacks, 398
Squid
    command-line administration, 297
    configuring proxy servers, 295–297
    configuring with SquidMan, 295–297
SquidMan utility, 295–297
    Clients tab, 296
    Direct tab, 296
    General tab, 295–296
    installing, 295
    Parent tab, 296
    preference screen settings, 295–296
    starting and stopping, 296, 297
    Template tab, 296

src-ip mask, pipes, 322
src-port mask, pipes, 322
Ss state, ps command, 36
ssh
    Carbon Copy Cloner (CCC), 172
    non-standard ports, 278
    passwordless ssh authentication, 174
SSH (Secure Shell), 412–414
    authentication, 413
    combining with PPP as VPN link, 419–422
    configuring Timbuktu security, 412
    disabling, 476
    enabling, 412–413
    id_dsa/id_dsa.pub keys, 414
    Mac OS X Server security, 475–477
    passphrases, 413, 414
    password-based authentication, 413
    public/private key pairs, 413
    Remote Login feature, 412, 413
    securing, 413–414
    setting up, 420–421
$SSH_ORIGINAL_COMMAND, 176
SSID suppression, 337
SSIs (server-side includes), 381
    blocking hosts based on robots.txt, 387
SSL (Secure Sockets Layer), 185
    configuring Entourage to use, 199
    e-mail security, 196–199
    Mail port settings for, 197
    OpenSSL tool, 391
    securing LDAP, 431–432
    self-signed SSL certificates, 197
    tightening security with TLS, 391
    use SSL on clients, 474
    verifying authenticity of server, 197
SSL certificates
    generating self-signed certificate, 475
    Mac OS X Server security, 474–475
    reimporting, 475
    securely binding clients to Open Directory, 442
    securing LDAP, 431–432
    web server security, OS X, 461–463
stacked switches, 289
    Fibre Channel, 561
staff group, Mac OS X, 81
standard user, 51
StartupItems tool, 45
STAT column, ps command, 36
stay_setuid flag, sudoers file, 71

stdinpass option, hdiutil, 253, 255
stealth mode, enabling, 309–310
stealth scanning, 491
sticky bit, POSIX, 87, 356
storage pools, Xsan, 560
StorNext, Xsan interoperability, 559
stream ciphers, 574
stroke utility, port scanning, 311
su command, 69
    reviewing command-line logs, 123
subnet mask
    client IP addresses, 314
subnets, 286
subpath expression, sandbox, 164
sudo command, 69
    using ipfw, 317
sudo kill command, 422
sudoers file, 69–74
    aliases, 72
    Cmnd_Alias, 70, 73
    combining PPP and SSH as VPN link, 419
    editing, 69, 72
    escaping characters, 73
    flags defining privileges, 70–71
    for webscripters, 74
    granting resource access to users/aliases, 73
    Host_Alias, 70, 73
    location of, 69
    NOPASSWD tag, 74
    PASSWD tag, 74
    pushing file to other users on network, 74
    rules conflicting in, 74
    Runas_Alias, 70, 73
    syntax of, 74
    User_Alias, 72
    wildcards, 73
SUID applications, 75–76
    listing all SUID or SGID files, 76
suid bit, 87–88
SuperDuper, 512–513
superuser see root user
SUS3 (Single Unix Standard, version 3), 85
swap files, 10
Swatch, 130
switches, 289
    managed switches, 289–291
    rogue access points, 290
    stacked switches, 289

switching accounts
    Fast User Switching, 8
symbolic link type, POSIX, 83
symbolic links
    securing directory listings, 397
SymLinksIfOwnerMatch directive, 397
symmetric-key cryptography, 573, 574
SYN scan, 489, 491
SYN/ACK packet, 491
SYN/stealth scan, 491–492
Sync tab, MobileMe, 515
synchronization
    Bluetooth-PDA-Sync, 18
synchronized profiles
    mapping drives within Windows, 456
syslog service option, AirPort, 330
syslogd daemon, 30, 115
System keychain, 237
System Preferences
    Accounts preference pane, 4–8
    Bluetooth preference pane, 16–18
    configuring VPN connection, 416
    customizing, 4
    Print & Fax preference pane, 18
    Security preference pane, 9–14
    Sharing preference pane, 20–21
        viewing daemons running on Mac, 38
    Software Update preference pane, 14–16
System Preferences pane
    Require password to unlock option, 10
System Preferences policy, 450, 452
System Private Interface, 160
System Processes option, Activity Monitor, 33
system.log file, 125
    rotating logs, 127
SystemStarter tool, 45

T

t option, mount command, 75
t permission, POSIX
    sticky bit preventing deletion, 87
T state, ps command, 36
tape libraries, backups using, 530–531
tar command, 518
targetpw flag, sudoers file, 71
targets
    defining, Nessus, 500
    Metasploit, 503

Task Manager, Windows, 131–132
TCP (Transmission Control Protocol) see TCP/IP
TCP connect scan, 489
TCP/IP, 277–279
    moving packets, 278
    ports, 278
teaming (link aggregation), 291
Telnet, 412
telnet application, 395
Template tab, SquidMan utility, 296
Terminal window
    finding log files, 118
    opening, 31
    reviewing command-line logs, 123
testing
    see also network scanning
    firewalls, 310–311
    software updates, 15
text editors
    flags defining privileges in sudoers file, 71
TGT, Kerberos, 427
threads, 30
Threads column, Activity Monitor, 34
threats see malware
throttling
    address masking, 322
    dummynet, 321
ticket, Kerberos, 427
ticket, NTLMv1, 371
Timbuktu Pro, 408–412
    adding new users, 409–410
    configuring master password, 411
    configuring maximum security options, 411, 412
    configuring password rules, 410, 411
    configuring services, 412
    connecting to client system, 410
    installing, 408
    Master Password feature, 411
    testing new user accounts, 410–412
    User setup screen, 409
time
    setting time automatically, AirPort, 331
Time Capsule, 512
TIME column, ps command, 35
time keyword, mtree, 110
time limits, setting for access, 61–62
Time Machine, 506–512
    backup security, 507

choosing backup device, 507
device exclusions, 508
disabling backups, 510
excluding directories, 510
invisible items, 508
network volume backups, 511–512
restoring files from, 510–511
setting data not to be backed up, 508
setting data to be backed up, 509
viewing files not backed up by default, 509
Time Machine preference pane, 506
time synchronization, 427
TLS (Transport Layer Security), 185
    web site security, 391–392
tmp folder
    troubleshooting cut/copy/paste issues, 43
top command
    action before using, 31
    MREGS column, 37
    PRTS column, 36–38
    RPRVT column, 37
    RSHRD column, 37
    sorting output, 37
traceroute command, 284
traffic shaping, 321
transferring files *see* file sharing
transport layer, 278
Transport Layer Security *see* TLS
trash
    Secure Empty Trash feature, 23–24
Triple-DES, 573
Tripwire, 493–494
Trojan horses, 214, 215
    virus replication, 143
TrueCrypt, 270–271
trusted applications, 312
    keychain access, 145
    viewing, 312
TrustedBSD's MAC framework, 157
TTY column, ps command, 35
tty_tickets flag, sudoers file, 71
Turn On FileVault button
    enabling FileVault for users, 260
two-tier (client-server) networks, 282, 354
type keyword, mtree, 110
type option, hdiutil, 253, 255, 256

U

u option, ps command, 35
U state, ps command, 36
UDIF image format, diskutil, 256
UDP (User Datagram Protocol), 277
    UDP traffic and subnets, 286
UDTO image format, diskutil, 256
uid keyword, mtree, 109
umask
    applying new umask value, 86
    Mac OS X default value, 85
    NSUmask value, 86
umask command, 77
Umask Doctor, 86
uname keyword, mtree, 109
UNC (universal naming convention), 456
underscore (_) character
    accounts beginning with, 65
Universal Access policy, 450
Universally Unique IDentifier (UUID), 65
Unix files
    # character, 69
    % character, 70
unload verb, launchd, 312
unsetg command, Metasploit, 502
unsolicited messages *see* spam
updates
    Software Update preference pane, 14
Upgrade Storage feature, MobileMe, 517
Use a master password option, Firefox, 192
use command, Metasploit, 502
Use secure virtual memory option, 10
user access
    controlling use of Finder, 56
    copying Parental Controls settings, 62–63
    granular control of managed settings in Leopard, 63
    limiting to web sites, 58–59
    limiting communication via iChat and Mail, 59–61
    managing, 62
    restricting with sudoers, 69–74
    restricting to applications, 57
    securing mount points, 74–75
    setting time limits for, 61–62
user accounts
    adding aliases, 64
    administrative user, 51
    Advanced Options, 64
    generateduid key, 65

group accounts, 53
guest accounts, 53
hardening, 49
hidden service users and groups, 65
local directory services, 65–69
root users, 53
setting up parental controls, 56–62
sharing accounts, 52–53
standard user, 51
storage of, 65
types of, 51–53
User Authentication screen
    configuring PPTP-based VPN, 417
User column, Activity Monitor, 34
user data, FileVault encrypting, 257–265
User Datagram Protocol *see* UDP
user input, filtering characters, 399
User Settings window, 8
User setup screen, Timbuktu Pro, 409
user shells, Sandbox securing, 166–171
User_Alias, sudoers file, 72, 74
users
    adding to groups, 53–54
    administrative users, 8
    creating Open Directory users, 444–446
    disabling superuser account, 55, 56
    enabling FileVault for users, 260–262
    enabling root user, 6
    enabling superuser account, 54–55
    encrypting beyond home directory, 13
    Fast User Switching, 8
    granting resource access to, 73
    identifying who ran programs, 120
    Log out option, 10
    Mac OS X security, 4
    multiple users in workgroup setting, 7
    multiuser operating systems, 50
    Other User Processes option, 33
    setting up alias for sudo, 73
    usability and user security, 50
user-specific logs, 121–122
UTI mechanism
    application identification, 142
utility scripts, Retrospect, 527–528
UUID (Universally Unique IDentifier), 65

V

v option, mount command, 75
validation
    input validation, PHP, 383–384

var/log directory
    finding log files, 118
verbose mode, mount command, 75
verification
    application integrity, 143
    applications, 153–156
version command, Metasploit, 502
Vi, running commands from, 76
Vipul's Razor, 210
virtual machines, backups, 509
virtual memory, 10
    Activity Monitor utility, 35
    Use secure virtual memory option, 10
Virtual Network Computing *see* VNC
virtual private network *see* VPN
virus definitions, 220
virus scanner, ClamXav, 224
viruses, 213
    antivirus software, 218–228
    CommuniGate Pro, 211–212
    Elk Cloner, 216
    macro viruses, 215, 216
    mail server-based solutions for, 207–212
    malware and, 213, 215
    outsourcing spam and virus filtering, 212
    replication, 143
    retrovirus, 215, 216
    W97M virus, 217
VirusScan, McAfee, 220
visudo command, 72
    flags defining privileges in sudoers file, 71
VLAN (virtual LAN) support
    managed switches, 289
Vmirror, 562
VNC (Virtual Network Computing)
    Screen Sharing and, 402, 403
VNC client access
    enabling Remote Management, 408
    enabling Screen Sharing, 404
volumes
    changes to, 248
    hard links security issues, 108
    restricting access using mount points, 74, 75
    showing volumes mounted on system, 75
    Xsan, 560
VPN (virtual private network), 414–422
    adding VPN connection, 415
        configuring routing, 422

disconnecting, 422
setting up PPP, 421–422
setting up SSH, 420–421
setting up VPN account, 419–420
configuring VPN connection, 416
connecting to, 414–415
connecting to Cisco VPN, 417–418
Select the Interface screen, 415
serveradminm command, 477
setting up L2TP, 415–416
setting up PPTP, 416–417
VPN link
combining PPP and SSH as, 419–422
VPN protocols, 415
VPN tunnels, 398, 414, 419
vulnerability scanning, 489–492
Nessus, 497
SAINT, 503–504

W

w (write) permission, POSIX, 83
alpha/decimal/binary formats, 84
problem with 644 permission, 85
W97M virus, 217
WAPs (wireless access points), 326
AirPort, 327–328
finding access points while traveling, 346
wardriving, 337
safeguards against cracking wireless networks, 349
WDS (wireless distribution system), 328
WDS network, 328
changing form of encryption, 329
web browser security, 185–196
see also security
Firefox, 189–196
plug-ins, 188
Safari, 185–189
attacks on the Mac, 187
installation of unwanted software, 188
web browsers
performance issues with plug-in, 187
web pages
404 error code, 389
web server security
see also security
blocking hosts based on robots.txt, 387–388
controlling search engine access, 386

Mac OS X Server, 459–462
realms, 459–461
SSL certificates, 461–463
securing web server, 377–382
changing log file location, 379
disabling CGI, 381
disabling unnecessary services in Apache, 382
httpd service, 378–379
proxy servers, 381
replacing default web site files, 379
restricting Apache access, 380
running on nonstandard port, 380
web servers
enabling Apache web server, 377
enumerating, 395–396
securing files on, 396–398
Web services, OS X, turning on, 377, 378
Web Sharing box, OS X, 377, 378
Web Sharing service, 39
web site security
see also security
code injection attacks, 398–399
controlling directory access, 388–391
cross-site scripting (XSS) attacks, 398–399
enumerating web servers, 395–396
htaccess file, 388–391
implementing digital certificates, 392
information privacy, 392–396
Perl scripts, 385–386
PHP, 382–384
protecting information from Google, 394–395
replacing default web site files, 379
reviewing safety of module, 382
scripts, 384–386
securing directory listings, 396–397
securing files on web server, 396–398
securing PHP, 383
securing robots.txt, 386–388
securing web servers, 377–382
SQL Injection attacks, 398
tightening with TLS, 391–392
web sites
hosting, 378
limiting access to, 58–59
WEBDAV-Digest, 438
webscripters, sudoers file for, 74
weekly.out log file, 128
WEP

AirPort protocols, 327
WEP keys
    cracking, 347–348
    generation of 40-bit keys, 343
whatis command, 128
When Junk Mail Arrives options, 203
white listing
    application configuring, 150
    using in Entourage, 205–206
white-box testing, 485
WHOIS lookup, 392
    Network Utility performing, 487
    querying whois databases, 488
Whois tab, Network Utility, 393, 394
wildcards, sudoers file, 73
Windowed Processes option, Activity
        Monitor, 33
Windows clients
    providing directory services for, 453–454
Windows methods to log events, 130–133
    Event Viewer, 130–131
    Performance counters, 132, 133
    Task Manager, 131–132
Windows Sharing
    when to enable and dangers, 303
Windows users, providing password for, 361
Windows, mapping drives within, 456
WinMagic SecureDoc, 271–272
WINS Server option
    sharing files with AirPort, 364
wireless access points (WAPs)
    key generation process, 343
    network structure impacting security
        level, 341
    Newsham 21-bit attack, 343
wireless access points see WAPs
wireless distribution system see WDS
wireless hacking tools, 342–347
    EtherPeek, 347
    Ettercap, 347
    iStumbler, 344–346
    KisMAC, 342–344
    MacStumbler, 346
wireless networks, 325–327
    AirPort, 327–328
    client computers, 339–340
    configuring encryption type, AirPort, 332
    cracking WEP keys, 347–348
    cracking WPA-PSK, 348–349
    hiding, 337–338
    IEEE 802.11 protocol, 326

network structure impacting security
        level, 341
    packet interception, 326
    safeguards against cracking, 349–350
    securing computer-to-computer
        networks, 340–341
    security issues, 325
    viewing details about, 345
wireless security
    on OS X Server using RADIUS, 471–473
Wireless tab, AirPort Utility, 331, 332
    SSID suppression, 337
wLAN see wireless networks
workflows, Automator
    script malware attacks, 217
Workgroup Manager
    configuring policies, 449
    creating Open Directory groups, 446–447
    creating Open Directory users, 445–446
    enabling FileVault for users, 261
    file sharing security, NFS, 466
    Managed Client OS X (MCX), 149–152
    managed preferences, 451
workgroup setting, multiple users in, 7
worm worm, 216
worms, 214, 215
    Code Red worm, 216
    Duh worm, 144
    iKee worm, 144
    Melissa worm, 216
    MyDoom worm, 216
    Nimda worm, 216
    OSX.Leap.A worm, 214
    payload, 214
    worm worm, 216
WPA2, AirPort protocols, 327
WPA2 Enterprise, 327
WPA-PSK, cracking, 348–349
Write Attributes access right, ACEs, 92
write blocking, forensics, 538
Write Ext Attributes access right, 92
write mode, POSIX permissions, 82
    alpha/decimal/binary formats, 84
    file sharing, 355
Write Only permission, ACE, 99
Write Report option, MacForensicsLab,
        555–556
Write/Add Files access right, ACEs, 92
write-permissions category, ACEs, 92–93
writesecurity privilege, 91

write-tmp-only sandbox profile, 160

X

x (execute) permission, POSIX, 83
    alpha/decimal/binary formats, 84
x option, ps command, 35
Xgrid Sharing service, 39
    when to enable and dangers, 304
XMPP protocol, iChat server, 478
Xsan
    affinities, storage pools, 561
    configuration files, 559
    Fibre Channel, 561
    full disk encryption, 266
    LUN (logical unit number), 560
    metadata, 560–561
    permissions, 561
    quotas, 562
    security, 559–562
    storage, 560
    storage pools, 560
    StorNext interoperability, 559
    volumes, 560

X-Spam-Status, 203
XSS (cross-site scripting) attacks, 398–399
XSS holes, 399

Y

Yahoo Mac Forensics group, 537
Yasu
    running maintenance scripts with, 127–128
yellow triangle, Firefox
    indicating allowed application is not signed, 151

Z

Z state, ps command, 36
Zero Out Data option
    securely erasing disks, 22
zero-day exploits, 221
zombies, 215, 216
zone transfers, DNS, 489

You Need the Companion eBook

Your purchase of this book entitles you to buy the companion PDF-version eBook for only $10. Take the weightless companion with you anywhere.

We believe this Apress title will prove so indispensable that you'll want to carry it with you everywhere, which is why we are offering the companion eBook (in PDF format) for $10 to customers who purchase this book now. Convenient and fully searchable, the PDF version of any content-rich, page-heavy Apress book makes a valuable addition to your programming library. You can easily find and copy code—or perform examples by quickly toggling between instructions and the application. Even simultaneously tackling a donut, diet soda, and complex code becomes simplified with hands-free eBooks!

Once you purchase your book, getting the $10 companion eBook is simple:

1. Visit **www.apress.com/promo/tendollars/**.
2. Complete a basic registration form to receive a randomly generated question about this title.
3. Answer the question correctly in 60 seconds, and you will receive a promotional code to redeem for the $10.00 eBook.

233 Spring Street, New York, NY 10013

All Apress eBooks subject to copyright protection. No part may be reproduced or transmitted in any form or by any means, electronic or mechanical, including photocopying, recording, or by any information storage or retrieval system, without the prior written permission of the copyright owner and the publisher. The purchaser may print the work in full or in part for their own noncommercial use. The purchaser may place the eBook title on any of their personal computers for their own personal reading and reference.

Offer valid through 11/10.